Marion Hanson

(Intermediate)
present heaven - place Christians go
when they die
     (new earth)
eternal heaven - place where we will
live forever after the final resurrection

"One thing's for sure: Earth can't keep its promises, but aren't you glad Heaven does? And oh the joy of one day enjoying not only new glorified bodies but hearts free of sin! Randy does an awesome job of answering people's toughest questions about what lies on the other side of death. Heaven provides a clear and very readable guide to grasping all that the Savior has in store for those who trust in him."

JONI EARECKSON TADA, founder and CEO, Joni and Friends

"Randy Alcorn's thorough mind and careful pen have produced a treasury about Heaven that will inform my own writing for years."

JERRY B. JENKINS, novelist

"When Randy Alcorn speaks, I listen; when he writes, I read. This is not only so because Alcorn is a uniquely gifted communicator but because his walk matches his talk. To put it plainly, he is the real deal!"

HANK HANEGRAAFF, president of the Christian Research Institute International and host of the *Bible Answer Man* radio broadcast

"Seldom have I had the chance to witness both true genius and genuine humility in the same person. Randy Alcorn is a fully devoted follower of Christ. I believe God has sovereignly prepared Randy, over his lifetime, for the writing of this book on Heaven. He has long reflected upon this subject, and this book is the fruit of his biblically disciplined study and his sacred imagination. Randy is a wonderfully original thinker, yet a thorough-going biblicist. Other than the Bible itself, this book may well be the single most life-changing book you'll ever read. It has certainly refueled my soul and given me a fresh sense of purpose and drive. Having read this book, I will never be the same."

STU WEBER, pastor and author of *Tender Warrior*

"This is the best book on Heaven I've ever read."

RICK WARREN, pastor and author of *Purpose-Driven Life*

"I just turned the last page of Randy Alcorn's Heaven . . . *and I feel so full. My heart brims with excitement about my future home and with love for the creative God who designed it for me. My mind has been delighted to consider scriptural truths I've previously glossed over. My spirit yearns to walk in God's company. We all need to know what awaits us beyond the grave. Drawing from God's Word, Randy Alcorn has explained and carefully illustrated these plans in an easy-to-follow format. Do not miss this book.* Heaven *will change your life, your perspective, and perhaps even your eternal destiny."*

ANGELA HUNT, author of *The Debt*

Randy Alcorn's Heaven *is biblically thorough and helps bring together loose ends on this very encouraging subject. This is a great book!*

DR. GENE A. GETZ, Director, Center for Church Renewal; former pastor, seminary professor, and author of *Sharpening the Focus of the Church*

Tyndale House Publishers, Inc.
Carol Stream, Illinois

HEAVEN

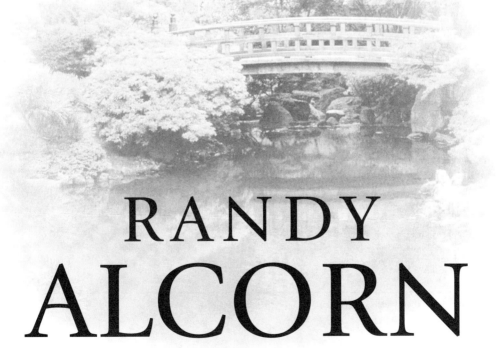

RANDY
ALCORN

Visit Tyndale's exciting Web site at www.tyndale.com

TYNDALE and Tyndale's quill logo are registered trademarks of Tyndale House Publishers, Inc.

Heaven

Library of Congress Cataloging-in-Publication Data

Alcorn, Randy C.
  Heaven / Randy Alcorn.
    p. cm.
  Includes bibliographical references and index.
  ISBN 978-0-8423-7942-7
  ISBN 978-0-8423-7944-1 (pbk.)
  1. Heaven—Christianity.   I. Title.
  BT846.3.A43 2004
  236′.24—dc2   2004011329

Printed in the United States of America

16   15   14   13   12   11
24   23   22   21   20   19

To Kevin Butler, Jessi Hickman, Gary Stump,
Cami Norquist, Jerry Hardin, Greg Coffey,
Lucille Alcorn, Leona Bryant, David Reeves,
Daniel Traugott, Lynley Herbert, Stephenie Saint,
Rachel Terveen, Eli Hubbard, Jonathan Coburn,
Emily Kimball, Al Baylis, III, John Swartzendruber,
Bob Whitson, Owen Raynor, Joyce Kelley, Zach Evans,
Ryan Dekker, Cody Ogle, Philip Higgins, Dawn Lechler,
Sally Turpin, Laura Libby, Mike Cimmarrusti, Kyle Speer,
Matthew Pearson, Jonathan Murphy, Brad and Steffanie Jones,
Eric Kuemmel, Cheyenne Fiveash, Elizabeth Wall,
Kelley Lance Courtney, Alison Heth,
and countless others
who departed "prematurely"
(yet in God's good time)
to a world far greater than this one
but far less than the one to come,
which all of us who know King Jesus
will behold together, slack-jawed,
on the New Earth's first morning.

CONTENTS

PART I
A THEOLOGY OF HEAVEN

SECTION ONE
REALIZING OUR DESTINY

SECTION TWO
UNDERSTANDING THE PRESENT HEAVEN

SECTION THREE
GRASPING REDEMPTION'S FAR REACH

SECTION FOUR
ANTICIPATING RESURRECTION

PART II
QUESTIONS AND ANSWERS ABOUT HEAVEN

PART III
LIVING IN LIGHT OF HEAVEN

ACKNOWLEDGMENTS

Thanks to the hundreds of people who, after reading my books, have written me to ask questions about Heaven. Many have shared their stories of loved ones dying, of facing their own deaths, and of God's grace preparing them for Heaven. Some have sought answers to the deepest questions within and have pushed me further in my study of God's Word.

To scholars (and friends) Gerry Breshears, Justin Taylor, and Gregg Allison, who graciously gave me the theological critique I sought: Thanks, men, for sharpening iron and being willing to see the manuscript at its worst so you could help me bring it to its best. And thanks, Justin, for passing on to me all those great resources.

Thanks to my good friend Stu Weber for giving me such strong encouragement after reading the original manuscript. It helped renew my strength to tackle the revisions with hope for the impact of the final product.

I usually mention my buddy Steve Keels in the acknowledgments, but this time he actually deserves it. Thanks, Steve, for being a model of true friendship. I loved our long hours discussing the world to come, and I look forward to many more (both here and there). And if—as you've told me—I'll be your gardener on the New Earth, I'll consider it a privilege.

Thanks for the contributions of Randy Butler, Larry Gadbaugh, Marshall Beretta, Keith Krell, Barry Arnold, Matt Guerino, Ruthanna Metzgar, Skeets Norquist, Amy Campbell, Scott Teeny, Dave Sheets, Dave Martin, and Paul Martin. My friends Angie Hunt and Dave Jackson from ChiLibris shared helpful insights regarding animals. Sarah Ballenger chased down stray endnotes. Diane Meyer offered great encouragement—thanks, sis.

I deeply appreciated and benefited from conversations with my family: Nanci, the world's best wife, and our sons and daughters, Dan and Angela Stump and Dan and Karina Franklin. Special thanks to Karina, who did considerable early editing of the rough manuscript. Nanci, I'm deeply grateful God used your encouraging words on the first drafts to keep me at this huge task.

Thanks to the musicians of Sovereign Grace Ministries, who draw worshipful attention to the God of Heaven, and to my friend John G. Elliott, whose song "The Praise Goes On and On" and other wonderful Christ-centered music kept me company during much of this several-year project.

I appreciate the diligence, insights, and friendship of my Tyndale House editors, Dave Lindstedt and Lynn Vanderzalm. It was a long haul for all of us, Dave and Lynn—thanks for being faithful. Thanks, Carol Traver, for all your labors. Thanks also to the copy editors: Michal Needham, MaryLynn Layman, Heather House, and Jeff Erickson. Special thanks to my friend Ron Beers, publisher at Tyndale House, who first asked, "Would you write a big book on Heaven?" Without Ron's prompting, I might not have undertaken this project.

Thanks to my friends and EPM staffers Bonnie Hiestand, Kathy Norquist, Janet Albers, Linda Jeffries, and Sharon Misenhimer for all you did to free me to work on this book. Thanks to the following people, who kindly typed up many of the citations from over 150 sources: Amy Campbell, Kelsey Carl, Polly Carl, Judy Drais, Lori Durbin, Femy Guilleux, Andrew Hale, Shawnda Holzer, Tina Ide, LeannaRuth Jensen, Debby Lehr, Christy Miesner, Pauline Merit, Christie Strait, Donna Thomson, Parm Tunnell, and Sherie Way.

I'm grateful to some of my Western Seminary "Theology of Heaven" class members, whose papers stimulated various insights: Danny Jenkins, Andrew McClellan, Mark Baker, Kathryn Barram, Holley Clough, Jan Dwyer, Geoff Hart, Richard Herold, and James Warrick.

Special thanks to Randy and Sue Monnes for generously opening to me their cozy riverside cabin in Sandy, Oregon, for a number of weeks. And to my friends Melissa and Mike King, who made me feel at home as their neighbors.

My deepest gratitude to the hundreds of people on our prayer team, who read my e-mails and took the time to pray for me and for this book. If lives are touched for eternity by it, you will have played a major role. God will reward your faithfulness.

Thanks above all to King Jesus, who stayed with me in long, lonely hours of composition and rewrites, seemingly endless revisions, and labor to search the Scriptures and get all the details right. I knew this would be a massive and taxing project, but I didn't anticipate the extent to which it would drive me to my knees. What great comfort Jesus Christ brought me in the middle of many nights, as I asked and received his empowerment.

Thank you, my grace-giving Lord. Every joy Heaven offers is a derivative of you, who are joy itself. Heaven will be a thrilling adventure because you are a thrilling person. Thanks for being the source of all great adventures, including those awaiting us in the new universe.

I can hardly wait.

ABOUT THIS BOOK

Bookstores overflow with accounts of near-death and after-death experiences, complete with angels giving guided tours of Heaven. A few of these books may have authentic components, but many are unbiblical and misleading.

We Christians who believe God's Word are partly to blame for this. Why? We have failed to explore and explain the Bible's magnificent teachings about Heaven. No wonder a flood of unbiblical thinking has rushed in to fill the vacuum. Because the human heart cries out for answers about the *afterlife*, our silence on Heaven is particularly striking.

The truth is, in our seminaries, churches, and families, we have given amazingly little attention to the place where we will live forever with Christ and his people—the New Earth, in the new universe. This eternal Heaven is the central subject of this book. It's a subject I've found to be fascinating, thrilling, and life-changing.

TEST THIS BOOK BY SCRIPTURE

From the beginning, I want to make it clear that it's vitally important that this book be true to Scripture. I believe that most of my conclusions, even those that significantly depart from current evangelical thinking, will stand up to biblical scrutiny. Inevitably, however, some may not. In the context of prophetic statements, the apostle Paul says, "Test everything. Hold on to the good" (1 Thessalonians 5:21). It's up to you to test by God's Word what I say, hold on to the good, and reject the bad.

Through biblical study and extensive reading, dialogue, and critique, I've tried to detect any conclusions that don't pass Scripture's test, to eliminate them before this book was published. But despite my best efforts, some errors undoubtedly have slipped through. I call on readers to be like the Bereans, who "examined the Scriptures every day to see if what Paul said was true" (Acts

17:11). Don't throw out the baby of truth with the bathwater of what you regard as my mistakes—but, by all means, *do* throw out the bathwater!

I invite you to contact me if you believe you have biblical grounds for disagreeing with anything in this book. I am open to correction—in fact, I *seek* it, and I will make any warranted changes in future editions. This revised version of the book contains a number of changes I made based on input from readers of the first edition. I am grateful for their questions and criticisms. (Keep in mind, though, when you write to me, that "I've never heard this before . . ." and "I've always thought that . . ." and "Our denomination teaches . . ." are not biblical grounds for disagreement.)

Many things in this book will be new even to readers who are veteran students of Scripture. New ideas are rightly suspect because they are often heretical. However, when biblical truths have been long neglected or ignored, attempts to present them may sound far-fetched. They may appear to be adding to or misinterpreting Scripture, when in fact they are simply portraying what Scripture has said all along but we've failed to grasp. In these pages I will introduce some biblical truths that I believe have been long ignored or spiritualized and thereby stripped of their richness and significance.

STRUCTURE AND CONTENT

Examining the table of contents will give you a good feel for this book. In part 1, "A Theology of Heaven," I will explain the difference between the present Heaven (where Christians go when they die) and the ultimate, eternal Heaven (where God will dwell with his people on the New Earth). Don't be afraid of the word *theology*—it simply means a study of God's relation to the world—and don't underestimate your ability to understand what God has revealed to you in his Word. We'll discuss whether the current Heaven is a physical place; whether people there remember life on Earth; whether they pray for loved ones on Earth and can actually see what's going on here; and we'll answer the question, If people in Heaven are aware of events on Earth, including suffering, how could it be Heaven?

The backbone of part 1 is a discussion of the book's central subject, the New Earth. I'll present foundational biblical truths concerning God's larger plan in redemption, especially in the doctrine of the resurrection of the dead and what that means for the New Earth. I will answer questions such as, What will it mean to see God? What will our relationships with people be like? What will it mean to rule the earth with Christ?

Part 2, "Questions and Answers about Heaven," addresses specific questions about life on the New Earth that arise out of the foundational teachings in part 1—questions such as, Will the New Earth be like Eden? Will there be animals on the New Earth? What kind of city is the New Jerusalem? What will our bodies be like? Will we eat and drink? Will we work? use machinery? play? study and learn? create art and music and culture?

You may find that the material in the first part of the book is paradigm shifting. If you don't understand the foundational principles, however, you will come to the second half with a different set of assumptions, and what I'm saying may not make sense. The soundness of my conclusions in the question and answer section depends on the biblical basis I present in part 1.

I sometimes skip around when reading a book, going straight to the chapters that deal with what interests me most. If you do this, I hope you'll then go back to the foundational chapters to see what the book's logic is built upon. If you are patient enough to read this book consecutively, I think you'll be rewarded. Part 3, "Living in Light of Heaven," encourages us to let the doctrine of Heaven transform us and fill us with joyful anticipation.

If I were dealing with the subject of Heaven in order of *importance*, I would begin with a discussion of God's presence in Heaven and our relationship with him, because being with God and seeing his face is the central joy of Heaven and the source of all other joys. But there's a major obstacle: Because of our wrong assumptions about the eternal state, we bring misguided perspectives to what it will mean to see God or be with him. We succumb to the vague, ethereal notions of eastern religions rather than build our understanding on the concrete, physical depictions of biblical and historical Christianity. We fail to envision God as forever incarnate in the risen Christ, and we fail to recognize the New Earth as a physical environment, civilization, and culture in which God will dwell with us. Consequently, I must lay the biblical groundwork before I discuss what it will mean to live with God forever and answer other key questions about Heaven.

"I'VE NEVER THOUGHT THIS WAY BEFORE"

A friend asked me the central premise of this book. When I explained it briefly, he looked at me wide-eyed, incredulous. I rephrased it, using different Scriptures and illustrations. Suddenly, the light went on for him. He said, "The more you restate it in different ways, the more Scripture you use, the more it makes sense. But I've *never* thought this way before. I don't think many people have. You'll need to make your case carefully, or people just won't believe it."

I will try to make the case carefully and biblically. There is plenty in this book for everyone to disagree with. But I hope you'll find that most of it rings true to Scripture and opens up exciting doors to imagining and anticipating everything that awaits God's children in the magnificent world to come.

THE SUBJECT OF HEAVEN

Do not let your hearts be troubled. Trust in God; trust also in me. In my Father's house are many rooms; if it were not so, I would have told you. I am going there to prepare a place for you. And if I go and prepare a place for you, I will come back and take you to be with me that you also may be where I am.

John 14:1-3

The sense that we will live forever *somewhere* has shaped every civilization in human history. Australian aborigines pictured Heaven as a distant island beyond the western horizon. The early Finns thought it was an island in the faraway east. Mexicans, Peruvians, and Polynesians believed that they went to the sun or the moon after death.[1] Native Americans believed that in the afterlife their spirits would hunt the spirits of buffalo.[2] The *Gilgamesh* epic, an ancient Babylonian legend, refers to a resting place of heroes and hints at a tree of life. In the pyramids of Egypt, the embalmed bodies had maps placed beside them as guides to the future world.[3] The Romans believed that the righteous would picnic in the Elysian fields while their horses grazed nearby. Seneca, the Roman philosopher, said, "The day thou fearest as the last is the birthday of eternity." Although these depictions of the afterlife differ, the unifying testimony of the human heart throughout history is belief in life after death. Anthropological evidence suggests that every culture has a God-given, innate sense of the eternal—that this world is not all there is.[4]

EARLY CHRISTIANS' PREOCCUPATION WITH HEAVEN

The Roman catacombs, where the bodies of many martyred Christians were buried, contain tombs with inscriptions such as these:

- In Christ, Alexander is not dead, but lives.
- One who lives with God.
- He was taken up into his eternal home.[5]

One historian writes, "Pictures on the catacomb walls portray Heaven with beautiful landscapes, children playing, and people feasting at banquets."[6]

In AD 125, a Greek named Aristides wrote to a friend about Christianity, explaining why this "new religion" was so successful: "If any righteous man among the Christians passes from this world, they rejoice and offer thanks to God, and they escort his body with songs and thanksgiving as if he were setting out from one place to another nearby."[7]

In the third century, the church father Cyprian said, "Let us greet the day which assigns each of us to his own home, which snatches us from this place and sets us free from the snares of the world, and restores us to paradise and the kingdom. Anyone who has been in foreign lands longs to return to his own native land. . . . We regard paradise as our native land."[8]

These early Christian perspectives sound almost foreign today, don't they? But their beliefs were rooted in the Scriptures, where the apostle Paul writes, "To me, to live is Christ and to die is gain. . . . I desire to depart and be with Christ, which is better by far" (Philippians 1:21, 23). He also wrote, "As long as we are at home in the body we are away from the Lord. . . . We . . . would prefer to be away from the body and at home with the Lord" (2 Corinthians 5:6, 8).

When Jesus told his disciples, "In my Father's house are many rooms. . . . I am going there to prepare a place for you" (John 14:2), he deliberately chose common, physical terms (*house, rooms, place*) to describe where he was going and what he was preparing for us. He wanted to give his disciples (and us) something tangible to look forward to—an actual place where they (and we) would go to be with him.

This place is not an ethereal realm of disembodied spirits, because human beings are not suited for such a realm. A *place* is by nature physical, just as human beings are by nature physical. (We are also spiritual.) What we are suited for—what we've been specifically designed for—is a place like the one God made for us: Earth.

In this book, we'll see from Scripture an exciting yet strangely neglected truth—that God never gave up on his original plan for human beings to dwell on Earth. In fact, the climax of history will be the creation of new heavens and a New Earth, a resurrected universe inhabited by resurrected people living with the resurrected Jesus (Revelation 21:1-4).

OUR TERMINAL DISEASE

As human beings, we have a terminal disease called *mortality*. The current death rate is 100 percent. Unless Christ returns soon, we're all going to die. We don't like to think about death; yet, worldwide, 3 people die every second, 180 every minute, and nearly 11,000 every hour. If the Bible is right about what happens to us after death, it means that more than 250,000 people every day go either to Heaven or Hell.†

David said, "Show me, O Lord, my life's end and the number of my days; let me know how fleeting is my life. You have made my days a mere handbreadth; the span of my years is as nothing before you. Each man's life is but a breath" (Psalm 39:4-5). Picture a single breath escaping your mouth on a cold day and dissipating into the air. Such is the brevity of life here. The wise will consider what awaits us on the other side of this life that so quickly ends.

God uses suffering and impending death to unfasten us from this earth and to set our minds on what lies beyond. I've lost people close to me. (Actually, I haven't *lost* them, because I know where they are—rather, I've lost *contact* with them.) I've spent a lot of time talking to people who've been diagnosed with terminal diseases. These people, and their loved ones, have a sudden and insatiable interest in the afterlife. Most people live unprepared for death. But those who are wise will go to a reliable source to investigate what's on the other side. And if they discover that the choices they make during their brief stay in this world will matter in the world to come, they'll want to adjust those choices accordingly.

Ancient merchants often wrote the words *memento mori*—"think of death"—in large letters on the first page of their accounting books.[9] Philip of Macedon, father of Alexander the Great, commissioned a servant to stand in his presence each day and say, "Philip, you will die." In contrast, France's Louis XIV decreed that the word *death* not be uttered in his presence. Most of us are more like Louis than Philip, denying death and avoiding the thought of it except when it's forced upon us. We live under the fear of death.

Jesus came to deliver us from the fear of death, "so that by his death he might destroy him who holds the power of death—that is, the devil—and free those who all their lives were held in slavery by their fear of death" (Hebrews 2:14-15).

In light of the coming resurrection of the dead, the apostle Paul asks, "Where, O death, is your victory? Where, O death, is your sting?" (1 Corinthians 15:55).

---

†To underscore the fact that Heaven and Hell are real places, I am deliberately capitalizing them throughout the book, as I would other proper nouns, such as Chicago, Nigeria, Europe, or Saturn. I also capitalize the New Earth, just as I would New England. Not to do so would imply that Heaven and Hell and the New Earth aren't *real* places. But they are—they're as real as the places we were born and the places we now live.

What delivers us from the fear of death? What takes away death's sting? Only a relationship with the person who died on our behalf, the one who has gone ahead to make a place for us to live with him. If we don't know Jesus, we *will* fear death and its sting—and we should.

SEEING THE SHORE

Perhaps you've come to this book burdened, discouraged, depressed, or even traumatized. Perhaps your dreams—your marriage, career, or ambitions—have crumbled. Perhaps you've become cynical or have lost hope. A biblical understanding of the truth about Heaven can change all that.

In 1952, young Florence Chadwick stepped into the waters of the Pacific Ocean off Catalina Island, determined to swim to the shore of mainland California. She'd already been the first woman to swim the English Channel both ways. The weather was foggy and chilly; she could hardly see the boats accompanying her. Still, she swam for fifteen hours. When she begged to be taken out of the water along the way, her mother, in a boat alongside, told her she was close and that she could make it. Finally, physically and emotionally exhausted, she stopped swimming and was pulled out. It wasn't until she was on the boat that she discovered the shore was less than half a mile away. At a news conference the next day she said, "All I could see was the fog. . . . I think if I could have seen the shore, I would have made it."[10]

Consider her words: "I think if I could have seen the shore, I would have made it." For believers, that shore is Jesus and being with him in the place that he promised to prepare for us, where we will live with him forever. The shore we should look for is that of the New Earth. If we can see through the fog and picture our eternal home in our mind's eye, it will comfort and energize us.

If you're weary and don't know how you can keep going, I pray this book will give you vision, encouragement, and hope. No matter how tough life gets, if you can see the shore and draw your strength from Christ, you'll make it.

I pray this book will help you see the shore.

PART I

A THEOLOGY OF HEAVEN

REALIZING OUR DESTINY

CHAPTER 1

ARE YOU LOOKING
FORWARD TO HEAVEN?

The man who is about to sail for Australia or New Zealand as a settler, is naturally anxious to know something about his future home, its climate, its employments, its inhabitants, its ways, its customs. All these are subjects of deep interest to him. You are leaving the land of your nativity, you are going to spend the rest of your life in a new hemisphere. It would be strange indeed if you did not desire information about your new abode. Now surely, if we hope to dwell for ever in that "better country, even a heavenly one," we ought to seek all the knowledge we can get about it. Before we go to our eternal home we should try to become acquainted with it.

J. C. Ryle

Jonathan Edwards, the great Puritan preacher, often spoke of Heaven. He said, "It becomes us to spend this life only as a journey toward heaven . . . to which we should subordinate all other concerns of life. Why should we labor for or set our hearts on anything else, but that which is our proper end and true happiness?"[11]

In his early twenties, Edwards composed a set of life resolutions. One read, "Resolved, to endeavor to obtain for myself as much happiness, in the other world, as I possibly can."[12]

Some may think it odd and inappropriate that Edwards was so committed to pursuing happiness for himself in Heaven. But Pascal was right when he said, "All men seek happiness. This is without exception. Whatever different means they employ, they all tend to this end."[13] And if we all seek happiness, why not do as Edwards did and seek it where it can actually be found—in the person of Jesus and the place called Heaven?

Tragically, however, most people do not find their joy in Christ and Heaven. In fact, many people find no joy at all when they think about Heaven.

A pastor once confessed to me, "Whenever I think about Heaven, it makes me depressed. I'd rather just cease to exist when I die."

"Why?" I asked.

"I can't stand the thought of that endless tedium. To float around in the clouds with nothing to do but strum a harp . . . it's all so terribly boring. Heaven doesn't sound much better than Hell. I'd rather be annihilated than spend eternity in a place like that."

Where did this Bible-believing, seminary-educated pastor get such a view of Heaven? Certainly not from Scripture, where Paul said to depart and be with Christ was *far better* than staying on a sin-cursed Earth (Philippians 1:23). My friend was more honest about it than most, yet I've found that many Christians share the same misconceptions about Heaven.

After reading my novel *Deadline,* which portrays Heaven as a real and exciting place, a woman wrote me, "I've been a Christian since I was five. I'm married to a youth pastor. When I was seven, a teacher at my Christian school told me that when I got to Heaven, I wouldn't know anyone or anything from earth. I was terrified of dying. I was never told any different by anyone. . . . It's been really hard for me to advance in my Christian walk because of this fear of Heaven and eternal life."

Let those words sink in: "This *fear* of heaven and eternal life." Referring to her recently transformed perspective, she said, "You don't know the weight that's been lifted off of me. . . . Now I can't wait to get to Heaven."

OUR UNBIBLICAL VIEW OF HEAVEN

When an English vicar was asked by a colleague what he expected after death, he replied, "Well, if it comes to that, I suppose I shall enter into eternal bliss, but I really wish you wouldn't bring up such depressing subjects."[14]

Over the past fifteen years, I've received thousands of letters and have had hundreds of conversations concerning Heaven. I've spoken about Heaven at churches and conferences. I've written about Heaven and taught a seminary course titled "A Theology of Heaven." There's a great deal I don't know, but one thing I *do* know is what people think about Heaven. And frankly, I'm alarmed.

I agree with this statement by John Eldredge in *The Journey of Desire:* "Nearly every Christian I have spoken with has some idea that eternity is an unending church service. . . . We have settled on an image of the never-ending sing-along in the sky, one great hymn after another, forever and ever, amen. And our heart sinks. *Forever and ever? That's it? That's the good news?* And then we sigh and feel guilty that we are not more 'spiritual.' We lose heart, and we turn once more to the present to find what life we can."[15]

Gary Larson captured a common misperception of Heaven in one of his *Far Side* cartoons. In it a man with angel wings and a halo sits on a cloud, doing nothing, with no one nearby. He has the expression of someone marooned on a desert island with absolutely nothing to do. A caption shows his inner thoughts: "Wish I'd brought a magazine."

In *The Adventures of Huckleberry Finn*, Mark Twain portrays a similar view of Heaven. The Christian spinster Miss Watson takes a dim view of Huck's fun-loving spirit. According to Huck, "She went on and told me all about the good place. She said all a body would have to do there was go around all day long with a harp and sing, forever and ever. So I didn't think much of it. . . . I asked her if she reckoned Tom Sawyer would go there, and she said, not by a considerable sight. I was glad about that, because I wanted him and me to be together."[16]

The pious Miss Watson had nothing to say about Heaven that appealed to Huck. (And nothing, if we're honest, that appeals to *us*.) What would have attracted him was a place where he could do meaningful and pleasurable things with enjoyable people. In fact, that's a far more accurate depiction of what Heaven will actually be like. If Miss Watson had told Huck what the Bible says about living in a resurrected body and being with people we love on a resurrected Earth with gardens and rivers and mountains and untold adventures—now *that* would have gotten his attention!

When it came to Heaven and Hell, Mark Twain never quite got it. Under the weight of age, he said in his autobiography, "The burden of pain, care, misery grows heavier year by year. At length ambition is dead, pride is dead, vanity is dead, longing for release is in their place. It comes at last—the only unpoisoned gift earth ever had for them—and they vanish from a world where they were of no consequence; where they achieved nothing; where they were a mistake and a failure and a foolishness."[17]

What a contrast to the perspective that Charles Spurgeon, his contemporary, had on death: "To come to Thee is to come home from exile, to come to land out of the raging storm, to come to rest after long labour, to come to the goal of my desires and the summit of my wishes."[18]

We do not desire to eat gravel. Why? Because God did not design us to eat gravel. Trying to develop an appetite for a disembodied existence in a nonphysical Heaven is like trying to develop an appetite for gravel. No matter how sincere we are, and no matter how hard we try, it's not going to work. Nor should it.

What God made us to desire, and therefore what we *do* desire if we admit it, is exactly what he promises to those who follow Jesus Christ: a resurrected life in a resurrected body, with the resurrected Christ on a resurrected Earth. Our desires correspond precisely to God's plans. It's not that we want something, so we engage in wishful thinking that what we want exists. It's the opposite—the reason we want it is precisely because God has planned for it to exist. As we'll see, resurrected people living in a resurrected universe isn't our idea—it's *God's*.

Nineteenth-century British theologian J. C. Ryle said, "I pity the man who never thinks about heaven."[19] We could also say, "I pity the man who never thinks *accurately* about Heaven." It's our inaccurate thinking, I believe, that causes us to choose to think so little about Heaven.

THEOLOGICAL NEGLECT OF HEAVEN

John Calvin, the great expositor, never wrote a commentary on Revelation and never dealt with the eternal state at any length. Though he encourages meditation on Heaven in his *Institutes of the Christian Religion*, his theology of Heaven seems strikingly weak compared to his theology of God, Christ, salvation, Scripture, and the church. This is understandable in light of the pressing theological issues of his day, but surprisingly few theologians in the centuries since Calvin have attempted to fill in the gaps. A great deal has been written about eschatology—the study of the end times—but comparatively little about Heaven. (Only a small number of the books on Heaven I've collected are still in print.)

Theologian Reinhold Niebuhr wrote an in-depth two-volume set titled *The Nature and Destiny of Man*. Remarkably, he had nothing to say about Heaven.[20]

William Shedd's three-volume *Dogmatic Theology* contains eighty-seven pages on eternal punishment, but only two on Heaven.[21]

> While Christians still accept heaven as an article of faith, their vigor in defining the nature of eternal life has much diminished. In spite of the current revival of religious interest in America and Europe, the desire to discuss the details of heavenly existence remains a low priority.
>
> **COLLEEN MCDANNELL and BERNHARD LANG**

In his nine-hundred-page theology, *Great Doctrines of the Bible*, Martyn Lloyd-Jones devotes less than two pages to the eternal state and the New Earth.[22]

Louis Berkhof's classic *Systematic Theology* devotes thirty-eight pages to creation, forty pages to baptism and communion, and fifteen pages to what theologians call "the intermediate state" (where people abide between death and resurrection). Yet it contains only two pages on Hell and one page on the eternal state.

When all that's said about the eternal Heaven is limited to page 737 of a 737-page systematic theology like Berkhof's, it raises a question: Does Scripture really have so little to say? Are there so few theological implications to this subject? The biblical answer, I believe, is an emphatic *no!*

In *The Eclipse of Heaven*, theology professor A. J. Conyers writes, "Even to one without religious commitment and theological convictions, it should be an unsettling thought that this world is attempting to chart its way through some of the most perilous waters in history, having now decided to ignore what was for nearly two millennia its fixed point of reference—its North Star. The certainty of judgment, the longing for heaven, the dread of hell: these are not prominent considerations in our modern discourse about the important matters of life. But they once were."[23]

Conyers argues that until recently the doctrine of Heaven was enormously important to the church.[24] Belief in Heaven was not just a nice auxiliary sentiment. It was a central, life-sustaining conviction.

Sadly, even for countless Christians, that is no longer true.

OFF OUR RADAR SCREENS

"An overwhelming majority of Americans continue to believe that there is life after death and that heaven and hell exist," according to a Barna Research Group poll.[25] But what people actually believe about Heaven and Hell varies widely. A Barna spokesman said, "They're cutting and pasting religious views from a variety of different sources—television, movies, conversations with their friends."[26] The result is a highly subjective theology of the afterlife, disconnected from the biblical doctrine of Heaven.

I attended a fine Bible college and seminary, but I learned very little about Heaven. I don't recall a single classroom discussion about the New Earth. In my Hebrews-to-Revelation class, we never made it to Revelation 21–22, the Bible's most definitive passage on the eternal Heaven. In my eschatology class, we studied various views of the Rapture and the Millennium, but almost no attention at all was given to the New Earth. In fact, I learned more about the strengths and weaknesses of belief in a mid-Tribulation Rapture than about Heaven and the New Earth combined.

Heaven suffers as a subject precisely because it comes last, not only in theological works but in seminary and Bible college classrooms. Teachers often get behind in their eschatology classes, enmeshed in the different views of Hell, Israel and the church, the Tribulation, and the Millennium. No time is left for discussing the new heavens and New Earth.

Imagine you're part of a NASA team preparing for a five-year mission to Mars. After a period of extensive training, the launch date finally arrives. As the rocket lifts off, one of your fellow astronauts says to you, "What do you know about Mars?"

Imagine shrugging your shoulders and saying, "Nothing. We never talked about it. I guess we'll find out when we get there." It's unthinkable, isn't it? It's inconceivable that your training would not have included extensive study of and preparation for your ultimate destination. Yet in seminaries, Bible schools, and churches across the United States and around the world, there is very little teaching about our ultimate destination: the new heavens and New Earth.

Many Christians who've gone to church all their adult lives (especially those under fifty) can't recall having heard a single sermon on Heaven. It's occasionally mentioned, but rarely emphasized, and *almost never* is it developed as a topic. We're told how to *get* to Heaven, and that it's a better destination than Hell, but we're taught remarkably little about Heaven itself.

Pastors may not think it's important to address the subject of Heaven because their seminary didn't have a required course on it—or even an elective. Similarly, when pastors don't preach on Heaven, their congregations assume that the Bible doesn't say much about it.

In 1937, Scottish theologian John Baillie wrote, "I will not ask how often during the last twenty-five years you and I have listened to an old-style warning against the flames of hell. I will not even ask how many sermons have been preached in our hearing about a future day of reckoning when men shall reap according as they have sown. It will be enough to ask how many preachers, during these years, have dwelt on the joys of heavenly rest with anything like the old ardent love and impatient longing."[27]

If this was the case then, how much truer is it now? Heaven has fallen off our radar screens. How can we set our hearts on Heaven when we have an impoverished theology of Heaven? How can we expect our children to be excited about Heaven—or to stay excited about it when they grow up? Why do we talk so little about Heaven? And why is the little we have to say so vague and lifeless?

WHERE DO WE GET OUR MISCONCEPTIONS?

I believe there's one central explanation for why so many of God's children have such a vague, negative, and uninspired view of Heaven: the work of Satan.

Jesus said of the devil, "When he lies, he speaks his native language, for he is a liar and the father of lies" (John 8:44). Some of Satan's favorite lies are about Heaven. Revelation 13:6 tells us the satanic beast "opened his mouth to blaspheme God, and to slander his name and his dwelling place and those who live in heaven." Our enemy slanders three things: God's person, God's people, and God's place—namely, Heaven.[†]

After being forcibly evicted from Heaven (Isaiah 14:12-15), the devil became bitter not only toward God, but toward mankind and toward Heaven itself, the place that was no longer his. It must be maddening for him that we're now entitled to the home he was kicked out of. What better way for the devil and his demons to attack us than to whisper lies about the very place on which God tells us to set our hearts and minds?

Satan need not convince us that Heaven doesn't exist. He need only convince us that Heaven is a place of boring, unearthly existence. If we believe that lie, we'll be robbed of our joy and anticipation, we'll set our minds on this life and not the next, and we won't be motivated to share our faith. Why should we share the "good news" that people can spend eternity in a boring, ghostly place that even *we're* not looking forward to?

In *The Country of the Blind*, H. G. Wells writes of a tribe in a remote valley deep in a towering mountain range. During a terrible epidemic, all the villagers lose their sight. Eventually, entire generations grow up having no awareness of sight or the world they're unable to see. Because of their handicap, they do not know their true condition, nor can they understand what their world looks like. They cannot imagine what realms might lie beyond their valley.

Spiritually speaking, we live in the Country of the Blind. The disease of sin has blinded us to God and Heaven, which are real yet unseen. Fortunately, Jesus has come to our valley from Heaven to tell us about his father, the world beyond, and the world to come. If we listen to him—which will require a concerted effort not to listen to the lies of the devil—we will never be the same. Nor will we ever want to be.

Satan hates the New Heaven and the New Earth as much as a deposed dictator hates the new nation and new government that replaces his. Satan cannot stop Christ's redemptive work, but he can keep us from seeing the breadth and depth of redemption that extends to the earth and beyond. He cannot keep Christ from defeating him, but he can persuade us that Christ's victory is only partial, that God will abandon his original plan for mankind and the earth.

[†]The NASB supplies words not in the original (here, in italics), which make the three things that Satan slanders appear to be only two: "And he opened his mouth in blasphemies against God, to blaspheme His name and His tabernacle, *that is*, those who dwell in heaven." It equates God's dwelling place, his Tabernacle, with the people who live in Heaven. Hence it retains the two familiar ideas of the objects of Satan's slander—God and his people—while not recognizing the less familiar one, God's dwelling place, Heaven. The NASB reading offers an alternative understanding of the passage.

Because Satan hates us, he's determined to rob us of the joy we'd have if we believed what God tells us about the magnificent world to come.

RESISTING NATURALISM'S SPELL

C. S. Lewis depicts another source of our misconceptions about Heaven: naturalism, the belief that the world can be understood in scientific terms, without recourse to spiritual or supernatural explanations.

In *The Silver Chair*, Puddleglum, Jill, and Eustace are captured in a sunless underground world by an evil witch who calls herself the queen of the underworld. The witch claims that her prisoners' memories of the overworld, Narnia, are but figments of their imagination. She laughs condescendingly at their child's game of "pretending" that there's a world above and a great ruler of that world.

When they speak of the sun that's visible in the world above, she asks them what a sun is. Groping for words, they compare it to a giant lamp. She replies, "When you try to think out clearly what this *sun* must be, you cannot tell me. You can only tell me it is like the lamp. Your *sun* is a dream; and there is nothing in that dream that was not copied from the lamp."

When they speak of Aslan the lion, king of Narnia, she says they have seen cats and have merely projected those images into the make-believe notion of a giant cat. They begin to waver.

The queen, who hates Aslan and wishes to conquer Narnia, tries to deceive them into thinking that whatever they cannot perceive with their senses must be imaginary—which is the essence of naturalism. The longer they are unable to see the world they remember, the more they lose sight of it.

She says to them, hypnotically, "There never was any world but mine," and they repeat after her, abandoning reason, parroting her deceptions. Then she coos softly, "There is no Narnia, no Overworld, no sky, no sun, no Aslan." This illustrates Satan's power to mold our weak minds as we are trapped in a dark, fallen world. We're prone to deny the great realities of God and Heaven, which we can no longer see because of the Curse.

Finally, when it appears they've succumbed to the queen's lies, Puddleglum breaks the spell and says to the enraged queen, "Suppose we *have* only dreamed, or made up, all those things—trees and grass and sun and moon and stars and Aslan himself. Suppose we have. Then all I can say is that . . . the made-up things seem a good deal more important than the real ones. Suppose this black pit of a kingdom of yours *is* the only world. Well, it strikes me as a pretty poor one. And that's a funny thing, when you come to think of it. We're just babies making up a game, if you're right. But four babies playing a game can make a play-world which licks your real world hollow."[28]

The truth is exactly the opposite of naturalism's premise—in fact, the dark world's lamps are copies of the sun, and its cats are copies of Aslan. Heaven isn't an extrapolation of earthly thinking; Earth is an extension of Heaven, made by the Creator King. The realm Puddleglum and the children believe in, Narnia and its sun and its universe, is real, and the witch's world—which she tempts them to believe is the only real world—is in fact a lesser realm, corrupted and in bondage.

When the queen's lies are exposed, she metamorphoses into the serpent she really is, whereupon Rilian, the human king and Aslan's appointed ruler of Narnia, slays her. The despondent slaves who'd lived in darkness are delivered. Light floods in, and their home below becomes a joyous place again because they realize there is indeed a bright world above and Aslan truly rules the universe. They laugh and celebrate, turning cartwheels and popping firecrackers.

Sometimes we're like Lewis's characters. We succumb to naturalistic assumptions that what we see is real and what we don't see isn't. God can't be real, we conclude, because we can't see him. And Heaven can't be real because we can't see it. But we must recognize our blindness. The blind must take by faith that there are stars in the sky. If they depend on their ability to see, they will conclude there are no stars.

We must work to resist the bewitching spell of naturalism. Sitting here in a dark world, we must remind ourselves what Scripture tells us about Heaven. We will one day be delivered from the blindness that separates us from the real world. We'll realize then the stupefying bewitchment we've lived under. By God's grace, may we stomp out the bewitching fires of naturalism so that we may clearly see the liberating truth about Christ the King and Heaven, his Kingdom.

CHAPTER 2

IS HEAVEN BEYOND
OUR IMAGINATION?

*To speak of "imagining heaven" does not imply or entail that heaven is a
fictional notion, constructed by deliberately disregarding the harsher realities
of the everyday world. It is to affirm the critical role of the God-given human
capacity to construct and enter into mental pictures of divine reality, which are
mediated through Scripture and the subsequent tradition of reflection and
development. We are able to inhabit the mental images we create, and thence
anticipate the delight of finally entering the greater reality to which they
correspond.*

Alister McGrath

When Marco Polo returned to Italy from the court of Kublai Khan, he described a world his audience had never seen—one that could not be understood without the eyes of imagination. Not that China was an imaginary realm, but it was very different from Italy. Yet as two locations on planet Earth inhabited by human beings, they had much in common. The reference points of Italy allowed a basis for understanding China, and the differences could be spelled out from there.[29]

The writers of Scripture present Heaven in many ways, including as a garden, a city, and a kingdom. Because gardens, cities, and kingdoms are familiar to us, they afford us a bridge to understanding Heaven. However, many people make the mistake of assuming that these are *merely* analogies with no actual correspondence to the reality of Heaven (which would make them poor analogies). Analogies can be pressed too far, but because Scripture makes it clear that Jesus is preparing a place for us, and God's Kingdom will come to Earth, and a physical resurrection awaits us, there is no reason to spiritualize or allegorize all earthly descriptions of Heaven. Indeed, some of them may be simple, factual statements. Too often we've been taught that Heaven is a non-physical realm, which cannot have real gardens, cities, kingdoms, buildings, banquets, or bodies. So we fail to take seriously what Scripture tells us about Heaven as a familiar, physical, tangible *place*.

As human beings, whom God made to be both physical and spiritual, we are not designed to live in a non-physical realm—indeed, we are incapable of even imagining such a place (or, rather, *non*-place). An incorporeal state is not only unfamiliar to our experience, it is also incompatible with our God-given constitution. We are not, as Plato supposed, merely spiritual beings temporarily encased in bodies. Adam did not become a "living being"—the Hebrew word *nephesh*—until he was both body *and* spirit (Genesis 2:7). We are physical beings as much as we are spiritual beings. That's why our bodily resurrection is essential to endow us with eternal righteous humanity, setting us free from sin, the Curse, and death.

THE IMPORTANCE OF USING OUR IMAGINATION

We cannot anticipate or desire what we cannot imagine. That's why, I believe, God has given us glimpses of Heaven in the Bible—to fire up our imagination and kindle a desire for Heaven in our hearts. And that's why Satan will always discourage our imagination—or misdirect it to ethereal notions that violate Scripture. As long as the resurrected universe remains either undesirable or unimaginable, Satan succeeds in sabotaging our love for Heaven.

After reading my novels that portray Heaven, people often tell me, "These pictures of Heaven are exciting. But are they based on Scripture?" The answer, to the best of my understanding, is yes. Scripture provides us with a substantial amount of information, direct and indirect, about the world to come, with enough detail to help us envision it, but not so much as to make us think we can completely wrap our minds around it. I believe that God expects us to use our imagination, even as we recognize its limitations and flaws. If God didn't want us to imagine what Heaven will be like, he wouldn't have told us as much about it as he has.

Rather than ignore our imagination, I believe we should fuel it with Scripture, allowing it to step through the doors that Scripture opens. I did not come to the Bible with the same view of Heaven that I came away with. On the contrary, as a young Christian, and even as a young pastor, I viewed Heaven in the same stereotypical ways I now reject. It was only through years of scriptural study, meditation, and research on the subject that I came to the view of Heaven I now embrace.

Nearly every notion of Heaven I present in this book was stimulated and reinforced by biblical texts. Though some of my interpretations and speculations are no doubt mistaken, they are not baseless. Rightly or wrongly, I have drawn most of them from my understanding of the explicit and implicit teachings of

Scripture. Discussions of Heaven tend to be either hyperimaginative or utterly unimaginative. Bible believers have tended toward the latter, yet both approaches are inadequate and dangerous. What we need is a biblically inspired imagination.

We should ask God's help to remove the blinders of our preconceived ideas about Heaven so we can understand Scripture. The apostle Paul said, "Reflect on what I am saying, for the Lord will give you insight into all this" (2 Timothy 2:7). I encourage you to pray, "Open my eyes that I may see wonderful things in your law" (Psalm 119:18).

I've collected more than 150 books on Heaven, many of them very old and out of print, and I've read nearly all of them. One thing I've found is that books about Heaven are notorious for saying we can't know what Heaven is like, but it will be more wonderful than we can imagine. However, the moment we say that we can't imagine Heaven, we dump cold water on all that God has revealed to us about our eternal home. If we can't envision it, we can't look forward to it. If Heaven is unimaginable, why even try?

Everything pleasurable we know about life on Earth we have experienced through our senses. So, when Heaven is portrayed as beyond the reach of our senses, it doesn't invite us; instead, it alienates and even frightens us. Our misguided attempts to make Heaven "sound spiritual" (i.e., non-physical) merely succeed in making Heaven sound unappealing.

PICTURING HEAVEN

By the time you finish reading this book, you will have a biblical basis for envisioning the eternal Heaven. You will understand that in order to get a picture of Heaven—which will one day be centered on the New Earth—you don't need to look up at the clouds; you simply need to look around you and imagine what all this would be like without sin and death and suffering and corruption.

When I anticipate my first glimpse of Heaven, I remember the first time I went snorkeling. I saw countless fish of every shape, size, and color. And just when I thought I'd seen the most beautiful fish, along came another even more striking. Etched in my memory is a certain sound—the sound of a gasp going through my rubber snorkel as my eyes were opened to that breathtaking underwater world.

I imagine our first glimpse of Heaven will cause us to similarly gasp in amazement and delight. That first gasp will likely be followed by many more as we continually encounter new sights in that endlessly wonderful place. And that will be just the beginning, because we will not see our real eternal home—

the New Earth—until after the resurrection of the dead. And it will be far better than anything we've seen.

So look out a window. Take a walk. Talk with your friend. Use your God-given skills to paint or draw or build a shed or write a book. But imagine it—all of it—in its original condition. The happy dog with the wagging tail, not the snarling beast, beaten and starved. The flowers unwilted, the grass undying, the blue sky without pollution. People smiling and joyful, not angry, depressed, and empty. If you're not in a particularly beautiful place, close your eyes and envision the most beautiful place you've ever been—complete with palm trees, raging rivers, jagged mountains, waterfalls, or snow drifts.

Think of friends or family members who loved Jesus and are with him now. Picture them with you, walking together in this place. All of you have powerful bodies, stronger than those of an Olympic decathlete. You are laughing, playing, talking, and reminiscing. You reach up to a tree to pick an apple or orange. You take a bite. It's so sweet that it's startling. You've never tasted anything so good. Now you see someone coming toward you. It's Jesus, with a big smile on his face. You fall to your knees in worship. He pulls you up and embraces you.

At last, you're with the person you were made for, in the place you were made to be. Everywhere you go there will be new people and places to enjoy, new things to discover. What's that you smell? A feast. A party's ahead. And you're invited. There's exploration and work to be done—and you can't wait to get started.

I have a biblical basis for all of these statements, and many more. After examining what Scripture says, I hope that next time you hear someone say, "We can't begin to imagine what Heaven will be like," you'll be able to tell them, "*I* can."

But before we go further, we need to address some frequently raised objections.

IF "NO EYE HAS SEEN," HOW CAN WE KNOW?

A pastor visiting my office asked what I was writing. "A big book on Heaven," I said.

"Well," he replied, "since Scripture says 'No eye has seen, no ear has heard, no mind has conceived what God has prepared for those who love him,' what will you be talking about? Obviously, we can't know what God has prepared for us in Heaven." (He was referring to 1 Corinthians 2:9.)

I said to him what I always say: "You didn't complete the sentence. You also have to read verse ten." Here's how the complete sentence reads: " 'No eye has seen, no ear has heard, no mind has conceived what God has prepared for those who love him'—*but God has revealed it to us by his Spirit*" (emphasis added). The context makes it clear that this revelation is God's Word (v. 13), which tells us what God has prepared for us. After reading a few dozen books about Heaven, I came to instinctively cringe whenever I saw 1 Corinthians 2:9. It's a wonderful verse; it's just that it's nearly always misused. It says *precisely the opposite* of what it's cited to prove![†]

What we otherwise could not have known about Heaven, because we're unable to see it, God says *he has revealed to us through his Spirit*. This means that God has explained to us what Heaven is like. Not exhaustively, but accurately. God tells us about Heaven in his Word, not so we can shrug our shoulders and remain ignorant, but because he wants us to understand and anticipate what awaits us.

Other verses are likewise pulled out to derail discussions about Heaven. For example, "The secret things belong to the Lord our God" (Deuteronomy 29:29). Heaven is regarded as a "secret thing." But the rest of the verse—again, rarely quoted—completes the thought: "But the things revealed belong to us and to our children forever."

We should accept that many things about Heaven are secret and that God has countless surprises in store for us. But as for the things God *has* revealed to us about Heaven, these things belong to us and to our children. It's critically important that we study and understand them. That is *precisely* why God revealed them to us!

> Although fundamentalists would discard the suggestion that heaven no longer is an active part of their belief system, eternal life has become an unknown place or a state of vague identity. Conservative Christians . . . do not return to the rich heavenly images of previous generations. The drama of the future is decidedly this-worldly; it occurs during the period before and during the millennium, not in a heavenly world.
>
> **COLLEEN MCDANNELL and BERNHARD LANG**

Another "silencer" is 2 Corinthians 12:2-4. Paul says that fourteen years earlier he was "caught up to paradise," where he "heard inexpressible things, things that man is not permitted to tell." Some people use this verse to say we

---

[†]Another problem with using 1 Corinthians 2:9 is that it isn't talking about Heaven. In its context, it refers to the salvation-related hidden wisdom of God. Some would argue that God's hidden wisdom broadly includes wisdom about Heaven, but my point is that even if the verse did refer to Heaven, it says the opposite of what it is typically cited to prove, because verse 10 indicates that God has *revealed* these hidden truths.

should not discuss what Heaven will be like. But all it says is that God didn't permit Paul to talk about his visit to Heaven. In contrast, God *commanded* the apostle John to talk about his prolonged visit to Heaven, which he did in detail in the book of Revelation. Likewise, Isaiah and Ezekiel wrote about what they saw in Heaven.

Although it's inappropriate for us to speculate on what Paul might have seen in Heaven, it's certainly appropriate to discuss what John saw, *because God chose to reveal it to us*. If he didn't intend for us to understand it, why would he bother telling us about it? (When was the last time you wrote someone a letter using words you didn't expect them to comprehend?) So, we *should* study, teach, and discuss God's revelation about Heaven given to us in his Word.

Certainly, not everything the Bible says about Heaven is easily envisioned. Consider Ezekiel's description of the living creatures and their wheels, and the manifestation of God's glory that leaves the prophet groping for words (Ezekiel 1:4-28). Still, many other passages concerning Heaven are much easier to grasp.

Isaiah 55:9 is another verse often cited in support of a "don't ask, don't tell" approach to Heaven: "As the heavens are higher than the earth, so are my ways higher than your ways and my thoughts than your thoughts." God's thoughts are indeed higher than ours, but when he reduces his thoughts into words and reveals them in Scripture, he expects us to study them, meditate on them, and understand them—again, not exhaustively, but accurately.

SETTING OUR HEARTS AND MINDS ON HEAVEN

"Set your hearts on things above, where Christ is seated at the right hand of God" (Colossians 3:1). This is a direct command to set our hearts on Heaven. And to make sure we don't miss the importance of a heaven-centered life, the next verse says, "Set your minds on things above, not on earthly things." God commands us to set our hearts and minds on Heaven.

To long for Christ is to long for Heaven, for that is where we will be with him. God's people are "longing for a better country" (Hebrews 11:16). We cannot set our eyes on Christ without setting our eyes on Heaven, and we cannot set our eyes on Heaven without setting our eyes on Christ. Still, it is not only Christ but "things above" we are to set our minds on.

The Greek word translated "set your hearts on" is *zeteo*, which "denotes man's general philosophical search or quest."[30] The same word is used in the Gospels to describe how "the Son of Man came to *seek* . . . what was lost" (Luke 19:10, emphasis added). It's also used for how a shepherd looks for his lost sheep (Matthew 18:12), a woman searches for a lost coin (Luke 15:8), and a merchant searches for a fine pearl (Matthew 13:45). It is a diligent, active, single-minded investigation. So we can understand Paul's admonition in Colossians 3:1 as follows: "Diligently, actively, single-mindedly pursue the things above"—in a word, *Heaven*. (Now you have a clear biblical reason for reading this book!)

The verb *zeteo* is in the present tense, suggesting an ongoing process. "Keep seeking heaven." Don't just have a conversation, read a book, or listen to a sermon and feel as if you've fulfilled the command. Since you'll spend the next lifetime living in Heaven, why not spend this lifetime seeking Heaven, so you can eagerly anticipate and prepare for it?

The command, and its restatement, implies there is nothing automatic about setting our minds on Heaven. In fact, most commands assume a resistance to obeying them, which sets up the necessity for the command. We are told to avoid sexual immorality because it is our tendency. We are not told to avoid jumping off buildings because normally we don't battle such a temptation. The command to think about Heaven is under attack in a hundred different ways every day. Everything militates against it. Our minds are so much set on Earth that we are unaccustomed to heavenly thinking. So we must work at it.

What have you been doing daily to set your mind on things above, to *seek* Heaven? What should you do differently?

Perhaps you're afraid of becoming "so heavenly minded you're of no earthly good." Relax—you have nothing to worry about! On the contrary, many of us are so earthly minded we are of no heavenly *or* earthly good. C. S. Lewis observed, "If you read history, you will find that the Christians who did most for the present world were just those who thought most of the next. The Apostles themselves, who set on foot the conversion of the Roman Empire, the great men who built up the Middle Ages, the English Evangelicals who abolished the Slave Trade, all left their mark on Earth, precisely because their minds were occupied with Heaven. It is since Christians have largely ceased to think of the other world that they have become so ineffective in this. Aim at Heaven and you will get earth 'thrown in': aim at earth and you will get neither."[31]

> Most of us find it very difficult to want "Heaven" at all—except in so far as "Heaven" means meeting again our friends who have died. One reason for this difficulty is that we have not been trained: our whole education tends to fix our minds on this world. Another reason is that when the real want for Heaven is present in us, we do not recognize it.
>
> **C. S. LEWIS**

We need a generation of heavenly minded people who see human beings and the earth itself not simply as they are, but as God intends them to be.

FUELING OUR IMAGINATION

We must begin by reasoning from God's revealed truth. But that reasoning will call upon us to use our Scripture-enhanced imagination. As a nonfiction writer and Bible teacher, I begin by seeing what Scripture actually says. As a novelist, I take that revelation and add to it the vital ingredient of imagination. As C. S. Lewis said, "While reason is the natural organ of truth, imagination is the organ of meaning."[32] In the words of Francis Schaeffer, "The Christian is the really free man—he is free to have imagination. This too is our heritage. The Christian is the one whose imagination should fly beyond the stars."[33]

Schaeffer always started with God's revealed truth. But he exhorted us to *let that truth fuel our imagination*. Imagination should not fly *away* from the truth but fly *upon* the truth.

If you're a Christian suffering with great pains and losses, Jesus says, "Be of good cheer" (John 16:33, NKJV). The new house is nearly ready for you. Moving day is coming. The dark winter is about to be magically transformed into spring. One day soon you will be home—for the first time. Until then, I encourage you to meditate on the Bible's truths about Heaven. May your imagination soar and your heart rejoice.

CHAPTER 3

IS HEAVEN OUR DEFAULT DESTINATION . . . OR IS HELL?

The safest road to hell is the gradual one—the gentle slope, soft underfoot, without sudden turnings, without milestones, without signposts.

C. S. Lewis

For every American who believes he's going to Hell, there are 120 who believe they're going to Heaven.[34] This optimism stands in stark contrast to Christ's words in Matthew 7:13-14: "Enter through the narrow gate. For wide is the gate and broad is the road that leads to destruction, and many enter through it. But small is the gate and narrow the road that leads to life, and only a few find it."

What would keep us out of Heaven is universal: "All have sinned and fall short of the glory of God" (Romans 3:23). Sin separates us from a relationship with God (Isaiah 59:2). God is so holy that he cannot allow sin into his presence: "Your eyes are too pure to look on evil; you cannot tolerate wrong" (Habakkuk 1:13). Because we are sinners, we are not entitled to enter God's presence. We cannot enter Heaven as we are.

So Heaven is *not* our default destination. No one goes there automatically. Unless our sin problem is resolved, the only place we will go is our true default destination . . . Hell.

I am addressing this issue now because throughout this book I will talk about being with Jesus in Heaven, being reunited with family and friends, and enjoying great adventures in Heaven. The great danger is that readers will *assume* they are headed for Heaven. Judging by what's said at most funerals, you'd think nearly *everyone's* going to Heaven, wouldn't you? But Jesus made it clear that most people are *not* going to Heaven: "Small is the gate and narrow the road that leads to life, and only a few find it."

We dare not "wait and see" when it comes to what's on the other side of death. We shouldn't just cross our fingers and hope that our names are written in the Book of Life (Revelation 21:27). We can know, we *should* know, before we die. And because we may die at any time, we need to know *now*—not next month or next year. "Why, you do not even know what will happen tomorrow. What is your life? You are a mist that appears for a little while and then vanishes" (James 4:14).

It's of paramount importance to make sure you are going to Heaven, not Hell. The voice that whispers, "There's no hurry; put this book down; you can always think about it later," is not God's voice. He says, "Now is the day of salvation" (2 Corinthians 6:2) and "Choose for yourselves this day whom you will serve" (Joshua 24:15).

HELL: HEAVEN'S AWFUL ALTERNATIVE

Hell will be inhabited by people who haven't received God's gift of redemption in Christ (Revelation 20:12-15). After Christ returns, there will be a resurrection of believers for eternal life in Heaven and a resurrection of unbelievers for eternal existence in Hell (John 5:28-29). The unsaved—everyone whose name is not written in the Lamb's Book of Life—will be judged by God according to the works they have done, which have been recorded in Heaven's books (Revelation 20:12-15). Because those works include sin, people on their own, without Christ, cannot enter the presence of a holy and just God and will be consigned to a place of everlasting destruction (Matthew 13:40-42). Christ will say to those who are not covered by his blood, "Depart from me, you who are cursed, into the eternal fire prepared for the devil and his angels" (Matthew 25:41).

Hell will not be like it's often portrayed in comic strips, a giant lounge where between drinks people tell stories of their escapades on Earth. Rather, it will be a place of utter misery (Matthew 13:42; 13:50; 22:13; 24:51; 25:30; Luke 13:28). It will be a place of conscious punishment for sins, with no hope of relief. This is why Dante, in the *Inferno*, envisioned this sign chiseled above Hell's gate: "Abandon every hope, you who enter."[35]

The reality of Hell should break our hearts and take us to our knees and to the doors of those without Christ. Today, however, even among many Bible believers, Hell has become "the *H* word," seldom named, rarely talked about. It doesn't even appear in many evangelistic booklets. It's common to deny or ignore the clear teaching of Scripture about Hell. Hell seems disproportionate, a divine overreaction. In the words of one professor and contributor to an evangelical publication, "I consider the concept of hell as endless torment in body and mind an outrageous doctrine. . . . How can Christians possibly project a deity of such cruelty and vindictiveness whose ways include inflicting everlasting torture upon his creatures, however sinful they may have been? Surely a God who would do such a thing is more nearly like Satan than like God."[36]

Many imagine that it is civilized, humane, and compassionate to deny the existence of an eternal Hell, but in fact it is arrogant that we, as creatures, would dare to take what we think is the moral high ground in opposition to what God the Creator has clearly revealed.

We don't want to believe that any others deserve eternal punishment, because if they do, so do we. But if we understood God's nature and ours, we would be shocked not that some people could go to Hell (where else would sinners go?), but that any would be permitted into Heaven. Unholy as we are, we are disqualified from saying that infinite holiness doesn't demand everlasting punishment. By denying the endlessness of Hell, we minimize Christ's work on the cross. Why? Because we lower the stakes of redemption. If Christ's crucifixion and resurrection didn't deliver us from an eternal Hell, his work on the cross is less heroic, less potent, less consequential, and thus less deserving of our worship and praise. As theologian William G. T. Shedd put it, "The doctrine of Christ's vicarious atonement logically stands or falls with that of eternal punishment."[37]

> I had far rather walk, as I do, in daily terror of eternity, than feel that this was only a children's game in which all the contestants would get equally worthless prizes in the end.
>
> **T. S. ELIOT**

Satan has obvious motives for fueling our denial of eternal punishment: He wants unbelievers to reject Christ without fear; he wants Christians to be unmotivated to share Christ; and he wants God to receive less glory for the radical nature of Christ's redemptive work.

WHAT DID JESUS SAY ABOUT HELL?

Many books deny Hell. Some embrace universalism, the belief that all people will ultimately be saved. Some consider Hell to be the invention of wild-eyed prophets obsessed with wrath. They argue that Christians should take the higher road of Christ's love. But this perspective overlooks a conspicuous reality: *In the Bible, Jesus says more than anyone else about Hell* (Matthew 10:28; 13:40-42; Mark 9:43-44). He refers to it as a literal place and describes it in graphic terms—including raging fires and the worm that doesn't die. Christ says the unsaved "will be thrown outside, into the darkness, where there will be weeping and gnashing of teeth" (Matthew 8:12). In his story of the rich man and Lazarus, Jesus taught that in Hell, the wicked suffer terribly, are fully conscious, retain their desires and memories and reasoning, long for relief, cannot be comforted, cannot leave their torment, and are bereft of hope (Luke 16:19-31). The Savior could not have painted a more bleak or graphic picture.

How long will Hell last? "They will go away to eternal punishment," Jesus said of the unrighteous, "but the righteous to eternal life" (Matthew 25:46). Here, in the same sentence, Christ uses the same word translated "eternal" (*aionos*) to describe the duration of *both* Heaven and Hell. Thus, if Heaven will be consciously experienced forever, Hell *must* be consciously experienced forever.

C. S. Lewis said, "I have met no people who fully disbelieved in Hell and also had a living and life-giving belief in Heaven."[38] The biblical teaching on both destinations stands or falls together.

If I had a choice, that is if Scripture were not so clear and conclusive, I would certainly not believe in Hell. Trust me when I say I do not *want* to believe in it. But if I make what I want—or what others want—the basis for my beliefs, then I am a follower of myself and my culture, not a follower of Christ. "There seems to be a kind of conspiracy," writes novelist Dorothy Sayers, "to forget, or to conceal, where the doctrine of hell comes from. The doctrine of hell is not 'mediaeval priestcraft' for frightening people into giving money to the church: it is Christ's deliberate judgment on sin. . . . We cannot repudiate Hell without altogether repudiating Christ."[39] In *The Problem of Pain*, C. S. Lewis writes of Hell, "There is no doctrine which I would more willingly remove from Christianity than this, if it lay in my power. But it has the full support of Scripture and, specially, of our Lord's own words; it has always been held by Christendom; and it has the support of reason."[40]

IS IT UNLOVING TO SPEAK OF HELL?

If you were giving some friends directions to Denver and you knew that one road led there but a second road ended at a sharp cliff around a blind corner, would you talk only about the safe road? No. You would tell them about both, especially if you knew that the road to destruction was wider and more traveled. In fact, it would be terribly unloving *not* to warn them about that other road.

For the same reason, we must not believe Satan's lie that it's unloving to speak to people about Hell. The most basic truth is that there are only two possible destinations after death: Heaven and Hell. Each is just as real and just as eternal as the other. Unless and until we surrender our lives to Jesus Christ, we're headed for Hell. The most loving thing we can do for our friends and our family is to warn them about the road that leads to destruction and tell them about the road that leads to life.

It would upset us, but would we think it unloving if a doctor told us we had a potentially fatal cancer? And would the doctor not tell us if the cancer could be eradicated? Why then do we not tell unsaved people about the cancer of sin and evil and how the inevitable penalty of eternal destruction can be avoided by the atoning sacrifice of Jesus Christ?

Teresa of Avila, a sixteenth-century Carmelite nun, had an agonizing vision of Hell. She later wrote of the torment she endured:

> I was terrified by all this, and, though it happened nearly six years ago, I still am as I write: even as I sit here, fear seems to be depriving my body of its natural warmth. I never recall any time when I have been suffering trials or pains and when everything that we can suffer on earth has seemed to me of the slightest importance by comparison with this. . . . It has been of the greatest benefit to me, both in taking from me all fear of the tribulations and disappointments of this life and also in strengthening me to suffer them and to give thanks to the Lord, Who, as I now believe, has delivered me from such terrible and never-ending torments.[41]

If we understood Hell even the slightest bit, none of us would ever say, "Go to Hell." It's far too easy to go to Hell. It requires no change of course, no navigational adjustments. We were born with our autopilot set toward Hell. It is nothing to take lightly—Hell is the single greatest tragedy in the universe.

God loves us enough to tell us the truth—there are two eternal destinations, not one, and we must choose the right path if we are to go to Heaven. All roads do not lead to Heaven. Only one does: Jesus Christ. He said, "No one comes to the Father except through me" (John 14:6). All other roads lead to Hell. The high stakes involved in the choice between Heaven and Hell will cause us to appreciate Heaven in deeper ways, never taking it for granted, and always praising God for his grace that delivers us from what we deserve and grants us forever what we don't.

EARTH: THE IN-BETWEEN WORLD

God and Satan are not equal opposites. Likewise, Hell is not Heaven's equal opposite. Just as God has no equal as a person, Heaven has no equal as a place.

Hell will be agonizingly dull, small, and insignificant, without company, purpose, or accomplishment. It will not have its own stories; it will merely be a footnote on history, a crack in the pavement. As the new universe moves gloriously onward, Hell and its occupants will exist in utter inactivity and insignificance, an eternal non-life of regret and—perhaps—diminishing personhood.

Scripture says of those who die without Jesus, "They will be punished with everlasting destruction and shut out from the presence of the Lord and from the majesty of his power" (2 Thessalonians 1:9). Because God is the source of all good, and Hell is the absence of God, Hell must also be the absence of all good. Likewise, community, fellowship, and friendship are good, rooted in the triune God himself. But in the absence of God, Hell will have no community, no camaraderie, no friendship. I don't believe Hell is a place where demons take delight in punishing people and where people commiserate over their fate. More likely, each person is in solitary confinement, just as the rich man is portrayed alone in Hell (Luke 16:22-23). Misery loves company, but there will be nothing to love in Hell.

Earth is an in-between world touched by both Heaven and Hell. Earth leads directly into Heaven or directly into Hell, affording a choice between the two. The best of life on Earth is a glimpse of Heaven; the worst of life is a glimpse of Hell. For Christians, this present life is the closest they will come to Hell. For unbelievers, it is the closest they will come to Heaven.

> Resolved, that I will live so as I shall wish I had done when I come to die. . . . Resolved, to endeavor to my utmost to act as I can think I should do, if, I had already seen the happiness of heaven, and hell torments.
>
> **JONATHAN EDWARDS**

The reality of the choice that lies before us in this life is both wonderful and awful. Given the reality of our two possible destinations, shouldn't we be willing to pay any price to avoid Hell and go to Heaven? And yet, the price has already been paid. "You were bought at a price" (1 Corinthians 6:20). The price paid was exorbitant—the shed blood of God's Son, Jesus Christ.

Consider the wonder of it: God determined that he would rather go to Hell on our behalf than live in Heaven without us. He so much wants us *not* to go to Hell that he paid a horrible price on the cross so that we wouldn't have to.

As it stands, however, apart from Christ, our eternal future will be spent in Hell.

Jesus asks a haunting question in Mark 8:36-37: "What good is it for a man to gain the whole world, yet forfeit his soul? Or what can a man give in exchange for his soul?"

The price has been paid. But still, we must choose. Like any gift, forgiveness can be offered, but it isn't ours until we choose to receive it. A convicted criminal can be offered a pardon by the governor, but if he or she rejects the pardon, it's not valid. A pardon must be accepted. Similarly, Christ offers each of us the gift of forgiveness and eternal life—but just because the offer is made doesn't make it ours. To have it, we must choose to accept it.

But is it really possible to know you will go to Heaven when you die? Before diving further into the subject of Heaven, we'll address this question in the following chapter.

CHAPTER 4

CAN YOU KNOW YOU'RE GOING TO HEAVEN?

Soon you will read in the newspaper that I am dead. Don't believe it for a moment. I will be more alive than ever before.

D. L. Moody

Earth recedes. . . . Heaven opens before me!

D. L. Moody (on his deathbed)

Ancient cities kept rolls of their citizens. Guards were posted at the city gates to keep out criminals and enemies by checking their names against the list. This is the context for Revelation 21:27: "Nothing impure will ever enter [the city], nor will anyone who does what is shameful or deceitful, but only those whose names are written in the Lamb's book of life."

Ruthanna Metzgar, a professional singer, tells a story that illustrates the importance of having our names written in the book. Several years ago, she was asked to sing at the wedding of a very wealthy man. According to the invitation, the reception would be held on the top two floors of Seattle's Columbia Tower, the Northwest's tallest skyscraper. She and her husband, Roy, were excited about attending.

At the reception, waiters in tuxedos offered luscious hors d'oeuvres and exotic beverages. The bride and groom approached a beautiful glass and brass staircase that led to the top floor. Someone ceremoniously cut a satin ribbon draped across the bottom of the stairs. They announced the wedding feast was about to begin. Bride and groom ascended the stairs, followed by their guests.

At the top of the stairs, a maitre d' with a bound book greeted the guests outside the doors.

"May I have your name please?"

"I am Ruthanna Metzgar and this is my husband, Roy."

He searched the *M*'s. "I'm not finding it. Would you spell it please?"

Ruthanna spelled her name slowly. After searching the book, the maitre d' looked up and said, "I'm sorry, but your name isn't here."

"There must be some mistake," Ruthanna replied. "I'm the singer. I sang for this wedding!"

The gentleman answered, "It doesn't matter who you are or what you did. Without your name in the book you cannot attend the banquet."

He motioned to a waiter and said, "Show these people to the service elevator, please."

The Metzgars followed the waiter past beautifully decorated tables laden with shrimp, whole smoked salmon, and magnificent carved ice sculptures. Adjacent to the banquet area, an orchestra was preparing to perform, the musicians all dressed in dazzling white tuxedos.

The waiter led Ruthanna and Roy to the service elevator, ushered them in, and pushed G for the parking garage.

After locating their car and driving several miles in silence, Roy reached over and put his hand on Ruthanna's arm. "Sweetheart, what happened?"

"When the invitation arrived, I was busy," Ruthanna replied. "I never bothered to RSVP. Besides, I was the singer. Surely I could go to the reception without returning the RSVP!"

Ruthanna started to weep—not only because she had missed the most lavish banquet she'd ever been invited to, but also because she suddenly had a small taste of what it will be like someday for people as they stand before Christ and find their names are not written in the Lamb's Book of Life.[42]

Throughout the ages, countless people have been too busy to respond to Christ's invitation to his wedding banquet. Many assume that the good they've done—perhaps attending church, being baptized, singing in the choir, or helping in a soup kitchen—will be enough to gain entry to Heaven. But people who do not respond to Christ's invitation to forgive their sins are people whose names aren't written in the Lamb's Book of Life. To be denied entrance to Heaven's wedding banquet will not just mean going down the service elevator to the garage. It will mean being cast outside into Hell, forever.

In that day, no explanation or excuse will count. All that will matter is whether our names are written in the book. If they're not, we'll be turned away.

Have you said yes to Christ's invitation to join him at the wedding feast and spend eternity with him in his house? If so, you have reason to rejoice—Heaven's gates will be open to you.

If you have been putting off your response, your RSVP, or if you presume that you can enter Heaven without responding to Christ's invitation, one day you will deeply regret it.

PREPARING FOR THE JOURNEY

An Indiana cemetery has a tombstone, more than one hundred years old, with the following epitaph:

> *Pause, stranger, when you pass me by:*
> *As you are now, so once was I.*
> *As I am now, so you will be.*
> *So prepare for death and follow me.*

An unknown passerby scratched these additional words on the tombstone:

> *To follow you I'm not content,*
> *Until I know which way you went.*[43]

Can we really know in advance where we're going when we die? The apostle John, the same one who wrote about the new heavens and New Earth, said in one of his letters, "I write these things to you who believe in the name of the Son of God so that *you may know that you have eternal life*" (1 John 5:13, emphasis added). We *can* know for sure that we have eternal life. We can know for sure that we will go to Heaven when we die.

Do you?

People who want to get to Florida don't simply get in the car and start driving, hoping the road will somehow get them there. Instead, they look at a map and chart their course. They do this in advance, rather than waiting until they arrive at the wrong destination or discover they've spent three days driving the wrong direction. If you want to get somewhere, guesswork is a poor strategy. The goal of getting to Heaven is worthy of greater advanced planning than we would give to any other journey—yet some people spend far more time preparing for a trip to Disney World.

Many books on Heaven seem to assume every reader is Heaven-bound. The Bible says otherwise. I owe it to all my readers to share with them God's map to Heaven and offer them his Good News.

WHAT YOU NEED TO KNOW AND DO

To sin is to fall short of God's holy standards. Sin is what ended Eden's Paradise. And all of us, like Adam and Eve, are sinners. *You* are a sinner. That's the first thing you need to know. Sin deceives us and makes us think that wrong is right and right is wrong (Proverbs 14:12).

Sin has consequences, but God has provided a solution for our sin: "The wages of sin is death, but the gift of God is eternal life in Christ Jesus our Lord" (Romans 6:23). Jesus Christ, the Son of God, loved us so much that he became a man to deliver us from our sin (John 3:16). He came to identify with us in our humanity and our weakness, but he did so without being tainted by our sin, self-deception, and moral failings (Hebrews 2:17-18; 4:15-16).

We're told that "God made him [Christ] who had no sin to be sin for us, so that in him we might become the righteousness of God" (2 Corinthians 5:21). This means that even though we are under God's wrath for our sins, Jesus died on the cross as our representative, our substitute. God then poured out his wrath on Christ instead of on us. Christ, who stood in our place, conveyed his righteousness to us so that we are declared innocent of all our sins and declared righteous, so we may enter the very presence of God in Heaven and be at home with him there.

No other prophet or religious figure—only Jesus, the Son of God—is worthy to pay the penalty for our sins demanded by God's holiness (Revelation 5:4-5, 9-10). Only when our sins are dealt with in Christ can we enter Heaven. We cannot pay our own way. "Salvation is found in no one else [but Jesus], for there is no other name under heaven given to men by which we must be saved" (Acts 4:12).

Being himself God and therefore all-powerful, Jesus Christ rose from the grave, defeating sin and conquering death (1 Corinthians 15:3-4, 54-57). When Christ died on the cross for us, he said, "It is finished" (John 19:30). The Greek word translated "it is finished" was commonly written across certificates of debt when they were canceled. It meant "paid in full." Christ died so that the certificate of debt, consisting of all our sins, could once and for all be marked "paid in full."

Because of Jesus Christ's sacrificial death on the cross on our behalf, God freely offers us forgiveness. "He does not treat us as our sins deserve or repay us according to our iniquities. . . . As far as the east is from the west, so far has he removed our transgressions from us" (Psalm 103:10-12).

Forgiveness is not automatic. If we want to be forgiven, we must recognize and repent of our sins: "He who conceals his sins does not prosper, but whoever confesses and renounces them finds mercy" (Proverbs 28:13). Forgiveness is established by our confession: "If we confess our sins, he is faithful and just and will forgive us our sins and purify us from all unrighteousness" (1 John 1:9).

Christ offers to everyone the gift of forgiveness, salvation, and eternal life: "Whoever is thirsty, let him come; and whoever wishes, let him take the free gift of the water of life" (Revelation 22:17).

There's no righteous deed we can do that will earn us a place in Heaven (Titus 3:5). We come to Christ empty-handed. We can take no credit for salvation: "For it is by grace you have been saved, through faith—and this not from yourselves, it is the gift of God—not by works, so that no one can boast" (Ephesians 2:8-9).

This gift cannot be worked for, earned, or achieved in any sense. It's not dependent on our merit or effort but solely on Christ's generous and sufficient sacrifice on our behalf. Ultimately, God's greatest gift is himself. We don't just need salvation, we need Jesus the Savior. It is the person, God, who graciously gives us the place, Heaven.

JOINING THE BODY OF CHRIST: THE CHURCH

You may think that you don't deserve forgiveness after all you've done. That's exactly right. *No one* deserves forgiveness. If we deserved it, we wouldn't need it. That's the point of grace. On the cross, Jesus experienced the Hell we deserve, so that for eternity we can experience the Heaven we don't deserve.

Once forgiven, we can look forward to spending eternity in Heaven with Christ and our spiritual family (John 14:1-3; Revelation 20:11–22:6). We need never fear that God will find a skeleton in our closet and say, "If I'd known you did *that*, I wouldn't have let you into Heaven." Every sin is washed away by the blood of Christ. Moreover, God is all-knowing. He has seen us at our worst and still loves us. No sin is bigger than the Savior. If God wasn't willing to forgive sin on the basis of Christ's sacrifice, Heaven would be empty.

Jesus said, "Watch out that no one deceives you" (Matthew 24:4). There are countless groups, religious and secular, that will assure you Heaven is your automatic destination or that it can be attained by your hard work and abstention from certain sins. This is false—there is no salvation except by Jesus and his redemptive work.

False teachers can be attractive and persuasive, often quoting the Bible out of context. But they should be rejected because they contradict God's Word (Acts 17:11). False doctrine is one reason the Christian life should not and cannot be lived in isolation. We must become part of a family of Christians called a church, where God's Word is believed and taught. You may feel self-conscious around other Christians because of your past. You shouldn't. A Christ-centered church is not a showcase for saints but a hospital for sinners. The people you're joining are human, imperfect, and needy. Most church people aren't self-righteous. Those who are should be pitied, because they don't understand God's grace.

A good church will teach God's Word and provide love, help, and support. If you have further questions about Jesus and about Heaven, you can find answers there. (If you're looking for such a church in your area but can't find one, use the address at the end of this book to contact our organization, and we'll gladly help you.)

To those who presumed they would go to Heaven because they were religious, Jesus said, "Not everyone who says to me, 'Lord, Lord,' will enter the kingdom of Heaven, but only he who does the will of my Father who is in heaven. Many will say to me on that day, 'Lord, Lord, did we not prophesy in your name, and in your name drive out demons and perform many miracles?' Then I will tell them plainly, 'I never knew you. Away from me, you evildoers!'" (Matthew 7:21-23). Those who assume their religious activities alone will get them to Heaven have a terrible surprise ahead.

Do not merely assume that you are a Christian and are going to Heaven. Make the conscious decision to accept Christ's sacrificial death on your behalf. When you choose to accept Christ and surrender control of your life to him, you can be certain that your name is written in the Lamb's Book of Life.

WATER FOR THE THIRSTY

After showing us the new heavens and New Earth, Jesus says near the end of the Bible, "I am the Alpha and the Omega, the Beginning and the End. To him who is thirsty I will give to drink without cost from the spring of the water of life" (Revelation 21:6). But then Jesus adds these sobering words: "He who overcomes will inherit all this, and I will be his God and he will be my son. But the cowardly, the unbelieving, the vile, the murderers, the sexually

> There have been times when I think we do not desire heaven but more often I find myself wondering whether, in our heart of hearts, we have ever desired anything else.
>
> **C. S. LEWIS**

immoral, those who practice magic arts, the idolaters and all liars—their place will be in the fiery lake of burning sulfur" (Revelation 21:7-8).

For those who know Christ, their place is Heaven. For those who do not know Christ, their place is Hell. Jesus said, "I am the way and the truth and the life. No one comes to the Father except through me" (John 14:6). There is no middle ground. Either you are a follower of Jesus or you are not. Christ said, "He who is not with me is against me" (Luke 11:23).

The Bible ends with yet one more invitation, suggesting that God wants to give every reader one last chance: "The Spirit and the bride say, 'Come!' And let him who hears say, 'Come!' Whoever is thirsty, let him come; and whoever wishes, let him take the free gift of the water of life" (Revelation 22:17). It is

Jesus—and Heaven—we thirst for. Jesus and Heaven are offered to us at no cost because he already paid the price for us.

God invites you to come. The church invites you to come. As a follower of Jesus, I invite you to come.

Why would you not come? What reason could be good enough to turn away from Jesus and from eternal life in the new heavens and New Earth? In the words of C. S. Lewis, "All your life an unattainable ecstasy has hovered just beyond the grasp of your consciousness. The day is coming when you will wake to find, beyond all hope, that you have attained it, or else, that it was within your reach and you have lost it forever."[44]

You are made for a person and a place. Jesus is the person. Heaven is the place. They are a package—you cannot get Heaven without Jesus or Jesus without Heaven. We will explore Heaven's joys and wonders throughout this book. But we dare not presume we can enter Heaven apart from Christ.

"Seek the Lord while he may be found; call on him while he is near" (Isaiah 55:6).

Have you confessed your sins? asked Christ to forgive you? placed your trust in Christ's death and resurrection on your behalf? asked Jesus to be your Lord and empower you to follow him?

Wouldn't it be tragic if you read this book on Heaven but didn't get to go there?

UNDERSTANDING THE PRESENT HEAVEN

CHAPTER 5

WHAT IS THE NATURE OF
THE PRESENT HEAVEN?

Pippin: "I didn't think it would end this way . . ."
Gandalf: "End? No, the journey doesn't end here. Death is just another path
. . . one that we all must take. The grey rain-curtain of this world rolls back,
and all turns to silver glass . . . and then you see it."
Pippin: "What? Gandalf? See what?"
Gandalf: "White shores . . . and beyond. The far green country under a swift
sunrise."
Pippin: "Well, that isn't so bad."
Gandalf: "No . . . no, it isn't."

Peter Jackson's film The Return of the King

The apostle Paul considered it vital for us to know what happens when we die: "Brothers, we do not want you to be ignorant about those who fall asleep, or to grieve like the rest of men, who have no hope" (1 Thessalonians 4:13).

Using the euphemism "those who fall asleep," Paul speaks of those who have died. If we are alive at Christ's return, he assures us we will be "caught up together with them in the clouds to meet the Lord in the air. And so we will be with the Lord forever. Therefore encourage each other with these words" (1 Thessalonians 4:17-18).

Most of this book will be centered on the eternal Heaven—the place where we will live forever after the final resurrection. But because we've all had loved ones die, and we ourselves will die unless Christ returns first, we should consider what Scripture teaches about the present Heaven—the place Christians go when they die.

THE TEMPORARY NATURE OF THE PRESENT HEAVEN

When a Christian dies, he or she enters into what is referred to in theology as the intermediate state, a transitional period between our past lives on Earth and our future resurrection to life on the New Earth. Usually when we refer to "Heaven," we mean the place that Christians go when they die. This is what I am calling the *present* or intermediate Heaven. When we tell our children "Grandma's now in Heaven," we're referring to the present Heaven.

By definition, an intermediate state or location is *temporary*. Life in the Heaven we go to when we die, where we'll dwell prior to our bodily resurrection, is "better by far" than living here on Earth under the Curse, away from the direct presence of God (Philippians 1:23). Still, the intermediate or present Heaven is *not* our final destination. Though it will be a wonderful place, the present Heaven is not the place we are made for—the place God promises to refashion for us to live in forever. God's children are destined for life as resurrected beings on a resurrected Earth. We must not lose sight of our true destination. If we do, we'll be confused and disoriented in our thinking about where, and in what form, we will spend eternity.

WILL WE LIVE IN HEAVEN FOREVER?

The answer to the question, Will we live in Heaven forever? depends on what we mean by Heaven. Will we be with the Lord forever? Absolutely. Will we always be with him in exactly the same place that Heaven is now? No. In the present Heaven, we'll be in Christ's presence, and we'll be joyful, but we'll be looking forward to our bodily resurrection and permanent relocation to the New Earth.

It bears repeating because it is so commonly misunderstood: *When we die, believers in Christ will not go to the Heaven where we'll live forever.* Instead, we'll go to an intermediate Heaven. In that Heaven—where those who died covered by Christ's blood are now—we'll await the time of Christ's return to the earth, our bodily resurrection, the final judgment, and the creation of the new heavens and New Earth. If we fail to grasp this truth, we will fail to understand the biblical doctrine of Heaven.

It may seem strange to say that the Heaven we go to at death isn't eternal, yet it's true. "Christians often talk about living with God 'in heaven' forever," writes theologian Wayne Grudem. "But in fact the biblical teaching is richer than that: it tells us that there will be new heavens and a new earth—an entirely renewed creation—and we will live with God there. . . . There will also be a new kind of unification of heaven and earth. . . . There will be a joining of heaven and earth in this new creation."[45]

Let me suggest an analogy to illustrate the difference between the present Heaven and the eternal Heaven. Suppose you lived in a homeless shelter in Miami. One day you inherit a beautiful house, fully furnished, on a gorgeous hillside overlooking Santa Barbara, California. With the home comes a wonderful job doing something you've always wanted to do. Not only that, but you'll also be near close family members who moved from Miami many years ago.

On your flight to Santa Barbara, you'll change planes in Dallas, where you'll spend an afternoon. Some other family members, whom you haven't seen in years, will meet you at the Dallas airport and board the plane with you to Santa Barbara. You look forward to seeing them.

Now, when the Miami ticket agent asks you, "Where are you headed?" would you say "Dallas"? No. You would say Santa Barbara, because that's your final destination. If you mentioned Dallas at all, you would only say, "I'm going to Santa Barbara *by way of* Dallas."

When you talk to your friends in Miami about where you're going to live, would you focus on Dallas? No. You might not even mention Dallas, even though you will be a Dallas-dweller for several hours. Even if you spent a week in Dallas, it wouldn't be your focus. Dallas is just a stop along the way. Your true destination—your new permanent home—is Santa Barbara.

> At the age of eighty-three I asked myself what I knew about the home of God, and I was truly shocked to admit I knew very little. . . . Increasing age and the fact that I shall soon be making my own pilgrimage, have begotten within my soul an intense desire to explore this fascinating subject.
>
> **IVOR POWELL**

Similarly, the Heaven we will go to when we die, the present Heaven, is a temporary dwelling place, a stop along the way to our final destination: the New Earth.

Another analogy is more precise but difficult to imagine, because for most of us it's outside our experience. Imagine leaving the homeless shelter in Miami and flying to the intermediate location, Dallas, and then turning around and *going back home* to your place of origin, which has been completely renovated—a New Miami. In this New Miami, you would no longer live in a homeless shelter, but in a beautiful house in a glorious pollution-free, crime-free, sin-free city. So you would end up living not in a different home, but in *a radically improved version of your old home.*

This is what the Bible promises us—we will live with Christ and each other forever, not in the intermediate, or present, Heaven, but on the New Earth, where God will be at home with his people.

DOES HEAVEN REALLY CHANGE?

Only God is eternal and self-existent. All else is created. Heaven is not synonymous with God, nor is it part of his essential being. Therefore, God must have created Heaven. It is not a place where he *must* dwell, but it is where he *chooses* to dwell. Because Heaven is a place where angels live, where finite beings come and go, it appears to be a finite environment, a specific location.

Because God created Heaven, it had a beginning and is therefore neither timeless nor changeless. It had a past (the time prior to Christ's incarnation, death, and resurrection), it has a present (the Heaven where believers go when they die), and it will have a future (the eternal Heaven, or New Earth). The past Heaven, the present Heaven, and the future or eternal Heaven can all be called Heaven, yet *they are not synonymous*, even though they are all God's dwelling places.

Books on Heaven often fail to distinguish between the intermediate and eternal states, using the one word—*Heaven*—as all-inclusive. But this has dulled our thinking and keeps us from understanding important biblical distinctions. In this book, when referring to the place believers go after death, I use terms such as *the present Heaven* or *the intermediate Heaven*. I'll refer to the eternal state as *the eternal Heaven* or *the New Earth*. I hope you can see why this is such an important distinction. The present Heaven is a temporary lodging, a waiting place until the return of Christ and our bodily resurrection. The eternal Heaven, the New Earth, is our true home, the place where we will live forever with our Lord and each other. The great redemptive promises of God will find their ultimate fulfillment on the New Earth, not in the present Heaven.

When we speak about the future New Earth, as we'll do in most of this book, much of what we say about it may not be true of the intermediate Heaven. (For instance, we will eat and drink in our resurrection bodies on the New Earth, but that doesn't mean people eat and drink in the present Heaven.) And when we describe the present Heaven, it will not necessarily correspond with what the eternal Heaven, the New Earth, will be like. Once we abandon our assumptions that Heaven cannot change, it all makes sense. *God* does not change; he's immutable. But God clearly says that Heaven *will* change. It will eventually be relocated to the New Earth (Revelation 21:1). Similarly, what we now refer to as Hell will also be relocated. After the Great White Throne Judgment, Hell will be cast into the eternal lake of fire (Revelation 20:14-15).

DISTINGUISHING THE PRESENT AND FUTURE HEAVENS

The questions, What is Heaven like? and, What *will* Heaven be like? have two different answers. The present, intermediate Heaven is in the angelic realm, distinctly separate from Earth (though as we'll see, likely having more physical qualities than we might assume). By contrast, the future Heaven will be in the human realm, on Earth. Then the dwelling place of God will also be the dwelling place of humanity, in a resurrected universe: "I saw a new heaven and a new earth. . . . I saw the Holy City, the new Jerusalem, coming down out of heaven from God. . . . And I heard a loud voice from the throne saying, 'Now the dwelling of God is with men, and he will live with them. They will be his people, and God himself will be with them and be their God'" (Revelation 21:1-3). Heaven, God's dwelling place, will one day be on the New Earth.

Notice that the New Jerusalem, which *was* in Heaven, will come down out of Heaven from God. Where does it go? To the New Earth. From that time on, "the dwelling of God" will be with redeemed mankind *on Earth*.

Some would argue that the New Earth shouldn't be called Heaven. But it seems clear to me that if God's special dwelling place is by definition Heaven, and we're told that "the dwelling of God" will be with mankind on Earth, then Heaven and the New Earth will be essentially the same place. We're told that "the throne of God and of the Lamb" is in the New Jerusalem, which is brought down to the New Earth (Revelation 22:1). Again, it seems clear that wherever God dwells with his people and sits on his throne would be called Heaven.

I concur with theologian Anthony Hoekema, who writes, "The 'new Jerusalem' . . . does not remain in a 'heaven' far off in space, but it comes down to the renewed earth; there the redeemed will spend eternity in resurrection bodies. So heaven and earth, now separated, will then be merged: the new earth will also be heaven, since God will dwell there with his people. Glorified believers, in other words, will continue to be in heaven while they are inhabiting the new earth."[46]

That God would come down to the New Earth to live with us fits perfectly with his original plan. God could have taken Adam and Eve up to Heaven to visit with him in his world. Instead, he came down to walk with them in their world (Genesis 3:8). Jesus says of anyone who would be his disciple, "My Father will love him, and we will come to him and make our home with him" (John 14:23). This is a picture of God's ultimate plan—not to take us up to live in a realm made for him, but to come down and live with us *in the realm he made for us.*

Most views of Heaven are anti-incarnational. They fail to grasp that Heaven will be God dwelling with us—resurrected people—on the resurrected

Earth. The Incarnation is about God inhabiting space and time as a human being—the new heavens and New Earth are about God making space and time his *eternal* home. As Jesus is God incarnate, so the New Earth will be Heaven incarnate. Think of what Revelation 21:3 tells us—God will relocate his people and come down from Heaven to the New Earth to live with them: "God himself will be with them." Rather than our going up to live in God's home forever, *God will come down* to live in *our* home forever. Simply put, though the present Heaven is "up there," the future, eternal Heaven will be "down here." If we fail to see that distinction, we fail to understand God's plan and are unable to envision what our eternal lives will look like.

Several books on Heaven state that the New Jerusalem will not descend to Earth but will remain "suspended over the earth."[47] But Revelation 21:2 doesn't say this. When John watches the city "coming down" from Heaven, there's no reason to believe it stops before reaching the New Earth. The assumption that it remains suspended over the earth arises from the notion that Heaven and Earth must always be separate. But Scripture indicates they will be joined. Their present incompatibility is due to a temporary aberration—Earth is under sin and the Curse. Once that aberration is corrected, Heaven and Earth will be fully compatible again (Ephesians 1:10).

Utopian idealists who dream of mankind creating "Heaven on Earth" are destined for disappointment. But though they are wrong in believing that humans can achieve a utopian existence apart from God, the reality of Heaven on Earth—God dwelling with mankind in the world he made for us—will in fact be realized. It is *God's* dream. It is God's plan. He—not we—will accomplish it.

DO WE REMAIN CONSCIOUS AFTER DEATH?

"The dust returns to the ground it came from, and the spirit returns to God who gave it" (Ecclesiastes 12:7). At death, the human spirit goes either to Heaven or Hell. Christ depicted Lazarus and the rich man as conscious in Heaven and Hell immediately after they died (Luke 16:22-31). Jesus told the dying thief on the cross, "Today you will be with me in paradise" (Luke 23:43). The apostle Paul said that to die was to be with Christ (Philippians 1:23), and to be absent from the body was to be present with the Lord (2 Corinthians 5:8). After their deaths, martyrs are pictured in Heaven, crying out to God to bring justice on Earth (Revelation 6:9-11).

These passages make it clear that there is no such thing as "soul sleep," or a long period of unconsciousness between life on Earth and life in Heaven. The phrase "fallen asleep" (in 1 Thessalonians 4:13 and similar passages) is a euphemism for death, describing the body's outward appearance. The spirit's depar-ture from the body ends our existence on Earth. The physical part of us "sleeps" until the resurrection, while the spiritual part of us relocates to a conscious exis-tence in Heaven (Daniel 12:2-3; 2 Corinthians 5:8). Some Old Testament pas-sages (e.g., Ecclesiastes 9:5) address outward appearances and do not reflect the fullness of New Testament revelation concerning immediate relocation and consciousness after death.

Every reference in Revelation to human beings talking and worshiping in Heaven prior to the resurrection of the dead demonstrates that our spiritual be-ings are conscious, not sleeping, after death. (Nearly everyone who believes in soul sleep believes that souls are disembodied at death; it's not clear how dis-embodied beings *could* sleep, because sleeping involves a physical body.)

WILL WE BE JUDGED WHEN WE DIE?

When we die, we face judgment, what is called the judgment of faith. The out-come of this judgment determines whether we go to the present Heaven or the present Hell. This initial judgment depends not on our works but on our faith. It is not about what we've done during our lives but about what Christ has done for us. If we have accepted Christ's atoning death for us, then when God judges us after we die, he sees his Son's sacrifice for us, not our sin. Salvation is a free gift, to which we can contribute absolutely nothing (Ephesians 2:8-9; Titus 3:5).

This first judgment is not to be confused with the final judgment, or what is called the judgment of works. Both believers and unbelievers face a final judg-ment. The Bible indicates that all believers will stand before the judgment seat of Christ to give an account of their lives (Romans 14:10-12; 2 Corinthians 5:10). It's critical to understand that this judgment is a judgment of works, not of faith (1 Corinthians 3:13-14). Our works do not affect our salvation, but they do affect our reward. Rewards are about our work for God, empowered by his Spirit. Rewards are conditional, dependent on our faithfulness (2 Timothy 2:12; Revelation 2:26-28; 3:21).[†]

Unbelievers face a final judgment of works as well. The Bible tells us it will come at the great white throne, at the end of the old Earth and just before the beginning of the New Earth (Revelation 20:11-13).

[†]I deal at length with the topic of eternal rewards in my books *In Light of Eternity* (Colorado Springs: WaterBrook, 1999), *Money, Possessions, and Eternity* (Wheaton, Ill.: Tyndale, 2003), and *The Law of Rewards* (Wheaton, Ill.: Tyndale, 2003).

Opinions vary about when the judgment of works for believers will occur. Some people picture it occurring immediately after the judgment of faith, a "one at a time" judgment happening as each believer dies. Others think it happens in the present Heaven, between our death and the return of Christ. Those who believe in a pretribulational Rapture often envision the judgment of works happening between the Rapture and the physical return of Christ, while the Tribulation is taking place on Earth. Still others believe it happens at the same time as the Great White Throne Judgment of unbelievers, after the Millennium.

IS THE PRESENT HEAVEN PART OF OUR UNIVERSE OR ANOTHER?

The present Heaven is normally invisible to those living on Earth. For those who have trouble accepting the reality of an unseen realm, consider the perspective of cutting-edge researchers who embrace string theory. Scientists at Yale, Princeton, and Stanford, among others, postulate that there are ten unobservable dimensions and likely an infinite number of imperceptible universes.[48] If this is what leading scientists believe, why should anyone feel self-conscious about believing in *one* unobservable dimension, a realm containing angels and Heaven and Hell?

The Bible teaches that sometimes humans are allowed to see into Heaven. When Stephen was being stoned because of his faith in Christ, he gazed into Heaven: "Stephen, full of the Holy Spirit, looked up to heaven and saw the glory of God, and Jesus standing at the right hand of God. 'Look,' he said, 'I see heaven open and the Son of Man standing at the right hand of God'" (Acts 7:55-56). Scripture tells us not that Stephen dreamed this, but that he actually *saw* it.

Wayne Grudem points out that Stephen "did not see mere symbols of a state of existence. It was rather that his eyes were opened to see a spiritual dimension of reality which God has hidden from us in this present age, a dimension which none the less really does exist in our space/time universe, and within which Jesus now lives in his physical resurrected body, waiting even now for a time when he will return to earth."[49]

I agree with Grudem that the present Heaven is a space/time universe. He may be right that it's part of our own universe, or it may be in a different universe. It could be a universe next door that's normally hidden but sometimes opened. In either case, it seems likely that God didn't merely create a vision for Stephen in order to make Heaven *appear* physical. Rather, he allowed Stephen to see an intermediate Heaven that *was* (and is) physical.

The prophet Elisha asked God to give his servant, Gehazi, a glimpse of the invisible realm. He prayed, "'O Lord, open his eyes so he may see.' Then the Lord opened the servant's eyes, and he looked and saw the hills full of horses and chariots of fire all around Elisha" (2 Kings 6:17). It could be argued that these horses and chariots (with angelic warriors) exist beside us in our universe, but we are normally blind to them. Or they may be in a universe beside ours that opens up into ours so that angelic beings—and horses, apparently—can move between universes.

A third possibility—to me, the least convincing one in these instances—is that such descriptions are merely metaphorical, not to be taken literally. But Acts 7 and 2 Kings 6 are narrative accounts, historical in nature, not apocalyptic or parabolic literature. The text is clear that Stephen and Gehazi saw things actual and physical. This supports the view that Heaven is a physical realm. Physical and spiritual are neither opposite nor contradictory. In fact, the apostle Paul refers to the resurrection body as a "spiritual body" (1 Corinthians 15:44). God is a spirit, and angels are spirit beings, but both can—and on the New Earth will—live in a physical environment.

If a blind man momentarily gained his sight and described an actual tree that he saw, other blind people—especially if they lived in a world where everyone was blind—might automatically assume the tree was nonliteral, a mere symbol of some spiritual reality. But they would be wrong. Likewise, we should not assume that the Bible describes Heaven in physical ways merely to accommodate us. It is fully possible that the present Heaven is a physical realm.

Because the question of the physical nature of the present Heaven is important and controversial, we'll take a closer look at it in the next chapter.

CHAPTER 6

IS THE PRESENT HEAVEN A PHYSICAL PLACE?

For the entrance of the greater world is wide and sure, and they who see the straitness and the painfulness from which they have been delivered must wonder exceedingly as they are received into those large rooms with joy and immortality.

Amy Carmichael

After reading one of my books, a missionary wrote to me, deeply troubled that I thought Heaven might be a physical place. In our correspondence, no matter how many Scripture passages I pointed to, it didn't matter. He'd always been taught that Heaven was "spiritual" and therefore not physical. To suggest otherwise was, in his mind, to commit heresy.

My concern was not so much that he believed the present Heaven isn't physical. (Maybe he's right.) Rather, it was that he seemed convinced that if Heaven *were* physical, it would be less sacred and special. He viewed physical and spiritual as opposites. When I asked him to demonstrate from Scripture why Heaven cannot be a physical place, he told me the answer was very simple: because "God is spirit" (John 4:24). He believed that verse settled the question once and for all.

But saying that God is spirit is very different from saying that Heaven is spirit. Heaven, after all, is not the same as God. God created Heaven; therefore, he did not always dwell there. Though God chooses to dwell in Heaven, he does not need a dwelling place. However, as finite humans, we do. It's no problem for the all-powerful God, a spirit, to dwell in a spiritual realm or a physical realm or a realm that includes both. The real question is whether people, being by nature both spiritual and physical, can dwell in a realm without physical properties.

The physical New Earth will be our ultimate dwelling place, but until then we shouldn't find it surprising if God chooses to provide a waiting place that's also physical. For us to exist as human beings, we occupy space. It seems reasonable to infer that the space we occupy would be physical. If the present, intermediate Heaven is a place where God, angels, and humans dwell, it makes sense that Heaven would be accommodated to mankind, because God needs no accommodation. We know that angels can exist in a physical world because they exist in this one, not just in Heaven. In fact, angels sometimes, perhaps often, take on human form (Hebrews 13:2).

If we are to draw inferences about the nature of Heaven, we shouldn't derive them from the nature of God. After all, he is a one-of-a-kind being who is infinite, existing outside of space and time. Rather, we should base our deductions on the nature of humanity. It's no problem for the infinite God to dwell wherever mankind dwells. The question is whether finite humans can exist as God does—outside of space and time. I'm not certain we can. But I am certain that *if* we can, it is only as a temporary aberration that will be permanently corrected by our bodily resurrection in preparation for life on the New Earth.

Why are we so resistant to the idea that Heaven could be physical? The answer, I believe, is centered in an unbiblical belief that the spirit realm is good and the material world is bad, a view I am calling *Christoplatonism*. (For a discussion of Christoplatonism's false assumptions, see appendix A.) For our purposes in this chapter, I will summarize this belief that looms like a dark cloud over the common view of Heaven.

Plato, the Greek philosopher, believed that material things, including the human body and the earth, are evil, while immaterial things such as the soul and Heaven are good. This view is called Platonism. The Christian church, highly influenced by Platonism through the teachings of Philo (ca. 20 BC–AD 50) and Origen (AD 185–254), among others, came to embrace the "spiritual" view that human spirits are better off without bodies and that Heaven is a disembodied state. They rejected the notion of Heaven as a physical realm and spiritualized or entirely neglected the biblical teaching of resurrected people inhabiting a resurrected Earth.

Christoplatonism has had a devastating effect on our ability to understand what Scripture says about Heaven, particularly about the eternal Heaven, the New Earth. A fine Christian man said to me, "This idea of having bodies and eating food and being in an earthly place . . . it just sounds so *unspiritual*." Without knowing it, he was under the influence of Christoplatonism. If we believe, even subconsciously, that bodies and the earth and material things are unspiritual, even evil, then we will inevitably reject or spiritualize any biblical revelation about our bodily resurrection or the physical characteristics of the New Earth. That's exactly what has happened in most Christian churches, and it's a large reason for our failure to come to terms with a biblical doctrine of Heaven. Christoplatonism has also closed our minds to the possibility that the present Heaven may actually be a physical realm. If we look at Scripture, however, we'll see considerable evidence that the present Heaven has physical properties.

HEAVEN AS SUBSTANCE, EARTH AS SHADOW

In his seventeenth-century classic *Paradise Lost*, John Milton describes Eden as a garden full of aromatic flowers, delicious fruit, and soft grass, lushly watered. He also connects Eden with Heaven, the source of earthly existence, portraying Heaven as a place of great pleasures and the source of Earth's pleasures. In Milton's story, the angel Raphael asks Adam,

> *What if Earth*
> *Be but the shadow of Heav'n, and things therein*
> *Each to other like, more then on Earth is thought?*[50]

Though the idea of Earth as Heaven's shadow is seldom discussed, even in books on Heaven, it's a concept that has biblical support. For example, the temple in Heaven is filled with smoke from the glory of God (Revelation 15:8). Is this a figurative temple with figurative smoke? Or is there an actual fire creating literal smoke in a real building? We're told there are scrolls in Heaven, elders who have faces, martyrs who wear clothes, and even people with "palm branches in their hands" (Revelation 7:9). There are musical instruments in the present Heaven (Revelation 8:6), horses coming into and out of Heaven (2 Kings 2:11; Revelation 19:14), and an eagle flying overhead in Heaven (Revelation 8:13). Perhaps some of these objects are merely symbolic, with no corresponding physical reality. But is that true of *all* of them?

Many commentators dismiss the possibility that any of these passages in Revelation should be taken literally, on the grounds that it is apocalyptic literature, which is known for its figures of speech. But the book of Hebrews isn't apocalyptic, it's epistolary. It says that earthly priests "serve at a sanctuary that is a copy and shadow of what is in heaven" (Hebrews 8:5). Moses was told, in building the earthly tabernacle, "See to it that you make everything according to the pattern shown you on the mountain" (Hebrews 8:5). If that which was built after the pattern was physical, might it suggest the original was also physical?

The book of Hebrews seems to say that we should see Earth as a *derivative* realm and Heaven as the *source* realm. If we do, we'll abandon the assumption that something existing in one realm cannot exist in the other. In fact, we'll consider it likely that what exists in one realm exists in at least some form in the other. We should stop thinking of Heaven and Earth as opposites and instead view them as overlapping circles that share certain commonalities.

Christ "went through the greater and more perfect tabernacle that is not man-made, that is to say, not a part of this creation" (Hebrews 9:11). "Christ did not enter a man-made sanctuary that was only a copy of the true one; he entered heaven itself" (Hebrews 9:24). The earthly sanctuary was a copy of the true one in Heaven. In fact, the New Jerusalem that will be brought down to the New Earth is currently in the intermediate or present Heaven (Hebrews 12:22). If we know that the New Jerusalem will be physically on the New Earth, and we also know that it is in the present Heaven, *does that not suggest the New Jerusalem is currently physical?* Why wouldn't it be? Unless we start with an assumption that Heaven *can't* be physical, it seems that this evidence would persuade us that it is indeed physical.

These verses in Hebrews suggest that God created Earth in the image of Heaven, just as he created mankind in his image. C. S. Lewis proposed that "the hills and valleys of Heaven will be to those you now experience not as a copy is to an original, nor as a substitute is to the genuine article, but as the flower to the root, or the diamond to the coal."[51]

> · The church is constantly being tempted to accept this world as her home . . . but if she is wise she will consider that she stands in the valley between the mountain peaks of eternity past and eternity to come. The past is gone forever and the present is passing as swift as the shadow on the sundial of Ahaz. Even if the earth should continue a million years not one of us could stay to enjoy it. We do well to think of the long tomorrow.
>
> **A. W. TOZER**

Often our thinking is backwards. Why do we imagine that God patterns Heaven's holy city after an earthly city, as if Heaven knows nothing of community and culture and has to get its ideas from us? Isn't it more likely that earthly realities, including cities, are derived from heavenly counterparts? We tend to start with Earth and reason up toward Heaven, when instead we should start with Heaven and reason down toward Earth. It isn't merely an accommodation to our earthly familial structure, for instance, that God calls himself a father and us children. On the contrary, he created father-child relationships to display his relationship with us, just as he created human marriage to reveal the love relationship between Christ and his bride (Ephesians 5:32).

In my novel *Safely Home,* I envision the relationship between Earth and Heaven:

Compared to what he now beheld, the world he'd come from was a land of shadows, colorless and two-dimensional. This place was fresh and captivating, resonating with color and beauty. He could not only see and hear it, but feel and smell and taste it. Every hillside, every mountain, every waterfall, every frolicking animal in the fields seemed to beckon him to come join them, to come from the outside and plunge into the inside. This whole world had the feel of cool water on a blistering August afternoon. The light beckoned him to dive in with abandon, to come join the great adventure.

"I know what this is," Quan said.

"Tell me," said the Carpenter.

"It's the substance that casts all those shadows in the other world. The circles there are copies of the spheres here. The squares there are copies of the cubes here. The triangles there are copies of the pyramids here. Earth was a flatland. This is . . . well, the inside is bigger than the outside, isn't it? How many dimensions are there?"

"Far more than you have seen yet," the King said, laughing.

"This is the Place that defines and gives meaning to all places," Li Quan said. "I never imagined it would be like this."[52]

DOES "PARADISE" SUGGEST A PHYSICAL PLACE?

During the Crucifixion, when Jesus said to the thief on the cross, "Today you will be with me in paradise" (Luke 23:43), he was referring to the present Heaven. But why did he call it *paradise*, and what did he mean?

The word *paradise* comes from the Persian word *pairidaeza,* meaning "a walled park" or "enclosed garden." It was used to describe the great walled gardens of the Persian king Cyrus's royal palaces. In the Septuagint, the Greek translation of the Old Testament, the Greek word for paradise is used to describe the Garden of Eden (e.g., Genesis 2:8; Ezekiel 28:13). Later, because of the Jewish belief that God would restore Eden, *paradise* became the word to describe the eternal state of the righteous, and to a lesser extent, the present Heaven.[53]

The word *paradise* does not refer to wild nature but to nature under mankind's dominion. The garden or park was not left to grow entirely on its own. People brought their creativity to bear on managing, cultivating, and presenting the garden or park. "The idea of a walled garden," writes Oxford professor Alister McGrath, "enclosing a carefully cultivated area of exquisite plants and animals, was the most powerful symbol of paradise available to the human imagination, mingling the images of the beauty of nature with the orderliness of human construction. . . . The whole of human history is thus enfolded in the subtle interplay of sorrow over a lost paradise, and the hope of its final restoration."[54]

In the Judaism of the New Testament era, "The site of reopened Paradise is almost without exception the earth. . . . The belief in resurrection gave assurance that all the righteous, even those who are dead, would have a share in the reopened paradise."[55]

Paradise was not generally understood as mere allegory, with a metaphorical or spiritual meaning, but as an actual physical place where God and his people lived together, surrounded by physical beauty, enjoying great pleasures and happiness.

God says, "To him who overcomes, I will give the right to eat from the tree of life, which is in the paradise of God" (Revelation 2:7). The same physical tree of life that was in the Garden of Eden will one day be in the New Jerusalem on the New Earth (Revelation 22:2). Now it is (present tense) in the intermediate or present Heaven. Shouldn't we assume it has the same physical properties it had in the Garden of Eden and will have in the New Jerusalem? If it doesn't, could it be called the tree of life?

We are told that after the Fall, God "drove the man out; and at the east of the garden of Eden He stationed the cherubim and the flaming sword which turned every direction to guard the way to the tree of life" (Genesis 3:24, NASB). It appears that Eden's Paradise, with the tree of life, retained its identity as a physical place but was no longer accessible to mankind. It was guarded by cherubim, who are residents of Heaven, where God is "enthroned between the cherubim" (2 Kings 19:15).

Eden was not destroyed. What was destroyed was mankind's ability to live in Eden. There's no indication that Eden was stripped of its physicality and transformed into a "spiritual" entity. It appears to have remained just as it was, a physical paradise removed to a realm we can't gain access to—most likely the present Heaven, because we know for certain that's where the tree of life now is (Revelation 2:7).

God is not done with Eden. He preserved it not as a museum piece but as a place that mankind will one day occupy again—and to a certain extent may now occupy in the present Heaven. Because we're told that the tree of life will be located in the New Jerusalem, on both sides of a great river (Revelation 22:2), it seems likely that the original Eden may be a great park at the center of the city. If we know the tree that distinguished Eden will be there, why not Eden itself?

This would fit perfectly with the statement in Revelation 2:7 that the tree of life is presently in Paradise.

Though the rest of the earth fell under human sin, Eden was for some reason treated differently. Perhaps it had come from Heaven, God's dwelling place, and was transplanted to Earth. We don't know. But we do know this: God came to Eden to visit with Adam and Eve (Genesis 3:8), which he would no longer do after Adam and Eve were banished from the Garden after the Fall. Whether or not Eden was created along with the rest of the earth, clearly it was special to God, and it remains special to him. The tree of life's presence in the New Jerusalem establishes that elements of Eden, as physical as the original, will again be part of the human experience. The presence of the tree of life in the present Heaven suggests that Heaven too has physical properties and is capable of containing physical objects.

DO PEOPLE HAVE INTERMEDIATE BODIES IN THE PRESENT HEAVEN?

Unlike God and the angels, who are in essence spirits (John 4:24; Hebrews 1:14), human beings are by nature both spiritual *and* physical (Genesis 2:7). God did not create Adam as a spirit and place it inside a body. Rather, he first created a body, *then* breathed into it a spirit. There never was a moment when a human being existed without a body. Neurophysiological studies reveal an intimate connection between the body and what has historically been referred to as the soul—which includes the mind, emotions, will, intentionality, and capacity to worship.† It appears that we are not essentially spirits who inhabit bodies, but we are essentially as much physical as we are spiritual. We cannot be fully human without both a spirit *and* a body.

Given the consistent physical descriptions of the present Heaven and those who dwell there, it seems possible—though this is certainly debatable—that between our earthly life and our bodily resurrection, God may grant us some physical form that will allow us to function as human beings while in that unnatural state "between bodies," awaiting our resurrection. Just as the intermediate state is a bridge between life on the old Earth and the New Earth, perhaps intermediate bodies, or at least a physical form of some sort, serve as bridges between our present bodies and our resurrected bodies.

---

†Some regard the spirit as a third component with body and soul, whereas others see it as simply another word for the immaterial person.

The apostle Paul says, "Meanwhile we groan, longing to be clothed with our heavenly dwelling, because when we are clothed, we will not be found naked. For while we are in this tent, we groan and are burdened, because we do not wish to be unclothed but to be clothed with our heavenly dwelling, so that what is mortal may be swallowed up by life" (2 Corinthians 5:2-4). Some take this to mean that the intermediate state is a condition of disembodied nakedness. They may well be right. Others, however, believe that Paul is longing to be with Christ (Philippians 1:21), but he cannot long for a state of Platonic nakedness, which he considers repugnant. Thus, they understand Paul to be saying that at death we are immediately clothed by a heavenly dwelling (whether Heaven itself or an intermediate form), in which we will await our resurrection.

> Women sometimes have the problem of trying to judge by artificial light how a dress will look by daylight. That is very like the problem for all of us: to dress our souls not for the electric lights of the present world but for the daylight of the next. The good dress is the one that will face that light. For that light will last longer.
>
> **C. S. LEWIS**

There is evidence that suggests the latter position could be correct. For instance, the martyrs in Heaven are described as wearing clothes (Revelation 6:9-11). Disembodied spirits don't wear clothes. Many consider the clothes purely symbolic of being covered in Christ's righteousness. Of course, they could also be real clothes with symbolic meaning, just as the Ark of the Covenant had symbolic meaning but was also a real, physical object.

Because these martyrs are also called "souls" (Revelation 6:9), some insist that they must be disembodied spirits. But the Greek word *psuche,* here translated "soul," does not normally mean disembodied spirit. On the contrary, it is typically used of a whole person, who has both body and spirit, or of animals, which are *physical* beings. It is used in Revelation 12:11 to describe the martyrs, who "did not love their *lives* [*psuche*] so much as to shrink from death." Because *death* relates to their physical bodies, not their spirits (which would not die), the emphasis is more on their bodies than on their spirits. According to the *Theological Dictionary of the New Testament,* "[*Psuche*] does not carry with it any clear distinction between a noncorporeal and a corporeal state. . . . The reference is not to a part of man that has survived death, but to the total existence of man."[56]

It appears the apostle John had a body when he visited Heaven, because he is said to have grasped, held, eaten, and tasted things there (e.g., Revelation 10:9-10). To assume this is all figurative language is not a restriction demanded by the text but only by our presupposition that Heaven isn't a physical place. (For a discussion of literal and figurative interpretation, see appendix B.)

In the apostle Paul's account of being caught up to the present Heaven (which he calls "the third heaven"), he expresses uncertainty about whether he'd had a body there or not: "Whether in the body or apart from the body I do not know, but God knows" (2 Corinthians 12:3). The fact that he thought he *might* have had a body in Heaven is significant. He certainly didn't dismiss the thought as impossible, as Plato would have. His uncertainty might suggest that he sensed he had a physical form in Heaven that was body-like but somehow different from his earthly body. If he had been nothing but spirit in Heaven, it's unlikely he would say he wasn't certain whether or not he'd had a body there.

If those in Heaven are granted temporary forms—and I recognize it only as a possibility—it would in no way minimize the absolute necessity or critical importance of our future bodily resurrection, which Paul emphatically establishes in 1 Corinthians 15:12-32. In fact, it would only be on the basis of the certainty of a future resurrection that temporary bodies *might* be given—just as in Old Testament times the certainty of Christ's future death and resurrection permitted those people, who otherwise would have been Hell-bound, to enter Paradise.

We do *not* receive resurrection bodies immediately after death. Resurrection is not one-at-a-time. If we have intermediate forms in the intermediate Heaven, they won't be our true bodies, which have died. Continuity is *only* between our original and resurrection bodies. *If* we are given intermediate forms, they are at best temporary vessels (comparable to the human-appearing bodies that angels sometimes take on), distinct from our true bodies, which remain dead until our resurrection.

A fundamental article of the Christian faith is that the resurrected Christ now dwells in Heaven. We are told that his resurrected body on Earth was physical, and that this same, physical Jesus ascended to Heaven, from which he will one day return to Earth (Acts 1:11). It seems indisputable, then, to say that there is at least one physical body in the present Heaven.

If Christ's body in the present Heaven has physical properties, it stands to reason that others in Heaven might have physical forms as well, even if only temporary ones. It also makes sense that other aspects of the present Heaven would have physical properties—so that, for example, when Christ is seen standing at the right hand of God (Acts 7:56), he is actually standing on something. Otherwise we would have to conclude that the resurrected (and thus, embodied) Christ has been floating for two thousand years in a realm without material substance. (He *could*, of course, but *does* he?) If we know there is physical substance in Heaven (namely, Christ's body), can we not also assume that other references to physical objects in Heaven, including physical forms and clothing, are literal rather than figurative?

ENOCH, ELIJAH, AND MOSES

Enoch and Elijah appear to have been taken to Heaven in their physical bodies. "Enoch walked with God; and he was not, for God took him" (Genesis 5:24, NASB). Apparently Enoch's body was not left behind to bury. The Septuagint translates it as Enoch "was not found." Hebrews 11:5 explicitly says that Enoch didn't die: "By faith Enoch was taken away so that he did not see death, 'and was not found, because God had taken him'" (NKJV). Similarly, Elijah was taken to Heaven without dying and without leaving a body behind: "Elijah went up by a whirlwind into heaven. And Elisha . . . saw him no more" (2 Kings 2:11-12, NKJV).

We do not know how bodies under the Curse could be taken to Heaven, but doesn't it appear that they were, since no bodies were left behind? Our spirits are also under the Curse, but based on Christ's redemptive work they are allowed entrance to Heaven. Perhaps God extended the same grace to allow the bodies of Enoch and Elijah into the intermediate Heaven. If that is the case, they may even now be living in pre-resurrected bodies in Heaven, just as Christ is living there in his resurrected body.

Given that at least one and perhaps three people now have bodies in Heaven, isn't it possible that others might be given physical forms as well?

Moses and Elijah appeared physically with Christ at the Transfiguration (Luke 9:28-36). Because they'd already gone to Heaven (Moses having died and Elijah having been taken from Earth in a whirlwind), if souls in the present Heaven are disembodied, God would've had to create temporary bodies for them when they came from Heaven to be with Jesus on the mountain. If so, they would have gone from being disembodied to embodied, and after the Transfiguration become disembodied again to await the final resurrection.

A second possibility is that Moses and Elijah came to Earth in the same temporary bodies they already had in Heaven. (In Elijah's case, his temporary body might even have been his original earthly body, which had never died.) If Moses and Elijah came to Earth with the same temporary bodies they had in Heaven, they could have returned to Heaven just as they were. Did their joining Christ on Earth require them to become *something* else, or did it simply involve their coming *somewhere* else? Was it that they were temporarily *embodied*, or merely temporarily *relocated*?

The physical presence of Moses and Elijah at the Transfiguration seems to demonstrate beyond question that God at least sometimes creates intermediate bodies for people to inhabit prior to the resurrection of the dead—even if only for Moses and Elijah, and only while they were on Earth. The question is whether these temporary bodies were granted only to Moses and Elijah while they were on the mountain, or whether temporary bodies are granted to everyone in the present Heaven.

WHAT CAN WE LEARN FROM THE RICH MAN AND LAZARUS?

In the New Testament account of the rich man and Lazarus, Jesus ascribes physical properties to people who have died (Luke 16:19-31):

> There was a rich man who was dressed in purple and fine linen and lived in luxury every day. At his gate was laid a beggar named Lazarus, covered with sores and longing to eat what fell from the rich man's table. Even the dogs came and licked his sores.
>
> The time came when the beggar died and the angels carried him to Abraham's side. The rich man also died and was buried. In hell, where he was in torment, he looked up and saw Abraham far away, with Lazarus by his side. So he called to him, "Father Abraham, have pity on me and send Lazarus to dip the tip of his finger in water and cool my tongue, because I am in agony in this fire."
>
> But Abraham replied, "Son, remember that in your lifetime you received your good things, while Lazarus received bad things, but now he is comforted here and you are in agony. And besides all this, between us and you a great chasm has been fixed, so that those who want to go from here to you cannot, nor can anyone cross over from there to us."
>
> He answered, "Then I beg you, father, send Lazarus to my father's house, for I have five brothers. Let him warn them, so that they will not also come to this place of torment."
>
> Abraham replied, "They have Moses and the Prophets; let them listen to them."
>
> "No, father Abraham," he said, "but if someone from the dead goes to them, they will repent."
>
> He said to him, "If they do not listen to Moses and the Prophets, they will not be convinced even if someone rises from the dead."

Some believe this story is nothing more than a parable intended to convey a central idea about the after-death consequences of our choices made on Earth. They believe that Lazarus and the rich man were not real people, and that references to fire, thirst, finger, and tongue are not intended as physical realities.

I certainly don't believe that every biblical account should be taken literally (for a more complete discussion of this, see appendix B, "Literal and Figurative Interpretation"), and I certainly agree there is much figurative language in this passage. However, I also think it's a mistake to dismiss the parable as strictly figurative based on assumptions that the afterlife consists of disembodied people in a non-physical realm.

Jesus could easily have portrayed the rich man and Lazarus in other ways. He could have said, "When Lazarus died, his spirit drifted without a body into a realm without sin and pain." But he didn't. It seems unlikely that Jesus would have depicted the afterlife in such concrete detail if it had nothing to teach us concerning the nature of Heaven and Hell.

Did you know that this is the only parable Jesus told in which he gave a specific name to someone in the story? Naming Lazarus suggests that Jesus was speaking of a real man who had that name. Furthermore, if the events in this story didn't actually happen, if Jesus made up the name for the poor man, why would he choose the name *Lazarus*—the name of his close friend, who was actually a rich man, not a poor man? Jesus knew *that* Lazarus, the brother of Mary and Martha, would die and Jesus would raise him from the dead. Using Lazarus's name would inevitably create confusion—two different Lazaruses who die and live again, one in Paradise, the other on Earth? When Jesus could have chosen from hundreds of other names, it seems doubtful he would have invented a name that would unnecessarily confuse. The best explanation for why Jesus called the man Lazarus may be this: He was a real man, and *that was his name*. If so, it increases the probability that Jesus was telling us about what actually happened to two men after they died.

Consider the story's major components:

- When Lazarus died, angels carried him to Paradise.
- The rich man died and went to a place of torment.
- Lazarus is with Abraham (and, by inference, others); the rich man is by himself (no one else is mentioned).
- The intermediate Heaven and Hell are separated by a fixed chasm. But in this case, people on both sides could see and communicate with each other, at least on a limited basis. (It's possible this was granted to Abraham and the rich man as an exception, not the norm. We shouldn't build a doctrine on it because it's not supported by other references.)
- Both the rich man and Abraham reasoned and communicated, and they maintained their distinct identities from Earth (as did

Lazarus), indicating direct continuity from their earthly lives to their afterlives.

- The rich man and Lazarus are depicted as having physical forms. The rich man had a tongue and a thirst that he wished to satisfy with water. Lazarus had a finger, and there was water available to him in Paradise, into which he might dip his finger. Of course, these references may be entirely figurative. But they might also suggest the possession of transitional physical forms, existing in a physical Paradise, to sustain and manifest human identity between death and resurrection.
- The rich man certainly remembers—and possibly sees—his lost brothers. He expresses concern for their welfare and asks that Lazarus be sent to warn them. This indicates consciousness after death and clear memory of Earth and people on Earth.
- Abraham says that no one can cross the gap between Heaven and Hell.

The problem with a strictly literal interpretation of this passage is that it presses too far, suggesting things that are unlikely and not taught elsewhere, such as that people in Heaven and Hell talk to each other. The problem with a strictly figurative interpretation is that it makes it difficult to know what, if anything, to take seriously. If no real conclusions can be derived from the story, what is the value of all its details?

Perhaps we should consider an interpretive position that doesn't insist that every detail is literal but also recognizes that Jesus intended for us to picture people in the afterlife as real humans with thoughts and capacities (and perhaps even forms), and with the same identity, memories, and awareness from their lives and relationships on Earth. Surely Jesus intended us to envision both Heaven and Hell as real places where there are real people who came from Earth. Every one of these teachings is directly or indirectly suggested in other passages—but none as graphically or memorably as this one.

In the intermediate Heaven or Hell, we will await the time that Jesus foretold, "when all who are in their graves will hear his voice and come out—those who have done good will rise to live, and those who have done evil will rise to be condemned" (John 5:28-29). Until that day comes, Scripture teaches that those who die will go to a real place, either the present Heaven or the present Hell, as conscious human beings with memory of their lives and relationships on Earth. Those in Hell will live in misery, hopelessness, and apparent isolation, while those in Heaven will live in comfort, joy, and rich relationship with God and others.

CHAPTER 7

WHAT IS LIFE LIKE IN THE PRESENT HEAVEN?

When I was a boy, the thought of Heaven used to frighten me more than the thought of Hell. I pictured Heaven as a place where time would be perpetual Sundays, with perpetual services from which there would be no escape.

David Lloyd George

We can learn a great deal about the present Heaven from three key verses in Revelation: "When [the Lamb] opened the fifth seal, I saw under the altar the souls of those who had been slain because of the word of God and the testimony they had maintained. They called out in a loud voice, 'How long, Sovereign Lord, holy and true, until you judge the inhabitants of the earth and avenge our blood?' Then each of them was given a white robe, and they were told to wait a little longer, until the number of their fellow servants and brothers who were to be killed as they had been was completed" (6:9-11).

I offer here twenty-one brief observations concerning this passage:

1. When these people died on Earth, they relocated to Heaven (v. 9).
2. These people in Heaven were the same ones killed for Christ while on Earth (v. 9). This demonstrates direct continuity between our identity on Earth and our identity in Heaven. The martyrs' personal history extends directly back to their lives on Earth. Those in the present Heaven are not different people; they are the same people relocated—"righteous men made perfect" (Hebrews 12:23).
3. People in Heaven will be remembered for their lives on Earth. These were known and identified as ones slain "because of . . . the testimony they had maintained" (v. 9).
4. "They called out" (v. 10) means they are able to express themselves audibly. This could suggest they exist in physical form, with vocal cords or other tangible means to express themselves.
5. People in the present Heaven can raise their voices (v. 10). This

indicates that they are rational, communicative, and emotional—even passionate—beings, like people on Earth.

6. They called out in "a loud voice," not "loud voices." Individuals speaking with one voice indicate that Heaven is a place of unity and shared perspective.

7. The martyrs are fully conscious, rational, and aware of each other, God, and the situation on Earth.

8. They ask God to intervene on Earth and to act on their behalf: "How long . . . until you judge the inhabitants of the earth and avenge our blood?"(v. 10).

9. Those in Heaven are free to ask God questions, which means they have an audience with God. It also means they need to learn. In Heaven, people desire understanding and pursue it.

10. People in the present Heaven know what's happening on Earth (v. 10). The martyrs know enough to realize that those who killed them have not yet been judged.

11. Heaven dwellers have a deep concern for justice and retribution (v. 10). When we go to Heaven, we won't adopt a passive disinterest in what happens on the earth. On the contrary, our concerns will be more passionate and our thirst for justice greater. Neither God nor we will be satisfied until his enemies are judged, our bodies raised, sin and Satan defeated, Earth restored, and Christ exalted over all.

12. The martyrs clearly remember their lives on Earth (v. 10). They even remember that they were *murdered.*

13. The martyrs in Heaven pray for judgment on their persecutors who are still at work hurting others. They are acting in solidarity with, and in effect interceding for, the suffering saints on Earth. This suggests that saints in Heaven are both seeing and praying for saints on Earth.

14. Those in Heaven see God's attributes ("Sovereign . . . holy and true") in a way that makes his judgment of sin more understandable.

15. Those in Heaven are distinct individuals: "Then each of them was given a white robe" (v. 11). There isn't one merged identity that obliterates uniqueness, but a distinct "each of them."

16. The martyrs' wearing white robes suggests the possibility of actual physical forms, because disembodied spirits presumably don't wear robes. The robes may well have symbolic meaning, but it doesn't mean they couldn't also be physical. The martyrs appear to have physical forms that John could actually see.

17. God answers their question (v. 11), indicating communication and

process in Heaven. It also demonstrates that we won't know everything in Heaven—if we did, we would have no questions. The martyrs knew more after God answered their question than before they asked it. There is learning in the present Heaven.

18. God promises to fulfill the martyrs' requests, but says they will have to "wait a little longer" (v. 11). Those in the present Heaven live in anticipation of the future fulfillment of God's promises. Unlike the eternal Heaven—where there will be no more sin, Curse, or suffering on the New Earth (Revelation 21:4)—the present Heaven coexists with and watches over an Earth under sin, the Curse, and suffering.

19. There is time in the present Heaven (vv. 10-11). The white-robed martyrs ask God a time-dependent question: "How long, Sovereign Lord . . . until you judge the inhabitants of the earth and avenge our blood?" (v. 10). They are aware of time's passing and are eager for the coming day of the Lord's judgment. God answers that they must "wait a little longer" until certain events transpire on Earth. Waiting requires the passing of time.

20. The people of God in Heaven have a strong familial connection with those on Earth, who are called their "fellow servants and brothers" (v. 11). We share the same Father, "from whom every family in heaven and on earth is named" (Ephesians 3:15, ESV). There is not a wall of separation within the bride of Christ. We are one family with those who've gone to Heaven ahead of us. After we go to Heaven, we'll still be one family with those yet on Earth. These verses demonstrate a vital connection between the events and people in Heaven and the events and people on Earth.

21. Our sovereign God knows down to the last detail all that is happening and will happen on Earth (v. 11), including every drop of blood shed and every bit of suffering undergone by his children. Voice of the Martyrs estimates that more than 150,000 people die for Christ each year, an average of more than four hundred per day. God knows the name and story of each one. He knows exactly how many martyrs there will be, and he is prepared to return and set up his Kingdom when the final martyr dies.

I've made these observations on the present Heaven based on only three verses. Unless there is some reason to believe that the realities of this passage apply *only* to one group of martyrs and to no one else in Heaven—and I see no such indication—then we should assume that what is true of them is also true of our loved ones already there, and will be true of us when we die.

DO HEAVEN'S INHABITANTS REMEMBER LIFE ON EARTH?

As we've seen, the martyrs depicted in Revelation 6 clearly remember at least some of what happened on Earth, including that they underwent great suffering. If they remember their martyrdom, there's no reason to assume they would forget other aspects of their earthly lives. In fact, we'll all likely remember much more in Heaven than we do on Earth, and we will probably be able to see how God and angels intervened on our behalf when we didn't realize it.

In Heaven, those who endured bad things on Earth are comforted for them (Luke 16:25). This comfort implies memory of what happened. If there was no memory of the bad things, what would be the need for or nature of such comfort?

After we die, we will give an account of our lives on Earth, down to specific actions and words (2 Corinthians 5:10; Matthew 12:36). Given our improved minds and clear thinking, our memory should be more—not less—acute concerning our life on Earth. Certainly, we must remember the things we'll give an account for. Because we'll be held accountable for more than we presently remember, presumably our memory will be far better.

The doctrine of eternal rewards hinges on specific acts of faithfulness done on Earth that survive the believer's judgment and are brought into Heaven with us (1 Corinthians 3:14). In Heaven, the Bride's wedding dress stands for "the righteous acts of the saints" done on Earth (Revelation 19:7-8). Our righteous deeds on Earth will not be forgotten but "will follow" us to Heaven (Revelation 14:13). The positions of authority and the treasures we're granted in Heaven will perpetually remind us of our life on Earth, because what we do on Earth will earn us those rewards (Matthew 6:19-21; 19:21; Luke 12:33; 19:17, 19; 1 Timothy 6:19; Revelation 2:26-28).

God keeps a record in Heaven of what people do on Earth, both unbelievers and believers. We know that record will outlast our life on Earth—for believers, at least until the judgment seat of Christ (2 Corinthians 5:10); for unbelievers, right up until the Great White Throne Judgment (Revelation 20:11-13), just preceding the coming of the new heavens and New Earth. For those now in Heaven, these records of life on Earth still exist. In chapter 32 we'll take a look at the "scroll of remembrance" mentioned in Malachi 3:16, which even now is being written in Heaven concerning those living on Earth.

Memory is a basic element of personality. If we are truly *ourselves* in Heaven, there must be continuity of memory from Earth to Heaven. We will not be different people, but the same people marvelously relocated and transformed. Heaven cleanses us but does not revise or extinguish our origins or history. Undoubtedly we will remember God's works of grace in our lives that comforted, assured, sustained, and empowered us to live for him.

DO PEOPLE IN THE PRESENT HEAVEN SEE WHAT IS HAPPENING ON EARTH?

If the martyrs in Heaven know that God hasn't yet brought judgment on their persecutors (Revelation 6:9-11), it seems evident that the inhabitants of the present Heaven can see what's happening on Earth, at least to some extent. When Babylon is brought down, an angel points to events happening on Earth and says, "Rejoice over her, O heaven! Rejoice, saints and apostles and prophets! God has judged her for the way she treated you" (Revelation 18:20). That the angel specifically addresses people living in Heaven indicates they're aware of what's happening on Earth.

Further, there is "the roar of a great multitude in heaven shouting: Hallelujah!" and praising God for specific events of judgment that have just taken place on Earth (Revelation 19:1-5). Again, the saints in Heaven are clearly observing what is happening on Earth.

Because Heaven's saints return with Christ to set up his millennial kingdom (Revelation 19:11-14), it seems unthinkable to imagine they would have remained ignorant of the culmination of human history taking place on Earth. The picture of saints in Heaven blissfully unaware of what is transpiring on Earth seems insubstantial. After all, God and his angels (and the saints themselves) are about to return for the ultimate battle in the history of the universe, after which Christ will be crowned king. Those on Earth may be ignorant of Heaven, but those in Heaven are *not* ignorant of Earth.

In the Old Testament account of King Saul wrongly appealing to the witch of Endor to call upon Samuel to come back from the afterlife, the medium was terrified when God actually sent Samuel. Interestingly, Samuel remembered what Saul had done before Samuel died, and he was aware of what had happened since he died (1 Samuel 28:16-19). Though God could have briefed Samuel on all this, it seems likely the prophet knew simply because those in Heaven are aware of what happens on Earth.

When called from Heaven to the Transfiguration on Earth, Moses and Elijah "appeared in glorious splendor, talking with Jesus. They spoke about his departure, which he was about to bring to fulfillment at Jerusalem" (Luke 9:31). They seemed fully aware of the drama they'd stepped into, of what was currently transpiring on Earth, and of God's redemptive plan about to be accomplished. (And surely they returned to Heaven remembering what they'd discussed with Jesus.)

Hebrews 12:1 tells us to "run with perseverance the race marked out for us," creating the mental picture of the Greek competitions, which were watched intently by throngs of engrossed fans sitting high up in the ancient stadiums. The "great cloud of witnesses" refers to the saints who've gone before us, whose accomplishments on the playing field of life are now part of our rich history. The imagery seems to suggest that those saints, the spiritual "athletes" of old, are now watching us and cheering us on from the great stadium of Heaven that looks down on the field of Earth. (The witnesses are said to "surround" us, not merely to have preceded us.) Even if, as some argue, the word *witnesses* may refer to their faithful service for God more than to the idea of their watching us, other passages clearly demonstrate Heaven's awareness of Earth.

> We who have gone through the day of sadness,
> shall enjoy together that day of gladness.
>
> **RICHARD BAXTER**

The unfolding drama of redemption, awaiting Christ's return, is currently happening on Earth. Earth is center court, center stage, awaiting the consummation of Christ's return and the establishment of his Kingdom. This seems a compelling reason to believe that the current inhabitants of Heaven would be able to observe what's happening on Earth.

In Heaven, Christ watches closely what transpires on Earth, especially in the lives of God's people (Revelation 2–3). If the Sovereign God's attention is on Earth, why wouldn't the attention of his heavenly subjects be focused here as well? When a great war is transpiring, are those in the home country uninformed and unaware of it? When a great drama is taking place, do those who know the writer, producer, and cast—and have great interest in the outcome— refrain from watching?

Angels saw Christ on Earth (1 Timothy 3:16). There are clear indications that the angels know what is happening on Earth (1 Corinthians 4:9; 1 Timothy 5:21). If angels, why not saints? It seems the people of God in Heaven would have as much of a vested interest in the spiritual events happening on Earth as angels do. Wouldn't we expect that the body and bride of Christ in Heaven would be intensely interested in the rest of the body and bride of Christ still living on Earth?

Abraham and Lazarus saw the rich man in Hell (Luke 16:23-26). If it is possible, at least in some cases, to see Hell from Heaven, why would people be unable to see Earth from Heaven?

Christ said, "There will be more rejoicing in heaven over one sinner who repents than over ninety-nine righteous persons who do not need to repent" (Luke 15:7). Similarly, "there is rejoicing in the presence of the angels of God over one sinner who repents" (Luke 15:10). Notice it does not speak of rejoicing *by* the angels but *in the presence* of angels. Who is doing this rejoicing in Heaven? I believe it logically includes not only God but also the saints in Heaven, who would so deeply appreciate the wonder of human conversion—especially the conversion of those they knew and loved on Earth. If they rejoice over conversions happening on Earth, then obviously *they must be aware of what is happening on Earth*—and not just generally, but specifically, down to the details of individuals coming to faith in Christ.

DO PEOPLE IN HEAVEN PRAY FOR THOSE ON EARTH?

Based on the scriptural evidence, I believe that departed saints currently in the present Heaven do intercede in prayer—at least sometimes—for those of us still on Earth.

Christ, the God-man, is in Heaven, at the right hand of God, interceding for people on Earth (Romans 8:34), which tells us there is at least one person who has died and gone to Heaven and is now praying for those on Earth. The martyrs in Heaven also pray to God (Revelation 6:10), asking him to take specific action on Earth. They are praying for God's justice on the earth, which has intercessory implications for Christians now suffering here. The sense of connection and loyalty to the body of Christ—and concern for the saints on Earth—would likely be enhanced, not diminished, by being in Heaven (Ephesians 3:15). In any case, Revelation 6 makes it clear that some who have died and are now in Heaven are praying concerning what's happening on Earth.

If prayer is simply talking to God, presumably we will pray more in Heaven than we do now—not less. And given our righteous state in Heaven, our prayers will be more effective than ever (James 5:16). Revelation 5:8 speaks of the "prayers of the saints" in a context that may include saints in Heaven, not just on Earth. We are never told to pray *to* the saints, but only to God. Yet the saints may well be praying for us.

If people in Heaven are allowed to see at least some of what transpires on Earth (and clearly they are, as we've seen), then it would seem strange for them *not* to intercede in prayer.

If we believe that Heaven is a place of ignorance or disinterest about Earth, we will naturally assume that people in Heaven don't pray for people on Earth. However, if we believe that people in Heaven are aware of events on Earth, and that they talk to God about his plan, his purpose, and his people, we will naturally assume they *do* pray for people on Earth. In my opinion, Scripture argues for the second assumption, not the first. I believe the burden of proof falls on those who would argue that people in Heaven don't pray for those on Earth. Where is this idea taught in Scripture? Often this deduction is based on a faulty premise—that for people in Heaven to be happy, they can't know what's happening on Earth. Let's take a closer look at that argument.

CAN IT BE HEAVEN IF PEOPLE ARE AWARE OF ANYTHING BAD ON EARTH?

Many books on Heaven maintain that those in Heaven cannot be aware of people and events on Earth because they would be made unhappy by all the suffering and evil; thus, Heaven would not truly be Heaven.

I believe this argument is invalid. After all, God knows exactly what's happening on Earth, yet it doesn't diminish Heaven for him. Likewise, it's Heaven for the angels, even though they also know what's happening on Earth. In fact, angels in Heaven see the torment of Hell, but it doesn't negate their joy in God's presence (Revelation 14:10). Abraham and Lazarus saw the rich man's agonies in Hell, but it didn't cause Paradise to cease to be Paradise (Luke 16:23-26). Surely then, nothing they could see on Earth could ruin Heaven for them. (Again, the parable does not suggest that people in Heaven normally gaze into Hell.)

It's also possible that even though joy would predominate in the present Heaven, there could be periodic sadness because there's still so much evil and pain on Earth. Christ grieved for people when he was on Earth (Matthew 23:37-39; John 11:33-36). Does he no longer grieve just because he's in Heaven? Or does he still hurt for his people when they suffer? Acts 9:4-5 gives a clear answer. Jesus said, "Saul, Saul, why do you persecute me?" When Saul asked who he was, he replied, "I am Jesus, whom you are persecuting." Doesn't Christ's identification with those being persecuted on Earth suggest he's currently hurting for his people, even as he's in Heaven?

If Jesus, who is in Heaven, feels sorrow for his followers, might not others in Heaven grieve as well? It's one thing to no longer cry because there's nothing left to cry about, which will be true on the New Earth. But it's something else to no longer cry when there's still suffering on Earth. Going into the presence of Christ surely does not make us *less* compassionate.

We must also keep in mind that Revelation 21:4, the verse most often quoted on the subject of sorrow in Heaven, refers specifically to the eternal Heaven, the New Earth. "He will wipe every tear from their eyes. There will be no more death or mourning or crying or pain, for the old order of things has passed away." Christ's promise of no more tears or pain comes *after* the end of the old Earth, after the Great White Throne Judgment, after "the old order of things has passed away" and there's no more suffering on Earth. = *eternal heaven*

The present Heaven and the eternal Heaven are not the same. We can be assured there will be no sorrow on the New Earth, our eternal home. But though the present Heaven is a far happier place than Earth under the Curse, Scripture doesn't state there can be no sorrow there. At the same time, people in Heaven are not frail beings whose joy can only be preserved by shielding them from what's really going on in the universe. Happiness in Heaven is not based on ignorance but on perspective. Those who live in the presence of Christ find great joy in worshiping God and living as righteous beings in rich fellowship in a sinless environment. And because God is continuously at work on Earth, the saints watching from Heaven have a great deal to praise him for, including God's drawing people on Earth to himself (Luke 15:7, 10). But those in the present Heaven are also looking forward to Christ's return, their bodily resurrection, the final judgment, and the fashioning of the New Earth from the ruins of the old. Only then and there, in our eternal home, will all evil and suffering and sorrow be washed away by the hand of God. Only then and there will we experience the fullness of joy intended by God and purchased for us by Christ at an unfathomable cost.

Meanwhile, we on this dying Earth can relax and rejoice for our loved ones who are in the presence of Christ. As the apostle Paul tells us, though we naturally grieve at losing loved ones, we are not "to grieve like the rest of men, who have no hope" (1 Thessalonians 4:13). Our parting is not the end of our relationship, only an interruption. We have not "lost" them, because we know where they are. They are experiencing the joy of Christ's presence in a place so wonderful that Christ called it Paradise. And one day, we're told, in a magnificent reunion, they and we "will be with the Lord forever. Therefore encourage each other with these words" (1 Thessalonians 4:17-18).

they're gone on a trip.
no phones.

GRASPING REDEMPTION'S FAR REACH

CHAPTER 8

THIS WORLD IS NOT
OUR HOME . . . OR IS IT?

God will make the new earth his dwelling place. . . . Heaven and earth will
then no longer be separated as they are now, but they will be one. But to leave
the new earth out of consideration when we think of the final state of believers
is greatly to impoverish biblical teaching about the life to come.

Anthony Hoekema

M any books on Heaven say nothing about the New Earth. Sometimes a few
paragraphs, vaguely worded, are tacked on at the end. Other books address the New Earth but undercut its true nature: "Is this new earth like our present earth? Probably not."[57] But if it isn't, why does God call it a New *Earth*? One
author says, "The eternal phase of Heaven will be so unlike what we are familiar
with that our present language can't even describe it."[58] Certainly our present language can't *fully* describe it, but it *does* in fact describe it (e.g., Revelation 21–22).

Many religions, including Buddhism and Hinduism, characterize the afterlife as vague and intangible. Christianity specifically refutes this notion. Biblical Christianity doesn't give up on humanity *or* the earth.

Paul Marshall writes, "Our destiny is an earthly one: a new earth, an earth
redeemed and transfigured. An earth reunited with heaven, but an earth, nevertheless."[59]

OUR LONGING FOR EDEN

We are homesick for Eden.[60] We're nostalgic for what is implanted in our hearts.
It's built into us, perhaps even at a genetic level. We long for what the first man and
woman once enjoyed—a perfect and beautiful Earth with free and untainted relationships with God, each other, animals, and our environment. Every attempt at
human progress has been an attempt to overcome what was lost in the Fall.

John Eldredge, in *The Journey of Desire*, tells a parable of a sea lion who had lost
the sea and lived in a desert where it was dry and dusty. But something inside him
longed for what he'd been made for: "How the sea lion came to the barren lands, no

one could remember. It all seemed so very long ago. So long, in fact, it appeared as though he had always been there. Not that he belonged in such an arid place. How could that be? He was, after all, a sea lion. But as you know, once you have lived so long in a certain spot, no matter how odd, you come to think of it as home."[61]

Our ancestors came from Eden. We are headed toward a New Earth. Meanwhile, we live out our lives on a sin-corrupted Earth, between Eden and the New Earth, but we must never forget that this is not our natural state. Sin and death and suffering and war and poverty are not natural—they are the devastating results of our rebellion against God.

We long for a return to Paradise—a perfect world, without the corruption of sin, where God walks with us and talks with us in the cool of the day. Because we're human beings, we desire something tangible and physical, something that will not fade away. And that is exactly what God promises us—a home that will not be destroyed, a kingdom that will not fade, a city with unshakable foundations, an incorruptible inheritance.

Adam was formed from the dust of the earth, forever establishing our connection to the earth (Genesis 2:7). Just as we are made *from* the earth, so too we are made *for* the earth. But, you may object, Jesus said he was going to prepare a place for us and would take us there to live with him forever (John 14:2-3). Yes. But *what is that place?* Revelation 21 makes it clear—it's the New Earth. That's where the New Jerusalem will reside when it comes down out of Heaven. Only *then* will we be truly home.

CLUES TO THE NATURE OF THE ETERNAL HEAVEN

I heard a pastor say on the radio, "There's nothing in our present experience that can suggest to us what Heaven is like." But if the eternal Heaven will be a New Earth, doesn't that suggest that the current Earth must be bursting with clues about what Heaven will be like?

Scripture gives us images full of hints and implications about Heaven. Put them together, and these jigsaw pieces form a beautiful picture. For example, we're told that Heaven is a city (Hebrews 11:10; 13:14). When we hear the word *city*, we shouldn't scratch our heads and think, "I wonder what that means?" We understand cities. Cities have buildings, culture, art, music, athletics, goods and services, events of all kinds. And, of course, cities have *people* engaged in activities, gatherings, conversations, and work.

Heaven is also described as a country (Hebrews 11:16). We know about countries. They have territories, rulers, national interests, pride in their identity, and citizens who are both diverse and unified.

If we can't imagine our present Earth without rivers, mountains, trees, and flowers, then why would we try to imagine the New Earth without these features? We wouldn't expect a non-Earth to have mountains and rivers. But God doesn't promise us a non-Earth. He promises us a *New* Earth. If the word *Earth* in this phrase means anything, it means that we can expect to find earthly things there—including atmosphere, mountains, water, trees, people, houses—even cities, buildings, and streets. (These familiar features are specifically mentioned in Revelation 21–22.)

We're told we'll have resurrection bodies (1 Corinthians 15:40-44). When God speaks of us having these bodies, do we shrug our shoulders and say, "I can't imagine what a new body would be like"? No, of course we can imagine it. We know what a body is—we've had one all our lives! (And we can remember when ours looked better, can't we?) So we *can* imagine a new body.

In Heaven, we'll rest (Revelation 14:13). We know what it means to rest. And to *want* to rest (Hebrews 4:10-11).

We're told we will serve Christ on the New Earth, working for his glory (Revelation 22:3). We know what it means to work. And to *want* to work.

Scripture speaks of a New Jerusalem made of precious stones. Some of the jewels listed in Revelation 21:19-21 are among the hardest substances known. They indicate the material solidity of the New Earth.

The problem is not that the Bible doesn't tell us much about Heaven. It's that we don't pay attention to what it tells us.

Some of the best portrayals I've seen of the eternal Heaven are in children's books. Why? Because they depict earthly scenes, with animals and people playing, and joyful activities. The books for adults, on the other hand, often try to be philosophical, profound, ethereal, and otherworldly. But that kind of Heaven is precisely what the Bible *doesn't* portray as the place where we'll live forever.

John Eldredge says, "We can only hope for what we desire."[62] To this I would add a corollary: *We can only desire what we can imagine.* If you think you can't imagine Heaven—or if you imagine it as something drab and unappealing—you can't get excited

> God promises that the glory of his people will demand a glorious creation to live in. So the fallen creation will obtain the very freedom from futility and evil and pain that the church is given. So when God makes all things new, he makes us new spiritually and morally, he makes us new physically, and then he makes the whole creation new so that our environment fits our perfected spirits and bodies.
>
> **JOHN PIPER**

about it. You can't come with the childlike eagerness that God so highly values (Mark 10:15).

Abraham "was looking forward to the city with foundations, whose architect and builder is God" (Hebrews 11:10). If he was looking forward to it, don't you think he was imagining what it would be like? Abraham's descendants "were longing for a better country—a heavenly one" (Hebrews 11:16). And, as Christ's followers, "we do not have an enduring city, but we are looking for the city that is to come" (Hebrews 13:14); "we are looking forward to the new heavens and new earth he has promised" (2 Peter 3:13, NLT).

Are we looking forward to, longing for, and looking for an unearthly realm? No—we're longing for new heavens and a New Earth . . . a new *universe*.

IS THE ETERNAL HEAVEN AN ACTUAL PLACE?

Many people can't resist spiritualizing what the Bible teaches about Heaven. According to an evangelical theologian, "While heaven is both a place and a state, it is primarily a state."[63] But what does this mean? Is any other place primarily a state?

Another theologian writes, "Paul does not think of heaven as a place, but thinks of it in terms of the presence of God."[64] But when a person is "present," doesn't that suggest there's a place?

One book puts *place* in quotation marks whenever it uses the word to describe Heaven or Hell. It says Paradise is "a spiritual condition more than a spatial location."[65] But Jesus didn't say that Heaven was "primarily a state" or a "spiritual condition." He spoke of a *house* with many *rooms* in which he would prepare a *place* for us (John 14:2). In Revelation 21–22, the New Earth and New Jerusalem are portrayed as actual places, with detailed physical descriptions.

Jesus told the disciples, "I will come back and take you to be with me that you also may be where I am" (John 14:3). He uses ordinary, earthly, spatial terms to describe Heaven. The word *where* refers to a place, a location. Likewise, the phrase *come back and take you* indicates movement and a physical destination.

If Heaven isn't a place, would Jesus have said it was? If we reduce Heaven to something less than or other than a place, we strip Christ's words of their meaning.

ARE WE JUST A-PASSING THROUGH?

The old gospel song, "This world is not my home, I'm just a-passing through," is a half-truth. We may pass from the earth through death, but eventually we'll be back to live on the restored Earth.

Earth has been damaged by our sin (Genesis 3:17). Therefore, the earth as it is now (under the Curse) is not our home. The world as it was, and as it will be, *is* our home. We have never known a world without sin, suffering, and death. Yet we yearn for such a life and such a world. When we see a roaring waterfall, beautiful flowers, a wild animal in its native habitat, or the joy in the eyes of our pets when they see us, we sense that this world is—or at least was *meant to be*—our home.

We are pilgrims in this life, not because our home will never be on Earth, but because our eternal home is not *currently* on Earth. It was and it will be, but it's not now.

Will the Eden we long for return? Will it be occupied by familiar, tangible, physical features and fully embodied people? The Bible clearly answers *yes*.

The biblical doctrine of the New Earth implies something startling: that if we want to know what the ultimate Heaven, our eternal home, will be like, the best place to start is by looking around us. We shouldn't close our eyes and try to imagine the unimaginable. We should open our eyes, because the present Earth is as much a valid reference point for envisioning the New Earth as our present bodies are a valid reference point for envisioning our new bodies. After all, we're living on the remnants of a perfect world, as the remnants of a perfect humanity. We shouldn't read into the New Earth anything that's wrong with this one, but can we not imagine what it would be like to be unhindered by disease and death? Can we not envision natural beauty untainted by destruction?

The idea of the New Earth as a physical place isn't an invention of short-sighted human imagination. Rather, it's the invention of a transcendent God, who made physical human beings to live on a physical Earth, *and* who chose to become a man himself on that same Earth. He did this that he might redeem mankind *and* Earth. Why? In order to glorify himself and enjoy forever the company of men and women in a world he's made for us.

THE THREE PHASES OF EARTH'S HISTORY

In order to have a biblical worldview, we must have a sense of our past, present, and future, and how they relate to each other. Without understanding God's original plan for mankind and the earth, we cannot understand his future plan. Without the bookends of past and future in place, the book itself—our present lives—won't stand up.

The following chart shows the three phases of Earth's history: humanity's past on the original Earth; our present experience on the fallen Earth; and our promised future on the New Earth.[†]

The chart portrays human history and human destiny. It demonstrates the continuity of past, present, and future, and the continuity between life on the old Earth and life on the New Earth. By comparing each series of statements, you'll see the distinct differences between these three periods. I encourage you to study this chart and contemplate the significance of each phase of Earth's history.

THREE ERAS OF MANKIND AND EARTH

PAST Genesis 1–2	PRESENT Genesis 3—Revelation 20	FUTURE Revelation 21–22
Original mankind	Fallen mankind; some believe and are transformed	Resurrected mankind
Original Earth	Fallen Earth, with glimmers of original	New (resurrected) Earth
God delegates reign to innocent mankind	Disputed reign with God, Satan, and fallen mankind	God delegates reign to righteous mankind
Mankind given dominion, with intended stewardship of Earth	Mankind's dominion thwarted, frustrated, and twisted	Mankind's dominion fulfilled; redeemed stewardship of Earth
God in Heaven, visiting Earth	God in Heaven, separate yet active (indwells believers by his Spirit)	God living forever with mankind on the New Earth
No Curse (universal perfection and blessing)	Sin and the Curse (withdrawal of blessing, or blessing selectively given, plus common grace)	No more Curse (greater blessing, deeper perfection, grace unending)
No shame	Shame	No shame or potential for shame

[†]An important limitation of this chart is its inability to fully reflect the "already and not yet" paradox of our being raised with Christ and seated with him in Heaven, the present reality of our righteousness in Christ, and the fact that God's new creation has already started with the death and resurrection of Christ.

PAST Genesis 1–2	PRESENT Genesis 3—Revelation 20	FUTURE Revelation 21–22
Tree of life in Eden (mankind can eat)	Tree of life in Paradise (mankind cut off from)	Tree of life in New Jerusalem (mankind can eat again forever)
River of life	Rivers and nature, with glimmers of past and future	River of life flows from the throne
Before redemption	Unfolding drama of redemption	After redemption
Sin unknown	Sin corrupts; its power and penalty assaulted, defeated by Christ	Sin forever removed
No death	Death permeates all	Death forever removed
Mankind created from the earth	Mankind dies, returns to the earth; new life to some	Mankind resurrected from the earth to live on the New Earth
First Adam reigns	First Adam falls; mankind reigns corruptly, with glimpses of good; second Adam comes	Last Adam reigns as God-man, with mankind as co-heirs and delegated kings
Serpent, Satan, on Earth	Serpent, Satan, judged but still present on Earth	Serpent, Satan, removed from Earth, thrown into eternal fire
God walking with humans in the Garden	Humans cut off from God	God dwells face-to-face with humans
God's glory evident to all, in all	God's glory obscured, seen in glimpses	God's glory forever manifested in all
Unhindered individual worship	Worship hampered by sin	Unhindered corporate worship
God's goodness known	God's goodness known by some, doubted by others	God's goodness forever celebrated

PAST Genesis 1–2	PRESENT Genesis 3—Revelation 20	FUTURE Revelation 21–22
Creation and mankind perfect	Creation and mankind tainted by sin	Creation and mankind restored to perfection
Mankind names, tends, rules the animals	Animals and mankind hurt each other	Animals and mankind live in complete harmony
Ground fertile, vegetation lush	Ground cursed, vegetation diseased	Ground fertile, vegetation thrives
Abundant food and water	Hunger and thirst, toil for food and water	Abundant food and water
Restfulness, satisfaction in labor	Restlessness, toil in labor	Enhanced restfulness, joy in labor
Innocence, closeness to God	Sin (alienation from God); some declared righteous in Christ	Righteousness (intimacy with God); complete righteousness in Christ
Paradise	Paradise lost, sought; glimmers seen, foretastes	Paradise regained and magnified
Mankind in ideal place	Mankind banished, struggles and wanders in fallen place(s)	Man restored to ideal place
Mankind able either to sin or not to sin	Mankind enslaved to sin, empowered not to sin	Mankind unable to sin, permanently empowered
Naked in innocence	Clothed due to unrighteousness	Clothed with righteousness
One marriage (Adam and Eve)	Many marriages	One marriage (Christ and church)
Marriage perfect	Marriage flawed by sin, blame, manipulation	Marriage perfect, unhindered
Beginning of human culture	Contamination and advancement of culture	Purification and eternal expansion of culture

PAST Genesis 1–2	PRESENT Genesis 3—Revelation 20	FUTURE Revelation 21–22
Mankind learns, creates in purity	Mankind learns, creates in impurity (Cain, Babel)	Mankind learns, creates in wisdom and purity
Mankind rules and expands Paradise	Mankind banished from Paradise, longs for return to Paradise	Mankind has unlimited, free access to Paradise
God's plan for mankind and Earth revealed	God's plan delayed and enriched	God's plan for mankind and Earth realized

In Genesis 3, the earth's first radical transition (mankind's fall and first judgment) can be seen as one bookend of human history. In Revelation 20, we see the second bookend in the earth's last radical transition (Christ's return and last judgment), creating a picture of great symmetry.

In Genesis, God plants the Garden on Earth; in Revelation, he brings down the New Jerusalem, with a garden at its center, to the New Earth. In Eden, there's no sin, death, or Curse; on the New Earth, there's no *more* sin, death, or Curse. In Genesis, the Redeemer is promised; in Revelation, the Redeemer returns. Genesis tells the story of Paradise lost; Revelation tells the story of Paradise regained. In Genesis, humanity's stewardship is squandered; in Revelation, humanity's stewardship is triumphant, empowered by the human and divine King Jesus.

These parallels are too remarkable to be anything but deliberate. These mirror images demonstrate the perfect symmetry of God's plan. We live in the in-between time, hearing echoes of Eden and the approaching footfalls of the New Earth.

Paul Marshall concludes, "This world is our home: we are made to live here. It has been devastated by sin, but God plans to put it right. Hence, we look forward with joy to newly restored bodies and to living in a newly restored heaven and earth. We can love this world because it is God's, and it will be healed, becoming at last what God intended from the beginning."[66]

The earth matters, our bodies matter, animals and trees matter, *matter* matters, because God created them and intends them to manifest his glory. And as we'll see in the following chapters, the God who created them has not given up on them any more than he has given up on us.

CHAPTER 9

WHY IS EARTH'S REDEMPTION ESSENTIAL TO GOD'S PLAN?

It is quite striking that virtually all of the basic words describing salvation in the Bible imply a return to an originally good state or situation. Redemption is a good example. To redeem is to "buy free," literally to "buy back." . . . The point of redemption is to free the prisoner from bondage, to give back the freedom he or she once enjoyed.

Albert Wolters

The entire physical universe was created for God's glory. But humanity rebelled, and the universe fell under the weight of our sin. Yet the serpent's seduction of Adam and Eve did not catch God by surprise. He had in place a plan by which he would redeem mankind—and all of creation—from sin, corruption, and death. Just as he promises to make men and women new, he promises to renew the earth itself.

Behold, I will create new heavens and a new earth. (Isaiah 65:17)

"As the new heavens and the new earth that I make will endure before me," declares the Lord, "so will your name and descendants endure." (Isaiah 66:22)

In keeping with his promise we are looking forward to a new heaven and a new earth, the home of righteousness. (2 Peter 3:13)

Then I saw a new heaven and a new earth, for the first heaven and the first earth had passed away. (Revelation 21:1)

Many other passages allude to the new heavens and New Earth without using those terms. God's redemptive plan climaxes not at the return of Christ, nor in the millennial kingdom, but on the New Earth. Only then will all wrongs be made right. Only then will there be no more death, crying, or pain (Revelation 21:1-4).

Consider this: If God's plan was merely to take mankind to the present Heaven, or to a Heaven that was the dwelling place of spirit beings, there would be no need for new heavens and a New Earth. Why refashion the stars of the heavens and the continents of the earth? God could just destroy his original creation and put it all behind him. But he won't do that. Upon creating the heavens and the earth, he called them "very good." Never once has he renounced his claim on what he made. He isn't going to abandon his creation. He's going to restore it. We won't go to Heaven and leave Earth behind. Rather, God will bring Heaven and Earth together into the same dimension, with no wall of separation, no armed angels to guard Heaven's perfection from sinful mankind (Genesis 3:24). God's perfect plan is "to bring all things in heaven and on earth together under one head, even Christ" (Ephesians 1:10).

God's redemptive goals are far less modest than we imagine. He surrenders no territory to the enemy. C. S. Lewis said of Milton's *Paradise Lost*, "Reading [it] makes us feel what it is like to live in a universe where every square inch, every split second, is claimed by God and counterclaimed by God."[67]

Christ died not merely to make the best of a bad situation. He died so that mankind, Earth, and the universe itself would be renewed to forever proclaim his glory.

GOD'S EARTHLY RENEWAL PLAN

God has never given up on his original creation. Yet somehow we've managed to overlook an entire biblical vocabulary that makes this point clear. *Reconcile. Redeem. Restore. Recover. Return. Renew. Regenerate. Resurrect.* Each of these biblical words begins with the *re-* prefix, suggesting a return to an original condition that was ruined or lost. (Many are translations of Greek words with an *ana* prefix, which has the same meaning as the English *re-.*) For example, *redemption* means to buy back what was formerly owned. Similarly, *reconciliation* means the restoration or reestablishment of a prior friendship or unity. *Renewal* means to make new again, restoring to an original state. *Resurrection* means becoming physically alive again, after death.

These words emphasize that God always sees us in light of what he intended us to be, and he always seeks to *restore us* to that design. Likewise, he sees the earth in terms of what he intended it to be, and he seeks to restore it to its original design.

Religion professor Albert Wolters, in *Creation Regained*, writes, "[God] hangs on to his fallen original creation and salvages it. He refuses to abandon the work of his hands—in fact, he sacrifices his own Son to save his original project. Humankind, which has botched its original mandate and the whole creation along with it, is given another chance in Christ; we are reinstated as God's managers on earth. The original good creation is to be restored."[68]

If God had wanted to consign us to Hell and start over, he could have. He could have made a new Adam and Eve and sent the old ones to Hell. But he didn't. Instead, he chose to redeem what he started with—the heavens, Earth, and mankind—to bring them back to his original purpose. God is the ultimate salvage artist. He loves to restore things to their original condition—and make them even better. God's purpose in our salvation is reflected in a phrase from the hymn "Hallelujah, What a Savior!": "ruined sinners to reclaim."[69] *Reclaim* is another *re-* word. It recognizes that God had a prior claim on humanity that was temporarily lost but is fully restored and taken to a new level in Christ. "The earth is the Lord's, and everything in it, the world, and all who live in it" (Psalm 24:1). God has never surrendered his title deed to the earth. He owns it—and he will not relinquish it to his enemies.

In *The Lion, the Witch, and the Wardrobe*, C. S. Lewis portrays the White Witch, who parallels the devil, as having a hold on Narnia that makes that world "always winter, but never Christmas." Those loyal to Aslan, though they've never seen him, eagerly await his appearing, for only he can make the world right again by assuming his role as rightful king. (First, however, he will shed his redemptive blood on the Stone Table.)

It's not only the *individuals* of Narnia who need Aslan to come, it is the entire *world* of Narnia. Similarly, Scripture tells us, "The reason the Son of God appeared was to destroy the devil's work" (1 John 3:8).

Notice Aslan's intention. He is the king, the son of the great Emperor beyond the Sea. Yet he delegates the responsibility of ruling the world to sons of Adam and daughters of Eve: Peter, Edmund, Susan, and Lucy. They are the rulers of Narnia. Likewise, God intends for *us*, sons and daughters of Adam and Eve, to be rulers of his New Earth, which he powerfully delivers from its always-winter-never-Christmas curse.

It's impossible to understand the ministry of Christ without the larger view of redemption's sweeping salvage plan. Albert Wolters points out that most of Christ's miracles "are miracles of *restoration*—restoration to health, restoration to life, restoration to freedom from demonic possession. Jesus' miracles provide us with a sample of the meaning of redemption: a freeing of creation from the shackles of sin and evil and a reinstatement of creaturely living as intended by God."[70] God placed mankind on Earth to fill it, rule it, and develop it to God's glory. But that plan has never been fulfilled. Should we therefore conclude that God's plan was ill-conceived, thwarted, or abandoned? No. These conclusions do not fit the character of an all-knowing, all-wise, sovereign God.

God determined from the beginning that he will redeem mankind and restore the earth. Why? So his original plan will be fulfilled.

Scripture shows us God's purpose with remarkable clarity; yet for many years as a Bible student and later as a pastor, I did not think in terms of renewal and restoration. Instead, I believed God was going to destroy the earth, abandon his original design and plan, and start over by implementing a new plan in an unearthly Heaven. Only in the past fifteen years have my eyes been opened to what Scripture has said all along.

What lies behind our notion that God is going to destroy the earth and be done with it? I believe it's a weak theology of God. Though we'd never say it this way, we see him as a thwarted inventor whose creation failed. Having realized his mistake, he'll end up trashing most of what he made. His consolation for a failed Earth is that he rescues a few of us from the fire. But this idea is emphatically refuted by Scripture. God has a magnificent plan, and he will *not* surrender Earth to the trash heap.

As Wolters says, "Redemption is not a matter of an addition of a spiritual or supernatural dimension to creaturely life that was lacking before; rather, it is a matter of bringing new life and vitality to what was there all along. . . . The only thing redemption adds that is not included in the creation is the remedy for sin, and that remedy is brought in solely for the purpose of recovering a sinless creation. . . . Grace *restores* nature, making it whole once more."[71]

THE NEW EARTH IS THE OLD EARTH RESTORED

Peter preached that Christ "must remain in heaven until the time comes for God to restore everything, as he promised long ago through his holy prophets" (Acts 3:21). We're told that a time is coming when God will restore *everything*. This is an inclusive promise. It encompasses far more than God merely restoring disembodied people to fellowship in a spirit realm. (Because living in a spirit realm is not what humans were made for and once enjoyed, it would not qualify as "restoring.") It is God restoring mankind to what we once were, what he designed us to be—fully embodied, righteous beings. And restoring the entire physical universe to what it once was.

Where will the restoration that Peter preached about be realized? The answer, he tells us, is found in the promises given "long ago through [God's] holy prophets." Read the prophets and the answer becomes clear—God will restore everything *on Earth*. The prophets are never concerned about some far-off realm of disembodied spirits. They are concerned about the land, the inheritance, the city of Jerusalem, and the earth they walked on. Messiah will come from Heaven to Earth, not to take us away from Earth to Heaven, but to restore Earth to what he intended so he can live with us here forever.

Luke tells the story of the prophetess Anna, a woman in her eighties, who worshiped at the Temple night and day, fasting and praying. Upon seeing the baby Jesus, she immediately approached Mary and Joseph and "gave thanks to God and spoke about the child to all who were looking forward to the redemption of Jerusalem" (Luke 2:36-38).

Notice Luke's exact wording. What were God's people looking forward to? *Redemption.* Their own redemption? Of course. But it was much more than that. It was the redemption of not only themselves, but also their families and community and even their city, Jerusalem. And the redemption of Jerusalem would also be the redemption of Israel. As the entire world was promised blessing through Abraham, the redemption of Jerusalem and Israel speaks of the redemption of the earth itself.

And who would be the agent of that redemption? Jesus, this child, the Messiah who would become King not only of redeemed individuals, but also King of a redeemed Jerusalem, and King of a redeemed earth. This is the gospel of the Kingdom. Anything less is a narrow view of God's redemptive plan.

So, will the earth we know come to an end? Yes. To a *final* end? No.

Revelation 21:1 says the old Earth will pass away. But when people pass away, they do not cease to exist. As we will be raised to be new people, so the earth will be raised to be a New Earth.

Did Peter invent the notion of all things being restored? No—he not only learned it from the

> Whatever sin has touched and polluted, God will redeem and cleanse. If redemption does not go as far as the curse of sin, then God has failed. Whatever the extent of the consequences of sin, so must the extent of redemption be.
>
> **STEVEN J. LAWSON**

prophets, he heard it directly from Christ. When Peter, hoping for commendation or reward, pointed out to Jesus that the disciples had left everything to follow him, the Lord didn't rebuke him. Instead, he said, "At the renewal of all things, when the Son of Man sits on his glorious throne, you who have followed me will also sit on twelve thrones, judging the twelve tribes of Israel" (Matthew 19:27-28).

Note Christ's word choice. He did not say "after the *destruction* of all things" or "after the *abandonment* of all things" but "at the *renewal* of all things." This is not a small semantic point—it draws a line in the sand between two fundamentally different theologies. Mankind was designed to live on the earth to God's glory. That's exactly what Christ's incarnation, death, and resurrection secured—a renewed humanity upon a renewed Earth. Jesus explicitly said "all things" would be renewed. The word *paligenesia*, translated "renewal" in Matthew 19:28, comes from two words which together mean "new genesis" or "coming back from death to life."[72] When Jesus said that "all things" would be renewed, the disciples would have understood him to mean "all things" that were part of the only lives they knew—those on Earth. Apart from those aspects of our present earthly lives that are inherently sinful or are fulfilled by a greater reality (more on this later), "all things" appears to be comprehensive.

J. R. R. Tolkien portrays a similar view of renewal in *The Hobbit*, when the dwarf king, Thorin Oakenshield, speaks his last words to Bilbo Baggins, whom he has wronged: "Farewell. . . . I go now to the halls of waiting to sit beside my fathers, until the world is renewed. Since I leave now all gold and silver, and go where it is of little worth, I wish to part in friendship from you, and I would take back my words and deeds at the Gate."[73]

Tolkien reflects biblical theology in the phrase "until the world is renewed." Thorin says he goes "to the halls of waiting to sit beside my fathers." This would be the intermediate Heaven. But he would wait there "until the world is renewed." This would be the eternal Heaven—not to be lived in a netherworld but in a resurrected world.

The predominant belief that the ultimate Heaven God prepares for us will be unearthly could not be more unbiblical. Earth was made for people to live on, and people were made to live on Earth. According to the prophets, the apostle Peter, and Christ himself, our destiny is to live forever on a restored and renewed Earth.

In the movie *The Passion of the Christ*, when Jesus is headed toward Calvary, on his knees under the weight of the cross, he says to his shocked and grief-torn mother, "Behold, I make all things new." These words are straight from Revelation 21:5, where they are spoken by the risen Jesus concerning the New Earth, where a renewed humanity will live on a renewed Earth, joyful in the presence of their resurrected Savior, who made it all possible by paying a price that was inconceivably great.

REDEMPTION = RETURN

Redemption buys back God's original design. In the words of one writer, "Adam and Eve (and their children) were to extend the blessings of Paradise throughout the entire world. . . . Salvation, therefore, restores man to his original calling and purpose, and guarantees that man's original mandate—to exercise dominion under God over the whole earth—will be fulfilled."[74]

If, due to the Fall, God would have given up on his original purpose for mankind to fill the earth and rule it (Genesis 1:28), he surely wouldn't have repeated the same command to Noah after the Flood: "Be fruitful and increase in number and fill the earth" (Genesis 9:1). Still, until sin and the Curse are permanently removed, people would be incapable of exercising proper stewardship of the earth.

Our present purpose is inseparable from God's stated eternal purpose for us to rule the earth forever as his children and heirs. That is at the core of the Westminster Shorter Catechism's defining statement: "Man's chief end is to glorify God, and to enjoy him forever."[75] We will glorify God and find joy in him as we do what he has made us to do: serve him as resurrected beings and carry out his plan for developing a Christ-centered, resurrected culture in a resurrected universe.

"For as in Adam all die, so in Christ all will be made alive. But each in his own turn: Christ, the firstfruits; then, when he comes, those who belong to him. Then the end will come, when he hands over the kingdom to God the Father after he has destroyed all dominion, authority and power. For he must reign until he has put all his enemies under his feet" (1 Corinthians 15:22-25).

Most scholars agree that the point of this passage is not that Christ will someday cease to reign, but that his reign will continue *until* and *after* his enemies are conquered and judged. (When a prince handed over to his father a kingdom he had conquered, it was common for the king to entrust rulership of that kingdom back to his son.)

Christ's mission is both to redeem what was lost in the Fall and to destroy all competitors to God's dominion, authority, and power. When everything is put under his feet, when God rules all and mankind rules the earth as kings under Christ, the King of kings, at last all will be as God intends. The period of rebellion will be over forever, and the universe, and all who serve Christ, will participate in the Master's joy!

GOD'S GLORY ON GOD'S EARTH

The physical heavens are constantly declaring God's glory (Psalm 19:1-2). Even now, in reference to an Earth under the Curse, God says, "The glory of the Lord fills the whole earth" (Numbers 14:21). But the universe will behold an even greater display of God's glory, one that will involve redeemed men and women and redeemed nations on a redeemed earth. It is on Earth, God promises, that "the glory of the Lord will be revealed, and all mankind together will see it" (Isaiah 40:5). That God will be glorified on Earth is central to innumerable passages, including these two:

> Surely his salvation is near those who fear him, that his glory may dwell in our land. (Psalm 85:9)

> I saw the glory of the God of Israel coming from the east . . . and the land was radiant with his glory. (Ezekiel 43:2)

In both these passages, the word translated as "land" (*erets*) is the word for "earth." Ezekiel saw God's glory at the gates of Jerusalem—manifested not in some immaterial realm but on the earth.

To understand why Peter preached that God promised through the prophets that he would "restore everything" (Acts 3:21), consider this sampling of passages that promise God's glory will be manifested to all the nations of the earth, particularly in the New Jerusalem:

> The nations will fear the name of the Lord, all the kings of the earth will revere your glory. For the Lord will rebuild Zion and appear in his glory. (Psalm 102:15-16)

> They will neither harm nor destroy on all my holy mountain, for the earth will be full of the knowledge of the Lord as the waters cover the sea. In that day the Root of Jesse will stand as a banner for the peoples; the nations will rally to him, and his place of rest will be glorious. (Isaiah 11:9-10)

> "They will proclaim my glory among the nations. And they will bring all your brothers, from all the nations, to my holy mountain in Jerusalem as an offering to the Lord—on horses, in chariots and wagons, and on mules and camels," says the Lord. (Isaiah 66:19-20)

> This is what the Lord Almighty says: "In a little while I will once more shake the heavens and the earth, the sea and the dry land. I will shake all nations, and the desired of all nations will come, and I will fill this house with glory," says the Lord Almighty. (Haggai 2:6-7)

God's Kingdom and dominion are not about what happens in some remote, unearthly place; instead, they are about what happens on the earth, which God created for his glory. God has tied his glory to the earth and everything connected with it: mankind, animals, trees, rivers, *everything*. "Holy, holy, holy is the Lord Almighty; the whole earth is full of his glory" (Isaiah 6:3). The Hebrew here can be translated "the fullness of the earth is his glory." His glory is manifested in his creation. The earth is not disposable. It is essential to God's plan. God promises that ultimately the whole Earth will be filled with his glory (Psalm 72:19; Habakkuk 2:14).

God has his hands on the earth. He will not let go—even when it requires that his hands be pierced by nails. Both his incarnation and those nails secured him to Earth and its eternal future. In a redemptive work far larger than most imagine, Christ bought and paid for our future and the earth's.

A VISION OF THE NEW EARTH

Another significant passage that describes the New Earth is Isaiah 60. Although it doesn't contain the term *New Earth* (as do Isaiah 65 and 66), we can be certain that's what Isaiah intended because his precise language is used in John's depiction of the New Earth in Revelation 21–22. Thus, Isaiah 60 serves as the best biblical commentary on Revelation 21–22.

At the beginning of Isaiah's remarkable prophetic message, God says to his people in Jerusalem, "The Lord rises upon you and his glory appears over you. Nations will come to your light, and kings to the brightness of your dawn" (vv. 2-3). God's people will have a glorious future in which the earth's nations and kings will participate in and benefit from a renewed and glorious Jerusalem. It won't be only some nations, but all of them: "All assemble and come to you" (v. 4).

This will be a time of unprecedented rejoicing: "Then you will look and be radiant, your heart will throb and swell with joy" (v. 5). On the renewed Earth, the nations will bring their greatest treasures into this glorified city: "The wealth on the seas will be brought to you, to you the riches of the nations will come" (v. 5).

There will be animals on the New Earth, from various nations: "Herds of camels will cover your land, young camels of Midian and Ephah" (v. 6). Redeemed people will travel from far places to the glorified Jerusalem: "And all from Sheba will come, bearing gold and incense and proclaiming the praise of the Lord" (v. 6).

People who dwell on islands will worship God, and ships will come from

"Tarshish, bringing your sons from afar, with their silver and gold, to the honor of the Lord your God, the Holy One of Israel, for he has endowed you with splendor" (v. 9).

Most of us are unaccustomed to thinking of nations, rulers, civilizations, and culture in Heaven—but Isaiah 60 is one of many passages that demonstrate that the New Earth will in fact be *earthly*.

Isaiah speaks words that John applies directly to the New Jerusalem (in Revelation 21:25-26): "Your gates will always stand open, they will never be shut, day or night, so that men may bring you the wealth of the nations—their kings led in triumphal procession" (v. 11).

The magnificence of nations will be welcomed into the King's great city: "The glory of Lebanon will come to you, the pine, the fir and the cypress together" (v. 13). The hearts of the nations will be transformed in their attitudes toward God, his people, and his city: "The sons of your oppressors will come bowing before you; all who despise you will bow down at your feet and will call you the City of the Lord" (v. 14). God promises the New Jerusalem, "I will make you the everlasting pride and the joy of all generations" (v. 15). This is not a temporary period of fleeting prosperity but an "everlasting" condition. It will not be limited to one time period but will be for "all generations."

The New Jerusalem will be the beneficiary of all people groups and their rulers: "You will drink the milk of nations and be nursed at royal breasts" (v. 16). The fulfillment of all these promises will testify to God's greatness: "Then you will know that I, the Lord, am your Savior, your Redeemer, the Mighty One of Jacob" (v. 16). God promises something that has never yet been true of the earthly Jerusalem: "I will make peace your governor and righteousness your ruler. No longer will violence be heard in your land, nor ruin or destruction within your borders, but you will call your walls Salvation and your gates Praise" (vv. 17-18).

Isaiah then tells us what John connects directly to the New Earth (in Revelation 21:23; 22:5): "The sun will no more be your light by day, nor will the brightness of the moon shine on you, for the Lord will be your everlasting light, and your God will be your glory. Your sun will never set again, and your moon will wane no more; the Lord will be your everlasting light, and your days of sorrow will end" (vv. 19-20).

Of the New Jerusalem, we're told that "nothing impure will ever enter it, nor will anyone who does what is shameful or deceitful, but only those whose names are written in the Lamb's book of life" (Revelation 21:27). Isaiah tells us the same, using inclusive language that could not apply to the old Earth under the Curse: "Then will all your people be righteous" (60:21). Isaiah adds, "and they will possess the land [*erets*] forever." The earth will be theirs, not for a glorious decade or century or millennium, but *forever*.[76]

Though Isaiah's reference to animal sacrifices and a temple (v. 7) raise questions, it's clear that the passage as a whole is a prophetic depiction of the future New Earth. There is no interpretive reason to believe that the descriptions in Isaiah 60 of the New Earth will be fulfilled any less literally than those in Isaiah 52–53.[†] Because Isaiah's words about the Messiah's first coming were so meticulously fulfilled, down to specific physical details, shouldn't we assume that his prophecies in subsequent chapters concerning life on the New Earth will likewise be literally and specifically fulfilled?

Christ's millennial reign may prefigure the fulfillment of God's promises about Jerusalem's future. But we will see their ultimate fulfillment only in the New Jerusalem on the New Earth, when the Curse is gone, death is no more, and God's people will live on the earth forever.

REDEMPTION OF NATIONS AND CULTURE

Both Isaiah and John, using similar language, state that on the New Earth "the kings of the earth will bring their splendor into" the New Jerusalem and "the glory and honor of the nations will be brought into it" (Revelation 21:24, 26; cf. Isaiah 60:3, 5).

Though John doesn't elaborate in Revelation, Isaiah is specific about what will be brought to the Holy City. He mentions the cultural products of once-pagan nations: the ships of Tarshish and the trees of Lebanon and the camels of Ephah and the gold and incense of Sheba, which will be brought in by its people "proclaiming the praise of the Lord" (Isaiah 60:6). Treasures that were once linked to idolatry and rebellion will be gathered into the city and put to God-glorifying use. Both Isaiah and Revelation indicate that the products of human culture will play an important role on the New Earth.

In his excellent treatment of Isaiah and the New Jerusalem, *When the Kings Come Marching In*, Richard Mouw points out that the same ships of Tarshish and trees of Lebanon mentioned in Isaiah 60 are regarded in Isaiah 2 as objects of human pride that God promises to bring down (vv. 12-13, 16-18).[77] Isaiah speaks of a day of judgment in which "men will flee to caves in the rocks and to holes in the ground from dread of the Lord and the splendor of his majesty,

---

[†]Isaiah 52–53 details the Messiah's death, saying he was pierced for our transgressions, sacrificed as a lamb, was numbered with the transgressors, bore our sins, interceded for the transgressors, etc.

when he rises to shake the earth" (2:19). This language is strongly evocative of the depiction of God's end times judgment, in which men try to hide "in caves and among the rocks of the mountains" (Revelation 6:15).

In Isaiah 10:34, the prophet tells us that God "will cut down the forest thickets with an ax; Lebanon will fall before the Mighty One." Because people put their pride and hope in "their" forests and ships, God will demonstrate his superiority by bringing down the forests and sinking the ships.

Now, if the trees of Lebanon and ships of Tarshish are singled out as being destroyed in God's future judgment, how can they, as Isaiah 60 indicates, turn up again in the Holy City as instruments of service to the Lord?

This is the paradox of Scripture's simultaneous teachings of destruction and renewal. That which is now used for prideful and even idolatrous purposes will be used to the glory of God when the hearts of mankind are transformed and creation itself is renewed.[78]

There is nothing wrong with ships, lumber, gold, or camels. What God will destroy in his judgment is the idolatrous *misuse* of these good things. Then, having destroyed our perversions of his good gifts, he will, in his re-creation of the earth, restore these things as good and useful tools for his glory.

Later, we'll return to the subject of culture on the New Earth. But for now, it will suffice that Isaiah and John help us envision the New Earth as not only a world of natural wonders, but as one that also includes multinational citizens and cultural treasures.

Significantly, the vivid description of the New Earth in Isaiah 60 is immediately followed by the explicitly messianic passage that Jesus used as his inaugural text for his ministry (Luke 4:16-19): "The Spirit of the Sovereign Lord is on me, because the Lord has anointed me to preach good news to the poor. He has sent me to bind up the brokenhearted, to proclaim freedom for the captives and release from darkness for the prisoners" (Isaiah 61:1).

It was the incarnation, atonement, and resurrection of Jesus Christ that brought redemption to mankind, Jerusalem, and the earth. Christ's mission was to reclaim and set free not only the earth's inhabitants, but the earth itself. He came not only to redeem mankind as individuals, but also as nations and cultures, and to redeem not only the work of his own hands (e.g., the forests of Lebanon), but also the works of his *creatures'* hands (e.g., the ships of Tarshish).

Theologian A. A. Hodge says it beautifully:

Heaven, as the eternal home of the divine Man and of all the redeemed members of the human race, must necessarily be thoroughly human in its structure, conditions, and activities. Its joys and activities must all be rational, moral, emotional, voluntary and active. There must be the exercise of all the faculties, the gratification of all tastes, the development of all talent capacities, the realization of all ideals. The reason, the intellectual curiosity, the imagination, the aesthetic instincts, the holy affections, the social affinities, the inexhaustible resources of strength and power native to the human soul must all find in heaven exercise and satisfaction. Then there must always be a goal of endeavor before us, ever future. . . . Heaven will prove the consummate flower and fruit of the whole creation and of all the history of the universe.[79]

CHAPTER 10

WHAT WILL IT MEAN FOR THE CURSE TO BE LIFTED?

Everything will be glorified, even nature itself. And that seems to me to be the biblical teaching about the eternal state: that what we call heaven is life in this perfect world as God intended humanity to live it. When he put Adam in Paradise at the beginning, Adam fell, and all fell with him, but men and women are meant to live in the body, and will live in a glorified body in a glorified world, and God will be with them.

Martyn Lloyd-Jones

When Adam and Eve fell into sin, Satan appeared to have ruined God's plan for a righteous, undying humanity to rule the earth to God's glory. Yet immediately after the Fall, God promised a redeemer, the seed of the woman, who would one day come and crush the serpent: "I will put enmity between you and the woman, and between your offspring and hers; he will crush your head, and you will strike his heel" (Genesis 3:15).

While the wound of sin was still fresh, before the first scar had formed, God unveiled his plan to send a fully human redeemer who would be far more powerful than Satan. In a courageous act of intervention to deliver mankind, this redeemer would deliver a mortal wound to the usurping devil, and in the process would be wounded himself.

"Since one of the results of sin had been death," writes Anthony Hoekema, "the promised victory must somehow involve the removal of death. Further, since another result of sin had been the banishment of our first parents from the Garden of Eden, from which they were supposed to rule the world for God, it would seem that the victory should also mean man's restoration to some kind of regained paradise, from which he could once again properly and sinlessly rule the earth. . . . In a sense, therefore, the expectation of a New Earth was already implicit in the promise of Genesis 3:15."[80]

Later, it's revealed that this redeemer would be the seed of Abraham (Genesis 22:18), of the tribe of Judah (Genesis 49:10) and the house of David (2 Samuel 7:12-13). Genesis 3:15 is the first of many passages anticipating a suffering servant who would battle Satan and redeem God's people (e.g., Isaiah 42:1-4;

49:5-7; 52:13-15; 53). That suffering servant would be Christ, the Messiah, who came to make all things new.

God did not sit idly by or shrug his shoulders at sin, death, and the Curse. He did not relinquish his claim on mankind and the earth. No sooner did ruin descend on humanity and Earth than God revealed his plan to defeat Satan and retake them for his glory.

TAKING OUR INHERITANCE

Our interest in the end times usually extends to the period immediately preceding and following the return of Christ. But God's plan culminates after the final judgment, when King Jesus says, "Come, you who are blessed by my Father; take your inheritance, the kingdom prepared for you since the creation of the world" (Matthew 25:34). Where is this kingdom? Exactly where it has been from the beginning—on Earth.

What is the inheritance Jesus speaks of? Just as the children of kings inherit kingdoms, and kingdoms consist of land and property, so Earth is humanity's God-given property.

God hasn't changed his mind; he hasn't fallen back to Plan B or abandoned what he originally intended for us at the creation of the world. When Christ says "take your inheritance, the kingdom prepared for you since the creation of the world," it's as if he's saying, "This is what I wanted for you all along. This is what I went to the cross and defeated death to give you. Take it, rule it, exercise dominion, enjoy it; and in doing so, share my happiness."

God doesn't throw away his handiwork and start from scratch—instead, he uses the same canvas to repair and make more beautiful the painting marred by the vandal. The vandal doesn't get the satisfaction of destroying his rival's masterpiece. On the contrary, God makes an even greater masterpiece out of what his enemy sought to destroy.

Satan wants us to give up on God, on our purpose and calling, and on our planet. God reminds us, "The one who is in you is greater than the one who is in the world" (1 John 4:4). Satan seeks to destroy the earth. God seeks to restore and renew the earth, rule it, and hand it back over to his children. God will win the battle for us and for the earth.

UNITING HEAVEN AND EARTH

God's plan of the ages is "to bring all things in heaven and on earth together under one head, even Christ" (Ephesians 1:10). "All things" is broad and inclusive—nothing will be left out. This verse corresponds precisely to the culmination of history that we see enacted in Revelation 21, the merging together of the once separate realms of Heaven and Earth, fully under Christ's lordship.

The hymn "This Is My Father's World" expresses this truth in its final words: "Jesus who died shall be satisfied, and earth and heaven be one."[81] Just as God and mankind are reconciled in Christ, so too the dwellings of God and mankind—Heaven and Earth—will be reconciled in Christ. As God and man will be forever united in Jesus, so Heaven and Earth will forever be united in the new physical universe where we will live as resurrected beings. To affirm anything less is to understate the redemptive work of Christ. Yet, strangely, in the schools and churches I've been a part of—and in the vast majority of the 150 books about Heaven I've read—this central truth has *rarely* been affirmed. Many people with whom I've spoken have told of similar experiences.

Heaven is God's home. Earth is our home. Jesus Christ, as the God-man, forever links God and mankind, and thereby forever links Heaven and Earth. As Ephesians 1:10 demonstrates, this idea of Earth and Heaven becoming one is explicitly biblical. Christ will make Earth into Heaven and Heaven into Earth. Just as the wall that separates God and mankind is torn down in Jesus, so too the wall that separates Heaven and Earth will be forever demolished. There will be one universe, with all things in Heaven and on Earth together under one head, Jesus Christ. "Now the dwelling of God is with men, and he will live with them" (Revelation 21:3). God will live with us on the New Earth. That will "bring all things in heaven and on earth together."

God's plan is that there will be no more gulf between the spiritual and physical worlds. There will be no divided loyalties or divided realms. There will be one cosmos, one universe united under one Lord—forever. This is the unstoppable plan of God. This is where history is headed.

When God walked with Adam and Eve in the Garden, Earth was Heaven's backyard. The New Earth will be even more than that—it will be Heaven itself. And those who know Jesus will have the privilege of living there.

WHO WILL REIGN OVER THE EARTH?

The Bible's central storyline revolves around a question: Who will reign over the earth? Earth's destiny hangs in the balance. Because it is the realm where God's glory has been most challenged and resisted, it is therefore also the stage on which his glory will be most graphically demonstrated. By reclaiming, restoring, renewing, and resurrecting Earth—and empowering a regenerated mankind to reign over it—God will accomplish his purpose of bringing glory to himself.

In Scripture, those said to have thrones include God the Father (Hebrews 12:2; Revelation 22:1), Christ the Son (Luke 1:32; Hebrews 1:8), God's human children (Revelation 4:4; 11:16), and Satan (Revelation 2:13). God's claim to his throne is absolute. The claim of human beings to their thrones is valid, but *only* if they remain in submission to God, who delegated dominion to them as his heirs and subrulers. Satan's claim to the throne is false.

Ultimately, Satan will be eternally dethroned. People who reject God will be eternally dethroned. God will be permanently enthroned. Righteous human beings, first enthroned by God to reign over the earth from Eden, then dethroned by their own sin and Satan, will be reenthroned forever with God. "And they will reign for ever and ever" (Revelation 22:5).

Christ will become the unchallenged, absolute ruler of the universe and then will turn over to his Father the Kingdom he has won (1 Corinthians 15:28). Redeemed humans will be God's unchallenged, delegated rulers of the New Earth. God and humanity will live together in eternal happiness, forever deepening their relationships, as the glory of God permeates every aspect of the new creation.

THE LAST ADAM DEFEATS SATAN

Satan successfully tempted the first Adam in Eden. The theological consequences of Adam's sin (and the redeeming work of the last Adam, Jesus Christ, the new head of the human race) are laid out in Romans 5:12-19. When Satan tempted the last Adam in the wilderness (which is what Eden's garden had become), Christ resisted him. But the evil one was desperate to defeat Christ, to kill him as he had the first Adam (Matthew 4:1-11; Luke 4:1-13).

Satan appeared to succeed when the last Adam died. But Jesus didn't die because he had sinned. He died because, as God's Son, he chose to pay the price for mankind's sins, tracing all the way back to the first Adam and forward to the final generation of the fallen Earth. Satan's apparent victory in Christ's death was what assured the devil's final defeat. When Christ rose from the dead, he dealt Satan a fatal blow, crushing his head, assuring both his destruction and the resurrection of mankind and the earth. Satan's grip on this world was loosened. It's still strong, but once he is cast into the lake of fire and God refashions the old Earth into the New Earth, mankind and Earth will slip forever from Satan's grasping hands, never again to be touched by him (Revelation 20:10).

Christ has already defeated Satan, but the full scope of his victory has not yet been manifested on Earth. At Christ's ascension, God "seated him at his right hand in the heavenly realms, far above all rule and authority, power and dominion, and every title that can be given, not only in the present age but also in the one to come. And God placed all things under his feet and appointed him to be head over everything" (Ephesians 1:20-22).

These words are all-inclusive, and they are past tense, not future. Christ rules the universe. And yet it is only upon Christ's physical return to the earth that Satan will be bound.

This is the "already and not yet" paradox that characterizes life on the present Earth. Heaven's king is even now "ruler of the kings of the earth" (Revelation 1:5). "On his robe and on his thigh this name is written: King of kings and Lord of lords" (Revelation 19:16).

Through Christ's redemptive work, he "disarmed the powers and authorities" and "made a public spectacle of them, triumphing over them" (Colossians 2:15). His death stripped Satan of ultimate power (Hebrews 2:14). "The Son of God appeared for this purpose, to destroy the works of the devil" (1 John 3:8, NASB).

Note that it says Christ came not to destroy the world he created, but to destroy the works of the devil, which were to twist and pervert and ruin what God had made. Redemption will forever destroy the devil's work by removing its hold on creation, and reversing its consequences. It is Satan's desire to destroy the world. God's intent is not to destroy the world but to deliver it from destruction. His plan is to redeem this fallen world, which he designed for greatness.

Redeemed mankind will reign with Christ over the earth. The gates of Satan's false kingdom will not prevail against Christ's church (Matthew 16:18).

The outcome of the great war is not in question. It is certain. Christ will reign victoriously forever. The only question we must answer is this: Will we fight on his side or against him? We answer this question not just once, with our words, but daily, with our choices.

REMOVING THE CURSE

"No longer will there be any curse" (Revelation 22:3). If the Bible said nothing else about life in the eternal Heaven, the New Earth, these words would tell us a vast amount.

No more Curse.

What would our lives be like if the Curse were lifted? One day we will know firsthand—but even now there's much to anticipate.

After Adam sinned, God said, "Cursed is the ground [earth] because of you" (Genesis 3:17). When the Curse is reversed, we will no longer engage in "painful toil" (v. 17) but will enjoy satisfying caretaking. No longer will the earth yield "thorns and thistles" (v. 18), defying our dominion and repaying us for corrupting it. No longer will we "return to the ground . . . [from which we] were taken" (v. 19), swallowed up in death as unrighteous stewards who ruined ourselves and the earth.

Our welfare is inseparable from Earth's welfare. Our destiny is inseparable from Earth's destiny. That's why the curse on mankind required that the earth be cursed and why the earth will also be resurrected when we are resurrected.

The Curse will be reversed.

As a result of the Curse, the first Adam could no longer eat from the tree of life, which presumably would have made him live forever in his sinful state (Genesis 3:22). Death, though a curse in itself, was also the only way out from under the Curse—and that only because God had come up with a way to defeat death and restore mankind's relationship with him.

Christ came to remove the curse of sin and death (Romans 8:2). He is the second Adam, who will undo the damage wrought by the first Adam (1 Corinthians 15:22, 45; Romans 5:15-19). In the Cross and the Resurrection, God made a way not only to restore his original design for mankind but also to expand it. In our resurrection bodies, we will again dwell on Earth—a New Earth—completely free of the Curse. Unencumbered by sin, human activity will lead naturally to a prosperous and magnificent culture.

Under the Curse, human culture has not been eliminated, but it has been severely hampered by sin, death, and decay. Before the Fall, food was readily available with minimal labor. Time was available to pursue thoughtful aesthetic ideas, to work for the sheer pleasure of it, to please and glorify God by developing skills and abilities. Since the Fall, generations have lived and died after spending most of their productive years eking out an existence in the pursuit of food, shelter, and protection against theft and war. Mankind has been dis-

> Because of man's fall into sin, a curse was pronounced over this creation. God now sent his son into this world to redeem that creation from the results of sin. The work of Christ, therefore, is not just to save certain individuals, not even to save an innumerable throng of blood-bought people. The total work of Christ is nothing less than to redeem this entire creation from the effects of sin. That purpose will not be accomplished until God has ushered in the new earth, until Paradise Lost has become Paradise Regained.
>
> **ANTHONY HOEKEMA**

tracted and debilitated by sickness and sin. Our cultural development has likewise been stunted and twisted, and sometimes misdirected—though not always. Even though our depravity means we have no virtue that makes us worthy of our standing before God, we are nevertheless "made in God's likeness" (James 3:9). Consequently, some things we do, even in our fallenness, such as painting, building, performing beautiful music, finding cures for diseases, and other cultural, scientific, commercial, and aesthetic pursuits, are good.

The removal of the Curse means that people, culture, the earth, and the universe will again be as God intended. The lifting of the Curse comes at a terrible price: "Christ redeemed us from the curse of the law by becoming a curse for us" (Galatians 3:13, ESV). God's law shows us how far short we fall. But Jesus took on himself the curse of sin, satisfying God's wrath. By taking the Curse upon himself and defeating it through his resurrection, Jesus guaranteed the lifting of the Curse from mankind and from the earth.

The removal of the Curse will be as thorough and sweeping as the redemptive work of Christ. In bringing us salvation, Christ has already undone some of the damage in our hearts, but in the end he will finally and completely restore his entire creation to what God originally intended (Romans 8:19-21). Christ will turn back the Curse and restore to humanity all that we lost in Eden, and he will give us much more besides.

FAR AS THE CURSE IS FOUND

Jesus came not only to save spirits from damnation. That would have been, at most, a partial victory. No, he came to save his whole creation from death. That means our bodies too, not just our spirits. It means the earth, not just humanity. And it means the universe, not just the earth.

Christ's victory over the Curse will not be partial. Death will not just limp away wounded. It will be annihilated, utterly destroyed: "[God] will destroy the shroud that enfolds all peoples, the sheet that covers all nations; he will swallow up death forever. The Sovereign Lord will wipe away the tears from all faces; he will remove the disgrace of his people from all the earth" (Isaiah 25:7-8).

Isaac Watts's magnificent hymn "Joy to the World" is theologically on target:

> *No more let sins and sorrows grow*
> *Nor thorns infest the ground;*
> *He comes to make His blessings flow*
> *Far as the curse is found.*

God will lift the Curse, not only morally (in terms of sins) and psychologically (in terms of sorrows), but also physically (in terms of thorns in the ground).

How far does Christ's redemptive work extend? *Far as the curse is found.* If redemption failed to reach the farthest boundaries of the Curse, it would be incomplete. The God who rules the world with truth and grace won't be satisfied until every sin, every sorrow, every thorn is reckoned with.

In the Reformed tradition, Albert Wolters embraces an expansive redemptive worldview: "Biblical religion . . . views the whole course of history as a movement from a garden to a city, and it fundamentally affirms that movement. . . . Redemption in Jesus Christ reaches just as far as the fall. The horizon of creation is at the same time the horizon of sin and of salvation. To conceive of either the fall or Christ's deliverance as encompassing less than the whole of creation is to compromise the biblical teaching of the radical nature of the fall and the cosmic scope of redemption."[82]

Jesus came not only to rescue people from ultimate destruction. He came also to rescue the entire universe from ultimate destruction. He will transform our dying Earth into a vital New Earth, fresh and uncontaminated, no longer subject to death and destruction.

The Curse is real, but it is *temporary*. Jesus is the cure for the Curse. He came to set derailed human history back on its tracks. Earth won't be put out of its misery; it will be infused with a greater life than it has ever known, at last becoming all that God meant for it to be.

We have never seen the earth as God made it. Our planet as we know it is a shadowy, halftone image of the original. But it does whet our appetites for the New Earth, doesn't it? If the present Earth, so diminished by the Curse, is at times so beautiful and wonderful; if our bodies, so diminished by the Curse, are at times overcome with a sense of the earth's beauty and wonder; then *how magnificent will the New Earth be?* And what will it be like to experience the New Earth in something else we've never known: perfect bodies?

A mature Christian Bible student wrote me a note after reading a draft of this book: "I realize now that I have always thought that when we die we go immediately to our eternal home. After I was there, that would be the end of the story. I wouldn't care about what happened to Earth and everything on it. Why *should* I care about a doomed planet?"

Without Christ, both the earth and mankind would be doomed. But Christ came, died, and rose from the grave. He brought deliverance, not destruction. Because of Christ, we are not doomed, and neither is the earth.

Earth cannot be delivered from the Curse by being destroyed. It can only be delivered by being *resurrected*. As we'll see in the next section, Christ's resurrection is the forerunner of our own, and our resurrection is the forerunner of the earth's.

ANTICIPATING RESURRECTION

CHAPTER 11

WHY IS RESURRECTION
SO IMPORTANT?

*Make no mistake: if He rose at all it was as His body; if the cells' dissolution
did not reverse, the molecules reknit, the amino acids rekindle, the Church
will fall. . . . Let us not mock God with metaphor, analogy, sidestepping
transcendence; making of the event a parable, a sign painted in the faded
credulity of earlier ages: let us walk through the door.*

John Updike

In the late 1990s, a group of scholars assembled to evaluate whether Jesus actually said the things attributed to him by the Gospel writers. Although they employed remarkably subjective criteria in their evaluation of Scripture, members of the self-appointed "Jesus Seminar" were widely quoted by the media as authorities on the Christian faith.

Marcus Borg, a Jesus Seminar leader, said this of Christ's resurrection: "As a child, I took it for granted that Easter meant that Jesus literally rose from the dead. I now see Easter very differently. For me, it is irrelevant whether or not the tomb was empty. Whether Easter involved something remarkable happening to the physical body of Jesus is irrelevant."[83]

As a child, Borg was right. As an adult—though considered a spokesman for Christianity—he couldn't be more wrong. What Borg calls irrelevant—the physical resurrection of Christ's body—the apostle Paul considered absolutely essential to the Christian faith. Paul wrote to the Corinthians, "If Christ has not been raised, your faith is futile; you are still in your sins. . . . [and] we are to be pitied more than all men" (1 Corinthians 15:17, 19).

The physical resurrection of Jesus Christ is the cornerstone of redemption—both for mankind and for the earth. Indeed, without Christ's resurrection and what it means—an eternal future for fully restored human beings dwelling on a fully restored Earth—there is no Christianity.

RESURRECTION IS PHYSICAL

The major Christian creeds state, "I believe in the resurrection of the body." But I have found in many conversations that Christians tend to spiritualize the resurrection of the dead, effectively denying it.[†] They don't reject it as a doctrine, but they deny its essential *meaning*: a permanent return to a physical existence in a physical universe.

Of Americans who believe in a resurrection of the dead, two-thirds believe they will not have bodies after the resurrection.[84] But this is self-contradictory. A non-physical resurrection is like a sunless sunrise. There's no such thing. Resurrection *means* that we will have bodies. If we didn't have bodies, we wouldn't be resurrected!

The biblical doctrine of the resurrection of the dead begins with the human body but extends far beyond it. R. A. Torrey writes, "We will not be disembodied spirits in the world to come, but redeemed spirits, in redeemed bodies, in a redeemed universe."[85] If we don't get it right on the resurrection of the body, we'll get nothing else right. It's therefore critical that we not merely affirm the resurrection of the dead as a point of doctrine but that we *understand* the meaning of the resurrection we affirm.

Genesis 2:7 says, "The Lord God formed the man from the dust of the ground and breathed into his nostrils the breath of life, and the man became a living being." The Hebrew word for "living being" is *nephesh*, often translated "soul." The point at which Adam became *nephesh* is when God joined his body (dust) and spirit (breath) together. Adam was not a living human being until he had both material (physical) and immaterial (spiritual) components. Thus, the essence of humanity is not just spirit, but *spirit joined with body*. Your body does not merely house the real you—it is as much a part of who you are as your spirit is.

If this idea seems wrong to us, it's because we have been deeply influenced by Christoplatonism.[‡] From a christoplatonic perspective, our souls merely occupy our bodies, like a hermit crab inhabits a seashell, and our souls could naturally—or even ideally—live in a disembodied state.

It's no coincidence that the apostle Paul's detailed defense of the physical resurrection of the dead was written to the church at Corinth. More than any other New Testament Christians, the Corinthian believers were immersed in the Greek philosophies of Platonism and dualism, which perceived a dichotomy between the spiritual and the physical. The biblical view of human nature,

---

[†]For Paul's exposition of the resurrection of the dead, see 1 Corinthians 15:12-58.
[‡]The basic principles of Christoplatonism are explained in chapter 6, and a more complete explanation of Christoplatonism's false assumptions can be found in appendix A.

however, is radically different. Scripture indicates that God designed our bodies to be an integral part of our total being. Our physical bodies are an essential aspect of who we are, not just shells for our spirits to inhabit.

Death is an abnormal condition because it tears apart what God created and joined together. God intended for our bodies to last as long as our souls. Those who believe in Platonism or in preexistent spirits see a disembodied soul as natural and even desirable. The Bible sees it as unnatural and undesirable. We are unified beings. That's why the bodily resurrection of the dead is so vital. And that's why Job rejoiced that *in his flesh he would see God* (Job 19:26).

When God sent Jesus to die, it was for our bodies as well as our spirits. He came to redeem not just "the breath of life" (spirit) but also "the dust of the ground" (body). When we die, it isn't that our real self goes to the present Heaven and our fake self goes to the grave; it's that part of us goes to the present Heaven and part goes to the grave to await our bodily resurrection. We will never be all that God intended for us to be until body and spirit are again joined in resurrection. (If we do have physical forms in the intermediate state, clearly they will not be our original or ultimate bodies.)

Any views of the afterlife that settle for less than a bodily resurrection—including Christoplatonism, reincarnation, and transmigration of the soul—are explicitly unchristian. The early church waged major doctrinal wars against Gnosticism and Manichaeism, dualistic worldviews that associated God with the spiritual realm of light and Satan with the physical world of darkness. These heresies contradicted the biblical account that says God was pleased with the *entire* physical realm, all of which he created and called "very good" (Genesis 1:31). The truth of Christ's resurrection repudiated the philosophies of Gnosticism and Manichaeism. Nevertheless, two thousand years later, these persistent heresies have managed to take hostage our modern theology of Heaven.

Our incorrect thinking about bodily resurrection stems from our failure to understand the environment in which resurrected people will live—the New Earth. Anthony Hoekema is right: "Resurrected bodies are not intended just to float in space, or to flit from cloud to cloud. They call for a *new earth* on which to live and to work, glorifying God. The doctrine of the resurrection of the body, in fact, makes no sense whatever apart from the doctrine of the new earth."[86]

CONTINUITY IS CRITICAL

Paul says that if Christ didn't rise from the dead, we're still in our sins (1 Corinthians 15:17)—meaning we'd be bound for Hell, not Heaven.

Paul doesn't just say that if there's no *Heaven*, the Christian life is futile. He says that if there's no *resurrection of the dead*, then the hope of Christianity is an illusion, and we're to be pitied for placing our faith in Christ. Paul has no interest in a Heaven that's merely for human spirits. Ultimately, there is no Heaven for human spirits unless Heaven is also for human bodies.

> Christianity is not a platonic religion that regards material things as mere shadows of reality, which will be sloughed off as soon as possible. Not the mere immortality of the soul, but rather the resurrection of the body and the renewal of all creation is the hope of the Christian faith.
>
> **JOHN PIPER**

Wishful thinking is not the reason why, deep in our hearts, we desire a resurrected life on a resurrected Earth instead of a disembodied existence in a spiritual realm. Rather, it is precisely because God intends for us to be raised to new life on the New Earth that we desire it. It is God who created us to desire what we are made for. It is God who "set eternity in the hearts of men" (Ecclesiastes 3:11). It is God who designed us to live on Earth and to desire the earthly life. And it is our bodily resurrection that will allow us to return to an earthly life—this time freed from sin and the Curse.

That's God's idea, not ours. Our desires simply correspond to God's intentions, because he implanted his intentions into us in the form of our desires.

"Therefore, if anyone is in Christ, he is a new creation; the old has gone, the new has come!" (2 Corinthians 5:17). Becoming a new creation sounds as if it involves a radical change, and indeed it does. But though we become *new* people when we come to Christ, we still remain the *same* people.

When I came to Christ as a high school student, I became a new person, yet I was still the same person I'd always been. My mother saw a lot of changes, but she still recognized me. She still said, "Good morning, Randy," not "Who are *you*?" My dog never once growled at me—he knew who I was. I was still Randy Alcorn, though a substantially transformed Randy Alcorn. This same Randy will undergo another change at death, and yet another change at the resurrection of the dead. But through all the changes *I will still be who I was and who I am.* There will be continuity from this life to the next. I will be able to say with Job, "In my flesh I will see God; I myself will see him with my own eyes—I, and not another" (Job 19:26-27).

Conversion does not mean eliminating the old but transforming it. Despite the radical changes that occur through salvation, death, and resurrection, we remain who we are. We have the same history, appearance, memory, interests, and skills. This is the principle of *redemptive continuity*. God will not scrap his original creation and start over. Instead, he will take his fallen, corrupted children and restore, refresh, and renew us to our original design.

Theologian Herman Bavinck, writing in the early twentieth century, argued that a parallel continuity exists between the old and New Earth: "God's honor consists precisely in the fact that he redeems and renews the same humanity, the same world, the same Heaven, and the same earth that have been corrupted and polluted by sin. Just as anyone in Christ is a new creation in whom the old has passed away and everything has become new (2 Corinthians 5:17), so this world passes away in its present form as well, in order out of its womb, at God's word of power, to give birth and being to a new world."[87]

The New Earth will still be Earth, but a changed Earth. It will be converted and resurrected, but it will still be Earth and recognizable as such. Just as those reborn through salvation maintain continuity with the people they were, so too the world will be reborn in continuity with the old world (Matthew 19:28). In fact, writes Bavinck, "the rebirth of humans is completed in the rebirth of creation. The kingdom of God is fully realized only when it is visibly extended over the earth as well."[88]

If we don't grasp redemptive continuity, we cannot understand the nature of our resurrection. "There must be continuity," writes Anthony Hoekema, "for otherwise there would be little point in speaking about a resurrection at all. The calling into existence of a completely new set of people totally different from the present inhabitants of the earth would not be a resurrection."[89]

Continuity is evident in passages that discuss resurrection, including 1 Corinthians 15:53: "For the perishable must clothe itself with the imperishable, and the mortal with immortality." It is *this* (the perishable and mortal) which puts on *that* (the imperishable and immortal). Likewise, it is *we*, the very same people who walk this earth, who will walk the New Earth. "And so *we* will be with the Lord forever" (1 Thessalonians 4:17, emphasis added).

Pointing out that God says he is, not was, the God of the patriarchs, Christ says to those denying the resurrection of the dead, "He is not the God of the dead but of the living" (Matthew 22:32).

THE NATURE OF OUR NEW BODIES

The empty tomb is the ultimate proof that Christ's resurrection body was the same body that died on the cross. If *resurrection* meant the creation of a new body, Christ's original body would have remained in the tomb. When Jesus said to his disciples after his resurrection, "It is I myself," he was emphasizing to them that he was the same person—in spirit *and* body—who had gone to the cross (Luke 24:39). His disciples saw the marks of his crucifixion, unmistakable evidence that this was the same body.

Jesus said, "Destroy this temple, and I will raise it again in three days" (John 2:19). John clarifies that "the temple he had spoken of was his body" (v. 21). The body that rose is the body that was destroyed. Hence, Hank Hanegraaff says, "There is a one-to-one correspondence between the body of Christ that died and the body that rose."[90]

In its historic crystallization of orthodox doctrine, the Westminster *Larger Catechism* (1647) states, "The self-same bodies of the dead which were laid in the grave, being then again united to their souls forever, shall be raised up by the power of Christ."[91] The Westminster Confession, one of the great creeds of the Christian faith, says, "All the dead shall be raised up, with the self-same bodies, and none other."[92] "Self-same bodies" affirms the doctrine of continuity through resurrection.

This, then, is the most basic truth about our resurrected bodies: They are the same bodies God created for us, but they will be raised to greater perfection than we've ever known. We don't know everything about them, of course, but *we do know a great deal.* Scripture does not leave us in the dark about our resurrection bodies.

Because we each have a physical body, we already have the single best reference point for envisioning a *new* body. It's like the new upgrade of my word processing software. When I heard there was an upgrade available, I didn't say, "I have no idea what it will be like." I knew that for the most part it would be like the old program, only better. Sure, it has some new features that I didn't expect, and I'm glad for them. But I certainly recognize it as the same program I've used for a decade.

Likewise, when we receive our resurrected bodies, we'll no doubt have some welcome surprises—maybe even some new features (though no glitches or programming errors)—but we'll certainly recognize our new bodies as being *ours.* God has given us working models to guide our imagination about what our new bodies will be like on the New Earth.

CHRIST'S RESURRECTED LIFE IS THE MODEL FOR OURS

Not only do we know what our present bodies are like, we also have an example in Scripture of what a resurrection body is like. We're told a great deal about Christ's resurrected body, and we're told that our bodies will be like his.

Beloved, we are God's children now; it does not yet appear what we shall be, but we know that when he appears we shall be like him, for we shall see him as he is. (1 John 3:2, RSV)

Strangely, though Jesus in his resurrected body proclaimed, "I am not a ghost" (Luke 24:39, NLT), countless Christians think they will be ghosts in the eternal Heaven. I know this because I've talked with many of them. They think they'll be disembodied spirits, or wraiths. The magnificent, cosmos-shaking victory of Christ's resurrection—by definition a physical triumph over physical death in a physical world—escapes them. If Jesus had been a ghost, if *we* would be ghosts, then *redemption wouldn't have been accomplished.*

Jesus walked the earth in his resurrection body for forty days, showing us how we would live as resurrected human beings. In effect, he also demonstrated *where* we would live as resurrected human beings—on Earth. Christ's resurrection body was suited for life on Earth, not primarily life in the intermediate Heaven. As Jesus was raised to come back to live on Earth, so we will be raised to come back to live on Earth (1 Thessalonians 4:14; Revelation 21:1-3).

The risen Jesus walked and talked with two disciples on the Emmaus road (Luke 24:13-35). They asked him questions; he taught them and guided them in their understanding of Scripture. They saw nothing different enough about him to tip them off to his identity until "their eyes were opened" (v. 31). This sug-

> The Jesus who says, "Touch me and see; a ghost does not have flesh and bones, as you see I have,"... this is the Jesus who draws back the curtain on the heavenly life and shows us what it will be like: embodied!
>
> **BRUCE MILNE**

gests that God had prevented them from recognizing Jesus earlier, which they otherwise would have. The point is that they didn't see anything amiss. They saw the resurrected Jesus as a normal, everyday human being. The soles of his feet didn't hover above the road—they walked on it. No one saw bread going down a transparent esophagus when he swallowed.

We know the resurrected Christ looked like a man because Mary called him "sir" when she assumed he was the gardener (John 20:15). Though at first she didn't recognize his voice, when he called her by name, she recognized him (v. 16). It was then that she "turned toward him." Because modest women didn't look male strangers in the eye, this phrase suggests that she hadn't gotten a good look at him before.

The times Jesus spent with his disciples after his resurrection were remarkably normal. Early one morning, he "stood on the shore" at a distance (John 21:4). He didn't hover or float—or even walk on water, though he could have. He stood, then called to the disciples (v. 5). Obviously his voice sounded human, because it traveled across the water and the disciples didn't suspect it was anyone but a human. It apparently didn't sound like the deep, otherworldly voices that movies assign to God or angels.

Jesus had started a fire, and he was already cooking fish that he'd presumably caught himself. He cooked them, which means he didn't just snap his fingers and materialize a finished meal. He invited them to add their fish to his and said, "Come and have breakfast" (John 21:12).

In another appearance to the disciples, Christ's resurrection body seamlessly interacted with the disciples' mortal bodies (John 20:19-23). Nothing indicates that his clothes were strange or that there was a halo over his head. He drew close enough to breathe on them (v. 22).

On the other hand, though the doors were locked, Christ suddenly appeared in the room where the disciples were gathered (v. 19). Christ's body could be touched and clung to and could consume food, yet it could apparently "materialize" as well. How is this possible? Could it be that a resurrection body is structured in such a way as to allow its molecules to pass through solid materials or to suddenly become visible or invisible? Though we know that Christ could do these things, we're not explicitly told we'll be able to. It may be that some aspects of his resurrection body are unique because of his divine nature.†

By observing the resurrected Christ, we learn not only about resurrected bodies but also about resurrected relationships. Christ communicates with his disciples and shows his love to them as a group and as individuals. He instructs them and entrusts a task to them (Acts 1:4-8). If you study his interactions with Mary Magdalene (John 20:10-18), Thomas (20:24-29), and Peter (21:15-22), you will see how similar they are to his interactions with these same people before he died. The fact that Jesus picked up his relationships where they'd left off is a foretaste of our own lives after we are resurrected. We will experience continuity between our current lives and our resurrected lives, with the same memories and relational histories.

Once we understand that Christ's resurrection is the prototype for the resurrection of mankind and the earth, we realize that Scripture has given us an interpretive precedent for approaching passages concerning human resurrection

---

†Even if Christ's resurrection body has capabilities that ours won't, we know we'll still be able to stretch the capacities of our perfected human bodies to their fullest, which will probably seem supernatural to us compared to what we've known.

and life on the New Earth. Shouldn't we interpret passages alluding to resurrected people living on the New Earth as literally as those concerning Christ's resurrected life during the forty days he walked on the old Earth?

THE GLORIFIED CHRIST

> The Lord Jesus Christ . . . will transform our lowly bodies so that they will be like his glorious body. (Philippians 3:20-21)

We've established that Christ's resurrected body, before his ascension, was quite normal in appearance. But what is Christ's "glorious body" like? We are given a picture on the Mount of Transfiguration: "There he was transfigured before them. His face shone like the sun, and his clothes became as white as the light" (Matthew 17:2). The Transfiguration appears to have given us a preview of Christ's glorified body.

John describes the glorified Christ he saw in the present Heaven:

> I turned around to see the voice that was speaking to me. And when I turned I saw seven golden lampstands, and among the lampstands was someone "like a son of man," dressed in a robe reaching down to his feet and with a golden sash around his chest. His head and hair were white like wool, as white as snow, and his eyes were like blazing fire. His feet were like bronze glowing in a furnace, and his voice was like the sound of rushing waters. In his right hand he held seven stars, and out of his mouth came a sharp double-edged sword. His face was like the sun shining in all its brilliance. When I saw him, I fell at his feet as though dead. Then he placed his right hand on me and said: "Do not be afraid. I am the First and the Last. I am the Living One; I was dead, and behold I am alive for ever and ever! And I hold the keys of death and Hades." (Revelation 1:12-18)

Now, in comparison to both Matthew 17 and Revelation 1, it appears that the risen Christ, before his ascension, was not yet fully glorified. If he would have been glorified, surely his identity would have been immediately apparent to Mary Magdalene (John 20:14), the disciples on the Emmaus road (Luke 24:15-16), and Peter and the apostles when they saw him on the shore (John 21:4).

Consider one of the apostle Paul's reports of encountering the glorified Christ on the road to Damascus: "A great light from heaven suddenly shone around me. And I fell to the ground and heard a voice saying to me, 'Saul, Saul, why are you persecuting me?' And I answered, 'Who are you, Lord?' And he said to me, 'I am Jesus of Nazareth, whom you are persecuting.' Now those who were with me saw the light but did not understand the voice of the one who was speaking to me. . . . I could not see because of the brightness of that light" (Acts 22:6-11, ESV).

It appears that Paul's unredeemed eyes were not yet ready to behold the glorified Christ. This is in contrast to Stephen, who saw the glorified Christ at God's right hand, but apparently was *not* blinded: "But Stephen, full of the Holy Spirit, looked up to heaven and saw the glory of God, and Jesus standing at the right hand of God. 'Look,' he said, 'I see heaven open and the Son of Man standing at the right hand of God'" (Acts 7:55-56).

Certainly, the glorified Christ will be by far the most glorious being in Heaven. Yet, as we will see, Scripture indicates that we too, in a secondary and derivative way, will reflect God's glory in physical brightness.

Scripture speaks of the likeness of Adam and the likeness of Christ, making some distinction between them: "And just as we have borne the likeness of the earthly man, so shall we bear the likeness of the man from heaven" (1 Corinthians 15:49). Christ will remain a man, but his deity that was once veiled in his humanity will shine through it. Because of the Fall and the Curse, we have never been or seen human beings who are fully functional as God's image-bearers, conveying the brightness and majesty of his being. But that day is coming. Christ, the God-man, the new head of our human race, will be the ultimate image-bearer, fully conveying the brightness and majesty of the Almighty.

Note, however, that the difference between Adam and Christ, which Paul speaks of in 1 Corinthians 15:45–49, is *not* that one was a physical being and the other wasn't. It was that Adam was under sin and the Curse, and Christ was untouched by sin and the Curse. Jesus was and is a human being, "in every respect like us" (Hebrews 2:17, NLT), except with respect to sin. So although we should recognize that our resurrection bodies will be glorious in ways that our current bodies are not, we should also realize that those bodies will continue to be—in both the same and in greater ways—the functional physical bodies that God designed for us from the beginning.

OF THE DUST OF THE EARTH

After reading the first printing of this book, one Bible teacher expressed his disagreement with my belief that there will be a fundamental continuity between our present bodies and our resurrection bodies. His understanding is that our resurrection bodies will not be earthly, as our present bodies are. He believes they will not contain DNA or any genetic or physical ties to our current bodies.

In support of his position, he cited 1 Corinthians 15:47-48, which says, "The first man was of the dust of the earth, the second man from heaven. As was the earthly man, so are those who are of the earth; and as is the man from heaven, so also are those who are of heaven."

Paul's point here, I believe, is *not* that Christ's body *wasn't* "of dust" but that Adam's *was*. Indeed, if Christ's body wasn't "of dust," if he had no genetic relationship with Adam, then he would not be fully human, and he would not be Messiah, the Son of Man. He is—not merely was, but *is*—a descendant of Adam. He is the last Adam, not a non-Adam (1 Corinthians 15:45).

When viewed in context, "dust of the earth" seems to refer to more than the first man's origin, and at points appears to be associated with mortality and corruption. The man of dust, who was human only, succumbed to temptation; the man from Heaven, who is both human and divine, could not and did not.

Can one be "of dust" yet not under sin and death? Yes. Adam was, until the Fall. But he was subject to temptation, with the potential to succumb, whereas one day, when fully redeemed, human beings will not be.

Christ, as the last Adam, is certainly more than Adam, and far greater than Adam, for he came from Heaven. But he did in fact become a man, and was therefore of the earth. God originally made man from the earth. That is intrinsic to humanity, and Christ is fully human.

Christ's resurrection and glorification did not negate his genetic tie to his ancestors. They do not mean he is no longer a Jew, no longer of Abraham's seed, or no longer fully human. He who is tied to the earth in terms of his humanity will rule the earth for eternity.

Christ is and will forever remain both God (from Heaven) and man (of earth).

I will grant that if 1 Corinthians 15:47 were the only verse we had, then it could be legitimately interpreted as saying our resurrection bodies won't be physical or organically related to our current bodies. But it is *not* the only passage we have, and the other passages simply do not allow us to conclude that Christ's resurrection body did not have actual physical continuity to the old, and was in that sense "not of dust." Surely the risen and glorified Christ remains a descendant of Adam, Abraham, and David. Indeed, it is difficult to understand how he could hold to his claim to Messiahship if this were not the case.

The nail prints in Christ's hands and feet are the strongest possible affirmation that the same earthly body that was crucified is now the same heavenly body that was raised. "It is I myself! Touch me and see; a ghost does not have flesh and bones as you see I have" (Luke 24:39).

"Heavenly" transcends "earthly" but does not negate it. The earthly becomes heavenly, not losing its original properties but gaining much more. (It loses the properties that came with the Curse, of course, but *those were not its original properties.*)

In 1 Corinthians 15, the Resurrection is repeatedly depicted as overcoming the Curse. Our bodies in their present condition are referred to as perishable, corrupted, dishonorable, and weak in relationship to the death which results in burial. The passage culminates in verses 51-57, which speak of the sounding of the last trumpet, at which time the perishable will put on the imperishable, and the mortal will put on immortality. Then death will be swallowed up in victory. Its sting will be forever removed. Why? Because *sin* will be removed ("the sting of death is sin").

This great passage about bodily resurrection does not simply focus on a new state and a new life, but also on *the reversal of the Curse, and the conquest of sin and death*. With all its allusions to what is new, it is nonetheless *a passage of restoration of the old*. It introduces glorious newness—but before anything else, it conquers all that sin and death and the Curse bring to humanity, human relationships and activities (including culture), and the earth itself. God will restore us and the earth to what he made us to be. Then, in resurrection and glorification, he will take what was and make it far greater yet.

THE PROMISE OF IMPERISHABLE BODIES

When Paul speaks of our resurrection bodies, he says, "The body that is sown is perishable, it is raised imperishable; it is sown in dishonor, it is raised in glory; it is sown in weakness, it is raised in power; it is sown a natural body, it is raised a spiritual body. If there is a natural body, there is also a spiritual body" (1 Corinthians 15:42-44).

The following chart summarizes the contrasts in this passage:

EARTHLY BODY	RESURRECTION BODY
Sown a perishable body	Raised an imperishable body
Sown in dishonor	Raised in glory
Sown in weakness	Raised in power
Sown a natural body	Raised a spiritual body

When Paul uses the term "spiritual body" (1 Corinthians 15:44), he is not talking about a body made of spirit, or an incorporeal body—there is no such thing. *Body* means corporeal: flesh and bones. The word *spiritual* here is an adjective describing *body*, not negating its meaning. A spiritual body is first and foremost a real body or it would not qualify to be called a body. Paul could have simply said, "It is sown a natural body, it is raised a spirit," if that were the case. Judging from Christ's resurrection body, a spiritual body appears most of the time to look and act like a regular physical body, with the exception that it may have (and in Christ's case it *does* have) some powers of a metaphysical nature; that is, beyond normal physical abilities.

Paul goes on to say, "And just as we have borne the likeness of the earthly man, so shall we bear the likeness of the man from heaven. I declare to you, brothers, that flesh and blood cannot inherit the kingdom of God, nor does the perishable inherit the imperishable. . . . We will be changed. For the perishable must clothe itself with the imperishable, and the mortal with immortality. When the perishable has been clothed with the imperishable, and the mortal with immortality, then the saying that is written will come true: 'Death has been swallowed up in victory.' 'Where, O death, is your victory? Where, O death, is your sting?'" (1 Corinthians 15:49-50, 52-55).

When Paul says that "flesh and blood cannot inherit the kingdom of God," he's referring to our flesh and blood *as they are now*: cursed and under sin. Our present bodies are fallen and destructible, but our future bodies—though still bodies in the fullest sense—will be untouched by sin and indestructible. They will be like Christ's resurrection body—both physical *and* indestructible.

One Bible student told me that he couldn't believe that the risen Christ might have DNA. But why not? Who created DNA in the first place? Christ explicitly said that his body was of flesh and bones. Flesh and bones have DNA. There is no reason to believe that his new body doesn't. Is Christ a *former* descendant of Abraham and David, or is the glorified Christ in Heaven still their descendant? I believe his claim to rulership in the Millennium and on the New Earth depends in part on the fact that he remains, and will always remain, an actual, physical descendant of Abraham and David.

A body need not be destructible in order to be real. Our destructibility is an aberration of God's created norm. Death, disease, and the deterioration of age are products of sin. Because there was no death before the Fall, presumably Adam and Eve's original bodies were either indestructible or self-repairing (perhaps healed by the tree of life, as suggested in Revelation 22:2). Yet they were truly flesh and blood.

Scripture portrays resurrection as involving both fundamental continuity and significant dissimilarity. We dare not minimize the dissimilarities—for our glorification will certainly involve a dramatic and marvelous transformation. But, in my experience, the great majority of Christians have underemphasized continuity. They end up thinking of our transformed selves as no longer being ourselves, and the transformed Earth as no longer being the earth. In some cases, they view the glorified Christ as no longer being the same Jesus who walked the earth—a belief that early Christians recognized as heresy.

Many of us look forward to Heaven more now than we did when our bodies functioned well. Joni Eareckson Tada says it well: "Somewhere in my broken, paralyzed body is the seed of what I shall become. The paralysis makes what I am to become all the more grand when you contrast atrophied, useless legs against splendorous resurrected legs. I'm convinced that if there are mirrors in heaven (and why not?), the image I'll see will be unmistakably 'Joni,' although a much better, brighter Joni."[93]

Inside your body, even if it is failing, is the blueprint for your resurrection body. You may not be satisfied with your current body or mind—but you'll be thrilled with your resurrection upgrades. With them you'll be better able to serve and glorify God and enjoy an eternity of wonders he has prepared for you.

CHAPTER 12

WHY DOES ALL CREATION AWAIT OUR RESURRECTION?

The kingdom of God . . . does not mean merely the salvation of certain individuals nor even the salvation of a chosen group of people. It means nothing less than the complete renewal of the entire cosmos, culminating in the new heaven and the new earth.

Anthony Hoekema

The gospel is far greater than most of us imagine. It isn't just good news for us—it's good news for animals, plants, stars, and planets. It's good news for the sky above and the earth below. Albert Wolters says, "The redemption in Jesus Christ means the restoration of an original good creation."[94]

BROADENING OUR VIEW OF REDEMPTION

Many of us have come to think of redemption far too narrowly. That's why we're fooled into thinking that Heaven must be fundamentally different from Earth—because in our minds, Earth is bad, irredeemable, beyond hope. However, "the teaching that the new creation involves a radically new beginning," writes theologian Cornelius Venema, "would suggest that sin and evil have become so much a part of the substance of the present created order that it is unrelievedly and radically evil. . . . It would even imply that the sinful rebellion of the creation had so ruined God's handiwork as to make it irretrievably wicked."[95]

But let's not forget that God called the original earth "very good"—the true earth, as he designed it to be (Genesis 1:31).

The breadth and depth of Christ's redemptive work will escape us as long as we think it is limited to humanity. In Colossians 1:16-20, notice that God highlights his plan for the church, but then he goes beyond it, emphasizing "all things," "everything," "things on earth," and "things in Heaven":

For by him [Jesus] *all things* were created: *things in heaven and on
earth*, visible and invisible, whether thrones or powers or rulers or
authorities; *all things* were created by him and for him. He is before *all
things*, and in him *all things* hold together. And he is the head of the
body, the church; he is the beginning and the firstborn from among
the dead, so that in *everything* he might have the supremacy. For God
was pleased to have all his fullness dwell in him, and through him to
reconcile to himself *all things*, whether *things on earth* or *things in
heaven*, by making peace through his blood, shed on the cross.
(emphasis added)

God was pleased to reconcile to himself *all things, on Earth and in Heaven*. The
Greek words for "all things," *ta panta*, are extremely broad in their scope.[96]

Eugene Peterson captures the universal implications of Christ's redemption
when he paraphrases Colossians 1:18-20 in *The Message*: "He was supreme in
the beginning and—leading the resurrection parade—he is supreme in the end.
From beginning to end he's there, towering far above everything, everyone. So
spacious is he, so roomy, that everything of God finds its proper place in him
without crowding. Not only that, but all the broken and dislocated pieces of the
universe—people and things, animals and atoms—get properly fixed and fit together in vibrant harmonies, all because of his death, his blood that poured
down from the Cross."

The power of Christ's resurrection is enough not only to remake us, but also
to remake every inch of the universe—mountains, rivers, plants, animals, stars,
nebulae, quasars, and galaxies. Christ's redemptive work extends resurrection
to the far reaches of the universe. This is a stunning affirmation of God's greatness. It should move our hearts to wonder and praise.

ALL CREATION WAITS IN EAGER EXPECTATION

Do you ever sense creation's restlessness? Do you hear groaning in the cold
night wind? Do you feel the forest's loneliness, the ocean's agitation? Do you
hear longing in the cries of whales? Do you see blood and pain in the eyes of
wild animals, or the mixture of pleasure and pain in the eyes of your pets? Despite vestiges of beauty and joy, something on this earth is terribly wrong. Not
only God's creatures but even inanimate objects seem to feel it. But there's also
hope, visible in springtime after a hard winter. As Martin Luther put it, "Our
Lord has written the promise of the resurrection not in books alone, but in

every leaf in springtime."[97] The creation hopes for, even anticipates, *resurrection*. That's exactly what Scripture tells us.

> The creation waits in eager expectation for the sons of God to be revealed. For the creation was subjected to frustration, not by its own choice, but by the will of the one who subjected it, in hope that the creation itself will be liberated from its bondage to decay and brought into the glorious freedom of the children of God.
>
> We know that the whole creation has been groaning as in the pains of childbirth right up to the present time. Not only so, but we ourselves, who have the firstfruits of the Spirit, groan inwardly as we wait eagerly for our adoption as sons, the redemption of our bodies. (Romans 8:19-23)

The "redemption of our bodies" refers to the resurrection of the dead. Paul says that not only we but "the whole creation" awaits the earthwide deliverance that will come with our bodily resurrection. Not only mankind in general but believers in particular (those with God's Spirit within) are aligned with the rest of creation, which intuitively reaches out to God for deliverance. We know what God intended for mankind and the earth, and therefore we have an object for our longing. We groan for what creation groans for—redemption. God subjected the whole creation to frustration by putting the Curse not only on mankind but also on the earth (Genesis 3:17). Why? Because human beings and the earth are inseparably linked. And as together we fell, together we shall rise. God will transform the fallen human race into a renewed human race and the present Earth into the New Earth.

What does it mean that creation waits for God's children to be revealed? Our Creator, the Master Artist, will put us on display to a wide-eyed universe. Our revelation will be an unveiling, and we will be seen as what we are, as what we were intended to be—God's image-bearers. We will glorify him by ruling over the physical universe with creativity and camaraderie, showing respect and benevolence for all we rule. We will be revealed at our resurrection, when our adoption will be finalized and our bodies redeemed. We will be fully human, with righteous spirits and incorruptible bodies.

AS MANKIND GOES, SO GOES CREATION

John Calvin writes in his commentary on Romans 8:19, "I understand the passage to have this meaning—that there is no element and no part of the world which is being touched, as it were, with a sense of its present misery, that does not intensely hope for a resurrection."[98]

What is "the whole creation" that groans for our resurrection? The phrase appears to be completely inclusive of "the heavens and the earth" that God created in the beginning (Genesis 1:1). So it is the heavens and the earth that eagerly await our resurrection. This includes Earth and everything on it, as well as the planets of our solar system and the far reaches of our galaxy and beyond. If it was created, Paul includes it in "the whole creation."

Why does the creation wait eagerly for our resurrection? For one simple but critically important reason: *As mankind goes, so goes all of creation.* Thus, just as all creation was spoiled through our rebellion, the deliverance of all creation hinges on our deliverance. The glorification of the universe hinges on the glorification of a redeemed human race. The destiny of all creation rides on our coattails.

> Though the Witch knew the Deep Magic, there is a magic deeper still which she did not know. Her knowledge goes back only to the dawn of time. But if she could have looked a little further back, into the stillness and the darkness before Time dawned . . . she would have known that when a willing victim who had committed no treachery was killed in a traitor's stead, the Table would crack and Death itself would start working backwards.
>
> **C. S. LEWIS**

What possible effect could our redemption have on galaxies that are billions of light years away? The same effect that our fall had on them. Adam and Eve's sin did not merely create a personal catastrophe or a local, Edenic catastrophe; it was a catastrophe of cosmic—not just global—proportions.

Astronomy has been my hobby since childhood. Years before I came to know Christ, I was fascinated by the violent collisions of galaxies, explosions of stars, and implosions into neutron stars and black holes. The second law of thermodynamics, entropy, tells us that all things deteriorate. This means that everything was once in a better condition than it is now. Children and stars can both be born, but both ultimately become engaged in a downward spiral. Even the remotest parts of the universe reveal vast realms of fiery destruction. On the one hand, these cataclysms declare God's greatness. On the other hand, they reflect something that is out of order on a massive scale.

It seems possible that even the second law of thermodynamics (at least as it is popularly understood) may have been the product of mankind's fall. If true, it demonstrates the mind-boggling extent of the Curse. The most remote galaxy, the most distant quasar, was somehow shaken by mankind's sin.[†]

Adherents of some views of the origin of the universe believe that entropy (i.e., all things tend toward deterioration and disorder) has *always* been operative. But we should not look at things as they are now and assume they've always been this way. In 2 Peter 3:4-7, the Bible rejects the uniformitarian view that "processes acting in the same manner as at present and over long spans of time are sufficient to account for all current . . . features [in the universe] and all past . . . changes."[99] We are so accustomed to the cycle of death in nature that we assume it is natural and has always been as it is. The Bible appears to say otherwise: "Death came through a man [Adam]" (1 Corinthians 15:21). I see no biblical evidence for the assumption that God designed his creation to fall into death, or that animal death predated mankind's fall. Do artists deliberately inject decay into their work? Would an omnipotent Artist do so? Both Genesis and Romans 8 suggest otherwise. (I am well aware that many will disagree with me on this, but I state it based on my understanding of Romans 8.)

Isn't it reasonable to suppose that the pristine conditions of God's original creation were such that humans and animals would not die, stellar energy would be replenished, and planets would not fall out of orbit? What if God intended that our dominion over the earth would ultimately extend to the entire physical universe? Then we would not be surprised to see the whole creation come under our curse, because it would all be under our stewardship.

"Even after the fall," writes theologian Erich Sauer, "the destiny and the redemption of the earth remain indissolubly united with the existence and development of the human race. The redemption of the earth is, in spite of all, still bound up with man. . . . *Man* is the instrument for the redemption of the earthly creation. And because this remains God's way and goal, there can be a new heaven and a new earth only *after* the great white throne, i.e., after the completion and conclusion of the history of human redemption."[100]

WAS THERE REALLY NO DEATH?

God made seasons, and I wouldn't be surprised if in Eden the colors of autumn leaves were more brilliant than we see on the present Earth. This "death" of

---

[†]Some people argue that walking, breathing, digestion, and solar heating of the earth all involve the law of entropy. When I speak of that law, however, I mean specifically the parts related to death, decay, and the deterioration of things, especially living beings, as a departure from their ideal created state.

leaves in the fall could be part of a living tree's beauty, not its curse. Did leaves ever fall in Eden? Once they fell, did they rot? Eventually wouldn't the earth have been covered with leaves? God made us to consume vegetation, which doesn't involve harm or suffering. Why shouldn't he allow it to decompose through natural processes? Did Adam and Eve step ankle deep in human and animal waste because it did not decay? Was there no compost to enrich the garden? Wine requires fermentation, a form of decay. Did bread not rise?[101]

All of these natural processes could easily have been part of God's original design. What I believe was *not* part of his ideal world was the suffering and death of living creatures. I see no evidence that suffering and death could be part of a world God called "very good."

I realize this raises inevitable objections. Were there no carnivores before the Fall? From the shape of their teeth and claws to the position of their eyes to their digestive systems, it could be argued that carnivores were designed by their creator to stalk, capture, and kill their prey. Were foxes designed to keep rodents in check, and falcons made to dive to catch and eat fish? Did the lion "eat straw like the ox" as we are told he will one day (Isaiah 11:7)? Was it true in Eden as it will be on the New Earth, "[Animals] will neither harm nor destroy" (Isaiah 11:9)? Many think otherwise, but I believe the answer is yes.

I realize that if there was no food chain, then the animal world of Eden was different than the animal world we know today. Indeed, our entire ecosystem was likely changed more by the Fall than we can imagine. We don't know what the animals in Eden looked like. Did God change their form as part of the Curse—or as a way to help them survive after the Curse? Is it possible that originally cheetahs ran for the sheer joy of it rather than to chase their prey? Could a lion have been capable of tearing apart other animals but have no desire to do so? Could he be powerful, even with sharp teeth, without being a killer? I think so. There is a special beauty in great power that refrains from doing harm, as Jesus himself demonstrated.

However, the debates about entropy, plant death, animal death, and the earth's age should not deter us from a central agreement that, as Paul says, "the whole creation" has come under mankind's curse, and God will deliver the whole creation by our resurrection.

FROM THE FALL TO OUR RESURRECTION

How will the effects of our bodily resurrection be felt by the entire universe? In exactly the same way that all creation suffered from our fall into sin. There is a metaphysical and moral link between mankind and the physical universe.

Romans 8 is a profound theological statement in that it extends the doctrine of the Fall far beyond what we might have expected. But in doing so—and we often miss this—it extends the doctrine of Christ's redemption every bit as far.

We should expect that anything affected by the Fall will be restored to its original condition. Things will no longer get worse. When they change, they will only get better. That will be true of our bodies and our minds and human culture in the new universe. And there are no grounds to imagine that the link between mankind and the universe will cease. Why shouldn't it continue for all eternity?

"We know," Paul says, "that the whole creation has been groaning" (Romans 8:22). Consider the shocking cruelty in the animal world, where mothers sometimes devour their offspring, and most of those that survive are mercilessly killed by predators. If "the whole creation" is as comprehensive as it appears, then there is not an amoeba or chromosome or DNA strand or galaxy unaffected by mankind's fall. That is the bad news. Paul follows with the good news—that what went down with mankind in the Fall will come back up with us when Christ's redemptive work is completed. The God who raised Jesus will in turn raise his people and the universe.

There is such a close biblical connection between the inhabitants of the earth and Earth itself that the phrase "the world" (*kosmos*) is sometimes synonymous with *people*: "God so loved the world," and "God was reconciling the world to himself in Christ" (John 3:16; 2 Corinthians 5:19). In John's Gospel, "the world" often refers to fallen humanity in rebellion against God. And it is people, not the planet, who believe in Christ. Still, there are words for mankind that don't connect us to the earth, unlike *kosmos*, which does. In Romans 8 we see that the redemptive work of Christ not only rescues people who believe in him, it rescues the world itself. Just as we will die, the earth will be destroyed; and just as we will be raised, the earth will be renewed.

John Piper writes, "What happens to our bodies and what happens to the creation go together. And what happens to our bodies is not annihilation but redemption. . . . Our bodies will be redeemed, restored, made new, not thrown away. And so it is with the heavens and the earth."[102]

THE PAINS AND PROMISE OF CHILDBIRTH

It's fair to say that most Christians believe there will be no carryover into Heaven of our present culture, art, technology, or the products of human creativity. Indeed, it's common to doubt if we will even remember our lives on Earth or the people whom God used to influence and shape us, including our families and closest friends.

If our assumptions about the end of the world were correct, what analogy would we expect Paul to use for what will happen to creation? An old man dying? A mortally wounded soldier gasping his final breaths? Those images would fit well with a belief that the universe will come to a violent, final end. But Paul doesn't use analogies of death and destruction. He uses the analogy of childbirth: "The whole creation has been groaning as in the pains of childbirth right up until the present time" (Romans 8:22).

There are pains in childbirth for mother and child, but the result is a continuation, a fulfillment of a process that has long been underway. The pains of childbirth are analogous to the present sufferings of mankind, animals, and the entire universe. But those sufferings are temporary because of the imminent miracle of birth. A far better world will be born out of this one, and a far better humanity will be born out of what we now are.

The fallen but redeemed children of God will be transformed into something new: sinless, wise stewards of the earth. Today the earth is dying; but before it dies—or in its death—it will give birth to the New Earth. The New Earth will be the child of the old Earth, just as the new human race will be the children of the old race. Yet it is still *us*, the same human beings, and it will also be the same Earth.

Romans 8 contains a powerful theology of suffering. There's the groaning of those dying without hope, and in contrast, the groaning of those in childbirth. Both processes are painful, yet they are very different. The one is the pain of hopeless dread, the other the pain of hopeful anticipation. The Christian's pain is very real, but it's the pain of a mother anticipating the joy of holding her child.

It is no coincidence that the first two chapters of the Bible (Genesis 1–2) begin with the creation of the heavens and the earth and the last two chapters (Revelation 21–22) begin with the re-creation of the heavens and the earth.

All that was lost at the beginning will be restored at the end. And far more will be added besides.

CHAPTER 13

HOW FAR-REACHING IS THE RESURRECTION?

Why does God go to all the trouble to dirty his hands, as it were, with our decaying, sin-stained flesh, in order to reestablish it as a resurrection body and clothe it with immortality? . . . Because his Son paid the price of death so that the Father's purpose for the material universe would be fulfilled, namely, that he would be glorified in it, including in our bodies forever and ever.

John Piper

Jesus became a man and lived as a man on Earth, in order to redeem mankind. His victory had to take place on Earth—the dwelling place of mankind—and it has to culminate on Earth, where Christ will return to set up his Kingdom with his redeemed and resurrected people.

We were created *from* the earth to live *on* the earth. Our hope isn't that we'll be delivered *from* our bodies but *into* our new bodies, and into the new world where we'll live with Jesus.

The only unearthly eternal destination spoken of in Scripture is Hell, not Heaven. Yet even in Hell the condemned will have a physical presence. Jesus said that all people will be resurrected, some to life, some to condemnation (John 5:28-29). While some will forever experience the physical pleasures of Heaven, others will experience the physical torments of Hell.

THE RESURRECTION OF OUR DEEDS

Anticipating eternal life as resurrected beings in a resurrected universe has present, practical implications. "Therefore [in light of our eventual resurrection], my dear brothers, stand firm. Let nothing move you. Always give yourselves fully to the work of the Lord, because you know that your labor in the Lord is not in vain" (1 Corinthians 15:58).

How do we know that our labor in the Lord is not in vain? Because of our bodily resurrection. Just as we will be carried over from the old world to the new, so will our labor. In a sense, not only our bodies but our service for Christ will be resurrected. J. B. Phillips renders 1 Corinthians 15:58 as follows: "Let nothing move you as you busy yourselves in the Lord's work. Be sure that nothing you do for him is ever lost or ever wasted."[103]

Bruce Milne writes, "Every kingdom work, whether publicly performed or privately endeavoured, partakes of the kingdom's imperishable character. Every honest intention, every stumbling word of witness, every resistance of temptation, every motion of repentance, every gesture of concern, every routine engagement, every motion of worship, every struggle towards obedience, every mumbled prayer, everything, literally, which flows out of our faith-relationship with the Ever-Living One, will find its place in the ever-living heavenly order which will dawn at his coming."[104]

If the creation itself will be resurrected, could this also include some of the works of our hands? "If any man builds on this foundation [Christ] using gold, silver, costly stones, wood, hay or straw, his work will be shown for what it is, because the Day will bring it to light. It will be revealed with fire, and the fire will test the quality of each man's work. If what he has built survives, he will receive his reward. If it is burned up, he will suffer loss; he himself will be saved, but only as one escaping through the flames" (1 Corinthians 3:12-15).

We have the assurance of Scripture that all believers will survive the fire of testing and be raised. But it is not only ourselves that will outlast this world and be carried over to the new one. It is what we do with our lives. Our righteous works will follow us to Heaven (Revelation 14:13). Not only will some things that God has made survive his judgment, but so will some things *we* have done. Products of faithful lives will endure. They will be purified and "laid bare," so their beauty will be forever seen. God's fire will not destroy the whole Earth; it will destroy all that displeases him. But there is much that pleases him, and these things will endure the fire, to be reconstituted after the final resurrection of the dead. Not only will acts of obedience and spiritual sacrifices be carried over from one world to the next, but everything else good will also last forever.

Moses prayed, "Establish the work of our hands" (Psalm 90:17). The Hebrew word translated "establish," as indicated in the margin notes of the *New American Standard Bible*, means "make permanent." So Moses was asking God to give permanence to what he did with his hands.

If the components of our disintegrated bodies will endure the fire and be reassembled in resurrected bodies, what about the gold, silver, and costly stones of our works? Paul appears to be saying more than just that we will be rewarded for what we did on Earth. He appears to be saying that what we did on Earth will itself endure. Does he mean that these things too will be resurrected?

In my book *The Law of Rewards*, I make a case from these passages and many others that what's done in this life has a direct carryover to the next life.[105] *Resurrection* is not a figurative expression. It indicates durability. If our physical bodies will survive, doesn't it suggest that other physical things might also survive?

USING OUR IMAGINATION ABOUT THE RESURRECTION

Biblically, the resurrection of the dead extends much further than most of us have been taught. How much further might the power of resurrection go? Let's use our biblically informed imaginations. Could a child's story written out of love for Jesus survive this world, either in Heaven's handwriting or the child's own? Might certain works of art, literature, and music survive either literally (on the canvas and paper they were written on) or at least be re-created in Heaven? Obviously, we can't be certain, but isn't the idea consistent with what we've seen of the nature of resurrection?

If our bodies and the works of our hands that please God will be resurrected, why not a chair, cabinet, or wardrobe made by Jesus in his carpenter's shop in Nazareth? Couldn't God reassemble those molecules as easily as our own? Are they not as much a part of God's "very good" creation as our bodies, and animals, lakes, and trees? What about things we made to God's glory? Could these be resurrected or reassembled?

In my novel *Safely Home*, I portray a faithful Chinese servant who builds a chair for Jesus, a chair on which no one else ever sits. It represents Christ's presence in his home. Might Jesus resurrect such a chair and use it on the New Earth? If Jesus will resurrect people and flowers, might he also resurrect a specific flower arrangement given to a sick person that prompted a spiritual turning point? Might he resurrect a song or book written to his glory? or a letter written to encourage a friend or stranger? or a blanket a grandmother made for her grandchild? or a child's finger painting? or a man's log cabin built for his pioneer family? or a photograph album lovingly assembled by a devoted mother? or a baseball bat that a man handcrafted for his grandson's eleventh birthday?

Some may think it silly or sentimental to suppose that nature, animals, paintings, books, or a baseball bat might be resurrected. It may appear to trivialize the coming resurrection. I would suggest that it does exactly the opposite: It *elevates* resurrection, emphasizing the power of Christ to radically renew mankind—and far more. God promises to resurrect not only humanity but also the creation that fell as a result of our sin. Because God will resurrect the earth itself, we know that the resurrection of the dead extends to things that are inanimate. Even some of the works of our hands, done to God's glory, will survive. I may be mistaken on the details, but Scripture is clear that in some form, at least, what's done on Earth to Christ's glory will survive. Our error has not been in overestimating the extent of God's redemption and resurrection but *underestimating* it.

Close your eyes and picture something special hanging on your living-room wall or posted on your refrigerator. You may see these things in Heaven, and not just in your memory. Picture the kinds of things done by his children that God, the ultimate father, would put on display. God rewards with permanency what is precious to his heart. What pleases him will not forever disappear.

If we understand the meaning of *resurrection*, it will revolutionize our thinking about the eternal Heaven. God, whose grace overflows, may be lavish in what he chooses to resurrect.

Let's pray with Moses, "Make *permanent* the works of our hands."

REFORMING OUR VOCABULARY TO FIT THE RESURRECTION

A radio preacher, speaking about a Christian woman whose Christian husband had died, said, "Little did she know that when she hugged her husband that morning, she would never hug him again."

Though the preacher's words were well intentioned, they were not true. He could have said, "She'd never again hug her husband in this life," or better, "She would not be able to hug her husband again until the next world." Because of the coming resurrection of the dead, we *will* be able to hug each other again— on the New Earth.

Someone might say, "We all know what the preacher meant." But I'm not sure we really do—or that *he* really did. I'm not trying to be picky, but we need to carefully reform our vocabulary to express what's actually true. If we don't, we will ultimately fail to *think* biblically and continue to embrace predominant stereotypes of Heaven.

"That's the last time I'll ever see him in his body," a man said of his son who died. No. Because they were both Christians, they will see each other again in their resurrection bodies.

"I'll never see my daughter again on this earth." But if she is a believer, and you are, then the statement is wrong. You *will* see her again on this earth. You and she will be transformed, and the earth will be transformed, but it will still *really* be you and your daughter on an Earth that *really* is the same Earth.

We do not just say what we believe—we end up believing what we say.

That's why I propose that we should consciously correct our vocabulary so it conforms to revealed biblical truth. It's hard for us to think accurately about the New Earth because we're so accustomed to speaking of Heaven as the opposite of Earth. It may be difficult to retrain ourselves, but we should do it. We must teach ourselves to embrace the principle of continuity of people and the earth in the coming resurrection that Scripture teaches.

> We need a clear understanding of the doctrine of the new earth, therefore, in order to see God's redemptive program in cosmic dimensions. We need to realize that God will not be satisfied until the entire universe has been purged of all the results of man's fall.
>
> **ANTHONY HOEKEMA**

Because ethereal notions of Heaven have largely gone unchallenged, we often think of Heaven as less real and less substantial than life here and now. (Hence, we don't think of Heaven as a place where people will hug, and certainly not in *these* bodies.) But in Heaven we won't be shadow people living in shadowlands—to borrow C. S. Lewis's imagery. Instead, we'll be fully alive and fully physical in a fully physical universe.

In one sense, we've never seen our friend's body as truly as we will see it in the eternal Heaven. We've never been hugged here as meaningfully as we'll be hugged there. And we've never known this earth to be all that we will then know it to be.

Jesus Christ died to secure for us a resurrected life on a resurrected Earth. Let's be careful to speak of it in terms that deliver us from our misconceptions and do justice to the greatness of Christ's redemptive work.

RESURRECTION DAY

What will it be like on our resurrection day, when we return with Christ to this old Earth, when we are given new bodies in the knowledge that we will together colonize a New Earth (whether that is immediately, or after a thousand years)? At the end of my novel *Safely Home*, I tried to catch a flavor of what it may be like:

> The battle cry of a hundred million warriors erupted from one end of the heavens to the other. There was war on that narrow isthmus between heaven and hell, a planet called Earth. The air was filled with the din of combat—the wails of oppressors being slain and the joyous celebrations of the oppressed, rejoicing that at long last their liberators had arrived.

Some of the warriors sang as they slew, swinging swords to hew the oppressors with one arm and, with the other, pulling victims up onto their horses.

The long arm of the King moved with swiftness and power. The hope of reward that kept the sufferers sane was vindicated at last. No child of heaven was touched by the sword this day, for the universe could not tolerate the shedding of one more drop of righteous blood.

Heaven released fury. Earth bled fear. It was the old world's last night.

At the Lion's nod, Michael raised his mighty sword and brought it down upon the great dragon. His muscles bulging at the strain, Michael picked up his evil twin and cast the writhing beast into a great pit. The mauler of men, the hunter of women, the predator of children, the persecutor of the righteous shrieked in terror. The vast army of heaven's warriors cheered.

The battalions of Charis gazed upon the decimated face of the earth, the scorched soil of the old world. Nothing had survived the fires of this holocaust of things. Nothing but the King's Word, his people, and the deeds of gold and silver and precious stones they had done for him during the long night since Eden's twilight.

Soldiers dropped their weapons, the crippled tossed their crutches and ran, the blind opened their eyes and saw. They pointed and shouted and danced, throwing their arms around each other, for each knew that any now left on earth were under the King's blood and could be fully trusted. The King gathered children upon his lap. He wiped away their tears. . . .

The sound of a great multitude, like the roar of rushing waters and loud peals of thunder, shouted, "Hallelujah! For our Lord God Almighty reigns. Let us rejoice and be glad and give him glory! For the wedding of the Lamb has come, and his bride has made herself ready." . . .

All eyes turned to the King. The entire universe fell silent, antici-pating his words.

"I will turn the wasteland into a garden," the King announced. "I will bring here the home I have made for you, my bride. There will be a new world, a life-filled blue-green world, greater than all that has ever been. The Shadowlands are mine again, and I shall transform them. My kingdom has come. My will shall be done. Winter is over. Spring is here at last!"

A great roar rose from the vast crowd. The King raised his hands.

Upon seeing those scars, the cheering crowds remembered the unthinkable cost of this great celebration.

Warriors slapped each other on the back. The delivered hugged their deliverers, enjoying a great reunion with those once parted from them.

The multitudes innumerable began to sing the song for which they had been made, a song that echoed off a trillion planets and reverberated in a quadrillion places in every nook and cranny of the creation's expanse. Audience and orchestra and choir all blended into one great symphony, one grand cantata of rhapsodic melodies and sustaining harmonies. All were participants. Only one was an audience, the Audience of One. The smile of the King's approval swept through the choir like fire across dry wheat fields.

When the song was complete, the Audience of One stood and raised his great arms, then clapped his scarred hands together in thunderous applause, shaking ground and sky, jarring every corner of the cosmos. His applause went on and on, unstopping and unstoppable.

Every one of them realized something with undiminished clarity in that instant. They wondered why they had not seen it all along. What they knew in that moment, in every fiber of their beings, was that this Person and this Place were all they had ever longed for . . . and ever would.[106]

SEEING THE EARTH RESTORED

CHAPTER 14

WHERE AND WHEN WILL
OUR DELIVERANCE COME?

*There is not one inch in the entire area of our human life about which Christ,
who is Sovereign of all, does not cry out, "Mine!"*

Abraham Kuyper

If God were to end history and reign forever in a distant Heaven, Earth would
be remembered as a graveyard of sin and failure. Instead, Earth will be redeemed and resurrected. In the end it will be a far greater world, even for having
gone through the birth pains of suffering and sin—yes, *even sin*. The New
Earth will justify the old Earth's disaster, make good out of it, putting it in perspective. It will preserve and perpetuate Earth's original design and heritage.

Isaiah and the prophets make clear the destiny of God's people. They will
live in peace and prosperity, as free people in their promised land. But what
about the recipients of these promises who have died—including people who
lived in times of enslavement and captivity, war, poverty, and sickness? For
many, life was short, hard, and sometimes cruel. Did these poor people ever live
to see peace and prosperity, a reign of righteousness, or the end of wickedness?

No.

Have any of their descendants lived to see such a place?

No. "All these people were still living by faith when they died. They did not
receive the things promised; they only saw them and welcomed them from a
distance. And they admitted that they were aliens and strangers on earth. People who say such things show that they are looking for a country of their
own.... They were longing for a better country—a heavenly one.... [God] has
prepared a city for them" (Hebrews 11:13-14, 16).

THE OLD TESTAMENT HOPE FOR A NEW EARTH

The "country of their own" spoken of in Hebrews 11 is a real country, with a
real capital city, the New Jerusalem. It is an actual place where these "aliens and

strangers on earth" will ultimately live in actual bodies. If the promises God made to them were promises regarding Earth (and they were), then the heavenly "country of their own" must ultimately include Earth. The fulfillment of these prophecies requires exactly what Scripture elsewhere promises—a resurrection of God's people *and* God's Earth.

What thrilled these expectant believers was not that God would rule in Heaven—he already did. Their hope was that one day he would rule on Earth, removing sin, death, suffering, poverty, and heartache. They believed the Messiah would come and bring Heaven to Earth. He would make God's will be done on Earth as it is in Heaven.

The hope of the ancient Israelites was not only for their distant offspring but also for *themselves.* They longed for God's rule on Earth, not just for a hundred years or a thousand, but forever.

It's commonly taught that the Old Testament concept of Heaven is stunted. However, though it's certainly true that very little is said about the intermediate Heaven, where believers go when they die, *the Old Testament actually says a great deal about the eternal Heaven.* (We saw some of it in Isaiah 60 and other passages, and there's a lot more.) Unfortunately, we often don't realize it. Why? Because when we read passages about a future earthly kingdom, we assume they don't refer to Heaven. But because God will dwell with his people on the New Earth, these Scripture passages *do* refer to Heaven.

> Since where God dwells, there heaven is, we conclude that in the life to come heaven and earth will no longer be separated, as they are now, but will be merged. Believers will therefore continue to be in heaven as they continue to live on the new earth.
>
> **ANTHONY HOEKEMA**

"But your dead will live; their bodies will rise. You who dwell in the dust, wake up and shout for joy. . . . The earth will give birth to her dead" (Isaiah 26:19). Just as Adam was made from the dust of the earth, we will be remade from the dust to which we returned at death. God's people are not looking for deliverance *from* Earth, but deliverance *on* Earth. That's exactly what we will find after our bodily resurrection.

THE QUESTION OF THE MILLENNIUM

Many have reduced the coming reign of Christ on Earth to a thousand-year millennial kingdom on the old Earth. Consequently, they have failed to understand the biblical promise of an eternal reign on the New Earth. Because of this, it's necessary for us to take a closer look at the Millennium, which has been the subject of considerable debate throughout church history.

Revelation 20 refers six times to the Millennium, describing it like this:

- The devil is bound for a thousand years (v. 2).
- For a thousand years, the nations are no longer deceived (v. 3).
- The saints come to life and reign with Christ for a thousand years (v. 4).
- The rest of the dead don't come to life until after the thousand years are ended (v. 5).
- The saints will be priests and kings for a thousand years (v. 6).
- Satan will be loosed at the end of the thousand years, and he will prompt a final human rebellion against God (vv. 7-8).

Theologians differ over whether the Millennium should be understood as a literal thousand-year reign, and when it will occur in relation to the second coming of Christ. Christians generally hold one of three views about the Millennium: postmillennial, premillennial, or amillennial.

From a *postmillennial* viewpoint, Christ's Kingdom is spreading throughout the world, and God's justice will prevail across the earth prior to Christ's return. After his reign is established through his people for a long duration (not necessarily a literal thousand years), Christ will physically return to an already substantially redeemed world.

From a *premillennial* viewpoint—which would include much of dispensational theology and the teaching of a variety of scholars throughout church history—the Millennium will be a literal thousand-year reign of Christ, which will begin immediately upon his return when he defeats his enemies in the battle of Armageddon. During these thousand years, God's promises of the Messiah's earthly reign will be fulfilled. Redeemed Jews will live in their homeland, and (according to some teachings) the church will govern the world with Christ. The Millennium will end with a final rebellion, and the old Earth will be replaced by, or transformed into, the New Earth.

From an *amillennial* viewpoint—including most Reformed theology and the teaching of many scholars throughout church history—the Millennium isn't a literal thousand years, nor is it a future state. Rather, the events depicted in Revelation 20:3-7 are happening right now as Christ's church reigns with him over the earth, in victorious triumph empowered by his death and resurrection. The saints rule over the earth from the present Heaven, where they dwell with Christ.

Theologians who hold to amillennial or premillennial viewpoints differ on specific details even within their own camps. For instance, according to dispensational premillennialism, the Rapture will occur prior to the Tribulation, and both will occur prior to the final return of Christ to Earth. According to historic premillennialism, the Rapture is an inseparable part of Christ's single, physical return to Earth, which will occur after the Tribulation.[107]

Though I don't believe the case for postmillennialism is strong (either biblically or in light of human history), both premillennialism and amillennialism have many biblical points in their favor.[†] I personally believe there will be a literal thousand-year reign of Christ on the present Earth (though I'm not dogmatic on this point), but I also understand and respect the strong interpretive arguments that have been made in support of amillennialism.

Although the Millennium is a subject of interest to many, it's not the subject of this book. I mention it only to point out that our beliefs about the Millennium need not affect our view of the New Earth. The Millennium question relates to whether the old Earth will end after the return of Christ, or a thousand years later after the end of the Millennium. But regardless of when the old Earth ends, the central fact is that *the New Earth will begin*. The Bible is emphatic that God's ultimate Kingdom and our final home will *not* be on the old Earth but on the New Earth, where at last God's original design will be fulfilled and enjoyed *forever*—not just for a thousand years. Hence, no matter how differently we may view the Millennium, we can still embrace a common theology of the New Earth.

THE PROMISED NEW WORLD

A dominant theme in Old Testament prophecies involves God's plan for an earthly kingdom of righteousness. This pertains to the earth in general and Jerusalem in particular. Isaiah, for example, repeatedly anticipates this coming new world.

The Messiah "will reign on David's throne and over his kingdom . . . forever" (Isaiah 9:7). David's throne was an earthly one, with an earthly past and an earthly future.

In Isaiah 11:1-10, we're told of the Messiah's mission to Earth: "He will defend the poor and the exploited. He will rule against the wicked and destroy them" (v. 4, NLT). With the lifting of the Curse, the Messiah will bring peace to the animal kingdom: "The wolf will live with the lamb, the leopard will lie

---

[†]I highly recommend studying the various views of the Millennium from the perspective of their advocates, not their detractors. An excellent resource is *The Meaning of the Millennium: Four Views,* Robert G. Clouse, ed. (Downers Grove, Ill.: InterVarsity, 1978).

down with the goat" (v. 6). (This fulfills the deliverance spoken of in Romans 8.) Isaiah says there will be no harm or destruction in Jerusalem (v. 9). The Messiah "will stand as a banner for the peoples," and "the nations will rally to him" (v. 10). His "place of rest will be glorious" (v. 10). (This anticipates Revelation 21–22.)

Where will this happen? Not "up there" in a distant Heaven, but "down here" on Earth, in Jerusalem. As we saw in chapter 9, Isaiah 60 speaks of the city gates always being open, because there are no longer any enemies. In words nearly identical to those of John concerning the New Earth (Revelation 21:24-26), it speaks of nations and kings bringing in their wealth. It tells of God's light replacing the sun's and promises that "your days of sorrow will end" (Isaiah 60:19-20)—two prophecies clearly fulfilled in Revelation.

But Isaiah 60 is not alone in these powerful portrayals of everlasting national and global renewal. "As a bridegroom rejoices over his bride, so will your God rejoice over you. . . . You who call on the Lord, give yourselves no rest, and give him no rest till he establishes Jerusalem and makes her the praise of the earth. . . . Pass through, pass through the gates! Prepare the way for the people. . . . Raise a banner for the nations" (Isaiah 62:5-7, 10).

"See, your Savior comes! See, his reward is with him, and his recompense accompanies him" (Isaiah 62:11). This statement reappears in Revelation 22:12, in the words of Jesus Christ: "Behold, I am coming soon! My reward is with me, and I will give to everyone according to what he has done."

The preoccupation with God's establishment of an earthly kingdom couldn't be more clear than it is in Isaiah 65: "'Behold, I will create new heavens and a new earth. . . . But be glad and rejoice forever in what I will create, for I will create Jerusalem to be a delight and its people a joy. I will rejoice over Jerusalem and take delight in my people; the sound of weeping and of crying will be heard in it no more. . . . They will build houses and dwell in them; they will plant vineyards and eat their fruit. . . . The wolf and the lamb will feed together, and the lion will eat straw like the ox, but dust will be the serpent's food. They will neither harm nor destroy on all my holy mountain,' says the Lord" (vv. 17-19, 21, 25).

Throughout church history, some Bible students have believed that the thousand-year kingdom spoken of in Revelation 20 is literal. Others believe it is figurative. I cannot resolve that debate. My point here is not to say that Isaiah 60 and 65 *don't* refer to a literal thousand-year reign of Christ on the old Earth. Rather, I am saying that they *do* refer to the eternal reign of Christ on the New Earth.

It is common for prophetic statements to have partial fulfillment in one era and complete fulfillment in another. It may be that these passages will have a partial and initial fulfillment in a literal millennium, explaining why the passages contain a few allusions to death, which is incompatible with the New Earth. But, in context, these prophecies go far beyond a temporary kingdom on an Earth that is still infected by sin, curse, and death, and that ends with judgment and destruction. They speak of an eternal kingdom, a messianic reign over a renewed Earth that lasts forever, on which sin, curse, and death have no place at all.

The New Earth will be the setting for God's Kingdom. The New Jerusalem will be where people come to pay him tribute: "'As the new heavens and the new earth that I make will endure before me,' declares the Lord, 'so will your name and descendants endure. . . . All mankind will come and bow down before me,' says the Lord" (Isaiah 66:22-23).

Those who insist that Revelation 21–22 should be understood figuratively must then also take all the Isaiah passages figuratively. But Jewish scholars understood them literally. There's every indication Jesus took them literally. The heart cry of the nation was for the Messiah to come and set up his physical Kingdom on Earth.

> [Christ's resurrection] is not a matter of a "spirit appearance," but the utterly unprecedented, unique, world-transforming, heaven-anticipating, sovereign action of the Creator in the first installment of remaking the world.
>
> **BRUCE MILNE**

It's worth restating that we should expect Isaiah's prophecies about the Messiah's second coming and the New Earth to be literally fulfilled because his detailed prophecies regarding the Messiah's first coming were literally fulfilled (e.g., Isaiah 52:13; 53:4-12). When Jesus spoke to his disciples before ascending to Heaven, he said it was not for them to know *when* he would restore God's Kingdom on Earth (Acts 1:6-8), but he did not say they wouldn't know *if* he would restore God's Kingdom. After all, restoring the Kingdom of God on Earth was his ultimate mission.

The angel Gabriel promised Mary concerning Jesus, "The Lord God will give him the throne of his father David, and he will reign over the house of Jacob forever; his kingdom will never end" (Luke 1:32-33). David's throne is not in Heaven but on Earth. It is God's reign on Earth, not in Heaven, that is the focus of the unfolding drama of redemption. That earthly reign will be forever established on the New Earth.

God has a future plan for the earth and a future plan for Jerusalem. His plan involves an actual kingdom over which he and his people will reign—not merely for a thousand years but forever (Revelation 22:5). It will be the long-delayed but never-derailed fulfillment of God's command for mankind to exercise righteous dominion over the earth.

THE MESSIAH'S EARTHLY KINGDOM

God's people were right to expect the Messiah to bring an earthly kingdom. That's exactly what God promised: "All kings shall fall down before Him; All nations shall serve Him" (Psalm 72:11, NKJV). An explicitly messianic passage tells us, "His rule will extend from sea to sea and from the River to the ends of the earth" (Zechariah 9:10).

God promises that he has a great future in store for Jerusalem, in which, he says, "I will extend peace to her like a river, and the wealth of nations like a flooding stream" (Isaiah 66:12). Nations at peace will bring their cultural treasures into a healed Jerusalem, precisely as Revelation 21:24 portrays.

Every time Jewish people greet each other with *Shalom*, they express the God-given cry of the heart to live in a world where there's no sin, suffering, or death. There was once such a world, enjoyed by only two people and some animals. But there will again be such a world, enjoyed by all its inhabitants, including everyone who knows Christ.

Isaiah 66 says that peace will come to Jerusalem and Jerusalem will become a center of all nations. " 'I . . . am about to come and gather all nations and tongues, and they will come and see my glory.' . . . 'As the new heavens and the new earth that I make will endure before me,' declares the Lord, 'so will your name and descendants endure. . . . All mankind will come and bow down before me,' says the Lord" (Isaiah 66:18, 22-23).

This prophecy, like the others, is clearly fulfilled in the later chapters of Revelation. Jerusalem will again be a center of worship. Because this Jerusalem will reside on the New Earth, wouldn't we expect it to be called the New Jerusalem? That's exactly what it is called (see Revelation 3:12; 21:2).

Scripture's repeated promises about land, peace, and the centrality of Jerusalem among all cities and nations will be fulfilled. If a millennial reign on Earth precedes the New Earth, it could offer a foretaste. However, regardless of the proper understanding of the Millennium, the ultimate fulfillment of a host of Old Testament prophecies will be on the New Earth, where the people of God will "possess the land *forever*" (Isaiah 60:21, emphasis added).

CHAPTER 15

WILL THE OLD EARTH BE
DESTROYED . . . OR RENEWED?

In his redemptive activity, God does not destroy the works of his hands, but cleanses them from sin and perfects them, so that they may finally reach the goal for which he created them. Applied to the problem at hand, this principle means that the new earth to which we look forward will not be totally different from the present one, but will be a renewal and glorification of the earth on which we now live.

Anthony Hoekema

Will the present Earth and the entire universe be utterly destroyed, and the New Earth and new universe made from scratch? Or will the original universe be renewed and transformed into the new one? At first glance, some Scriptures seem to answer "utterly destroyed":

In the beginning you laid the foundations of the earth, and the heavens are the work of your hands. They will perish, but you remain; they will all wear out like a garment. Like clothing you will change them and they will be discarded. (Psalm 102:25-26)

[Jesus said,] "Heaven and earth will pass away, but my words will never pass away." (Luke 21:33)

The day of the Lord will come like a thief. The heavens will disappear with a roar; the elements will be destroyed by fire, and the earth and everything in it will be laid bare. (2 Peter 3:10)

Then I saw a new heaven and a new earth, for the first heaven and the first earth had passed away, and there was no longer any sea. (Revelation 21:1)

In contrast, there are passages that speak of the earth remaining forever (Ecclesiastes 1:4; Psalm 78:69). However, the same Hebrew word translated "forever" in these passages is used elsewhere in ways that don't mean forever (e.g., Deuteronomy 15:17). It is clear that the earth *as it is now* will not remain forever—but what does that really mean?

BURNED UP OR REFINED?

Scripture says that the fire of God's judgment will destroy "wood, hay or straw," yet it will purify "gold, silver, [and] costly stones," which will all survive the fire and be carried over into the new universe (1 Corinthians 3:12-15). Similarly, the apostle John notes that when believers die, what they have done on Earth to Christ's glory "will follow them" into Heaven (Revelation 14:13). These are earthly things that will outlast the present Earth. "Those purified works on the earth," writes Albert Wolters, "must surely include the products of human culture. There is no reason to doubt that they will be transfigured and transformed by their liberation from the curse, but they will be in essential continuity with our experience now—just as our resurrected bodies, though glorified, will still be bodies."[108]

As we have seen in a number of passages that use words such as *renewal* and *regeneration*, the same Earth destined for destruction is also destined for restoration. Many have grasped the first teaching but not the second. Therefore, they misinterpret words such as *destroy* to mean absolute or final destruction, rather than what Scripture actually teaches: a temporary destruction that is reversed through resurrection and restoration.

A variety of theologians take this view of temporary, not final, destruction. Wayne Grudem, in his discussion of 2 Peter 3:10, which speaks of "everything" in the earth being "laid bare," suggests that Peter "may not be speaking of the earth as a planet but rather the surface things on the earth (that is, much of the ground and the things on the ground)."[109]

Anthony Hoekema says, "If God would have to annihilate the present cosmos, Satan would have won a great victory. . . . Satan would have succeeded in so devastatingly corrupting the present cosmos and the present earth that God could do nothing with it but to blot it totally out of existence. But Satan did not win such victory. On the contrary, Satan has been decisively defeated. God will reveal the full dimensions of that defeat when he shall renew this very earth on which Satan deceived mankind and finally banish from it all the results of Satan's evil machinations."[110]

John Piper argues that God did not create matter to throw it away. He writes, "When Revelation 21:1 and 2 Peter 3:10 say that the present earth and heavens will 'pass away,' it does not have to mean that they go out of existence, but may mean that there will be such a change in them that their present condition passes away. We might say, 'The caterpillar passes away, and the butterfly emerges.' There is a real passing away, and there is a real continuity, a real connection."[111]

My wife, Nanci, and I will never forget driving home from church on May 18, 1980, and seeing a cloud of volcanic ash billowing overhead. It was the eruption of Mount Saint Helens, seventy miles from our home. For weeks, ash fell so thick every day that we repeatedly had to hose off windshields and driveways. Many people in the Portland area wore surgical masks to keep from choking. The destruction of the once-beautiful mountain and its surrounding area was catastrophic. Great trees were charred and had fallen like giant matchsticks. The devastation appeared comprehensive. Experts predicted that it would certainly be decades, possibly centuries, before the area came back to life. Yet within only a few years it had begun to be restored, demonstrating healing properties that God has built into his creation, evident even under the Curse.

> According to Scripture the present world will neither continue forever nor will it be destroyed and replaced by a totally new one. Instead it will be cleansed of sin and re-created, reborn, renewed, made whole. While the kingdom of God is first planted spiritually in human hearts, the future blessedness is not to be spiritualized. Biblical hope, rooted in incarnation and resurrection, is creational, this-worldly, visible, physical, bodily hope. The rebirth of human beings is completed in the glorious rebirth of all creation, the New Jerusalem whose architect and builder is God himself.
>
> **HERMAN BAVINCK**

After seeing such utter devastation replaced by new beauty—even apart from God's supernatural intervention—I have no trouble envisioning God remaking a charred Earth into a new one, fresh and vibrant.

As we saw in chapter 12, Romans 8:19-23 inseparably links the destinies of mankind and Earth. As such, the earth will be raised to new life in the same way our bodies will be raised to new life.

REDEMPTION MEANS RESTORATION

Even if the term *New Earth* appeared nowhere in Scripture, even if we didn't have dozens of other passages such as Isaiah 60 that refer to it so clearly, Acts 3:21 would be sufficient. It tells us that Christ will "remain in heaven until the time comes for God to restore everything, as he promised long ago through his holy prophets." When Christ returns, God's agenda is not to destroy everything and start over, but to "restore everything." The perfection of creation once lost will be fully regained, and then some. The same Peter who spoke these words in Acts 3 wrote the words about the earth's destruction in 2 Peter 3—apparently he saw no conflict between them.

Albert Wolters says, "Redemption means *restoration*—that is, the return to the goodness of an originally unscathed creation and not merely the addition of something supracreational. . . . This restoration affects the *whole* of creational life and not merely some limited area within it."[112] It will be as if an artist wiped away the old paint, stained and cracking, and started a new and better painting, but using the same images on the same canvas.

Still, many cannot reconcile the idea of redemption through restoration with the statements of 2 Peter 3:10 that "the heavens will disappear with a roar," and "the elements will be destroyed by fire," and "the earth and everything in it will be laid bare." John Piper says of this passage, "What Peter may well mean is that at the end of this age there will be cataclysmic events that bring this world to an end as we know it—not putting it out of existence, but wiping out all that is evil and cleansing it by fire and fitting it for an age of glory and righteousness and peace that will never end."[113]

I think the key to understanding the qualified meaning of these images of destruction in 2 Peter lies within the passage itself. The passage draws a parallel between the earth in the time of Noah, which was "destroyed" through the Flood, and the time to come when the present world will be destroyed in judgment again, this time not by water but by fire (2 Peter 3:6-7). The stated reference point for understanding the future destruction of the world is the Flood. The Flood was certainly cataclysmic and devastating. But did it obliterate the world, making it cease to exist? No. Noah and his family and the animals were delivered from God's judgment in order to reinhabit a new world made ready for them by God's cleansing judgment. Flooding the whole world didn't destroy all the mountains (Genesis 8:4). Though many people believe that the Tigris and Euphrates rivers near Eden (Genesis 2:14) weren't the same rivers as those we know today, the fact that they were given the same names as the originals suggests some continuity.

The cleansing with fire will be more thorough than the Flood in that it will permanently eliminate sin. But just as God's judgment by water didn't make the earth permanently uninhabitable, neither will God's judgment by fire.

The King James Version translates 2 Peter 3:10 this way: "The earth also and the works that are therein shall be burned up." But the word translated "burned up" does not appear in the oldest Greek manuscripts, which contain a word that means "found" or "shown." The New International Version translates it "laid bare," and the English Standard Version renders it "exposed." God's fire of judgment will consume the bad but refine the good, exposing things as they really are.

Theologian Cornelius Venema explains, "The word used in the older and better manuscripts conveys the idea of a process that does not so much destroy or burn up, but uncovers or lays open for discovery the creation, now in a renewed state of pristine purity."[114] Likewise rejecting "burned up" as the best translation, Albert Wolters argues that "translations of this text have often been influenced by a world view that denies the continuity between the present and future state of creation."[115] Venema makes the connection between 2 Peter 3 and Romans 8 when he observes, "Second Peter 3:5-13 confirms . . . the basic ideal also expressed, though in different language, in Romans 8. The new heavens and earth will issue from God's sovereign and redemptive work. . . . It will involve the renewal of all things, not the creation of all new things . . . [and] it follows that the life to come in the new creation will be as rich and full of activity in the service of the Lord as was intended at the beginning."[116]

Several prominent ancient theologians acknowledged the continuity between the present Earth and the New Earth. Jerome often said that Heaven and Earth would not be annihilated but would be transformed into something better. Augustine wrote similarly, as did Gregory the Great, Thomas Aquinas, and many medieval theologians.[117]

THE MEANING OF "NEW"

As we've seen, the expression "Heaven and Earth" is a biblical designation for the entire universe. So when Revelation 21:1 speaks of "a new heaven and a new earth," it indicates a transformation of the entire universe. The Greek word *kainos*, translated "new," indicates that the earth God creates won't merely be new as opposed to old, but new in quality and superior in character. According to Walter Bauer's lexicon, *kainos* means new "in the sense that what is old has become obsolete, and should be replaced by what is new. In such a case the new is, as a rule, superior in kind to the old."[118]

It means, therefore, "not the emergence of a cosmos totally other than the present one, but the creation of a universe which, though it has been gloriously renewed, stands in continuity with the present one."[119]

Paul uses the same word, *kainos*, when he speaks of a believer becoming "a new creation" (2 Corinthians 5:17). The New Earth will be the same as the old Earth, just as a new Christian is still the same person he was before. Different? Yes. But also the same.

When a house burns to the ground, the components of the house do not cease to exist, but take on another form. According to the first law of thermo-dynamics (conservation of energy), the fire doesn't obliterate the wood but transforms it into different substances, including charcoal and carbon dioxide. What we consider annihilation is not what it appears.

Resurrection, however, goes beyond that. A new house is not made out of the materials of a house that burned, but out of new materials. Though it may be on the same ground, made according to the same blueprint, it's a different house. Resurrection, however, is about continuity—the *same* body that was destroyed is reconstructed into the new.

As God may gather the scattered DNA and atoms and molecules of our bodies, he will regather all he needs of the scorched and disfigured Earth. As our old bodies will be raised to new bodies, so the old Earth will be raised to become the New Earth. So, will the earth be destroyed or renewed? The answer is *both*—but the "destruction" will be temporal and partial, whereas the renewal will be eternal and complete.

The doctrine of the new creation, extending not only to mankind, but to the world, the natural realm, and even nations and cultures, is a major biblical theme, though you would never know it judging by how little attention it receives among Christians.

In an important essay, theologian Greg Beale argues that "new creation is a plausible and defensible centre for New Testament theology." He states, "The Bible begins with original creation which is corrupted, and the rest of the Old Testament is a redemptive-historical process working toward a restoration of the fallen creation in a new creation. The New Testament then sees these hopes beginning fulfillment and prophesies a future time of fulfillment in a consummated new creation, which Revelation 21:1–22:5 portrays."[120]

Hence, as we've seen from Isaiah and throughout the Old Testament, the doctrine of the new heavens and New Earth is not some late-developing after-thought but a central component of redemptive history and intention. It is the paradigm of biblical perspective—inclusive of but broader than the themes of kingdom, covenant, resurrection, and salvation. As Beale puts it, "New creation is the New Testament's hermeneutical and eschatological centre of gravity."[121]

Summarizing theologian William Dumbrell's views of new creation, Beale says, "All of the Old Testament works toward the goal of new creation, and the New Testament begins to fulfill that primary goal. . . . Redemption is always subordinate to creation in that it is the means of reintroducing the conditions of the new creation. All events since the fall are to be seen as a process leading to the reintroduction of the original creation. Dumbrell is correct in understanding new creation as the dominating notion of biblical theology because new creation is the goal or purpose of God's redemptive-historical plan; new creation is the logical main point of Scripture."[122]

The earth's death will be no more final than our own. The destruction of the old Earth in God's purifying judgment will immediately be followed by its resurrection to new life. Earth's fiery "end" will open straight into a glorious new beginning. And as we'll see later, it will just keep getting better and better.

Hermeneutics - study of the methodological principles of interpretation

Eschatology - branch of theology concerned with final events in the history of the world or mankind; concerning the Second Coming, the resurrection of the dead or the Last judgment is the study of end times.

CHAPTER 16

WILL THE NEW EARTH BE FAMILIAR . . . LIKE HOME?

The life we now have as the persons we now are will continue in the universe in which we now exist.

Dallas Willard

Sometimes when we look at this world's breathtaking beauty—standing in a gorgeous place where the trees and flowers and rivers and mountains are wondrous—we feel a twinge of disappointment. Why? Because we know we're going to leave this behind. In consolation or self-rebuke, we might say, "This world is not my home." If we were honest, however, we might add, "But part of me sure wishes it was."

What we really want is to live forever in a world with all the beauty and none of the ugliness—a world without sin, death, the Curse, and all the personal and relational problems and disappointments they create.

Those who emphasize our citizenship in Heaven—and I'm one of them—sometimes have an unfortunate habit of minimizing our connection to the earth and our destiny to live on it and rule it. We end up thinking of eternity as a non-earthly spiritual state in which Earth is but a distant memory, if we remember it at all.

This faulty theology accuses God of failure. Why? Because it assumes he will never accomplish a lasting state of righteousness on Earth. (Even the Millennium ends in rebellion.) Instead, he finally has to resort to making mankind less human (disembodied) and destroying the earth he made. God's magnificent sovereign plan of the ages is reduced, in our minds, to a failed experiment.

WHAT OUR HOME WILL REALLY BE LIKE

The correction to the heresy of believing God's plan has failed is the biblical doctrine of the new heavens and New Earth. Theologian René Pache writes, "The emphasis on the present heaven is clearly rest, cessation from earth's battles and comforts from earth's sufferings. The future heaven is centered more on activity and expansion, serving Christ and reigning with Him. The scope is much larger, the great city with its twelve gates, people coming and going, nations to rule. In other words, the emphasis in the present heaven is on the absence of earth's negatives, while in the future heaven it is the presence of earth's positives, magnified many times through the power and glory of resurrected bodies on a resurrected Earth, free at last from sin and shame and all that would hinder both joy and achievement."[123]

Understanding and anticipating the physical nature of the New Earth corrects a multitude of errors. It frees us to love the world that God has made, without guilt, while saying no to the world corrupted by our sin. It reminds us that God himself gave us the earth, gave us a *love* for the earth, and will delight to give us the New Earth.

Think for a moment what this will mean for Adam and Eve. When the New Earth comes down from Heaven, the rest of us will be going home, but Adam and Eve will be *coming* home. Only they will have lived on three Earths—one unfallen, one fallen, and one redeemed. Only they will have experienced, at least to a degree, the treasure of an original, magnificent Earth that was lost and is now regained.

When we open our eyes for the first time on the New Earth, will it be unfamiliar? Or will we recognize it as home?

As human beings, we long for home, even as we step out to explore undiscovered new frontiers. We long for the familiarity of the old, even as we crave the innovation of the new. Think of all the things we love that are new: moving into a new house; the smell of a new car; the feel of a new book; a new movie; a new song; the pleasure of a new friend; the enjoyment of a new pet; new presents on Christmas; staying in a nice new hotel room; arriving at a new school or a new workplace; welcoming a new child or grandchild; eating new foods that suit our tastes. We love newness—yet in each case, what is new is attached to something familiar. We don't really like things that are utterly foreign to us. Instead, we appreciate fresh and innovative variations on things that we already know and love. So when we hear that in Heaven we will have new bodies and live on a New Earth, that's how we should understand the word *new*—a restored and perfected version of our familiar bodies and our familiar Earth and our familiar relationships.

A common misunderstanding about the eternal Heaven is that it will be unfamiliar. But that couldn't be further from the truth. The following chart compares widespread assumptions about Heaven with biblically based characteristics of Heaven:

WHAT WE ASSUME ABOUT HEAVEN	WHAT THE BIBLE SAYS ABOUT HEAVEN
Non-Earth	New Earth
Unfamiliar; otherworldly	Familiar; earthly
Disembodied	Resurrected (embodied)
Foreign	Home (all the comforts of home with all the innovations of an infinitely creative God)
Leaving favorite things behind	Retaining the good; finding the best ahead
No time and space	Time and space
Static	Dynamic
Neither old (like Eden) nor new and earthly; just strange and unknown	Both old and new
Nothing to do; floating on the clouds	A God to worship and serve; a universe to rule; purposeful work to accomplish; friends to enjoy
No learning or discovery; instant and complete knowledge	An eternity of learning and discovering
Boring	Fascinating
Loss of desire	Continuous fulfillment of desire
Absence of the terrible (but presence of little we desire)	Presence of the wonderful (everything we desire and nothing we don't)

What we have assumed about Heaven has reduced it to a place we look forward to only as an alternative to an intolerable existence here on the present Earth. Only the elderly, disabled, suffering, and persecuted might desire the Heaven we imagine. But the Bible portrays life in God's presence, in our resurrected bodies in a resurrected universe, as so exciting and compelling that even the youngest and healthiest of us should daydream about it.

No wonder Satan doesn't want us to learn the truth about Heaven. If we fall in love with the place and look forward to the future that God has for us, we'll fall more in love with God, and we'll be emboldened to follow him with greater resolve and perspective.

When we see Heaven for the first time with our own eyes, I imagine our responses may mirror those I've depicted in my novel *Edge of Eternity* when Nick's companions finally pass through the gates of the City of Light (I've borrowed several expressions from C. S. Lewis):

"This is it . . . the country for which I was made!"

"At last, the real world!"

"I've been born. All my life on Earth was but a series of labor pains preparing me for this."

"This is joy itself. Every foretaste of joy in the Shadowlands was but the stab, the pang, the inconsolable longing for this place!"

"How could anyone be satisfied with less than this?"[124]

The moment we set foot on the New Earth, we'll know it's exactly where we belong. But we don't have to wait until we die to learn about Heaven.

As a bride lives daily in anticipation of the bridegroom's arrival, coming to take her to the house he's built for her, we should think daily about Jesus and about Heaven. Instead of feeling abandoned, the bride feels honored because she knows that she will live in the home the bridegroom has lovingly constructed with her in mind. She may experience some loneliness and difficulty, but she knows he hasn't forgotten her and what he's doing for her will assure her future happiness. Her present happiness depends on trusting him, believing that he will come to take her home, where they'll joyfully live together forever.

THE FAMILIARITY OF HOME

When the Bible tells us that Heaven is our home, what meanings should we attach to the word *home*?

Familiarity is one. I have countless pleasurable memories from childhood. Even those who endured childhood traumas usually have some good memories too. When I ride my bike through my old neighborhood (only a few miles away from my current home), that fond familiarity comes over me like a wave. The hills, the houses, the fences and fields, the schoolyard where I played football and shot baskets. When I gaze at the house I grew up in, every room in that house, every inch of that property, reverberates with memories of my father, mother, brother, friends, dogs, cats, frogs, and lizards. When I go past my childhood home, I step back into a place inseparable from who I was and am, inseparable from my family and friends.

A place with loved ones—that's a central quality of home. The hominess of the house I live in now is inseparable from my wife, Nanci, and my daughters, Angela and Karina, who are married and have their own homes but often come to visit. The girls' husbands are sons to us now, and we love having them here. As I write, we're anticipating our first grandchildren, and we're already preparing the place for them. Memories of extended family and friends who've stayed with us also contribute to the hominess of this place.

Everything here speaks of time spent with significant people: playing together, talking together, eating together, reading together, crying together, praying together, charting the course of our lives together. Home is where we're with the ones we love.

Heaven will be just like that. We'll be with people we love, and we'll love no one more than Jesus, who purchased with his own blood the real estate of the New Earth. It won't be long before we settle in there. Because we've already lived on Earth, I think it will seem from the first that we're coming home. Because we once lived on Earth, the New Earth will strike us as very familiar.

> The resurrection of the body . . . declares that God will make good and bring to perfection the human project he began in the Garden of Eden.
>
> **TIMOTHY GEORGE**

Home is a place where we fit right in. It's the place we were made for. Most houses we live in on Earth weren't really made just for us. But the New Earth will be. When Nanci was pregnant with each of our girls, she and I prepared a place for them. We decorated the room, picked out the right wallpaper, set up the crib just so, and selected the perfect blankets. The quality of the place we prepared for our daughters was limited only by our skills, resources, and imagination.

In Heaven, what kind of a place can we expect our Lord to have prepared for us? Because he isn't limited and he loves us even more than we love our children, I think we can expect to find the best place ever made by anyone, for anyone, in the history of the universe. The God who commends hospitality will not be outdone in his hospitality to us.

A good carpenter envisions what he wants to build. He plans and designs. Then he does his work, carefully and skillfully, fashioning it to exact specifications. He takes pride in the work he's done and delights in showing it to others. And when he makes something for his bride or his children, he takes special care and delight.

Jesus is the carpenter from Nazareth. He knows how to build. He's had experience building entire worlds (billions of them, throughout the universe). He's also an expert at *repairing* what has been damaged—whether people or worlds. He does not consider his creation disposable. This damaged creation cries out to be repaired, and it is his plan to repair it. He's going to remodel the old Earth on a grand scale. How great will be the resurrected planet that he calls the New Earth—the one he says will be our home . . . and *his*.

NEW SONG, NEW CAR, NEW EARTH

By calling the New Earth *Earth*, God emphatically tells us it will be earthly, and thus familiar. Otherwise, why call it Earth?

When Scripture speaks of a "new song," do we imagine it's wordless, silent, or without rhythm? Of course not. Why? Because then it wouldn't be a song. If I promised you a new car, would you say, "If it's new, it probably won't have an engine, transmission, doors, wheels, stereo, or upholstery"? If a new car didn't have these things, it wouldn't be a car. If we buy a new car, we know it will be a better version of what we already have, our old car. Likewise, the New Earth will be a far better version of the old Earth.

The word *new* is an adjective describing a noun. The noun is the main thing. A new car is first and foremost a car. A new body is mainly a body. A New Earth is mainly an Earth.

The New Earth will not be a non-Earth but a real Earth. The Earth spoken of in Scripture is the Earth we know—with dirt, water, rocks, trees, flowers, animals, people, and a variety of natural wonders. An Earth without these would not be Earth.

The Greek word translated "earth" is *ge*, from which we get "geology." It is used of land, soil, and the world itself. Walter Bauer defines *ge* as "the surface of the earth as the habitation of humanity."[125] *Ge* connotes physicality. It's not a figurative, airy, symbolic, or abstract word. It's tangible, concrete. It speaks of an earthly realm where there are physical human beings, animals, vegetation, and natural resources.

Many of the Scripture passages using *ge* contain references to people, who dwell on the earth. Mankind and Earth are inseparable. The New Earth will be populated by redeemed people. Without people, the earth would be incomplete. Without the earth, people would be incomplete.

We're told the "first earth" will pass away (Revelation 21:1). The word for "first" is *prote*, suggesting a vital connection between the two Earths. The first Earth serves as the prototype or pattern for the New Earth. There's continuity between old and new. We should expect new trees, new flowers, new rocks, new rivers, new mountains, and new animals. (*New*, not *non-*.)

As our current bodies are the blueprints for our resurrection bodies, this present Earth is the blueprint for the New Earth.

DOES EARTHLINESS DEMEAN HEAVEN?

In Greek mythology, Mount Olympus is an earthly Heaven, where gods indulge in scandalous behavior, making Heaven seem cheap and man-made. Islam portrays Heaven as a place where a man is given countless concubines—promiscuity as an eternal reward. We rightly recoil at this. It may partly account for why some people resist the notion of a New Earth, assuming that earthliness somehow demeans God and Heaven.

Scripture portrays God as holy and transcendent. Because Heaven is his dwelling place, it seems inappropriate to think of Heaven in earthly terms. But even before Christ's incarnation, God came to the Garden to walk with Adam and Eve. And Christ's incarnation and resurrection took it much further—one member of the transcendent triune God became *permanently* immanent. Jesus is in physical form, in a human resurrection body, for all eternity. (He may choose to exercise his divine omnipresence in a way we can't comprehend, or he may experience it within the Godhead through Father and Spirit, but there is no indication that Jesus the risen Savior will cease to be the eternal God-man.) His marriage to us is not an unequal yoke of a spiritual God to physical people—not only are we also spiritual, but Jesus, by incarnation and resurrection, is also physical.

Before the Incarnation, Heaven was transcendent. By virtue of the Incarnation, Heaven became immanent. The coming New Earth will be God's dwelling place, as pure and holy as Heaven has ever been. Thus, it *cannot* be inappropriate to think of Heaven in earthly terms, because it is Scripture itself that compels us to do so. In the words of Paul Marshall, "What we need is not to be rescued from the world, not to cease being human, not to stop caring for the world, not to stop shaping human culture. What we need is the power to do these things according to the will of God. We, as well as the rest of creation, need to be redeemed."[126]

HOMESICK AT HOME

Do you recall a time when you were away from your earthly home and desperately missed it? Maybe it was when you were off at college or in the military or traveling extensively overseas or needed to move because of a job. Do you re-member how your heart ached for home? That's how we should feel about Heaven. We are a displaced people, longing for our home. C. S. Lewis said, "If I find in myself a desire which no experience in this world can satisfy, the most probable explanation is that I was made for another world."[127]

Augustine wrote, "I am groaning with inexpressible groaning on my wan-derer's path, and remembering Jerusalem with my heart lifted up towards it—Jerusalem my homeland, Jerusalem my mother."[128]

Nothing is more often misdiagnosed than our homesickness for Heaven. We think that what we want is sex, drugs, alcohol, a new job, a raise, a doctor-ate, a spouse, a large-screen television, a new car, a cabin in the woods, a condo in Hawaii. What we really want is the person we were made for, Jesus, and the place we were made for, Heaven. Nothing less can satisfy us. C. S. Lewis said, "The settled happiness and security which we all desire, God withholds from us by the very nature of the world: but joy, pleasure, and merriment He has scat-tered broadcast. We are never safe, but we have plenty of fun, and some ecstasy. It is not hard to see why. The security we crave would teach us to rest our hearts in this world and oppose an obstacle to our return to God."[129]

In his discussion of Christian orthodoxy, G. K. Chesterton wrote, "The modern philosopher had told me again and again that I was in the right place, and I had still felt depressed even in acquiescence. . . . When I heard that I was in the wrong place . . . my soul sang for joy, like a bird in spring. I knew now . . . why I could feel homesick at home."[130]

I like Chesterton's picture of feeling homesick at home. We can say, "Heaven will be our eternal home," or "Earth will be our eternal home," but we shouldn't say, "Heaven, not Earth, will be our eternal home," because the Heaven in which we'll live will be centered on the New Earth.

A Christian I met in passing once told me it troubled him that he really didn't long for Heaven. Instead, he yearned for an Earth that was like God meant it to be. He didn't desire a Heaven out there somewhere, but an Earth under his feet, where God was glorified. He felt guilty and unspiritual for this desire. At the time, my eyes hadn't been opened to Scripture's promise of the New Earth. If I could talk with that man again (I hope he reads this book), I'd tell him what I should have told him the first time—that his longing was bibli-cal and right. In fact, the very place he's always longed for, an Earth where God was fully glorified, is the place where he will live forever.

To say "This world is not your home" to a person who's fully alive and alert to the wonders of the world is like throwing a bucket of water on kindling's blaze. We should fan the flames of that blaze to help it spread, not seek to put it out. Otherwise, we malign our God-given instinct to love the earthly home God made for us. And we reduce "spirituality" into a denial of art, culture, science, sports, education, and all else human. When we do this, we set ourselves up for hypocrisy—for we may pretend to disdain the world while sitting in church, but when we get in the car we turn on our favorite music and head home to barbecue with friends, watch a ball game, play golf, ride bikes, work in the garden, or curl up savoring a cup of coffee and a good book. We do these things not because we are sinners but because we are *people*. We will still be people when we die and go to Heaven. This isn't a disappointing reality—it's God's plan. He made us as we are—except the sin part, which has nothing to do with friends, eating, sports, gardening, or reading.

We get tired of ourselves, of others, of sin and suffering and crime and death. Yet we love the earth, don't we? I love the spaciousness of the night sky over the desert. I love the coziness of sitting next to Nanci on the couch in front of the fireplace, blanket over us and dog snuggled next to us. These experiences are not Heaven—but they are *foretastes* of Heaven. What we love about this life are the things that resonate with the life we were made for. The things we love are not merely the best this life has to offer—they are previews of the greater life to come.

CELEBRATING OUR RELATIONSHIP
WITH GOD

CHAPTER 17

WHAT WILL IT MEAN
TO SEE GOD?

I shall rise from the dead. . . . I shall see the Son of God, the Sun of Glory, and shine myself as that sun shines. I shall be united to the Ancient of Days, to God Himself, who had no morning, never began. . . . No man ever saw God and lived. And yet, I shall not live till I see God; and when I have seen him, I shall never die.

John Donne

I f I were dealing with aspects of Heaven in their order of *importance*, I would have begun with a chapter about God and our eternal relationship with him. However, I thought it was first necessary to establish a clear picture of our physical, resurrected life on the New Earth. Without the foundation laid in earlier chapters, the idea of "seeing God" would inevitably be skewed by christoplatonic assumptions about the nature of the afterlife. If we don't base our perspective of Heaven on a clear understanding of our coming bodily resurrection and the truth about the physical nature of the New Earth, our concept of being with God will be more like that of Eastern mysticism than of biblical Christianity.

The magnificent theme of beholding God's face shouldn't be poisoned by dull stereotypes and vague, lifeless caricatures. I hope we can now approach the topic of our eternal relationship with God with the richness and vitality it deserves.

"O God, you are my God, earnestly I seek you; my soul thirsts for you, my body longs for you, in a dry and weary land where there is no water" (Psalm 63:1). We may imagine we want a thousand different things, but God is the one we really long for. His presence brings satisfaction; his absence brings thirst and longing. *Our longing for Heaven is a longing for God*—a longing that involves not only our inner beings, but our bodies as well. Being with God is the heart and soul of Heaven. Every other heavenly pleasure will derive from and be secondary to his presence. God's greatest gift to us is, and always will be, himself.

THE BEATIFIC VISION

Ancient theologians often spoke of the "beatific vision." The term comes from three Latin words that together mean "a happy-making sight." The sight they spoke of was God. Revelation 22:4 says of God's servants on the New Earth, "They will see his face." To see God's face is the loftiest of all aspirations—though sadly, for most of us, it's not at the top of our wish list. (If we understand what it means, it will be.)

To be told we'll see God's face is *shocking* to anyone who understands God's transcendence and inapproachability. In ancient Israel, only the high priest could go into the Holy of Holies, and he but once a year. Even then, according to tradition, a rope was tied around the priest's ankle in case he died while inside the Holy of Holies. Why? Well, God struck down Uzzah for *touching* the Ark of the Covenant (2 Samuel 6:7). Who would volunteer to go into the Holy of Holies to pull out the high priest if God slew him?

When Moses said to God, "Show me your glory," God responded, "'I will cause all my goodness to pass in front of you. . . . But,' he said, 'you cannot see my face, for no one may see me and live.' . . . 'When my glory passes by, I will put you in a cleft in the rock and cover you with my hand until I have passed by. Then I will remove my hand and you will see my back; but my face must not be seen'" (Exodus 33:18-23).

Moses saw God but not God's face. The New Testament says that God "lives in unapproachable light, whom no one has seen or can see" (1 Timothy 6:16). To see God's face was utterly unthinkable.

That's why, when we're told in Revelation 22:4 that we'll see God's face, it should astound us. For this to happen, it would require that we undergo something radical between now and then. The obstacles to seeing God are daunting: "Without holiness no one will see the Lord" (Hebrews 12:14). It's only because we'll be fully righteous in Christ, completely sinless, that we'll be able to see God and live.

Not only will we see his face and live, but we will likely wonder if we ever lived before we saw his face! To see God will be our greatest joy, the joy by which all others will be measured.

I imagine what this will be like in my novel *Edge of Eternity*, when Nick Seagrave at last sees Jesus Christ:

> The King stepped from the great city, just outside the gate, and put
> his hand on my shoulder. I was aware of no one and nothing but him.
> I saw before me an aged, weathered King, thoughtful guardian of an
> empire. But I also saw a virile Warrior-Prince primed for battle, eager

to mount his steed and march in conquest. His eyes were keen as sharpened swords yet deep as wells, full of the memories of the old and the dreams of the young.[131]

This is the wonder of our redemption—to be welcomed into the very presence of our Lord and to see him face-to-face. What will we see in his eyes? Though we cannot experience its fullness yet, we can gain a foretaste now: "We have confidence to enter the Most Holy Place by the blood of Jesus" (Hebrews 10:19); "Let us then with confidence draw near to the throne of grace" (Hebrews 4:16, ESV). We shouldn't read these verses casually, for they tell us something wonderful beyond comprehension—that the blood of Jesus has bought us full access to God's throne room and his Most Holy Place. Even now, he welcomes us to come there in prayer. In eternity, when we're resurrected beings, he will not only permit us to enter his presence in prayer, but he will welcome us to *live* in his presence as resurrected beings.

FACES OF FATHER AND SON

David says, "One thing I ask of the Lord, this is what I seek: that I may dwell in the house of the Lord all the days of my life, to gaze upon the beauty of the Lord and to seek him in his temple" (Psalm 27:4). David was preoccupied with God's person, and also with God's place. He longed to be where God was and to gaze on his beauty. To see God's face is to behold his beauty, which is the source of all lesser beauties.

God, who is transcendent, became immanent in Jesus Christ, who is Immanuel, "God with us" (Matthew 1:23). God the Son pitched his tent among us, on our Earth, as one of us (John 1:14). So whenever we see Jesus in Heaven, *we will see God*. Because Jesus Christ is God, and a permanent manifestation of God, he could say to Philip, "Anyone who has seen me has seen the Father" (John 14:9). Certainly, then, a primary way we will see the Father on the New Earth is through his Son, Jesus. Jonathan Edwards emphasized Christ as the member of the Godhead we will see: "The seeing of God in the glorified body of Christ is the most perfect way of seeing God with the bodily eyes that can be; for in seeing a real body that one of the persons of the Trinity has assumed to be his body, and that he dwells in for ever as his own in which the divine majesty and excellency appears as much as 'tis possible for it to appear in outward form or shape."[132]

Yet Jesus said, "Blessed are the pure in heart, for they will see God" (Matthew 5:8). And in Revelation 22:4, when it says "they will see his face, and his name will be on their foreheads," it appears to be referring to seeing the face of God the Father.

"God is spirit" (John 4:24). Biblical references to God's body parts (e.g., "the eyes of the Lord" or "God's arms") are figures of speech. Yet in some sense, it seems that Moses saw the bright essence of God himself, even without seeing God's face. Is brightness really part of God the Father's essence, or is it a form in which he chooses to reveal himself to physical eyes? I don't pretend to understand how we will see the Father's face, but it seems that in some sense we will.

SEEING GOD WITH OUR NEW BODIES

Near the end of *The City of God,* Augustine addresses whether we will see God with physical eyes—or only with spiritual eyes—in our resurrection bodies: "It is possible, it is indeed most probable, that we shall then see the physical bodies of the new heaven and the new earth in such a fashion as to observe God in utter clarity and distinctness, seeing him everywhere present and governing the whole material scheme of things. . . . Perhaps God will be known to us and visible to us in the sense that he will be spiritually perceived by each of us in each one of us, perceived in one another, perceived by each in himself; he will be seen in the new heaven and earth, in the whole creation as it then will be; he will be seen in every body by means of bodies, wherever the eyes of the spiritual body are directed with their penetrating gaze."[133]

A book on Heaven says, "The redeemed will see God—not, to be sure, with physical eyes."[134] But why not? The scene depicted in Revelation 22:3-4 comes *after* our bodily resurrection: "The throne of God . . . will be in the city, and his servants will . . . see his face." As physical beings we will certainly have physical eyes—how else should we expect to see God? Our resurrection bodies will have physical-spiritual eyes, untainted by sin, disease, or death. They will see far better than Moses' eyes, which allowed him to see an indirect manifestation of God's glory.

> The kingdom must not be understood as merely the salvation of certain individuals or even as the reign of God in the hearts of his people; it means nothing less than the reign of God over his entire created universe. . . . The kingdom is not man's upward climb to perfection but God's breaking into human history to establish his reign and to advance his purposes.
>
> **ANTHONY HOEKEMA**

Will the Christ we worship in Heaven as God also be a man? Yes. "Jesus Christ is the same yesterday [when he lived on Earth] and today [when he lives in the present Heaven] and forever [when he will live on the New Earth, in the eternal Heaven]" (Hebrews 13:8). Christ didn't put on a body as if it were a coat. He didn't contain two separable components, man and God, to be switched on and off at will. Rather, he was and is and will be always a man *and* God.

When Christ died, he might have appeared to shed his humanity; but when he rose in an indestructible body, he declared his permanent identity as the God-man. J. I. Packer writes, "By incarnation the Son became more than he was before, and a human element became integral to the ongoing life of the Triune God. . . . Christ's glorified humanity, which is the template and link for the glorification that is ours, must go on forever."[135] This is a mystery so great it should leave us breathless.

Job, in his anguish, cried out in a vision of striking clarity: "I know that my Redeemer lives, and that in the end he will stand upon the earth. And after my skin has been destroyed, yet in my flesh I will see God; I myself will see him with my own eyes—I, and not another. How my heart yearns within me!" (Job 19:25-27). The anticipation of seeing God face-to-face, in our resurrected bodies, is heartfelt and ancient. "And we all, with unveiled face, beholding the glory of the Lord, are being transformed into the same image from one degree of glory to another" (2 Corinthians 3:18, ESV). Our glorification will increase as we behold God in his glory.

We need not wait till the New Earth to catch glimpses of God. We're told his "invisible qualities" can be "clearly seen" in "what has been made" (Romans 1:20). Consider the trees, flowers, sun, rain, and the people around you. Yes, there's devastation all around us and within us. Eden has been trampled, burned, and savaged. Yet the stars in the sky nevertheless declare God's glory (Psalm 19:1), as do animals, art, and music. But our vision is hampered by the same curse that infects all creation. One day both we and the universe will be forever cured of sin. In that day, *we will see God.*

SEEING GOD: OUR PRIMARY JOY

In Heaven, the barriers between redeemed human beings and God will forever be gone. To look into God's eyes will be to see what we've always longed to see: the person who made us for his own good pleasure. Seeing God will be like seeing everything else for the first time. Why? Because not only will we see God, he will be the lens through which we see everything else—people, ourselves, and the events of this life.

What is the essence of eternal life? "That they may know you, the only true God, and Jesus Christ, whom you have sent" (John 17:3). Our primary joy in

Heaven will be knowing and seeing God. Every other joy will be derivative, flowing from the fountain of our relationship with God. Jonathan Edwards said, "God himself is the great good which they are brought to the possession and enjoyment of by redemption. He is the highest good, and the sum of all that good which Christ purchased. . . . The redeemed will indeed enjoy other things . . . but that which they shall enjoy in the angels, or each other, or in anything else whatsoever, that will yield them delight and happiness, will be what will be seen of God in them."[136]

Asaph says, "Whom have I in heaven but you? And earth has nothing I desire besides you" (Psalm 73:25). This may seem an overstatement—there's *nothing* on Earth this man desires but God? But he's affirming that the central desires of our heart are for God. Yes, we desire many other things—but in desiring them, it is really *God* we desire. Augustine called God "the end of our desires." He prayed, "You have made us for yourself, O Lord, and our hearts are restless until they rest in you."[137]

Suppose you're sick. Your friend brings a meal. What meets your needs—the meal or the friend? *Both.* Of course, without your friend, there would be no meal; but even without a meal, you would still treasure your friendship. Hence, your friend is both your higher pleasure *and* the source of your secondary pleasure (the meal). Likewise, God is the source of all lesser goods, so that when they satisfy us, it's God himself who satisfies us. (In fact, it's God who satisfies you by giving you the friend who gives you the meal.)

When I speak elsewhere in the book of the multifaceted joys of the resurrected life in the new universe, some readers may think, *But our eyes should be on the giver, not the gift; we must focus on God, not on Heaven.* This approach sounds spiritual, but it erroneously divorces our experience of God from life, relationships, and the world—all of which God graciously gives us. It sees the material realm and other people as God's competitors rather than as instruments that communicate his love and character. It fails to recognize that because God is the ultimate source of joy, and all secondary joys emanate from him, to love secondary joys on Earth *can be*—and in Heaven *always will be*—to love God, their source.

Though Christoplatonism frowns upon the pleasures of the physical world, mistaking asceticism for spirituality, Scripture says we are to put our hope not in material things but "in God, who richly provides us with everything for our enjoyment" (1 Timothy 6:17). If he provides everything for our enjoyment, we shouldn't feel guilty for enjoying it, should we?

Paul says it is demons and liars who portray the physical realm as unspiritual, forbid people from the joys of marriage, including sex, and "order them to abstain from certain foods, which God created to be received with thanksgiving by those who believe and who know the truth. For everything God created is good, and nothing is to be rejected if it is received with thanksgiving, because it is consecrated by the word of God and prayer" (1 Timothy 4:3-5).

Because of the current darkness of our hearts, we must be careful not to make idols out of God's provisions. But once we're freed from sin and we're in God's presence, we'll never have to worry about putting people or things above God. That would be unthinkable. (Were we thinking clearly, it would be unthinkable to us *now*.)

God isn't displeased when we enjoy a good meal, marital sex, a football game, a cozy fire, or a good book. He's not up in Heaven frowning at us and saying, "Stop it—you should only find joy in me." This would be as foreign to God's nature as our heavenly Father as it would be to mine as an earthly father if I gave my daughters a Christmas gift and started pouting because they enjoyed it too much. No, I gave the gift to bring joy to them and to me—if they didn't take pleasure in it, I'd be disappointed. Their pleasure in my gift to them draws them closer to me. I am *delighted* that they enjoy the gift.

Of course, if children become so preoccupied with the gift that they walk away from their father and ignore him, that's different. Though preoccupation with a God-given gift can turn into idolatry, enjoying that same gift with a grateful heart can draw us closer to God. In Heaven we'll have no capacity to turn people or things into idols. When we find joy in God's gifts, we will be finding our joy in him.

All secondary joys are *derivative* in nature. They cannot be separated from God. Flowers are beautiful for one reason—God is beautiful. Rainbows are stunning because God is stunning. Puppies are delightful because God is delightful. Sports are fun because God is fun. Study is rewarding because God is rewarding. Work is fulfilling because God is fulfilling.

Ironically, some people who are the most determined to avoid the sacrilege of putting things before God miss a thousand daily opportunities to thank him, praise him, and draw near to him, because they imagine they shouldn't enjoy the very things he made to help us know him and love him.

God is a lavish giver. "He who did not spare his own Son, but gave him up for us all—how will he not also, along with him, graciously give us all things?" (Romans 8:32). The God who gave us his Son delights to graciously give us "all things." These "all things" are in addition to Christ, but they are never *instead* of him—they come, Scripture tells us, "along with him." If we didn't have Christ, we would have nothing. But because we have Christ, we have everything. Hence, we can enjoy the people and things God has made, and in the process enjoy the God who designed and provided them for his pleasure and ours.

God welcomes prayers of thanksgiving for meals, warm fires, games, books, relationships, and every other good thing. When we fail to acknowledge God as the source of all good things, we fail to give him the recognition and glory he deserves. We separate joy from God, which is like trying to separate heat from fire or wetness from rain.

The movie *Babette's Feast* depicts a conservative Christian sect that scrupulously avoids "worldly" distractions until a woman's creation of a great feast opens their eyes to the richness of God's provision. *Babette's Feast* beautifully illustrates that we shouldn't ignore or minimize God's lavish, creative gifts, but we should enjoy them and express heartfelt gratitude to God for all of life's joys. When we do this, instead of these things drawing us *from* God, they draw us *to* God. That's precisely what all things and all beings in Heaven will do—draw us to God, never away from him.

Every day we should see God in his creation: in the food we eat, the air we breathe, the friendships we enjoy, and the pleasures of family, work, and hobbies. Yes, we must sometimes forgo secondary pleasures, and we should never let them eclipse God. And we should avoid opulence and waste when others are needy. But we should thank God for all of life's joys, large and small, and allow them to draw us to him.

That's exactly what we'll do in Heaven . . . so why not start now?

SEEING GOD IN EVERYTHING GOOD

They feast on the abundance of your house; you give them drink from your river of delights. For with you is the fountain of life. (Psalm 36:8-9)

This passage portrays the joy that God's creatures find in feasting on Heaven's abundance, and drinking deeply of his delights. Notice that this abundance and the river of delights flow from and are completely dependent on their source: God. He alone is the fountain of life, and without him there could be neither life nor joy, neither abundance nor delights.

God doesn't want to be replaced or depreciated. He wants to be recognized as the source of all our joys, and he wants us to draw closer to him through partaking of his creation. My taking pleasure in a good meal or a good book is taking pleasure in God. It's not a substitute for God, nor is it a distraction from him. In the words of the Westminster Shorter Catechism, it's what I was made for: "Man's chief end is to glorify God, and to enjoy him forever."[138]

In Jeremiah 31:34, God describes his future Kingdom: "No longer will a man teach his neighbor, or a man his brother, saying, 'Know the Lord,' because they will all know me, from the least of them to the greatest." There will always be more to see when we look at God, because his infinite character can never be exhausted. We could—and will—spend countless millennia exploring the depths of God's being and be no closer to seeing it all than when we first started. This is the magnificence of God and the wonder of Heaven.

Theologian Sam Storms writes, "We will constantly be more amazed with God, more in love with God, and thus ever more relishing his presence and our relationship with him. Our experience of God will never reach its consummation. We will never finally arrive, as if upon reaching a peak we discover there is nothing beyond. Our experience of God will never become stale. It will deepen and develop, intensify and amplify, unfold and increase, broaden and balloon."[139]

Beholding and knowing God, we will spend eternity worshiping, exploring, and serving him, seeing his magnificent beauty in everything and everyone around us. Augustine wrote in *The City of God*, "We shall in the future world see the material forms of the new heavens and the new earth in such a way that we shall most distinctly recognize God everywhere present and governing all things, material as well as spiritual."[140] In the new universe, as we study nature, as we pursue science and mathematics and every realm of knowledge, we'll see God in everything, for he's behind it all.

Many commoners in history would have thought it the ultimate experience to gain an audience with their human king, to meet him face-to-face. How much greater will it be to see God in his glory? There could be no higher privilege, no greater thrill. All our explorations and adventures and projects in the eternal Heaven—and I believe there will be many—will pale in comparison to the wonder of seeing God. Yet everything else we do will help us to see God better, to know him and worship him better.

Eden's greatest attraction was God's presence. The greatest tragedy of sin and the Curse was that God no longer dwelt with his people. His presence came back in a small but real way in the Holy of Holies in the Tabernacle and the Temple. After the Exile, Ezekiel saw God's *shekinah* glory—his visible presence—leave the Temple and the city, a sad day for Israel (Ezekiel 11:23).

God's shekinah glory returned in Christ, who *tabernacled* among us (took up temporary residence); "We have seen his glory" (John 1:14). God's glory resides now in his people, the temple he indwells (1 Corinthians 3:17). But one day Christ will come and make a new people, a New Earth, and a new universe in which he will dwell among his people, fully and freely.

God promised Simeon, a "righteous and devout" old man who lived in Jerusalem at the time of Christ's birth, that he would not die until he had seen the Messiah. The culminating joy of Simeon's life was to see Jesus when Joseph and

Mary brought him to the Temple (Luke 2:25-32). We too have been promised that we'll see Jesus. As Simeon lived his earthly life in anticipation of seeing Jesus, so should we. All else—in this world and the next—will be secondary to beholding our Lord. To see Jesus—what could be greater? "We shall be like him, for we shall see him as he is" (1 John 3:2).

The apostle John was Christ's dearest friend on Earth. But when John saw Jesus in Heaven, he "fell at his feet as though dead" (Revelation 1:17). We will see Christ in his glory. The most exhilarating experiences on Earth, such as white-water rafting, skydiving, or extreme sports, will seem tame compared to the thrill of seeing Jesus.

Being with him. Gazing at him. Talking with him. Worshiping him. Embracing him. Eating with him. Walking with him. Laughing with him. Imagine it!

Will we ever tire of praising him? Augustine writes, "God himself, who is the Author of virtue, shall be our reward. As there is nothing greater or better than God himself, God has promised us himself. God shall be the end of all our desires, who will be seen without end, loved without cloy, and praised without weariness."[141]

THE BLIND BOY AND THE KING

In *The Happiness of Heaven*, published in 1871, Father J. Boudreau tells of a kindhearted king who finds a blind, destitute orphan boy while hunting in a forest. The king takes the boy to his palace, adopts him as his son, and provides for his care. He sees that the boy receives the finest education. The boy is extremely grateful, and he loves the king, his new father, with all his heart.

When the boy turns twenty, a surgeon performs an operation on his eyes, and for the first time he is able to see.

This boy, once a starving orphan, has for some years been a royal prince, at home in the king's palace. But something wonderful has happened, something far greater than the magnificent food, gardens, libraries, music, and wonders of the palace. The boy is finally able to *see* the father he loves. Boudreau writes, "I will not attempt to describe the joys that will overwhelm the soul of this fortunate young man when he first sees that king, of whose manly beauty, goodness, power, and magnificence he has heard so much. Nor will I attempt to describe the other joys which fill his soul when he beholds his own personal beauty, and the magnificence of his princely garments whereof he had also heard so much heretofore. Much less will I attempt to picture his exquisite and unspeakable happiness when he sees himself adopted into the royal family, honored and loved by all, together with all the pleasures of life within his reach. . . . All this taken together is a beatific vision for him."[142]

The boy's rescue by his father is analogous to our conversion. We come to know God's love and enjoy his presence. When we die, we'll be with the Lord, and that will be wonderful, though it's uncertain whether we will yet fully see God's face. The great day we await is the establishing of the new heavens and New Earth, where, we are told, as resurrected beings we will actually *see God's face*.

"The vision of God has a transforming power," writes Boudreau. "Thus the soul, because she only sees God as He is, is filled to overflowing with all knowledge; she becomes beautiful with the beauty of God, rich with His wealth, holy with His holiness, and happy with His unutterable happiness."[143]

CHAPTER 18

WHAT WILL IT MEAN FOR GOD TO DWELL AMONG US?

If the goodness, beauty, and wonder of creatures are so delightful to the human mind, the fountainhead of God's own goodness (compared with the trickles of goodness found in creatures) will draw excited human minds entirely to itself.
Thomas Aquinas

In Eden, God came down to Earth, the home of mankind, whenever he wished (Genesis 3:8). On the New Earth, God and mankind will be able to come to each other whenever they wish. We will not have to leave home to visit God, nor will God leave home to visit us. God and mankind will live together forever in the same home—the New Earth.

God declares this truth in Scripture:

I will put my dwelling place among you, and I will not abhor you.
I will walk among you and be your God, and you will be my people.
(Leviticus 26:11-12)

My dwelling place will be with them; I will be their God, and they will be my people. (Ezekiel 37:27)

I will live with them and walk among them, and I will be their God, and they will be my people. (2 Corinthians 6:16)

THE MARRIAGE OF GOD AND MAN, HEAVEN AND EARTH

The marriage of the God of Heaven with the people of Earth will also bring the marriage of Heaven and Earth. There will not be two universes—one the primary home of God and angels, the other the primary home of humanity. Nothing will separate us from God, and nothing will separate Earth and Heaven. Once God and mankind dwell together, there will be no difference between

Heaven and Earth. Earth will become Heaven—and it will truly be Heaven on Earth. The New Earth will be God's locus, his dwelling place. This is why I do not hesitate to call the New Earth "Heaven," for where God makes his home is Heaven. The purpose of God will at last be achieved: "To bring all things in heaven and on earth together under one head, even Christ" (Ephesians 1:10).

In fact, there may not be two universes even now. In *The Divine Conspiracy*, philosophy and theology professor Dallas Willard argues that there is only one universe, and it's where we'll live forever:

> We can be sure that heaven in the sense of our afterlife is just our future in this universe. There is not another universe besides this one. God created the heavens and the earth. That's it. And much of the difficulty in having a believable picture of heaven and hell today comes from the centuries-long tendency to "locate" them in "another reality" outside the created universe.
>
> But time is within eternity, not outside it. The created universe is within the kingdom of God, not outside it. And if there is anything we know now about the "physical" universe, it surely is that it would be quite adequate to eternal purposes. And given that it has been produced, which is not seriously in doubt, all that one might require of an utterly realistic future for humanity in it is surely possible.[144]

It might be better, then, if we think of the location of the present Heaven as not in another universe but simply as a part of ours that we are unable to see, due to our spiritual blindness. If that's true, when we die we don't go to a different universe but to a place within our universe that we're currently unable to see.

Just as blind people cannot see the world, even though it exists all around them, we are unable to see Heaven in our fallen condition. Is it possible that before sin and the Curse, Adam and Eve saw clearly what is now invisible to us? Is it possible that Heaven itself is but inches away from us? Does death restore a visual acuity we once had? Willard says, "When we pass through what we call death, we do not lose the world. Indeed, we see it for the first time as it really is."[145]

THE JOY OF A GOD-CENTERED HEAVEN

Consider this statement: "God himself will be with them" (Revelation 21:3). Why does it emphatically say God *himself*? Because God won't merely send us a delegate. He will actually come to live among us on the New Earth. As Steven J. Lawson explains, "God's glory will fill and permeate the entire new Heaven, not just one centralized place. Thus, wherever we go in Heaven, we will be in the immediate presence of the full glory of God. Wherever we go, we will enjoy the complete manifestation of God's presence. Throughout all eternity, we will never be separated from direct, unhindered fellowship with God."[146]

God's glory will be the air we breathe, and we'll always breathe deeper to gain more of it. In the new universe, we'll never be able to travel far enough to leave God's presence. If we could, we'd never want to. However great the wonders of Heaven, God himself is Heaven's greatest prize. Father Boudreau writes, "The beatitude of Heaven consists essentially in the vision, love, and enjoyment of God himself."[147]

In Heaven we'll at last be freed of self-righteousness and self-deceit. We'll no longer question God's goodness; we'll see it, savor it, enjoy it, and declare it to our companions. Surely we will wonder how we ever could have doubted his goodness. For then our faith will be sight—*we shall see God.*

Many contemporary approaches to Heaven either leave God out or put him in a secondary role. *The Five People You Meet in Heaven*, a best-selling novel, portrays a man who feels lonely and unimportant.[148] He dies, goes to Heaven, and meets five people who tell him his life really mattered. He discovers forgiveness and acceptance. It sounds good, but the book fails to present Jesus Christ as the object of saving faith. Instead, it portrays a Heaven that isn't about God, but about us. A Heaven that's not about God's glory, but our healing. And a Heaven that's not about God's unfathomable grace to undeserving sinners, but our goodness and self-importance. Man is the cosmic center; God plays a supporting role. This sort of Heaven, of which the Bible knows nothing, is a place of therapeutic self-preoccupation rather than preoccupation with the person of Christ.

Jonathan Edwards said in a 1733 sermon, "God is the highest good of the reasonable creature, and the enjoyment of him is the only happiness with which our souls can be satisfied. To go to heaven fully to enjoy God, is infinitely better than the most pleasant accommodations here. Fathers and mothers, husbands, wives, children, or the company of earthly friends, are but shadows. But the enjoyment of God is the substance. These are but scattered beams, but God is the sun. These are but streams, but God is the fountain. These are but drops, but God is the ocean."[149]

HEAVEN RELOCATED TO EARTH

Not only will God come to dwell with us on Earth, he will also bring with him the New Jerusalem, an entire city of people, structures, streets, walls, rivers, and trees that is now in the present, intermediate Heaven. If you've ever seen a house being relocated, you appreciate what a massive undertaking it is. God will relocate an entire city—Heaven's capital city, the New Jerusalem—from Heaven to Earth. It's a vast complex containing, perhaps, hundreds of millions of residences. He will bring with it Heaven's human inhabitants and angels as well.

It appears that God has already fashioned the New Jerusalem: "He has prepared a city for them" (Hebrews 11:16). It doesn't say that God *will* prepare a city or even that he *is preparing* it, but that he *has* prepared it. This suggests that the New Jerusalem, complete or nearly complete, is already there in the present Heaven. When God fashions the New Earth, he will relocate the city from Heaven to the New Earth. It's possible that those in the present Heaven are already living in it. Or it may be set aside, awaiting simultaneous habitation by *all* its occupants when transferred to the New Earth. Imagine the thrill of beholding and exploring God's city together!

> We are certain that when the mists of death are cleared away, the whole city will stand visible and proud. Our inheritance is as sure as morning.
>
> **CALVIN MILLER**

God's new center of government will be the New Earth. This will be the ultimate answer to the Lord's Prayer, "Thy will be done in earth, as it is in heaven" (Matthew 6:10, KJV). God's will shall be done on the New Earth as it now is in Heaven. Indeed, the New Earth shall be a part of Heaven, for the veil between the worlds, first torn apart by the Cross and Christ's resurrection, will be permanently removed. There will be no barrier between Earth and Heaven, or between mankind and God.

BEING WITH GOD

Many books and programs these days talk about messages from the spirit realm, supposedly from people who've died and now speak through channelers or mediums. They claim to have come from Heaven to interact with loved ones, yet almost never do they talk about God or express wonder at seeing Jesus. But no one who had actually been in Heaven would neglect to mention what Scripture shows is the main focus. If you had spent an evening dining with a king, you wouldn't come back and talk about the place settings. When the apostle John was shown Heaven and wrote about it to the church, he recorded the details—but first and foremost, from beginning to end, he kept talking about Jesus.

The 1998 movie *What Dreams May Come* portrays Heaven as a beautiful place, yet shows it as lonely because a man's wife isn't there. Remarkably, someone else is entirely absent from the movie's depiction of Heaven: *God*.

Going to Heaven without God would be like a bride going on her honeymoon without her groom. A Heaven without God would be like a palace without a king. If there's no king, there's no palace. If there's no God, there's no Heaven. Teresa of Avila said, "Wherever God is, there is Heaven."[150] The corollary is obvious: Wherever God is not, there is Hell. As John Milton put it, "Thy presence makes our Paradise, and where Thou art is Heaven."[151] Heaven will simply be a physical extension of God's goodness. To be with God—to know him, to see him—is the central, irreducible draw of Heaven.

The presence of God is the essence of Heaven (just as the absence of God is the essence of Hell). Because God is beautiful beyond measure, if we knew nothing more than that Heaven was God's dwelling place, it would be more than enough. The best part of life on the New Earth will be enjoying God's presence, having him actually dwell among us (Revelation 21:3-4). Just as the Holy of Holies contained the dazzling presence of God in ancient Israel, so will the New Jerusalem contain his presence—but on a much larger scale—on the New Earth. The Holy of Holies in the Temple at Jerusalem was a perfect thirty-foot cube. The New Jerusalem itself will be a perfect cube, one that stretches fourteen hundred miles in each direction (Revelation 21:16).

In the New Jerusalem, there will be no temple (Revelation 21:22). Everyone will be allowed unimpeded access into God's presence. "Blessed are those who . . . may go through the gates into the city" (Revelation 22:14).

Heaven's greatest miracle will be our access to God. In the New Jerusalem, we will be able to come physically, through wide open gates, to God's throne.

BEING WITH JESUS

Jesus promised his disciples, "I will come back and take you to be with me that you also may be where I am" (John 14:3). For Christians, to die is to "be present with the Lord" (2 Corinthians 5:8, NKJV). The apostle Paul says, "I desire to depart and be with Christ, which is better by far" (Philippians 1:23). He could have said, "I desire to depart and be in Heaven," but he didn't—his mind was on being with his Lord Jesus, which is the most significant aspect of Heaven.

Samuel Rutherford said, "O my Lord Jesus Christ, if I could be in heaven without thee, it would be a hell; and if I could be in hell, and have thee still, it would be a heaven to me, for thou art all the heaven I want."[152] Martin Luther said, "I had rather be in hell with Christ, than be in heaven without him."[153] A place with Christ cannot be Hell, only Heaven. A place without Christ cannot be Heaven, only Hell.

We'll worship Jesus as the Almighty and bow to him in reverence, yet we'll never sense his disapproval—because we'll never disappoint him. He'll never be unhappy with us. We'll be able to relax in Heaven. The other shoe will never drop. No skeletons will fall out of our closets. Christ bore every one of our sins. He paid the ultimate price so that we would be forever free from sin—and the fear of sin. All barriers between us and him will be forever gone. He will be our best friend.

When Jesus prays that we will be with him in Heaven, he explains why: "Father, I want those you have given me to be with me where I am, and *to see my glory*, the glory you have given me because you loved me before the creation of the world" (John 17:24, emphasis added). When we accomplish something, we want to share it with those closest to us. Likewise, Jesus wants to share with us his glory—his person and his accomplishments. There's no contradiction between Christ acting for his glory and for our good. The two are synonymous. Our greatest pleasure, our greatest satisfaction, is to behold his glory. As John Piper says, "God is most glorified in us when we are most satisfied in him."[154]

Christ's desire for us to see his glory should touch us deeply. What an unexpected compliment that the Creator of the universe has gone to such great lengths, at such sacrifice, to prepare a place for us where we can behold and participate in his glory.

Jesus indwells us now, and perhaps he will then, but he will also physically reside on the earth with us. Have you ever imagined what it would be like to walk the earth with Jesus, as the disciples did? Have you ever wished you had that opportunity? You *will*—on the New Earth. Whatever we will do with Jesus, we'll be doing with the second member of the triune God. What will it be like to run beside God, laugh with God, discuss a book with God, sing and climb and swim and play catch with God? Jesus promised we would eat with him in his Kingdom. This is an intimacy with God unthinkable to any who don't grasp the significance of the Incarnation. To eat a meal with Jesus will be to eat a meal *with God*.

HOW CAN MILLIONS OF PEOPLE ALL BE WITH JESUS AND RECEIVE PERSONAL ATTENTION?

After the first edition of this book, this question was one of the most frequently asked. It's worth considering.

Though it's possible we may cover vast distances at immense speeds in God's new universe, I don't believe we'll be capable of being two places at once. Why? Because we'll still be finite. Only God is infinite.

Because the resurrected Christ is both man and God, the issue of whether he can be in more than one place at the same time involves a paradox not only in the future, but also in the present.

On the one hand, Jesus is a man, and man is finite and limited to one location. On the other hand, Jesus is God, and God is infinite and omnipresent. In a sense, then, one of these truths has to yield somewhat to the other. I suggest that perhaps Christ's humanity defined the extent of his presence in his first coming and life on Earth (humanity thereby trumping deity by limiting omnipresence).

> Since God will make the new earth his dwelling place, and since where God dwells therein heaven is, we shall then continue to be in heaven while we are on the new earth. For heaven and earth will then no longer be separated as they are now, but they will be one. But to leave the new earth out of consideration when we think of the final state of believers is greatly to impoverish biblical teaching about the life to come.
>
> **PETER TOON**

But Christ's deity may well define the extent of his presence in his second coming and life on the New Earth (deity thereby trumping the normal human inability to be in two places at once). Jesus has and always will have a single resurrected body, in keeping with his humanity. Yet that body *glorified* may allow him a far greater expression of his divine attributes than during his life and ministry here on Earth.

Since we can accurately say that Jesus' functioning as a man does not prohibit him from being God, we must also say that Jesus' functioning as God does not prohibit him from being a man. So, although we cannot conceive exactly how it could happen, I believe it's entirely possible that Jesus could in the future remain a man while fully exercising the attributes of God, including, at least in some sense, omnipresence.

Don't we already see that now? Where is Christ? At the right hand of God (Hebrews 12:2). Just before dying, Stephen saw him there (Acts 7:55). Jesus will remain there until he returns to the earth. In terms of his human body, Christ is in one location, and only one.

But despite his fixed location at God's right hand, Jesus is here now, with each of us, just as he promised to be (Matthew 28:20). He dwells in our hearts, living within us (Ephesians 3:17; Galatians 2:20). If even now, in this sin-stained world, he indwells those who are saints and yet sinners, how much more will he be able to indwell us in the world to come when no sin shall separate us from him? That indwelling will in no way be obscured by sin.

On the New Earth, isn't it likely we might regularly hear him speak to us directly as he dwells in and with us, wherever we are? Prayer might be an unhindered two-way conversation, whether we are hundreds of miles away in another part of the New Jerusalem, thousands of miles away on another part of the New Earth, or thousands of light years away in the new universe.

Consider the promise that when Christ returns "every eye will see him" (Revelation 1:7). How is that physically possible? By the projection of his image? But every eye will see *him*, not merely his image. Will he be in more than one place at one time?

If God took on human form any number of times, as recorded in Scripture, couldn't Christ choose to take on a form to manifest himself to us at a distant place? If he did that, might he not take on a temporary form very similar in appearance to his actual physical form, which may at that moment be sitting on the throne in the New Jerusalem? Might Jesus appear to us and walk with us in a temporary but tangible form that is an expression of his real body? Or might the one body of Jesus be simultaneously present with his people in a million places?

Might we walk with Jesus (not just spiritually, but also physically) while millions of others are also walking with him? Might we not be able to touch his hand or embrace him or spend a long afternoon privately conversing with him—not just with his spirit, but his whole person?

It may defy our logic, but God is capable of doing far more than we imagine. Being with Christ is the very heart of Heaven, so we should be confident that we will have unhindered access to him.

WILL GOD SERVE US?

Jesus said, "It will be good for those servants whose master finds them watching when he comes. I tell you the truth, he will dress himself to serve, will have them recline at the table and will come and wait on them" (Luke 12:37).

This is an amazing passage. Jesus says that the Master will do something culturally unthinkable—become a servant to his servants. Why? Because he loves them, and also out of appreciation for their loyalty and service to him. The King becomes a servant, making his servants kings! Notice that he won't merely command his other servants to serve them. He will do it himself.

We will be in Heaven only because "the Son of Man did not come to be served, but to serve, and to give his life as a ransom for many" (Matthew 20:28). We must assent to Christ's service for us (John 13:8). But even in Heaven, it appears, Jesus will sometimes serve us. What greater and more amazing reward could be ours in the new universe than to have Jesus choose to serve us?

If it was our idea that God would serve us, it would be blasphemy. But it's *his* idea. As husbands serve their wives and parents serve their children, God desires to serve us. "On this mountain the Lord Almighty will prepare a feast of rich food for all peoples" (Isaiah 25:6). God will be the chef—he'll prepare us a meal. In Heaven, God will overwhelm us with his humility and his grace.

Both God the Father and God the Son are portrayed as reigning on thrones in Heaven. But what will be the Holy Spirit's role? The answer isn't spelled out in detail, but we can surmise that he'll be involved in creating the new heavens and New Earth (Genesis 1:2; Isaiah 32:15). He may continue to indwell believers (John 16:7). He'll empower us to rule wisely with Christ (Deuteronomy 34:9; Judges 3:10). He may still move our hearts to glorify and worship the Father and the Son (John 16:14; Revelation 19:1-10). He'll continue forever as their companion in the Triune Godhead (Genesis 1:26; Hebrews 9:14).[155]

WHOM WOULD YOU CHOOSE?

If you had the opportunity to spend the evening with any person who's ever lived, whom would you choose? Probably someone fascinating, knowledgeable, and accomplished. High on my list would be C. S. Lewis, A. W. Tozer, Jonathan Edwards, Hudson Taylor, and Charles Spurgeon. Or how about Ruth, David, Mary, Paul, or Adam and Eve? I'd enjoy meeting Eric Liddell, the great runner and Christ-follower portrayed in *Chariots of Fire.*

Perhaps you'd choose someone beautiful and talented. Maybe you'd hope that at the end of the evening he or she would have enjoyed your company enough to want to spend time with you again.

Is Jesus the first person you would choose? Who is more beautiful, talented, knowledgeable, fascinating, and interesting than he?

The good news is, *he chose you.* If you're a Christian, you'll be with him for eternity and enjoy endless fascinating conversations and experiences. Incredibly, he'll also enjoy your company and mine. After all, he paid the ultimate price just so he could have us over to his place for eternity.

Most of us would love to spend the evening with a great author, musician, artist, or head of state. God is the master artist who created the universe, the inventor of music, the author and main character of the unfolding drama of redemption. Head of state? He's king of the entire universe. Yet if someone says,

"I want to go to Heaven to be with God forever," others wonder, *Wouldn't that be boring?*

What are we thinking?

The very qualities we admire in others—every one of them—are true of God. He's the source of everything we find fascinating. Who made Bach, Beethoven, and Mozart? Who gave them their gifts? Who created music itself and the ability to perform it?

All that is admirable and fascinating in human beings comes from their creator.

HIDDEN WITH CHRIST IN GOD

In a sense, we're already in Heaven with Christ: "Since, then, you have been raised with Christ, set your hearts on things above, where Christ is seated at the right hand of God. Set your minds on things above, not on earthly things. For you died, and *your life is now hidden with Christ in God.* When Christ, who is your life, appears, then you also will appear with him in glory" (Colossians 3:1-4, emphasis added).

Our intimate link with Christ in his redemptive work makes us inseparable from him, even now. As we walk with him and commune with him in this world, we experience a faint foretaste of Heaven's delights and wonders.

Though it's true that Christ is with us and within us while we're on Earth, it also works in the other direction—we're united with Christ, so much so that we are seated with him in Heaven: "God raised us up with Christ and seated us with him in the heavenly realms in Christ Jesus" (Ephesians 2:6).

Notice that the following description, written to believers alive on Earth, is in the present perfect (not future) tense, which expresses a completed action: "You have come to Mount Zion, to the heavenly Jerusalem, the city of the living God. You have come to thousands upon thousands of angels in joyful assembly, to the church of the firstborn, whose names are written in heaven. You have come to God, the judge of all men, to the spirits of righteous men made perfect" (Hebrews 12:22-23).

In a metaphysical sense, we've already entered Heaven's community. By seeing ourselves as part of the heavenly society, we can learn to rejoice *now* in what Heaven's residents rejoice in. They rejoice in God, his glory, his grace, and his beauty. They rejoice in repentant sinners, the saints' faithfulness and Christlikeness, and the beauty of God's creation. They rejoice in the ultimate triumph of God's Kingdom and the coming judgment of sin.

Heaven, then, isn't only our future home. It's our home already, waiting over the next hill. If we really grasp this truth, it will have a profound effect on our holiness. A man who sees himself seated with Christ in Heaven, in the very presence of a God to whom the angels cry out, "Holy, holy, holy," won't spend his evenings viewing Internet pornography.

No wonder the devil is so intent on keeping us from grasping our standing in Christ—for if we see ourselves in Heaven with Christ, we'll be drawn to worship and serve him here and now, creating ripples in Heaven's waters that will extend outward for all eternity.

CHAPTER 19

HOW WILL WE WORSHIP GOD?

*What is the essence of heaven? . . . [It is the] beatific vision, love, and
enjoyment of the triune God. For the three divine persons have an infinitely
perfect vision and love and enjoyment of the divine essence and of one another.
And in this infinite knowing, loving and enjoying lies the very life of the
triune God, the very essence of their endless and infinite happiness. If the
blessed are to be endlessly and supremely happy, then, they must share in the
very life of the triune God, in the divine life that makes Them endlessly and
infinitely happy.*

E. J. Fortman

Have you ever—in prayer or corporate worship or during a walk on the beach—for a few moments experienced the very presence of God? It's a tantalizing encounter, yet for most of us it tends to disappear quickly in the distractions of life. What will it be like to behold God's face and never be distracted by lesser things? What will it be like when every lesser thing unfailingly points us back to God?

Today, many Christians have come to depreciate or ignore the beatific vision, supposing that beholding God would be of mere passing interest, becoming monotonous over time. But those who know God know that he is anything *but* boring. Seeing God will be dynamic, not static. It will mean exploring new beauties, unfolding new mysteries—forever. We'll explore God's being, an experience delightful beyond comprehension. The sense of wide-eyed wonder we see among Heaven's inhabitants in Revelation 4–5 suggests an ever-deepening appreciation of God's greatness. That isn't all there is to Heaven, but if it were, it would be more than enough.

In Heaven, we'll be at home with the God we love and who loves us wholeheartedly. Lovers don't bore each other. People who love God could never be bored in his presence. Remember, the members of the triune Godhead exist in eternal relationship with each other. To see God is to participate in the infinite delight of their communion.

ALL-ENCOMPASSING WORSHIP

Most people know that we'll worship God in Heaven. But they don't grasp how thrilling that will be. Multitudes of God's people—of every nation, tribe, people, and language—will gather to sing praise to God for his greatness, wisdom, power, grace, and mighty work of redemption (Revelation 5:13-14). Overwhelmed by his magnificence, we will fall on our faces in unrestrained happiness and say, "Praise and glory and wisdom and thanks and honor and power and strength be to our God for ever and ever. Amen!" (Revelation 7:9-12).

People of the world are always striving to celebrate—they just lack ultimate *reasons* to celebrate (and therefore find lesser reasons). As Christians, we have those reasons—our relationship with Jesus and the promise of Heaven. "Now the dwelling of God is with men, and he will live with them. They will be his people, and God himself will be with them and be their God" (Revelation 21:3). Does this excite you? If it doesn't, you're not thinking correctly.

I find it ironic that many people stereotype life in Heaven as an interminable church service. Apparently, church attendance has become synonymous with boredom. Yet meeting God—when it truly happens—will be far more exhilarating than a great meal, a poker game, hunting, gardening, mountain climbing, or watching the Super Bowl. Even if it were true (it isn't) that church services must be dull, *there will be no church services in Heaven.* The church (Christ's people) will be there. But there will be no temple, and as far as we know, no services (Revelation 21:22).

Will we always be engaged in worship? Yes and no. If we have a narrow view of worship, the answer is no. But if we have a broad view of worship, the answer is yes. As Cornelius Venema explains, worship in Heaven will be all-encompassing: "No legitimate activity of life—whether in marriage, family, business, play, friendship, education, politics, etc.—escapes the claims of Christ's kingship. . . . Certainly those who live and reign with Christ forever will find the diversity and complexity of their worship of God not less, but richer, in the life to come. Every legitimate activity of new creaturely life will be included within the life of worship of God's people."[156]

Will we always be on our faces at Christ's feet, worshiping him? No, because Scripture says we'll be doing many other things—living in dwelling places, eating and drinking, reigning with Christ, and working for him. Scripture depicts people standing, walking, traveling in and out of the city, and gathering at feasts. When doing these things, we won't be on our faces before Christ. Nevertheless, all that we do will be an act of worship. We'll enjoy full and unbroken fellowship with Christ. At times this will crescendo into greater heights of praise as we assemble with the multitudes who are also worshiping him.

Worship involves more than singing and prayer. I often worship God while reading a book, riding a bike, or taking a walk. I'm worshiping him now as I write. Yet too often I'm distracted and fail to acknowledge God along the way. In Heaven, God will always be first in my thinking.

Even now, we're told, "Be joyful always; pray continually; give thanks in all circumstances" (1 Thessalonians 5:16-18). That God expects us to do many other things, such as work, rest, and be with our families, shows that we must be able to be joyful, pray, and give thanks *while doing other things*.

Have you ever spent a day or several hours when you sensed the presence of God as you hiked, worked, gardened, drove, read, or did the dishes? Those are foretastes of Heaven—not because we are doing nothing but worshiping, but because we are worshiping God *as we do everything else*.

In Heaven, where everyone worships Jesus, no one says, "Now we're going to sing two hymns, followed by announcements and prayer." The singing isn't ritual but spontaneous praise (Revelation 5:11-14). If someone rescued you and your family from terrible harm, especially at great cost to himself, no one would need to tell you, "Better say thank you." On your own, you would shower him with praise. Even more will you sing your Savior's praises and tell of his life-saving deeds.

In 2003 when Saddam Hussein's statues were being torn down in Baghdad, a television commentator said something so striking that I wrote it down. He said, "These people are used to coming out in the streets and praising Saddam. If they didn't, they were punished. He had a policy of compulsory adulation."

God seeks worshipers (John 4:23). But he has no policy of compulsory adulation. His children's response to him is voluntary. Once we see God as he really is, no one will need to beg, threaten, or shame us into praising him. We will overflow in gratitude and praise. We are *created* to worship God. There's no higher pleasure. At times we'll lose ourselves in praise, doing nothing but worshiping him. At other times we'll worship him when we build a cabinet, paint a picture, cook a meal, talk with an old friend, take a walk, or throw a ball.

WHY WORSHIP CAN'T BE BORING

Some subjects become less interesting over time. Others become more fascinating. Nothing is more fascinating than God. The deeper we probe into his being, the more we want to know. One song puts it this way: "As eternity unfolds, the thrill of knowing Him will grow."[157]

We'll never lose our fascination for God as we get to know him better. The thrill of knowing him will never subside. The desire to know him better will motivate everything we do. To imagine that worshiping God could be boring is to impose on Heaven our bad experiences of so-called worship. Satan is determined to make church boring, and when it is, we assume Heaven will be also. But church can be exciting, and worship exhilarating. That's what it will be in Heaven. We will see God and understand why the angels and other living creatures delight to worship him.

> Hearts on earth may say in the course of a joyful experience, "I don't want this ever to end." But invariably it does. The hearts of those in heaven say, "I want this to go on forever." And it will. There is no better news than this.
>
> **J. I. PACKER**

Have you known people who couldn't be boring if they tried? Some people are just fascinating. It seems I could listen to them forever. But not really. Eventually, I'd feel as if I'd gotten enough. But we can never get enough of God. There's no end to what he knows, no end to what he can do, no end to who he is. He is mesmerizing to the depths of his being, and those depths will never be exhausted. No wonder those in Heaven always redirect their eyes to him—they don't want to miss anything.

At times throughout the day, as I work in my office, I find myself on my knees thanking God for his goodness. When I eat a meal with my wife, talk with a friend, or take our dog for a walk, I worship God for his goodness. The world is full of praise-prompters—the New Earth will overflow with them. I've found great joy in moments where I've been lost in worship—many of them during church services—but they're too fleeting. If you've ever had a taste of true worship, you crave *more* of it, never less.

"Speak to one another with psalms, hymns and spiritual songs. Sing and make music in your heart to the Lord, always giving thanks to God the Father for everything, in the name of our Lord Jesus Christ" (Ephesians 5:19-20). The music we make isn't congregational singing. It's in our hearts and in our daily lives. Has someone ever done something for you that makes you so grateful that you just can't stop saying thank you? This is how we should feel about God.

The holiness of God that overwhelmed Isaiah will be utterly engrossing to hearts made holy. J. C. Ryle writes, "Without holiness on earth, we shall never be prepared to enjoy heaven. Heaven is a holy place, the Lord of heaven is a holy being, the angels are holy creatures. Holiness is written on everything in heaven. . . . How shall we ever be at home and happy in heaven if we die unholy?"[158]

In Heaven, worshiping God won't be restricted to a time posted on a sign, telling us when to start and stop. It will permeate our lives, energize our bodies, and fuel our imaginations.

CHRIST AND HIS BRIDE

Jonathan Edwards said of people in Heaven, "As they increase in the knowledge of God and of the works of God, the more they will see of his excellency; and the more they see of his excellency . . . the more will they love him; and the more they love God, the more delight and happiness . . . will they have in him."[159]

Jesus called his disciples *friends* (John 15:15). He likewise regards us with deep affection. Good friendship is characterized by growth. Friendship with the God of Heaven has the most room for growth because of his inexhaustible greatness. Yet our relationship with Christ goes even beyond friendship.

"Blessed are those who are invited to the wedding supper of the Lamb!" (Revelation 19:9). It's amazing enough that we'll be invited to the King's wedding. What's beyond amazing is that we'll be his bride. (Think about *that* for a few million years!) There is an intimacy between husband and wife that includes close friendship yet also transcends it.

The return of Christ will signal not only the Father rescuing his children but also the Bridegroom rescuing his bride. As the church, we're part of the ultimate Cinderella story—rescued from a home where we labor, often without appreciation or reward. One day we'll be taken into the arms of the Prince and whisked away to live in his palace. When "the wedding of the Lamb has come" (Revelation 19:7), the New Jerusalem, consisting not only of buildings but of God's people, will come down out of Heaven, "prepared as a bride beautifully dressed for her husband" (Revelation 21:2); "And his bride has made herself ready. Fine linen, bright and clean, was given her to wear" (Revelation 19:7-8). The eyes of the universe will be on the Bridegroom, but also on the bride for whom he died.

I have vivid memories of my wife's and daughters' pure beauty in their wedding dresses. The church, Christ's bride, should likewise be characterized by purity, as a fitting gift to our Bridegroom, the crown prince who has been utterly faithful to us.

If I were to ask you, "What does the fine linen the bride is wearing stand for?" you might be inclined to say, "The righteousness of Christ that covers us." Significantly, however, the text says something different: "Fine linen stands for the righteous acts of the saints" (Revelation 19:8). It's only because of the Bridegroom's work that the chosen princess, the church, can enter the presence of her Lord. Yet her wedding dress is woven through her many acts of faithfulness while away from her Bridegroom on the fallen Earth. The picture is compelling. Each prayer, each gift, each hour of fasting, each kindness to the needy, all of these are the threads that have been woven together into this wedding dress. Her works have been empowered by the Spirit, and she has spent her life on Earth sewing her wedding dress for the day when she will be joined to her beloved Bridegroom.

This gives us a wonderful reason to stay alive, even though we are apart from our beloved. Why? Because we aren't yet finished sewing our wedding dress. The wedding approaches, yet there's more for us to do to present ourselves pure before our Lord. We're eager for his return, but we don't sit idly by. Part of us wants fewer days between now and the wedding, because we're so eager to be with our beloved in our new home. But another part wants more days to better prepare for the wedding, to sew our dress through acts of faithful service to God.

The imagery is beautiful but potentially disturbing. A pure bride doesn't want to appear scantily clad at the altar before her beloved Bridegroom and a multitude of guests. But if she has been diligent to prepare, her dress will be substantial and complete.

ABSORBING, BUT NOT ABSORBED

We must distinguish the biblical promise of seeing God from the beliefs of Buddhism, Hinduism, or New Age mysticism, in which individuality is obliterated or assimilated into Nirvana. Though God will be absorbing, we will not be absorbed by him. Though we may feel lost in God's immensity, we will not lose our identity when we see him. Instead, we will find it. "Whoever loses his life for me will find it" (Matthew 16:25).

"The people of God will not be absorbed into or partake in an immediate way of the being of God," writes Cornelius Venema. "God's people will see him without any of the sinful limitations of the present. No sin-induced stupor, no failure of hearing, no blindness of vision will obscure the beauty of God from their knowledge."[160]

We will not know God exhaustively, but we will know him accurately. We will no longer twist and distort the truth about God.

Some have portrayed the beatific vision as a pursuit in which every person seeks God individually. It is characteristic of our Western cultural independence that we think of Heaven in highly individualized ways. But God also views us corporately, as Christ's bride, as part of a great eternal community in which we'll love our Lord together and undertake cooperative pursuits for his glory. We will always be individuals, but Heaven will not be a place of individualism.

We aren't individual brides of Christ; we are collectively the bride of Christ. Christ is not a polygamist. He will be married to one bride, not millions. We belong to each other and need each other. We should guard not only our own purity, but each other's. We *are* our brother's keeper.

The fact that countless professing Christians are not part of a local church testifies to our over-individualized spirituality. Scripture teaches that we need each other and should not withdraw from each other's fellowship, instruction, or accountability. It's unbiblical to imagine that we can successfully seek God on our own (Hebrews 10:25). Because we will be part of a community of saints that constitutes the bride of Christ for eternity, and because we will worship and serve him together, to prepare properly for Heaven we must be part of a church now.

NO RIVALRY BETWEEN CHRIST AND HEAVEN

A man said to a few of us at a gathering, "I find myself longing for Heaven." After he left, someone said to me, "Shouldn't he be longing for *God*, not Heaven?" This may sound spiritual, but is it? Scripture speaks positively of "longing for a better country" (Hebrews 11:16). I don't know the man's heart, but his statement was biblically warranted. The right kind of longing for Heaven *is* a longing for God, and longing for God is longing for Heaven. If we understand what Heaven is (God's dwelling place) and who God is, we will see no conflict between the two. A woman who longs to be reunited with her husband could well say, "I just want to go home."

I'm often asked the following question in various ways: "Why talk about Heaven when we can just talk about Jesus?" The answer is that the two go together. We were made for a person (Christ) and a place (Heaven). There is no rivalry between Christ and Heaven.

Any bride in love with her husband wants to be with him more than anything. But if he goes away to build a beautiful place for her, won't she get excited about it? Won't she think and talk about that place? Of course. Moreover, he *wants* her to! If he tells her, "I'm going to prepare a place for you," he's implying, "I want you to look forward to it." Her love and longing for the place he's preparing—where she will live with him—is inseparable from her love and longing for her husband.

Some erroneously assume that the wonders, beauties, adventures, and marvelous relationships of Heaven must somehow be in competition with the one who has created them. God has no fear that we'll get too excited about Heaven. After all, the wonders of Heaven aren't *our* idea, they're *his*. There's no dichotomy between anticipating the joys of Heaven and finding our joy in Christ. It's all part of the same package. The wonders of the new heavens and New Earth will be a primary means by which God reveals himself and his love to us.

Picture Adam and Eve in the Garden of Eden. Eve says to Adam, "Isn't this place magnificent? The sun feels wonderful on my face, the blue sky's gorgeous. These animals are a delight. Try the mango—it's delicious!"

Can you imagine Adam responding, "Your focus is all wrong, Eve. You shouldn't think about beauty, refreshment, and mouthwatering fruit. All you should think about is God."

Adam would never say that, because in thinking about these things, Eve *would be* thinking about God. Likewise, our enjoyment of what God has provided us should be inseparable from worshiping, glorifying, and appreciating him. God is honored by our thankfulness, gratitude, and enjoyment of him.

I've heard it said that "God, not Heaven, is our inheritance." Well, God *is* our inheritance (Psalm 16:6), but so is Heaven (1 Peter 1:3-4). God and Heaven—the person and the place—are so closely connected that they're sometimes referred to interchangeably. The Prodigal Son confessed, "I have sinned against heaven" (Luke 15:18, 21). John the Baptist said, "A man can receive only what is given him from heaven" (John 3:27). Why didn't he say *God* instead of *Heaven?* Because God has made himself that closely identified with Heaven. It's his place. And that's *his* idea, not ours. He could have offered us his person without his place. But he didn't.

So, thinking about Heaven shouldn't be viewed as an obstacle to knowing God but as a *means* of knowing Him. The infinite God reveals himself to us in tangible, finite expressions. Next to the incarnate Christ, Heaven will tell us more about God than anything else. Some people have told me, "I just want to be with Jesus—I don't care if Heaven's a shack." Well, Jesus cares. He *wants* us to anticipate Heaven and enjoy the magnificence of it, not to say, "I don't care about it" or "I'd be just as happy in a shack." When you go to visit your parents in the house you grew up in, it's no insult to tell them "I love this place." It's a compliment. They'll delight in it, not resent it.

Every thought of Heaven should move our hearts toward God, just as every thought of God will move our hearts toward Heaven. That's why Paul could tell us to set our hearts on Heaven, not just "set your hearts on God." To do one is to do the other. Heaven will not be an idol that competes with God but a lens by which we see God.

If we think unworthy thoughts of Heaven, we think unworthy thoughts of

God. That's why the conventional caricatures of Heaven do a terrible disservice to God and adversely affect our relationship with him. If we come to love Heaven more—the Heaven God portrays in Scripture—we will inevitably love God more. If Heaven fills our hearts and minds, God will fill our hearts and minds.

Those who love God should think more often of Heaven, not less.

RULING ON THE NEW EARTH

CHAPTER 20

WHAT DOES GOD'S ETERNAL KINGDOM INVOLVE?

Why do we not know the country whose citizens we are? Because we have wandered so far away that we have forgotten it. But the Lord Christ, the king of the land, came down to us, and drove forgetfulness from our heart. God took to Himself our flesh so that He might be our way back.

Augustine

If you were to describe a kingdom, what elements would you include? A king, certainly, and subjects to be ruled, but what else? In order to be rightly described as a kingdom, wouldn't it also have to include territory, a government, and a culture? Why is it, then, that when we think of God's Kingdom, we often think only of the King and his subjects, but we leave out the territory and the culture? We spiritualize God's Kingdom, perceiving it as otherworldly and intangible. But Scripture tells us otherwise.

DIDN'T JESUS SAY HIS KINGDOM WASN'T EARTHLY?

When Jesus said to the Pharisees, "I am not of this world" (John 8:23), he did not mean "I am not *in* or *on* this world." Rather, he was speaking of his place of origin. His Kingdom is not *of* the world because it is not *from* the world. It did not originate here. Furthermore, it's uncontaminated by the fallen Earth and operates by different principles.

When Jesus was on trial, he said to Pilate, "My kingdom is not of this world. If it were, my servants would fight to prevent my arrest by the Jews. But now my kingdom is from another place. . . . You are right in saying I am a king. In fact, for this reason I was born, and for this I came into the world" (John 18:36-37). When Jesus said, "My kingdom is not of this world," he did not mean that his Kingdom wouldn't be *on* this earth after it is transformed. He meant that his Kingdom isn't *of* this earth as it is now, under the Curse. Although Christ's Kingdom isn't *from* the earth, it extends *to* the earth, and one day it will fully *include* the earth and be centered on it. Christ's Kingdom touches this world through his indwelling Spirit, the presence of the church, and his providential reign. Thus, Jesus could say, "The kingdom of God is near you" (Luke 10:9). He could say of little children, "The kingdom of heaven belongs to such as these" (Matthew 19:14).

It's important to distinguish between what's "worldly" and what's earthly and physical. God's creation is *earthly* (Genesis 1:31). The product of fallen human culture is *worldly* (Romans 12:1-2; Titus 2:12). Similarly, what is of the body is God-made, whereas what is of the "flesh" (*sarx*) is under the sin principle that dominates our fallen humanity (Romans 7:5, 18). However, *flesh* isn't a universally negative word. Jesus is said repeatedly to have had *sarx*, or "flesh" (1 Timothy 3:16; Hebrews 2:14; 2 John 1:7), but he didn't have sin; therefore, *flesh* and *sin* cannot be synonymous. Although our physical bodies are under sin and can be instruments of sin, they aren't the ultimate source of sin. We're commanded to "offer the parts of your body to [God] as instruments of righteousness" (Romans 6:13). In so doing, our bodies are restored to their original purpose of being instruments of a righteous spirit, heart, or mind. And that is what they'll be forever after our bodily resurrection.

JESUS, WORTHY KING OF THE NEW EARTH

Revelation 5:1-10 depicts a powerful scene in the present Heaven. God the Father, the ruler of Heaven, sits on the throne with a sealed scroll in his right hand. What's sealed—with seven seals, to avoid any possibility that the document has been tampered with—is the Father's will, his plan for the distribution and management of his estate. In this case, the entitlement of the estate is the earth, which includes its people. God had intended for the world to be ruled by humans. But who will come forward to open the document and receive the inheritance?

John writes, "I wept and wept because no one was found who was worthy to open the scroll or look inside" (Revelation 5:4).

Because of human sin, mankind and the earth have been corrupted. No man is worthy to take the role God intended for Adam and his descendants. Adam proved unworthy, as did Abraham, David, and every other person in history. But right when it appears that God's design for mankind and the earth will forever be thwarted, the text continues in high drama: "Then one of the elders said to me, 'Do not weep! See, the Lion of the tribe of Judah, the Root of David, has triumphed. He is able to open the scroll and its seven seals.' Then I saw a Lamb, looking as if it had been slain, standing in the center of the throne, encircled by the four living creatures and the elders. . . . He came and took the scroll from the right hand of him who sat on the throne. And when he had taken it, the four living creatures and the twenty-four elders fell down before the Lamb. . . . And they sang a new song: 'You are worthy to take the scroll and to open its seals, because you were slain, and with your blood you purchased men for God from every tribe and language and people and nation'" (Revelation 5:5-9).

> An old theologian once said, "Who chides a servant for taking away the first course of a feast when the second consists of far greater delicacies?" Who then can regret that this present world passes away when he sees that an eternal world of joy is coming? The first course is grace, but the second is glory, and that is as much better as the fruit is better than the blossom.
>
> **CHARLES SPURGEON**

Every finite being, angelic and human, stands in amazement at this man and what he has done. The Father, who sits on Heaven's throne, will never die. Instead, the heir, the beloved firstborn son, has died. He was slain that he might "purchase men for God"—and not just a small representation of fallen humanity, but "from every tribe and language and people and nation" (Revelation 5:9).

The passage culminates with a statement about Christ's followers: "You have made them to be a kingdom and priests to serve our God, and they will reign on the earth" (Revelation 5:10).

Psalm 2 speaks of Christ ruling "with an iron scepter" and dashing the nations to pieces "like pottery" (v. 9), a reference to the Messiah's return, judgment, and perhaps his millennial reign. But once we enter the new heavens and New Earth, there's no iron rule or dashing to pieces, for there's no more rebellion, sin, or death. The vanquishing of sin doesn't mean the end of Christ's rule. It means the end of his *contested* rule and the beginning of his eternally uncontested rule, when he will delegate earthly rule to his co-heirs.

If we understood God's unaltered plan for his people to exercise dominion over the earth, it wouldn't surprise us to find on the New Earth that nations still exist and kings come into the New Jerusalem bringing tribute to the King of kings (Revelation 21:24, 26).

THE IMPORTANCE OF LAND

An essential component of any kingdom is *land*. I don't always agree with David Chilton, but I believe he's correct when he says in *Paradise Restored*, "When God created Adam, He placed him into a land, and gave him dominion over it. Land is basic to dominion; therefore, salvation involves a restoration to land and property. . . . This is why Biblical law is filled with references to property, law, and economics; and this is why the Reformation laid such stress on this world, as well as the next. Man is not saved by being delivered out of his environment. Salvation does not rescue us from the material world, but from sin, and from the effects of the Curse. The Biblical ideal is for every man to own property—a place where he can have dominion and rule under God."[161]

We are pilgrims on this earth that is passing away, but eventually we'll be pioneers and settlers on the New Earth. The earth is our proper dwelling place: "For the upright will live in the land, and the blameless will remain in it; but the wicked will be cut off from the land" (Proverbs 2:21-22). "The righteous will never be uprooted, but the wicked will not remain in the land" (Proverbs 10:30).

Christ says, "I will write on him [who overcomes] the name of my God and the name of the city of my God, the new Jerusalem, which is coming down out of heaven from my God; and I will also write on him my new name" (Revelation 3:12).

Consider how the theme that Earth belongs to God and his people (not to the unrighteous who sometimes rule it now) is carried throughout Psalms, Proverbs, and Isaiah:

You made [mankind] ruler over the works of your hands; you put everything under his feet. (Psalm 8:6)

The earth is the Lord's, and everything in it, the world, and all who live in it. (Psalm 24:1)

He himself shall dwell in prosperity, and his descendants shall inherit the earth. (Psalm 25:13, NKJV)

For evildoers shall be cut off; but those who wait on the Lord, they shall inherit the earth. . . .The meek shall inherit the earth, and shall delight themselves in the abundance of peace. . . . For those blessed by Him shall inherit the earth, but those cursed by Him shall be cut off. (Psalm 37:9, 11, 22, NKJV)

How awesome is the Lord Most High, the great King over all the earth! (Psalm 47:2)

I will preserve You and give You as a covenant to the people, to restore the earth, to cause them to inherit the desolate heritages. (Isaiah 49:8, NKJV)

The man who makes me his refuge will inherit the land and possess my holy mountain. (Isaiah 57:13)

In Isaiah 57:13, the Hebrew word *erets*, here translated "land," is the same word translated "earth" in many other contexts, including those just cited. *Erets* is the fourth most frequently used noun in the Old Testament, appearing more than 2,500 times.[162] The frequency of the word's use reflects its centrality. The Old Testament is filled with the idea of place, earth, land. Earth is the place of all mankind; Israel, especially Jerusalem, is the place of God's covenant people.

God gave management of the earth to Adam and Eve. All people would be their descendants, taking up their management responsibilities in turn. Then came the Fall and the Flood. Later, when God made his covenant with Abraham, what did he promise him first? Land (Genesis 12:1, 7). Though the whole Earth was under the Curse, God granted Abraham a piece of land that could be lived on, ruled, and managed in a way that would bring glory to God and blessing to all other lands and nations.

"If you belong to Christ, then you are Abraham's seed, and heirs according to the promise" (Galatians 3:29). New covenant Christians, not just Israel, are heirs of the promises made to Abraham—and these promises center on possessing the land.

After saying that mankind would rise from the dust of the earth and rule Christ's Kingdom on Earth (Daniel 12:2-3), God promises Daniel, "You will rise to receive your allotted inheritance" (Daniel 12:13). Inheritance typically involves not just money but also land, a place lived on and managed by human beings. After our bodily resurrection, we will receive a physical inheritance. The New Earth is the ultimate Promised Land, the eternal Holy Land in which all God's people will dwell.

THE GOAL OF HISTORY

God is the sovereign ruler of the universe, yet he chooses not to rule the universe alone. He delegates responsibilities to angels, who exist in a hierarchy of command under Michael the archangel (Jude 1:9; Revelation 12:7). God made human beings in his image, as creators and rulers, to carry out his divine will. He does not grudgingly pass on to us management responsibilities. On the contrary, he delights to entrust Earth's rule to us. He has uniquely created and gifted us to handle such responsibilities and to find joy in them.

We've been born into the family of an incredibly wealthy landowner.

There's not a millimeter of cosmic geography that doesn't belong to him, and by extension to his children, his heirs. Our Father has a family business that stretches across the whole universe. He entrusts to us management of the family business, and that's what we'll do for eternity: manage God's assets and rule his universe, representing him as his image-bearers, children, and ambassadors.

While we face our daily challenges, the knowledge that a New Earth is coming should reassure us and give us perspective. It means there's not only hope but purpose in our suffering. It means that though injustice is widespread, it will not last. God will make all things right, rewarding his people for trusting him. He will turn this upside-down world right side up, placing it in the care of his beloved children.

The promise of a New Earth reminds us that the events of human history aren't meaningless. Rather, they are heading toward the fulfillment of a divine plan, involving a New Earth with culture and citizens that glorify God.

"We cannot understand biblical revelation, human history, or the events of our own lives if we don't grasp God's plan for the new heavens and New Earth," writes theologian Herman Ridderbos. "[Christ's] redemption acquires the significance of an all-inclusive divine drama, of a cosmic struggle . . . the goal of which is to bring back the entire created cosmos under God's dominion and rule."[163]

Remember God's explicitly stated plan: "to bring all things in heaven and on earth together under one head, even Christ" (Ephesians 1:10). His design is through Christ "to reconcile to himself all things, whether things on earth or things in heaven, by making peace through his blood, shed on the cross" (Colossians 1:20).

We're mistaken to leave such verses in the hands of universalists, who isolate them and disregard the emphatic biblical statements that some will spend eternity in Hell. But we must not ignore the broad redemptive significance of these passages. Anthony Hoekema is correct when he insists that "we must see [history] as moving toward the goal of a finally restored and glorified universe."[164]

Consider this prophetic statement: "The kingdom of the world has become the kingdom of our Lord and of his Christ, and he will reign for ever and ever" (Revelation 11:15). It doesn't say that Christ will destroy this world's kingdom. It doesn't even say he'll replace this world's kingdom. No, the kingdom of this world will actually *become* the Kingdom of Christ. God won't obliterate earthly kingdoms but will *transform them into his own*. And it's that new earthly kingdom (joined then to God's heavenly Kingdom) over which "he will reign for ever and ever."

This is a revolutionary viewpoint, standing in stark contrast to the prevalent myth that God's Kingdom will demolish and replace the kingdoms of Earth rather than cleanse, redeem, and resurrect them into his eternal Kingdom. This brings us back again to that remarkable statement about the New Jerusalem: "The nations will walk by its light, and the kings of the earth will bring their splendor into it. On no day will its gates ever be shut. . . . The glory and honor of the nations will be brought into it" (Revelation 21:24-26).

Bruce Milne says of this text, "Nothing of ultimate worth from the long history of the nations will be omitted from the heavenly community. Everything which authentically reflects the God of truth, all that is of abiding worth from within the national stories and the cultural inheritance of the world's peoples, will find its place in the New Jerusalem."[165]

As the magi, kings of foreign nations, once came to the old Jerusalem seeking to worship the Messiah King, on the New Earth countless magi will journey to the New Jerusalem. Hearts filled with worship, they will humbly offer King Jesus the tribute of their cultural treasures. He will be pleased to receive them. The King will delight to entrust the rule of the nations to those who served him faithfully when Earth lived under sin's shadow, before its triumphant and eternal deliverance.

CHAPTER 21

WILL WE ACTUALLY RULE WITH CHRIST?

In the messianic kingdom the martyrs will reclaim the world as the possession which was denied to them by their persecutors. In the creation in which they endured servitude, they will eventually reign.

Irenaeus

God created Adam and Eve to be king and queen over the earth. Their job was to rule the earth, to the glory of God.

They failed.

Jesus Christ is the second Adam, and the church is his bride, the second Eve. Christ is king, the church is his queen. Christ will exercise dominion over all nations of the earth: "He will rule from sea to sea and from the River to the ends of the earth. . . . All kings will bow down to him and all nations will serve him" (Psalm 72:8, 11). As the new head of the human race, Christ—with his beloved people as his bride and co-rulers—will at last accomplish what was entrusted to Adam and Eve. God's saints will fulfill on the New Earth the role God first assigned to Adam and Eve on the old Earth. "They will reign for ever and ever" (Revelation 22:5).

Richard Mouw writes, "Over and over again the Scriptures make this plain: the political power which has been so corrupted and twisted in the hands and hearts of sinful rulers must be returned to its rightful source."[166]

The Kingdom that God will bring to Earth will crush the last of Earth's kingdoms. Daniel prophesied, "The rock that struck the statue became a huge mountain and filled the whole earth. . . . In the time of those kings, the God of heaven will set up a kingdom that will never be destroyed, nor will it be left to another people. It will crush all those kingdoms and bring them to an end, but it will itself endure forever" (Daniel 2:35, 44).

Human kingdoms will rise and fall until Christ sets up a kingdom that forever replaces them, where mankind rules in righteousness. "He was given authority, glory and sovereign power; all peoples, nations and men of every language worshiped him. His dominion is an everlasting dominion that will not pass away, and his kingdom is one that will never be destroyed" (Daniel 7:14).

Because Christ will be the King of kings, this will be the Kingdom of kingdoms—the greatest kingdom in human history. Yes, *human history*, for our history will not end at Christ's return or upon our relocation to the New Earth. It will continue forever, to the glory of God.

"Rejoice greatly. . . . See, your king comes to you, righteous and having salvation, gentle and riding on a donkey, on a colt, the foal of a donkey. . . . He will proclaim peace to the nations. His rule will extend from sea to sea and from the River to the ends of the earth" (Zechariah 9:9-10). Matthew 21:5 makes it clear that Zechariah's prophecy concerns the Messiah. Just as the first part of the prophecy was literally fulfilled when Jesus rode a donkey into Jerusalem, we should expect that the second part will be literally fulfilled when Jesus brings peace to the nations and rules them all. Jesus will return to Earth as "King of kings and Lord of lords" (Revelation 19:11-16). We're promised that "the Lord will be king over the whole earth" (Zechariah 14:9).

Bible-believing Jews in the first century were not foolish to think that the Messiah would be King of the earth. They were wrong about the Messiah's identity when they rejected Christ, and they were wrong to overlook his need to come as a suffering servant to redeem the world; but they were *right* to believe that the Messiah would forever rule the earth. He will!

Prior to Christ's return, his Kingdom will be intermingled with the world's cultures (Matthew 13:24-30). But his followers will be growing in character and proving their readiness to rule. Through adversity and opportunity, as well as in their artistic and cultural accomplishments, they will be groomed for their leadership roles in Christ's eternal Kingdom. Their society-transforming creative skills will be put on prominent display in the new universe, where they will "shine like the sun in the kingdom of their Father" (Matthew 13:43).

WHY ARE WE SURPRISED THAT WE'LL RULE THE EARTH?

Because I teach on the subject of redeemed humanity ruling the earth, I've had many opportunities to observe people's responses. Often they're surprised to learn that we will reign in eternity over lands, cities, and nations. Many are skeptical—it's a foreign concept that seems fanciful. Nothing demonstrates how far we've distanced ourselves from our biblical calling like our lack of knowledge about our destiny to rule the earth. Why are we so surprised, when it is spoken of throughout the Old Testament and repeatedly reaffirmed in the New Testament?

Because crowns are the primary symbol of ruling, every mention of crowns as rewards is a reference to our ruling with Christ. In his parables, Jesus speaks of our ruling over cities (Luke 19:17). Paul addresses the subject of Christians ruling as if it were Theology 101: "Do you not know that the saints will judge the world? . . . Do you not know that we will judge angels?" (1 Corinthians 6:2-3). The form of the verb in this question implies that we won't simply judge them a single time but will continually rule them.

If Paul speaks of this future reality as if it were something every child should know, why is it so foreign to Christians today? Elsewhere he says, "If we endure, we will also reign with him" (2 Timothy 2:12). God's decree that his servants will "reign for ever and ever" on the New Earth (Revelation 22:5) is a direct fulfillment of the commission he gave to Adam and Eve: "Be fruitful and increase in number; fill the earth and subdue it. Rule over the fish of the sea and the birds of the air and over every living creature that moves on the ground" (Genesis 1:28). This mandate is confirmed by David: "You put us in charge of everything you made, giving us authority over all things" (Psalm 8:6, NLT).

When we consider that mankind's reign on the earth is introduced in the first chapters of the Bible, mentioned throughout the Old Testament, discussed by Jesus in the Gospels, by Paul in the Epistles, and repeated by John in the Bible's final chapters, it is remarkable that we would fail to see it. Remembering again that a "crown" speaks of ruling authority, consider the following examples from one small portion of Scripture, Revelation 2–5:

Be faithful, even to the point of death, and I will give you the crown of life. (2:10)

To him who overcomes and does my will to the end, I will give authority over the nations. (2:26)

I am coming soon. Hold on to what you have, so that no one will take your crown. (3:11)

To him who overcomes, I will give the right to sit with me on my throne, just as I overcame and sat down with my Father on his throne. (3:21)

The twenty-four elders fall down before him who sits on the throne. . . . They lay their crowns before the throne. (4:10)

[You] have redeemed us to God by Your blood out of every tribe and tongue and people and nation, and have made us kings and priests to our God; and we shall reign on the earth. (5:9-10, NKJV)

Who does God say will reign? People of every tribe and language and people and nation. Where will they reign? On Earth, not in some intangible heavenly realm. Where on Earth? Likely with people of their own tribe, language, and nation—cultural distinctives that we're told still exist on the New Earth (Revelation 21:24, 26; 22:2).

Wayne Grudem states that "when the author of Hebrews says that we do 'not yet' see everything in subjection to man (Hebrews 2:8), he implies that all things will eventually be subject to us, under the kingship of the man Christ Jesus. . . . This will fulfill God's original plan to have everything in the world subject to the human beings that he had made. In this sense, then, we will 'inherit the earth' (Matthew 5:5) and reign over it as God originally intended."[167]

OUR INHERITANCE: OWNING AND RULING THE LAND

When an earthly father dies, he bequeaths his estate to his offspring. His children are heirs. To what? To their father's property. If he owned land, they become landowners. If he was a king, they are heirs to his entire kingdom. When an earthly king dies, his firstborn takes his place. Sometimes the new king is surrounded by siblings who are his co-heirs and therefore co-rulers. As heirs, the king's children rule on their father's behalf, even if he still lives. They share in his glory. They go to battle to defend his kingdom, which is also *their* kingdom. In battle, they share in his sufferings.

It's the same in our relationship with God. "The Spirit himself testifies with our spirit that we are God's children. Now if we are children, then we are heirs—heirs of God and co-heirs with Christ, if indeed we share in his sufferings in order that we may also share in his glory" (Romans 8:16-17).

Of course, the King of the universe, God, never dies. But he has delegated sovereignty to his firstborn son, Jesus. Christ, in turn, gladly shares his dominion with the redeemed—his siblings—who are co-heirs of the Father's throne. They will rule with Christ over the Kingdom.

The right to exercise power comes from ownership. A king owns his kingdom, which consists of land. The extent of his rule is the extent of what he owns. Because God owns the entire universe, the Kingdom that falls into the lap of his heirs, his children, encompasses the entire universe. (That it all came under the Curse for Adam's sin demonstrates its tie to humanity.)

Christ, the firstborn, is the primary ruler, but we are called "co-heirs with Christ." God entrusts us to rule one prime piece of territory—Earth, which he created specifically for us.

God has not arbitrarily assigned us to rule the earth. It's our land, our kingdom, granted to us by our Father. It's a kingdom once lost by us to a usurping pseudo-king, Satan, but which was won back for us by the mighty valor of Christ, who shed his blood to purchase our freedom—and with it our inheritance, the earth.

This is the drama of redemption. If we fail to understand our status as God's children and heirs and rulers of the earth, we will fail to comprehend God's redemptive work. But if we do understand our role in God's plan, we'll realize that he would not deliver us from Earth to live forever in a disembodied realm. In fact, the inheritance that God grants us is the very same Earth over which epic battles have been fought since Satan's first attack in Eden. Our inheritance is not only physical but also eternal: "The days of the blameless are known to the Lord, and their inheritance will endure forever" (Psalm 37:18).

Currently, on this earth under the Curse, we serve Christ and "share in his sufferings." Why? Because the earth is under siege. It's being claimed by a false king, Satan, and his false princes, the fallen angels. It's being claimed by human kings, rebels who set themselves up against God and violate his standards by declaring their independence from him. Those who are co-heirs with Christ engage in spiritual warfare to reclaim the hearts of mankind for God's glory. "For our struggle is not against flesh and blood, but against the rulers, against the authorities, against the powers of this dark world and against the spiritual forces of evil in the heavenly realms" (Ephesians 6:12). After the final battle is won by Christ, we will rule the earth with him as co-heirs of his Kingdom.

SHOULD WE WANT TO RULE?

The government of the New Earth won't be a democracy. It won't be majority rule, and it won't be driven by opinion polls. Instead, every citizen of Heaven will have an appointed role, one that fulfills him or her and contributes to the whole. No one will "fall through the cracks" in God's Kingdom. No one will feel worthless or insignificant.

When I write and speak on this subject, people often respond, "But I don't *want* to rule. That's not my idea of Heaven."

Well, it's *God's* idea of Heaven.

We are part of God's family. Ruling the universe is the family business. To want no part of it is to want no part of our Father. It may sound spiritual to say we don't care to rule, but because God's the one who wants us to rule, the spiritual response is to be interested in his plans and purposes.

Whom will we rule? Other people. Angels. If God wishes, he may create new beings for us to rule. Who will rule over us? Other people.

There will be a social hierarchy of government, but there's no indication of a relational hierarchy. In other words, the apostle Paul will be in a position of greater leadership than most of us, but that doesn't mean he'll be inaccessible. There will be no pride, envy, boasting, or anything sin-related. Our differences will be a manifestation of God's creativity. As we're different in race, nationality, gender, personality, gifting, and passions, so we'll be different in positions of service.

> The future heaven is centered more on activity and expansion, serving Christ and reigning with Him. . . . The emphasis in the present heaven is on the absence of earth's negatives, while in the future heaven it is the presence of earth's positives, magnified many times through the power and glory of resurrected bodies on a resurrected earth, free at last from sin and shame and all that would hinder both joy and achievement.
>
> **RENÉ PACHE**

All of us will have some responsibility in which we serve God. Scripture teaches that our service for him now on Earth will be evaluated to help determine how we'll serve him on the New Earth. The humble servant will be put in charge of much, whereas the one who lords it over others in the present world will have power taken away: "For everyone who exalts himself will be humbled, and he who humbles himself will be exalted" (Luke 14:11). If we serve faithfully on the present Earth, God will give us permanent management positions on the New Earth. "Whoever can be trusted with very little can also be trusted with much" (Luke 16:10). The Owner has his eye on us—if we prove faithful, he'll be pleased to entrust more to us.

We've been conditioned to associate governing with self-promoting arrogance, corruption, inequality, and inefficiency. But these are perversions, not inherent properties of leadership. Ruling involves responsibility—perhaps that's why some people don't look forward to it. Some people live in anticipation of retirement, when responsibilities will be removed. Why would they want to take on an eternal task of governing? But what they think they want now and what they'll really want as resurrected beings—with strong bodies and minds in a society untouched by sin—may be quite different.

Imagine responsibility, service, and leadership that's pure joy. The responsibility that God will entrust to us as a reward can only be good for us, and we'll find delight in it. To rule on the New Earth will be to enable, equip, and guide, offering wisdom and encouragement to those under our authority. We've so often seen leadership twisted that we've lost a biblical view of what ruling, or exercising dominion, really means. God, ruler of the universe, is living proof that ruling can and should be good.

Some people have a deep fear of public speaking, and they imagine that ruling means they'll be miserable, having to be "up front" and speak to groups. But the fear, anxiety, dread, and turmoil we associate with certain activities on the present Earth will be *gone* on the New Earth. If God wants us to do something, we'll be wired and equipped to do it. Our service will not only bring him glory but also bring us joy.

This applies to countless other questions about Heaven, such as, Will we have to sing even if we don't like to? The question assumes facts not in evidence—that whatever we dislike now we'll dislike then. But doesn't experience tell us otherwise? Aren't there foods we love now that we hated as children? Aren't there books we love now that would've bored us when we were younger? Had we been able to decide as children everything we would do or not do as adults, wouldn't we have robbed ourselves of countless joys? We mustn't assume that everything we don't like doing now we still won't like doing in Heaven.

Of course, not all positions of responsibility over others involve people. Adam and Eve governed animals before there were any other people. Some of us may be granted the privilege of caring for animals. (My wife would love that, especially being responsible for dogs!) Perhaps some will care for forests. Ruling will likely involve the management of all of God's creation, not just people.

Perhaps God will offer us choices of where we might want to serve him. On the New Earth, we'll do what we want, but we'll want what God wants, and that will bring us our greatest joy.

Some of the most qualified people to lead in Heaven will be those who don't want to lead now. Some who are natural leaders here but have not been faithful will not be leaders in Heaven. Remember, it's not the proud and confident who will inherit the earth and rule it; it's the *meek* (Matthew 5:5). And even the meek will be stripped of their wrong motives and the temptation to exploit others. We'll have no more skepticism and disillusionment about government. Why? Because we'll be governed by Christlike rulers, and all of us will be under the grand and gracious government of Christ himself.

WHOSE IDEA IS OUR RULERSHIP?

Many people have told me they're uncomfortable with the idea that mankind will rule the earth, govern cities, and reign forever. It sounds presumptuous and self-important. I would agree—if it was *our* idea to reign over the universe, it would indeed be presumptuous. But it was *not* our idea, it was God's. And it's not a minor or peripheral doctrine; it's at the very heart of Scripture.

A reader of one of my previous books sent a letter expressing amazement at something I said. "You take the stewardship parables literally," he wrote. "You actually think some believers will rule over cities in Heaven!"

Yes, I do, though I never would have come up with this understanding on my own. But because dozens of passages affirm that we will rule the earth, I am compelled to believe them. The man who wrote the letter has read the same Scriptures, but he doesn't connect them with the teachings about our bodily resurrection, the New Earth, and reigning with Christ. If he did, he'd see that a largely (though not exclusively) literal understanding of the stewardship parables—which refer to our reigning over cities—fits *perfectly* with the teaching of countless other passages. The fact that it doesn't conform to his own view of Heaven suggests his view is in need of revision. (As I have studied the subject of Heaven, I've often had to revise my own viewpoint to bring it in line with what the Bible teaches.)

We must learn to take Scripture seriously when it speaks of our reigning over the earth. By telling ourselves that we mustn't interpret Scripture literally, often we end up rejecting its plain meaning. Our assumptions generally dictate our interpretations. If we imagine, for example, that the eternal Heaven is disembodied and unearthly, then concepts of government, culture, social structures, and delegated tasks will naturally strike us as naive, if not bizarre. But if we understand the doctrine of the resurrection of the dead and the reality of the New Earth, these concepts make perfect sense.

Others may perceive that the New Earth will need no government or that differing levels of authority (e.g., some ruling over ten cities while others rule over five or one or none) are inherently corrupt or unfair. But the need for government didn't come about as a result of sin. God governed the universe before Satan fell. Likewise, he created mankind as his image-bearers, with the capacity for ruling, and before Adam and Eve sinned, God specifically commanded them to rule the earth. Ruling isn't a bad thing, it's a good thing. God has called us to it and has equipped us for it—to rule the earth, rule it well, and find pleasure in ruling it. Because we're sinners, power tends to corrupt us. But on the New Earth there will be no sin. Therefore, all ruling will be just and benevolent, devoid of abuse, corruption, or lust for power.

Some Christians err by demeaning and ignoring politics, thereby failing to exercise their God-given stewardship. Others put too much confidence in politics, failing to understand God's insistence that he alone will establish a perfect government on Earth. When have we ever experienced the "peace on Earth" promised at Christ's birth? We haven't yet, but we will (Zechariah 9:9-10; Ezekiel 37:26-28; Isaiah 42:1-4; Matthew 12:18-21). Meanwhile, God calls us to cultural reform and development. Christians should be involved in the political process, and we can do much good, but we should never forget that the only government that will succeed in global reform is Christ's government.

Jesus said, "I confer on you a kingdom, just as my Father conferred one on me, so that you may eat and drink at my table in my kingdom and sit on thrones, judging the twelve tribes of Israel" (Luke 22:29-30).

This is an astounding statement, one that should cause us to pause in wonder. Christ is conferring to us a kingdom? A *kingdom*? To *us*?

God's purpose and plan will not fully be achieved until Christ confers upon us the Kingdom he has won. This will take place after our bodily resurrection, when we will eat and drink at a table with the resurrected Christ on a resurrected Earth. (Some scholars limit this reign to the Millennium, but parallel passages indicate an eternal reign.) That this is an actual rule on a physical, earthly kingdom, not a "spiritual" rule in a disembodied state, is demonstrated by the references to our eating and drinking at a table with Christ.

LOOKING FORWARD TO WHAT GOD HAS FOR US

The Master will say, "Well done, good and faithful servant. You have been faithful over a little; I will set you over much. Enter into the joy of your master" (Matthew 25:23, ESV).

Commenting on this passage, Dallas Willard writes, "That 'joy' is, of course, the creation and care of what is good, in all its dimensions. A place in God's creative order has been reserved for each one of us from before the beginnings of cosmic existence. His plan is for us to develop, as apprentices to Jesus, to the point where we can take our place in the ongoing creativity of the universe."[168]

The idea of entering into the Master's joy is a telling picture of Heaven. It's not simply that being with the Master produces joy in us, though certainly it will. Rather, it's that our Master himself is joyful. He takes joy in himself, in his children, and in his creation. His joy is contagious. Once we're liberated from the sin that blocks us from God's joy and our own, we'll enter into his joy. Joy will be the very air we breathe. The Lord is inexhaustible—therefore his joy is inexhaustible.

God is grooming us for leadership. He's watching to see how we demonstrate our faithfulness. He does that through his apprenticeship program, one that prepares us for Heaven. Christ is not simply preparing a place for us; he is preparing us for that place.

We all have dreams but often don't see them realized. We become discouraged and lose hope. But as Christ's apprentices, we must learn certain disciplines. Apprentices in training must work hard and study hard to prepare for the next test or challenge. Apprentices may wish for three weeks of vacation or more pay to pursue outside interests. But the Master may see that these would not lead to success. He may override his apprentices' desires in order that they might learn perspective and patience, which will serve them well in the future. While the young apprentices experience the death of their dreams, the Master is shaping them to dream greater dreams that they will one day live out on the New Earth with enhanced wisdom, skill, appreciation, and joy.

Through the challenges you now face, what dreams might God be preparing you to live out on the New Earth?

CHAPTER 22

HOW WILL WE RULE
GOD'S KINGDOM?

*Our liveliness in all duties, our enduring of tribulation, our honoring of God,
the vigor of our love, thankfulness, and all our graces, yea, the very being of
our religion and Christianity, depend on the believing, serious thoughts of
our rest [heaven].*

Richard Baxter

When we read that God promises us "an inheritance that can never perish,
spoil or fade—kept in heaven for you" (1 Peter 1:4), we may think of this
inheritance as Heaven or its pleasures. But God not only gives pleasures to his
heirs, he also gives us power—positions of authority in his eternal Kingdom. Our
vested interest in the New Earth couldn't be greater. It was purchased on the
cross by the blood of God's Son. The New Earth isn't a blissful realm that we'll
merely visit, as vacationers go to a theme park. Rather, it's a realm we'll joyfully
rule with Jesus, exercising dominion as God's image-bearers.

In Romans 8:16-17, Paul writes, "The Spirit himself testifies with our
spirit that we are God's children. Now if we are children, then we are heirs—
heirs of God and co-heirs with Christ, if indeed we share in his sufferings in
order that we may also share in his glory." While we're on Earth, we serve
Jesus, rejecting Earth's value system, but not because we despise the earth or
have no interest in it. On the contrary, we reject much of what this fallen
Earth offers us *precisely because we want all of what God offers us on the redeemed
Earth*. We will forever please our Father by ruling over the earth that he'll refashion for us to live on forever. As co-rulers with Christ, we'll share in the
glory of the sovereign ruler himself.

Some might protest, "How dare we imagine such a future for ourselves!"
Certainly it would be blasphemous for fallen humans to claim a share of God's
throne if it was *our* idea. But again, it's not our idea; it's God's idea. It's his sovereign plan, laid out before the foundation of the world, which he has gone to
sacrificial lengths to implement. If we reject the idea that God has called us to

rule the earth, then we reject his explicitly stated plan and his sovereignly orchestrated purpose. *How dare we?*

It's in the context of our being heirs and co-heirs with Christ, heirs and future rulers of the earth, that Paul writes of all creation groaning as it waits to be
"liberated from its bondage to decay and brought into the glorious freedom of
the children of God" (Romans 8:21). In this same context, Paul offers us perspective on how to view the hardships of life in a fallen world: "I consider that
our present sufferings are not worth comparing with the glory that will be revealed in us" (Romans 8:18).

WHY GOD CREATED MANKIND AND THE EARTH

In *The End for which God Created the World*, Jonathan Edwards writes, "God
has a disposition to communicate himself, to spread abroad his own fullness.
His purpose was for his goodness to over-spill his own Being, as it were. He
chose to create the heavens and the earth so that his glory could come pouring
out from himself in abundance. He brought a physical reality into existence in
order that it might experience his glory and be filled with it and reflect it—every
atom, every second, every part and moment of creation. He made human beings in his own image to reflect his glory, and he placed them in a perfect environment which also reflected it."[169]

Earth exists for the same reason that mankind and everything else exists: to
glorify God. God is glorified when we take our rightful, intended place in his
creation and exercise the dominion that he bestowed on us. God appointed human beings to rule the earth: "Then God said, 'Let Us make man in Our image,
according to Our likeness; let them have dominion over the fish of the sea, over
the birds of the air, and over the cattle, over all the earth and over every creeping
thing that creeps on the earth.' So God created man in His own image; in the
image of God He created him; male and female He created them. Then God
blessed them, and God said to them, 'Be fruitful and multiply; fill the earth and
subdue it; have dominion over the fish of the sea, over the birds of the air, and
over every living thing that moves on the earth'" (Genesis 1:26-28, NKJV).

God's intention for humans was that we would occupy the whole Earth and
reign over it. This dominion would produce God-exalting societies in which we
would exercise the creativity, imagination, intellect, and skills befitting beings
created in God's image, thereby manifesting his attributes. To be made in
God's image involves a communicative mandate: that through our creative in-
dustry as God's subcreators, we should together make the invisible God visible,
thus glorifying him in the sight of all creation.

Culture encompasses commerce, the arts, sciences, athletics—anything and everything that God-empowered, creative human minds can conceive and strong human bodies can implement. In *The King of the Earth*, theologian Erich Sauer writes of the phrase in Genesis 1:26 "let them have dominion": "These words plainly declare the vocation of the human race to rule. They also call him to progressive growth in culture. Far from being something in conflict with God, cultural achievements are an essential attribute of the nobility of man as he possessed it in Paradise. Inventions and discoveries, the sciences and the arts, refinement and ennobling, in short, the advance of the human mind, are throughout the will of God. They are the taking possession of the earth by the royal human race (Genesis 1:28), the performance of a commission, imposed by the Creator, by God's ennobled servants, a God-appointed ruler's service for the blessing of this earthly realm."[170]

This reigning, expanding, culture-enriching purpose of God for mankind on Earth was never revoked or abandoned. It has only been interrupted and twisted by the Fall. But neither Satan nor sin is able to thwart God's purposes. Christ's redemptive work will ultimately restore, enhance, and expand God's original plan.

John, the same apostle who writes, "Do not love the world or anything in the world" (1 John 2:15), also writes, "For God so loved the world that he gave his one and only Son" (John 3:16). Because God hates sin, he rejects the sinful world that fallen humanity tries to create: "the cravings of sinful man, the lust of his eyes and the boasting of what he has and does" (1 John 2:16). But God loves the world he created, and he'll restore it as part of his grand plan for humanity's redemption.

"Don't you know that friendship with the world is hatred toward God? Anyone who chooses to be a friend of the world becomes an enemy of God" (James 4:4). How do we understand passages such as this? Consider the predicament of decent German citizens under the Nazi regime. Did they love their homeland, Germany, or did they hate it? Both, simultaneously. They hated the Nazi government, the arrogance, depravity, bigotry, brutality, and persecution. Yet they knew there was a better Germany, even though it was buried beneath the prevailing tide of fascism. They were loyal to that *better* Germany, and they could still see signs of it in the beautiful countryside, a concerto, the eyes of a kind neighbor, Germans jailed for resisting the Nazis, and faithful citizens quietly intervening to save Jews. Paradoxically, it was *their very love for Germany that fueled their opposition to* Nazi *Germany*. Likewise, our love for God's Earth fuels our opposition to fallen Earth.

We need to think carefully when we read Scriptures that talk about "the world." I recommend adding the words *as it is now, under the Curse*, to keep the biblical distinctions clear in our minds:

> Friendship with the world [*as it is now, under the Curse*] is hatred toward God. (James 4:4)

> Do not be conformed to this world [*as it is now, under the Curse*]. (Romans 12:2, NKJV)

> The wisdom of this world [*as it is now, under the Curse*] is foolishness with God. (1 Corinthians 3:19, NKJV)

The world as it was, and the world as it will be, is exceedingly good. The world *as it is now*, inhabited by humanity *as we are now*, is twisted. But this is a temporary condition, with an eternal remedy: Christ's redemptive work.

Paul says that Christ "gave himself for our sins to rescue us from the present evil age" (Galatians 1:4). Not all worlds and all ages are evil, but only this world in this present age. When Jesus calls Satan "the prince of this world" (John 14:30; 16:11) and Paul calls Satan "the god of this age" (2 Corinthians 4:4), it's a relative and temporary designation. God is still God over the universe, still sovereign over Earth and over Satan. But the devil is the usurper who has tried to steal Earth's throne from man, God's delegated king of the earth. In his time, God will take back the throne, as the God-man Jesus Christ, at last restoring and raising Earth.

Paul encourages us not to become engrossed in the world as it is because "this world in its present form is passing away" (1 Corinthians 7:31). God will not bring an end to the earth—rather, he will bring to an end this temporary rebellion. He will transform Earth into a realm of unsurpassed magnificence, for his glory and for our good.

GOD'S KINGDOM . . . AND OURS

In Daniel 7 we're given a prophetic revelation of four earthly kingdoms, beginning with Nebuchadnezzar's Babylon, that will one day be forever replaced by a fifth kingdom. "There before me was one like a son of man, coming with the clouds of heaven. He approached the Ancient of Days and was led into his presence. He was given authority, glory and sovereign power; all peoples, nations and men of every language worshiped him. His dominion is an everlasting dominion that will not pass away, and his kingdom is one that will never be destroyed" (Daniel 7:13-14).

Because the four pagan kingdoms are on Earth, the implication is that the fifth kingdom—God's eternal Kingdom—will also be on Earth.

Daniel said of the four earthly kingdoms, "In my vision at night I looked, and there before me were the four winds of heaven churning up the great sea. Four great beasts, each different from the others, came up out of the sea" (Daniel 7:2). These nations might appear to rise to power arbitrarily, but their emergence is orchestrated by Heaven, and their ruling authority is granted by God for they are "given authority to rule" (v. 6), and later "their dominion was taken away" (v. 12, ESV).

In contrast to the tenuous and temporary rule of the nations, we're told that the Messiah's dominion—in context, a kingdom on *Earth*—will be "everlasting" and "will not pass away" and "will never be destroyed" (v. 14).

Notice the continuity between the ultimate earthly kingdom of the Messiah and the previous earthly kingdoms of Babylon, Medo-Persia, Greece, and Rome, from which eventually comes the kingdom of the Antichrist. The kingdom with the everlasting dominion is not a dominion over a *different* realm but over the *same* realm—Earth. In speaking of these kingdoms, God is not comparing apples (Earth) with oranges (a spirit realm), but apples with apples.

Christ will not merely destroy the earth where fallen kings once ruled. Rather, he will rule over the same Earth, transformed and new.

At Daniel's request, an angel provides an interpretation of his vision: "The four great beasts are four kingdoms that will rise from the earth" (v. 17). Then the angel makes an extraordinary statement: "But the saints of the Most High will receive the kingdom and will possess it forever—yes, for ever and ever" (v. 18). This statement makes clear both the kingdom's location (Earth) and its duration (eternal).

Some theologians reduce Daniel 7 to a promise that God's saints

> Heaven, as the eternal home of the divine Man and of all the redeemed members of the human race, must necessarily be thoroughly human in its structure, conditions, and activities. Its joys and activities must all be rational, moral, emotional, voluntary and active. There must be the exercise of all the faculties, the gratification of all tastes, the development of all talent capacities, the realization of all ideals. . . . Heaven will prove the consummate flower and fruit of the whole creation and of all the history of the universe.
>
> **A. A. HODGE**

will reign with Christ during the Millennium. But the text couldn't be clearer—it says "for ever and ever," not a thousand years. Many other passages also affirm an earthly reign that will last forever (e.g., Joshua 14:9; 2 Samuel

7:16; Isaiah 34:17; 60:21; Jeremiah 17:25; Micah 4:7; Revelation 22:5). The angel Gabriel told Mary that Christ "will reign over the house of Jacob forever; his kingdom will never end" (Luke 1:33). Regardless of whether one believes in a literal Millennium, passages such as the ones cited here shouldn't be understood as millennial references. They refer instead to an everlasting Kingdom.

But where is that eternal Kingdom located? If the other four kingdoms, spanning centuries, rose "from the earth," and if the Antichrist will rule on the earth, where will God's Kingdom be in order to replace those kingdoms? *On the earth.*

Under God's covenant with Israel, the people never looked for the Messiah to reign in Heaven. That would be nothing new, because God already reigns in Heaven. Establishing God's Kingdom was never about an immaterial spirit realm. It always concerned the one place in the universe made for mankind, the one place where God's reign has been disputed: *Earth.*

It's a common but serious mistake to spiritualize the eternal Kingdom of God. Many people imagine that God will replace the earthly kings and their kingdoms with a transcendent sovereignty over the spiritual realm of Heaven. But again, that would be nothing new. Furthermore, the clear meaning of Daniel 7 is that the coming reign of God and his people will take place *on Earth.* It will directly and decisively replace the corrupt reigns of prior kings of the earth.

The ongoing succession of Earth's unrighteous rulers should make us hunger for the day when our righteous God will rule, not just in Heaven but on Earth. At stake is whether God's will shall be done on Earth. The answer is that it *will* be done on Earth, for all eternity, under the reign of Christ and redeemed mankind, his servant kings.

God has never abandoned his original plan that righteous human beings will inhabit and rule the earth. That's not merely an argument from silence. Daniel 7:18 explicitly reveals that "the saints of the Most High will receive the kingdom and will possess it forever." What is "the kingdom"? Earth.

Earth is unique. It's the one planet—perhaps among billions—where God chose to act out the unfolding drama of redemption and reveal the wonders of his grace. It's on the New Earth, the capital planet of the new universe, that he will establish an eternal Kingdom.

Daniel 7:21-22 says that an earthly ruler "was waging war against the saints and defeating them, *until* the Ancient of Days came and pronounced judgment in favor of the saints of the Most High, and the time came when they possessed the kingdom" (emphasis added).

The same earthly kingdoms ruled by ungodly human beings will ultimately be ruled by godly human beings. Christ's promise wasn't figurative—the meek really *will* inherit the earth (Matthew 5:5). And they will rule what they inherit.

THE KINGDOM TRANSFER

Daniel 7:25 tells us that the saints will be handed over to the earth's kingdoms, which will persecute them for a season. But then a stunning reversal will occur. "Then the sovereignty, power and greatness of the kingdoms under the whole heaven will be handed over to the saints, the people of the Most High. His kingdom will be an everlasting kingdom, and all rulers will worship and obey him" (v. 27).

The Kingdom will be God's, yet he will appoint his saints as rulers under him, and they "will worship and obey him."

What is the "greatness of the kingdoms under the whole heaven" that will be "handed over to the saints"? I believe it includes all that makes the nations great. That would include, among other things, their cultural, artistic, athletic, scientific, and intellectual achievements. All of these will not be lost or destroyed but "handed over to the saints" as they rule God's eternal Kingdom on the New Earth. We will become the stewards, the managers of the world's wealth and accomplishments.

Consider the marvels of this revelation. God's children who suffered under ungodly earthly kings *will forever take their place as earthly kings.* The great cultural accomplishments of ungodly nations will be handed over to God's people to manage and (I assume) develop and expand.

The very Earth to which Satan once laid claim will be stripped from his grasp and given over to those whom he hates and seeks to destroy—God's saints. Notice it doesn't say that the earth's kingdoms will be destroyed, but that they will be "handed over" to the saints, placed under their just rule. All the wrongs done on Earth by tyrants will be a thing of the past. No more persecution and injustice. The Earth that was first put under mankind's dominion and was twisted by the Fall will be redeemed, restored, and put under the righteous rule of a redeemed and restored mankind.

If the Bible made no other reference to believers ruling over an earthly kingdom, the emphatic message of Daniel 7 would suffice: *The saints of God will rule the earth forever.*

Many people believe that if God rules the universe, there's no room for other rulers. But this can't be true, because we're told that "all rulers will worship and obey him" (v. 27). As we've seen from Isaiah 60 and Revelation 21, there will still be nations on the New Earth, and they will still have rulers. But they will be *righteous* rulers, subordinate to Christ. People of every national and ethnic group ("tribe and language and people and nation") will worship the Lamb (Revelation 5:9). Some will rule over cities; others will rule over nations.

AN EVER-EXPANDING GOVERNMENT

God says of the reigning Messiah, "Of the increase of his government and peace there will be no end" (Isaiah 9:7). What does this mean? If it was simply that the Messiah's reign will never cease, it would more likely say, "His government shall never end." That's true, of course, but it's not the point of the text. If it means only that his government shall be all-encompassing, it might say, "Of his governmental authority there will be no limit." That's also true, but again it's not the point. The key word in Isaiah 9:7 is *increase*. Nearly every major English translation of the Bible renders the Hebrew word *marbiyth* as "increase" or "expansion." In other words, Christ's government of the New Earth and the new universe will be *ever-expanding*.

How could that be? Even if the New Earth were many times the size of the present one, wouldn't every inch of it immediately or eventually be under his control and under ours as his representatives? If so, it wouldn't be ever-expanding. So what can it mean? There are two ways in which a government can increase: (1) by expanding into previously ungoverned territories; or (2) by creating new territories (an option not available to us as humans).

It may be that Christ's government will always increase because he will continually create new worlds to govern (and, perhaps, new creatures to inhabit those new worlds). Or perhaps it will always increase because the new universe, though still finite, may be so vast that what Christ creates in a moment will never be exhaustively known by finite beings. From what we know of our current universe, with billions of galaxies containing millions of billions of stars and untold planets, this is certainly possible. The restoration of the current universe alone will provide unimaginable territories for us to explore and establish dominion over to God's glory.

Mankind's fall may have initiated a divine moratorium on creation. By analogy, imagine a skilled artist who encounters difficulties with one great painting, his magnum opus. For the time being, he sets aside everything else to focus on this one work to bring it to completion. He's still a creator, still an artist. A hundred other dream projects await him. Once his consuming central creation is finally done, he will return to his practiced habit of creating new works of art. (Of course, the analogy breaks down because God isn't limited to one "painting," one act of creation, at a time.)

If Christ expands his rule by creating new worlds, whom will he send to govern them on his behalf? His redeemed people. Some may rule over towns, some cities, some planets, some solar systems or galaxies. Sound far-fetched? Not if we understand both Scripture and science. Consider how our current universe is constantly expanding. Each moment, the celestial geography dramatically increases. As old stars burn out, new stars are being born. Is God their creator? Yes. Suppose the new heavens also expand, creating new geography in space and ever increasing the size of God's Kingdom. Will he fill that empty space with new creation? Will he dispatch exploratory and governing expeditions to these worlds, where his glory will be seen in new and magnificent creations?

The proper question is not, Why would God create new worlds? That's obvious. God is by nature a creator and ruler. He is glorified by what he creates and rules. He delights to delegate authority and dominion to his children to rule his creation on his behalf. "Of the increase of his government and peace there shall be no end."

Is there anything in Scripture—anything we know about God—that would preclude him from expanding his creation and delegating authority to his children to rule over it? I can't think of anything. Can you?

THE SAINTS WILL RULE

God's throne is referred to forty times in the book of Revelation, appearing in sixteen of the twenty-two chapters. In *The Biblical Doctrine of Heaven*, Wilbur Smith writes, "The basic undertone of all that is revealed in the Apocalypse concerning the activities of heaven may be summed up in this one word *throne*."[171] Revelation isn't primarily a book about the Antichrist or the Tribulation; it's a book about God reigning. He reigns over the fallen universe now, and he will reign uncontested over the new universe, with mankind reigning by his side. Concerning the repeated references to our reigning over God's universe, Dr. Henry Grattan Guinness writes, "We must not regard this as a figure of speech, but as the description of an actual reality."[172]

Humans are made to be kingdom builders, but history demonstrates that when we try to build without God as King, our "utopias" become hell on Earth. "Tragically," writes Bruce Milne, "humanity failed to fulfill its calling as God's vice-regents. Instead we have tumbled down to the dust from which we were taken and groveled on the earth instead of reaching to the skies."[173] Pascal writes that man endures "the miseries of a dethroned monarch." He asks, "What can this incessant craving, and this impotence of attainment mean, unless there was once a happiness belonging to man, of which only the faintest traces remain, in that void which he attempts to fill with everything within his reach?"[174]

By rebelling against the King of kings, mankind abdicated dominion over the earth. But Christ will restore us to the throne occupied so briefly by Adam and Eve. He will hand over to us the Kingdom. He said to his disciples, "Do not be afraid, little flock, for your Father has been pleased to give you the kingdom" (Luke 12:32).

SERVICE AS A REWARD

Those coming out of the Great Tribulation will be specially rewarded by being given a place "before the throne of God," where they will "serve him day and night" (Revelation 7:14-15). Notice that the Master rewards his faithful servants not by taking away responsibilities but by giving them greater ones.

Service is a reward, not a punishment. This idea is foreign to people who dislike their work and only put up with it until retirement. We think that faithful work should be rewarded by a vacation for the rest of our lives. But God offers us something very different: more work, more responsibilities, increased opportunities, along with greater abilities, resources, wisdom, and empowerment. We will have sharp minds, strong bodies, clear purpose, and unabated joy. The more we serve Christ now, the greater our capacity will be to serve him in Heaven.

Reigning over cities will certainly not be "having nothing to do." I believe that those who rule cities on the New Earth will have leisure (rest) and will fully enjoy it, but they will have plenty to do. Dallas Willard suggests, "Perhaps it would be a good exercise for each of us to ask ourselves: Really, how many cities could I now govern under God? If, for example, Baltimore or Liverpool were turned over to me, with power to do what I want with it, how would things turn out? An honest answer to this question might do much to prepare us for our eternal future in this universe."[175]

Will everyone be given the opportunity to rule in the new universe? The apostle Paul said that eternal rewards are available "not only to me, but also to all who have longed for his appearing" (2 Timothy 4:8). The word *all* is encouraging. "The Lord will reward everyone for whatever good he does, whether he is slave or free" (Ephesians 6:8). The word *everyone* is again encouraging. It won't be just a select few rewarded with positions of leadership.

Should we be excited that God will reward us by making us rulers in his Kingdom? Absolutely. Jesus said, "Rejoice and be glad, because great is your reward in heaven" (Matthew 5:12).

God will choose who reigns as kings, and I think some great surprises are in store for us. Christ gives us clues in Scripture as to the type of person he will choose: "Blessed are the poor in spirit, for theirs is the kingdom of heaven. . . . Blessed are the meek, for they will inherit the earth. . . . Blessed are those who are persecuted because of righteousness, for theirs is the kingdom of heaven"

(Matthew 5:3, 5, 10); "'God opposes the proud but gives grace to the humble.' Humble yourselves, therefore, under God's mighty hand, that he may lift you up in due time" (1 Peter 5:5-6).

Look around you to see the meek and the humble. They may include street sweepers, locksmith's assistants, bus drivers, or stay-at-home moms who spend their days changing diapers, doing laundry, packing lunches, drying tears, and driving carpools for God.

I once gave one of my books to a delightful hotel bellman. I discovered he was a committed Christian. He said he'd been praying for our group, which was holding a conference at the hotel. Later, I gave him a little gift, a rough wooden cross. He seemed stunned, overwhelmed. With tears in his eyes he said, "You didn't need to do that. I'm only a bellman." The moment he said it, I realized that this brother had spent his life serving. It will likely be someone like him that I'll have the privilege of serving under in God's Kingdom. He was "only a bellman" who spoke with warmth and love, who served, who quietly prayed in the background for the success of a conference in his hotel. I saw Jesus in that bellman, and there was no "only" about him.

Who will be the kings of the New Earth? I think that bellman will be one of them. And I'll be honored to carry his bags.

PART II

QUESTIONS AND ANSWERS ABOUT HEAVEN

WHAT WILL THE RESURRECTED EARTH BE LIKE?

CHAPTER 23

WILL THE NEW EARTH BE AN EDENIC PARADISE?

This world—including its natural wonders—gives us foretastes and glimpses of the next world. These people—including ourselves—give us foretastes and glimpses of the new people to come. This life—including its culture—gives us foretastes and glimpses of the next life.

If we take literally the earthly depictions of life on the New Earth, it allows us to make a direct connection with our current lives. When I'm eating with people here, enjoying food and friendship, it's a bridge to when I'll be eating there, enjoying food and friendship. This isn't making a leap into the dark of a shadowy afterlife; it's just taking a few natural steps in the light Scripture gives us.

Every joy on earth—including the joy of reunion—is an inkling, a whisper of greater joy. The Grand Canyon, the Alps, the Amazon rain forests, the Serengeti Plain—these are rough sketches of the New Earth. One day we may say, as a character in one of my novels said, "The best parts of the old world were sneak previews of this one. Like little foretastes, like licking the spoon from Mama's beef stew an hour before supper."[176]

All our lives we've been dreaming of the New Earth. Whenever we see beauty in water, wind, flower, deer, man, woman, or child, we catch a glimpse of Heaven. Just like the Garden of Eden, the New Earth will be a place of sensory delight, breathtaking beauty, satisfying relationships, and personal joy.

God himself prepared mankind's first home on Earth. "Now the Lord God had planted a garden in the east, in Eden; and there he put the man he had formed. And the Lord God made all kinds of trees grow out of the ground—trees that were pleasing to the eye and good for food" (Genesis 2:8-9). The phrase "planted a garden" shows God's personal touch, his intimate interest in the creative details of mankind's home. In the same way that God paid attention to the details of the home he prepared for Adam and Eve in Eden, Christ is paying attention to the details as he prepares for us an eternal home in Heaven (John 14:2-3). If he prepared Eden so carefully and lavishly for mankind in the six days of creation, what has he fashioned in the place he's been preparing for us in the two thousand years since he left this world?

God poured himself, his creativity, and his love into making Eden for his creatures. But at that time, that's all we were: his creatures, his image-bearers. Now that we are both his children and his *bride,* chosen out of the human race to live with him forever, would we expect more or less than Eden? More, of course. And that's exactly what the New Earth will be.

WILL THE NEW EARTH BE A RETURN TO EDEN?

Some people assume that the New Earth will "start over" with Eden's original paradise. However, Scripture demonstrates otherwise. The New Earth, as we've seen, includes a carryover of culture and nations. History won't start over with the New Earth any more than history started over when Adam and Eve were banished from the Garden. Eden was part of history. There was direct continuity from the pre-Fall world to the post-Fall world. Similarly, there will be direct continuity between the dying old Earth and the resurrected New Earth. The earthshaking Fall divided history, but it didn't end history. The resurrection of all things will divide Earth's history, but it won't end it.

Culture won't regress to Eden, where musical instruments hadn't yet been invented or where metalworking and countless other skills hadn't yet been developed (Genesis 4:20-22). The fact that God mentions in Scripture these and other examples of technological progress suggests that he approved of the use of creativity and skills to develop society, even though people were hampered by the Curse.

Some people expect the New Earth to be a return to Eden, with no technology or the accomplishments of civilization. But that doesn't fit the biblical picture of the great city, the New Jerusalem. Nor is it logical. Would we expect on the New Earth a literal reinvention of the wheel?

Consider this analogy: a young man has been sick from infancy and is suddenly healed. Does he become a baby again? No. He's a well young man. He doesn't go back and start over from the point his health went bad. Rather, he continues from where he is, going on from there. He doesn't abandon the knowledge and skills he's developed. He's simply far more capable of using them now that he's been healed.

Having used such an illustration, Albert Wolters says,

> By analogy, salvation in Jesus Christ, conceived in the broad creational
> sense, means a restoration of culture and society in their present stage of

development. That restoration will not necessarily oppose literacy or urbanization or industrialization or the internal combustion engine, although these historical developments have led to their own distortions or evils. Instead, the coming of the kingdom of God demands that these developments be reformed, that they be made answerable to their creational structure, and that they be subjected to the ordinances of the Creator.[177]

Will the New Earth start over as a new Eden, or will it contain the cumulative benefits of human knowledge, art, and technology?

Life in the new creation will not be a repristination of all things—a going back to the way things were at the beginning. Rather, life in the new creation will be a restoration of all things—involving the removal of every sinful impurity and the retaining of all that is holy and good. Were the new creation to exclude the diversity of the nations and the glory of the kings of the earth, it would be impoverished rather than enriched, historically regressive and reactionary rather than progressive. To express the point in the form of a question: is it likely that the music of Bach and Mozart, the painting of Rembrandt, the writing of Shakespeare, the discoveries of science, etc., will be altogether lost upon life in the new creation?[178]

HOW DOES EDEN ANTICIPATE THE NEW EARTH?

Eden wasn't just a garden. It was an entire land of natural wonders. The Pishon River, originating in Eden, flowed "through the entire land of Havilah. . . . (The gold of that land is good; aromatic resin and onyx are also there)" (Genesis 2:11-12). The precious onyx stone was located not only near Eden but actually *in* Eden (Ezekiel 28:13).

Later in Israel's history, God commanded the high priest to wear two onyx stones with the names of the twelve tribes written on them. God calls these "memorial stones" (Exodus 28:9-12). Not just the names but the stones themselves were apparently memorials. But what would onyx stones memorialize? The Genesis and Ezekiel passages suggest the answer: Eden.

The onyx stones on the high priest's shoulders served to remind the people of Eden, the perfect Earth that should be kept alive in the hearts, dreams, and hopes of God's people.[179] God wanted his people to look at the Temple and the high priest—a symbol of mankind reconciled to God—and to remember Eden, where people lived in communion with God. The stones suggested that in redeeming mankind, God would restore them to Eden.

The final biblical reference to onyx stones, and the only one in the New Testament, tells us they will be on the foundations of the New Jerusalem's walls (Revelation 21:19-20). The onyx of Eden and on the high priest's shoulders—representing two places where God dwelled with his people—will be displayed in the Holy City, where God will forever live with his people. Hence, the onyx on the high priest and in the Temple simultaneously points us to our past in Eden *and* our future on the New Earth.

Just as Eden is our backward-looking reference point, the New Earth is our forward-looking reference point. We should expect the New Earth to be like Eden, only better. That's exactly what Scripture promises. Notice the earth's restoration to Edenlike qualities prophesied in these passages:

> Indeed, the Lord will comfort Zion; he will comfort all her waste places. And her wilderness He will make like Eden, and her desert like the garden of the Lord; joy and gladness will be found in her, thanksgiving and sound of a melody. (Isaiah 51:3, NASB)

> They will say, "This desolate land has become like the garden of Eden; and the waste, desolate and ruined cities are fortified and inhabited." (Ezekiel 36:35, NASB)

> The wilderness and the wasteland shall be glad for them, and the desert shall rejoice and blossom as the rose. (Isaiah 35:1, NKJV)

> Instead of the thorn shall come up the cypress tree, and instead of the brier shall come up the myrtle tree. (Isaiah 55:13, NKJV)

Commenting on such passages, theologian Anthony Hoekema writes, "Prophecies of this nature should be understood as descriptions of the new earth, which God will bring into existence after Christ comes again—a new earth which will last, not just for a thousand years, but forever. . . . Keeping the doctrine of the new earth in mind . . . will open up the meaning of large portions of Old Testament prophetic literature in surprisingly new ways."[180]

WHAT WILL NEW NATURE BE LIKE?

We've never seen men and women as they were intended to be. We've never seen animals the way they were before the Fall. We see only marred remnants of what once was.

Likewise, we've never seen nature unchained and undiminished. We've only seen it cursed and decaying. Yet even now we see a great deal that pleases and excites us, moving our hearts to worship.

If the "wrong side" of Heaven can be so beautiful, what will the right side look like? If the smoking remains are so stunning, what will Earth look like when it's resurrected and made new, restored to the original?

C. S. Lewis and J. R. R. Tolkien saw core truth in the old mythologies, and in their books they give us a glimpse of people and beasts and trees that are vibrantly alive. What lies in store for us is what we have seen only in diminished glimpses. As Lewis and Tolkien realized, "Pagan fables of paradise were dim and distorted recollections of Eden."[181]

> In the truest sense, Christian pilgrims have the best of both worlds. We have joy whenever this world reminds us of the next, and we take solace whenever it does not.
>
> **C. S. LEWIS**

The earthly beauty we now see won't be lost. We won't *trade* Earth's beauty for Heaven's but *retain* Earth's beauty and *gain* even deeper beauty. As we will live forever with the people of this world—redeemed—we will enjoy forever the beauties of this world—redeemed.

C. S. Lewis said, "We want something else which can hardly be put into words—to be united with the beauty we see, to pass into it, to receive it into ourselves, to bathe in it, to become part of it."[182]

And so we shall.

WILL THIS EARTH'S PLACES BE RESURRECTED TO THE NEW EARTH?

In becoming new, will the old Earth retain much of what it once was? The New Earth will still be just as much Earth as the new us will still be us. "The world into which we shall enter in the Parousia of Jesus Christ is . . . not another world; it is this world, this heaven, this earth; both, however, passed away and renewed. It is these forests, these fields, these cities, these streets, these people, that will be the scene of redemption."[183]

Shouldn't we expect, then, that some of the same geological features of the old Earth will characterize the new? Shouldn't we expect the New Earth's sky to be blue? Might God refashion the rain forests or the Grand Canyon? If the earth becomes the New Earth, might Lake Louise become the New Lake Louise?

Might we travel to a familiar place and say, "This is the very spot we stood on," in the same sense we'll be able to say, "These are the very hands I used to help the needy"?

In *The Last Battle,* C. S. Lewis portrays the girl Lucy as she mourns the loss of Narnia, a great world created by Aslan, a beloved world that she assumed had been forever destroyed. Jewel the unicorn mourns too, calling his beloved Narnia "The only world I've ever known."

Although Lucy and her family and friends are on the threshold of Aslan's country (Heaven), she still looks back at Narnia and feels a profound loss. But as she gets deeper into Aslan's country, she notices something totally unexpected. What happens next, I believe, reflects the biblical revelation of the New Earth:

"Those hills," said Lucy, "the nice woody ones and the blue ones behind—aren't they very like the southern border of Narnia."

"Like!" cried Edmund after a moment's silence. "Why they're exactly like. Look, there's Mount Pire with his forked head, and there's the pass into Archenland and everything!"

"And yet they're not like," said Lucy. "They're different. They have more colours on them and they look further away than I remembered and they're more . . . more . . . oh, I don't know. . . ."

"More like the real thing," said the Lord Digory softly.

Suddenly Farsight the Eagle spread his wings, soared thirty or forty feet up into the air, circled round and then alighted on the ground.

"Kings and Queens," he cried, "we have all been blind. We are only beginning to see where we are. From up there I have seen it all— Ettinsmuir, Beaversdam, the Great River, and Cair Paravel still shining on the edge of the Eastern Sea. Narnia is not dead. This is Narnia."

"But how can it be?" said Peter. "For Aslan told us older ones that we should never return to Narnia, and here we are."

"Yes," said Eustace. "And we saw it all destroyed and the sun put out."

"And it's all so different," said Lucy.

"The Eagle is right," said the Lord Digory. "Listen, Peter. When Aslan said you could never go back to Narnia, he meant the Narnia you were thinking of. But that was not the real Narnia. That had a beginning and an end. It was only a shadow or a copy of the real Narnia, which has always been here and always will be here: just as our own world, England and all, is only a shadow or copy of something in Aslan's real world. You need not mourn over Narnia, Lucy. All of the old Narnia that mattered, all the dear creatures, have been drawn into the real Narnia through the

Door. And of course it is different; as different as a real thing is from a shadow or as waking life is from a dream." . . .

The difference between the old Narnia and the new Narnia was like that. The new one was a deeper country: every rock and flower and blade of grass looked as if it meant more. I can't describe it any better than that: if you ever get there, you will know what I mean.

It was the Unicorn who summed up what everyone was feeling. He stamped his right forehoof on the ground and neighed and then cried:

"I have come home at last! This is my real country! I belong here. This is the land I have been looking for all my life, though I never knew it till now. The reason why we loved the old Narnia is that it sometimes looked a little like this."[184]

Lewis captured the biblical theology of the old and New Earth, and the continuity between them, better than any theologian I've read. Did you catch his message? Our world is a Shadowlands, a copy of something that once was, Eden, and yet will be, the New Earth. All of the old Earth that matters will be drawn into Heaven, to be part of the New Earth.

Through The Chronicles of Narnia series, we and our children can learn to envision the promised Heaven on Earth in a biblical and compelling way.[†] We can learn to anticipate nature, culture, and humanity that will be, as the Lord Digory put it, "more like the real thing." Lewis goes even further later in *The Last Battle*:

"Why!" exclaimed Peter. "It's England. And that's the house itself— Professor Kirk's old home in the country where all our adventures began!"

"I thought that house had been destroyed," said Edmund.

"So it was," said the Faun. "But you are now looking at the England within England, the real England just as this is the real Narnia. And in that inner England no good thing is destroyed."[185]

Based on what Scripture tells us of the New Earth and the New Jerusalem, and that certain things will be restored, I think what Lewis envisions is very possible. On the New Earth we will see the *real* Earth, which includes the good things not only of God's natural creation but also of mankind's creative expression to God's glory. On the New Earth, no good thing will be destroyed.

[†]I encourage parents to read The Chronicles of Narnia series aloud to their family or to listen to the complete books in radio theatre audio productions copublished by Tyndale and Focus on the Family.

WILL WE MISS THE OLD EARTH?

The New Earth will be a place of healing (Revelation 22:2). Christ's healing ministry was thus a foretaste of Heaven, the place where all hurts are healed, all suffering forever eclipsed by joy. Whenever Jesus healed people, the act spoke of wholeness and health, the original perfection of Adam and Eve, and the coming perfection of resurrected bodies and spirits. Every healing was a memorial to the Eden that was and a signpost to the New Earth that will be.

As we set our minds and hearts on Heaven, we should not only go back to the Garden of Eden but also move forward to the Holy City, where we will experience both the riches of nature unruined and human creativity unleashed.

Everything changes when we grasp that all we love about the old Earth will be ours on the New Earth—either in the same form or another. Once we understand this, we won't regret leaving all the wonders of the world we've seen or mourn not having seen its countless other wonders. Why? Because *we will yet be able to see them.*

God is no more done with the earth than he's done with us.

CHAPTER 24

WHAT IS THE NEW JERUSALEM?

S cripture describes Heaven as both a country (Luke 19:12; Hebrews 11:14-16) and a city (Hebrews 12:22; 13:14; Revelation 21:2). Fifteen times in Revelation 21 and 22 the place God and his people will live together is called a city. The repetition of the word and the detailed description of the architecture, walls, streets, and other features of the city suggest that the term *city* isn't merely a figure of speech but a literal geographical location. After all, where do we expect physically resurrected people to live if not in a physical environment?

Everyone knows what a city is—a place with buildings, streets, and residences occupied by people and subject to a common government. Cities have inhabitants, visitors, bustling activity, cultural events, and gatherings involving music, the arts, education, religion, entertainment, and athletics. If the capital city of the New Earth doesn't have these defining characteristics of a city, it would seem misleading for Scripture to repeatedly call it a city.

The city at the center of the future Heaven is called the New Jerusalem. The city is portrayed as a walled city; its security is beyond question. It is perched on the peak of a hill that no invading army could ascend. The city's walls are so thick that they couldn't be breached by any siege engine and so high that no human could hope to scale them. (Of course, the city won't ever be under attack, but its structure will remind us of God's might and commitment to protect his people.)

When I think of the walls of the New Jerusalem, I remember the morning a pastor came to see me. His teenage son Kevin, who was also his best friend, had died four months earlier. This pastor had recently attended a seminary course I taught, "A Theology of Heaven." By God's grace the class had comforted and encouraged this man.

As the pastor sat in my office, he opened his hand to reveal a beautiful reddish, polished stone. I'd never seen anything like it. He said it was jasper, which I recognized as a stone that will make up the walls of the New Jerusalem (Revelation

21:18). The stone was a reminder of his son Kevin and of the assurance that he and his son will live together again in a glorious city with jasper walls.

The pastor insisted I keep the jasper stone. He said, "I want you to know I'm praying for you as you write your book about Heaven. And I want you to have this stone to remind you of Heaven's reality."

I often look at the stone and hold it in my hand. The more I do, the more beautiful it becomes. It's not ghostly; it's solid and substantial—just like the place that awaits us.

WHAT ARE THE CITY'S DIMENSIONS?

The city's exact dimensions are measured by an angel and reported to be 12,000 stadia, the equivalent of 1,400 miles or 2,200 kilometers, in length, width, and height (Revelation 21:15-16). Even though these proportions may have symbolic importance, this doesn't mean they can't be literal. In fact, Scripture emphasizes that the dimensions are given in "man's measurement" (Revelation 21:17). If the city really has these dimensions (and there's no reason it couldn't), what more could we expect God to say to convince us? (I deal with whether the dimensions are literal in appendix B, "Literal and Figurative Interpretation.")

A metropolis of this size in the middle of the United States would stretch from Canada to Mexico and from the Appalachian Mountains to the California border. The New Jerusalem is all the square footage anyone could ask for.

Even more astounding is the city's 1,400-mile height. Some people suggest this is the reach of the city's tallest towers and spires, rising above buildings of lesser height. If so, they argue that it's more like a pyramid than a cube.

We don't need to worry that Heaven will be crowded. The ground level of the city will be nearly two million square miles. This is forty times bigger than England and fifteen thousand times bigger than London. It's ten times as big as France or Germany and far larger than India. But remember, that's just the ground level.

Given the dimensions of a 1,400-mile cube, if the city consisted of different levels (we don't know this), and if each story were a generous twelve feet high, the city could have over 600,000 stories. If they were on different levels, billions of people could occupy the New Jerusalem, with many square miles per person.

If these numbers are figurative, not literal (and that is certainly possible), surely they are still meant to convey that the home of God's people will be extremely large and roomy.

The cube shape of the New Jerusalem reminds us of the cube shape of the Most Holy Place in the Temple (1 Kings 6:20), the three dimensions perhaps suggestive of the three persons of the Trinity. God will live in the city, and it is his presence that will be its greatest feature.

WHAT IS THE SIGNIFICANCE OF THE CITY'S GATES?

The city has "a great, high wall with twelve gates, and with twelve angels at the gates. On the gates were written the names of the twelve tribes of Israel. There were three gates on the east, three on the north, three on the south and three on the west" (Revelation 21:12-13). A city's gates were important for several reasons. First, they were a place of defense from enemies. Typically the gates of the city were shut tight at night to keep out dangers. Even Disneyland, "the happiest place on earth," closes its gates at night. However, Scripture tells us, "On no day will [the New Jerusalem's] gates ever be shut" (Revelation 21:25). Why can the gates remain open? Because the city's twelve gates are attended by twelve angels. Of course, there will be no enemies outside the city's gates—the entire New Earth will be filled with the knowledge of God (Habakkuk 2:14). And citizens from outside the gates will regularly travel in through them (Revelation 21:24, 26).

All enemies of the Kingdom will be forever cast into the lake of fire, far away from the New Earth. So the gates will remain open, with no need for searches or metal detectors. Any citizen of the New Earth is always welcome, always free to come to the capital city—and even to access the King's throne! The open gates guarded by angels remind us that our safety has been bought and permanently secured by our God.

The city's open gates are a great equalizer. There's no elitism in Heaven; everyone will have access because of Christ's blood. His death is the admission ticket to every nook and cranny of the New Jerusalem. People won't have to prove their worth or buy their way through the gates. All people will have access to the city's parks, museums, restaurants, libraries, concerts—anything and everything the city has to offer. Nobody will have to peek over the fence or look longingly through the windows.

The gates are where people enter and leave the city. The vast distances

> From opposite standpoints of the Christian world, from different quarters of human life and character, through various expressions of their common faith and hope, through diverse modes of conversion, through different portions of the Holy Scripture will the weary travelers enter the Heavenly City and meet each other—"not without surprise"—on the shores of the same river of life.
>
> **DWIGHT L. MOODY**

involved—three gates on each of the city's sides, which measure more than 1,400 miles—suggest each gate may go out into a different country, perhaps each with radically different terrain. Imagine the people of every nationality, color, and dress going in and out of the city, some people leaving on a task or mission, some going on an adventure, others coming to a banquet or going to visit friends and loved ones.

People have always gathered at city gates to share news and tell stories. Will people on the New Earth be less relational than we are now? No, we'll be freed to be more relational, without the fears, inadequacies, and sins that currently plague us. We'll be eager to hear other people's stories, and we'll all have our own stories to tell—and we'll be able to tell them better than we ever have. No one will have to wonder if they're being told the truth, since there will be no deceit (Revelation 21:8).

Are we to take the references to the city's walls and gates at face value? Some people say no: "These descriptions, of course, are not meant to be taken literally. They are vivid poetic metaphors for a reality which is indestructible, gleaming, incalculably precious. . . . If invited for a walk, most of us would prefer a leafy country lane to a street paved with gold. One is natural and instantly appealing; the other seems lifeless and manufactured."[186]

As we'll deal with in appendix B, we shouldn't dismiss the physical descriptions of the great city. Streets can be made of actual gold and still have symbolic meaning. My wedding ring reminds me of my commitment to my wife, but that doesn't mean it isn't a literal ring. The open gates of Heaven will remind us of God's accessibility, but that doesn't mean they aren't literal gates. I think it would be more enjoyable than most commentators suppose to walk on a street paved with gold. I've had great walks on asphalt—what's wrong with gold? We are wrong to assume we must either walk on gold streets or leafy country lanes. Why not both?

WHAT WILL IT BE LIKE FOR THE CITY'S CITIZENS?

To be part of a city is to be a citizen, which involves both responsibilities and privileges. The apostle Paul reminded the Philippians, who were proud of their Roman citizenship, "Our citizenship is in heaven" (Philippians 3:20). Note the verb in the statement: Our citizenship "is," not "will be," in Heaven. Although our citizenship in Heaven is present, our residence there is future. People born far from their father's native country are still citizens of that country, even though they have never lived there. One day as children and heirs of Heaven's king, we will enter into full possession of our native land, which we will rule to our Father's glory.

God's people were once nomadic, wandering in the wilderness of Sinai for forty years. Finally they settled down in cities. The New Jerusalem will be a solid, permanent city, secured by far more than tent stakes.

A building's greatest strength is its foundation. The New Jerusalem has not one foundation, but twelve, each decorated with a different gem (Revelation 21:14, 19-20). Furthermore, this city is built by God himself. In Old Testament times, Abraham "was looking forward to the city with foundations, whose architect and builder is God" (Hebrews 11:8-10). The New Jerusalem is that city. Whatever God builds will last.

People have told me they can't get excited about the New Jerusalem because they don't like cities. But this city will be different—it will have all the advantages we associate with earthly cities but none of the disadvantages. The city will be filled with natural wonders, magnificent architecture, thriving culture—but it will have no crime, pollution, sirens, traffic fatalities, garbage, or homelessness. It will truly be Heaven on Earth.

If you think you hate cities, you'll quickly change your mind when you see this one. Imagine moving through the city to enjoy the arts, music, and sports without pickpockets, porn shops, drugs, or prostitution. Imagine sitting down to eat and raising glasses to toast the King, who will be glorified in every pleasure we enjoy.

The Artist's fingerprints will be seen everywhere in the great city. Every feature speaks of his attributes. The priceless stones speak of his beauty and grandeur. The open gates speak of his accessibility. All who wish to come to him at his throne may do so at any time. We can learn a lot about people by walking through their houses. The whole universe will be God's house—and the New Jerusalem will be his living room. God will delight to share with us the glories of his capital city—and ours.

CHAPTER 25

WHAT WILL THE GREAT CITY BE LIKE?

Why did Magellan and Columbus and all the other explorers and their crews go off seeking "the new world"? Because *we were made to seek out new worlds.* We were *made* to be seekers and explorers. As we seek and explore God's creation, we'll grow in our knowledge of God, becoming increasingly motivated to explore the wonders of God himself.

The demands and distractions of our present life teach us to set aside or stifle our longing to explore, yet it still surfaces. On the New Earth, that desire won't be thwarted or trumped by pragmatic considerations. Rather, it will be stimulated and encouraged by God, each other, and all that's within us.

However, the first place we may wish to explore will be the largest city that has ever existed—the capital city of the New Earth. The New Jerusalem will be a place of extravagant beauty and natural wonders. It will be a vast Eden, integrated with the best of human culture, under the reign of Christ. More wealth than has been accumulated in all human history will be spread freely across this immense city.

HOW EXTRAVAGANT WILL THE CITY BE?

Presumably many other cities will be on the New Earth, such as those Jesus mentioned in the stewardship parables (Luke 19:17-19). The kings of nations who bring their treasures into the New Jerusalem must come from and return to somewhere, presumably countryside and cities lying beyond the New Jerusalem. But no city will be like this one, for it will be called home by the King of kings.

Heaven's capital city will be filled with visual magnificence. "It shone with the glory of God, and its brilliance was like that of a very precious jewel, like a jasper, clear as crystal" (Revelation 21:11). John goes on to describe the opulence: "The wall was made of jasper, and the city of pure gold, as pure as glass. The foundations of the city walls were decorated with every kind of precious stone" (Revelation 21:18-19). John then names twelve stones, eight of which correspond to the stones of the high priest's breastpiece (Exodus 28:17-20).

The precious stones and gold represent incredible wealth, suggestive of the exorbitant riches of God's splendor. "The twelve gates were twelve pearls, each gate made of a single pearl. The great street of the city was of pure gold, like transparent glass" (Revelation 21:21). Each gate tower is carved from a single, huge pearl. "Among the ancients, the pearl was highest in value among the precious stones."[187] The text doesn't say this, but commentators often suggest that because a pearl is formed through the oyster's pain, the pearl may symbolize Christ's suffering on our behalf as well as the eternal beauty that can come out of our temporary suffering.

WHAT IS THE RIVER OF LIFE?

John describes a natural wonder in the center of the New Jerusalem: "the river of the water of life, as clear as crystal, flowing from the throne of God and of the Lamb down the middle of the great street of the city" (Revelation 22:1-2). Why is water important? Because the city is a center of human life and water is an essential part of life. Ghosts don't need water, but human bodies do. We all know what it's like to be thirsty, but the original readers, who lived in a bone-dry climate, readily grasped the wonder of constantly available fresh water, pure and uncontaminated, able to satisfy the deepest thirst.

Notice that the source of this powerful stream is the throne of God, occupied by the Lamb. He's the source of all natural beauties and wonders. They derive their beauty from the Artist. The great river reflects his thirst-quenching, need-satisfying nature. He always meets his people's needs and fulfills their longings.

On the New Earth, we won't have to leave the city to find natural beauty. It will be incorporated into the city, with the river of life as its source. The river flows down the city's main street. Likely it has countless tributaries flowing throughout the rest of the city. Can you picture people talking and laughing beside this river, sticking their hands and faces down into the water and drinking? This fully accessible natural wonder on the city's main street is amazing—something that would be featured in any travel brochure.

The city has many other streets, of course, but none like this, for this one leads directly to the king's throne. The fact that the water is flowing down from it suggests the throne's high elevation. One need only follow the street—or the river—up to its source to arrive at the city's centerpiece: the Lamb's throne.

WHAT IS THE TREE OF LIFE?

After John describes the river of life, he mentions another striking feature: "On each side of the river stood the tree of life, bearing twelve crops of fruit, yielding its fruit every month. And the leaves of the tree are for the healing of the nations" (Revelation 22:2).

The tree of life is mentioned three times in Genesis 2, in Eden, and again four times in Revelation, three of those in the final chapter. These instances seem to refer to Eden's literal tree of life. We're told the tree of life is presently in Paradise, the intermediate Heaven (Revelation 2:7). The New Jerusalem itself, also in the present Heaven, will be brought down, tree of life and all, and placed on the New Earth (Revelation 21:2). Just as the tree was apparently relocated from Eden to the present Heaven, it will be relocated again to the New Earth.

In Eden, the tree appears to have been a source of ongoing physical life. The presence of the tree of life suggests a supernatural provision of life as Adam and Eve ate the fruit their Creator provided. Adam and Eve were designed to live forever, but to do so they likely needed to eat from the tree of life. Once they sinned, they were banned from the Garden, separated from the tree, and subject to physical death, just as they had experienced spiritual death. Since Eden, death has reigned throughout history. But on the New Earth, our access to the tree of life is forever restored. (Notice that there's no mention of a tree of the knowledge of good and evil to test us. The redeemed have already known sin and its devastation; they will desire it no more.)

In the New Earth, we will freely eat the fruit of the same tree that nourished Adam and Eve: "To him who overcomes, I will give the right to eat from the tree of life, which is in the paradise of God" (Revelation 2:7). Once more human beings will draw their strength and vitality from this tree. The tree will produce not one crop but twelve. The newness and freshness of Heaven is demonstrated in the monthly yield of fruit. The fruit is not merely to be admired but consumed.

The description of the tree of life in Revelation 22 mirrors precisely what's prophesied in the Old Testament: "Fruit trees of all kinds will grow on both banks of the river. Their leaves will not wither, nor will their fruit fail. Every month they will bear, because the water from the sanctuary flows to them. Their fruit will serve for food and their leaves for healing" (Ezekiel 47:12).

> Then shall I see, and hear, and know
> All I desired or wished below;
> And every power find sweet employ
> In that eternal world of joy.
> **ISAAC WATTS**

[handwritten margin notes: what about those living outside the city. In other country etc. Do they have the tree of life? River flowing?]

Commentator William Hendriksen suggests, "The term 'tree of life' is collective, just like 'avenue' and 'river.' The idea is not that there is just one single tree. No, there is an entire park: whole rows of trees alongside the river; hence, between the river and the avenue. And this is true with respect to all the avenues of the city. Hence, the city is just full of parks, cf. Rev. 2:7. Observe, therefore, this wonderful truth: the city is full of rivers of life. It is also full of parks containing trees of life. These trees, moreover, are full of fruit."[188]

This broader view of the tree of life would account for the fact that the tree grows on both sides of a great river at once and yields twelve different kinds of fruit. (Of course, even if Hendriksen is wrong in supposing that the tree of life is collective, it is reasonable that just as there were other trees in Eden, there will be other trees on the New Earth.)

John also tells us that "the leaves of the tree are for the healing of the nations" (Revelation 22:2). For the third time in Revelation 21–22, the inhabitants of the New Earth are referred to as nations. Nations will not be eliminated but healed. But since we won't experience pain or disease in Heaven, what's the point of leaves for healing? Perhaps they, like the tree's fruit, will have life-sustaining or life-enhancing properties that will help people maintain health and energy. Our physical life and health, even our healing, comes not from our intrinsic immortal nature but from partaking of God's gracious provision in the fruit and leaves of the tree of life. Hence, our well-being is not granted once for all but will be forever sustained and renewed as we depend on him and draw from his provision.

Some people find it hard to understand why perfectly healthy people will need food, water, and health-giving vegetation on the New Earth. It appears that we will still have needs, but they will all be met. The organic nature of edible fruit and medicinal leaves emphasizes the tie of mankind to Earth, suggesting that eternal life won't be as different from life in Eden as is often assumed.

WILL THE NEW EARTH HAVE OTHER NATURAL WONDERS?

What Scripture tells us about the river of life and the tree of life and its fruits is indicative of the natural wonders that will be part of the New Earth. Just as "the tree" probably includes many trees, "the river" likely becomes many rivers, which in turn form lakes. Since this is the New Earth, we should expect geographical properties of Earth: mountains, waterfalls, and other natural wonders.

In describing the New Earth, John speaks of "a mountain great and high" (Revelation 21:10). Note that John calls it *a* mountain, not *the* mountain. We know that the New Earth has at least one mountain, and we can assume it has hundreds or thousands of them.

Just as our resurrection bodies will be better than our current ones, the New Earth's natural wonders will presumably be more spectacular than those we now know. We can expect more magnificent mountains and more beautiful lakes and flowers than those on this earth. If we imagine the New Earth to have fewer and less beautiful features than the old, we picture the earth's regression. The least we should expect is retention. But in fact, I believe there's every reason to anticipate *progression*. The depiction of the precious metals and stones and vast architecture is lavish beyond imagination, as are the descriptions of trees on both sides of the great river, bearing new fruit each month. Everything God tells us suggests we will look back at the present Earth and conclude, creatively speaking, that God was just "warming up" and getting started.

Look at God's track record in creating natural wonders in this universe. On Mars, the volcano Olympus Mons rises 79,000 feet, nearly three times higher than Mount Everest. The base of Olympus Mons is 370 miles across and would cover the entire state of Nebraska. The Valles Marineris is a vast canyon that stretches one-sixth of the way around Mars. It's 2,800 miles long, 370 miles wide, and 4.5 miles deep. Hundreds of our Grand Canyons could fit inside it.

The New Earth may have far more spectacular features than these. Imagine what we might find on the new Mars or the new Saturn and Jupiter and their magnificent moons. I remember vividly the thrill of first seeing Saturn's rings through my new telescope when I was eleven years old. It exhilarated me and stirred my heart. Five years later, I heard the gospel for the first time and came to know Jesus, but the wonders of the heavens helped lead me to God. How many times in the new universe will we be stunned by the awesomeness of God's creation?

Remember, God will make the new heavens, which will correspond to the old and which will therefore include renewed versions of the planets, stars, nebulae, and galaxies God created in the first heavens.

The New Earth's waterfalls may dwarf Niagara—or the New Niagara Falls may dwarf the one we know now. We will find rock formations more spectacular than Yosemite's, peaks higher than the Himalayas, forests deeper and richer than anything we see in the Pacific Northwest.

Some current earthly phenomena may not occur on the New Earth, including earthquakes, floods, hurricanes, and volcanoes. These may be aberrations due to the Curse. God's Kingdom is described as one "that cannot be shaken" (Hebrews 12:28). However, it may be that the foundations of the New Earth's buildings will be such that they would remain solid in the most violent storms or earthquakes. In that case, we might ride out an earthquake as if we were on a roller coaster—experiencing the thrill of the event without the danger. We could praise God for the display of his magnificent power.

On the present Earth, God shows himself through natural wonders and weather (Job 9:5-7; 38:34-35). Since the old Earth is the prototype of the new, there's every reason to believe he will show his greatness and beauty the same way on the New Earth.

WILL THE NEW JERUSALEM'S BEAUTY BE NATURAL OR DESIGNED?

As I mentioned earlier, some people read the Bible's description of Heaven's capital city and think they will be uncomfortable in that vast architecture. Tolkien seems to address this in his Lord of the Rings trilogy, where he portrays differing concepts of Elvish beauty and Dwarvish beauty. Elves, people of the woods and waters, celebrate and protect the natural beauty of Middle Earth. Dwarves, in contrast, are miners and builders who dig deep for precious stones and construct vast buildings. The Elves are uncomfortable with Dwarvish architecture, and the Dwarves feel uncomfortable deep in the forest.

Legolas the Elf and Gimli the Dwarf forge a great friendship. They come to appreciate the previously undiscovered beauties of each other's world. Legolas beholds the underground wonders of Moria, a gigantic and awesome architectural accomplishment, testifying to the ingenuity and beauty of what Dwarves can carve out of stone. Similarly, Gimli comes to appreciate the spectacular natural beauties of Lothlorien and of Galadriel, the Elven queen.

As I read Revelation 21–22, I'm struck with how the Elven paradise reflects the Edenic elements of the New Jerusalem—rivers, trees, fruits, and mountains—while the Dwarves' view of beauty reflects the vast detailed architecture and precious stones of Heaven's capital. Which kind of beauty is better? We needn't choose between them. The New Earth will be filled with both. Whatever God's people create is also God's creation, for it is he who shapes and gifts and empowers us to create.

It's likely that our tastes will differ enough that some of us will prefer to gather in the main streets and auditoriums for the great cultural events, while others will want to withdraw to feed ducks on a lake or to leave the city with their companions to pursue adventures in some undeveloped place. Wherever we go and whatever we do, we'll never leave the presence of the King. For although he dwells especially in the New Jerusalem, he will yet be fully present in the far reaches of the new universe—in which every subatomic particle will shout his glory.

CHAPTER 26

WILL THERE BE SPACE AND TIME?

A number of books suggest that our existence in Heaven will be without space or time. One book describes Heaven as "a mode of existence where space and time are meaningless concepts."[189] Is that true?

WHAT WILL THE NEW CELESTIAL HEAVENS BE LIKE?

What does the Bible mean by the term *new heavens*? Let's look at a few passages.

The Old Testament uses no single word for *universe* or *cosmos*. When Genesis 1:1 speaks of God's creating "the heavens and the earth," the words are synonymous with what we mean by *universe*. *Heavens* refers to the realms above the earth: atmosphere, sun, moon, and stars, and all that's in outer space. Then in Isaiah, God says, "Behold, I will create new heavens and a new earth" (Isaiah 65:17). This corresponds to Genesis 1:1, indicating a complete renewal of the same physical universe God first created.

Revelation 21:1-2 says, "I saw a new heaven and a new earth, for the first heaven and the first earth had passed away. . . . I saw the Holy City, the new Jerusalem, coming down out of heaven from God." Because "new heaven" (singular) is used here, some think it's God's dwelling place that passes away and is renewed. But the present Heaven is described as unshakable in ways the physical universe isn't (Hebrews 12:26-28). The "new heaven" in Revelation 21:1 apparently refers to exactly the same atmospheric *and* celestial heavens as "heavens" does in Genesis 1:1. It also corresponds to the "new heaven(s)" of Isaiah 65:17, Isaiah 66:22, and 2 Peter 3:13. In Revelation 21:2, we see God's dwelling place isn't replaced but *relocated* when the New Jerusalem is brought down to the New Earth.

The new heavens will surely be superior to the old heavens, which themselves are filled with untold billions of stars and perhaps trillions of planets. God's light casts the shadows we know as stars, the lesser lights that point to

God's substance. As the source is greater than the tributary, God, the Light, is infinitely greater than those little light-bearers we know as stars.

The Bible's final two chapters make clear that every aspect of the new creation will be greater than the old. Just as the present Jerusalem isn't nearly as great as the New Jerusalem, no part of the present creation—including the earth and the celestial heavens—is as great as it will be in the new creation.

While some passages suggest that the universe will wear out and the stars will be destroyed, others indicate that the stars will exist forever (Psalm 148:3-6). Is this a contradiction? No. We too will be destroyed by death, yet we will last forever. The earth will be destroyed in God's judgment, yet it will last forever. In exactly the same way, the stars will be destroyed, yet they will last forever. Based on the redemptive work of Christ, God will resurrect them.

Earth is the first domain of mankind's stewardship, but it is not the only domain. Because the whole universe fell under mankind's sin, we can conclude that the whole universe was intended to be under mankind's dominion. If so, then the entire new universe will be ours to travel to, inhabit, and rule—to God's glory.

Do I seriously believe the new heavens will include new galaxies, planets, moons, white dwarf stars, neutron stars, black holes, and quasars? Yes. The fact that they are part of the first universe and that God called them "very good," at least in their original forms, means they will be part of the resurrected universe. When I look at the Horsehead Nebula and ask myself what it's like there, I think that one day I'll know. Just as I believe this "self-same body"—as the Westminster Confession put it—will be raised and the "self-same" Earth will be raised, I believe the "self-same" Horsehead Nebula will be raised. Why? Because it is part of the present heavens, and therefore will be raised as part of the new heavens.

Will the new planets be mere ornaments, or does God intend for us to reach them one day? Even under the Curse, we've been able to explore the moon, and we have the technology to land on Mars. What will we be able to accomplish for God's glory when we have resurrected minds, unlimited resources, complete scientific cooperation, and no more death? Will the far edges of our galaxy be within reach? And what about other galaxies, which are plentiful as blades of grass in a meadow? I imagine we will expand the borders of righteous mankind's Christ-centered dominion, not as conquerors who seize what belongs to others, but as faithful stewards who will occupy and manage the full extent of God's physical creation.

WHAT IS THE MORNING STAR?

Jesus says of the overcomer, "I will also give him the morning star" (Revelation 2:28). The morning star is a celestial object—the planet Venus. Although most people consider Jesus' statement to be figurative, it could suggest that God might entrust to his children planets or stars (with their respective planetary systems) in the new heavens. If the new creation is indeed a resurrected version of the old, then there will be a new Venus, after all.

Currently Venus is a most inhospitable planet. Humans could never survive its incredible heat and corrosive atmosphere. However, it's possible that indestructible resurrected bodies could endure its atmosphere. It's also possible that when the Curse is lifted, Venus may become a beautiful paradise.

We know God will put one world under his children's authority—Earth. If the rest of the planets and the entire universe fell with and will rise with mankind, I can easily envision our inhabiting and governing other resurrected planets.

For those of us who love astronomy and for fantasy and science-fiction fans, this has exciting implications. I believe the great nebula of Orion, which has drawn hearts, including mine, to worship through its expansive beauty and wonder, will be refashioned as part of the new heavens. Will we see a new Saturn, new Jupiter, new Ganymede, new Pleiades, and a new Milky Way? I think that's the logical conclusion based on what Scripture reveals. In the same way that the New Earth will be refashioned and still be a true Earth, *with continuity to the old*, the new cosmic heavens will likewise be the old renewed.

In my novel *Dominion* I try to depict this in a scene in which Jesus takes a woman who has died to a new world:

> Eventually they arrived on a world more beautiful than Dani could fathom—cascading waterfalls, rainbows of a hundred colors, mountain peaks five times higher than any on earth. Oceans with blue-green water, and waves crashing upon rocks the size of mountains. Grassy meadows, fields of multicolored flowers—colors she had never seen before. This place seemed somehow familiar to her, yet how could it, since it was like nothing she'd ever seen? Still, she felt profoundly at home.
>
> "Why hasn't anyone told me of this place until now? I'd think it would be the talk of heaven!"
>
> The Carpenter smiled at her. "They did not tell you because they do not know of it. They've never been here."
>
> "What do you mean?"
>
> "You are the first to visit this world."
>
> "No," she said, then her face flushed. "How could that be?"
>
> "This is yours. As your father once built you that tree house, I fashioned this place just for you."

Nancy beamed. "He gave us our own worlds too," she said. "Beautiful as this is, mine seems the perfect one for me. The Master tells me each world he gives is tailor-made to the receiver."

"This is all for me?"

"Yes," the Carpenter said. "Do you like it?"

"Oh, I love it. And I haven't even begun to explore it! Thank you. Oh, thank you." She hugged him tight. He took delight in her delight.

"This is not the ultimate place I have prepared for you, my daughter. But it is a pleasant beginning, isn't it?"[190]

God has built into us the longing to see the wonders of his far-flung creation. The popularity of science fiction reflects that longing. Visiting a Star Trek convention demonstrates how this—like anything else—can become a substitute religion, but the fervor points to a truth: We do possess a God-given longing to know a greater intelligence and to explore what lies beyond our horizons.

In the Star Trek movie *Generations*, the character Guinan tells Captain Picard about a place called the Nexus. She describes it this way: "It was like being inside joy, as if joy was something tangible, and you could wrap yourself up in it like a blanket."

I don't believe in the Nexus. But I do believe in the new heavens and the New Earth. What will the new heavens be like? Like being inside joy, as if joy were something tangible, and you could wrap yourself up in it like a blanket.

Scottish novelist George MacDonald wrote to his dying daughter, "I do live expecting great things in the life that is ripening for me and all mine—when we shall have all the universe for our own, and be good merry helpful children in the great house of our father. Then, darling, you and I and all will have grand liberty wherewith Christ makes free—opening his hand to send us out like white doves to range the universe."[191]

What has God made in the heights of distant galaxies, never seen by human eyes? One day we'll behold those wonders, soaking them in with openmouthed awe. And if that won't be enough, we may see wonders God held back in his first creation, wonders that will cause us to marvel and drop to our knees in worship when we behold them in the new creation.

WILL WE LIVE IN A SPATIAL WORLD?

The doctrine of resurrection is an emphatic statement that we will forever occupy space. We'll be physical human beings living in a physical universe. The resurrected Christ said, "Touch me and see; a ghost does not have flesh and bones, as you see I have" (Luke 24:39). He walked on Earth; we will walk on Earth. He occupied space; we will occupy space.

We are finite physical creatures, and that means we *must* live in space and time. Where else would we live? Eden was in space and time, and the New Earth will be in space and time. We will be delivered from all evil, but space isn't evil. It's good. God made it. It's Christoplatonism that tries to persuade us something's wrong with space and time.

One writer says of Heaven, "It is certainly justifiable to abandon the scheme of time and space and to put in its place a divine simultaneity."[192] This has a high-sounding resonance, but what does it mean? That we can be a thousand places at once, doing ten thousand different things? Those are the Creator's attributes, not the creature's. There's no evidence that we could be several places at once. The promise of Heaven is not that we will become infinite—that would be to become inhuman. It's that we'll be far better finite humans than we have ever been. Even if we're able to move rapidly from one place to another or to pass our resurrected molecules through solid objects, as the risen Jesus did, we'll still be finite. (As I said before, I'm not certain we'll have that power, though it's possible.)

If we plan to get together with friends, the question is, "Where and when?" *Where* is space; *when* is time. The three gates on the west side of the New Jerusalem are a minimum of fourteen hundred miles from the gates on the east side. If I wait for you at a gate on the west side, you won't see me if you show up at a gate on the east side. (Even if the stated dimensions are figurative, the principle remains the same.) When we walk outside the city gate, we won't remain inside. People, even resurrected people, can be in only one place at one time. There's no suggestion that even the resurrected Jesus was in two places at once.

One author says, "Time and space will not be the same as known here on earth, and relationships will be of a different order. This be-

> We shall not cease from exploration
> And the end of all our exploring
> Will be to arrive where we began
> And know the place for the first time.
>
> **T. S. ELIOT**

ing so, it is clear that the life of the new humanity in their resurrection bodies of glory can be described only in symbolic terms."[193] But what's the biblical evidence for this claim? The biblical texts speak of time and space in the New Earth similarly to how they speak of them here and now. By reducing resurrected life to symbols, don't we undermine the meaning of humanity, Earth, and resurrection?

Jesus spoke of the uttermost parts or farthest ends of Heaven (Mark 13:27,

NKJV). Even the present Heaven appears to occupy space. But certainly the new heavens and the New Earth will. Resurrection doesn't eliminate space and time; it redeems them.

In the heavenly realms, even angels, whom we think of as disembodied spirits, can be hindered in space and time due to combat with fallen angels (Daniel 10:13). In other words, they can be delayed (time) from arriving at a particular destination (space).

People imagine they're making Heaven sound wondrous when they say there's no space and time there. (If it doesn't have space, it's not even a "there.") In fact, they make Heaven sound utterly alien and unappealing. We don't want to live in a realm—in fact, it couldn't even *be* a realm—that's devoid of space and time any more than a fish wants to live in a realm without water. If fish could think, try telling one, "When you die, you'll go to fish Heaven and—isn't this great?—there will be no water! You won't have fins, and you won't swim. And you won't eat because you won't need food. I'll bet you can't wait to get there!" After hearing our christoplatonic statements about Heaven, stripped of the meaning of resurrection, no wonder we and our children don't get excited about Heaven.

Sir Isaac Newton said of God, "He is eternal and infinite, omnipotent and omniscient; that is, his duration reaches from eternity to eternity; his presence from infinity to infinity."[194] God is the one "who inhabits eternity" (Isaiah 57:15, NKJV). Creatures inhabit time. Jesus, as the God-man, inhabits both. By being with him on the New Earth, we will share space and time with God.

WILL WE EXPERIENCE TIME IN HEAVEN?

Scripture says, "With the Lord a day is like a thousand years, and a thousand years are like a day" (2 Peter 3:8). Does this mean there will be no time in Heaven?

The natural understanding of a New Earth is that it would exist in space and time, with a future unfolding progressively, just as it does now. Yet people repeatedly say there will be "no time in Heaven." One theologian argues, "What a relief and what joy to know that in heaven there will be no more time."[195] Another writer says, "Heaven will be a place where time will stand still."[196]

Where do such ideas come from? A misleading translation in the King James Version of the Bible says that "there should be time no longer" (Revelation 10:6). This was the basis for theologians such as Abraham Kuyper to conclude there will be no time in Heaven. But other versions correctly translate this phrase "There will be no more delay!" (NIV, RSV), which means not that time itself will cease but that there is no time left before God's judgment is executed.

Other people are confused because they remember the phrase "Time shall be no more" and think it's from the Bible. It's actually from a hymn. Ironically, the same hymn speaks of "When the morning breaks . . ." Both the words *morning* and *when* are references to time.

John Newton's hymn "Amazing Grace" demonstrates a better grasp of time:

When we've been there ten thousand years,
Bright shining as the sun,
We've no less days to sing God's praise,
Than when we'd first begun.[197]

Scripture contains many other evidences of time in Heaven:

- Heaven's inhabitants track with events happening in time, right down to rejoicing the moment a sinner on Earth repents (Luke 15:7).
- Martyrs in Heaven are told to "wait a little longer" when they ask "how long" before Christ will judge the inhabitants of the earth and avenge the martyrs' blood (Revelation 6:10-11). Those in Heaven couldn't ask "how long" or be told "wait a little longer" unless time passes in Heaven.
- Paul spoke of Heaven in terms of "the coming ages" (Ephesians 2:7). He speaks not just of a future age but of ages (plural).
- God's people in Heaven "serve him day and night in his temple" (Revelation 7:15).
- The tree of life on the New Earth will be "yielding its fruit every month" (Revelation 22:2). There are days and months both in the present and eternal Heaven.
- God says, "The new heavens and the new earth that I make will endure before me. . . . From one New Moon to another and from one Sabbath to another, all mankind will come and bow down before me" (Isaiah 66:22-23). New Moons and Sabbaths require moon, sun, and time.
- God said, "Summer and winter, day and night will never cease" (Genesis 8:22). This wasn't the result of the Curse; it was God's original design.
- We're told that "there was silence in heaven for about half an hour" (Revelation 8:1).
- The book of Revelation shows the present Heaven's inhabitants operating within time. The descriptions of worship include successive actions, such as falling down at God's throne and casting crowns

before him (Revelation 4:10). There's a sequence of events; things occur one after another, not all at once.

- The inhabitants of Heaven sing (Revelation 5:9-12). Music in Heaven requires time. Meter, tempo, and rests are all essential components of music, and each is time-related. Certain notes are held longer than others. Songs have a beginning, middle, and end. That means they take place in time.

How can Scripture be any more clear about time in Heaven? (Right down to silence in Heaven for half an hour.) To say we'll exist outside of time is like saying we'll know everything. It confuses eternity with infinity. We'll live for eternity as finite beings. God can accommodate to us by putting himself into time, but we can't accommodate to him by becoming timeless. It's not in us to do so because we're not God.

Writers frequently distinguish between the Greek words *kronos* and *kairos*, viewing the former as "human time" or "quantity of time" and the latter as "God's time" or "quality of time." It's suggested that in eternity we'll live no longer in *kronos* but in *kairos*. However, it's unclear what this means. Will we still live in chronological sequence, where one word, step, or event follows the previous and is followed by the next? The Bible's answer is *yes*.

IS TIME BAD OR GOOD?

One writer maintains, "The end of the world is the end of time. Time will cease to exist. Time is a mark of the fallen state of the world."[198] But this would be true only if Adam and Eve existed outside of time—and they didn't. The sun rose and set in their perfect world. The sixth day of creation was followed by a day of rest. Time was *not* a mark of the world's fallen state.

God knows and can access past and future as readily as present. We can remember the past and anticipate the future, but we can live only in the present. Time is our environment. Just as a fish cannot live outside of water, so we cannot live outside of time and space.

Another author says, "Over everything on earth hangs the dark shadow of time."[199] But the shadow is not time. The shadow is death, which is a loss of resources and opportunity. People imagine time is an enemy because the clock seems to move so slowly when we're having a root canal and so quickly when we're doing what we love. But time isn't the problem, the Curse is. Time isn't the enemy, death is (1 Corinthians 15:26). Time predated sin and the Curse. When the Curse is lifted, time will remain. Without the Curse, time will never work against us. We won't run out of it. Time will bring gain, not loss. The passing of time will no longer threaten us. It will bring new adventures without a sense of loss for what must end.

We'll live *with* time, no longer *under* its pressure. When we see God face-to-face, time will pass, but we'll be lost in him. We'll be busy exploring his universe, working on projects, fellowshiping with him and each other, listening to and telling great stories. We'll delight in time because it's part of what God calls "very good." It's a dimension in which we'll enjoy God.

When we say good-bye in Heaven, we'll know people won't die before we see them next. Time will no longer be an hourglass in which the sands go from a limited past to a limited future. Our future will be unlimited. We'll no longer have to "number our days" (Psalm 90:12) or redeem the time, for time won't be a diminishing resource about to end.

Theologian Henry Berkhof anticipates that time itself will be resurrected to what God created it to be:

> Time is the mould of our created human existence. Sin led to the fact that we have no time, and that we spend a hurried existence between past and future. But the consummation as the glorification of existence will not mean that we are taken out of time and delivered from time, but that time as the form of our glorified existence will also be fulfilled and glorified. Consummation means to live again in the succession of past, present, and future, but in such a way that the past moves along with us as a blessing and the future radiates through the present so that we strive without restlessness and rest without idleness, and so that, though always progressing, we are always at our destination.[200]

Buddhism, which knows no resurrection, teaches that time will be extinguished. Christianity, solidly based on a resurrection of cosmic dimensions, teaches time will go on forever. For too long we've allowed an unbiblical assumption ("there will be no time in Heaven") to obscure overwhelming biblical revelation to the contrary. This has served Satan's purposes of dehumanizing Heaven and divorcing it from the existence we know. Since we cannot desire what we can't imagine, this misunderstanding has robbed us of desire for Heaven.

CHAPTER 27

WILL THE NEW EARTH HAVE SUN, MOON, OCEANS, AND WEATHER?

As we've seen, there will be direct continuity between this earth and the New Earth. But the Bible includes some passages that have led people to believe that the New Earth will have no sun, no moon, and no seas. Will that be the case? If so, won't we miss those aspects of our current lives?

WILL THE NEW EARTH HAVE A SUN AND MOON?

People who think the New Earth won't have a sun and moon generally refer to three passages:

> The city does not need the sun or the moon to shine on it, for the glory of God gives it light, and the Lamb is its lamp. (Revelation 21:23)

> There will be no more night. They will not need the light of a lamp or the light of the sun, for the Lord God will give them light. (Revelation 22:5)

> The sun will no more be your light by day, nor will the brightness of the moon shine on you, for the Lord will be your everlasting light, and your God will be your glory. Your sun will never set again, and your moon will wane no more; the Lord will be your everlasting light, and your days of sorrow will end. Then will all your people be righteous and they will possess the land forever. (Isaiah 60:19-21)

Notice that none of these verses actually says there will be no more sun or moon. (Reread them carefully.) They say that the New Jerusalem will not *need* their light, for sun and moon will be outshone by God's glory. The third passage says that at the time when God's people will possess the land forever, the sun won't set and the moon won't wane, yet neither will dominate the sky because of God's brighter light.

The emphasis isn't on the elimination of sun and moon, but on their being overshadowed by the greater light of God. Who needs a reading lamp when standing under the noonday sun? Who needs the sun when the light of God's presence pervades the city? The sun is local and limited, easily obscured by clouds. God's light is universal, all pervading; nothing can obstruct it.

God himself will be the light source for the New Jerusalem, restoring the original pattern that existed in Genesis 1 before the creation of sun and moon. Light preceded the light-holders, sun and moon, and apparently God's very being provided that light (Genesis 1:3). So it will be again—another example of how the last chapters of the Bible reestablish something from the first chapters.

Isaiah tells us, "The Lord will be your everlasting light" (60:19). But John goes further, saying, "The Lamb is its lamp" (Revelation 21:23). John tells us in his Gospel that Jesus is "the true light that gives light to every man" and the light that "shines in the darkness, but the darkness has not understood it" (John 1:9, 5). He records Christ's words, "I am the light of the world. Whoever follows me will never walk in darkness, but will have the light of life" (John 8:12). And John sees what Isaiah couldn't: The God who is the city's light is the Messiah himself.

Isaiah says to God, "Nations will come to your light, and kings to the brightness of your dawn" (Isaiah 60:3). The New Jerusalem will be a city illuminated not only by God's holiness but also by his grace.

WILL THERE BE NO MORE SUNSETS?

Some people comment, "If the New Earth will be full of the light of God, does that mean we won't see any more sunrises and sunsets?" Do you love sunrises and sunsets? Are you disappointed to think you might not see any again? Our sun is one of countless billions of suns. I think we'll see many more sunrises and sunsets, on many worlds. And when we're watching one of those spectacular sunrises, I don't think we'll wonder, *What am I missing?*

Note that the Revelation 22:5 passage quoted earlier says, "There will be no more night." Some people believe this is figurative, speaking of the moral perfection of the New Earth. Darkness is associated with crime, evil done under cover of night. Darkness is synonymous with distressed travelers unable to find their way. Prostitution, drunkenness, and idol worship often happened at night. In the modern era of electric lights, it's difficult to understand the utter dread of traveling in the dark and the threat of being locked out of the city gates that would close at night to prevent robbers, bands of marauders, or enemy soldiers from invading a city. To be outside the city at night was to be exceedingly vulnerable. This will no longer be.

Yet darkness isn't evil—God created it before the Fall (Genesis 1:5). Night is also associated with positive things: time with family after a hard day's work, opportunity to talk, rest, have dinner with loved ones, read Scripture, and pray.

Because God created the first celestial heavens to display his glory (Psalm 19:1), when he makes the new celestial heavens, they will perform this mission even better. That means *we'll have to be able to see them.* If that requires darkness, as it does now, then darkness we will have, if not on Earth, then somewhere from which we can behold God's glory in the new heavens.

I'm speculating, but I don't believe these passages demand constant and unvarying brightness, certainly not outside the New Jerusalem. There may be diffused light or twilight, without total darkness. Light may be constant in the Holy City but not necessarily in the cities and countries outside the city gates.

To view the new heavens, we might travel to the far side of the moon and other places where stargazing is unhindered by light and atmospheric distortion. Imagine the quality of telescopes that redeemed minds will design and build. We may be able to visit innumerable planets from which the wonders of the night sky can be viewed to the praise and glory of God.

How will our eyes be able to tolerate the bright light of the New Jerusalem? Our new bodies will be stronger than our present ones. We'll be designed for our highest purpose, to see God's face—brighter than the sun—without being blinded. Rather than turn away from that Light, we'll be drawn to it.

WILL THERE BE OCEANS?

One of the confusing—and to many people disappointing—statements of Scripture is that on the New Earth there will be "no longer any sea" (Revelation 21:1). When we read that, we think that there will be no more warm, inviting waters, no more surfing, tide pools, snorkeling and fun on the beach, and no more wonderful sea creatures. That's bad news.

But when Scripture says "there was no longer any sea," the core meaning is that there will be no more of the cold, treacherous waters that separate nations, destroy ships, and drown our loved ones. There will be no more creatures swallowing up seafarers and no more poisoned salt waters. That's good news.

Steven Lawson elaborates: "To the ancient peoples, the sea was frightful and fearsome, an awesome monster, a watery grave. They had no compass to guide them in the open sea. On a cloudy day, their ships were absolutely lost without the stars or the sun to guide them. Their frail ships were at the mercy of the tempestuous ocean's fearsome, angry storms. The loss of human life in the sea was beyond calculation. So the sea represented a vast barrier for nations, continents, and people groups."[201] Hence, the prospect of "no more sea" was very positive for the passage's original readers. Of course, God created the seas (Genesis 1:9-10). Like everything else he made, they were very good (Genesis 1:31). But the Curse had a devastating effect on creation. The seas as we now know them are deadly to human consumption. God's originally created seas surely wouldn't have poisoned people if they drank from them. It seems likely that the Curse resulted in the contamination of the oceans, as well as the threat to human life from floods, tidal waves, and tsunamis.

If a man would be alone, let him look at the stars. The rays that come from those heavenly worlds, will separate between him and what he touches. One might think the atmosphere was made transparent with this design, to give man, in the heavenly bodies, the perpetual presence of the sublime. Seen in the streets of cities, how great they are! If the stars should appear one night in a thousand years, how would men believe and adore; and preserve for many generations the remembrance of the city of God which had been shown! But every night come out these envoys of beauty, and light the universe with their admonishing smile.

RALPH WALDO EMERSON

Lawson also suggests there will no longer be seas because the seas as we know them are the result of God's judgment through the Flood. "Many scientists who are Christians believe that before the great flood of Noah's day, there was no sea. But in the Flood, the bottoms of the deep were opened up, allowing the release of great bodies of water, and the world was flooded. The oceans were then formed between the overturned land masses and the seas became a barrier separating what we now know to be continents, further dividing the human race. On the new earth, it appears there will be no sea because the earth will be restored to its original splendor."[202]

A case can be made that given the fallen state of nature, the salt seas function as a great antiseptic to cleanse the earth and make life possible here. The salt seas purge, cleanse, and preserve the earth. They absorb and cleanse the pollution and filth poured into them.[203] On the New Earth such cleansing will no longer be necessary.

Even if this passage means literally "no more ocean," of course this wouldn't require the absence of large bodies of water. Revelation tells us a great river flows right through the capital city (22:1-2). How much more water will there be outside the city? Flowing rivers go somewhere. We would expect lakes.

Some of the world's lakes are huge, sealike. The New Earth could have even larger lakes, especially if they have no oceans to flow into. Huge lakes could, in effect, be freshwater oceans.

Another reason I believe the New Earth will have large bodies of water is that, as I argue in chapter 39, the same animals that inhabit our current planet will inhabit the New Earth. Most animal species live underwater, not on land, and most of those live in the ocean. (It would certainly be no problem for God to refashion such creatures to live in fresh water.)

In a passage that definitely contains references to the New Earth, portions of which are cited in Revelation 21–22, Isaiah 60 says of the renewed Jerusalem, "the wealth on the seas will be brought to you, to you the riches of the nations will come" (v. 5). The passage goes on to speak of inhabited islands and their ships traveling the sea: "Surely the islands look to me; in the lead are the ships of Tarshish, bringing your sons from afar, with their silver and gold, to the honor of the Lord your God" (v. 9). Somehow the "no more sea" of Revelation 21 and the "wealth of the seas" and the great ships traveling them in Isaiah 60 are compatible.

As someone who loves to snorkel, explore ocean waters for hours at a time, and marvel at multicolored fish, great sea turtles, squid, rays, and eels, I sympathize with people's instinctive resistance to the words "there was no longer any sea." I've seen hundreds of different kinds of fish, some of them more spectacular than any land creature. I've done enough diving to know it's exhilarating, even worshipful, to be immersed in a God-made world normally beyond our reach. I remember one time snorkeling with one of my daughters, a friend, and his son. Suddenly we heard the melodic sounds of whales calling to each other. The sounds were so loud we expected whales to appear any moment. We floated, nearly motionless, just listening to musical beauty and power that defy words. I felt closer to God during that twenty minutes than at nearly any other time in my life.

I predict the New Earth will include large bodies of water where we'll dive, perhaps without tanks or masks. Can you imagine effortlessly holding your breath for hours? Imagine fresh water we can freely drink of, water in which we can open wide our eyes and play with God's creatures of the deep. Instead of salt water, it will be pure, refreshing, life-giving "sweet" water, just like the ocean water the noble mouse Reepicheep found in the waves near Aslan's country.[204]

WILL THERE BE SEASONS AND VARYING WEATHER?

Some people have never thought about Heaven's weather because they don't think of Heaven as a real place, certainly not on the New Earth. Or they assume the New Earth will have bright sunshine, no clouds, no rain . . . forever.

In a passage that promises rescue, security, and no more famine or fear for his people, God says, "I will bless them and the places surrounding my hill. I will send down showers in season; there will be showers of blessing. The trees of the field will yield their fruit and the ground will yield its crops" (Ezekiel 34:26-27).

Is rain a bad thing? No. It's good. We'll see trees bearing fruit on the New Earth. Will they be rained on? Presumably. Will rain turn to snow in higher elevations? Why not? If there's snow, will people play in it, throw snowballs, sled down hillsides? Of course. Just as resurrected people will still have eyes, ears, and feet, a resurrected Earth will have rain, snow, and wind.

As I write these words on a cold December day, a strong wind is blowing. Nearly bare trees are surrendering their last leaves. A row of fifty-foot-high trees, a stunning bluish green, are bending and flailing. It's a powerful, magnificent sight that moves me to worship God. We're expecting our first winter snow. The feeling of warmth and serenity here in the protection of our house is wonderful. It makes me ponder the protecting, sheltering, secure hand of God. I've often had similar feelings during pounding storms. Lightning, thunder, rain, and snow all declare God's greatness (Job 37:3-6). Is there any reason to conclude such things will not be part of the New Earth? None. Of course, no one will die or be hurt by such weather. No one will perish in a flood or be killed by lightning, just as no one will drown in the river of life.

When we live on the New Earth, could we go hiking in a snowstorm without fear of trauma or death? Could we jump off a cliff into a river three hundred feet below? Could we stand in an open field in flashing lightning and roaring thunder and experience the exhilaration of God's powerful hand? Must the New Earth be tamed, stripped of high peaks, deserts, waterfalls, and thunderstorms because these sometimes caused pain and death in this world? Nature, including variations in climate, will be a source of joy and pleasure, not destruction. If we stand amazed now at the wonders of God's great creation, we'll be even more amazed at the greater wonders of that greater creation.

I love the seasons, each of them. The crisp fall air, the brilliant yellows, oranges, and reds, the long good-bye to summer. The snow blankets of winter, the freshness and erupting beauty of spring, the inviting warmth of summer. Who are all those from? "God, who gives autumn and spring rains in season" (Jeremiah 5:24).

Will there still be seasons on the New Earth? Why wouldn't there be? Some people argue that because fall and winter are about dying, we won't experience them in Heaven because there will be no death there. I'm not convinced that seasons and their distinctive beauties are the result of the Fall. God is depicted as the seasons' Creator, and we're not told they didn't predate the Fall (Genesis 8:22). The "no more death" of Revelation 21 applies to living creatures, people and animals, but not necessarily to all vegetation. Even if it does, God can certainly create a cycle of seasonable beauty apart from death.

WILL WE MISS THINGS FROM THE OLD EARTH?

Have you ever bought an economy ticket for a flight but because of overbooking or some other reason been upgraded to first class? Did you regret the upgrade? Did you spend your time wondering, *What am I missing out on by not being in the back of the plane?*

The liabilities of economy class are removed in first class, but the assets aren't. You go from little legroom to lots of legroom, from an adequate chair to a comfortable one, maybe even one with a footrest. Rather than just a sandwich, you get a meal, on real plates. The flight attendants keep filling your cup, give you a great dessert, and offer a hot hand towel. In other words, it's not just that the bad things about economy seats are minimized; it's that all the good things are made better.

The upgrade from the old Earth to the New Earth will be vastly superior to that from economy to first class. (It may feel more like an upgrade to first class from the baggage hold.) Gone will be sin, the Curse, death, and suffering. In every way we will recognize that the New Earth is better—in no sense could it ever be worse.

If we would miss something from our old lives and the old Earth, it would be available to us on the New Earth. Why? Because we will experience all God intends for us. He fashions us to want precisely what he will give us, so what he gives us will be exactly what we want.

WHAT WILL OUR LIVES BE LIKE?

CHAPTER 28

WILL WE BE OURSELVES?

I n Dickens's *A Christmas Carol,* Ebenezer Scrooge was terrified when he saw a phantom.

> "Who are you?" Scrooge asked.
> "Ask me who I was," the ghost replied.
> "Who were you then?" said Scrooge. . . .
> "In life I was your partner, Jacob Marley."[205]

Disembodied spirits aren't who they once were. Continuity of identity ultimately requires bodily resurrection.

In the movie *2010,* David Bowman appears in ghostly form. When asked who he is, he replies, "I *was* David Bowman."

Unless we grasp the resurrection, we won't believe that we'll continue to be ourselves in the afterlife. We are physical beings. If the eternal Heaven is a disembodied state, then our humanity will either be diminished or transcended, and we will never again be ourselves after we die.

Contrast Jacob Marley and David Bowman with Job and Jesus. Job said, "In my flesh I will see God; . . . I, and not another" (Job 19:26-27). The risen Christ said, "Look at my hands and my feet. It is I myself! Touch me and see; a ghost does not have flesh and bones, as you see I have" (Luke 24:39).

Jesus called people in Heaven by name, including Lazarus in the present Heaven (Luke 16:25) and Abraham, Isaac, and Jacob in the eternal Heaven (Matthew 8:11). A name denotes a distinct identity, an individual. The fact that people in Heaven can be called by the same name they had on Earth demonstrates they remain the same people. In Heaven I'll be Randy Alcorn—without the bad parts—forever. If you know Jesus, you'll be you—without the bad parts—forever.

WILL WE BE UNIQUE?

Just as our genetic code and fingerprints are unique now, we should expect the same of our new bodies. Individual identity is an essential aspect of personhood. God is the creator of individual identities and personalities. He makes no two snowflakes, much less two people, alike. Not even "identical twins" are identical. Individuality preceded sin and the Curse. Individuality was God's plan from the beginning.

Heaven's inhabitants don't simply rejoice over nameless multitudes coming to God. They rejoice over each and every person (Luke 15:4-7, 10). That's a powerful affirmation of Heaven's view of each person as a separate individual whose life is observed and cared for one at a time.

When Moses and Elijah appeared out of Heaven to stand with Christ at his transfiguration, the disciples with Christ recognized Moses and Elijah as the distinct individuals they were, the same men they were on Earth, infused with holiness.

When we're told we'll sit at a banquet and eat with Abraham and Isaac and others, we will be sitting, eating beside, talking with, and laughing with not a general assembly, but particular individuals (Matthew 8:11).

In his book *The Problem of Pain*, C. S. Lewis expressed his awe at the diversity with which God created us: "If He had no use for all these differences, I do not see why He should have created more souls than one. . . . Your soul has a curious shape because it is a hollow made to fit a particular swelling in the infinite contours of the divine substance, or a key to unlock one of the doors in the house with many mansions. For it is not humanity in the abstract that is to be saved, but you—you, the individual reader, John Stubbs or Janet Smith. . . . Your place in heaven will seem to be made for you and you alone, because you were made for it—made for it stitch by stitch as a glove is made for a hand."[206]

What makes you *you*? It's not only your body but also your memory, personality traits, gifts, passions, preferences, and interests. In the final resurrection, I believe all of these facets will be restored and amplified, untarnished by sin and the Curse.

Do you remember a time when you really felt good about yourself? Not in pride or arrogance, but when you sensed you honored God, helped the needy, were faithful, humble, and servant-hearted, like Jesus? Do you remember when you encouraged someone? when you experienced who you were meant to be? when you were running or swimming or working and felt you were strong enough to go on forever (even though later you could hardly get out of bed)? That was a little taste of who you'll be in Heaven.

As C. S. Lewis expressed it in his space trilogy, we have become "bent" (sinful) versions of what God intended. Your deceitfulness, laziness, lust, deafness, disability, and disease are not the real you. They are temporary perversions that will be eliminated. They're the cancer that the Great Physician will surgically remove. His redemptive work is such that never again will they return.

When you're on the New Earth, for the first time you'll be the person God created you to be.

WILL WE BECOME ANGELS?

I'm often asked if people, particularly children, become angels when they die. The answer is no. Death is a relocation of the same person from one place to another. The place changes, but the person remains the same. The same person who becomes absent from his or her body becomes present with the Lord (2 Corinthians 5:8). The person who departs is the one who goes to be with Christ (Philippians 1:23).

Angels are angels. Humans are humans. Angels are beings with their own histories and memories, with distinct identities, reflected in the fact that they have personal names, such as Michael and Gabriel. Under God's direction, they serve us on Earth (Hebrews 1:14). Michael the archangel serves under God, and the other angels, in various positions, serve under Michael (Daniel 10:13; Revelation 12:7). In Heaven human beings will govern angels (1 Corinthians 6:2-3).

The fact that angels have served us on Earth will make meeting them in Heaven particularly fascinating. They may have been with us from childhood, protecting us, standing by us, doing whatever they could on our behalf (Matthew 18:10). They may have witnessed virtually every moment of our lives. Besides God himself, no one could know us better.

What will it be like not only to have them show us around the intermediate Heaven but also to walk and talk with them on the New Earth? What stories will they tell us, including what really happened that day at the lake thirty-five years ago when we almost drowned? They've guarded us, gone to fierce battle for us, served as God's agents in answer to prayers. How great it will be to get to know these brilliant ancient creatures who've lived with God from their creation. We'll consult them as well as advise them, realizing they too can learn from us, God's image-bearers. Will an angel who guarded us be placed under our management?

If we really believed angels were with us daily, here and now, wouldn't it motivate us to make wiser choices? Wouldn't we feel an accountability to holy beings who serve us as God's representatives?

Despite what some popular books say, there's no biblical basis for trying to make contact with angels now. We're to ask God, not angels, for wisdom (James 1:5). As Scripture says and as I portray in my novels *Dominion, Lord*

Foulgrin's Letters, and *The Ishbane Conspiracy*, Satan's servants can "masquerade as servants of righteousness" and bring us messages that appear to be from God but aren't (2 Corinthians 11:15).

Nevertheless, because Scripture teaches that one or more of God's angels may be in the room with me now, every once in a while I say "Thank you" out loud. And sometimes I add, "I look forward to meeting you." I can't wait to hear their stories.

We won't be angels, but we'll be *with* angels—and that'll be far better.

WILL WE HAVE EMOTIONS?

In Scripture, God is said to enjoy, love, laugh, take delight, and rejoice, as well as be angry, happy, jealous, and glad. Rather than viewing these actions and descriptors as mere anthropomorphisms, we should consider that our emotions are *derived from* God's. While we should always avoid creating God in our image, the fact remains we are created in his. Therefore, our emotions are a reflection of and sometimes (because of our sin) a *distortion of* God's emotions. To be like God means to have and express emotions. Hence, we should expect that in Heaven emotions will exist for God's glory and our good.

In Heaven we'll exercise not only intellect but also emotions (Revelation 6:10; 7:10). Even angels respond emotionally (Revelation 7:11-12; 18:1-24). Emotions are part of our God-created humanity, not sinful baggage to be destroyed. We should anticipate pure and accurately informed emotions guided by reality. Our present emotions are skewed by sin, but they'll be delivered from it.

Will we cry in Heaven? The Bible says, "He will wipe away every tear from their eyes; and there will no longer be *any* death; there will no longer be *any* mourning, or crying, or pain" (Revelation 21:4, NASB, emphasis added). These are the tears of suffering over sin and death, the tears of oppressed people, the cries of the poor, the widow, the orphaned, the unborn, and the persecuted. God will wipe away the tears of racial injustice. Such crying shall be no more.

The verse primarily addresses not tears per se but the tears coming from injustice and sorrow. Hence, we might shed tears of joy in Heaven. Can you imagine joy flooding your eyes as you meet Christ, for example, and as you're reunited with loved ones? I can.

We know that people in Heaven have lots of feelings—all good ones. We're told of banquets, feasts, and singing. People will laugh there (Luke 6:21). Feasting, singing, and rejoicing involve feelings. Feelings aren't part of the Curse; they're part of how God made human beings from the beginning. Our present emotions are bent by sin, but they will forever be straightened again when God removes the Curse.

Many people have a hard time with their feelings. In Heaven we'll be free to feel intensely, never afraid of our feelings.

One writer says of our life in Heaven, "We will live on a perpetual and exhilarating high akin to the feeling we have now when we shout 'Yes!' at a great victory."[207] I'm not so sure. Living constantly at a fever pitch of exhilaration would eclipse special moments of joy. Certainly in Heaven we won't experience sadness, but that doesn't require each moment's joy to be exactly equal to the rest. Will our emotions be more intense sometimes than others? I believe they will. We experience an ebb and flow to our lives. That rhythm is part of being human and finite—and we'll always be both.

WILL WE HAVE DESIRES?

We'll have many desires in Heaven, but they won't be *unholy* desires. Everything we want will be good. Our desires will please God. All will be right with the world, nothing forbidden. When a father cooks steaks on the barbecue grill, he wants his family to listen to them sizzle and eagerly desire to eat them. God created our desires and every object we desire. He loves it when our mouths water for what he's prepared for us. When we enjoy it, we'll be enjoying him.

One of the greatest things about Heaven is that we'll no longer have to battle our desires. They'll always be pure, attending to their proper objects. We'll enjoy food without gluttony and eating disorders. We'll express admiration and affection without lust, fornication, or betrayal. Those simply won't exist.

I tried to express that in my novel *Safely Home*. When one of the characters reaches Heaven, he has a conversation with the King: "I feel like I'm drinking from the Source of the Stream. Does this mean I'll feel no more longing?" The King—the Source—replies, "You will have the sweet longing of desire that can be fulfilled and shall be, again and again and again. [Heaven] is not the absence of longing but its fulfillment. Heaven is not the absence of itches; it is the satisfying scratch for every itch."[208]

Not long after we finish one meal, we start looking forward to the next. When a fun ride is over, we want to go on it again. Anticipation, desire, is a big part of joy. Since we'll be resurrected people in a resurrected universe, why would that change?

Christianity is unique in its perspective of our desires, teaching that they will be sanctified and fulfilled on the New Earth. Conversely, the Buddhist concept of deliverance teaches that one day people's desires will be eliminated.

That's radically different. Christianity teaches that Jesus takes our sins away while redeeming our desires. Desire is an essential part of humanity, a part that God built into people before sin cast its dark shadow on earth. I'm looking forward to having my desires redeemed. (Even now, as redeemed children of God, we get tastes of that, don't we?)

> When Christ calls me Home I shall go with the gladness of a boy bounding away from school.
>
> **ADONIRAM JUDSON**

Won't it be wonderful to be free from uncertainty about our desires? We often wonder, *Is it good or bad for me to want this thing or that award or his approval or her appreciation?* Sometimes I don't know which desires are right and which aren't. I long to be released from the uncertainty and the doubt. I long to be capable of always wanting what's good and right.

In C. S. Lewis's *The Last Battle*, his characters arrive in New Narnia. Lucy says, "I've a feeling we've got to the country where everything is allowed."[209] Augustine expressed a similar thought: "Love God and do as you please."[210] We will love God wholeheartedly—and therefore will want to do only what pleases him.

God placed just one restriction on Adam and Eve in Eden, and when they disregarded it, the universe unraveled. On the New Earth, that test will no longer be before us. God's law, the expression of his attributes, will be written on our hearts (Hebrews 8:10). No rules will be needed, for our hearts will be given over to God. David said, "Delight yourself in the Lord and he will give you the desires of your heart" (Psalm 37:4). Why? Because when we delight in God and abide in him, *whatever we want will be exactly what he wants for us.*

What we *should* do will at last be identical with what we *want* to do. There will be no difference between duty and joy.

WILL WE MAINTAIN OUR OWN IDENTITIES?

You will be *you* in Heaven. Who else would you be? If Bob, a man on Earth, is no longer Bob when he gets to Heaven, then, in fact, Bob did not go to Heaven. If when I arrive in Heaven I'm not the same person with the same identity, history, and memory, then *I* didn't go to Heaven.

The resurrected Jesus did not become someone else; he remained who he was before his resurrection: "It is I myself!" (Luke 24:39). In John's Gospel, Jesus deals with Mary, Thomas, and Peter in very personal ways, drawing on his previous knowledge of them (John 20:10-18, 24-29; 21:15-22). His knowledge and relationships from his pre-resurrected state carried over. When Thomas said, "My Lord and my God," he knew he was speaking to the same

Jesus he'd followed. When John said, "It is the Lord," he meant, "It's really him—the Jesus we have known" (John 21:4-7).

If we weren't ourselves in the afterlife, then we couldn't be held accountable for what we did in this life. The Judgment would be meaningless. If Barbara is no longer Barbara, she can't be rewarded or held accountable for anything Barbara did. She'd have to say, "But that wasn't me." The doctrines of judgment and eternal rewards depend on people's retaining their distinct identities from this life to the next.

Bruce Milne writes, "We can banish all fear of being absorbed into the 'All' which Buddhism holds before us, or reincarnated in some other life form as in the post-mortem prospect of Hinduism. . . . The self with which we were endowed by the Creator in his gift of life to us, the self whose worth was secured forever in the self-substitution of God for us on the cross, *that self* will endure into eternity. Death cannot destroy us."[211]

Some people read "you may participate in the divine nature" (2 Peter 1:4) and imagine that we will all become indistinguishable from God. But to imagine we'll lose our personal identities is a Hindu belief, not a Christian one. The verse in 2 Peter means that we're covered with Christ's righteousness. We'll participate in God's holiness yet fully retain our God-crafted individuality.

Our own personal history and identity will endure from one Earth to the next. "'As the new heavens and the new earth that I make will endure before me,' declares the Lord, 'so will your name and descendants endure'" (Isaiah 66:22). Jesus said to his disciples, "*I* will not drink of this fruit of the vine from now on until that day when *I* drink *it* anew with *you* in my Father's kingdom" (Matthew 26:29, emphasis added). The same Jesus will drink the same wine with the same disciples. It isn't that what *used to be us* will commune with *what used to be* Abraham, Isaac, and Jacob. Rather, we, the same people but fully cleansed, will eat at a table with the one and only Abraham, Isaac, and Jacob (Matthew 8:11).

In Heaven will we be called by our present names? The names of God's children are written in the Lamb's Book of Life (Revelation 20:15; 21:27). I believe those are our earthly names. God recognized as valid the names Adam gave the animals. God calls people by their earthly names, the names given by their parents. He calls people in Heaven by those same names—Abraham, Isaac, and Jacob, for instance. The names of the twelve sons of Israel and of the apostles, apparently the same names we know them by, are written on the city's gates and the foundations of its walls (Revelation 21:12-14). Our names reflect our individuality. To have the same name written in Heaven that was ours on Earth speaks of the continuity between this life and the next.

In addition to our earthly names, we'll receive new names in Heaven (Isaiah 62:2; 65:15; Revelation 2:17; 3:12). New names don't invalidate the old ones. Many people had multiple names in Scripture: Jacob is also Israel; Simon is also Peter; Saul is also Paul.

Imagine a beautiful rose garden. It's been perfectly designed and cultivated. But the rosebushes become diseased. The garden becomes a tangled mass. It's a sad, deteriorated remnant of the glorious garden it once was. Then the gardener determines to reclaim his garden. Day after day he prunes, waters, and fertilizes each bush. His desire isn't simply to restore the garden to its original beauty; it's to make it far more beautiful than ever.

When the gardener is done and the roses are thriving, beautiful, and fragrant, is the rose garden the same as it was? Is each individual rose the same? Yes and no. It's the same rose garden, restored to its previous beauty and beyond. Yet to look at it, it's hard to believe these are the same roses that were once a withered, tangled mess.

This is a picture of Creation, Fall, and Resurrection. When God is finished, we'll be ourselves without the sin—meaning that we'll be the best we can be.

WILL WE LOSE OURSELVES?

A man wrote me expressing his fear of losing his identity in Heaven: "Will being like Jesus mean the obliteration of self?" He was afraid that we'd all be alike, that he and his treasured friends would lose their distinguishing traits and eccentricities that make them special. But he needn't worry. We can all be like Jesus in character yet remain very different from each other in personality.

Distinctiveness is God's creation, not Satan's. What makes us unique will survive. In fact, much of our uniqueness may be uncovered for the first time.

At the very end of *Mere Christianity*, C. S. Lewis writes, "Until you have given up your self to Him you will not have a real self. Sameness is to be found most among the most 'natural' men, not among those who surrender to Christ. How monotonously alike all the great tyrants and conquerors have been: how gloriously different are the saints. . . . Nothing in you that has not died will ever be raised from the dead. Look for yourself, and you will find in the long run only hatred, loneliness, despair, rage, ruin, and decay. But look for Christ and you will find Him, and with Him everything else thrown in."[212]

CHAPTER 29

WHAT WILL OUR BODIES BE LIKE?

As we saw in chapter 11, our resurrected bodies will be real physical bodies, just as Christ's was and is. But what will our bodies look like? How will they function?

Our resurrection bodies will be free of the curse of sin, redeemed, and restored to their original beauty and purpose that goes back to Eden. The only bodies we've ever known are weak and diseased remnants of the original bodies God made for humans. But the bodies we'll have on the New Earth, in our resurrection, will be even more glorious than those of Adam and Eve.

WILL WE ALL HAVE BEAUTIFUL BODIES?

I heard someone say that in Heaven we'll all have sculpted bodies, without any fat. The comment reflects a yearning for our bodies to be healthy, fit, and beautiful.

I expect our bodies will be good-looking, but not with a weight-lifting, artificial-implant, skin-tuck, tanning-booth sort of beauty. The sculpted physique our culture admires would be regarded as freakish in other places and times. Some cultures consider what we call slimness as unhealthy and what we consider plumpness as a sign of vitality and prosperity. The same genetic tendencies that make some people unattractive by one culture's standards make them attractive in another.

Our new bodies, I expect, will have a natural beauty that won't need cosmetics or touch-ups. As for fat, because God created fat as part of our bodies, we'll surely have some, but in healthy proportion.

The most beautiful person you've ever seen is under the Curse, a shadow of the beauty that once characterized humanity. If we saw Adam and Eve as they were in Eden, they would likely take our breath away. If they would have seen us as we are now, they likely would have been filled with shock and pity.

God will decide what our perfect bodies look like, but we certainly shouldn't assume they'll all look alike. Different heights and weights seem as likely as different skin colors. Racial identities will continue (Revelation 5:9; 7:9), and this involves a genetic carryover from the old body to the new. I'm speculating, but it seems likely that people whose bodies were tall will have tall resurrection bodies; those who were short will likely be short. The naturally thin will be thin, and the naturally thick will be thick. But all of these sizes will be healthy and appealing, untouched by the Curse or disease or restrictions, and we'll each be perfectly happy with the form God designed for us.

Some people consider this topic unspiritual, but one of the church's greatest theologians, Augustine, didn't. He says in *The City of God*: "[The body] shall be of that size which it either had attained or should have attained in the flower of its youth, and shall enjoy the beauty that arises from preserving symmetry and proportion in all its members . . . overgrown and emaciated persons need not fear that they shall be in heaven of such a figure as they would not be even in this world if they could help it."[213]

We won't overeat or undereat on the New Earth. With health, vitality, and freedom, we'll all get plenty of activity. Will calories affect us the same way they do now? I don't know. But we certainly won't experience heart disease, diabetes, asthma, osteoporosis, arthritis, cancer, MS, HIV, or anything else that consumes the body. (No more insulin injections for me!)

Most people aren't longing so much for a perfect body as for the sense of well-being and approval they think goes with it. Of this we can be certain—no matter what we look like, our bodies will please the Lord, ourselves, and others. We won't gaze into the mirror wishing for a different nose or different cheeks, ears, or teeth. The sinless beauty of the inner person will overflow into the beauty of the outer person. We'll feel neither insecurity nor arrogance. We won't attempt to hide or impress. We won't have to *try* to look beautiful—we *will* be beautiful.

We'll be most grateful not about our appearance but our health and strength. We'll know that the Artist fashioned us just as he desired and that we'll never lose the health and beauty he's graciously given us.

WILL OUR RESURRECTION BODIES HAVE FIVE SENSES?

God designed us with five senses. They're part of what makes us human. Our resurrection bodies will surely have these senses. I expect they will increase in their power and sensitivity.

We'll stand on the New Earth and see it, feel it, smell it, taste its fruits, and hear its sounds. Not figuratively. Literally. We know this because we're promised resurrection bodies like Christ's. He saw and heard and felt and, as he cooked and ate fish, he presumably smelled and tasted it. We will too.

Heaven's delights will stretch our glorified senses to their limits. How will things look, and how far away will we be able to see them? Will our eyes be able to function alternately as telescopes and microscopes? Will our ears serve as sound-gathering disks? Will our sense of smell be far more acute, able to identify a favorite flower—or person—miles away, so we can follow the scent to the source?

Will our eyes be able to see new colors? We currently can't see ultraviolet and infrared, but we know they're real. Doesn't it seem likely that our resurrected eyes will see them? What did Adam and Eve see that we can't? Although we don't know the answers to these questions, it seems reasonable to suggest all of our resurrected senses will function at levels we've never known. David prayed, "I praise you because I am fearfully and wonderfully made" (Psalm 139:14). How much more will we praise God for the wonders of our resurrection bodies?

As we'll see in the following chapter, Scripture speaks repeatedly about eating in Heaven. What will our resurrected taste buds be able to taste? The best food here on Earth is tainted by the Curse. Our taste buds are still defective. Think of the best meal you've ever eaten, the best dessert you've ever tasted. Good as those were, they were just a hint of what's to come—a good enough hint to make us long for Heaven.

To be restored to the sensory abilities of Adam and Eve would be thrilling enough. But it seems likely our resurrected bodies will surpass theirs. What God remakes, he only improves.

God could add new senses to our old ones. What do I mean? I don't know—how could I explain a sense I've never experienced? If we'd never known sight, how could we sense what we were missing? If you'd never been able to smell lilacs or taste blueberry pie or hear Beethoven's Fifth Symphony, how would you grasp what it means to smell or taste or hear such things?

On the New Earth, I think we'll continually be discovering, to our delight, what we never knew existed, what we've been missing all our lives. No joy is greater than the joy of discovery. The God who always surpasses our expectations will forever give us more of himself and his creation to discover.

WILL OUR NEW BODIES HAVE NEW ABILITIES?

When it comes to doing what God wants, and what we want, sometimes our bodies fail us. The disciples intended to pray in Gethsemane but fell asleep. Jesus said to them, "The spirit is willing, but the body is weak" (Matthew 26:41). Our resurrection bodies, however, will never fail us. They'll work in perfect concert with our resurrected minds.

We should anticipate an unprecedented harmony of mind and body. Sometimes we get hints of this. H. A. Williams says, "When I play a game well, I have for that limited period of time an experience of the body's resurrection. For there is no hint of a dualism between mind and body with either of them trying to oppress or bully the other. I bring to the game my total undivided self."[214]

Christ's resurrection body had an ability to appear suddenly, apparently coming through a locked door to the apostles (John 20:19) and "disappearing" from the sight of the two disciples at Emmaus (Luke 24:31). When Christ left the earth, he defied gravity and ascended into the air (Acts 1:9).

It's possible that the risen Christ, who is man yet God, has certain physical abilities we won't have. Appearing and disappearing could be a limited expression of his omnipresence, and his ascension might be something our bodies couldn't imitate. On the one hand, because we're told in multiple passages that our resurrection bodies will be like Christ's, it may be possible at times to transcend the present laws of physics and/or travel in some way we're not now capable of. On the other hand, it's our God-given human nature to be embodied creatures existing in space and time. So it's likely that the same laws of physics that governed Adam and Eve will govern us. We can't be sure, but either way it will be wonderful.

We don't know the glorious plans God has for our bodies. We may have a whale's ability to dive or an eagle's ability to fly. Maybe we'll run like a cheetah or climb a mountain like a goat. (And who knows what cheetahs and goats may be able to do?)

Still, we shouldn't assume too much about flying and dematerializing in light of the fact that the eternal city will have streets and gates, implying normal ground traffic. Perhaps as our present inability to fly led to the invention of airplanes, our limitations as finite beings even in our resurrection will inspire us to exercise dominion over our environment by creating and perfecting new transportation modes. Perhaps some of what's been long dreamed of in science fiction awaits us in the new universe.

WILL OUR BODIES SHINE?

Some people have asked me if our resurrected bodies will shine. They cite two passages: "The righteous will shine like the sun in the kingdom of their Father" (Matthew 13:43) and "Those who have insight will shine brightly like the brightness of the expanse of heaven, and those who lead the many to righteousness, like the stars forever and ever" (Daniel 12:3, NASB).

On the one hand, Jesus didn't have a halo after his resurrection, and there's no reason to believe we will either. Christ's body appeared so earthly and normal that the disciples on the road to Emmaus didn't notice he was the resurrected Lord (Luke 24:13-24). However, at this point he was not yet glorified.

During Christ's transfiguration, his clothing "became as bright as a flash of lightning" (Luke 9:29). Since this portrays Christ as King, it makes sense to think he will literally shine in his kingdom on the New Earth. John says of the city, "the Lamb is its lamp" (Revelation 22:23). As noted earlier, John saw Christ in the present Heaven as a powerful shining being, not someone who would blend into a crowd (Revelation 1:12-18). Moses and Elijah, who joined Christ on the mountain, "appeared in glorious splendor" (Luke 9:31). After Moses received the Ten Commandments from God on the mountain, Moses' face shone (Exodus 34:29-30).

Many believe these descriptors are figures of speech. Yet in some cases (including Moses') it was clearly literal. Since God himself is consistently portrayed as existing in brilliant light, it shouldn't surprise us to think that in his presence we too will partake of his brightness. I believe that as resurrected beings, we will indeed bear this physical evidence of being God's image-bearers and living in God's presence. To be glorified appears to mean that, among other things, we may literally shine.

> This earthly body is slow and heavy in all its motions, listless and soon tired with action. But our heavenly bodies shall be as fire; as active and as nimble as our thoughts are.
>
> **BENJAMIN CALAMY**

If this seems hard to imagine, think of a person with drab, grayish, malnourished skin, and then imagine the same person as vibrant and healthy. Couldn't you say the person shines? Have you heard it said of someone "she's radiant"? I've met people so full of Jesus that they seem to have a physical brightness. If God himself is bright, then it seems appropriate that we, his image-bearers, will reflect his brightness. Now, moving beyond that analogy of our present condition, imagine people in the very presence of God, who are so righteous, so beautiful, so devoid of sin and darkness, so permeated by the very righteousness of God, that they have a literal physical radiance. That's not so hard to imagine, is it?

Shining speaks of glory, the outward display of greatness and majesty. *Glory* is a word associated with rulers. Kings had glory. We understandably hesitate to attribute glory to ourselves, but God doesn't hesitate to ascribe glory to us. As God's children we *should* bear his likeness. It's he, not we, who declares that we are royalty—kings and queens who will reign with Christ.

A. B. Caneday reminds us, "God is the original; we are the organic image, the living copy. We do not rightly speak of God as King by projecting onto him regal imagery because we think it is fitting for God. Rather, bowing before God who has dominion is proper, for man as king over creation, is the image of kingship; God, the true king, is the reality that casts the image of the earthly king."[215]

Hence, our glory as lesser kings and queens will serve to magnify his greater glory as the King of kings. We won't absorb and keep the glory given us, but we will reflect it and emanate it toward its proper object: Christ himself. This is evident in the fact that God's worshiping children will "lay their crowns before the throne" (Revelation 4:10).

What prepares us to participate in God's glory? Our current sufferings (Romans 8:17-18; 1 Peter 5:1-4). "For our light and momentary troubles are achieving for us an eternal glory that far outweighs them all" (2 Corinthians 4:17). Provided we draw our strength from Christ, the greater our troubles now, the greater our glory then.

WILL OUR BODIES BE PERFECT?

Whenever I spend time with severely handicapped people—physically, mentally, or both—I'm keenly aware of how wonderful it will be to have resurrected bodies. My friend David O'Brien is a brilliant man trapped in a body that groans for redemption. His cerebral palsy will be gone the moment he leaves this world for the present Heaven, but the biggest treat will be at his resurrection, when he will have a new body, forever free of disease. I picture David never having to repeat himself because others don't understand him. I see him running through fields on the New Earth. I look forward to running beside David . . . and probably behind him.

I often think of how paraplegics, quadriplegics, and people who have known constant pain will walk, run, jump, and laugh in the New Earth. Believers who are blind now will gawk at the New Earth's wonders. What a special pleasure for them.

Joni Eareckson Tada, a quadriplegic, says,

> I still can hardly believe it. I, with shriveled, bent fingers, atrophied muscles, gnarled knees, and no feeling from the shoulders down, will one day have a new body, light, bright, and clothed in righteousness—powerful and dazzling. Can you imagine the hope this gives someone spinal-cord injured like me? Or someone who is cerebral palsied, brain-injured, or who has multiple sclerosis? Imagine the hope this gives someone who is manic-depressive. No other religion, no other

philosophy promises new bodies, hearts, and minds. Only in the Gospel of Christ do hurting people find such incredible hope.[216]

Joni tells of speaking to a class of mentally handicapped Christians. They thought it was great when she said she was going to get a new body. But then she added, "And *you're* going to get new minds." The class broke out in cheers and applause. They knew just what they wanted—new minds.

My body and mind, for the moment, may be relatively healthy. But as an insulin-dependent diabetic, I've known what it is for both my body and my mind to fail me. They suffer under the Curse enough that I too know just what I want—a new body and a new mind, without sin, suffering and incapacity. Every year that goes by, I long more to be a resurrected person and to live on the resurrected Earth, with my resurrected brothers and sisters, and above all, with my Lord—the resurrected Jesus.

WILL WE BE MALE OR FEMALE?

One book about Heaven claims, "[T]here will be no male and female human beings. We shall all be children of God and sex will be no part of our nature."[217] The same book says, "Men will no longer be men nor will women be women."[218]

Similarly, another book says of those in Heaven, "[T]hey have reached that androgynous condition in which sex distinctions are transcended, or rather, in which the qualities of both sexes are blended together."[219]

Some people try to prove there will be no gender in Heaven by citing Paul's statement that in Christ there is neither "male nor female" (Galatians 3:28). But Paul refers to something that's already true on Earth: the equality of men and women in Christ. The issue isn't the obliteration of sexuality (you don't lose your gender at conversion).

Was Jesus genderless after his resurrection? Of course not. No one mistook him for a woman—or as androgynous. He's referred to with male pronouns.

We'll never be genderless because human bodies aren't genderless. The point of the resurrection is that we will have real human bodies essentially linked to our original ones. Gender is a God-created aspect of humanity.

In my novel *Deadline*, Finney addresses this matter with the angel Zyor:

> "But I am still a man here, and everyone I see is clearly male or female, more distinctly in fact than on earth. I had thought perhaps there would be no gender here. I had read that we would all be . . . like angels, like you."

Zyor looked surprised.

"You are like us in that you do not marry and bear children here. But as for your being a man, what else would you be? Elyon may unmake what men make, but he does not unmake what he makes. He made you male, as he made your mother and wife and daughters female. Gender is not merely a component of your being to be added in or extracted and discarded. It is an essential part of who you are."[220]

WILL WE WEAR CLOTHES?

Because Adam and Eve were naked and unashamed, some argue that in Heaven we won't need to wear clothes. But even in the present Heaven, before the final Resurrection, people are depicted as wearing clothes, white robes that depict our righteousness in Christ (Revelation 3:4; 6:11). It appears we'll wear clothes—not because there will be shame or temptation, but perhaps because they will enhance our appearance and comfort.

Wearing robes might strike us as foreign or formal. But to first-century readers, anything but robes would have seemed strange. Why? Because robes were what they normally wore. Rather than conclude that we'll all wear robes, a better deduction is that we'll all dress normally, as we did on the old earth. Am I saying some people will wear jeans, shorts, T-shirts, polo shirts, or flip-flops? Well, wouldn't those be just as normal for some twenty-first-century people as robes and sandals were for first-century people?

Robes weren't reserved for formal events; they were part of everyday garb. Of course, we might sometimes wear more and less formal clothes, for certain kinds of events. There's no indication that we'll have only one set of clothes to choose from.

Will we all wear white clothing? The white clothes may depict our righteousness (Revelation 7:9), as they did Christ's in his transfiguration. The emphasis on white may relate to cleanliness, which was extremely hard to maintain in that culture. Remarkably, the only person depicted in Heaven as wearing a robe that isn't white is Jesus Christ: "He is dressed in a robe dipped in blood" (Revelation 19:13). Just as Jesus wore clothes after his resurrection on the old Earth, he wears them now in the present Heaven, and will presumably wear them on the New Earth.

Will white be the only clothing color? No. There are angels wearing golden sashes (Revelation 15:6). Because resurrected people retain their individuality and nationality (we'll look more closely at this later) and because many ethnic groups wear colorful clothing, we should expect this on the New Earth.

The book of Revelation tells us we'll be priests and kings in Heaven. When you consider God's special adornment for the priests in the Old Testament (Exodus 28:4-43), it's likely God's royal and priestly people will wear beautiful clothes in Heaven.

WILL WE ALL APPEAR THE SAME AGE?

Will a child who dies at age six appear that age in Heaven? Will the man who dies at eighty appear to be eighty as he walks the New Earth?

People have asked questions like these throughout the centuries. Alister McGrath states,

> This issue caused the spilling of much theological ink, especially during the Middle Ages. . . . By the late thirteenth century, the church's emerging consensus was this: "As each person reaches their peak of perfection around the age of 30, they will be resurrected, as they would have appeared at that time—even if they never lived to reach that age." Peter Lombard's discussion of the matter is typical of his age: "A boy who dies immediately after being born will be resurrected in that form which he would have had if he had lived to the age of thirty." The New Jerusalem will thus be populated by men and women as they would appear at the age of 30 . . . but with every blemish removed.[221]

Thomas Aquinas, the great medieval theologian, argued that we will all be the age of Christ when he was crucified, about thirty-three. Aquinas pointed out,

> Human nature is deficient in a twofold manner: in one way because it has not yet obtained its ultimate perfection, and in a second way, because it has already receded from its ultimate perfection. Human nature is deficient in the first way in children, and in the second way in the aged. And therefore in each of these, human nature will be brought back by the resurrection of the state of its ultimate perfection, which is in the state of youth, toward which the movement of growth is terminated, and from which the movement of degeneration begins.[222]

Hank Hanegraaff suggests, "Our DNA is programmed in such a way that, at a particular point, we reach optimal development from a functional perspective. For the most part, it appears that we reach this stage somewhere in our twenties and thirties. . . . If the blueprints for our glorified bodies are in the

DNA, then it would stand to reason that our bodies will be resurrected at the optimal stage of development determined by our DNA."[223]

Does this mean that children who go to Heaven won't be children once they get there? Or that there will be no children on the New Earth? Isaiah 11:6-9 speaks of an Earth where "the leopard will lie down with the goat, the calf and the lion and the yearling together; and a little child will lead them. . . . The infant will play near the hole of the cobra, and the young child put his hand into the viper's nest. They will neither harm nor destroy on all my holy mountain."

Since the larger context of Isaiah is concerned with an eternal Kingdom of God on Earth, it seems inappropriate to restrict this passage to a thousand-year kingdom that ends in rebellion and destruction of human beings. The end of sin and the complete righteousness of all Earth's inhabitants won't come until the New Earth. But if Isaiah 11 is speaking of the New Earth, as does its parallel passage in Isaiah 65, who are the infants and young children playing with the animals? Is it possible that children, after they're resurrected on the New Earth, will be at the same level of development as when they died?

If so, these children would presumably be allowed to grow up on the New Earth—a childhood that would be enviable, to say the least! Believing parents, then, would presumably be able to see their children grow up—and likely have a major role in their lives as they do so. This would fit something I'll propose later, that on the New Earth many opportunities lost in this life will be wonderfully restored. Although it's not directly stated and I am therefore speculating, it's possible that parents whose hearts were broken through the death of their children will not only be reunited with them but will also experience the joy of seeing them grow up . . . in a perfect world.

It's also possible that on the New Earth we will appear ageless. C. S. Lewis portrays this in *The Great Divorce*, saying of Heaven's inhabitants, "No one in that company struck me as being of any particular age. One gets glimpses, even in our country, of that which is ageless—heavy thought in the face of an infant, and frolic childhood in that of a very old man."[224]

In my novels I suggest the possibility that in Heaven we'll see people as we most remember them on earth. So I'll see my parents as older, and they'll see me as younger. I'll see my children as younger, and they'll see me as older. I don't mean that physical forms will actually change but that the resurrection body will convey the real person we have known, and we will see each other through different eyes.

The New Earth will be a place of both maturity and perfection. Regardless of what age we appear, I believe that our bodies will demonstrate the qualities of youthfulness that Jesus so valued in children. God could easily have made a way for people to come into the world fully developed, not as maturing children. But he didn't. He put special qualities into children, ones we—and he—delight in. I fully expect all of us to have such qualities as curiosity, gratefulness, longing to learn and explore, and eagerness to hear stories and gather close to loved ones.

We'll be unburdened by the Curse that shrivels not just our bodies but also our spirits, robbing many of youthfulness. Jonathan Edwards stated, "The heavenly inhabitants . . . remain in eternal youth."[225] Heaven will be full of children . . . even if we look like adults. What we love about children is their joy, exuberance, curiosity, laughter, and spontaneity. In Heaven, whether or not anyone is the size and appearance of a child, we'll all be childlike in the ways that will bring joy to us and to our Father.

CHAPTER 30

WILL WE EAT AND DRINK ON THE NEW EARTH?

Words describing eating, meals, and food appear over a thousand times in Scripture, with the English translation "feast" occurring another 187 times. Feasting involves celebration and fun, and it is profoundly relational. Great conversation, storytelling, relationship-building, and laughter often happen during mealtimes. Feasts, including Passover, were spiritual gatherings that drew direct attention to God, his greatness, and his redemptive purposes.

People who love each other like to eat meals together. Jesus said to his disciples, "I confer on you a kingdom, just as my Father conferred one on me, so that you may eat and drink at my table in my kingdom" (Luke 22:29-30). Scripture says, "On this mountain the Lord Almighty will prepare a feast of rich food for all peoples, a banquet of aged wine—the best of meats and the finest of wines" (Isaiah 25:6).

WILL WE LITERALLY EAT AND DRINK?

Not all Christians believe that we will eat and drink in Heaven. Some people cite Romans 14:17: "The kingdom of God is not a matter of eating and drinking, but of righteousness, peace and joy in the Holy Spirit." But this passage isn't about the afterlife. Paul is speaking about our walk with God and the importance of not making other people stumble over what we eat and drink.

If we don't have intermediate bodies, then we won't eat in the intermediate Heaven. (If we do have temporary bodies, we might eat, but not necessarily.) However, it's interesting that manna is referred to as "the bread of angels" (Psalm 78:25). When angels, and God himself, took on human form, they ate human food (Genesis 18:1-2, 5-8). In the present Heaven is the tree of life, from which God says overcomers may eat (Revelation 2:7). Perhaps they won't eat from it until it's on the New Earth. Nevertheless, the fact that a tree with possibly edible fruit is currently located in the present Heaven at least raises the question of whether people can eat there now. However, since it's pre-resurrection, it seems likely there's no eating in the present Heaven.

Strangely, however, many people also believe we won't eat or drink in the eternal Heaven. They assume the biblical language about eating and drinking and banquets is figurative and that we will eat only "in a spiritual sense."[226] But how does one eat in a spiritual sense? And why is there a need to look for a spiritual sense when resurrected people in actual bodies will live on a resurrected Earth? Once again Christoplatonism lurks behind this understanding.

The resurrected Jesus invited his disciples, "Come and have breakfast." He prepared them a meal and then ate bread and fish with them (John 21:4-14). He proved that resurrection bodies are capable of eating food, *real* food. Christ could have abstained from eating. The fact that he didn't is a powerful statement about the nature of his resurrection body, and by implication, ours, since Christ "will transform our lowly bodies so that they will be like his glorious body" (Philippians 3:21).

Other passages indicate that we'll eat at feasts with Christ in an earthly kingdom. Jesus said to his disciples, "I tell you I will not drink again of the fruit of the vine until the kingdom of God comes" (Luke 22:18). On another occasion Jesus said, "Many will come from the east and the west, and will take their places at the feast with Abraham, Isaac and Jacob in the kingdom of heaven" (Matthew 8:11). Where will the kingdom of God come? To Earth. Where will God's Kingdom reach its ultimate and eternal state? On the New Earth.

An angel in Heaven said to John, "Blessed are those who are invited to the wedding supper of the Lamb!" (Revelation 19:9). What do people do at any supper—especially a wedding supper? Eat and drink, talk, tell stories, celebrate, laugh, and have dessert. Wedding feasts in the Middle East often lasted a full week. When we attend the wedding supper of the Lamb, we won't be guests—we'll be the bride!

Part of the conclusive evidence for the true physical resurrection of Christ is the fact that he ate and drank with his disciples:

> When he had said this, he showed them his hands and feet. And while they still did not believe it because of joy and amazement, he asked them, "Do you have anything here to eat?" They gave him a piece of broiled fish, and he took it and ate it in their presence. (Luke 24:40-43)

> God raised him from the dead on the third day and caused him to be seen. He was not seen by all the people, but by witnesses whom God

had already chosen—by us who ate and drank with him after he rose from the dead. (Acts 10:40-41)

Jesus said to them, "Bring some of the fish you have just caught. . . . Come and have breakfast." None of the disciples dared ask him, "Who are you?" They knew it was the Lord. Jesus came, took the bread and gave it to them, and did the same with the fish. This was now the third time Jesus appeared to his disciples after he was raised from the dead. When they had finished eating . . . (John 21:10-15)

These passages emphatically link eating and drinking to the resurrected state. The fact that it's so often repeated means it's not viewed as incidental. Scripture goes out of its way to prevent us from embracing the very misconceptions so many of us have: that life in Heaven will be "spiritual," not physical, and that we will not partake of any of the basic pleasures of this life.

Yet another biblical passage gives us insight about eating in Heaven. One day while eating in the home of a Pharisee, Jesus said to his host, "When you give a luncheon or dinner, . . . invite the poor, the crippled, the lame, the blind, and you will be blessed. Although they cannot repay you, you will be repaid at the resurrection of the righteous" (Luke 14:12-14). When Jesus made this reference to the resurrection of the dead, a man at the same dinner said to him, "Blessed is the man who will eat at the feast in the kingdom of God" (Luke 14:15). Since they were eating together at the time, the obvious meaning of "eat" and "feast" is literal. If the man who said this was wrong to envision literal eating after the bodily resurrection, Jesus had every opportunity to correct him. But he didn't. In fact, he built on the man's words to tell a story about someone who prepared a banquet and invited many guests (Luke 14:16-24). Clearly, both the man and Jesus were talking about actual eating at actual banquets, like the one they were at. One translation has the man at the dinner state, "What a privilege it would be to have a share in the Kingdom of God!" (Luke 14:15, NLT). But the Greek words do not mean "have a share in" the Kingdom; they mean "eat" in the Kingdom.

I don't always take the Bible literally. Scripture contains many figures of speech. But it's incorrect to assume that because some figures of speech are used to describe Heaven, all that the Bible says about Heaven, therefore, is figurative. When we're told we'll have resurrection bodies like Christ's and that he ate in his resurrection body, why should we assume he was speaking figuratively when he refers to tables, banquets, and eating and drinking in his Kingdom?

Speaking of eating, drinking, and the physical properties of life on the New

Earth, Wayne Grudem writes, "There is no strong reason to say these expressions are merely symbolic, without any literal reference. Are symbolic banquets and symbolic wine and symbolic rivers and trees somehow superior to real banquets and real wine and real rivers and trees in God's eternal plan? These things are just some of the excellent features of the perfection and final goodness of the physical creation that God has made."[227]

We're commanded, "Glorify God in your body" (1 Corinthians 6:20, NKJV). What will we do for eternity? Glorify God in our bodies. We're told, "Whether you eat or drink or whatever you do, do it all for the glory of God" (1 Corinthians 10:31). What will we do for eternity? Eat, drink, and do all to the glory of God.

An evangelical author tells us, "In Heaven, Scripture indicates that we shall neither eat nor drink."[228] But Scripture tells us no such thing. In fact, it couldn't show more clearly that we will eat and drink on the New Earth.

WILL WE EXPERIENCE HUNGER, AND WILL WE DIGEST FOOD?

Will we get hungry on the New Earth? Some people say no because we're told, "Never again will they hunger; never again will they thirst" (Revelation 7:16). But this doesn't mean that we'll lack an appetite or desire; it means our desires will be met. We will never go hungry or go thirsty. To find pleasure in eating assumes we desire to eat. Hunger and thirst are good things if food and drink are freely available, and God assures us that on the New Earth they always will be.

Did Adam and Eve hunger in Eden? Presumably. Will we thirst on the New Earth? "For the Lamb at the center of the throne will be their shepherd; he will lead them to springs of living water" (Revelation 7:17). God doesn't say we won't need to drink. Rather, he says he will lead us to drink. The natural stimulus to motivate drinking is thirst. We will presumably thirst for water, as we will thirst for God. But our thirst will never go unsatisfied. God created hunger and thirst, and he intends for them to be satisfied, not obliterated.

Paul quotes the Corinthians: "You say, 'Food is for the stomach, and the stomach is for food.' This is true, though someday God will do away with both of them" (1 Corinthians 6:13, NLT). Some people think God is saying here that we won't eat and won't have stomachs or digestive systems. But in context Paul is simply saying that the old body will die, so we shouldn't let the desires of that body control us. Naturally, if we're not embodied in the intermediate Heaven, we won't have stomachs or eat food there. But Paul isn't saying that our resurrected bodies won't have stomachs and that we won't eat food on the New Earth.

Some people argue that we won't eat or drink in Heaven because they're aghast at the thought of digestion and elimination. Could God make it so our new bodies wouldn't go through the same digestive and elimination processes they do now? Certainly. Will he? We don't know. But no aspect of our God-created physiology can be bad. To imagine otherwise is Christoplatonism again. Did Adam and Eve experience digestion and elimination in a perfect world? Of course. Jesus never sinned, but his body functioned just as ours do.

HOW WILL FOOD TASTE?

Only two people lived before the Fall. This means only two people have ever eaten food at its best, with their capacity to taste at its best.

The great wine Christ made and served at the wedding of Cana was a fore-taste of that best of wines he will provide for us on the New Earth. Even in this cursed world, Scripture is filled with more feasts than fasts. Who created our taste buds? Who determined what we like and what we don't? God did. The food we eat is from God's hand. Our resurrected bodies will have resurrected taste buds. We can trust that the food we eat on the New Earth, some of it familiar and some of it brand-new, will taste better than anything we've ever eaten here.

Food isn't just functional. We could get nourishment, after all, by mixing everything together in a blender, with no regard to color or texture or taste. Food is also for our enjoyment—not only its consumption but also its preparation and presentation. Shouldn't we expect boundless creativity in these as well? (If you've seen the marvelous movie *Babette's Feast*, you know what I mean.)

Reformer John Calvin wrote, "If we consider to what end God created foods, we shall find that he wished not only to provide for our necessities, but also for our pleasure and recreation. . . . With herbs, trees and fruits, besides the various uses he gives us of them, it was his will to rejoice our sight by their beauty, and to give us yet another pleasure in their odours."[229]

We won't "need" fine meals; we don't *need* them now. But we enjoy them now for the same reason we'll enjoy them then—because God made us to enjoy them and to glorify him as we eat and drink (1 Corinthians 10:31).

WILL WE EAT MEAT?

God's provision of food for people and animals was clearly indicated when he said, "I give you every seed-bearing plant on the face of the whole earth and every tree that has fruit with seed in it. They will be yours for food. And to all the beasts of the earth and all the birds of the air and all the creatures that move on the ground—everything that has the breath of life in it—I give every green plant for food" (Genesis 1:29-30).

It appears that neither people nor animals ate meat until after the Flood, when God said, "Everything that lives and moves will be food for you. Just as I gave you the green plants, I now give you everything" (Genesis 9:3). It makes sense that people and animals wouldn't eat meat before the Fall, when living beings didn't die. But why weren't animals eaten between the Fall and the Flood? Perhaps it was still unthinkable so close to Eden, when animals were to be cared for, not killed and eaten. Consider that the genealogies of Genesis 5 indicate that Noah's father, Lamech, was born before Adam died! Perhaps until after the Flood, animals still held a remnant of intelligence not sufficiently dissipated by the Fall.

> You are going now, said they, to the paradise of God, wherein you shall see the tree of life, and eat of the never-fading fruit thereof.
>
> **JOHN BUNYAN**

As mentioned in chapter 12, some people argue that animals died before the Fall.[230] But this conclusion seems to be driven by assumptions about the earth's age and interpretations of the fossil record, not from biblical texts. Scripture ties all death to Adam: "Sin entered the world through one man, and death through sin" (Romans 5:12). The "creation was subjected to frustration" and is in "bondage to decay" because of humanity's sin and will be delivered through humanity's resurrection (Romans 8:19-23). Whether blessing or curse, whether life or death, what is first true of mankind *then* extends to animals. This suggests animal death did not precede human death.

If animal death preceded human sin and death, so did animal suffering. Indeed, advocates of this position picture not only animals devouring and killing each other before the Fall but also people eating animals. But how does this reconcile with Genesis 9:3, where God says, "Just as I gave you the green plants, I *now* give you everything" (emphasis added)?

Would God call "very good" a realm in which animals suffered, died, and devoured one another? Surely the repeated redemptive promise that one day animals will live in peace with each other is at least to a degree a return to Edenic conditions, though it's certainly more than that (Isaiah 11:6-9).

If, as I believe, animal death was the result of the Fall and the Curse, once the Curse has been lifted on the New Earth, animals will no longer die. Just as they fell under mankind, so they will rise under mankind (Romans 8:21). This suggests people may become vegetarians on the New Earth, as they apparently were in Eden and during the time before the Flood.

How then should we understand this great text: "On this mountain the Lord Almighty will prepare a feast of rich food for all peoples, a banquet of aged wine—the best of meats and the finest of wines" (Isaiah 25:6)? One possibility is that this refers to the Millennium, where Christ reigns but the world is still under the Curse and therefore animals still die. The other possibility is that it refers to the New Earth. But we are told on the New Earth "There will be no more death . . . or pain, for the old order of things has passed away" (Revelation 21:4). The text doesn't specify "no more *human* death or pain."

So how could there be meat without animal death? Many people—I'm not one of them—eat meat substitutes and prefer the taste to real meat. How hard would it be for God to create far better substitutes that do qualify as meat in every sense of taste and texture, without coming from dead animals? This may stretch the meaning of "meat" and may seem unnatural, but wouldn't it be more natural than animals dying when we're told there will be no more death?

During the Millennium or on the New Earth, or both, fishermen will spread their nets and catch fish (Ezekiel 47:9-10). Either this is catch-and-release, purely for sport, or it suggests fish will still be eaten. Jesus ate fish in a resurrected body. However, that was on an unresurrected Earth, still under the Curse. Hunting and killing animals is legitimate and sometimes necessary on the present Earth. However, to the degree that hunting animals involves their fear, suffering, or death, it wouldn't fit with the biblical description of the New Earth, where not only people but also animals live in peace and harmony: "The wolf and the lamb will feed together, and the lion will eat straw like the ox. . . . They will neither harm nor destroy" (Isaiah 65:25). We're told animals' eating habits will change—why not ours?

The food chain may seem natural to us, but I believe it violates God's original design. No more curse and death means no more food chain involving living creatures. As radical a shift as that may seem, it will likely be a return to God's original design.

So, on the New Earth, we may consume a wonderful array of fruits and vegetables, perhaps supplemented by "meat" that doesn't require death—something that tastes better but isn't animal flesh. If the product of the Curse and death can taste good to fallen taste buds, how much better will God's specially designed foods smell and taste to resurrected senses?

WILL WE DRINK COFFEE IN HEAVEN?

I'll address this question not simply for the benefit of coffee lovers but because it's a revealing test of whether we're more influenced by biblical teaching or

Christoplatonism. Someone may say, "I sure *hope* there'll be coffee in heaven." But it's a statement that few would attempt to defend biblically.

But consider the facts. God made coffee. Coffee grows on Earth, which God made for mankind, put under our management, and filled with resources for our use. When God evaluated his creation, he deemed coffee trees, along with all else, to be "very good." Many people throughout history have enjoyed coffee—even in a fallen world where neither coffee nor our taste buds are at their best.

God tells us that he "richly provides us with everything for our enjoyment" (1 Timothy 6:17). Does "everything" include coffee? Paul also says, "For everything God created is good, and nothing is to be rejected if it is received with thanksgiving, because it is consecrated by the word of God and prayer" (1 Timothy 4:4-5). Again, does "everything" include coffee?

Given these biblical perspectives—and realizing that caffeine addiction or anything else that's unhealthy simply won't exist on the New Earth—can you think of any persuasive reason why coffee trees and coffee drinking wouldn't be part of the resurrected Earth?

Will the New Earth have fewer resources for human enjoyment than Eden did or than the world under the Curse offers? If you're tempted to say, "But in Heaven our minds will be on spiritual things, not coffee," your Christoplatonism detector should go off. It's fine if you don't like coffee, but to suggest that coffee is inherently unspiritual is . . . well, heresy. It directly contradicts the Scriptures just cited. God made the physical and spiritual realms not to oppose each other but to be united in bringing glory to him.

On the New Earth, we will "drink . . . from the spring of the water of life" (Revelation 21:6). God will prepare for us "a banquet of aged wine . . . the finest of wines" (Isaiah 25:6). Not only will we drink water and wine, we'll eat from fruit trees (Revelation 22:2), and there's every reason to believe we'll drink juice made from the twelve fruits from the tree of life. So, along with drinking water, wine, and fruit juice, is there any reason to suppose we wouldn't drink coffee or tea? Can you imagine drinking coffee or tea with Jesus on the New Earth? If you can't, why not?

If for health reasons you shouldn't drink coffee now, then don't. But aside from personal preference, the only compelling reason for not having coffee in Heaven would be if coffee were sinful or harmful. But it won't be. If drinking coffee would be unspiritual on the New Earth, then it must be unspiritual now. And unless someone's a caffeine addict, under bondage to coffee and not to Christ, or if a person's health is at stake, there's simply no biblical basis for believing drinking coffee is sinful. Those who shouldn't consume alcohol or caffeine now will be freed from addiction on the New Earth. Adverse health effects simply won't exist.

Those who for reasons of allergies, weight problems, or addictions can't regularly consume peanuts, chocolate, coffee, and wine—and countless other foods and drinks—may look forward to enjoying them on the New Earth. To be free from sin, death, and bondage on the New Earth will mean that we'll enjoy more pleasures, not fewer. And the God who delights in our pleasures will be glorified in our grateful praise.

SHOULD WE LOOK FORWARD TO FEASTS?

You and I have never eaten food in a world untouched by the Fall and the Curse. The palate and taste buds were injured in the Fall, as were all food sources. The best-tasting food we've ever eaten wasn't nearly as good as it must have tasted in Eden or as it will on the New Earth.

The person who's eaten the widest variety of meals on Earth still hasn't tasted countless others. How many special dishes will you discover on the New Earth? As yet, you may not have tasted your favorite meal—and if you have, it didn't taste as good as it will there. The best meals you'll ever eat are all still ahead of you on the New Earth.

If it seems trivial or unspiritual to anticipate such things, remember that it's God who promises that on the New Earth we will sit at tables, at banquets and feasts, and enjoy the finest foods and drinks. And to top it off, our Father promises that he *himself* will prepare for us the finest foods (Isaiah 25:6).

Don't you think he *wants* us to look forward to eating at his table?

CHAPTER 31

WILL WE BE CAPABLE OF SINNING?

People have said to me, "Heaven will be perfect, but a sinless environment doesn't mean we can't sin; Adam and Eve proved that. They lived in a sinless place, yet they sinned."

It's true that Satan tempted them, but he too originally was a perfect being living in a perfect environment, beholding God himself. Not only was there no sin in Heaven; there was no sin in the universe. Yet Satan sinned. Hence, Heaven's perfection, it seems, doesn't guarantee there'll be no future sin.

Some people also argue that being human demands free choice, and therefore we *must* have the capacity to choose evil in Heaven. If that's true, then we could experience another Fall.

Clearly, this is a question of great importance.

CAN WE KNOW WE WON'T SIN?

Christ promises on the New Earth, "There will be no more death or mourning or crying or pain, for the old order of things has passed away" (Revelation 21:4). Since "the wages of sin is death" (Romans 6:23), the promise of no more death is a promise of *no more sin*. Those who will never die can never sin, since sinners always die. Sin causes mourning, crying, and pain. If those will never occur again, then *sin* can never occur again.

Consider the last part of Revelation 21:4: "For the old order of things has passed away." What follows the word *for* explains Heaven's lack of death, mourning, crying, and pain. These are part of an old order of things that will forever be behind us. The sin that caused them will be no longer. We need not fear a second Fall.

Scripture emphasizes that Christ died *once* to deal with sin and will never again need to die (Hebrews 9:26-28; 10:10; 1 Peter 3:18). We'll have the very righteousness of God (2 Corinthians 5:21). We won't sin in Heaven for the same reason God doesn't: He cannot sin. Our eternal inability to sin has been purchased by Christ's blood.

"For by a single offering [himself] he has perfected for all time those who are being sanctified" (Hebrews 10:14, ESV). On the cross, validated by his resurrection, our Savior purchased our perfection *for all time.*

"Nothing impure will ever enter it [the New Jerusalem], nor will anyone who does what is shameful or deceitful, but only those whose names are written in the Lamb's book of life" (Revelation 21:27). The passage doesn't say: "If someone becomes impure or shameful or deceitful, that person will be evicted." There's an absolute contrast between sinners and the righteous. That Satan and evildoers are cast forever into the lake of fire (Revelation 20:10 and 21:8) shows an eternal separation of evil from the New Earth. Heaven will be completely devoid of evil, with no threat of becoming tainted. Three times in the final two chapters of Scripture, we're told that those still in their sins have no access to Heaven, and never will (Revelation 21:8, 27; 22:15).

That evil will have no footing in Heaven and no leverage to affect us is further indicated by Jesus when he says, "The Son of Man will send out his angels, and they will weed out of his kingdom *everything* that causes sin and all who do evil. They will throw them into the fiery furnace. . . . *Then* the righteous will shine like the sun in the kingdom of their Father" (Matthew 13:41-43, emphasis added).

Hebrews 9:26 says with an air of finality that Christ sacrificed himself "to put away sin" (NASB) or "to do away with sin" (NIV). Sin will be a thing of the past.

We'll be raised "incorruptible" (1 Corinthians 15:52, NKJV). *Incorruptible* is a stronger word than *uncorrupted.* Our risen bodies, and by implication our new beings, will be immune to corruption. Since the wages of sin is death, if we cannot die, then we cannot sin.

"Anyone who has died has been freed from sin" (Romans 6:7). Christ will not allow us to be vulnerable to the very thing he died to deliver us from. Since our righteousness is rooted in Christ, who is eternally righteous, we can never lose it.

WILL WE HAVE FREE WILL IN HEAVEN?

Some people believe that if we have free will in Heaven, we'll have to be free to sin, as were the first humans. But Adam and Eve's situation was different. They were innocent but had not been made righteous *by Christ.* We, on the other hand, become righteous through Christ's atonement: "For just as through the disobedience of the one man the many were made sinners, so also through the obedience of the one man the many will be made righteous"

(Romans 5:19). To suggest we could have Christ's righteousness yet sin is to say Christ could sin. God completely delivers us from sin—including vulnerability to sin.

Even now we may "participate in the divine nature and escape the corruption in the world caused by evil desires" (2 Peter 1:4). In Heaven there will be no evil desires, and no corruption, and we will fully participate in the sinless perfection of God.

What does this mean in terms of human freedom? Some people suggest our free choice is a temporary condition for the present life and won't characterize us in Heaven. But it seems to me that the capacity to choose is part of what makes us human. It's hard to believe God would be pleased by our worship if we had no choice but to offer it. It's one thing for him to enable us to worship. It's another for him to force us to do so or to make it automatic and involuntary. Christ woos his bride; he doesn't "fix" her so she has no choice but to love him.

Imagine a husband who desires his wife's love, and to ensure that love, he injects her with a chemical to remove her free will, to *make* her love him. This is not love; it is coercion. Once we become what the sovereign God has made us to be in Christ and once we see him as he is, then we'll see all things—including sin—for what they are. God won't need to restrain us from it. Sin will have absolutely no appeal. It will be, literally, unthinkable.

The inability to sin doesn't inherently violate free will. My inability to be God, an angel, a rabbit, or a flower is not a violation of my free will. It's the simple reality of my nature. The new nature that'll be ours in Heaven—the righteousness of Christ—is a nature that cannot sin, any more than a diamond can be soft or blue can be red. God cannot sin, yet no being has greater free choice than God does.

Theologian Paul Helm says, "The freedom of heaven, then, is the freedom from sin; not that the believer just happens to be free from sin, but that he is so constituted or reconstituted that he cannot sin. He doesn't want to sin, and he does not want to want to sin."[231]

WILL WE EVER BE TEMPTED?

Will we be tempted to turn our backs on Christ? No. What would tempt us? Innocence is the absence of something (sin), while righteousness is the presence of something (God's holiness). God will never withdraw from us his holiness; therefore we cannot sin.

We'll *never* forget the ugliness of sin. People who've experienced severe burns aren't tempted to walk into a bonfire. Having known death and life, we who will experience life will never want to go back to death. We'll never be deceived into thinking God is withholding something good from us or that sin is in our best interests.

Satan won't have any access to us. But even if he did, we wouldn't be tempted. We'll know not only what righteousness is but also what sin is—or was. We'll always know sin's costs. Every time we see the scarred hands of King Jesus, we'll remember. We'll see sin as God does. It will be stripped of its illusions and will be utterly unappealing.

Because our hearts will be pure and we'll see people as they truly are, every relationship in Heaven will be pure. We'll all be faithful to the love of our life: King Jesus. We couldn't do anything behind his back even if we wanted to. But we'll never want to.

We'll love everyone, men and women, but we'll be *in love* only with Jesus. We'll never be tempted to degrade, use, or idolize each other. We'll never believe the outrageous lie that our deepest needs can be met in any person but Jesus.

Often we act as if the universe revolves around us. We have to remind ourselves it's all about Christ, not us. In Heaven we'll see reality as it is and will, therefore, never have to correct our thinking. This will be Heaven's Copernican revolution—a paradigm shift in which we'll never again see ourselves as our center of gravity. Jesus Christ will be our undisputed center, and we won't want it any other way.

WILL WE REALLY BE PERFECT?

Someone e-mailed me this question: "In Heaven, will some people still be annoying? After all, eternity's a long time!" Annoyance is sometimes caused by others' sin, our own, or both. Since sin will be eliminated, so will annoyance. That doesn't mean people won't have idiosyncrasies, only that they won't be rooted in sin, and none of us will degrade or dismiss others.

Jonathan Edwards said, "Even the very best of men, are, on earth, imperfect. But it is not so in heaven. There shall be no pollution or deformity or offensive defect of any kind, seen in any person or thing; but every one shall be perfectly pure, and perfectly lovely in heaven."[232]

In Heaven we'll be perfectly *human*. Adam and Eve were perfectly human until they bent themselves into sinners. Then they lost something that was an original part of their humanity—moral perfection. Since then, under sin's curse, we've been human but never perfectly human.

We can't remember a time when we weren't sinners. We've always carried sin's baggage. What relief it will be not to have to guard our eyes and our minds. We will not need to defend against pride and lust because there will be none.

In Heaven we won't just be better than we are now—we'll be better than Adam and Eve were before they fell. Our resurrection bodies may be very much like their bodies were before the Fall, but we'll be a redeemed humanity with knowledge of God, including his grace, far exceeding theirs.

Of course, Adam and Eve will be with us too, in their resurrection bodies. No one will know better than they what we've missed. They will have lived on the original Earth, the fallen Earth, *and* the New Earth. (That's why they rank high on my list of people I want to talk with.)

In Heaven we'll be perfectly human, but we'll still be finite. Our bodies will be perfect in that they won't be diseased or crippled. But that doesn't mean they won't have limits.

> How great shall be that felicity, which shall be tainted with no evil, which shall lack no good, and which shall afford leisure for the praises of God, who shall be all in all!
>
> **SAINT AUGUSTINE**

The term *perfect* is often misused when it describes our state in Heaven. I've heard it said, for instance, "We'll communicate perfectly, so we'll never be at a loss for words." I disagree. I expect we'll sometimes grasp for words to describe the wondrous things we'll experience. I expect I'll stand in speechless wonder at the glory of God. I'll be morally perfect, but that doesn't mean I'll be capable of doing anything and everything. (Adam and Eve were morally perfect, but that didn't mean they could automatically invent nuclear submarines or defy gravity. They were perfect yet finite, just as we will be.)

Someone asked me, "If we're sinless, will we still be human?" Although sin is part of us now, it's not essential to our humanity—in fact, it's foreign to it. It's what twists us and keeps us from being what we once were—and one day will be.

Our greatest deliverance in Heaven will be from *ourselves*. Our deceit, corruption, self-righteousness, self-sufficiency, hypocrisy—all will be forever gone.

Theologian and novelist Frederick Buechner anticipates the new "us" on the New Earth: "Everything is gone that ever made Jerusalem, like all cities, torn apart, dangerous, heartbreaking, seamy. You walk the streets in peace now. Small children play unattended in the parks. No stranger goes by whom you can't imagine a fast friend. The city has become what those who loved it always dreamed and what in their dreams she always was. The new Jerusalem. That seems to be the secret of Heaven. The new Chicago, Leningrad, Hiroshima, Beirut. The new bus driver, hot-dog man, seamstress, hairdresser. The new you, me, everybody."[233]

WHAT IS OUR HOPE OF LIVING WITHOUT SIN?

What's the hope we should live for? It's more than freedom from suffering. It's deliverance from *sin*, freeing us to be fully human. Paul says, "In this hope we were saved" (Romans 8:24). What hope? The words of the previous verse tell us: "the redemption of our bodies" (v. 23). That's the final resurrection, when death will be swallowed up and sin will be reversed, never again to touch us. This is what we should long for and live for. Resurrection will mean many things—including *no more sin*.

Is resurrected living in a resurrected world with the resurrected Christ and his resurrected people *your* daily longing and hope? Is it part of the gospel you share with others? Paul says that the resurrection of the dead is the hope in which we were saved. It will be the glorious climax of God's saving work that began at our regeneration. It will mark the final end of any and all sin that separates us from God. In liberating us from sin and all its consequences, the resurrection will free us to live with God, gaze on him, and enjoy his uninterrupted fellowship forever, with no threat that anything will ever again come between us and him.

May God preserve us from embracing lesser hopes. May we rejoice as we anticipate the height, depth, length, and breadth of our redemption.

CHAPTER 32

WHAT WILL WE KNOW
AND LEARN?

I t's common to hear people say, "We don't understand now, but in Heaven we'll know everything." One writer says that people in Heaven can "easily comprehend divine mysteries."[234] Is this true? Will we really know everything in Heaven?

WILL WE KNOW EVERYTHING?

God alone is omniscient. When we die, we'll see things far more clearly, and we'll know much more than we do now, but we'll *never* know everything.

The apostle Paul wrote: "Now we see but a poor reflection as in a mirror; then we shall see face to face. Now I *know* in part; then I shall *know fully*, even as I am fully known" (1 Corinthians 13:12, emphasis added). The italicized words are based on two different Greek words: *ginosko* and *epiginosko*. The prefix *epi* intensifies the word to mean "to really know" or "to know extensively." However, when the word is used of humans, it never means absolute knowledge.

In his *Systematic Theology*, Wayne Grudem says, "1 Cor. 13:12 does not say that we will be omniscient or know everything (Paul could have said we will know all things, *ta panta*, if he had wished to do so), but, rightly translated, simply says that we will know in a fuller or more intensive way, 'even as we have been known,' that is, without any error or misconceptions in our knowledge."[235]

The New Living Translation reads, "Now we see things imperfectly as in a poor mirror." Mirrors in Paul's time had serious flaws. Corinth was famous for its bronze mirrors, but the color was off and shapes were distorted. The mirror's image lacked the quality of seeing someone face-to-face. Knowing and seeing were nearly synonyms in Greek thought.[236] The more you saw, the more you knew.

One day we'll see God's face and therefore truly know him (Revelation 22:4). Under the Curse we see myopically. When we're resurrected, our vision will be corrected. We'll at last be able to see eternal realities once invisible to us (2 Corinthians 4:18).

God sees clearly and comprehensively. In Heaven we'll see far more clearly, but we'll never see comprehensively. The point of comparing our knowing to God's knowing is that we'll know "fully" in the sense of accurately but not exhaustively.

In Heaven we'll be flawless, but not knowing everything isn't a flaw. It's part of being finite. Righteous angels don't know everything, and they long to know more (1 Peter 1:12). They're flawless but finite. We should expect to long for greater knowledge, as angels do. And we'll spend eternity gaining the greater knowledge we'll seek.

WILL WE LEARN?

I heard a pastor say, "There will be no more learning in Heaven." One writer says that in Heaven, "Activities such as investigation, comprehending and probing will never be necessary. Our understanding will be complete."[237] In a Gallup poll of people's perspectives about Heaven, only 18 percent thought people would grow intellectually in Heaven.[238]

Does Scripture indicate that we will learn in Heaven? Yes. Consider Ephesians 2:6-7: "God raised us up with Christ and seated us with him in the heavenly realms in Christ Jesus, in order that in the coming ages he might show the incomparable riches of his grace." The word *show* means "to reveal." The phrase *in the coming ages* clearly indicates this will be a progressive, ongoing revelation, in which we learn more and more about God's grace.

I frequently learn new things about my wife, daughters, and closest friends, even though I've known them for many years. If I can always be learning something new about finite, limited human beings, surely I'll learn far more about Jesus. None of us will ever begin to exhaust his depths.

Jesus said to his disciples, "Learn from me" (Matthew 11:29). On the New Earth, we'll have the privilege of sitting at Jesus' feet as Mary did, walking with him over the countryside as his disciples did, always learning from him. In Heaven we'll continually learn new things about God, going ever deeper in our understanding.

Consider again those Greek words *ginosko* and *epiginosko*, translated "know" in 1 Corinthians 13:12, used of our present knowledge on Earth and our future knowledge in Heaven. *Ginosko* often means "to come to know," and therefore "to learn" (Matthew 10:26; John 12:9; Acts 17:19; Philippians 2:19). *Epiginosko* also means "to learn" (Luke 7:37; 23:7; Acts 9:30; 22:29).[239] That we will one day "know fully" could well be understood as "we will always keep on learning."

It was God—not Satan—who made us learners. God doesn't want us to stop learning. What he wants to stop is what prevents us from learning.

Puritan preacher Jonathan Edwards, who intensely studied Heaven, believed "the saints will be progressive in knowledge to all eternity."[240] He added, "The number of ideas of the saints shall increase to eternity."[241]

Will our knowledge and skills vary? Will some people in Heaven have greater knowledge and specialized abilities than others? Why not? Scripture never teaches sameness in Heaven. We will be individuals, each with our own memories and God-given gifts. Some of our knowledge will overlap, but not all. I'm not a mechanic or gardener, as you may be. I may or may not learn those skills on the New Earth. But even if I do, that doesn't mean I'll ever be as skilled a gardener or mechanic as you will be. After all, you had a head start on learning. Remember the doctrine of continuity: What we learn here carries over after death.

Don't you love to discover something new? On the New Earth, some of our greatest discoveries may relate to the lives we're living right now. Columnist and commentator Paul Harvey made a career of telling "the rest of the story." That's exactly what we'll discover in Heaven again and again—the rest of the story. We'll be stunned to learn how God orchestrated the events of our lives to influence people we may have forgotten about.

Occasionally we hear stories that provide us a small taste of what we'll learn in eternity. One morning after I spoke at a church, a young woman came up to me and asked, "Do you remember a young man sitting next to you on a plane headed to college? You gave him your novel *Deadline*." I give away a lot of my books on planes, but after some prompting, I remembered him. He was an unbeliever. We talked about Jesus, and I gave him the book and prayed for him as we got off the plane.

I was amazed when the young woman said to me, "He told me he never contacted you, so you wouldn't know what happened. He got to college, checked into the dorm, sat down, and read your book. When he was done, he confessed his sins and gave his life to Jesus. And I can honestly tell you, he's the most dynamic Christian I've ever met."

All I did was talk a little, give him a book, and pray for him. But if the young woman hadn't told me, I wouldn't have had a clue what had happened. That story reminded me how many great stories await us in Heaven and how many we may not hear until we've been there a long time. We won't ever know everything, and even what we will know, we won't know all at once. We'll be learners, forever. Few things excite me more than that.

WILL WE EXPERIENCE PROCESS?

The first humans lived in process, as God ordained them to. Adam knew more a week after he was created than he did on his first day.

Nothing is wrong with process and the limitations it implies. Jesus "grew in wisdom and stature" (Luke 2:52). Jesus "learned obedience" (Hebrews 5:8). Growing and learning cannot be bad; the sinless Son of God experienced them. They are simply part of being human.

Unless we cease to be human after our resurrection, we will go on growing and learning. If anything, sin makes us less human. When the parasite of sin is removed, full humanity will be restored—and improved.

The sense of wonder among Heaven's inhabitants shows Heaven is not stagnant but fresh and stimulating, suggesting an ever-deepening appreciation of God's greatness (Revelation 4–6). Heaven's riches are rooted in Heaven's God. We will find in Heaven a continual progression of stimulating discovery and fresh learning as we keep grasping more of God.

In *Hamlet*, Shakespeare called what lies beyond death "the undiscover'd country."[242] It's a country we yearn to discover—and by Christ's grace, we will. Jonathan Edwards—as fine a theological mind as the world has ever known—defended and developed this thought, which he considered critical. He wrote, "How soon do earthly lovers come to an end of their discoveries of each other's beauty; how soon do they see all there is to be seen! But in Heaven there is eternal progress with new beauties always being discovered."[243] He continued, "Happiness of heaven is progressive and has various periods in which it has a new and glorious advancement and consists very much in beholding the manifestations that God makes of himself in the work of redemption."[244] Edwards contended that we will continually become happier in Heaven in "a never-ending, ever-increasing discovery of more and more of God's glory with greater and greater joy in him."[245] He said there will never be a time when there is "no more glory for the redeemed to discover and enjoy."[246] There won't ever "come a time when the union between God and the church is complete" because we will always be learning something new about our Bridegroom.[247]

We can anticipate an eternity of growing in Christlikeness as we behold God's face and are continuously "transformed into his likeness with ever-increasing glory" (2 Corinthians 3:18). We can begin this joyful process here and now, and there's every indication it will continue forever.

After creating the new universe, Jesus says, "I am making everything new!" (Revelation 21:5). Notice the verb tense is not "I have made" or "I will make" but "I am making." This suggests an ongoing process of renovation. Christ is a creator, and his creativity is never exhausted. He will go right on making new things. Heaven is not the end of innovation; it is a new beginning, an eternal break from the stagnancy and inertia of sin.

WHAT WILL IT BE LIKE TO LEARN?

Could God impart knowledge so we immediately know things when we get to Heaven? Certainly. Adam and Eve didn't go to school. They were created, it appears, with an initial vocabulary. But Adam and Eve are the exceptions. Every other person has learned by experience and study, over time. And Adam and Eve were learners the rest of their lives. Nothing ever came automatically again.

When we enter Heaven, we'll presumably begin with the knowledge we had at the time of our death. God may enhance our knowledge and will correct countless wrong perceptions. I imagine he'll reveal many new things to us, then set us on a course of continual learning, paralleling Adam and Eve's. Once we're in resurrection bodies with resurrected brains, our capacity to learn may increase. Perhaps angel guardians or loved ones already in Heaven will be assigned to tutor and orient us.

We will also study. Martin Luther said, "If God had all the answers in his right hand, and the struggle to reach those answers in his left, I would choose God's left hand." Why? Because it's not only truth we want, it's also the pleasure of *learning* the truth. God reveals himself to us in the process of our learning, often in bite-sized chunks, fit for our finite minds. The great preacher Donald Gray Barnhouse once said that if he was told he had three years left on Earth, he would spend two years studying and one preaching. Expressing a similar desire, Billy Graham said that if he had his life to do over again, he would study more and preach less.

Will we study doctrine in Heaven? Doctrine is truth, which is an extension of God's nature, and therefore also cannot be exhausted. We will have eternity to explore it. Truth will be living and vital, never dry and dusty. We will dialogue about truth not to impress each other but to enrich each other and ourselves as we discover more and more about God.

To study creation is to study the Creator. Science should be worshipful discovery because the heavens and all creation declare God's glory. God reveals his character in flowers, waterfalls, animals, and planets. God's name is written large in nature, in his beauty organization, skill, precision, and attention to detail. He's the Master Artist. On the New Earth everything will be a lens through which we see him. Biology, zoology, chemistry, astronomy, physics—all will be the study of God.

Will we discover new ideas? I believe we will. Jesus, the God-man, was sometimes "astonished" at what he saw on this earth (Matthew 8:10). If there was ever a man incapable of surprise, wouldn't we have expected it to be the "one who came from heaven" (John 3:13)? But if Jesus could be astonished on this old Earth, surely we will often be astonished at what we see in God, people, and creation on the New Earth.

There's so much to discover in this universe, but we have so little time and opportunity to do it. The list of books I haven't read, music I've never heard, and places I haven't been is unending. There's much more to know. I look forward to discovering new things in Heaven—forever. At the end of each day I'll have the same amount of time left as I did the day before. The things I didn't learn that day, the people I didn't see, the things I was unable to do—I can still learn, see, or do the next day. Places won't crumble, people won't die, and neither will I.

> What we do now is not discarded once we enter eternity. What we learn now is not erased in heaven. . . . What we experience in joy and understanding and insight now is not destroyed, but is the foundation on which all our eternal experience and growth is based.
>
> **SAM STORMS**

I heard someone say, "There won't be any teaching in Heaven. There won't be any need." But that assumes we will be omniscient and that we won't learn, which contradicts both Scripture and the way God made us. I've benefited greatly from the stimulation of college and seminary courses I've attended and taught. Discussions among thoughtful students and teachers can be exhilarating. I see God in the insights other people share with me. Learning is exciting. Education on this fallen Earth may sometimes be bland and can even undermine truth, but in Heaven all education will be a platform to display God's fascinating truth, drawing us closer to him.

Consider how exciting intellectual development will be. Father Boudreau wrote, "The life of Heaven is one of intellectual pleasure. . . . There the intellect of man receives a supernatural light. . . . It is purified, strengthened, enlarged, and enabled to see God as He is in His very essence. It is enabled to contemplate, face to face, Him who is the first essential Truth. It gazes undazzled upon the first infinite beauty, wisdom, and goodness, from whom flow all limited wisdom, beauty, and goodness found in creatures. Who can fathom the exquisite pleasures of the human intellect when it thus sees all truth as it is in itself?"[248]

If seeing truth "as it is in itself" is that exciting for those of us who've had some education here on Earth, imagine what it will be like for those who never had the benefits of literacy and education.

Think of what it will be like to discuss science with Isaac Newton, Michael

Faraday, and Thomas Edison or to discuss mathematics with Pascal. Imagine long talks with Malcolm Muggeridge or Francis Schaeffer. Think of reading and discussing the writings of C. S. Lewis, J. R. R. Tolkien, G. K. Chesterton, or Dorothy Sayers with the authors themselves. How would you like to talk about the power of fiction at a roundtable with John Milton, Daniel Defoe, Victor Hugo, Fyodor Dostoyevsky, Leo Tolstoy, and Flannery O'Connor?

How about discussing God's attributes with Stephen Charnock, A. W. Pink, A. W. Tozer, and J. I. Packer? Or talking theology with Augustine, Aquinas, Calvin, and Luther? Then, when differences arise, why not invite Jesus in to clear things up?

Imagine discussing the sermons of George Whitefield, Jonathan Edwards, Charles Finney, and Charles Spurgeon with the preachers themselves. Or sitting down to hear insights on family and prayer from Susanna Wesley. Or talking about faith with George Mueller or Bill Bright, then listening to their stories. You could cover the Civil War era with Abraham Lincoln and Harriet Beecher Stowe. Or the history of missions with William Carey, Amy Carmichael, Lottie Moon, or Hudson and Maria Taylor. You could discuss ministry ideas with Brother Andrew, George Verwer, Luis Palau, Billy Graham, Joni Eareckson Tada, Chuck Colson, or Elisabeth Elliot.

We'll contemplate God's person and works, talking long over dinner and tea, on walks and in living rooms, by rivers and fires. Intellectual curiosity isn't part of the Curse—it is God's blessing on his image-bearers. He made us with fertile, curious minds so that we might seek truth and find him, our greatest source of pleasure. In Heaven our intellectual curiosity will surely surface—and be satisfied—only to surface and be satisfied again and again.

In 1546, Philip Melanchthon gave a memorial address about his departed friend Martin Luther. In it Melanchthon envisioned Luther in Heaven, fellowshiping with predecessors in the faith: "We remember the great delight with which he recounted the course, the counsels, the perils and escapes of the prophets, and the learning with which he discoursed on all the ages of the Church, thereby showing that he was inflamed by no ordinary passion for these wonderful men. Now he embraces them and rejoices to hear them speak and to speak to them in turn. Now they hail him gladly as a companion, and thank God with him for having gathered and preserved the Church."[249]

WILL WE FIND BOOKS IN HEAVEN?

We know that sixty-six books, those that comprise the Bible, will be in Heaven—"Your Word, O Lord, is eternal; it stands firm in the heavens"

(Psalm 119:89). Jesus said, "Heaven and earth will pass away, but my words will never pass away" (Matthew 24:35). Presumably, we will read, study, contemplate, and discuss God's Word.

There are also other books in Heaven: "I saw the dead, great and small, standing before the throne, and books were opened. Another book was opened, which is the book of life. The dead were judged according to what they had done as recorded in the books" (Revelation 20:12).

What are these books? They appear to contain documentation of everything ever done by anyone on earth. To say the least, they must be extensive.

While some people take these books figuratively, to represent God's omniscience, we should not assume these aren't real books. It would have been easy to tell us "the all-knowing God judged everyone."

The other book is the Book of Life, in which the names of God's people are written. John mentions it throughout the book of Revelation (Revelation 3:5; 13:8; 17:8; 20:12, 15; 21:27). It's mentioned in the Hebrew Scriptures as well (Exodus 32:32-33; Daniel 12:1). It's also referred to in later literature, such as the book of Jubilees and the Dead Sea Scrolls. The apostle Paul refers to it in Philippians 4:3.

Other passages describe a scroll in Heaven. Jesus opens a great scroll (Revelation 5:1, 5), and an angel holds a little scroll (Revelation 10:2). The psalm writer David said, "Record my lament; list my tears on your scroll—are they not in your record?" (Psalm 56:8). He asked that his tears be kept in Heaven's permanent record.

Malachi 3:16-18 is a remarkable passage that tells us God documents the faithful deeds of his children on Earth: "Then those who feared the Lord talked with each other, and the Lord listened and heard. A scroll of remembrance was written in his presence concerning those who feared the Lord and honored his name. 'They will be mine,' says the Lord Almighty, 'in the day when I make up my treasured possession. I will spare them, just as in compassion a man spares his son who serves him. And you will again see the distinction between the righteous and the wicked, between those who serve God and those who do not.'"

God is proud of his people for fearing him and honoring his name, and he promises that all will see the differences between those who serve him and those who don't. Those distinctions are preserved in this scroll in Heaven.

The king often had scribes record the deeds of his subjects so that he could remember and properly reward his subjects' good deeds (Esther 6:1-11). While God needs no reminder, he makes a permanent record so that the entire universe will one day know his justification for rewarding the righteous and punishing the wicked.

There's no hint that God will destroy any or all of the books and scrolls presently in Heaven. It's likely that these records of the faithful works of God's people on Earth will be periodically read throughout the ages.

The books contain detailed historical records of all of our lives on this earth. Each of us is part of these records. Obscure events, words heard by only a handful of people will be known. Your acts of faithfulness and kindness that no one else knows are well-known by God. He is documenting them in his books. He will reward you for them in Heaven.

How many times have we done small acts of kindness on Earth without realizing the effects? How many times have we shared Christ with people we thought didn't take it to heart but who years later came to Jesus partly because of the seeds we planted? How many times have we spoken up for unborn children and seen no result, but as a result someone chose not to have an abortion and saved a child's life? How many dishes have been washed and diapers changed and crying children sung to in the middle of the night, when we couldn't see the impact of the love we showed? And how many times have we seen no response, but God was still pleased by our efforts?

God is watching. He is keeping track. In Heaven he'll reward us for our acts of faithfulness to him, right down to every cup of cold water we've given to the needy in his name (Mark 9:41). And he's making a permanent record in Heaven's books.

WILL THERE BE OTHER BOOKS BESIDES GOD'S?

I believe that on the New Earth, we'll also read books, new and old, written by people. Because we'll have strong intellects, great curiosity, and unlimited time, it's likely that books will have a *greater* role in our lives in Heaven than they do now. The libraries of the New Earth, I imagine, will be fantastic.

We'll have no lack of resources to study and understand. I once helped a young friend search for her biological mother, going through old court records, looking for just the right clue. We finally found it. I had the privilege of introducing them to each other. It was a taste of Heaven—where not all reunions will happen all at once, I imagine, but as eternity unfolds.

Will we search for information and do research on the New Earth? Why not?

Unlike the histories we read on Earth, Heaven's books will be objective and accurate. No exaggeration or overstatement, no spinning to make certain people look better and others worse. We will be able to handle the failings of our ancestors, just as they'll have the right perspective on ours.

Every biblical genealogy is a testimony to God's interest in history, heritage, and the unfolding of events on Earth. Will God lose interest in Earth? Will we? No. The New Earth's history includes that of the old Earth. But a new history will be built and recorded, a new civilization, wondrous beyond imagination. And we who know the King will all be part of it.

Books are part of culture. I expect many new books, great books, will be written on the New Earth. But I also believe that some books will endure from the old Earth. Any book that contains falsehood and dishonors God will have no place in Heaven. But what about great books, nonfiction and fiction? Will we find A. W. Tozer's *The Knowledge of the Holy*, J. I. Packer's *Knowing God*, John Piper's *Desiring God*, John Bunyan's *Pilgrim's Progress*, and Charles Sheldon's *In His Steps* on the New Earth? I'll be amazed if we don't find them there, just as I'll be amazed if no one sings John Newton's "Amazing Grace" in Heaven.

Perhaps those of us who are writers will go back to some of our published works and rewrite them in light of the perspective we'll gain. Maybe we'll look at our other books and realize they're no longer important—and some of them never were. The New Earth, I think, will confirm many things I've written in this book. It will completely dismantle others. "What was I thinking?" I'll ask myself. (If I knew which parts those were right now, I'd cut them out!) And I'll marvel at how much better the New Earth is than I ever imagined.

WILL WHAT WAS WRITTEN ON EARTH SURVIVE?

On the New Earth, will you see once more the letter of encouragement you wrote to your teenage son? Or the letter you wrote sharing Christ with your father? Or the life-changing words you jotted on a student's paper? Many such things written in this life may prove more important than books.

Some old books may be republished in the New Jerusalem. Or if God desires, he could preserve the original or printed copies from this earth. I wonder if John Wycliffe himself will hold again his Bible manuscripts. Will Harriet Beecher Stowe see again her pages of *Uncle Tom's Cabin*? Will Tolkien's The Lord of the Rings endure the fire? Will we read again a version of C. S. Lewis's *Mere Christianity* or The Chronicles of Narnia?

Will God preserve some books from our present lives? Will they be kept on the New Earth in museums and libraries? Will the God who resurrects people and animals and stars and rivers and trees also resurrect certain personal possessions, including books, which are first burned, then restored? C. S. Lewis portrayed it this way:

My friend said, "I don't see why there shouldn't be books in Heaven. But you will find that your library in Heaven contains only some of the books you had on earth." "Which?" I asked. "The ones you gave away or lent." "I hope the lent ones won't still have all the borrowers' dirty thumb marks," said I. "Oh yes they will," said he. "But just as the wounds of the martyrs will have turned into beauties, so you will find that the thumb-marks have turned into beautiful illuminated capitals or exquisite marginal woodcuts."[250]

CHAPTER 33

WHAT WILL OUR DAILY
LIVES BE LIKE?

Puritan pastor Richard Baxter's 1649 book *The Saints' Everlasting Rest* was the most influential book on Heaven ever written. Baxter marveled that we don't set everything else aside to consider Heaven and make sure we're going there. But somehow Heaven hasn't captured our imaginations or shaped our lives.

What will life in Heaven really be like? What does Scripture say we'll actually do in our eternal home?

WILL WE REST?

When God created the world, he rested on the seventh day (Genesis 2:2). That's the basis for the biblical Sabbath, when all people and animals rested (Exodus 20:9-11). God set aside days and weeks of rest, and he even rested the earth itself every seventh year (Leviticus 25:4-5). This is the rest we can anticipate on the New Earth—times of joyful praise and relaxed fellowship.

Our lives in Heaven will include rest (Hebrews 4:1-11). " 'Blessed are the dead who die in the Lord from now on.' 'Yes,' says the Spirit, 'they will rest from their labor, for their deeds will follow them'" (Revelation 14:13).

Eden is a picture of rest—work that's meaningful and enjoyable, abundant food, a beautiful environment, unhindered friendship with God and other people and animals. Even with Eden's restful perfection, one day was set aside for special rest and worship. Work will be refreshing on the New Earth, yet regular rest will be built into our lives.

Part of our inability to appreciate Heaven as a place of rest relates to our failure to enter into a weekly day of rest now. By rarely turning attention from our responsibilities, we fail to anticipate our coming deliverance from the Curse to a full rest.

"Make every effort to enter that rest" (Hebrews 4:11). It's ironic that it takes such effort to set aside time for rest, but it does. For me, and for many of us, it's difficult to guard our schedules, but it's worth it. The day of rest points us to Heaven and to Jesus, who said, "Come to me, all you who are weary . . . , and I will give you rest" (Matthew 11:28).

What feels better than putting your head on the pillow after a hard day's work? (How about what it will feel like after a hard *life's* work?) It's good to sit back and have a glass of iced tea, feel the sun on your face, or tilt back in your recliner and close your eyes. It's good to have nothing to do but read a good book or take your dog for a walk or listen to your favorite music and tell God how grateful you are for his kindness. Rest is good. So good that God built it into his creation and his law.

Some people thrive on social interaction; others are exhausted by it. Some love solitude; others don't. On the New Earth, we'll likely all welcome the lively company of others but also crave times of restful solitude. We'll enjoy both.

We catch glimpses of being able to enjoy both work and rest at once. I used to feel this when body, mind, and the beauty around me sometimes "kicked in" on a ten-mile run. I've experienced the same thing bicycling, when I've felt I could ride forever and the pedaling I was doing was part of a great rest. I can be working intently at something I love yet find the work restful and refreshing.

God rested on the seventh day, before sin entered the world. He prescribed rest for sinless Adam and Eve, and he prescribed it for those under the curse of sin. Regular rest will be part of the life to come in the new universe. (Wouldn't it be wise to learn how to rest now?)

WILL WE SLEEP?

If our lives on the New Earth will be restful, will we need to sleep? Some people argue that we won't sleep because we'll have perfect bodies. But the same argument would apply to eating—yet we know we'll eat. Adam and Eve were created perfect, but did they sleep? Presumably. If so, *sleep cannot be an imperfection*. It's a matter of God's design for the rhythm of life.

Sleep is one of life's great pleasures. It's part of God's perfect plan for humans in bodies living on the earth. Troubled sleep and sleeplessness are products of sin and the Curse, but sleep itself is God's gift. I believe we will likely need it *and* enjoy it.

Some people say, "But there won't be fatigue." Why not? Couldn't resources be depleted and renewed in a perfect but finite world, just as they were in Eden? We'll rest and be refreshed in Heaven. What's more restful and refreshing than a good sleep? If we will eat, walk, serve, work, laugh, and play, why would we not sleep?

WILL WE WORK?

The idea of working in Heaven is foreign to many people. Yet Scripture clearly teaches it. When God created Adam, he "took the man and put him in the Garden of Eden to work it and take care of it" (Genesis 2:15). Work was part of the original Eden. It was part of a perfect human life on Earth.

Work wasn't part of the Curse. The Curse, rather, made work menial, tedious, and frustrating: "Cursed is the ground because of you; through painful toil you will eat of it all the days of your life. It will produce thorns and thistles for you, and you will eat the plants of the field. By the sweat of your brow you will eat your food" (Genesis 3:17-19).

However, on the New Earth work will be redeemed and transformed into what God intended: "No longer will there be any curse. The throne of God and of the Lamb will be in the city, and his servants will serve him" (Revelation 22:3). *Serve* is a verb. Servants are people who are active and occupied, carrying out tasks.

God himself is a worker. He didn't create the world and then retire. Jesus said, "My Father is always at his work to this very day, and I, too, am working" (John 5:17). Jesus found great satisfaction in his work. "'My food,' Jesus said, 'is to do the will of him who sent me and to finish his work'" (John 4:34). We'll also have work to do, satisfying and enriching work that we can't wait to get back to, work that'll never be drudgery. God is the primary worker, and as his image-bearers, we're made to work. We create, accomplish, set goals, and fulfill them—to God's glory.

In *The Happiness of Heaven*, Father Boudreau argued against Aquinas's belief that Heaven is a place of motionless absorption with an intellectual contemplation of God:

> We are active by nature. Action, therefore, both of mind and body, is a
> law of our being, which cannot be changed without radically changing,
> or rather destroying, our whole nature. Instead of destroying it, it
> follows that in Heaven we shall be far more active than we can possibly
> be here below. . . . The soul of Jesus Christ enjoyed the Beatific Vision,
> even while here on earth in mortal flesh. Was He, on that account,
> prevented from doing anything except contemplating the divine
> essence? He certainly was not. He labored and preached; He also drank
> and slept; He visited His friends and did a thousand other things.[251]

Consider Christ's activities: working in a carpenter shop, walking the countryside, fishing, sailing, meeting people, talking, teaching, eating—doing his life's work. Even after his resurrection he moved from place to place, connecting with his disciples and continuing his work. (A preview of life after our resurrection.) Consider the following verses, which convey a mini-theology of work:

Having all that you need, you will abound in every good work. (2 Corinthians 9:8)

Whatever you do, work at it with all your heart, as working for the Lord, not for men. (Colossians 3:23)

See to it that you complete the work you have received in the Lord. (Colossians 4:17)

He will be an instrument for noble purposes, made holy, useful to the Master and prepared to do any good work. (2 Timothy 2:21)

Since an overseer is entrusted with God's work, he must be blameless. (Titus 1:7)

Obey [your leaders] so that their work will be a joy. (Hebrews 13:17)

You call on a Father who judges each man's work impartially. (1 Peter 1:17)

I know your deeds, your hard work and your perseverance. (Revelation 2:2)

Since work began before sin and the Curse, and since God, who is without sin, is a worker, we should assume human beings will work on the New Earth. We should assume we'll be able to resume the work started by Adam and Eve, exercising godly dominion over the earth, ruling it for God's glory.

But we don't need to just assume this. Scripture directly tells us. When the faithful servant enters Heaven, he is offered not retirement but this: "Well done, good and faithful servant; you have been faithful over a few things, I will make you ruler over many things. Enter into the joy of your lord" (Matthew 25:23, NKJV).

What kind of work will we do in Heaven? Maybe you'll build a cabinet with Joseph of Nazareth. Or with Jesus. Maybe you'll tend sheep with David, discuss medicine with Luke, sew with Dorcas, make clothes with Lydia, design a new tent with Paul or Priscilla, write a song with Isaac Watts, ride horses with John Wesley, or sing with Keith Green. Maybe you'll write a theology of the Trinity, bouncing your thoughts off Paul, John, Polycarp, Cyprian, Augustine, Calvin, Wesley . . . and even Jesus.

Our work will be joyful and fulfilling, giving glory to God. What could be better? Generally, unemployed people aren't happy. Work is a blessing, and not just because of its financial rewards. Even in a world under the Curse, most of us have known satisfaction in our work. Spurgeon asked his congregation, "Do you know, dear friends, the deliciousness of work?"[252]

Jesus said to his Father, "I brought glory to you here on earth by doing everything you told me to do" (John 17:4, NLT). How will we glorify God for eternity? By doing everything he tells us to do. What did God first tell mankind to do? Fill the earth and exercise dominion over it. What will we do for eternity to glorify God? We'll exercise dominion over the earth, demonstrating God's creativity and ingenuity as his image-bearers, producing Christ-exalting culture.

WILL WE HAVE OUR OWN HOMES?

Perhaps you're familiar with Christ's promise in John 14: "In my Father's house are many mansions. . . . I go to prepare a place for you" (v. 2, KJV). The Vulgate, the Latin Bible, used the word *mansiones* in that verse, and the King James Version followed by using *mansions*. Unfortunately, that rendering is misleading if it makes us envision having massive lodgings on separate estates. The intended meaning seems to be that we'll have separate dwelling places on a single estate or even separate rooms within the same house.

New Testament scholar D. A. Carson says, "Since heaven is here pictured as the Father's house, it is more natural to think of 'dwelling-places' within a house as rooms or suites. . . . The simplest explanation is best: my Father's house refers to heaven, and in heaven are many rooms, many dwelling-places. The point is not the lavishness of each apartment, but the fact that such ample provision has been made that there is more than enough space for every one of Jesus' disciples to join him in his Father's home."[253]

The New International Version rendering of John 14:2 is this: "In my Father's house are many rooms. . . . I am going there to prepare a place for you." *Place* is singular, but *rooms* is plural. This suggests Jesus has in mind for each of us an individual dwelling that's a smaller part of the larger place. This place will be home to us in the most unique sense.

The term *room* is cozy and intimate. The terms *house* or *estate* suggest spaciousness. That's Heaven: a place both spacious and intimate. Some of us enjoy coziness, being in a private space. Others enjoy a large, wide-open space. Most of us enjoy both—and the New Earth will offer both.

Heaven isn't likely to have lots of identical residences. God loves diversity, and he tailor-makes his children *and* his provisions for them. When we see the particular place he's prepared for us—not just for mankind in general but for us in particular—we'll rejoice to see our ideal home.

> Christian, meditate much on heaven, it will help thee to press on, and to forget the toil of the way. This vale of tears is but the pathway to the better country: this world of woe is but the stepping-stone to a world of bliss. And, after death, what cometh? What wonder-world will open upon our astonished sight?
>
> **CHARLES SPURGEON**

When you're traveling late at night and you don't know where you're going to stay, nothing's more discouraging than finding a No Vacancy sign. There's no such sign in Heaven. If we've made our reservations by accepting God's gift in Christ, then Heaven is wide open to us. Jesus knew what it was like to have no vacancy in the inn and to sleep in a barn. On the New Earth, he'll have plenty of room for all of us.

I live in Oregon. When I've flown home from overseas and landed in New York, I feel I've come "home," meaning I'm in my home country. Then when I land in Oregon, I'm more home. When I come to my hometown, everything looks familiar. Finally, when I arrive at my house, I'm really home. But even there I have a special room or two. Scripture's various terms—*New Earth, country, city, place,* and *rooms*—involve such shades of meaning to the word *home.*

Nanci and I love our home. When we're gone long enough, we miss it. It's not just the place we miss, of course—it's family, friends, neighbors, church. Yet the place offers the comfort of the routine, the feel of the bed, the books on the shelf. It's not fancy, but it's home. When our daughters were young, our family spent two months overseas visiting missionaries in six different countries. It was a wonderful adventure, but three days before the trip ended, our hearts turned a corner, and home was all we could think of.

Our love for home, our yearning for it, is a glimmer of our longing for our true home.

A passage in Isaiah starts "Behold, I will create new heavens and a new earth" and ends with "They will neither harm nor destroy on all my holy mountain" (Isaiah 65:17-25). In between is a verse that appears to refer to life on the New Earth: "They will build houses and dwell in them; they will plant vineyards and eat their fruit" (Isaiah 65:21). This involves not only houses but land. (Some argue that because the previous verse appears to speak of death, this must refer only to the Millennium.)

The New Earth's citizens will build, plant, and eat, as human beings on Earth always have. Like Adam and Eve in Eden, we'll inherit a place that God has prepared for us. But we'll be free to build on it and develop it as we see fit, to God's glory.

WILL WE OPEN OUR HOMES TO GUESTS?

I believe Scripture teaches that on the New Earth we'll open our homes to guests. I base this on Christ's words in Luke 16.

After speaking of the shrewd servant's desire to use earthly resources so that "people will welcome me into their houses" (v. 4), Jesus told his followers to "use worldly wealth to gain friends" (v. 9). Jesus instructed them to use their earthly resources to gain friends by making a difference in their lives on Earth. The reason? "So that when it [life on Earth] is gone, you will be welcomed into eternal dwellings" (v. 9).

Our "friends" in Heaven appear to be those whose lives we've touched on Earth and who now have their own "eternal dwellings." Luke 16:9 seems to say these "eternal dwellings" of our friends are places where we'll stay and enjoy companionship—second homes to us as we move about the Kingdom.

Because many people mistakenly believe that Heaven won't be earthlike, it never occurs to them to take this passage literally. They think "eternal dwellings" is a general reference to Heaven. But surely Christ isn't saying we'll enter Heaven because we used our money wisely. In the parable, the eternal dwellings are Heaven's equivalent to the private homes that the shrewd servant could stay in on Earth.

Do I believe Jesus is suggesting we'll actually share lodging, meals, and fellowship with friends in God's Kingdom? Yes. I'm aware that some readers will think this far-fetched. But that's only because when we think of Heaven, we don't think of resurrected people living on a resurrected Earth, living in dwelling places, and eating and fellowshiping together. But isn't that *exactly* what Scripture teaches us?

The song "Thank You" pictures us in Heaven, meeting people who explain how our giving touched their lives. They say, "Thank you for giving to the Lord, I am so glad you gave." This is more than a nice sentiment. It's something that will actually happen. Every time we give to missions and to feed the hungry, we should think about people we'll meet in Heaven, people whose homes on the New Earth we'll likely one day visit.

Mincaye, the Auca Indian who speared Nate Saint, is now a follower of Jesus. When Mincaye was asked what he's going to do when he meets Nate Saint in Heaven, he replied, "I'm going to run and throw my arms around Nate Saint and thank him for bringing Jesus Christ to me and my people." He added that Nate Saint would welcome him home.[254]

How many wonderful meetings and reunions should we all anticipate? "Do not forget to entertain strangers, for by so doing some people have entertained angels without knowing it" (Hebrews 13:2). Perhaps we'll be welcomed into the homes not only of people but also of angels, who will reciprocate the hospitality we showed them on the old Earth.

Will Jesus be one of the guests you welcome into your dwelling place? When he lived on Earth, Jesus often visited the home of his friends Mary, Martha, and Lazarus. Just before Jesus went to the cross, he told his disciples, "I will not drink of this fruit of the vine from now on until that day when I drink it anew with you in my Father's kingdom" (Matthew 26:29). He spoke these words as he ate a meal with them in a private home. When he dines and drinks with his disciples on the New Earth, what better places to do that than in homes?

Jesus says, "Here I am! I stand at the door and knock. If anyone hears my voice and opens the door, I will come in and eat with him, and he with me" (Revelation 3:20). Although he speaks figuratively here, his interest in our lives will surely extend to visiting us in our homes.

Incredible as it seems, Jesus desires our company. He's preparing us a place in Heaven. He'll welcome us into his home. And we should expect to welcome him into ours.

WHAT WILL OUR RELATIONSHIPS BE LIKE?

CHAPTER 34

WILL WE DESIRE RELATIONSHIPS WITH ANYONE EXCEPT GOD?

Throughout the ages, Christians have anticipated eternal reunion with their loved ones. In 710, the Venerable Bede, a church historian, wrote these words about Heaven:

> A great multitude of dear ones is there expecting us; a vast and mighty crowd of parents, brothers, and children, secure now of their own safety, anxious yet for our salvation, long that we may come to their right and embrace them, to that joy which will be common to us and to them, to that pleasure expected by our fellow servants as well as ourselves, to that full and perpetual felicity. . . . If it be a pleasure to go to them, let us eagerly and covetously hasten on our way, that we may soon be with them, and soon be with Christ.[255]

WILL WE WANT ANYONE BESIDES CHRIST?

Christ is "the Alpha and the Omega, the First and the Last" (Revelation 22:13). He alone is sufficient to meet all our needs.

Yet, God has designed us for relationship not only with himself but also with others of our kind. After God created the world, he stepped back to look at his work and pronounced it "very good." However, before his creation was complete, he said that one thing—and only one—was not good. "It is not good for the man to be alone. I will make a helper suitable for him" (Genesis 2:18). God planned for Adam, and all mankind, to need human companionship. In other words, God made people to need and desire others besides himself.

To some people, this sounds like heresy. After all, Asaph prays, "Whom have I in heaven but you? And earth has nothing I desire besides you" (Psalm 73:25). This verse is sometimes used to prove that we should desire nothing but God, that it is wrong to desire "earthly things," including human relationships. But

God made us to desire earthly things such as food, water, shelter, warmth, work, play, rest, human friendship, and much more. That won't change in Heaven.

People have told me we shouldn't long for Heaven, only for God. If that were true, God would condemn rather than commend his people who "were longing for a better country—a heavenly one" (Hebrews 11:16). King David saw no contradiction between seeking God the person and seeking Heaven the place. The two were inseparable: "One thing have I asked of the Lord, that will I seek after: that I may dwell in the house of the Lord all the days of my life, to gaze upon the beauty of the Lord and to inquire in his temple" (Psalm 27:4, ESV). Notice that David says he seeks "one thing"—to be in God's magnificent place and to be with God's magnificent person.

As I said in chapter 17, we must understand that God is the source of all joy—all other joys are secondary and derivative. They come from him, find their meaning in him, and cannot be divorced from him. Likewise, while Christ is our primary treasure, he encourages us to store up other treasures in Heaven (Matthew 6:19-21).

Christ is Heaven's center of gravity, but we don't diminish his importance by enjoying natural wonders, angels, or people. On the contrary, we'll exalt him and draw closer to him as we enjoy all he created.

WILL WE NEED ONLY GOD IN HEAVEN?

Like the desert monks who withdrew into the desert to live apart from human companionship, some people still insist, "I need only God." But as spiritual as it sounds, this perspective is another form of Christoplatonism. Consider again the implications of the fact that God said, "It is not good for the man to be alone" (Genesis 2:18). Think of it—God was with Adam in the Garden, yet God said that wasn't good enough. God designed us to need each other. What we gain from each other is more of God because we're created in his image and are a conduit for his self-revelation.

Eden was the forerunner of the New Earth. Since meaningful human companionship turned God's assessment of "not good" into a declaration of "very good" on the first Earth, we shouldn't expect him to change his mind on the New Earth. Yet many people minimize human relationships in Heaven. Protestant reformer John Calvin said, "To be in Paradise and live with God is not to speak to each other and be heard by each other, but is only to enjoy God, to feel his good will, and rest in him."[256] To Calvin's credit, he longed for the joy to be found in God. But he imagined a false dichotomy between the joys of relating to God and relating to God's children. To take pleasure in another image-bearer doesn't offend God; it *pleases* him. To enjoy a conversation with a brother or sister does not require making that person an idol or competitor with God. God was supremely pleased that Adam and Eve enjoyed each other's company in Paradise. God is our father, and fathers delight in their children's close relationships.

Some people falsely assume that when we give attention to people, it automatically distracts us from God. But even now, in a fallen world, people can turn my attention toward God. Was Jesus distracted from God by spending time with people on Earth? Certainly not. In Heaven, no person will distract us from God. We will never experience any conflict between worshiping God himself and enjoying God's people.

Deep and satisfying human relationships will be among God's greatest gifts. Jonathan Edwards saw no conflict between anticipating our relationships with God and our loved ones:

> Every Christian friend that goes before us from this world is a
> ransomed spirit waiting to welcome us in heaven. There will be the
> infant of days that we have lost below, through grace to be found
> above. There the Christian father, and mother, and wife, and child,
> and friend, with whom we shall renew the holy fellowship
> of the saints, which was interrupted by death here, but shall be
> commenced again in the upper sanctuary, and then shall never end.
> There we shall have companionship with the patriarchs and fathers
> and saints of the Old and New Testaments, and those of whom the
> world was not worthy. . . . And there, above all, we shall enjoy and
> dwell with God the Father, whom we have loved with all our hearts
> on earth; and with Jesus Christ, our beloved Savior, who has always
> been to us the chief among ten thousands, and altogether lovely; and
> with the Holy Spirit, our Sanctifier, and Guide, and Comforter; and
> shall be filled with all the fullness of the Godhead forever![257]

Jesus affirmed that the greatest commandment was to love God, but that the second, inseparable from the first, was to love our neighbor (Matthew 22:37-39). He never considered these commands as incompatible. Neither should we. He saw the second flowing directly from the first. One of the highest ways we love God is by loving people. Jesus rebuked the religious leaders because they imagined they could love God without loving people (Luke 10:27-37). The spiritual-sounding "I will love only God and no one else" is not only unspiritual; it's impossible. For if we don't love people, who are created in God's image, we can't love God.

WHAT DID PAUL SAY ABOUT REUNION IN HEAVEN?

Paul says to his friends in Thessalonica, "We loved you so much" and "You had become so dear to us," then speaks of his "intense longing" to be with them (1 Thessalonians 2:8, 17). In fact, Paul anticipates his ongoing relationship with the Thessalonians as part of his heavenly reward: "What is our hope, our joy, or the crown in which we will glory in the presence of our Lord Jesus when he comes? Is it not you? Indeed, you are our glory and joy" (1 Thessalonians 2:19-20).

Isn't this emphatic proof that it's appropriate for us to deeply love people and look forward to being with them in Heaven? Paul sees no contradiction in referring to both Christ and his friends as his hope and joy and crown in Heaven.

Paul then asks, "How can we thank God enough for you in return for all the joy we have in the presence of our God because of you?" (3:9). The joy he takes in his friends doesn't compete with his joy in God—it's part of it. Paul thanks God for his friends. Whenever we're moved to thank God for people, we're experiencing exactly what he intended.

Paul also says to the Thessalonians, "You long to see us, just as we also long to see you. . . . How can we thank God enough for you in return for all the joy we have in the presence of our God because of you? Night and day we pray most earnestly that we may see you again" (3:6, 9-10). Paul finds joy in God's presence because of other Christians. He anticipates the day "when our Lord Jesus comes with all his holy ones" (3:13). He looks forward to being with Jesus *and* his people.

Paul tells the Thessalonians that we'll be reunited with believing family and friends in Heaven: "Brothers, we do not want you to be ignorant about those who fall asleep, or to grieve like the rest of men, who have no hope. . . . God will bring with Jesus those who have fallen asleep in him. . . . We who are still alive and are left will be caught up together with them. . . . And so we will be with the Lord forever. Therefore encourage each other with these words" (4:13-14, 17-18). Our source of comfort isn't only that we'll be with the Lord in Heaven but also that we'll be with each other.

Puritan Richard Baxter longed for that comfort: "I know that Christ is all in all; and that it is the presence of God that makes Heaven to be heaven. But yet it much sweetens the thoughts of that place to me that there are there such a multitude of my most dear and precious friends in Christ."[258]

In Philippians 1, Paul speaks with unapologetic affection to his brothers in Christ, describing himself as longing for them. Note that he clearly sees no incompatibility between his Christ-centered desire to be with Jesus (1:21) and his Christ-centered love for others:

I thank my God every time I remember you. In all my prayers for all
of you, I always pray with joy because of your partnership in the gospel
from the first day until now, being confident of this, that he who
began a good work in you will carry it on to completion until the day
of Christ Jesus. (Philippians 1:3-6)

Paul's delight in his brothers in Christ reminds us that the first and second
greatest commands are inseparable: "Love the Lord your God with all your
heart . . . and love your neighbor as yourself" (Luke 10:27). And if you love your
neighbor as yourself, how much more your family, which derives its identity
from God himself?

As if anticipating that someone might object by saying, "But God is the
only one we should find joy in and long for," Paul continues his thought in the
following verses:

It is right for me to feel this way about all of you, since I have you in
my heart; for whether I am in chains or defending and confirming the
gospel, all of you share in God's grace with me. God can testify how I
long for all of you with the affection of Christ Jesus. (Philippians 1:7-8)

Note the source of Paul's deep longing and affection for his brothers and sisters:
Christ Jesus himself. Though it is possible to put people over God (which is
idolatry), it is also possible, while putting God over people, to find in people a
wonderful expression of God himself, so great that it is completely appropriate
for us to have them in our hearts, to find joy *in them*, and long to be *with them*.

Such sentiments are not idolatry, and it is not wrong to have them. In fact,
something is wrong if we do not have them. For finding joy in God and longing
for God does not kill our joy in and longing for others. Rather, it fuels it. The
joy and longing we have for other people is directly derived from our joy in and
longing for God.

WHAT WILL WE REMEMBER?

One writer claims, "We will not even remember this old world we call Earth . . .
nor will we even recall it! It simply will not come into our minds."[259] This common misperception confuses people. They think we won't remember our
earthly lives, including the relationships so precious to us.

The people who believe we will not remember our present lives often cite
Isaiah 65:17 as their proof: "Behold, I will create new heavens and a new earth.

The former things will not be remembered, nor will they come to mind." However, this verse should be viewed in context. It's linked to the previous verse, in which God says, "For the past troubles will be forgotten and hidden from my eyes." This doesn't suggest literal lack of memory, as if the omniscient God couldn't recall the past. Rather, it's like God's comment to Jeremiah: "I . . . will remember their sins no more" (Jeremiah 31:34). It means that God *chooses* not to bring up our past sins or hold them against us. In eternity, past sins and sorrows won't preoccupy God or us. We'll be capable of choosing not to recall or dwell on anything that would diminish Heaven's joy.

In chapter 7 we learned that the martyrs now in the intermediate Heaven remember what happened on Earth, including that they endured great suffering (Revelation 6:9-11). Jesus promised that in Heaven, those who endured bad things on Earth would be comforted for them (Luke 16:25). The comfort implies memory of what happened. If we had no memory of the bad things, why would we need comfort? How would we feel it?

Our minds will be clearer in Heaven, not foggier. Memory is basic to personality. The principle of continuity requires that we will remember our past lives. Heaven cleanses our slate of sin and error, but it doesn't erase our memory of it. The lessons we learned here about God's love, grace, and justice surely aren't lost but will carry over to Heaven. Father Boudreau states, "For the sins which so often made us tremble, are washed away in the blood of Jesus, and are, therefore, no longer a source of trouble. The remembrance of them rather intensifies our love for the God of mercy, and therefore increases our happiness."[260]

It seems likely that recalling the reality of our past troubles, sorrows, and sins would set a sharp contrast to the glories of Heaven, as darkness does to light, as Hell does to Heaven. We would lose this contrast if we forgot what sorrow was. If we forgot we were desperate sinners, how could we appreciate the depth and meaning of Christ's redemptive work for us?

Even though God will wipe away the tears and sorrow attached to this world, he will *not* erase from our minds human history and Christ's intervention. Remember that Christ's resurrection body has nail-scarred hands and feet (John 20:24-29). Seeing those scars in Heaven will always remind us that our sins nailed Jesus to the cross. Heaven's happiness won't be dependent on our ignorance of what happened on Earth. Rather, it will be enhanced by our informed appreciation of God's glorious grace and justice as we grasp what really happened here.

The Greek word for truth, *aletheia*, is a negated form of the verb translated "to forget"; knowing the truth means *to stop forgetting*. While a word's history doesn't determine its present meaning, in this case it's certainly suggestive. A

Christian view of truth is based not on forgetting but on remembering. Truth is seeing God at work in all events in our past, present, and future.

The New Earth will include memorials to the twelve tribes and the apostles (Revelation 21:12-14). This indicates continuity and memory of history. If we're aware of others' pasts on the old Earth, surely we'll be aware of our own.

God's acts of sovereign faithful grace will never be erased from our minds. Heaven's happiness will be dependent not on our ignorance but on our perspective. We'll see and know as never before.

WILL WE RECOGNIZE EACH OTHER?

When asked if we would recognize friends in Heaven, George MacDonald responded, "Shall we be greater fools in Paradise than we are here?"[261]

Yet many people wonder whether we'll know each other in Heaven. What lies behind that question is Christoplatonism and the false assumption that in Heaven we'll be disembodied spirits who lose our identities and memories. How does someone recognize a spirit?

As we've seen, however, these assumptions are unbiblical. (See appendix A for further discussion.) Christ's disciples recognized him countless times after his resurrection. They recognized him on the shore as he cooked breakfast for them (John 21:1-14). They recognized him when he appeared to a skeptical Thomas (John 20:24-29). They recognized him when he appeared to five hundred people at once (1 Corinthians 15:6).

But what about Mary at the garden tomb or the two men on the road to Emmaus? They didn't recognize Jesus. Some people have argued from this that Jesus was unrecognizable. But a closer look shows otherwise.

Jesus said to Mary in the garden, " 'Woman . . . why are you crying? Who is it you are looking for?' Thinking he was the gardener, she said, 'Sir, if you have carried him away, tell me where you have put him, and I will get him'" (John 20:15).

Distressed, teary-eyed Mary, knowing Jesus was dead, and not making eye

> How happy is that love, in which there is an eternal progress in all these things; wherein new beauties are continually discovered, and more and more loveliness, and in which we shall forever increase in beauty ourselves; where we shall be made capable of finding out and giving, and shall receive, more and more endearing expressions of love forever: our union will become more close, and communication more intimate.
>
> **JONATHAN EDWARDS**

contact with a stranger, naturally assumed he was the gardener. But as soon as Jesus said her name, she recognized him: "She turned toward him and cried out in Aramaic, 'Rabboni!' (which means Teacher)" (John 20:16).

Some commentators emphasize that the disciples on the Emmaus road didn't recognize Jesus. But notice what the text says: "As they talked and discussed these things with each other, Jesus himself came up and walked along with them; but they *were kept from* recognizing him" (Luke 24:15-16, emphasis added). God miraculously intervened to keep them from recognizing him. The implication is that apart from supernatural intervention, the men would have recognized Jesus, as they did later: "Then their eyes were opened and they recognized him, and he disappeared from their sight" (Luke 24:31).

Another indication that we'll recognize people in Heaven is Christ's transfiguration. Christ's disciples recognized the bodies of Moses and Elijah, even though the disciples couldn't have known what the two men looked like (Luke 9:29-33). This may suggest that personality will emanate through a person's body, so we'll instantly recognize people we know *of* but haven't previously met. If we can recognize those we've never seen, how much more will we recognize our family and friends?

Scripture gives no indication of a memory wipe causing us not to recognize family and friends. Paul anticipated being with the Thessalonians in Heaven, and it never occurred to him he wouldn't know them. In fact, if we wouldn't know our loved ones, the "comfort" of an afterlife reunion, taught in 1 Thessalonians 4:14-18, would be no comfort at all. J. C. Ryle said of this passage, "There would be no point in these words of consolation if they did not imply the mutual recognition of saints. The hope with which he cheers wearied Christians is the hope of meeting their beloved friends again. . . . But in the moment that we who are saved shall meet our several friends in heaven, we shall at once know them, and they will at once know us."[262]

The continuity of our resurrection minds and bodies argues that we'll have no trouble recognizing each other—in fact, we'll have much *less* trouble. In Heaven we probably won't fail to recognize an acquaintance in a crowd, or forget people's names.

Missionary Amy Carmichael had strong convictions on this question:

Shall we know one another in Heaven? Shall we love and remember? I do not think anyone need wonder about this or doubt for a single moment. We are never told we shall, because, I expect, it was not necessary to say anything about this which our own hearts tell us. We do not need words. For if we think for a minute, we know. Would you be yourself if you did not love and remember? . . . We are told that we shall be like our Lord Jesus. Surely this does not mean in holiness only, but in everything; and does not He know and love and remember? He would not be Himself if He did not, and we should not be ourselves if we did not.[263]

CHAPTER 35

WILL THERE BE MARRIAGE, FAMILIES, AND FRIENDSHIPS?

Receiving a glorified body and relocating to the New Earth doesn't erase history, it culminates history. Nothing will negate or minimize the fact that we were members of families on the old Earth. My daughters will always be my daughters, although first and foremost they are and will be God's daughters. My grandchildren will always be my grandchildren. Resurrection bodies presumably have chromosomes and DNA, with a signature that forever testifies to our genetic connection with family.

Heaven won't be without families but will be one big family, in which all family members are friends and all friends are family members. We'll have family relationships with people who were our blood family on Earth. But we'll also have family relationships with our friends, both old and new. We can't take material things with us when we die, but we do take our friendships to Heaven, and one day they'll be renewed.

Many of us treasure our families. But many others have endured a lifetime of brokenheartedness stemming from twisted family relationships. In Heaven neither we nor our family members will cause pain. Our relationships will be harmonious—what we've longed for.

When someone told Jesus that his mother and brothers were wanting to see him, he replied, "My mother and brothers are those who hear God's word and put it into practice" (Luke 8:19-21). Jesus was saying that devotion to God creates a bond transcending biological family ties. Jesus also said that those who follow him will gain "brothers, sisters, mothers, children" (Mark 10:29-30). I think of this when I experience an immediate depth of relationship with a fellow Christian I've just met.

If you weren't able to have children on Earth or if you've been separated from your children, both now and later God will give you relationships that will meet your needs to guide, help, serve, and invest in others. Your parental longings will be fulfilled. If you've never had a parent you could trust, you'll find trustworthy parents everywhere in Heaven, reminding you of your Father. And you can start with some of those relationships here.

So, it's not at all true that there will be "no family in Heaven." On the contrary, there will be *one* great family—and none of us will ever be left out. Every time we see someone, it will be a family reunion.

WILL THERE BE MARRIAGE AND FAMILY?

One group of religious leaders, the Sadducees, tried to trick Jesus with a question about marriage in Heaven. They didn't believe in the resurrection of the dead. Attempting to make him look foolish, they told Jesus of a woman who had seven husbands who all died. They asked him, "Now then, at the resurrection, whose wife will she be of the seven, since all of them were married to her?" (Matthew 22:28).

Christ replied, "At the resurrection people will neither marry nor be given in marriage; they will be like the angels in heaven" (Matthew 22:30).

There's a great deal of regret and misunderstanding about this passage. A woman wrote me, "I struggle with the idea that there won't be marriage in heaven. I believe I'll really miss it."

But the Bible does *not* teach there will be no marriage in Heaven. In fact, it makes clear there *will* be marriage in Heaven. What it says is that there will be *one* marriage, between Christ and his bride—and we'll all be part of it. Paul links human marriage to the higher reality it mirrors: "For this reason a man will leave his father and mother and be united to his wife, and the two will become one flesh. This is a profound mystery—but I am talking about Christ and the church" (Ephesians 5:31-32).

The one-flesh marital union we know on Earth is a signpost pointing to our relationship with Christ as our bridegroom. Once we reach the destination, the signpost becomes unnecessary. That one marriage—our marriage to Christ—will be so completely satisfying that even the most wonderful earthly marriage couldn't be as fulfilling.

Earthly marriage is a shadow, a copy, an echo of the true and ultimate marriage. Once that ultimate marriage begins, at the Lamb's wedding feast, all the human marriages that pointed to it will have served their noble purpose and will be assimilated into the one great marriage they foreshadowed. "The purpose of marriage is not to replace Heaven, but to prepare us for it."[264]

Here on Earth we long for a perfect marriage. That's exactly what we'll have—a perfect marriage with Christ. My wife, Nanci, is my best friend and my closest sister in Christ. Will we become more distant in the new world? Of course not—we'll become closer, I'm convinced. The God who said "It is not good for the man to be alone" (Genesis 2:18) is the giver and blesser of our relationships. Life on this earth matters. What we do here touches strings that reverberate for all eternity. Nothing will take away from the fact that Nanci and I are marriage partners here and that we invest so much of our lives in each other, serving Christ together. I fully expect no one besides God will understand me better on the New Earth, and there's nobody whose company I'll seek and enjoy more than Nanci's.

The joys of marriage will be far greater because of the character and love of our bridegroom. I rejoice for Nanci and for me that we'll both be married to the most wonderful person in the universe. He's already the one we love most—there is no competition. On Earth, the closer we draw to him, the closer we draw to each other. Surely the same will be true in Heaven. What an honor it will be to always know that God chose us for each other on this old Earth so that we might have a foretaste of life with him on the New Earth.

People with good marriages are each other's best friends. There's no reason to believe they won't still be best friends in Heaven.

Jesus said the institution of human marriage would end, having fulfilled its purpose. But he never hinted that deep relationships between married people would end. In our lives here, two people can be business partners, tennis partners, or pinochle partners. But when they're no longer partners, it doesn't mean their friendship ends. The relationship built during one kind of partnership often carries over to a permanent friendship after the partnership has ended. I expect that to be true on the New Earth for family members and friends who stood by each other here.

God usually doesn't replace his original creation, but when he does, he replaces it with something that is far better, never worse. Mormons attempt to have marriages permanently bound for eternity, but this disregards Christ's direct statement. Being married to Christ will be the ultimate thrill.

What about our children? What about my relationship to my daughters and sons-in-law and closest friends? There's every reason to believe we'll pick right up in Heaven with relationships from Earth. We'll gain many new ones but will continue to deepen the old ones. I think we'll especially enjoy connecting with those we faced tough times with on Earth and saying, "Did you ever imagine Heaven would be so wonderful?"

The notion that relationships with family and friends will be lost in Heaven, though common, is unbiblical. It denies the clear doctrine of continuity between this life and the next and suggests our earthly lives and relationships have no eternal consequence. It completely contradicts Paul's intense anticipation of being with the Thessalonians and his encouraging them to look forward to rejoining their loved ones in Heaven.

WILL THERE BE SEX?

As we saw earlier, we'll maintain distinct genders in our resurrection bodies. We'll be male or female. But will there be sex in the sense of sexual relations? If human marriage existed on the New Earth, by all means I would expect it to include sex. Sexual relations existed before the Fall and were not the product of sin and the Curse; they were God's perfect design. Since the lifting of the Curse will normally restore what God originally made, we would expect sex to be part of that. Given what we know about continuity between this life and the next, marriage and sex seem natural carryovers.

However, as we've seen, Christ made it clear that people in Heaven wouldn't be married to each other. He wasn't talking merely about the present Heaven, but "in the resurrection." He was specifically saying there will be no marriage among resurrected people on the resurrected Earth.

Because sex was designed to be part of a marriage relationship, marriage and sex logically belong together. Because we're told that humans won't be married to each other, and sex is intended for marriage, then logically we won't be engaging in sex.

This appears to be, then, an exception to the principle of continuity. However, since there's a different sort of continuity between earthly marriage and the marriage of Christ to his church, there may also be some way in which the intimacy and pleasure we now know as sex will also be fulfilled in some higher form. I don't know what that would be, but I do know that sex was designed by God, and I don't expect him to discard it without replacing it with something better. There's a unique metaphysical power to sexual union. It's no coincidence that pagan worship often involved sexual acts. As immoral as these acts were, they recognized a transcendent spiritual nature to sex. This otherworldliness is again a signpost—and it suggests that sexual relations in this world foreshadow something greater in the next world.

Certainly we should reject all christoplatonic assumptions that sex, which God called "very good," would be unworthy of Heaven. Rather than viewing marriage and sex as bad things to be replaced by good ones, we should view them as good things somehow transformed or resurrected into better ones.

If we won't have sex in Heaven and if in Heaven there's no frustration of desire, then it appears we won't desire sex. This isn't because we won't have physical desires, of course—we'll desire food and water. But what we *will* desire—and always enjoy—is the relational intimacy that was the best part of sex. We may discover, as we look back, that sex prefigured what it means to be lost in intimacy with Christ. Once we're married to him, we'll be at the destination that marital sex pointed to as a signpost.

Will our resurrection bodies have sex organs? Since men will be men, and women will be women, and since there will be direct continuity between the old bodies and the new, there's every reason to believe they will. Is that inconsistent, since they wouldn't be fulfilling a function for which they were designed? Not necessarily. Jesus was a perfect man, yet he was single and abstained from sex. Unmarried people on Earth have been called to celibacy, but they are still fully human.

> If I knew that never again would I recognize that beloved one with whom I spent more than thirty-nine years here on earth, my anticipation of heaven would much abate. To say that we shall be with Christ and that that will be enough, is to claim that there we shall be without the social instincts and affections which mean so much to us here. . . . Life beyond cannot mean impoverishment, but the enhancement and enrichment of life as we have known it here at its best.
>
> **W. GRAHAM SCROGGIE**

The earth will have been filled with people conceived through procreation, and we will experience deep intimacy with Christ, our bridegroom. So the purposes of sex will have been fulfilled. We'll participate in what sex was always pointing to—deep and engaging relational intimacy. We won't imagine we're missing out.

A single woman told me she would feel great loss if she went to Heaven never having had a great romance. But our romance with Christ will far exceed any earthly romance. No romance is perfect, and many end in disappointment. Our romance with Christ will never disappoint.

Someone wrote, "What will fill the void of marital intimacy in Heaven?" There will be no void. We'll have greater marital intimacy with Jesus than we ever had in the best earthly marriages.

A man whose wife died of cancer wrote me, "We could no longer have sexual relations, but our depth of partnership became greater than ever. Our relationship came to transcend sex." This will presumably be true of our human relationships in Heaven.

In response to the disappointment some feel at the idea of no sexual intercourse in Heaven, C. S. Lewis wrote,

I think our present outlook might be like that of a small boy who, on being told that the sexual act was the highest bodily pleasure should immediately ask whether you ate chocolates at the same time. On receiving the answer "No," he might regard absence of chocolates as the chief characteristic of sexuality. In vain would you tell him that the reason why lovers in their carnal raptures don't bother about chocolates is that they have something better to think of. The boy knows chocolate: he does not know the positive thing that excludes it. We are in the same position. We know the sexual life; we do not know, except in glimpses, the other thing which, in Heaven, will leave no room for it.[265]

WILL WE BE REUNITED WITH INFANTS WHO HAVE DIED?

We'll be reunited in Heaven with all believing loved ones. But what about infants, small children, and those who are mentally handicapped or have died too young to believe in Christ?

In Adam, all mankind sinned (Romans 5:12). We're conceived sinners (Psalm 51:5). Thus, children, as well as the mentally handicapped, have a sin nature and are separated from God. If God were willing to tolerate a certain number of sins but no more, then children who die young may not have reached their limit, thereby qualifying for Heaven. But Scripture teaches that the presence of any sin is enough to separate us from God (James 2:10). To say "Well, of course children are saved" won't suffice—given their sin natures, there is no "of course" about it.

A doctrine of infant salvation appears to require that children are conceived saved, then remain saved until they reach a certain age, at which point they become lost. But Scripture teaches we're conceived lost and remain lost until we become saved.

Scripture makes no reference to an "age of accountability," and it certainly doesn't teach the moral innocence of children. Charles Spurgeon said, "Some ground the idea of the eternal blessedness of the infant upon its *innocence*. We do no such thing. We believe that the infant fell in the first Adam 'for in Adam all died.' . . . If infants be saved it is not because of any natural innocence. They enter heaven by the very same way that we do: they are received in the name of Christ."[266]

Any person's salvation comes only through Christ's work (1 Timothy 2:5). Unless a person is born again, he or she can't enter God's Kingdom (John 3:3). How could a child be born again without consciously choosing Christ?

Scripture opens the door to the answer to this question through its teaching that God has a special love for children. Christ taught that we need to become like children to enter God's Kingdom, and he made a point of embracing children when his disciples wanted to exclude them (Matthew 19:13-14). He said "Let the little children come to me, and do not hinder them" (Luke 18:16). Christ used children as examples of faith (Matthew 18:2-4). In Ezekiel 16:21, God expresses his anger at the killing of children and refers to them as "my children."

Jesus says that the angels assigned to children "continually see the face of My Father who is in heaven" (Matthew 18:10, NASB). Clearly, this is special treatment, suggesting there may be other acts of special treatment, including salvation apart from the normal process of confession and repentance. Because of such passages, I believe that God in his mercy and his special love for children covers them with Christ's blood.

In Psalm 8:2, David says, "From the lips of children and infants you have ordained praise" (quoted by Jesus in Matthew 21:16). The inclusion of infants is significant because they would not be *conscious* of giving praise; it would have to be something instinctive. So, although children are sinners who need to be saved, God may well have a just way to cover them with Christ's blood so they go to Heaven when they die.

An interesting passage tells us that John the Baptist was filled with the Holy Spirit in his mother's womb (Luke 1:15, NASB). This suggests that God conferred a righteous standing—or at least a special, spiritual, sanctifying work— on John even though he was too young to confess his sinfulness or consciously yield to God. If God did that with John, couldn't he do it with other children? Similarly, David says God had been his God since his mother bore him (Psalm 22:10). God told Jeremiah he'd known him since before he was formed in his mother's womb (Jeremiah 1:5).

The most common biblical argument used to support infant salvation is David's statement about his infant son who died: "I will go to him, but he will not return to me" (2 Samuel 12:23). It's possible that David was saying either that he would die and go to the grave (joining his son in death but not necessarily in Heaven) or that he would die and, in fact, join his son in Heaven. I personally think David, in his agony, was consoling himself with the belief he would one day join his son in Heaven.

Although I believe God makes special provision for children to welcome them into Heaven, I'm concerned that this doctrine—which is at most implied and certainly not directly taught in Scripture—has been twisted in a way to make many people feel indifferent about two heartrending situations: abortion and children dying of sickness and malnutrition. I've written more elsewhere on the dangerous aspects of this subject.[267]

Perhaps in Heaven many people will meet their children who were aborted or their children who died in miscarriages (even some miscarriages their mothers weren't aware of). Many parents will be reunited with children who died at an early age. Perhaps these children will grab our hands and show us around the present Heaven. Then one day, after the final resurrection, we'll enjoy each other's company on the New Earth—and experience its wonders together.

If children do go to Heaven when they die, why doesn't God tell us that directly? It may be that he anticipates the twisted logic and rationalization it might foster in us. It might take from us the sense of urgency to see our children come to faith in Christ. It might cause us to be less concerned about the sacred God-given task of extending physical and financial help to the underprivileged and getting the gospel to children around the world. We must do what God has called us to do, which includes protecting, rescuing, feeding, evangelizing, and discipling children.

In Heaven, both we and they will be grateful for all we did on their behalf.

WHO WILL OUR FRIENDS BE IN HEAVEN?

Augustine and Aquinas—two of history's most influential theologians—imagined that in Heaven people would focus exclusively on God and that relationships between human beings would be minimal or insignificant.[268]

These great theologians were swayed by Christoplatonism. For the most part, they didn't seem to grasp that the eternal Heaven will be on Earth, where people will live and work in a relational society, glorifying God not merely as individuals but as a family in rich relationship with each other.

Near the end of his life, however, Augustine significantly changed his view of Heaven. He said, "We have not lost our dear ones who have departed from this life, but have merely sent them ahead of us, so we also shall depart and shall come to that life where they will be more than ever dear as they will be better known to us, and where we shall love them without fear of parting."[269] He also said, "All of us who enjoy God are also enjoying each other in Him."[270]

Do you have a close friend who's had a profound influence on you? Do you think it is a coincidence that she was in your dorm wing or became your roommate? Was it accidental that your desk was near his or that his family lived next door or that your father was transferred when you were in third grade so that you ended up in his neighborhood? God orchestrates our lives. "From one man he made every nation of men, that they should inhabit the whole earth; and he determined the times set for them and the exact places where they should live" (Acts 17:26).

Since God determined the time and exact places you would live, it's no accident which neighborhood you grew up in, who lived next door, who went to school with you, who was part of your church youth group, who was there to help you and pray for you. Our relationships were appointed by God, and there's every reason to believe they'll continue in Heaven.

God's plan doesn't stop on the New Earth; it continues. God doesn't abandon his purposes; he extends and fulfills them. Friendships begun on Earth will continue in Heaven, getting richer than ever.

Will some friendships be closer than others? Augustine claimed, "In the city of God there will be no special friendships. . . . All special attachments will be absorbed into one comprehensive and undifferentiated community of love. . . . The universalized love of heaven permits no exclusive, restricted circles of friends."[271]

But how does this position stand up to Scripture?

Just because we'll be sinless doesn't mean we won't be drawn to certain people more than others. We'll like everyone, but we'll be closer to some than others. Jesus was closer to John than to any of the other disciples. Jesus was closer to Peter, James, and John than to the rest of the Twelve, and closer to the Twelve than to the seventy, and closer to the seventy than to his other followers. He was close to Lazarus and Martha, and closer still to their sister Mary. He was so close to his mother that while he was dying on the cross, he instructed John to care for her after his death. Since Christ was closer to some people than to others, clearly there can't be anything wrong with it.

In Heaven there won't be cliques, exclusiveness, arrogance, posturing, belittling, or jealousy. But when friends particularly enjoy each other's company, they are reflecting God's design. If, as you walk about the New Jerusalem, you see Adam and Eve holding hands as they look at the tree of life, would you begrudge them their special friendship?

Perhaps you're disappointed that you've never had the friendships you long for. In Heaven you'll have much closer relationships with some people you now know, but it's also true that you may never have met the closest friends you'll ever have. Just as someone may be fifty years old before meeting her best friend, you may live on the New Earth enjoying many friendships before meeting someone who will become your dearest friend. Maybe your best friend will be someone sitting next to you at the first great feast. After all, the sovereign God who orchestrates friendships will be in charge of the seating arrangements.

On the New Earth we'll experience the joy of familiarity in old relationships and the joy of discovery in new ones. As we get to know each other better, we'll get to know God better. As we find joy in each other, we'll find joy in him. No human relationships will overshadow our relationship with God. All will serve to enhance it.

CHAPTER 36

WHOM WILL WE MEET, AND WHAT WILL WE EXPERIENCE TOGETHER?

In Heaven, will we spend time with people whose lives are recorded in Scripture and church history? No doubt. Jesus told us we'll sit at the dinner table with Abraham, Isaac, and Jacob (Matthew 8:11). If we sit with them, we should expect to sit with others. What do people do at dinner tables? In Middle Eastern cultures dinner was—and is—not only about good food and drink but also a time for building relationships, talking together, and telling stories.

Who will we talk with in Heaven? I'd like to ask Mary to tell stories about Jesus as a child. I'd enjoy talking with Simeon, Anna, Elizabeth, and John the Baptist. I want to hear Noah's accounts of life on the ark. I'm eager to listen to Moses tell about his times with God on the mountain. I'd like to ask Elijah about being taken away in the chariot and Enoch (and Enoch's wife) about his being caught up by God.

I want to talk with Mary, Martha, and their brother Lazarus. I'll ask people to fill in the blanks of the great stories in Scripture and church history. I want to hear a few million new stories. One at a time, of course, and spread out over thousands of years. I imagine we'll relish these great stories, ask questions, laugh together, and shake our heads in amazement.

We'll each have our own stories to tell also—and the memories and skills to tell them well. Right now, today, we are living the lives from which such stories will be drawn. Are we living them with eternity in mind? We'll have new adventures on the New Earth from which new stories will emerge, but I suspect the old stories from this life will always interest us too.

I look forward to reconnecting with many old friends as well as my mom and dad. I look forward to thanking C. S. Lewis, Francis Schaeffer, and A. W. Tozer for how their writings changed me. I anticipate meeting William Carey, Hudson and Maria Taylor, Amy Carmichael, Jim Elliot, Charles

Spurgeon, Dwight L. Moody, Harriet Beecher Stowe, some of the *Amistad* slaves, and a host of others.

Who's on your list?

How are you serving Christ today so that you may be on someone else's list?

WILL WE PURSUE AND DEVELOP RELATIONSHIPS?

One of the things I'm looking forward to in Heaven is meeting people I've known only by phone and e-mail. For those friends I rarely see, we'll finally have time and access to enjoy each other's company.

I want to spend time again with the people who had an influence on me as a young Christian. I don't know how many of my ancestors were Christians. Perhaps not many. But I can't wait to meet the ones who were and to hear their stories.

I'm eager to meet the young women our family supported in the Dominican Republic. I want to talk to some Cambodian pastors and Chinese house church members who received Bibles from the ministries we gave to. What will it be like to meet the Sudanese people our church helped rescue from slavery and oppression? I want to thank them for their faith and example.

I want to spend time with my handicapped friends and watch them enjoy the freedom of new bodies and minds. I look forward to sharp intellectual exchanges with those who finished their course on Earth with Alzheimer's. (Maybe I'll be one of them.)

I want to spend time with the martyrs, some of whose stories I've read. Most of them didn't know each other on Earth, but Revelation 6:9-11 portrays them as close-knit in Heaven.

We'll surely have many new relationships, some based on common interests, experiences, and histories on Earth. If you have a special interest in first-century Rome, perhaps you'll enjoy developing relationships with those who lived in that place and time.

We'll talk with angels who saw the earth created and who watched their comrades rebel. We'll meet angels who guarded and served us while we were on Earth. Don't you look forward to asking them questions?

If our conversations would be limited only to the earth's past, we might run the reservoir dry after fifty thousand years. But the beauty is that Heaven will bring as many new developments as Earth ever did, and eventually far more. We won't *begin* to run out of things to think about or talk about. The reservoir won't run dry. It will be replenished daily, forever expanding.

IF OUR LOVED ONES ARE IN HELL, WON'T THAT SPOIL HEAVEN?

Many people have lost loved ones who didn't know Christ. Some people argue that people in Heaven won't know Hell exists. But this would make Heaven's joy dependent on ignorance, which is nowhere taught in Scripture.

So, how could we enjoy Heaven knowing that a loved one is in Hell? J. I. Packer offers an answer that's difficult but biblical:

> God the Father (who now pleads with mankind to accept the recon-
> ciliation that Christ's death secured for all) and God the Son (our
> appointed Judge, who wept over Jerusalem) will in a final judgment
> express wrath and administer justice against rebellious humans. God's
> holy righteousness will hereby be revealed; God will be doing the right
> thing, vindicating himself at last against all who have defied him. . . .
> (Read through Matt. 25; John 5:22-29; Rom. 2:5-16, 12:19; 2 Thess.
> 1:7-9; Rev. 18:1–19:3, 20:11-15, and you will see that clearly.) God
> will judge justly, and all angels, saints, and martyrs will praise him for
> it. So it seems inescapable that we shall, with them, approve the judg-
> ment of persons—rebels—whom we have known and loved.[272]

In Heaven, we will see with a new and far better perspective. We'll fully concur with God's judgment on the wicked. The martyrs in Heaven call on God to judge evil people on Earth (Revelation 6:9-11). When God brings judgment on the wicked city of Babylon, the people in Heaven are told, "Re-joice over her, O heaven! Rejoice, saints and apostles and prophets! God has judged her for the way she treated you" (Revelation 18:20).

Hell itself may provide a dark backdrop to God's shining glory and unfath-omable grace. Jonathan Edwards made this case, saying, "When the saints in glory, therefore, shall see the doleful state of the damned, how will this heighten their sense of the blessedness of their own state, so exceedingly differ-ent from it." He added, "They shall see the dreadful miseries of the damned, and consider that they deserved the same misery, and that it was *sovereign grace,* and nothing else, which made them so much to differ from the damned."[273]

We'll never question God's justice, wondering how he could send good peo-ple to Hell. Rather, we'll be overwhelmed with his grace, marveling at what he did to send bad people to Heaven. (We will no longer have any illusion that fallen people are good without Christ.)

In Heaven we'll see clearly that God revealed himself to each person and that he gave opportunity for each heart or conscience to seek and respond to him

(Romans 1:18–2:16). Those who've heard the gospel have a greater opportunity to respond to Christ (Romans 10:13-17), but every unbeliever, through sin, has rejected God and his self-revelation in creation, conscience, or the gospel.

Everyone deserves Hell. No one deserves Heaven. Jesus went to the cross to offer salvation to all (1 John 2:2). God is absolutely sovereign and doesn't desire any to die without Christ (1 Timothy 2:3-4; 2 Peter 3:9). Yet many will perish in their unbelief (Matthew 7:13).

We'll embrace God's holiness and justice. We'll praise him for his goodness and grace. God will be our source of joy. Hell's small and distant shadow will not interfere with God's greatness or our joy in him. (All of this should motivate us to share the gospel of Christ with family, friends, neighbors, and the whole world.)

We'll also understand the truth revealed in 2 Peter 3:9: "The Lord is not slow in keeping his promise, as some understand slowness. He is patient with you, not wanting anyone to perish, but everyone to come to repentance." We will marvel at the patience God showed us and all of our loved ones, and how he long withheld our due judgment to give us opportunity to repent.

Although it will inevitably sound harsh, I offer this further thought: in a sense, none of our loved ones will be in Hell—only some whom we *once* loved. Our love for our companions in Heaven will be directly linked to God, the central object of our love. We will see him in them. We will not love those in Hell because when we see Jesus as he is, we will love only—and will only *want* to love—whoever and whatever pleases and glorifies and reflects him. What we loved in those who died without Christ was God's beauty we once saw in them. When God forever withdraws from them, I think they'll no longer bear his image and no longer reflect his beauty. Although they will be the same people, without God they'll be stripped of all the qualities we loved. Therefore, paradoxically, in a sense they will *not* be the people we loved.

I cannot prove biblically what I've just stated, but I think it rings true, even if the thought is horrifying.

Not only in Heaven but also while we are still here on Earth, our God is "the Father of compassion and the God of all comfort" (2 Corinthians 1:3). Any sorrows that plague us now will disappear on the New Earth as surely as darkness disappears when the light is turned on. "He will wipe away every tear from their eyes, . . . neither shall there be mourning nor crying nor pain" (Revelation 21:4, ESV).

This is God's promise. Let's rest in it.

Of this we may be absolutely certain: Hell will have no power over Heaven; none of Hell's misery will ever veto any of Heaven's joy.

WILL WE EVER DISAGREE?

Because we're finite and unique and because we'll never know everything, we may not agree about everything in Heaven. We'll agree on innumerable matters and wonder how we ever thought otherwise. But we'll still likely have different tastes in food and clothes and music and thousands of other things. We will have discussions, perhaps even debates, about things we won't yet understand. Of course, there will be no personal attacks, no ill-informed biases, and no prideful refusal to grant a valid point.

Some of us will have insights others don't. Some will have a better understanding in one area, others in a different area. Our beliefs can be accurate but incomplete, since we'll not be omniscient. Adam was without sin, yet he needed more than himself. Even before sin, surely he and Eve brought different perspectives. Not all disagreement is rooted in sin.

The companionship of other finite beings involves discussion and dialogue, which creates progress through synergy. That synergy involves differences and even disagreements. Could Michael and Gabriel, two sinless beings, have different opinions on a military strategy? Could they think differently enough to disagree? Why not?

C. S. Lewis, J. R. R. Tolkien, and other friends in their group called The Inklings often argued ideas with each other. On the New Earth, could Jonathan Edwards, G. K. Chesterton, Francis Schaeffer, Charles Spurgeon, and John Wesley agree on 90 percent of the issues, yet still challenge one another's ideas in what's still unknown to them, stimulating each other to a greater understanding? Could they even say, "Let's think and talk to the King, approach an angel or two, bounce our ideas off Paul, Luther, and Augustine, and then meet again and share what we've learned"?

Even though Christ's insights would be absolutely accurate, that doesn't mean we'll always fully understand them. God has made us learners. That's part of being finite.

If we will always and automatically see all things alike, then why will there be rulers and judges on the New Earth? In a perfect world, why would there be a need for authority? Because that's the way God has made us. He's the ultimate authority, but he delegates authority to mankind. It's not sin that necessitates authority, it's simply God's design, existing first within his triune being (John 8:28). Since we're told that we'll judge angels, will there be disagreements to pass judgment on? If sinless people see differently, might they still need wise counsel?

Uniqueness and differences existed before sin and will exist after it. Only God has infinite wisdom and knowledge. We should expect some differences in perspective, but we should also expect an ability to resolve them without rancor or bruised egos. Imagine the ability to question and challenge without any malice and to be questioned and challenged without a hint of defensiveness. Wouldn't that be Heaven?

WILL WE SHARE DISCOVERIES TOGETHER?

Many friendships emerge from shared experiences. Doing things together bonds us. The same will be true on the New Earth. We'll be knit together as we discover together the wonders of God and his universe.

Suppose you're taking a two-week extended family vacation, but you arrive at the vacation destination four days after most of the other family members. They say, "You should have seen the sunset last Thursday. It was incredible." Or "You should have been here for the barbeque." They talk about the whale that breached two hundred feet from shore. "You should have seen it."

What's your reaction? You're happy the family's been having a good time, but you feel as if you've missed something. You've missed the bonding that came with the common experience.

Wouldn't it be great to travel to Heaven together, simultaneously? Wouldn't it be great to be like Lewis and Clark, discovering *together* the wonders of the new world? In fact, that's precisely what Scripture tells us will happen. Though we go to the present Heaven one at a time as we die, *all of us* will be charter citizens of the New Earth. We'll be resurrected together and set foot on the New Earth together.

> Throughout eternity we will live full, truly human lives, exploring and managing God's creation to his glory. Fascinating vistas will unfold before us as we learn to serve God in a renewed universe.
>
> **EDWARD DONNELLY**

We'll discover what no one else has ever seen. We'll share our discoveries together, grabbing each other by the hand and saying, "You can't believe what Jesus made—an animal I've never dreamed of. You've got to come see it!"

We'll discover some things on our own, and we'll enjoy things that others have discovered. We'll get to share our finds.

Unlike the hypothetical experience of your arriving late to your vacation destination, you won't have missed out on the beginning of the New Earth. You will be there *first*—with everyone else. When someone asks, "Remember when God made the New Earth and brought the New Jerusalem down out of Heaven and came to dwell among us in the new world he built for us?" all of us will nod our heads and say, "Sure, I remember—how could I ever forget? *I was there!*"

What will it be like for those who died weak and elderly to take their first steps in their resurrected bodies? In C. S. Lewis's *The Last Battle*, on entering heaven Lord Digory says he and Lady Polly have been "unstiffened."[274] He adds, "We stopped feeling old." I look forward to seeing my mother and father "unstiffened" again—and to being completely unstiffened myself!

How glorious it will be for grandchildren and grandparents—and great-grandchildren and great-grandparents who never knew each other before—to enjoy youth together in the cities, fields, hillsides, and waters of the New Earth. To walk together, discover together, be amazed together—and praise Jesus together.

WILL WE WITNESS TOGETHER GOD'S NEW CREATION?

In *The Magician's Nephew*, C. S. Lewis portrays two children, a few adults, and a horse transported from Earth to an unknown place. It's the darkness and silence that precedes the day of Narnia's creation. They watch in wonder as this beautiful new world is masterfully shaped by the creator, Aslan the lion, who sings it into existence.[275]

God asked Job, "Where were you when I laid the earth's foundation? . . . On what were its footings set, or who laid its cornerstone—while the morning stars sang together and all the angels shouted for joy?" (Job 38:4-7).

The picture is of angels, created beings, witnessing God's creation of the first Earth. I believe Scripture makes clear that we'll have the privilege that was experienced by the fictional characters in *The Magician's Nephew* and by the real angelic beings who witnessed the creation of the first Earth: We will actually witness the creation of the New Earth.

In John's vision, after he saw humanity's resurrection, he saw "a new heaven and a new earth, for the first heaven and the first earth had passed away. . . . I saw the Holy City, the new Jerusalem, coming down out of heaven from God" (Revelation 21:1-2).

Although Scripture doesn't state this, the New Earth's creation might unfold in stages just as the old Earth's creation did. The first Earth was raw and uninhabitable, dark and empty (Genesis 1:2). God then created light, and on subsequent days he created water, sky, clouds, dry ground, vegetation, seed-bearing plants and trees, sun and moon and stars, and the entire celestial heavens. Then he made the sea creatures, birds, and the rest of the animals, domestic and wild. Finally, he fashioned the man.

God may form the ground of the New Earth directly from the old. He may form the waters of the new from the old. Romans 8 implies he will form the plants and animals of the New Earth from the old Earth, just as he will form our resurrected bodies out of genetic material from our old ones.

This time, however, new mankind will preexist the New Earth. But as he did for Adam and Eve, God will prepare it for us before we step foot on it. Perhaps on the sixth day of the new creation, instead of being formed from the dust to begin civilization, new men and women—who have beheld the new creation—will be brought down in the great city to settle on the New Earth, to continue and expand civilization to the glory of God.

Perhaps we'll watch God at work for another creative week, beholding his unfolding wonders one by one. Of course, since the forming of the New Earth is a resurrection of the old Earth, not a creation from nothing, its creation may be instantaneous. Either way, it will be spectacular, and we will watch and *ooh* and *aah* and applaud.

Just as God presented Eve to Adam in Eden, so he will bring Christ's bride to the second Adam, Christ, on the New Earth.

We will behold the wondrous creation of the New Earth—and then we will descend to live in that place, reigning forever with our beloved King Jesus.

CHAPTER 37

HOW WILL WE RELATE
TO EACH OTHER?

Will relationships with people be less important to us in Heaven than they are now? If the reason we valued a relationship stemmed from sin and the Curse, of course, we'd want no part of it in that evil way. But on the New Earth all relationships will be rooted in righteousness. More than ever, we'll value human relationships that draw us toward God.

Joy comes from shared experiences, as every reading group, fan club, or social organization testifies. I remember a weekend I spent at a conference center high on a hill, in a thick forest. The view from the mountain was breathtaking. So what did I do? After ten minutes of enjoying it and thanking God for it, I called my wife. Then my daughters. Then my friend Steve. I just wanted to share the joy with those I loved.

God designed us to need other people. We are made in his image, and he himself is a plurality—Father, Son, and Holy Spirit. "Then God said, 'Let us make man in our image, in our likeness'" (Genesis 1:26). Father, Son, and Spirit take pleasure in each other's companionship. Jesus spoke to his Father while "full of joy through the Holy Spirit" (Luke 10:21). Similarly, God has created us to take pleasure in his companionship, and in each other's.

Any vision of the afterlife that doesn't involve a society of human beings in meaningful relationship denies God's decree that it isn't good for human beings to be without others of their kind. It also denies innumerable Scripture passages that clearly reveal human society on the New Earth (e.g., Revelation 21:24-26; 22:2).

HOW WILL WE TREAT EACH OTHER?

We'll experience all the best of human relationships, with none of the worst. The burdens and tragedies of life will be lifted from us. We'll be free of what displeases God and damages relationships. No abortion clinics or psychiatric wards.

No missing children. No rape or abuse. No drug rehabilitation centers. No bigotry, muggings, or killings. No worry, depression, or economic downturns. No wars. No unemployment. No anguish over failure and miscommunication. No pretense or wearing masks. No cliques. No hidden agendas, backroom deals, betrayals, secret ambitions, plots, or schemes.

Imagine mealtimes full of stories, laughter, and joy without fear of insensitivity, inappropriate behavior, anger, gossip, lust, jealousy, hurt feelings, or anything that eclipses joy. That will be Heaven.

Jonathan Edwards anticipated Heaven's joyful relationships:

> No inhabitants of that blessed world will ever be grieved with the thought that they are slighted by those that they love, or that their love is not fully and fondly returned. . . . There shall be no such thing as flattery or insincerity in heaven, but there perfect sincerity shall reign through all in all. Everyone will be just what he seems to be, and will really have all the love that he seems to have. It will not be as in this world, where comparatively few things are what they seem to be, and where professions are often made lightly and without meaning. But there, every expression of love shall come from the bottom of the heart, and all that is professed shall be really and truly felt.[276]

WILL ALL PEOPLE BE EQUAL?

All people are equal in worth, but they differ in gifting and performance. God is the creator of diversity, and diversity means "inequality" of gifting (1 Corinthians 12:14-20). Because God promises to reward people differently according to their differing levels of faithfulness in this life, we should not expect equality of possessions and positions in Heaven.

If everyone were equal in Heaven in all respects, it would mean we'd have no role models, no heroes, no one to look up to, no thrill of hearing wise words from someone we deeply admire. I'm not equal to Hudson Taylor, Susanna Wesley, George Mueller, or C. S. Lewis. I want to follow their examples, but I don't need to be their equals.

There's no reason to believe we'll all be equally tall or strong or that we'll have the same gifts, talents, or intellectual capacities. If we all had the same gifts, they wouldn't be special. If you can do some things better than I can, and I than you, then we'll have something to offer each other.

We live in a culture that worships equality, but we err when we reduce equality to sameness. It's illogical to assume everyone in Heaven will be able to compose a concerto with equal skill or be able to throw a ball as far as everyone else. In a perfect world, Adam was bigger and stronger than Eve, and Eve had beauty, sensitivities, and abilities Adam didn't. In other words, diversity— not conformity—characterizes a perfect world.

> We can sit for hours listening to the interesting conversation of a learned man. . . . If these pleasures are so exquisite here below, where, after all, the wisest know so little, what shall we say of those same pleasures in heaven?
>
> **J. BOUDREAU**

Scripture is clear that we'll have different rewards and positions in Heaven, according to our faithful service in this life. Since everyone will be happy, what could be the nature of these differences? Jonathan Edwards said, "The saints are like so many vessels of different sizes cast into a sea of happiness where every vessel is full: this is eternal life, for a man ever to have his capacity filled. But after all 'tis left to God's sovereign pleasure, 'tis his prerogative to determine the largeness of the vessel."[277]

A pint jar and a quart jar can both be full, but the larger jar contains more. Likewise, in Heaven all of us will be full of joy, but some may have a larger capacity for joy, having been stretched through their dependence on God in this life. John Bunyan said it well: "He who is most in the bosom of God, and who so acts for him here, he is the man who will be best able to enjoy most of God in the kingdom of heaven."

WILL WE HAVE PRIVACY?

Some people understand Heaven as a place of complete communal living, where we'll always be with others and there will be no privacy.

Scripture speaks of having our own individual dwelling places, which indicates privacy (Luke 16:9). In the context of the New Earth, God says, "To his servants he will give another name" (Isaiah 65:15). Similarly, Jesus says, "I will also give him a white stone with a new name written on it, known only to him who receives it" (Revelation 2:17). A name known only to the recipient and God is private, indicating God will relate to us as individuals, not just as one large group.

C. S. Lewis asked, "What can be more a man's own than this new name which even in eternity remains a secret between God and him? And what shall we take this secrecy to mean? Surely, that each of the redeemed shall forever know and praise some one aspect of the divine beauty better than any other creature can. Why else were individuals created but that God, loving all infinitely, should love each differently?"[278]

Our different personalities, rewards, positions, and names in Heaven speak not only of our individuality but also of how God finds unique reasons to love us. I love my wife and daughters, and I love different things about each.

We're like unique instruments, played by an orchestra to produce one beautiful sound, rich in its variety. We all have our unique part in glorifying God. We bring something singular and vital to the concert of praise.

WILL THERE BE PRIVATE OWNERSHIP?

The fourteenth-century *Theologica Germanica* says, "In Heaven there is no ownership. If any there took upon him to call anything his own, he would straightway be thrust out into hell and become an evil spirit."[279]

Similarly, several Christian authors state, without biblical references, that people won't own anything in heaven. But what about the different dwelling places believers will have in Heaven (Luke 16:4, 9)? What about the treasures Christ commanded us to store up for ourselves in Heaven (Matthew 6:20)? What about the different crowns and rewards God will hand out according to our works (2 Corinthians 5:10)?

Will your crown be as much mine as yours? Of course not. What about the white stone God promises to give to overcomers, with the individual's new name written on it, a name no one else will know (Revelation 2:17)? Will you and I have equal possession of those stones or names? No. What God gives you will be yours, not mine. The one he gives me will be mine, not yours. Is this ownership wrong or selfish? No. Ownership is never wrong when God distributes to us possessions *he* wants us to own.

God will give us an inheritance in Heaven (Colossians 3:24). Doesn't the word *inheritance* mean something tangible, belonging to us? This inheritance is given by the Father to the individual child in recognition of proven character and faithfulness.

God promised Daniel, "You will rise to receive your allotted inheritance" (Daniel 12:13). Those who serve Christ on Earth have waiting for them an allotted inheritance in Heaven. What's allotted to Daniel will be his, not mine or yours.

Speaking of the New Earth, Christ says, "He who overcomes will inherit all this" (Revelation 21:7). Those faithful in serving Christ will not simply *live* in the new universe; they will *own* it, ruling it to the glory of the ultimate owner, God.

Heaven isn't a socialist utopia in which private ownership is evil. Materialism, greed, envy, and selfishness are sins; ownership is not. An ancient scholar wrote, "God . . . is the only Haver."[280] This sounds spiritual, but God is also a giver. If he gives to us, then we too become "havers."

God owns not only all of Heaven but also everything on Earth (Deuteronomy 10:14). So what's "ours" is ultimately God's. But that's as true here and now as in Heaven. That God owns whatever's "mine" and "yours" doesn't mean there's no distinction between them. The early Christians generously shared their possessions (Acts 4:32-35). But this never negated private ownership. Peter told Ananias that his property belonged to him before he sold it, and the money belonged to him after he sold it (Acts 5:4). In Heaven we'll no doubt delight in sharing our treasures with others, but they will still be our treasures, generously given to us by God.

Jesus says that those who have properly stewarded God's assets on Earth will be granted ownership of assets in Heaven. "If you have not been trustworthy with someone else's property, who will give you property of your own?" (Luke 16:12). He also commanded us, "Store up for yourselves treasures in heaven" (Matthew 6:20). He suggested that by parting with treasures now, we invest them in Heaven, where they'll be waiting for us when we arrive.

WILL WE REGAIN LOST RELATIONAL OPPORTUNITIES?

Do you have family and friends you wish you could spend more time with? In Heaven you'll have unlimited time. I'm eager to spend time again with my childhood friend Jerry, who died years ago. I anticipate meeting him in Heaven and picking up right where we left off.[281]

A young woman visiting a missionary in Eastern Europe asked her, "Isn't it hard being so far away from your [grown] children and missing important events in their lives?"

"Sure," the missionary replied. "But in Heaven we'll have all the time together we want. Right now there's kingdom work that needs to be done." This woman knows where her true home is—and that life there will be real life and that relationships among God's people will resume in ways even better than what we've known here.

We may not be able to regain opportunities that we passed up due to unfaithfulness, but I believe we'll regain whatever we passed up in order to faithfully serve God. Jesus said, "Blessed are you who hunger now, for you will be satisfied. Blessed are you who weep now, for you will laugh. Blessed are you when men hate you, when they exclude you and insult you. . . . Rejoice in that day and leap for joy, because great is your reward in heaven" (Luke 6:21-23).

Perhaps in some way on the New Earth, the wives and children of the five missionaries killed by the Auca Indians will receive "comp time" with their loved ones. Consider the millions of Christians who've suffered and died in prison because of their faith, who were snatched away from their families, deprived of opportunities they craved with children and parents and spouses. Wouldn't it be just like Jesus to reward them on the New Earth with opportunities to do the very things they missed—and far better things as well? That would fit well with the words of Jim Elliot, one of the five murdered missionaries: "He is no fool who gives what he cannot keep to gain what he cannot lose."[282]

> I have held many things in my hands, and I have lost them all. But whatever I have placed in God's hands, that I still possess.
>
> **MARTIN LUTHER**

Heaven offers more than comfort; it offers *compensation*. In the same way that the hungry will fill up in Heaven and those who weep will laugh, will those who suffer tragedy experience a compensating victory? Maybe on the New Earth my friend Greg will experience a greater but not dissimilar form of the joy he'd have had on this earth if he had not died as a teenager, impaled on a fence post. Maybe all my mom missed because she died before our daughters became adults will be hers in Heaven. She was a faithful servant of God and loved her granddaughters, who were very young when she died. I think God allowed my mom to watch them get married and become mothers, but one day she'll do more than watch them. I think it's likely that when they're together on the New Earth, she'll enjoy all the time she missed with them—and they with her. Maybe those who lost infants to miscarriage and disease and accidents will be given make-up time with them in the new world.

If a father dies before his daughter's wedding and if he and she are Christians, then he'll be there for his daughter's ultimate wedding—to Christ. They will experience a far greater joy on the New Earth than the joy they could have experienced on the old Earth if he had lived longer. If he died before she became an accomplished pianist, he may hear her now from Heaven, but he'll hear her play far better on the New Earth—and she'll see him watching her, delight on his face. If he never lived to see his believing son play basketball, he'll not only see him play on Earth but also play with him on the New Earth. And his children will enjoy the pleasure of seeing the look of utter approval on their father's face . . . and their Father's face.

In the movie *Babette's Feast*, through the misfortunes of war Babette was forced to leave Paris, where she'd been an exquisite gourmet cook. She ended up as a maid for two women who led a small group of austere believers who frowned on such worldly things as good cooking. Babette comes into a large sum of money and spends it all on a single dinner party given for the elderly sisters she's come to love. It's a picture of God's extravagant grace. Babette realizes she'll never again be able to afford to give such a gift or prepare such a meal. Touched by Babette's generosity, Phillipa—herself a gifted singer who had little opportunity to develop her gift—consoles her: "Babette, this is not the end; I'm certain it's not. In Paradise you will be the great artist that God meant you to be! . . . Oh, how you will delight the angels!"[283]

For those who know God, this sentiment is biblical. He's a God who redeems lost opportunities—especially those lost through our faithful service. I believe that once the Curse is lifted and death is forever reversed, we may live out many of the "could have beens" taken from us on this old Earth.

I think it's probable that two friends who always dreamed of going to a special place, but never managed to, will be able to go to that very place on the New Earth. And the man who couldn't get out of his wheelchair to go biking with his son will never lack that opportunity again.

WHAT WILL OUR REUNIONS BE LIKE?

In *The Last Battle*, Lewis depicts wonderful reunions in Aslan's country, which includes the New Narnia. Character after character from the earlier stories reappears, many of them last seen centuries or millennia earlier: Reepicheep, Puddleglum, Rilian, Caspian, Trumpkin, Bree, Mr. Tumnis, and countless others. They're together again, many meeting for the first time. Lucy and the other children are thrilled to see them all. The reunions and introductions go on and on, and the reader doesn't want them to stop. When everyone parted by death is restored to life—in familiar resurrected bodies on a familiar resurrected world and in the very presence of their beloved Aslan—it's contagiously thrilling.

For us, the ultimate reunion will be followed by endless adventures together. We'll likely have many temporary partings followed by absolutely certain reunions. But never again will there be the separation of death, with its suffering and sorrow. Never again will we wonder if we'll see those we love. Bishop Ryle assured his flock, "Those whom you laid in the grave with many tears are in good keeping: you will yet see them again with joy. Believe it, think it, rest on it. It is all true."[284]

CHAPTER 38

WHAT WILL NEW EARTH SOCIETY BE LIKE?

A rt, music, literature, crafts, technology, clothing, jewelry, education, food preparation—all are part of society or culture, which is the creative accomplishment of God's image-bearers. Human creations are an extension of God's own creative works because he created us to reflect him by being creators.

Mankind glorifies God by taking what God made from nothing and shaping it into what is for mankind's good and God's glory. The entire universe—including angels and living creatures in Heaven—should look at our creative ingenuity, our artistic accomplishments, and see God in us, his image-bearers. If that's true now, how much more will it be true when there's nothing in us to dishonor him?

We should expect the old Earth's social dynamics to carry over to the New Earth, except when they are a product of our fallenness or when God reveals otherwise. It's true that with engines have come pollution and fatalities. With printing and publishing have come godless books and magazines. With television has come the glorification of immorality and materialism. Computers have led to Internet pornography. With the splitting of the atom came a destructive bomb and loss of human life. With medical advances have come abortion and euthanasia. Yet *none* of these negative byproducts is intrinsic to the cultural advances themselves. Imagine those advances used purely for righteous purposes, without sin to taint them.

What you are imagining is the New Earth.

WILL WE HAVE ETHNIC AND NATIONAL IDENTITIES?

Theologian Abraham Kuyper said, "We find it extremely difficult to form any idea of the social state in heaven."[285] If by "heaven" Kuyper meant the present Heaven, he was correct. Scripture gives us pictures and hints, certainly, but they're not conclusive. But if by "heaven" he meant the eternal Heaven, he was wrong.

We're shown that the eternal Heaven, on the New Earth, will be a physical environment with physical people who work, eat, converse, and hold positions of authority. People live both inside and outside the city, come into each other's homes, travel, and worship together. Leaders of nations will bring the splendor of different cultures into the city where Jesus Christ will reign on the throne. These are only some of the indicators of our "social state" in Heaven.

Will we have ethnic and national identities? Yes. Is the risen Jesus Jewish? Certainly. Will we know he's Jewish? Of course. Our resurrected DNA will be unflawed, but it will preserve our God-designed uniquenesses, racial and otherwise.

The elders sing to the Lamb: "You are worthy. . . . Your blood has ransomed people for God from every tribe and language and people and nation. And you have caused them to become God's Kingdom and his priests. And they will reign on the earth" (Revelation 5:9-10, NLT). Who will serve as the New Earth's kings and priests? Not people who were *formerly* of every tribe, language, people, and nation. Their distinctions aren't obliterated but continue into the intermediate Heaven and then into the eternal Heaven.

Tribe refers to a person's clan and family lineage. *People* refers to race. *Nation* refers to those who share a national identity and culture. Dutch theologian Herman Bavinck said of the New Earth, "All those nations—each in accordance with its own distinct national character—bring into the new Jerusalem all they have received from God in the way of glory and honor."[286]

Like the current earthly Jerusalem, the New Jerusalem will be a melting pot of ethnic diversity. But unlike the current city, the groups in the New Jerusalem will be united by their common worship of King Jesus. They will delight in each other's differences, never resent or be frightened by them.

Unfortunately, in this world under the Curse, there's often hostility between races and nations. They're divided by sin, intolerant of differences in appearance, language, and culture. Speaking of the racial divide between Jews and Gentiles, Paul says, "For [Christ] himself is our peace, who has made the two one and has destroyed the barrier, the dividing wall of hostility. . . . His purpose was to create in himself one new man out of the two, thus making peace, and in this one body to reconcile both of them to God through the cross, by which he put to death their hostility" (Ephesians 2:14-16).

Christ died for our sins of racism. His work on the cross put racism to death. The redemption of mankind and the earth will include the redemption of human relationships and the uniting of different people groups in Christ. Racist groups that purport to be Christian are the opposite of Christian. There will be no racial prejudice in Heaven. There will be no illusions of racial or national superiority, no disputes over borders.

Some scholars argue that the image of God has a corporate dimension: "There is no one human individual or group who can fully bear or manifest all that is involved in the image of God, so that there is a sense in which that image is collectively possessed. The image of God is, as it were, parceled out among the peoples of the earth. By looking at different individuals and groups we get glimpses of different aspects of the full image of God."[287]

If this is true, and I believe it may be, then racism is not only an injustice toward people but also a rejection of God's very nature. On the New Earth we'll never celebrate sin, but we'll celebrate diversity in the biblical sense. We'll never try to keep people out. We'll welcome them in, exercising hospitality to every traveler. Peace on Earth will be rooted in our common ruler, Christ the King, who alone is the source of "Glory to God in the highest, and on earth peace among men with whom He is pleased" (Luke 2:14, NASB).

Peace on Earth will be accomplished not by the abolition of our differences but by a unifying loyalty to the King, a loyalty that transcends differences—and is *enriched* by them. The kings and leaders of nations will be united because they share the King's righteousness, and they, with him, will rejoice in their differences as a tribute to his creativity and multifaceted character.

WHAT LANGUAGES WILL WE SPEAK?

Will there be one central language in Heaven, a language we'll all speak and understand? (The Evangelical Covenant Church in which I became a Christian claimed it would be Swedish.) Scripture says of those with different languages, "They cried out in a loud voice" (Revelation 7:10). This singular "voice" implies a shared language.

This could be a trade language, Heaven's equivalent to Swahili or English, second languages that many know in addition to their native languages, allowing them to communicate. Or the common language could be our primary one. It may be a universal language God grants us without having to learn it. There's no indication Adam and Eve had to learn Eden's language, though no doubt their vocabulary expanded with use. We may have a similar experience in Heaven.

God says of many different nations, "You have made them to be a kingdom" (Revelation 5:10). *One* kingdom, *one* world, *one* government. This implies one shared central language.

God could allow us to understand all languages even if we can't speak them.

(Science fiction portrays this with a "universal translator.") But Scripture seems to suggest more. The Babel account offers clues as to the importance of shared language in an ideal society. "Now the whole world had one language and a common speech. . . . Then they said, 'Come, let us build ourselves a city, with a tower that reaches to the heavens, so that we may make a name for ourselves.' . . . The Lord said, 'If as one people speaking the same language they have begun to do this, then nothing they plan to do will be impossible for them'" (Genesis 11:1, 4, 6).

God then confused their language and dispersed them, so their great city went unfinished. Notice that all people originally shared one language, which empowered them to cooperate together in great achievements. But because they were united in self-glorification rather than God-glorification, they embraced a false unity that would've empowered further rebellion and self-destruction. Because the people weren't united around their God-designed purpose to rule the earth for his glory, God removed a source of their destructive unity and power—their shared language.

In reversing the Curse, God will reverse Babel. Instead of people's building a city for their glory, God will build a city for them, uniting them for his glory. In Genesis 11 the people attempted to connect Earth to Heaven with their city, making Heaven one with Earth. In Revelation 21 God brings Heaven down to Earth, in his city, making Earth one with Heaven.

Once mankind is made righteous and entrusted with stewarding the New Earth, God will likely again restore a common language (perhaps the same as Eden's, which apparently existed until Babel). Why? To make communication easy, not frustrating, and to enhance cooperation and cultural accomplishments.

This common language would make it so that "nothing they plan to do will be impossible for them" (Genesis 11:6). When the human heart is evil, that's bad; when the human heart is righteous, that's good. On the New Earth, all we propose to do will be for God's glory and our good. God will no longer need to protect us from ourselves. We will never unite to destroy and exploit, only to create and enhance. A shared language will likely be God's gift to empower us.

Nonetheless, it seems likely that in addition to our common language, we will maintain our current languages. Although the confusion of languages at Babel was originally a curse, the gatherings in Heaven of people of every nation, tribe, and language show that God will unite forever the people divided at Babel—not by eliminating their differences, but by eliminating sin, suspicion, and hostility.

Some argue from the Babel account that the existence of a variety of nations and languages is an aberration of God's ideal. Therefore, they conclude, it makes no sense that there would be more than one nation on the New Earth. But this perspective fails to take into account God's ability to accomplish his purposes even through human rebellion. It is God (not human sin or a curse) who is given credit for the making of nations: "From one man he made every nation of men, that they should inhabit the whole earth; and he determined the times set for them and the exact places where they should live" (Acts 17:26). Even if it defies our logic (though in my opinion it shouldn't), Scripture is explicit about the fact that there will be different nations, and kings of those nations, on the New Earth (Revelation 21:24-26). Whether they will speak different languages is a matter of opinion, but the existence of different nations is directly revealed.

Through understanding other languages, we'll broaden our view of God. "Is it possible that in heaven, we will have a word or words for 'worship' that will include all the connotations from all the languages of the world?"[288] I think it's likely.

The diversity of languages provides a wider range of opportunity to glorify God: "We hear them declaring the wonders of God in our own tongues!" (Acts 2:11). In Heaven we may hear people use a certain word from their language to describe one of God's attributes, and we may suddenly respond, "Yes, that's it! *That's* what I was trying to understand!"

In Heaven will Cambodians place their hands together and bow their heads in greeting? Will Kenyans dance to their distinctive drumbeats? Will Argentineans love soccer? Will Cubans speak Spanish and Britons speak English and Brazilians speak Portuguese? Why wouldn't they?

We won't be omniscient, so it's doubtful we'll know all languages. But certainly we could learn them much faster. Those of us who aren't naturally gifted in languages may be amazed at our abilities. Language experts, including translators, may see their skills pick up where they left off and further develop at unprecedented rates. They'll have eternity to learn as many languages as they wish.

What purpose will different languages serve on the New Earth? Knowing a language is part of understanding who people are and what their culture is like. As we develop new friendships in Heaven, we might enjoy learning people's first language in order to know them better. Perhaps within days or weeks we'll be able to understand new languages. Maybe throughout the course of a dinner conversation we'll steadily pick up the language of new friends, creating a bond and appreciation for them and their culture and our God.

WILL HEAVEN HAVE REPRESENTATIVES FROM
ALL TRIBES AND LANGUAGES?

Tribes, peoples, and nations will all make their own particular contribution to the enrichment of life in the New Jerusalem (Revelation 5:9; 7:9; 21:24-26). Daniel prophesied that the Messiah would be "given dominion and glory and a kingdom, that all peoples, nations, and languages should serve him" (Daniel 7:14, ESV). Just as the church's diversity of gifts serves the good of others (1 Corinthians 12:7-11), so our diversity will serve everyone's good in the new universe. Cornelius Venema wrote, "Nothing of the diversity of the nations and peoples, their cultural products, languages, arts, sciences, literature, and technology—so far as these are good and excellent—will be lost upon life in the new creation."[289]

Consider what it will be like to see the Masai of Kenya, the Dinka of Sudan, the Hmong, Athabaskans, Tibetans, Aucans, Icelanders, Macedonians, Moldovans, Moroccans, and Peruvians. Hundreds of nations, thousands of people groups will gather to worship Christ. And many national and cultural distinctives, untouched by sin, will continue to the glory of God.

God brings good even out of evil. His judgment on Babel accomplished his good purpose of creating a diversity of nations and languages, which would bring him glory through Christ's redemptive work. "From one man he made every nation of men, that they should inhabit the whole earth; and he determined the times set for them and the exact places where they should live" (Acts 17:26). The nations are not afterthoughts or accidents.

Although Israel has been the apple of God's eye, Scripture is full of affirmations that God's desire is to be glorified in *all* nations of the earth. God promised to make Abraham "the father of many nations" and told him "through your offspring all nations on earth will be blessed" (Genesis 17:4; 22:18). Scholars make various theological distinctions between Israel and the church, but the New Jerusalem includes "the twelve tribes of Israel" (Revelation 21:12) and is also called the bride of Christ, which is the church (Revelation 21:9). Paul says to the church in Galatia, "the Jerusalem that is above . . . is our mother" (Galatians 4:26). God has one bride, yet she consists of a wide diversity of people who will be healed of their divisions while maintaining their distinctives, testifying to their Creator's richness.

Through general revelation, God has made known his presence in people groups and cultures: "In the past, he let all nations go their own way. Yet he has not left himself without testimony" (Acts 14:16-17). God is not a tribal deity. He transcends all cultures yet is evident in all. Each culture has a memory of a time when people knew about God. Consider, for instance, the ancient Chinese language. The character meaning "create" consists of other characters for "speak," "dust," "life," and "walk." The character meaning "devil" consists of "secret," "man," and "garden." The character meaning "boat" combines those of "vessel," "eight," and "people," highly suggestive of Noah's ark. Chinese believers consider these and many other examples as evidence that their five-thousand-year-old language goes back to a time when biblical truths were well known in their culture.[290]

That God will redeem people of every tribe and language suggests that he has special interest in the work of Bible translation, the broad international reach of the *JESUS* film, and all mission endeavors, especially toward unreached people groups.

When we see the extent and diversity of Christ's redemption, we'll praise him. When we picture in our minds what Scripture tells us about resurrected people, nations, and cultures on a resurrected Earth, in a resurrected universe— we will think bigger thoughts of God.

WILL ANCIENT CULTURES BE RESURRECTED TO THE NEW EARTH?

At Christ's return, the earth will be healed from sin's wounds. These include not only toxic waste and chemical pollution but also cultural and moral pollution. The healing of wounds implies the return to an original condition. If our new bodies will look enough like the old bodies to be recognizable, doesn't this suggest that the New Earth will look enough like the old Earth for us to recognize it?

The New Earth will still be just as much Earth as the new us will still be us. Our resurrection bodies will have our eyes, ears, mouth, and nose. Like Christ's body, ours will maintain their distinguishing features. If our new bodies will so closely correspond to the present ones, won't the New Earth just as closely correspond to the present one? Will there be a New Mount Saint Helens and New Himalayas and a New Alaska under the new northern lights? Will there be a New Bermuda, a New Canada, a New Australia?

My understanding of Scripture suggests that the New Earth will include not only resurrected geographical locations but also resurrected cultures. The kings of the nations will bring their tribute, splendor, and glory into the New Jerusalem (Revelation 21:24, 26). There will be not one nation but many. This reference gives us biblical basis to suppose that the best culture, history, art, music, and the languages of the old Earth will be redeemed, purified, and carried over to the New Earth.

Theologian Anthony Hoekema suggests, "Kings in those days were more than political rulers; they were the representatives and bearers of the cultures of the nations over which they ruled. John is here speaking about the cultural and artistic contributions of various national groups which shall then have made their home in the new Jerusalem. . . . [I]n the life to come various types of people will retain their unique gifts. These gifts will develop and mature in a sinless way, and will be used to produce new cultural products to the everlasting glory of God's name."[291]

> As the Lamb of God he will draw all of the goods, artifacts, and instruments of culture to himself; the kings of the earth will return their authority and power to the Lamb who sits upon the throne; Jesus is the one whose blood has purchased a multi-national community, composed of people from every tribe and tongue and nation. His redemptive ministry . . . is cosmic in scope.
>
> **RICHARD MOUW**

Surely these kings and cultures who bring their "splendor" and "glory" into the new world won't start from scratch. They'll bring into the new world a national and personal history, an ethnic identity, and a wealth of customs, art forms, and knowledge. All these will be purified, but that leaves plenty of room for distinctive cultural celebrations, holidays, meals, sports, and many customs.

Hoekema also says, "The fact that not only kings but nations are mentioned implies that the various cultural contributions of different ethnic groups will then no longer be in competition with each other, but will harmoniously enrich life in the Holy City. Christ, who is the lamp of that city, will then draw all these cultural products into his service, for the glory of his Father."[292]

This understanding fits perfectly with Daniel's vision of the Messiah's return to Earth: "He was given authority, honor, and royal power over all the nations of the world, so that people of every race and nation and language would obey him" (Daniel 7:14, NLT). There's a direct continuity between the kingdoms of the old Earth and God's eternal Kingdom on the New Earth. Earthly kingdoms will not be destroyed but "handed over" to God's people: "Then the sovereignty, power and greatness of the kingdoms under the whole heaven will be handed over to the saints" (Daniel 7:27).

Surely the greatness of the nations that will be handed over to God's people cannot be restricted only to those nations existing at Christ's return. Indeed, most of the nations Daniel speaks of—including Babylon, Medo-Persia, and Rome—faded away long ago. But in the sweeping breadth of his redemptive work, I believe that God will resurrect not only modern nations but also ancient ones, including, for instance, Babylon and Rome. I think it's likely we'll not merely meet the redeemed people of ancient civilizations but also walk among redeemed civilizations. Are ancient Assyrians, Sumerians, Phoenicians, Babylonians, and Greeks among God's redeemed? We know they are, for no nation, past or present, is excluded from "every tribe and language and people and nation" (Revelation 7:9). In Heaven, God has determined to have representatives from *every* tribe, people group, and culture.

Because Scripture explicitly tells us that resurrected nations will be part of the New Earth, I think there's every reason to believe we'll see a resurrected Egypt, Rome, India, and China, as well as resurrected cultures of every part of ancient Africa, South America, North America, Australia, Asia, and Europe, including small cultures about which we presently know very little.

I interpret "every tribe and language and people and nation" literally. God chose people in even predominantly pagan nations and reached them by sending men and women or angels, dreams, and visions. What people groups will be worshiping Christ on the New Earth? Celts, Goths, Huns, Lombards, Saxons, Vikings, Serbs, Croats, Slovenes, Canaanites, Hittites, Phoenicians, Sumerians, Assyrians, Persians, Mongols, Malaysians, Aztecs, Mayans, Incas—and countless other civilizations, ancient and modern. Representatives of nations and cultures that no longer exist today will be raised, to God's glory, in a purified form that includes whatever pleased God and excludes whatever didn't.

Do you have a special interest in Europe of the Middle Ages? Then perhaps you'll enjoy developing relationships with those who lived in that era. Perhaps on the New Earth you'll live in a beautified version of their culture. (We shouldn't assume that all ancient people would embrace every modern convenience, even when given the choice.)

Does this sound speculative? I imagine it only because of Scripture's own words. I base my observation on the texts I've cited here and elsewhere in this book. I didn't begin with a vivid imagination of Heaven—exactly the opposite. I studied the Scriptures about Heaven. Only over the years, over the decades, did they infuse my imagination.

I believe we have more than just biblical *permission* to imagine resurrected races, tribes, and nations living together on the New Earth; we have a biblical *mandate* to do so. So close your eyes and imagine those ancient civilizations. Not just what they were, but what they yet will be.

SECTION ELEVEN

WHAT ABOUT ANIMALS?

CHAPTER 39

WILL ANIMALS INHABIT
THE NEW EARTH?

People often ask me whether animals will be in Heaven. Their second question, which is discussed in the next chapter, is whether they'll ever see their pets again. To some people, these are merely sentimental questions. To others, they are very important. Children especially want to know the answers. What do we tell them when they ask?

Scripture says a great deal about animals, portraying them as Earth's second most important inhabitants. God entrusted animals to us, and our relationships with animals are a significant part of our lives.

Isaiah 11:6-9 speaks of a coming glorious era on Earth when "the leopard will lie down with the goat, the calf and the lion and the yearling together; and a little child will lead them. The cow will feed with the bear, their young will lie down together, and the lion will eat straw like the ox. The infant will play near the hole of the cobra, and the young child put his hand into the viper's nest. They will neither harm nor destroy on all my holy mountain, for the earth will be full of the knowledge of the Lord as the waters cover the sea."

Some interpreters contend that this passage speaks only of the Millennium, but as we've seen, Isaiah anticipates an *eternal* Kingdom of God on Earth. Isaiah 65:17 and 66:22 specifically speak of the New Earth. Sandwiched between them is a reference very similar to that in Isaiah 11: "'The wolf and the lamb will feed together, and the lion will eat straw like the ox. . . . They will neither harm nor destroy on all my holy mountain,' says the Lord" (65:25).

When will there be *no more harm* on the earth? Not on the old Earth or even in the Millennium, which will end in rebellion and warfare, but on the New Earth, where there will be no more sin, death, or suffering (Revelation 21:4). These descriptions of animals peacefully inhabiting the earth *may* have application to a millennial kingdom on the old Earth, but their primary reference appears to be to God's eternal Kingdom, where mankind and animals will enjoy a redeemed Earth.

DO ANIMALS HAVE SOULS?

When God made the animals, he made "the wild animals according to their kinds, the livestock according to their kinds, and all the creatures that move along the ground according to their kinds. And God saw that it was good" (Genesis 1:25). Animals were important in Eden; therefore, unless there's revelation to the contrary, the principle of continuity suggests that they'll be important on the New Earth.

Like humans, animals were formed from the ground. "Now the Lord God had formed out of the ground all the beasts of the field and all the birds of the air" (Genesis 2:19). When God breathed a spirit into Adam's body, made from the earth, Adam became *nephesh*, a "living being" or "soul" (Genesis 2:7). Remarkably, the same Hebrew word, *nephesh*, is used for animals and for people. We are specifically told that not only people, but animals have "the breath of life" in them (Genesis 1:30; 2:7; 6:17; 7:15, 22). God hand-made animals, linking them both to the earth and humanity.

Am I suggesting animals have souls? Certainly they do not have *human* souls. Animals aren't created in God's image, and they aren't equal to humans in any sense. Nonetheless, there's a strong biblical case for animals having non-human souls. I didn't take this seriously until I studied the usage of the Hebrew and Greek words *nephesh* and *psyche,* often translated "soul" when referring to humans. (*Nephesh* is translated *psyche* in the Septuagint.) The fact that these words are often used of animals is compelling evidence that they have non-human souls. That's what most Christians in the past believed. In their book *Beyond Death*, Gary Habermas and J. P. Moreland point out, "It wasn't until the advent of seventeenth-century Enlightenment . . . that the existence of animal souls was even questioned in Western civilization. Throughout the history of the church, the classic understanding of living things has included the doctrine that animals, as well as humans, have souls."[293]

I cannot emphasize strongly enough that humans and animals are different. Humans continue to exist after death, but that may not be the case for animals. However, to do justice to Scripture, we need to recognize that people and animals share something unique: They are living beings. Because God has a future plan for both mankind and Earth, it strongly suggests that he has a future plan for animals as well.

WHY DID GOD SAVE ANIMALS FROM THE FLOOD?

One of the most revealing Old Testament pictures of God's redemptive work is the Flood and Noah's ark. When God saved people from the destruction of the

Flood, he also took great care to save the animals, the people's companions and helpers. God commanded Noah, "You are to bring into the ark two of all living creatures, male and female, to keep them alive with you. Two of every kind of bird, of every kind of animal and of every kind of creature that moves along the ground will come to you to be kept alive" (Genesis 6:19-20).

After the Flood, God made a covenant with Noah, and in that new covenant God included animals. Notice the repeated emphasis on animals:

> God said to Noah and to his sons with him: "I now establish my covenant with you and with your descendants after you and *with every living creature* that was with you—*the birds, the livestock and all the wild animals*, all those that came out of the ark with you—*every living creature* on earth. . . . Never again will there be a flood to destroy the earth." And God said, "This is the sign of the covenant I am making between me and you and *every living creature* with you, a covenant for all generations to come. . . . I will remember my covenant between me and you and *all living creatures of every kind*. . . . Whenever the rainbow appears in the clouds, I will see it and remember the everlasting covenant between God and *all living creatures of every kind* on the earth." So God said to Noah, "This is the sign of the covenant I have established between me and *all life on the earth*." (Genesis 9:9-17, emphasis added)

God's plan for a renewed Earth after the Flood emphatically involved animals. Wouldn't we expect his plan for a renewed Earth after the future judgment to likewise include animals? If the rescue of mankind in the ark is a picture of redemption, doesn't the rescue of the animals in the ark also anticipate their restoration as part of God's redemptive purposes?

In 2 Peter 3:5-7, we see a direct parallel between God's past judgment of the earth with water and his future judgment with fire. Mankind was judged in the Flood, and on his coattails most animals also perished. Eight human beings were rescued from the Flood to inhabit the new post-Flood Earth, but God didn't limit his rescue to people. He rescued representatives of every animal species to also occupy this new Earth. This is a powerful picture of what Romans 8 states—mankind and animals and all creation are linked together not only in curse and judgment but also in blessing and deliverance. Together they will experience life on a New Earth.

Selected humans, animals, vegetation, and geographical features (including mountains) were preserved by God in his judgment by water. Shouldn't we expect the same in his judgment by fire?

WHAT DOES GOD SHOW US ABOUT ANIMALS' IMPORTANCE?

God uses animals to fulfill his purposes. He ordered ravens to feed Elijah (1 Kings 17:4, 6). He "provided a great fish to swallow Jonah" (Jonah 1:17). He sent a fish with a coin in its mouth to teach his disciples a lesson (Matthew 17:27).

Consider the story of Balaam and his donkey (Numbers 22). God sends an angel to stop Balaam from doing evil. Balaam doesn't see the angel, but the donkey does. She veers off the road, and Balaam beats her. The donkey sees the angel twice more. Each time she veers off, and each time Balaam beats her. "Then the Lord opened the donkey's mouth, and she said to Balaam, 'What have I done to you to make you beat me these three times?'" (v. 28). Significantly, the wording doesn't suggest God put words in the donkey's mouth, as in ventriloquism; he "opened the donkey's mouth," permitting her to verbalize what appear to be actual thoughts and feelings.

Finally, God opens Balaam's eyes to see the angel, who asks him, "Why have you beaten your donkey these three times? . . . If she had not turned away, I would certainly have killed you by now, but I would have spared her" (Numbers 22:32-33).

Note that the angel says the donkey saved Balaam's life. If she hadn't, the angel would've killed Balaam while saving the donkey. God sometimes protects animals while judging their human masters. Animals, it appears, can have thoughts and feelings and can be responsive to realities in the spiritual realm that people are blind to. Furthermore, God cares about the welfare of his animals and holds us accountable for them.

When God sent Jonah to rescue Nineveh, God expressed his concern not only for the people in Nineveh but for its "many cattle as well. Should I not be concerned about that great city?" (Jonah 4:11). After Jonah warned Nineveh of coming destruction, the king commanded his people: "Do not let any man or beast, herd or flock, taste anything; do not let them eat or drink. But let man and beast be covered with sackcloth. Let everyone call urgently on God" (Jonah 3:7-8). Both people *and* animals were commanded to fast and put on sack-cloth—explicitly spiritual rituals.

God's care for animals appears even in the Ten Commandments: "Six days a week are set apart for your daily duties and regular work, but the seventh day is a day of rest dedicated to the Lord your God. On that day no one in your household may do any kind of work. This includes you, your sons and daughters, your male and female servants, your livestock, and any foreigners living among you" (Exodus 20:9-10, NLT). Animals also need rest. God carved into stone his care for them.

Some people accuse God of disrespect for animals because of the sacrificial system. But it was only because animals, created with the breath of life, are so loved by God and mankind that they qualify for the highest representative role imaginable: symbolizing God's messianic Redeemer. Lambs were often beloved pets (2 Samuel 12:3). It was because of their value that their sacrifice revealed sin's horror and the exorbitant cost of redemption. Millions of lambs were slaughtered in Israel's history, each pointing to Christ's redemptive work.

HOW WILL PEOPLE AND ANIMALS RELATE?

In the Genesis account of creation, God said, "It is not good for the man to be alone. I will make a helper suitable for him" (Genesis 2:18). God then brought animals and birds to the man. Only afterward did God create the woman as a more suitable helper.

God placed animals under the man's benevolent care: "Rule over the fish of the sea and the birds of the air and over every living creature that moves on the ground" (Genesis 1:28). This relationship is celebrated: "You made [mankind] ruler over the works of your hands; you put everything under his feet: all flocks and herds, and the beasts of the field, the birds of the air, and the fish of the sea, all that swim the paths of the seas" (Psalm 8:6-8).

God created us to be stewards of animals. He holds us accountable for how we treat them. "The godly are concerned for the welfare of their animals" (Proverbs 12:10, NLT). We are caretakers for the animals, but they belong to God, not us: "For all the animals of the forest are mine, and I own the cattle on a thousand hills. Every bird of the mountains and all the animals of the field belong to me" (Psalm 50:10-11, NLT).

Some people regard emotional attachment to animals as a modern development. But many cultures' historical records demonstrate otherwise. The prophet Nathan spoke to King David of the poor man who had a little lamb "who shared his food, drank from his cup and even slept in his arms. It was like a daughter to him" (2 Samuel 12:3). There's no suggestion this man's affection for his pet was inappropriate. David, unaware the story was told to expose his own sin, angrily responded that the man who stole the precious pet deserved to die.

We needn't speculate how God might populate a perfect Earth. He populated Eden with animals, under the rule of people. God doesn't make mistakes. There's every reason to believe he'll restore this self-proclaimed "very good" arrangement on the New Earth. We should expect the New Earth to be a place where we'll fulfill our calling to be faithful rulers and stewards of animals.

God directed Adam to name the animals (Genesis 2:19-20). The process of naming involved a personal relationship with the name-bearer. Note that Adam wasn't instructed to name the plants, only his wife and the animals, indicating their special relationship.

Eden was perfect. But without animals Eden wouldn't be Eden. The New Earth is the new Eden—Paradise regained, with the curse of the first Adam reversed, transformed into the blessing of the last Adam (Romans 5:14-15). Would God take away from us in Heaven what he gave, for delight and companionship and help, to Adam and Eve in Eden? Would he revoke his decision to put animals with people, under their care? Since he'll fashion the New Earth with renewed people, wouldn't we expect him also to include renewed animals?

WILL ANIMALS PRAISE GOD?

Throughout Scripture we read that animals praise God. I don't know exactly how animals praise God, but our inability to understand it shouldn't keep us from believing it.

Consider the psalms. Psalm 148 commands all of creation to praise the Lord, including the animals: "Wild animals and all cattle, small creatures and flying birds, kings of the earth and all nations, you princes and all rulers on earth, young men and maidens, old men and children. Let them praise the name of the Lord, for his name alone is exalted; his splendor is above the earth and the heavens" (vv. 10-13). If in some sense fallen animals, shadows of what they once were, can praise God on this fallen Earth, how much more should we expect them to do so on the New Earth? "Let everything that has breath praise the Lord" (Psalm 150:6). Since animals are said to have breath, they are included among those directed to praise God.

Passages in Revelation also indicate that the animals will praise their creator: "Then I heard every creature in heaven and on earth and under the earth and on the sea, and all that is in them, singing: 'To him who sits on the throne and to the Lamb be praise and honor and glory and power, for ever and ever!'" (Revelation 5:13). What are these "creatures" said to do? To sing praises to God in worship. If "every creature in heaven and on earth" includes animals, then animals praise God.

The most striking example of animals praising God in Heaven is often overlooked because of word selection in our Bible translations. We're told eight times in Revelation of "living creatures" in the present Heaven: "Day and night they never stop saying: 'Holy, holy, holy is the Lord God Almighty, who was, and is, and is to come.'. . . The living creatures give glory, honor and thanks to him who sits on the throne" (Revelation 4:8-9).

The word translated "living creatures" is *zoon*. Throughout most of the New Testament the word is translated "animal" and is used to indicate animals sacrificed in the Temple and wild, irrational animals (Hebrews 13:11; 2 Peter 2:12; Jude 1:10). In the Old Testament, the Septuagint used *zoon* to translate the Hebrew words for animals, including the "living creatures" of the sea (Genesis 1:21; Ezekiel 47:9). In extrabiblical writings, *zoon* commonly referred to ordinary animals and was used of the Egyptians' divine animals and the mythological bird called the Phoenix (1 Clement 25:2-3). In virtually every case inside and outside of Scripture, this word means not a person, not an angel, but an *animal*.

The King James Version translates *zoon* "beasts" in Revelation, but the negative connotations of that word led subsequent translators to settle on "living creatures." The most natural translation would be simply "animals." That word

> The whole brute creation will then, undoubtedly, be restored, not only to the vigour, strength, and swiftness which they had at their creation, but to a far higher degree of each than they ever enjoyed.
>
> **JOHN WESLEY**

would likely have been chosen by translators if it didn't sound so strange for readers to envision talking animals praising God around his throne! The "living creatures" look like a lion, an ox, a man, and an eagle (Revelation 4:7). They appear to be the same creatures of Ezekiel 1:5-14 and Ezekiel 10:10-14, also called the cherubim, who are distinguished from angels (Revelation 15:7). The cherubim are first mentioned in Genesis 3:24, as Eden's guardians. Their images were carved out of gold and placed on the Ark of the Covenant, indicating their closeness to God.

Somehow we have failed to grasp that the "living creatures" who cry out "Holy, holy, holy" are *animals*—living, breathing, intelligent and articulate *animals* who dwell in God's presence, worshiping and praising him. They preexisted and are greater than the animals we know. Perhaps they're the prototype creatures of Heaven after whom God designed Earth's animals. But even though they're highly intelligent and expressive, they're still animals; that's what Scripture calls them.

When we grasp these passages, we'll see the error of one writer's statement, "Clearly animals do not fit into the main purpose of heaven, which is the articulation of God's praise."[294] On the contrary, the *primary* beings shown articulating God's praise in Heaven, along with angels and humans (the elders), are animals!

Although earthly animals aren't capable of verbalizing praise as these animals in Heaven do, the passages speaking of earthly animals praising God and the story of Balaam's donkey clearly suggest that animals have a spiritual dimension far beyond our understanding. The Bible tells us that animals, in their own way, praise God. By extending to them the blessings of mankind's redemption, just as he extended to them the curses of mankind's sin, God will grant them an important role on the New Earth.

Once we recognize that the living creatures are animals, we need not see other references to animals in the present Heaven as figurative. For instance, Elijah was taken up to Heaven in a chariot pulled by horses (2 Kings 2:11). Revelation suggests there are horses in the present Heaven (Revelation 6:2-8); in fact, there are enough horses for the vast armies of Heaven to ride (Revelation 19:11-14). There are also invisible horses in angelic armies dispatched to Earth (2 Kings 6:17).

These horses could be symbolic, but as we saw in chapter 6, we find many other references to physical objects in the present Heaven, including Christ's resurrection body. It's therefore possible that besides the "living creatures," horses as well as other animals could be in the present Heaven. Even if this isn't the case, however, we have every reason to expect animals will find their ultimate home on the New Earth.

WILL WE SEE GOD'S ATTRIBUTES IN ANIMALS?

"For since the creation of the world God's invisible qualities—his eternal power and divine nature—have been clearly seen, being understood from what has been made" (Romans 1:20). Often this verse is understood to refer to stars, mountains, lakes, and natural wonders. But we shouldn't overlook God's supreme creation besides mankind: animals. God's invisible qualities, his divine attributes, are evident in animals.

If this is true even now, how much more will it be true on the New Earth? What will it be like to look at lions, study them, touch them, and see their power, nobility, and royalty—*and see God in them*? What will it be like to look at lambs and see their loving gentleness, meekness, and servanthood, to ponder their role in first covenant sacrifices—*and see God in them*?

In the Old Testament God asks Job, "Do you give the horse his strength . . . ? Do you make him leap like a locust . . . ? He paws fiercely, rejoicing in his strength. . . . He laughs at fear, afraid of nothing" (Job 39:19-22). The horse's strength, courage, and determination testify to those virtues in its Maker.

What qualities of loyalty, devotion, ingenuity, and single-mindedness will we see in animals on the New Earth? What will we learn from mice, iguanas, or armadillos? Certainly we'll praise God for his creativity and humor (consider the duckbill platypus).

Once the Curse is lifted, we'll see more attributes of God in animals than we've ever thought about. Consider what's visible in otters, dogs, and countless other animals: God's playfulness. (Did you think human beings invented play on our own?) I for one have praised God for and been drawn to him by the playfulness, exuberance, love, and devotion in the dogs I've had over the years. They communicate the beauty of their Maker.

Adam, Noah, and Jesus are the three heads of the three Earths. When Adam was created, God surrounded him with animals. When Noah was delivered from the Flood, God surrounded him with animals. When Jesus was born, God surrounded him with animals. When Jesus establishes the renewed Earth, with renewed men and women, don't you think he'll surround himself with renewed animals?

CHAPTER 40

WILL ANIMALS, INCLUDING OUR PETS, LIVE AGAIN?

C hrist proclaims from his throne on the New Earth: "Behold, I am making all things new" (Revelation 21:5, ESV). It's not just people who will be renewed but also the earth and "all things" in it. Do "all things" include animals? Yes. Horses, cats, dogs, deer, dolphins, and squirrels—as well as the inanimate creation—will be beneficiaries of Christ's death and resurrection.

Christ's emphasis isn't on making new things but on making old things new. It's not about inventing the unfamiliar but about restoring and enhancing the familiar. Jesus seems to be saying, "I'll take all I made the first time, including people and nature and animals and the earth itself, and bring it back as new, fresh, and indestructible."

HOW CLOSELY ARE ANIMALS TIED TO OUR RESURRECTION?

Did Christ die for animals? Certainly not in the way he died for mankind. People are made in God's image, animals aren't. People sinned, animals didn't. Because animals didn't sin, they don't need a redeemer in the same way.

But in another sense, Christ died for animals indirectly because his death for humanity purchased redemption for what was brought down by humanity's sin, including animals. Romans 8 is explicit on this point: "The creation itself will be liberated from its bondage to decay and brought into the glorious freedom of the children of God. We know that the whole creation has been groaning as in the pains of childbirth. . . . We ourselves . . . groan inwardly as we wait eagerly for . . . the redemption of our bodies" (Romans 8:21-23).

This is a clear statement that our resurrection, the redemption of our bodies, will bring deliverance not only to us *but also to the rest of creation, which has been groaning in its suffering.* This seems to indicate that on the New Earth, after mankind's resurrection, animals who once suffered on the old Earth will join God's children in glorious freedom from death and decay.

If God created a new race of humans on the New Earth—rather than raising the people who had lived on the old Earth—would it fulfill the promise in Romans 8 of redemption, deliverance, and resurrection? No. Why? To have meaning, the people who are redeemed and resurrected into the new world must be the same people who suffered in the old world. Otherwise, their longing for redemption would go unmet. As goes mankind, so go the animals. If we take to its logical conclusions the parallel Paul makes between humans' and animals' groaning, then at least some of those animals who suffered on the old Earth must be made whole on the New Earth.

It's not some abstract "animalkind" that cries out. The creatures that groan and cry out for their resurrection are specific suffering people and specific animals. They cry out for their deliverance, not another's. I believe this suggests that God may remake certain animals that lived on the old Earth.

Many passages indicate that God will bring judgment on "men and animals" or "man and beast" because of mankind's sin (Exodus 9:22-25; Jeremiah 7:20; 21:6; Ezekiel 14:12-13, 17). God's blessings on the righteous include blessings not only on their children but also on the offspring of their animals (Deuteronomy 7:13-14; 28:1-4).

This fits the words anticipating Christ's coming: "And all flesh will see the salvation of God" (Luke 3:6, NASB). The Greek word translated "flesh" is *sarx*. Some Bible versions translate this as "all people" or "all mankind," but the word is more inclusive. "All flesh" includes animals. They too will behold and benefit from Christ's redemptive work.

Psalm 104 demonstrates God's intimate involvement with the lives of his animals and his purposes for them. The psalm speaks of birds, cattle, wild donkeys, rock badgers, and lions, saying "the earth is full of your creatures" (v. 24). It speaks of "the sea, vast and spacious, teeming with creatures beyond number—living things both large and small" (v. 25). It says, "These all look to you" (v. 27). Then the psalm writer adds, "When you take away their breath, they die and return to the dust" (v. 29). But then we're told something amazing: "When you send your Spirit, they are created, and you renew the face of the earth" (v. 30). The "they" seems to refer to the animals who've died and returned to the dust. What does God mean that he sends his Spirit and creates them? It appears that he's talking about re-creating animals after they've died. Why? To "renew the face of the earth." The same "they" who die are the "they" who are created or re-created as part of the earth's renewal (Matthew 19:28).

WILL EXTINCT ANIMALS LIVE ON THE NEW EARTH?

Someone wrote to me, "My children are hoping extinct animals will be in Heaven, maybe even dinosaurs." Is this merely a child's fantasy? I think it's a question based on a rational conclusion. Were dinosaurs part of God's original creation of a perfect animal world? Certainly. Will the restoration of Earth and the redemption of God's creation be complete enough to bring back extinct animals? Will extinct animals be included in the "all things" Christ will make new? I see every reason to think so and no persuasive argument against it. I think we should fully expect that extinct animals and plants will be brought back to life. By resurrecting his original creation, God will show the totality of his victory over sin and death.

It's apparent that the Curse that fell on the earth resulted in some species dying out. But God promises, "No longer will there be any curse" (Revelation 22:3). And because it seems that the Curse will not merely be nullified but reversed, it seems likely that God might restore extinct animals and plants on the New Earth.

Animals are created for God's glory. What could speak more of his awesome power than a tyrannosaurus? When talking to Job, God pointed out his greatness revealed in the giant land and sea creatures behemoth and leviathan (Job 40–41). Why shouldn't all people have the opportunity to enjoy these great wonders of God on the New Earth?

Imagine Jurassic Park with all of the awesome majesty of those huge creatures but none of their violence and hostility. Imagine riding a brontosaurus—or flying on the back of a pterodactyl. Unless God made a mistake when he created them—and clearly he didn't—why wouldn't he include them when he makes "everything new"?

WILL OUR PETS BE RESTORED ON THE NEW EARTH?

Humorist Will Rogers said, "If there are no dogs in heaven, then when I die I want to go where they went." This statement was, of course, based on sentiment, not theology. However, it reflects something biblical: a God-given affection for animals. I've often thanked God for my golden retriever, who, when I was a boy, crawled into my sleeping bag as I lay in my backyard gazing up at the stars. Although I didn't know God then, he touched my life through that dog. Nanci and I have experienced many hours of laughter and joy in animals.

Certainly people can go to unhealthy extremes with their animals. Still, though we understandably roll our eyes at pet psychologists or estates left to Siamese cats, we should ask ourselves why so many people find such companionship, solace, and joy in their pets. Is it because of sin? I believe it's because of how God has made animals, and us.

That's why the question of whether pets will be in Heaven is not, as some assume, stupid. Animals aren't nearly as valuable as people, but God is their Maker and has touched many people's lives through them. It would be simple for him to re-create a pet in Heaven if he wants to. He's the *giver* of all good gifts, not the *taker* of them. If it would please us to have a pet restored to the New Earth, that may be sufficient reason. Consider parents who've acquired a pet because of their child's request. God is better than we are at giving good gifts to his children (Matthew 7:9-11). And if we object that animals won't make us happy in Heaven, we betray our Christoplatonism again—for by finding happiness in God's creation, we will find happiness in him.

We know animals will be on the New Earth, which is a redeemed and renewed old Earth, in which animals had a prominent role. People will be resurrected to inhabit this world. As we saw, Romans 8:21-23 assumes animals as part of a suffering creation eagerly awaiting deliverance through humanity's resurrection. This seems to require that some animals who lived, suffered, and died on the old Earth must be made whole on the New Earth. Wouldn't some of those likely be our pets?

> Something better remains after death for these poor creatures . . . that these, likewise, shall one day be delivered from this bondage of corruption, and shall then receive an ample amends for all their present sufferings.
>
> **JOHN WESLEY**

It seems God could do one of three things on the New Earth: (1) create entirely new animals; (2) bring back to life animals that have suffered in our present world, giving them immortal bodies (this could be re-creating, not necessarily resurrecting); (3) create some animals brand-new, "from scratch," *and* bring back to life some old ones.[295]

I'm avoiding the term *resurrection* for fear that it could lead to theological error that fails to recognize the fundamental differences between people and animals—something that certain "animal rights" advocates are guilty of. However, in the broad sense of the terms, the words *redemption* and *resurrection* can appropriately apply not only to mankind but also to Earth, vegetation, and animals. A resurrected field, meadow, flower, or animal, of course, would in no sense be equal to resurrected humans; it's simply that just as Creation and the Fall rode on the coattails of mankind, so will redemption and resurrection.

In many of his writings, C. S. Lewis commented on the future of animals. He said, "It seems to me possible that certain animals may have an immortality, not in themselves, but in the immortality of their masters. . . . Very few animals indeed, in their wild state, attain to a 'self' or ego. But if any do, and if it is agreeable to the goodness of God that they should live again, their immortality would also be related to man—not, this time, to individual masters, but to humanity."[296] In *The Great Divorce,* Lewis portrayed Sarah Smith, a woman ordinary on Earth, as great in Heaven. On Earth she loved both people and animals. In Heaven she's surrounded by the very animals she cared for on Earth.[297]

In her excellent book about Heaven, Joni Eareckson Tada says, "If God brings our pets back to life, it wouldn't surprise me. It would be just like Him. It would be totally in keeping with His generous character. . . . Exorbitant. Excessive. Extravagant in grace after grace. Of all the dazzling discoveries and ecstatic pleasures heaven will hold for us, the potential of seeing Scrappy would be pure whimsy—utterly, joyfully, surprisingly superfluous. . . . Heaven is going to be a place that will refract and reflect in as many ways as possible the goodness and joy of our great God, who delights in lavishing love on His children."[298]

In a poem about the world to come, theologian John Piper writes,

> *And as I knelt beside the brook*
> *To drink eternal life, I took*
> *A glance across the golden grass,*
> *And saw my dog, old Blackie, fast*
> *As she could come. She leaped the stream—*
> *Almost—and what a happy gleam*
> *Was in her eye. I knelt to drink,*
> *And knew that I was on the brink*
> *Of endless joy. And everywhere*
> *I turned I saw a wonder there.*[299]

IS IT WRONG TO GRIEVE A PET'S DEATH?

Many people grieve deeply when their pets die. Some have told me they're embarrassed or even ashamed at this. Their loss is great, and they long for hope that they'll see their pets again.

If we regard pets as God-created companions entrusted to our care, it's only right that we should experience grief at their loss. Who made these endearing qualities in animals? God. Who made us to be touched by them? God. Do we love animals because of sin and the Curse? No. We love animals because God created us—and them—to love each other. We can turn people into idols, but it doesn't mean it's wrong to love people. The same is true of animals.

We know the stories of pets who've risked their lives and died for their owners because the animals' instinct for love and loyalty outweighed their instinct for self-preservation. It's noble for a person to lay down his or her life for others, so animals who do the same must also be noble. We needn't be embarrassed either to grieve their loss or to want to see them again. If we believe God is their creator, that he loves us and them, that he intends to restore his creatures from the bondage they experienced because of our sin, then we have biblical grounds for not only wanting but also expecting that we may be with them again on the New Earth.

Let's not "correct" our children and grandchildren when they pray that they'll be able to see their pets again. The answer to that prayer is up to God. But he loves to hear the prayers of his children, and there is scriptural reason to believe he may answer those prayers. Remember too that our children's instinctive grasp of Heaven—and what we should look forward to there—is sometimes better than ours. (Christoplatonism hasn't gripped them yet.)

WHAT FUTURE IS GOD PLANNING FOR ANIMALS?

On November 30, 1781, John Wesley, who spent a large part of his life on horseback, preached a remarkable message. He began by addressing the many passages that speak of God's provision for cattle and birds, and not muzzling the ox that treads the corn. Wesley asked, "If the Creator and Father of every living thing is rich in mercy towards all . . . how is it that misery of all kinds overspreads the face of the earth? . . . All the beasts of the field, and all the fowls of the air, were with Adam in paradise. And there is no question but their state was suited to their place: It was paradisiacal; perfectly happy."[300]

Wesley explained mankind's appointed role on Earth and how the animals benefited from mankind's faithfulness to God and suffered in human rebellion: "Man was God's vicegerent upon earth, the prince and governor of this lower world; and all the blessings of God flowed through him to the inferior creatures. Man was the channel of conveyance between his Creator and the whole brute creation . . . so when man made himself incapable of transmitting those blessings, that communication was necessarily cut off."

Wesley argued that animals originally had greater understanding, wills, passions, liberty, and choice. He said, "How beautiful many of them were, we may conjecture from that which still remains. . . . It is probable they sustained much loss . . . their vigour, strength, and swiftness. But undoubtedly they suffered far more in their understanding. . . . As man is deprived of *his* perfection, his loving obedience to God; so brutes are deprived of *their* perfection, their loving obedience to man."

After recounting mankind's sad record of cruelty to animals, Wesley asked,

But will "the creature," will even the brute creation, always remain in this deplorable condition? God forbid that we should affirm this; yea, or even entertain such a thought! . . . The whole brute creation will then, undoubtedly, be restored, not only to the vigour, strength, and swiftness which they had at their creation, but to a far higher degree of each than they ever enjoyed. They will be restored, not only to that measure of understanding which they had in paradise, but to a degree of it as much higher than that. . . . Whatever affections they had in the garden of God, will be restored with vast increase; being exalted and refined in a manner which we ourselves are not now able to comprehend.

Wesley envisioned a magnificent restoration of the animal kingdom on the New Earth: "And with their beauty their happiness will return. . . . In the new earth, as well as in the new heavens, there will be nothing to give pain, but everything that the wisdom and goodness of God can create to give happiness. As a recompense for what they [animals] once suffered . . . they shall enjoy happiness suited to their state, without alloy, without interruption, and without end."

Wesley then made an extraordinary speculation: "What, if it should then please the all-wise, the all-gracious Creator to raise them higher in the scale of beings? What, if it should please him . . . to make them . . . capable of knowing and loving and enjoying the Author of their being?"

MIGHT SOME ANIMALS TALK?

Most people who've enjoyed the children's stories of Beatrix Potter, C. S. Lewis, or others who wrote of talking animals have probably never seriously considered the possibility that some animals might actually have talked in Eden or that they might talk on the New Earth.

We're told that in Eden the serpent was "more crafty than any of the wild animals the Lord God had made" (Genesis 3:1). *More* crafty suggests that some of the other animals were also crafty. Animals were smart, probably smarter than we imagine; the most intelligent animals we see around us are but fallen remnants of what once was. The serpent's intelligence was demonstrated in reasoning and persuasive speech. People typically imagine that Satan possessed a dumb animal, the snake, but the text doesn't say that. Today Satan can speak through a human being but not an animal because people can talk and animals can't. But the fact that he spoke through an animal in Eden suggests the animal had the capacity to speak. There's no suggestion Eve was surprised to hear an animal speak, indicating other animals also may have spoken.

When God spoke through Balaam's donkey, was he merely putting words into her mouth, or did he temporarily give the donkey the ability to verbalize her instinct, perceptions, and feelings? On the New Earth, might God, as John Wesley surmised, restore or increase both the intelligence and the communicative abilities of animals? Whales and dolphins communicate in highly specific ways, as do many primates, in varying degrees. These are God-given abilities. We should assume they'll be enhanced on the New Earth or at very least restored to the capabilities they had in Eden, where it's possible more than one animal talked.

In a universe teeming with God's creativity, should talking animals or intelligent non-human beings (such as angels and "living creatures" that not only talk but worship) surprise us? If people will be smarter and more capable on the New Earth, should it surprise us that animals might also be smarter and more capable? Remember, both in the Fall (sin) and the rise (resurrection), *as goes mankind, so goes creation.*

When in John's vision of Heaven he says, "I heard an eagle that was flying in midair call out in a loud voice" (Revelation 8:13), it may be figurative language. But when the serpent spoke to Eve and when the donkey spoke to Balaam, the stories are recorded in historical narrative, not in apocalyptic literature. Nothing in the context of the Genesis account or the Balaam story indicates these shouldn't be taken literally. Furthermore, as we've seen, living creatures—*animals*—verbalize praise to God. And "every creature" in the universe is said to sing and give praise to the Lamb (Revelation 5:13). The word for creature in that verse is *ktisma*, which clearly means "animals" in its only other appearance in Revelation (8:9). Just because these passages are in the book of Revelation doesn't mean they cannot be literal.

C. S. Lewis gives us a creative glimpse of what the resurrected Earth might be like. In *The Magician's Nephew*, King Aslan declares the sons of Adam and daughters of Eve, now in Narnia on its first day, to be his kings and queens. The talking animals make crowns for the first king and queen and express their delight in being ruled by these humans.

One of the animals who watches this scene is a horse named Strawberry, who drew a London carriage on Earth. He toiled, and sometimes his master Frank, a cabbie and a good man, whipped him to make him move faster. Strawberry, whom Aslan renamed Fledge, marvels at the new King Frank in the New Narnia: "My old master's been changed nearly as much as I have! Why, he's a real master now."[301]

Aslan later says to King Frank and Queen Helen, "Be just and merciful and brave. The blessing is upon you."[302]

All the people celebrate.

All the animals rejoice.

Aslan, Lord of all, is pleased.

WHAT WILL WE DO IN HEAVEN?

CHAPTER 41

WILL HEAVEN EVER BE BORING?

A common misconception about eternity surfaced in an episode of *Star Trek: Voyager*. A member of the undying "Q continuum" longs for an end to his existence. Why? Because, he complains, everything that could be said and done has *already* been said and done, and now there's only repetition and utter boredom. He says, "For us, the disease is immortality." Finally he's allowed to end his existence.

Science-fiction writer Isaac Asimov writes, "I don't believe in an afterlife, so I don't have to spend my whole life fearing hell, or fearing heaven even more. For whatever the tortures of hell, I think the boredom of heaven would be even worse."

Sadly, even among Christians, it's a prevalent myth that Heaven will be boring. Sometimes we can't envision anything beyond strumming a harp and polishing the streets of gold. We've succumbed to Satan's strategies "to blaspheme God, and to slander his name and his dwelling place" (Revelation 13:6).

WHAT WILL WE DO TO AVOID BOREDOM?

People sometimes say, "I'd rather be having a good time in Hell than be bored in Heaven." Many people imagine Hell as a place where they'll hang around, shoot pool, and joke with friends. That could happen on the New Earth, but not in Hell.

Hell is a place of torment and isolation, where friendship and good times don't exist. Hell will be deadly boring. Everything good, enjoyable, refreshing, fascinating, and interesting is derived from God. Without God there's nothing interesting to do. King David wrote, "In Your presence is fullness of joy; at Your right hand are pleasures forevermore" (Psalm 16:11, NKJV). In the presence of God, there's nothing but joy.

In his book *Things Unseen*, pastor Mark Buchanan asks,

Why won't we be bored in heaven? Because it's the one place where both impulses—to go beyond, to go home—are perfectly joined and totally satisfied. It's the one place where we're constantly discovering—where everything is always fresh and the possessing of a thing is as good as the pursuing of it—and yet where we are fully at home—where everything is as it ought to be and where we find, undiminished, that mysterious something we never found down here. . . . And this lifelong melancholy that hangs on us, this wishing we were someone else somewhere else, vanishes too. Our craving to go beyond is always and fully realized. Our yearning for home is once and for all fulfilled. The *ahh!* of deep satisfaction and the *aha!* of delighted surprise meet, and they kiss.[303]

Our belief that Heaven will be boring betrays a heresy—that God is boring. There's no greater nonsense. Our desire for pleasure and the experience of joy come directly from God's hand. He made our taste buds, adrenaline, sex drives, and the nerve endings that convey pleasure to our brains. Likewise, our imaginations and our capacity for joy and exhilaration were made by the very God we accuse of being boring. Are we so arrogant as to imagine that human beings came up with the idea of having fun?

"Won't it be boring to be good all the time?" someone asked. Note the assumption: sin is exciting and righteousness is boring. We've fallen for the devil's lie. His most basic strategy, the same one he employed with Adam and Eve, is to make us believe that sin brings fulfillment. However, in reality, sin robs us of fulfillment. Sin doesn't make life interesting; it makes life empty. Sin doesn't create adventure; it blunts it. Sin doesn't expand life; it shrinks it. Sin's emptiness inevitably leads to boredom. When there's fulfillment, when there's beauty, when we see God as he truly is—an endless reservoir of fascination—boredom becomes impossible.

Those who believe that excitement can't exist without sin are thinking with sin-poisoned minds. Drug addicts are convinced that without their drugs they can't live happy lives. In fact—as everyone else can see—drugs make them miserable. Freedom from sin will mean freedom to be what God intended, freedom to find far greater joy in everything. In Heaven we'll be *filled*—as Psalm 16:11 describes it—with joy and eternal pleasures.

WHY WOULD ANYONE THINK WE'D BE BORED?

An elderly gentleman I led to Christ asked a question of a Christian employee in his care center: "Will we have fun in Heaven?"

"Oh, *no*," the woman replied, appearing dismayed that he'd even asked.

When he told me this story, I shook my head, because I've heard it so often. Why did this Christian woman respond as she did? Because, in accordance with the faulty assumptions of Christoplatonism, she instinctively linked fun with sin and boredom with holiness. But she couldn't be more wrong. God promises that we'll laugh, rejoice, and experience endless pleasures in Heaven.

Someone told me nobody will enjoy playing golf in Heaven because it would get boring always hitting holes in one. But why assume everyone's skills will be equal and incapable of further development? Just as our minds will grow in knowledge, our resurrection bodies can develop greater skills.

Another reason people assume Heaven is boring is that their Christian lives are boring. That's not God's fault; it's their own. God calls us to follow him in an adventure that should put us on life's edge. He's infinite in creativity, goodness, beauty, and power. If we're experiencing the invigorating stirrings of God's Spirit, trusting him to fill our lives with divine appointments, experiencing the childlike delights of his gracious daily kindnesses, then we'll know that God is exciting and Heaven is exhilarating. People who love God crave his companionship. To be in his presence will be the very opposite of boredom.

We think of ourselves as fun-loving, and of God as a humorless killjoy. But we've got it backward. It's not God who's boring; it's us. Did we invent wit, humor, and laughter? No. God did. We'll never begin to exhaust God's sense of humor and his love for adventure. The real question is this: How could God not be bored with *us*?

Most of us can envision ourselves being happy for a few days or a week, if that. But a year of complete and sustained happiness? Impossible, we think, because we've never experienced it. We think of life under the Curse as normal because that's all we've ever known. A hundred or a million years of happiness is inconceivable to us. Just as creatures who live in a flat land can't conceive of three-dimensional space, we can't conceive of unending happiness. Because that level of happiness is not possible here on the fallen Earth, we assume it won't be possible on the New Earth. But we're wrong. To properly envision Heaven, we must remove from our eyes the distorted lenses of death and the Curse.

WILL OUR WORK BE ENGAGING?

On the New Earth, God will give us renewed minds and marvelously constructed bodies. We'll be whole people, full of energy and vision. James Campbell says, "The work on the other side, whatever be its character, will be adapted to each one's special aptitude and powers. It will be the work he can do best; the work that will give the fullest play to all that is within him."[304]

Even under the Curse, we catch glimpses of how work can be enriching, how it can build relationships, and how it can help us to improve. Work stretches us in ways that make us smarter, wiser, and more fulfilled. The God who created us to do good works (Ephesians 2:10) will not cancel this purpose when he resurrects us to inhabit the new universe. The Bible's picture of resurrected people at work in a vibrant society on a resurrected Earth couldn't be more compelling: We're going to help God run the universe (Luke 19:11-27).

We're told that we will serve God in Heaven (Revelation 7:15; 22:3). Service is active, not passive. It involves fulfilling responsibilities in which we expend energy. Work in Heaven won't be frustrating or fruitless; instead, it will involve lasting accomplishment, unhindered by decay and fatigue, enhanced by unlimited resources. We'll approach our work with the enthusiasm we bring to our favorite sport or hobby.

> Imaginary evil is romantic and varied; real evil is gloomy, monotonous, barren, boring. Imaginary good is boring; real good is always new, marvelous, intoxicating.
>
> **SIMONE WEIL**

In Heaven, we'll reign with Christ, exercise leadership and authority, and make important decisions. This implies we'll be given specific responsibilities by our leaders and we'll delegate specific responsibilities to those under our leadership (Luke 19:17-19). We'll set goals, devise plans, and share ideas. Our best work days on the present Earth—those days when everything turns out better than we planned, when we get everything done on time, and when everyone on the team pulls together and enjoys each other— are just a small foretaste of the joy our work will bring us on the New Earth.

A disembodied existence would be boring, but the reality of our bodily resurrection puts boredom to death. Imagine the animals that zoologists will research and play with or the flowers that botanists will study. Gifted astronomers and explorers may go from star system to star system, galaxy to galaxy, studying the wonders of God's creation. If we think life on the New Earth will be boring, we just aren't getting it. Take a closer look at God and his Word, and all thoughts that we'll be bored in his presence will vanish.

WILL OUR LIFE'S WORK CONTINUE?

Because there will be continuity from the old Earth to the new, it's possible we'll continue some of the work we started on the old Earth. I believe we'll pursue some of the same things we were doing, or dreamed of doing, before our death.

Of course, people whose jobs depend on aspects of our fallen world that will no longer exist on the New Earth—such as dentists (decay), police officers (crime), funeral directors (death), insurance salespeople (disability), and many others—will change their work in Heaven, but that doesn't mean they'll be unemployed. What's now an interest or hobby may become their main vocation. Others, however, may continue with work similar to what they do now, whether as gardeners, engineers, builders, artists, animal trainers, musicians, scientists, craftspeople, or hundreds of other vocations. A significant difference will be that they'll work without the hindrances of toil, pain, corruption, and sin.

Author Victor Hugo, in reflecting on his life's work, spoke profoundly of anticipating his work in Heaven:

> I feel within me that future life. I am like a forest that has been razed; the
> new shoots are stronger and brighter. I shall most certainly rise toward the
> heavens the nearer my approach to the end, the plainer is the sound of
> immortal symphonies of worlds which invite me. For half a century I have
> been translating my thoughts into prose and verse: history, drama, philos-
> ophy, romance, tradition, satire, ode, and song; all of these I have tried.
> But I feel I haven't given utterance to the thousandth part of what lies
> within me. When I go to the grave I can say, as others have said, "My
> day's work is done." But I cannot say, "My life is done." My work will
> recommence the next morning. The tomb is not a blind alley; it is a
> thoroughfare. It closes upon the twilight, but opens upon the dawn.[305]

I'm convinced that Hugo was right in saying that every Christian's life's work, though not always his or her vocation, will continue on the New Earth. After all, our calling to glorify God will never end. It applies as much here and now as it will then and there, and it will likely be fulfilled in many old ways as well as new ones.

In *The Biblical Doctrine of Heaven*, Wilbur Smith suggests, "In heaven we will be permitted to finish many of those worthy tasks which we had dreamed to do while on earth but which neither time nor strength nor ability allowed us to achieve."[306] This is an encouraging thought. It saves us from frantically thinking that we have to do it all now, or from giving up in despair because of the limits of time, money, and strength, and the duties that keep us from certain things we'd love to do.

James Campbell took comfort in this same idea:

> This throws some measure of relieving light upon the painful mystery of
> a life brought to a sudden close in the fullness of its power. In the pres-
> ence of such a tragedy we instinctively ask, Why this waste? Is all the

training, discipline, and culture of this choice spirit to be lost? It cannot be; for in God's universe nothing is ever lost. No preparation is ever in vain. There is need up there for clear heads, warm hearts, and skilled hands. . . . If some kinds of work are over, others will begin; if some duties are laid down, others will be taken up. And any regret for labour missed down here, will be swallowed up in the joyful anticipation of the higher service that awaits every prepared and willing worker in the upper kingdom of the Father. . . . He will allow no heaven-born hope to be put to shame, but will bring to realization life's brightest visions.[307]

What will it be like to perform a task, to build and create, knowing that what we're doing will last? What will it be like to be always gaining skill, so that our best work will always be ahead of us? Because our minds and bodies will never fade and because we will never lack resources or opportunity, our work won't degenerate. Buildings won't last for only fifty years, and books won't be in print for only twenty years. They'll last forever.

WILL THERE BE CULTURAL DEVELOPMENTS?

Anthony Hoekema says, "In the beginning man was given the so-called cultural mandate—the command to rule over the earth and to develop a God-glorifying culture. Because of man's fall into sin, that cultural mandate has never been carried out in the way God intended. Only on the new earth will it be perfectly and sinlessly fulfilled. Only then shall we be able to rule the earth properly."[308]

Would there have been human culture without the Fall? Of course. Culture is the natural, God-intended product of his gifting, equipping, and calling for mankind to rule over creation. Scripture describes developments in farming, metallurgy, and the crafting of musical instruments (Genesis 4:20-22) shortly after the Fall. If God had no interest in those cultural improvements, he wouldn't make note of them. God created his image-bearers to glorify him in creative accomplishments, and he's pleased by them.

Only two people in human history, Adam and Eve, even began to taste what it was like to fulfill God's command to subdue the earth, and they didn't get far. Was God shortsighted, not anticipating the Fall? Did he give up on Adam and Eve after they sinned? No. He had a plan that would fulfill his original design in greater ways. Resurrected culture will reach ever-expanding heights that no society has yet seen.

In *The Promise of the Future*, theologian Cornelius Venema writes, "Every legitimate and excellent fruit of human culture will be carried into and contribute to the splendour of life in the new creation. Rather than the new creation being a radically new beginning, in which the excellent and noble fruits of humankind's fulfillment of the cultural mandate are wholly discarded—the new creation will benefit from, and be immensely enriched by, its receiving of these fruits."[309]

Bruce Milne shares a similar perspective: "The one who is Lord of the whole of life was never going to bring us at the end into an eternal existence of mental constriction, or of emotional and creative impoverishment. Creativity will surely be valued, for such an anticipation must be in keeping with the nature of him who set the morning stars a-singing when he created them at the beginning, and whose joyful, uninhibited cry echoes across the battlements of the new creation. 'See, I am making everything new!' . . . What creative possibilities await us in the unfolding of the eternal ages no present imagination can begin to unravel."[310]

We should stretch our vision of what's in store for us. God's redemptive work is far greater than we imagine because God himself is far greater than we imagine.

LIFEBOAT OR ARK THEOLOGY?

Paul Marshall speaks of the prevalent but misguided notion that we've permanently wrecked the world. He says that many assume, "What's important now is simply that we rescue people from the wreckage."[311] He calls this *lifeboat theology*: "It is as if the creation were the *Titanic*, and now that we've hit the iceberg of sin, there's nothing left for us to do but get ourselves into lifeboats. The ship is sinking rapidly, God has given up on it and is concerned only with the survival of his people. Any effort we make to salvage God's creation amounts to re-arranging the deck chairs. Instead, some say, our sole task is to get into the lifeboats, to keep them afloat, to pluck drowning victims out of the water, and to sail on until we get to heaven where all will be well."[312]

Marshall says that this is the assumption and perspective that drives many evangelical Christians. He proposes an alternative to lifeboat theology, which he calls *ark theology*: "Noah's ark saved not only people, but it preserved God's other creatures as well. The ark looked not to flee but to return to the land and begin again. Once the flood subsided, *everyone and everything was intended to return again to restore the earth*."[313] God's preservation of man and animals and the earth itself demonstrates he hasn't given up on his creation. In fact, he commanded Noah after the Fall to do exactly what he commanded Adam and Eve before the Fall: Fill the earth and rule it. Noah went out to plant a vineyard (Genesis 9:20), and mankind was back to work again on the earth.

Our gifts and special interests—the way we're wired—aren't accidents. *God* made us this way. He intricately designed each of us to uniquely express his glory. Speaking of God's sovereign distribution of a variety of spiritual gifts, the apostle Paul says, "To each one the manifestation of the Spirit is given for the common good" (1 Corinthians 12:7). We'll be a great community on the New Earth. The gifts, skills, passions, and tasks God grants each of us will not only be for his glory and our good but also for the good of our larger family. God will rejoice as we thrive together, interdependently, in the New Earth's continuously creative culture.

HOW WILL WE EXPRESS OUR CREATIVITY?

In this world, even under the Curse, human imagination and skill have produced some remarkable works. The statues of Easter Island. Stonehenge. Shakespeare's plays. Beethoven's Ninth Symphony. The Golden Gate Bridge. Baseball. Heart transplants. Prenatal surgery. Microwave ovens. DVDs. The space shuttle. Chocolate ice cream. Pecan pie. Sports cars. It's a list that never ends.

With the resources God will lavishly give us on the New Earth, what will we be able to accomplish together? When we think about this, we should be like children anticipating Christmas—sneaking out of bed to see what's under the Christmas tree.

Without creativity, music would be a dull succession of sounds. Without creativity, books would be colorless and superficial. They wouldn't engage our minds and hearts. Paintings would be lifeless or nonexistent. Our homes would be barracks, our buildings boxes. God's preparing a place for us, and he'll equip us to develop it to his glory.

I agree with Anthony Hoekema when he says, "The possibilities that now rise before us boggle the mind. Will there be 'better Beethovens' on the new earth? . . . better Rembrandts, better Raphaels? Shall we read better poetry, better drama, and better prose? Will scientists continue to advance in technological achievement, will geologists continue to dig out the treasures of the earth, and will architects continue to build imposing and attractive structures? Will there be exciting new adventures in space travel? . . . Our culture will glorify God in ways that surpass our most fantastic dreams."[314]

> The best is yet to be.
>
> **JOHN WESLEY**

I imagine that people will express creativity in designing clothes. The precious stones of the New Jerusalem suggest jewelry may have a place on the New Earth. Some people wear jewelry now for status, but on the New Earth, God-made jewels worn by people made in the image of God will reflect the Creator's beauty. Isaiah 65:21 suggests that we'll build houses and live in them on the New Earth. If so, we'll no doubt decorate them beautifully.

Buildings on the scale of the New Jerusalem reflect extensive cultural advancement. Human builders will learn from God's design, just as Leonardo da Vinci learned by studying the form and flight of birds while working on his flying machine. What will clear-thinking human beings—unhindered by sin and the barriers that separate us—be able to design and build? What would Galileo, da Vinci, Edison, or Einstein achieve if they could live even a thousand years unhindered by the Curse? What will we achieve when we have resurrected bodies with resurrected minds, working together forever?

Some researchers suggest that we now use only 10 percent of our brainpower. Adam and Eve could likely use 100 percent of theirs—and their brainpower was probably far greater than ours. (Contrary to evolutionary assumptions, according to Scripture, mankind's greatest capacity was in the past.) On the New Earth, God's gifts to us will never be lost to age, death, pettiness, insecurity, or laziness. Undistracted and undiminished by sin and the demands of survival, mankind will create and innovate at unprecedented levels, to God's eternal glory.

WILL WE SHAPE CULTURE INTO NEW FORMS?

In the Garden of Eden, God told Adam to name all the animals. And "whatever the man called each living creature, that was its name" (Genesis 2:19). Remarkably, from that point forward, God called animals by the names that Adam chose. This demonstrates the lofty and meaningful role that God grants us in molding and governing culture.

Adam wasn't just preserving creation; he was shaping it. Paul Marshall writes, "We have a creative task in the world. We must shape things in ways for which there is sometimes no clear direction. This is why imagination is not just a feature of the arts; it is a feature of human life itself. Without imagination, without experimentation, without openness to new questions and new possibilities, there can be no science and no technology. We are not challenging God when we do this, at least not when we do it in humility and faith. We are not stealing fire from the gods. We are taking up our responsibility before God to shape what he has placed in our hands."[315]

Angels could have maintained the world as God created it. But it takes God's image-bearers to develop, expand, and enrich the earth. That is culture. It includes art, science, and technology. The question of whether these creative disciplines will continue in eternity is settled if we believe the Bible when it says that both mankind and the earth will continue in physical form. If so, then culture *must* continue.

If this sounds like an overemphasis on the New Earth rather than a proper emphasis on God, consider Christ's words: "I will write on him the name of my God and the name of the city of my God, the new Jerusalem, which is coming down out of heaven from my God; and I will also write on him my new name" (Revelation 3:12). Jesus says he will put on us his name and *also* the name of the New Jerusalem—a *place* with people, buildings, and culture. God chooses to mark us not only with his person but also with his place.

God is a creator, and he created us to be creators. Hence, what we create is an extension of God's creation. He accepts, embraces, and delights in our creation—even as he did the names that Adam gave the animals. He delights in us just as we delight in our own children's creativity. In *Exploring Heaven*, Arthur Roberts reflects on how life will be after the curse of sin has been removed:

> The city of man has had intimations of a coming splendor. Civilization has brought health and safety. It has brought freedom from toil and provided creative enjoyment to millions of persons. How much more, freed from the curse of sin, will civilization flourish! Heaven will provide for urban as well as pastoral living. . . . Already the city of man is probing the galaxies. Already it has catalogued the human genome. . . . With the curse of sin gone, apocalypses past, surely human beings in heaven will become active stewards of the Lord in completing or extending the universe of things and ideas. The whole creation groans, said Paul, awaiting human redemption. Civilization is not old; it has barely begun![316]

CHAPTER 42

WILL THERE BE ARTS, ENTERTAINMENT, AND SPORTS?

M usic, dancing, storytelling, art, entertainment, drama, and books have played major roles in human culture. Will they remain a part of our lives on the New Earth? I'm convinced the answer is yes.

WILL WE SING AND MAKE MUSIC?

Have you ever sat in stunned silence after listening to music beautifully performed? If you're like me, you don't want to leave the presence of greatness. On the New Earth we never will. Our great God will be above all, beneath all, and at the center of all. We'll see his wonders not only in his natural creation but also in every human achievement.

"I will sing to the Lord all my life; I will sing praise to my God as long as I live" (Psalm 104:33). On Earth, creative, artistic, and skilled people sing and play instruments to glorify God. The apostle John speaks of trumpets and harps in the present Heaven (Revelation 8:7-13; 15:2). If we'll have musical instruments in our pre-resurrected state, how much more should we expect to find them on the New Earth?

The Bible is full of examples of people praising God with singing and musical instruments. In the Temple—a representation of God's presence—288 people sang and played a variety of instruments (1 Chronicles 25:1-8). The psalmist instructed the people to praise God with trumpets, harps, lyres, tambourines, strings, flutes, and cymbals (Psalm 150). Hezekiah said, "We will sing with stringed instruments all the days of our lives in the temple of the Lord" (Isaiah 38:20). Jesus sang with his disciples (Mark 14:26), and the apostle Paul instructed Christians to sing to the Lord (Ephesians 5:19). James says, "Those who have reason to be thankful should continually sing praises to the Lord" (James 5:13, NLT).

The 144,000 "who had been redeemed from the earth" sing a "new song" before God's throne (Revelation 14:2-3). People in Paradise sing a "song of

Moses," a song written on the cursed Earth—likely the song of Exodus 15, rejoicing in the redemption of Passover (Revelation 15:2-3). This suggests we'll sing both old and new songs, songs written on Earth and songs written in Heaven. The songs emphasize God's greatness, justice, truth, holiness, and uniqueness (Revelation 5:9-10).

Scripture songs will endure, but other music from Earth may also be preserved. Consider Handel's *Messiah*, Luther's "A Mighty Fortress Is Our God," the black spiritual "Swing Low, Sweet Chariot," and Isaac Watts's "Alas! and Did My Savior Bleed?" What about the thousands of great hymns and praise songs from hundreds of cultures? Imagine a remote tribe singing praises in a beautiful language you've never heard.

Although some lyrics will require theological corrections, others will be suitable as is, ready to be sung in God's presence. Just as new songs will express old and new insights about God, the old songs will express earthly insights that in the context of Heaven will have a greater depth of meaning.

Will secular songs survive? Not if they dishonor Christ. But what about songs that cried for perspective and deliverance? We might recall and even sing such songs to remind us of when we longed for God and when he answered. Maybe other old songs, less deep but not sin-corrupted, will be sung just for fun. Which of your favorite songs will survive the fire? If there's a specific reason why some won't, why listen to them now?

Music is transcendent—a bridge between this world and another. That's why people devote so much of themselves to it and gain such pleasure in it. We love the rich and varied rhythms and harmonies. In Heaven God will unleash our creativity, not confine it. As a musical novice, I might compose something worthy of Bach. And what kind of music do you suppose Bach will compose?

WILL WE DANCE?

Throughout the ages, people have danced to God's glory on Earth (Ecclesiastes 3:4; Jeremiah 31:12-14). After the parting of the Red Sea, Miriam and the women of Israel danced and played tambourines, singing praises to God (Exodus 15:20-21). King David leapt and danced and celebrated before the Lord (2 Samuel 6:16). The psalmist says, "You turned my wailing into dancing" (Psalm 30:11). When the Prodigal Son returned, the house was filled with music and dancing (Luke 15:25). How much more should we expect to dance on the New Earth?

God places music and dancing alongside the simple earthly joys of planting and enjoying fruit: "I will build you up again and you will be rebuilt, O Virgin

Israel. Again you will take up your tambourines and go out to dance with the joyful. Again you will plant vineyards on the hills of Samaria; the farmers will plant them and enjoy their fruit" (Jeremiah 31:4-5).

It's God, not Satan, who made us to dance. If you believe that Satan invented dancing or that dancing is inherently sinful, you give Satan too much credit and God too little. God placed within us an instinctive physical response to music. As music is a means of worship, so is dancing. True, some dancing dishonors God, just as some eating, drinking, prayer, and religious activities dishonor God. Unfortunately, much dancing has become associated with immorality and immodesty. But, of course, that kind of dancing won't exist on the New Earth.

WILL WE TELL STORIES?

God regularly reminds his people of his past acts of faithfulness: "I am the Lord your God who brought you out of Egypt, out of the land of slavery" (Exodus 20:2). History, when viewed accurately, teaches us about God and about ourselves. It's the record of our failure to rule the earth righteously, the record of God's sovereign and gracious redemption of us and our planet.

The angels will be able to recount the creation of the original universe (Job 38:1-7). But we'll have an even greater story to tell—the creation of the new universe (Revelation 21:1-4).

When we gather at meals and other times, we'll tell stories of past battles. We'll recite God's acts of grace in our lives. (Are we practicing this now?) Some of those acts of grace we didn't understand at the time; some we resented. But we'll see then with an eternal perspective.

Just as we're now captivated by a person's story of heroism or rescue from danger, we'll be enthralled by the stories we'll share in Heaven. I want to hear Jim Elliot, Ed McCully, Pete Fleming, Roger Youderian, and Nate Saint discuss their final day on the old Earth. I can't wait to hear John Newton's story and William Wilberforce's and Mary Magdalene's. Wouldn't you love to hear from the angel who strengthened Christ in Gethsemane (Luke 22:43)? Imagine sitting around campfires on the New Earth, wide-eyed at the adventures recounted. Yes, I mean telling real stories around real campfires. Why not? After all, friendship, camaraderie, laughter, stories, and cozy campfires are all good gifts from God.

Consider the wonderful ending to John's Gospel: "Jesus did many other things as well. If every one of them were written down, I suppose that even the whole world would not have room for the books that would be written" (John 21:25). The Gospels contain wonderful stories, but they record only a small fraction of what Jesus did. And that was only during the brief span of his life on the old Earth. How much more will there be to tell about his never-ending life with his people on the New Earth? We can look forward to endless adventures, encounters, profound sayings, and delightful experiences with Jesus. When he tells a story, we'll all be on the edge of our seats. On the New Earth, our resurrected eyes and ears will see and hear God's glory as never before, and our resurrected hearts will be moved to see his beauty everywhere. We will live in a land of fascinating observations, captivating insights, wondrous adventures, and spellbinding stories.

The greatest novels, plays, and movies are stories of redemption. Think of *Les Miserables* or The Chronicles of Narnia or The Lord of the Rings trilogy. They draw their shape and power from the ultimate redemption story. The greatest story ever told—and it will be told and retold from thousands of different viewpoints, emphasizing different details—will be permanently engraved in the hands and feet of Jesus. That story, above all, will be in our hearts and on our tongues.

WILL THERE BE ART, DRAMA, AND ENTERTAINMENT?

God is an inventor and the director of the unfolding drama of redemption. He created the universe, then wrote, directed, and took the leading role in history's greatest story. We who have lived our own dramas and participated in God's, we whose lives were enriched through drama, should recognize its value in the new universe. The quality of drama will likely be vastly improved. Imagine how new minds and bodies on the New Earth will stir us to worship, dialogue, action, and creativity.

Will we use the arts—including drama, painting, sculpture, music, and much more—to praise God? Will they provide enjoyment and entertainment for resurrected people? C. S. Lewis said, "When you painted on earth . . . it was because you caught glimpses of Heaven in the earthly landscape."[317] Ultimately, the new earthly landscape *will be* Heaven's landscape. But that won't eliminate art, which is a God-given gift to his image-bearers. Art will rise to ever-higher levels in the new universe.

Will we see movies in Heaven? Many current movies celebrate sin and therefore won't have a place there. But good movies, like good books, tell powerful stories. Movies on the New Earth might depict sin, as the Bible does, showing it to be wrong. But for any portrayal of sin, there would be a greater emphasis on God's redemptive work.

Professor Arthur Roberts writes of drama and the arts in Heaven: "Some people may find it difficult to envision drama or literature without plots involving villainy, deceit, violence, or adultery. . . . Such fears are understandable, because it is difficult to see beyond the horizon of our experience. These questions reflect an inadequate vision of resurrected life. . . . Do our aesthetic adventures depend upon sin for flavor? I think not. In heaven, as on earth, effective drama portrays a triumph of good over evil. I daresay the vastness and the openness of the renewed cosmos offers adventures adequate for epic tales, just at it provides raw material for the visual arts, for painting, for sculpture, for architecture."[318]

Rather than forget about our lives on the old Earth, I think we'll depict them in drama and literature with perspective and gratitude to God. Will people really write new books on the New Earth? Why not? Reading and writing aren't the result of sin; they're the result of God's making us his image-bearers. Unless we believe the present Earth will be greater than the New Earth, then surely the greatest books, dramas, and poetry are yet to be written. Authors will have new insights, information, and perspectives. I look forward to reading nonfiction books that depict the character of God and the wonders of his universe. I'm eager to read new biographies and fiction that tell powerful redemptive stories, moving our hearts to worship God.

We'll be resurrected people with minds, hands, and eyes. As we've seen, there will be books and buildings in Heaven. Put enough books in a building, and you have a library. Imagine great rows of books, hundreds of thousands, millions of them. Imagine oak desks and ladders reaching to great shelves heavy with books. (If you like the sound of that, you may spend a lot of time in such a library or serve the King by helping others find the right books.) Will you be one who writes new books? Perhaps.

I want to be part of a group that explores the vast reaches of the new cosmos. When my fellow explorers and I return home to Earth, the capital planet, and enter the gates of the capital city, we'll gather for food and drinks, and catch up on our stories. I'll listen to your stories; maybe you'll listen to mine. Perhaps I'll write about great planets of star systems far away. I'll tell how my explorations deepened my love for Jesus. And you'll play or sing for me the music of praise you composed while I was gone. I'll marvel at its beauty, and I'll see Jesus in it and in you. Maybe I'll write a book about the Omega galaxy, while you'll write one about the music of the heart. We'll exchange manuscripts, stimulate new insights, and draw each other closer to God.

WILL WE LAUGH?

"If you're not allowed to laugh in heaven, I don't want to go there." It wasn't Mark Twain who said that. It was Martin Luther.

Where did humor originate? Not with people, angels, or Satan. God created all good things, including good humor. If God didn't have a sense of humor, we as his image-bearers wouldn't. That he has a sense of humor is evident in his creation. Consider aardvarks and baboons. Take a good look at a giraffe. You have to smile, don't you?

When laughter is prompted by what's appropriate, God always takes pleasure in it. I think Christ will laugh with us, and his wit and fun-loving nature will be our greatest source of endless laughter.

There's nothing like the laughter of dear friends. The Bible often portrays us around the dinner table in God's coming Kingdom. What sound do you hear when friends gather to eat and talk? The sound of laughter. My wife, Nanci, loves football. She opens our home to family and friends for Monday night football. If you came to our house, you'd hear cheers and groans, but the dominant sound in the room, week after week, is laughter. God made us to laugh and to love to laugh. It's therapeutic. The new universe will ring with laughter.

Am I just speculating about laughter? No. I can point to Scripture passages worth memorizing. For example, Jesus says, "Blessed are you who hunger now, for you will be satisfied. Blessed are you who weep now, for you will laugh" (Luke 6:21). *You will laugh.*

When will we be satisfied? In Heaven. When will we laugh? In Heaven. Can we be certain of that? Yes. Jesus tells us precisely when this promise will be fulfilled: "Rejoice in that day and leap for joy, because great is your reward in heaven" (Luke 6:23).

Just as Jesus promises satisfaction as a reward in Heaven, he also promises laughter as a reward. Anticipating the laughter to come, Jesus says we should "leap for joy" now. Can you imagine someone leaping with joy in utter silence, without laughter? Take any group of rejoicing people, and what do you hear? Laughter. There may be hugging, backslapping, playful wrestling, singing, and storytelling. But always there is laughter. It is God's gift to humanity, a gift that will be raised to new levels after our bodily resurrection.

The reward of those who mourn now will be laughter later. Passages such as Luke 6 gave the early Christians strength to endure persecution in "an understanding of heaven as the compensation for lost earthly privileges."[319] In early Christian Greek tradition, Easter Monday was a "day of joy and laughter," called Bright Monday.[320] Only the followers of Christ can laugh in the face of persecution and death because they know that their present trouble isn't all there is. They know that someday all will be right and joyful.

By God's grace, we can laugh on Earth now, even under death's shadow. Jesus doesn't say, "If you weep, soon things on Earth will take a better turn, and then you'll laugh." Things won't always take a better turn on Earth. Sickness, loss, grief, and death will find us. Just as our reward will come in Heaven, laughter (itself one of our rewards) will come in Heaven, compensating for our present sorrow. God won't only wipe away all our tears, he'll fill our hearts with joy and our mouths with laughter.

> The happiness of heaven is not like the steady, placid state of a mountain lake where barely a ripple disturbs the tranquility of its water. Heaven is more akin to the surging, swelling waves of the Mississippi at flood stage.
>
> **SAM STORMS**

The fact that we could wonder whether there's laughter in Heaven shows how skewed our perspective is. C. S. Lewis said, "But in this world everything is upside down. That which, if it could be prolonged here, would be a truancy, is likeliest that which in a better country is the End of ends. Joy is the serious business of Heaven."[321]

Even those who are poor, diseased, or grieving may experience therapeutic laughter. People at memorial services often laugh, even in the face of death. And if we can laugh hard now—in a world full of poverty, disease, and disasters—then surely we will laugh more in Heaven.

The only laughter that won't have a place in Heaven is the sort that late-night comedians often engage in—laughter that mocks troubled people, makes light of human suffering, or glorifies immorality. Jesus makes a sobering comment in Luke 6:25. He addresses not only Heaven but also Hell, saying, "Woe to you who are well fed now, for you will go hungry. Woe to you who laugh now, for you will mourn and weep." When will those who laugh now mourn and weep? In the afterlife. All those who have not surrendered their lives to God, who have exploited and ignored the needy, who laugh at and ridicule the unfortunate, and who flout God's standards of purity will have all eternity to mourn and weep. They will never laugh again.

One of Satan's great lies is that God—and goodness—is joyless and humorless, while Satan—and evil—brings pleasure and satisfaction. In fact, it's Satan who is humorless. Sin didn't bring him joy; it forever stripped him of joy. In contrast, envision Jesus with his disciples. If you cannot picture him teasing them and laughing with them, you need to reevaluate your understanding of the Incarnation. We need a biblical theology of humor that prepares us for an eternity of celebration and spontaneous laughter.

C. S. Lewis depicts the laughter in Heaven when his characters attend the great reunion on the New Narnia: "And there was greeting and kissing and handshaking and old jokes revived (you've no idea how good an old joke sounds after you take it out again after a rest of five or six hundred years)."[322]

Who is the most intelligent, creative, witty, and joyful human being in the universe? Jesus Christ. Whose laughter will be loudest and most contagious on the New Earth? Jesus Christ's.

When we face difficulty and discouragement in this world, we must keep our eyes on the source of our joy. Remember, "Blessed are you who weep now, for *you will laugh*" (Luke 6:21, emphasis added).

WILL WE PLAY?

When we were children, we played—with each other and with dogs and cats and frogs. We enjoyed hiding, climbing trees, sledding, and throwing snowballs and baseballs. We played nonstop, never having to go earn a living. We played just because it was fun. Is God pleased by that? Yes, because he created and values a childlike spirit (Mark 10:14-15).

If it's fun for children to play in the mud and if we'll be childlike on the New Earth, is it a stretch to think we might play in the mud? If something in you says there won't be mud on the New Earth, that something is Christoplatonism. When Revelation 22 speaks of a flowing river, with the tree of life growing on both sides of it, what do you suppose will be at the edge of the river, where it meets the dirt of the bank? Mud!

A mother sent me her son's question: "Will there be toys in Heaven?" I believe the answer is yes. After all, we'll still be human, so why wouldn't we still have the human inclination and capacity to enjoy things? And we'll still have the capacity to craft and create objects, so why not toys? Are toys sinful? No. Could they have existed in an unfallen world, as the product of human creativity? Of course.

WILL THERE BE SPORTS?

Just as we can look forward to cultural endeavors such as art, drama, and music on the New Earth, we can assume that we'll also enjoy sports there. According to the principle of continuity, we should expect the New Earth to be characterized by familiar, earthly (though uncorrupted) things. Scripture compares the Christian life to athletic competitions (1 Corinthians 9:24, 27; 2 Timothy 2:5). Because sports aren't inherently sinful, we have every reason to believe that the same activities, games, skills, and interests we enjoy here will be available on the New Earth, with many new ones we haven't thought of. (Your favorite sport in Heaven may be one you've never heard of or one that hasn't yet been invented.) Sports and our enjoyment of them aren't a result of the Fall. I have no doubt that sinless people would have invented athletics, with probably more variations than we have today. Sports suit our minds and our bodies. They're an expression of our God-designed humanity.

What kinds of new sports and activities might we engage in on the New Earth? The possibilities are limitless. Perhaps we'll participate in sports that were once too risky. And just as we might have stimulating conversations with theologians and writers in Heaven, we might also have the opportunity to play our favorite sports with some of our favorite sports heroes. How would you like to, in your resurrection body, play golf with Payne Stewart or play basketball with David Robinson? How would you like to play catch with Andy Pettitte or go for a run with Jesse Owens or Eric Liddell?

Eric Liddell understood that glorifying God extends to every part of our lives. Explaining that God had called him not only to missions work in China but also to compete in the Olympics, Liddell said to his sister, "He made me fast, and when I run I feel God's pleasure. . . . To give up running would be to hold him in contempt."[323]

In a tennis tournament, I once played a five-hour singles match in which each of the three sets went to a tiebreaker. I came away exhausted, lost two toenails, and limped for two weeks. But did I regret a single minute of that five-hour match? Not one. There's joy in testing the limits of our bodies. Furthermore, those exhilarating five hours created a permanent bond with my opponent, who became my friend.

As we expend energy in our new bodies, it's possible we'll tire and need refreshment. After playing for hours, we may eat and drink to replenish our bodies, laughing about what happened on the field, enjoying each other's company, and praising God for the sheer pleasure of it all.

People have told me, "But there can't be athletics in Heaven because competition brings out the worst in people." It's true that some people's sin spills over during athletic competition. But in Heaven, there will be no worst in us to bring out. People further object: "But in sports, someone has to lose. And in Heaven no one could lose." Who says so? I've thoroughly enjoyed many tennis matches and ten-kilometer races that I've lost. Losing a game isn't evil. It's not part of the Curse. To say that "everyone would have to win in Heaven" underestimates the nature of resurrected humanity.

CAN THERE BE THRILLS WITHOUT RISK?

A sincere young man told me that no matter what I might say, Heaven *must* be boring. Why? "Because you can't appreciate good without bad, light without darkness, or safety without danger. If Heaven is safe, if there's no risk, it has to be boring."

His first mistake was assuming there's no good without bad. God said Earth was "very good" before there was sin or anything bad (Genesis 1:31). Adam and Eve enjoyed Eden's goodness before experiencing the badness of sin. This young man's next mistake was believing that a person has to *currently* see evil at work to appreciate good and to *currently* be in danger to appreciate safety.

My father lived through the Great Depression. He told me stories of sleeping outside in the cold, covered only with newspaper. Dad first told me these stories *fifty years* after the fact. He'd been able to sleep inside for half a century, but he vividly remembered the hard times. Suppose someone had said to him, "You can't appreciate having a warm fire and a warm bed unless there's the threat of sleeping out in the cold tonight." He'd say, "You think I'll ever forget those days?" His memories didn't make him miserable; they made him grateful.

After our bodily resurrection, we'll still remember the darkness and dangers of this life. We'll contrast our past experiences with the light and safety of the New Earth, and we'll be profoundly grateful.

The same young man went on to say, "I like mountain climbing and extreme sports. I enjoy working hard and sweating. But there won't be any challenges in Heaven. If there's no risk of falling and dying, it can't be really fun."

Where does Scripture say there won't be challenges or hard work in Heaven? Were there no challenges in Eden? The Bible says there will be no more evil or suffering—*not* that there won't be challenges.

Did Adam and Eve work hard? Did they sweat and get sore? Everyone who enjoys sports knows that there's a "good tired" and a "good sore." It's satisfying. It's part of knowing you've stretched yourself. Why wouldn't our resurrection bodies sweat? God didn't create sweat glands *after* the Fall, did he?

Why couldn't we tumble while climbing on the New Earth? Won't there be gravity? Adam and Eve couldn't die, but couldn't they skin their knees? God didn't originally create bodies without nerve endings, did he? Perhaps they could fall, do minor damage, and then heal quickly. We're told that on the New Earth there'll be no more death, crying, or pain (Revelation 21:4). But we're also told, "The leaves of the tree are for the healing of the nations" (Revelation 22:2). No one will suffer or die on the New Earth, but this passage suggests that there might be enough minor damage to require healing.

But even if there's absolutely *no* injury, fear of injury and death aren't essential to excitement, are they? If you knew that in thirty years there hadn't been a single fatality on a roller coaster, couldn't you still be thrilled by the ride? When our daughters were small, they experienced the thrill of rides at the fair as I held them tightly. The fun was in moving fast, spinning around, feeling the wind on their faces. In the same way, couldn't we parachute from a plane and have an exhilarating free fall even if we knew there was a zero percent chance of dying? (Some of us might consider that *more* fun, not less.)

I believe our resurrection bodies will have adrenaline and the ability to feel. On the New Earth we may experience adventures that make our current mountain climbs, surfing, skydiving, and upside-down roller coaster rides seem tame. Why do I say this? It's more than wishful thinking. It's an argument from design. We take pleasure in exhilarating experiences not because of sin but because *God wired us this way.* We weren't made to sit all day in dark rooms, watching actors pretend to live and athletes do what we can't. We were made to live vibrant lives. Some of us are physically limited, and others are emotionally unable to handle too much excitement. But those are just temporary conditions. There's a new world coming—and a new *us.*

Because God's design wasn't an accident—because he doesn't make mistakes—we can be sure that excitement and exhilaration will be more, not less, a part of our experience in Heaven than it is now.

Skydiving without a parachute? Maybe, maybe not. Scuba diving without an air tank? I hope so. Will we be able to tolerate diving to depths of hundreds of feet without special equipment? We know that our resurrection bodies will be superior. Won't it be fantastic to test their limits and to invent new technologies that extend our ability to explore and enjoy God in the mighty realms he makes?

Those who know God and believe his promise of bodily resurrection can dream great dreams.

One day we will *live* those dreams.

CHAPTER 43

WILL OUR DREAMS BE FULFILLED AND MISSED OPPORTUNITIES REGAINED?

M any people believe this life is all there is. Their philosophy? "You only go around once on this earth, so grab for whatever you can."

If you're a child of God, you do *not* just "go around once" on Earth. You don't get just one earthly life. You get another—one far better and without end. You'll inhabit the New Earth! You'll live with the God you cherish and the people you love as an undying person on an undying Earth. Those who go to Hell are the ones who go around only once on this earth.

We use the term *eternal life* without thinking what it means. *Life* is an earthly existence in which we work, rest, play, and relate to each other in ways that include the cultivation and enjoyment of culture. Yet we have redefined *eternal life* to mean an off-Earth existence stripped of the defining properties of what we know life to be. Eternal life will be enjoying forever what life on Earth is at its finest moments, what it was intended to be. Since in Heaven we'll finally experience life at its best, it would be more accurate to call our present existence the *beforelife* rather than what follows the *afterlife*.

WILL UNFULFILLED DREAMS BE REALIZED IN HEAVEN?

Without an eternal perspective, without understanding the reality that the best is yet to come, we assume that people who die young, who are handicapped, who aren't healthy, who don't get married, or who don't _____ [fill in the blank] will inevitably miss out on the best life has to offer. But the theology underlying those assumptions is fatally flawed. We're presuming that our present Earth, bodies, culture, relationships, and lives are superior to those of the New Earth.

What are we thinking?

One day Nanci read me letters we'd never before seen translated, written in 1920 by her grandmother Ana Swanson to her family in Sweden. Ana suffered severe health problems. While she was in Montana, cared for by relatives, her husband, Edwin, was in Oregon, working and caring for their seven children day and night. Ana's letters tell how Edwin wore himself out, got sick, and died. Because Ana was too weak to care for her younger children, they, including Nanci's mother, Adele, were given up for adoption. Ana's letters reflect her broken heart, her nagging guilt . . . and her faith in God.

Nanci and I were overcome with tears as we read those letters. What tragic lives. What inconsolable disappointment and pain. Ana and Edwin loved Jesus. They once had great dreams for their lives and family. But poor health, misfortune, separation, and death forever stripped them of each other, their children, and their dreams.

Or did it?

As Nanci and I talked, we considered what God might choose to give this broken family on the New Earth. Perhaps they'll go together to places they would have gone if health and finances had allowed. Certainly Ana won't be plagued by illness, fatigue, grief, anxiety, and guilt. Isn't it likely their gracious God, who delights in redemption and renewal and restoration, will give them wonderful family times they were robbed of on the old Earth? Perhaps the God of second chances won't merely comfort Ana by removing her grief for what she lost. Perhaps he will in some way actually restore what she lost. Our God won't just take away suffering; he'll compensate by giving us greater delights than if there had been no suffering. He doesn't merely wipe away tears; he replaces those tears with corresponding joys. Hence, "our present sufferings are not worth comparing with the glory that will be revealed in us" (Romans 8:18).

I believe the New Earth will offer us opportunities we wished for but never had. God's original plan was that human beings would live happy and fulfilling lives on Earth. If our current lives are our only chances at that, God's plan has been thwarted. Consider the injustice—many honest, faithful people never got to live fulfilling lives, while some dishonest and unfaithful people seemed to fare much better.

But God is not unjust, and this is *not* our only chance at life on Earth. The doctrine of the New Earth clearly demonstrates that. Do we have further biblical support for this? I believe we do, in the same passage we looked at earlier about laughter in Heaven.

Luke the physician tells of a great number of people who came to Jesus "to hear him and to be healed of their diseases. Those troubled by evil spirits were cured, and the people all tried to touch him, because power was coming from him and healing them all" (Luke 6:18-19). Consider what was going through

Christ's mind as he dealt with these image-bearers plagued by sickness, poverty, and spiritual oppression. He knew the world was full of people whom he wouldn't heal in this life. He also knew that the same people he healed would one day grow weak again and die, leaving their families wailing over their graves. What could Jesus say to such people? Luke tells us: "Blessed are you who are poor, for yours is the kingdom of God. Blessed are you who hunger now, for you will be satisfied. Blessed are you who weep now, for you will laugh. Blessed are you when men hate you, when they exclude you and insult you and reject your name as evil, because of the Son of Man. Rejoice in that day and leap for joy, because great is your reward in heaven" (Luke 6:20-23).

Jesus tells the hungry they'll be satisfied. Those whose eyes are swollen with tears will laugh. Those persecuted should leap for joy now. Why? Because of their great reward in Heaven later.

Where will Heaven be? In the parallel passage Jesus says, "Blessed are the poor in spirit, for theirs is the kingdom of heaven. Blessed are those who mourn, for they will be comforted. Blessed are

> For three things I thank God every day of my life: thanks that he has vouchsafed me knowledge of his works; deep thanks that he has set in my darkness the lamp of faith; deep, deepest thanks that I have another life to look forward to—a life joyous with light and flowers and heavenly song.
>
> **HELEN KELLER**

the meek, for they will inherit the earth" (Matthew 5:3-5). Earth is the setting for God's ultimate comfort, for his reversal of life's injustices and tragedies. We will live on what we inherit—the earth. All the blessings Jesus promised will be ours in the place we will live—the New Earth.

That's one reason I believe that on the New Earth Ana and Edwin Swanson and their children will be able to experience much of what they didn't on the old Earth. *God promises to make up for the heartbreaks of this earth.*

Are you living with the disappointment of unfulfilled dreams? In Heaven you'll find their fulfillment! Did poverty, poor health, war, or lack of time prevent you from pursuing an adventure or dream? Did you never get to finish building that boat or painting that picture or writing that book—or reading that pile of books? Good news. On the New Earth you will have a second chance to do what you dreamed of doing—and far more besides.

I tried to express this perspective in *Safely Home*, where I tell the story of Li Quan, a brilliant Chinese man whose dream was to write and teach in a university. Persecution for his faith in Christ robbed him of that opportunity. He worked instead as an assistant locksmith, in faithfulness and humility. He never saw his dreams fulfilled on Earth. But later in Heaven, as I imagined it, Christ gives Li Quan an assignment—to write and teach.[324]

We don't want to live as some other kind of creatures in some other world. What we want is to be sinless, healthy people living on Earth, but without war, conflict, disease, disappointment, and death. We want to live in the kind of world where our dreams, the deepest longings of our hearts, really do come true.

That is exactly what God's Word promises us.

Our failure to grasp this hurts us in countless ways. We become discouraged, supposing that if we're handicapped, we'll never know the joy of running in a meadow or the pleasure of swimming. Or if we aren't married—or don't have a good marriage—we'll never know the joy of marriage.

On the New Earth, in perfect bodies, we'll run through meadows and swim in lakes. We'll have the most exciting and fulfilling marriage there's ever been, a marriage so glorious and complete there will be no purpose for another. Jesus himself will be our bridegroom!

The smartest person God ever created in this world may never have learned to read because he or she had no opportunity. The most musically gifted person may never have touched a musical instrument. The greatest athlete may never have competed in a game. The sport you're best at may be a sport you've never tried, your favorite hobby one you've never thought of. Living under the Curse means we miss countless opportunities. The reversing of the Curse, and the resurrection of our bodies and our Earth, mean we'll regain lost opportunities and inherit many more besides.

WHAT JOY WILL WE FIND IN NEW OPPORTUNITIES?

Joni Eareckson Tada writes from her wheelchair, "I haven't been cheated out of being a complete person—I'm just going through a forty-year delay, and God is with me even through that. Being 'glorified'—I know the meaning of that now. It's the time, after my death here, when I'll be on my feet dancing."[325]

Peter Toon expresses the disappointment we often feel—and the hope we can have:

> The most tragic strain in human existence lies in the fact that the pleasure which we find in the things of this life, however good that pleasure may be in itself, is always taken away from us. The things for which men strive hardly ever turn out to be as satisfying as they expected, and in the rare cases in which they do, sooner or later they are snatched away. . . . For the Christian, all those partial, broken and fleeting perfections which he

glimpses in the world around him, which wither in his grasp and he snatches away from him even while they wither, are found again, perfect, complete and lasting in the absolute beauty of God.[326]

God is big enough not only to fulfill your dreams but also to expand them as you anticipate Heaven. When you experience disappointment and loss as you faithfully serve God here, remember: the loss is temporary. The gains will be eternal. Every day on the New Earth will be a new opportunity to live out the dreams that matter most.

Certainly, some of our dreams are unworthy, and they'll be forgotten. But I think there's every reason to believe most of our God-honoring dreams that were unfulfilled on the old Earth will be fulfilled on the New Earth. If a young girl dies, will she miss out on doing fun and significant things on Earth she otherwise would have done? The standard response is, "To be with Jesus is better by far." That answer is correct but incomplete. Why? Because God has a future for us not just in the present Heaven but also as resurrected people on the New Earth.

When we're young, we dream of becoming astronauts, professional athletes, or great musicians. As we get older, our dreams shrink and "realism" sinks in: We'll never be able to fulfill most of our dreams. The death of idealism robs us of our youthfulness and vitality. We become cynical and lose the sense of awe and wonder our dreams once infused us with.

But when we realize that God calls us to be like children and that he'll give us a new universe and unlimited time, then we suddenly "get it." We realize we'll have opportunity to fulfill our dreams. In fact, we'll develop bigger dreams than we ever had—and fulfill those too. Our dreams will expand, not shrink. When the Curse is reversed, shrunken dreams will be revived and enhanced. Perhaps that's part of what it means to become like a little child and why childlikeness is necessary for Heaven. Children aren't disillusioned, hopeless, and cynical. Their dreams are great and broad. They don't list a hundred reasons why their dreams can't come true. Their dreams fuel their imagination and bring them joy. And eternal life on a New Earth means opportunity to fulfill every worthy dream.

At the end of Peter Jackson's production of *The Return of the King*, Bilbo Baggins—extremely old, decrepit, and weak-minded—is invited to board an Elven ship to sail from Middle Earth to Valinor (a sort of intermediate Heaven). He smiles, and a youthful energy returns to his eyes as he says, "I think I'm quite ready for another adventure."

For the Christian, death is not the end of adventure but a doorway from a world where dreams and adventures shrink, to a world where dreams and adventures forever expand.

As we head toward our future on the New Earth, we'll lose time and countless opportunities here—but we'll regain them there. And the better we use our time and opportunity for God's glory now, the greater will be our opportunities there (Luke 16:11-12; 19:17).

HOW SHOULD THE PROMISE OF COMPENSATION AFFECT US?

The lack of an eternal perspective sets us up not only for discouragement but also for sin. We tell ourselves, *If I don't experience an intimate relationship now, I never will.* Or *If I don't have the means to go there, I never will.* Then we feel desperate, tempted to take shortcuts to get what we want (what we *think* we want). We're tempted toward fornication, dishonesty, or theft. Or we live in regret, greed, and envy. But if we understand that we'll actually live in a new heavens and New Earth, a new universe full of new opportunities, then we can forgo certain pleasures and experiences *now*, knowing we can enjoy them *later*.

As I say in my book *The Law of Rewards*, it's by giving up various pleasures, possessions, and power now that we obtain them in the next world. So, it's not only virtuous for us to make sacrifices for the needy now; it's also *wise.* Jesus said if we help the needy who can't repay us, "You will be repaid at the resurrection of the righteous" (Luke 14:14). The treasures we lay up in Heaven will be ours to enjoy forever (Matthew 6:19-20).

If we're Christians, we get two opportunities to live on Earth. This first one is but a dot. It begins, it ends. It's brief. The second opportunity will be a line, extending on forever. We all live *in* the dot. But if we're smart, we'll be living *for* the line.[327]

We're told "in keeping with his promise we are looking forward to a new heaven and a new earth, the home of righteousness" (2 Peter 3:13). Yet how many of us are truly looking forward to the New Earth? Consciously? Daily? In your idle moments, when your mind gravitates to whatever excites and interests you most, what do you think about? A new car? A movie? A business opportunity? A chance to get rich? An attractive man or woman? A fun vacation? Or the New Earth?

Likely, you look forward to many things more than the New Earth. Yet living there with Jesus should be right at the top of our lists.

Anticipating resurrected bodies and a resurrected Earth should greatly encourage all who live with illness, disability, and the liabilities of old age. Some of you are bedridden, some are in wheelchairs. Others are weary, confused, unable to do what you long to. But for those who know Jesus, *all that will change.* The Lord we long for, the world we long for, the relationships and body and mind we long for, will forever be ours.

IS THE BEST YET TO BE?

The opening lines of Robert Browning's poem "Rabbi Ben Ezra" resonate with many people:

> *Grow old along with me!*
> *The best is yet to be,*
> *The last of life, for which the first was made.*

Unfortunately, an older couple reaches a time when those blissful words ring hollow. Disease, senility, incapacitation, or accidents inevitably come, eventually bringing death. With death comes separation from one's beloved, a heartbreaking ending. Then Browning's lovely words may haunt us. Old age and the "last of life," romanticized in the poem, can be brutal, devastating, sad, and lonely.

Nanci and I both watched our dear mothers die, then watched helplessly as our fathers got old and frail, in body and mind. From a human perspective, it felt hopeless because they'd been at their physical and mental peaks many years earlier, and all they could do was slide. But a biblical perspective changed everything for us. Scripture reminded us that God had a purpose for our parents and that after a brief period of deterioration, they would go to Heaven and immediately be relieved of their hardships. Then one day God will raise them, and they'll have new minds and bodies, ready to start fresh again on a New Earth.

For believers, more accurate poetic lines would be,

> *The best is yet to be,*
> *The next of lives, for which the first was made.*

The last of our life before we die is in fact *not* the last of our life! We'll go right on living in another place. And one day, in the resurrection, we'll live again on Earth, a life so rich and joyful that this life will seem impoverished in comparison. Millions of years from now we'll still be young.

In our society many people look to cosmetic surgeries, implants, and other methods to remodel and renovate our crumbling bodies. We hold to youthfulness with a white-knuckled grip. Ultimately it's all in vain. But the gospel promises us eternal youthfulness, health, beauty, and happiness in the presence

of our God and our spiritual family. It's not ours now—but it will be, in the resurrection of the dead.

ARE WE PAST OUR PEAKS?

The following diagram illustrates the biblical view of the future for those who
know Christ. The part of the graph below that depicts life on the present Earth is
the only one that takes a dip, representing the physical and mental decline of old
age that so many experience under the Curse. But at the point of death, it's followed
by a dramatic upward movement in which the believer goes immediately to be with
Christ in the intermediate Heaven. However, even though that's a vast improve-
ment, it's not the believer's peak. We'll be resurrected, eventually living on a resurrected Earth. Our knowledge and life experiences, certainly, and probably our skills
and strength, will continue to develop. In other words, *we will never pass our peak.*

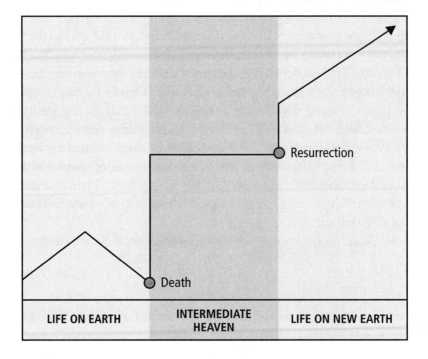

I write this book well aware that I won't be on Earth much longer. Oh, I
might last another thirty years. But it could be twenty, ten, five, or one—one
year, day, or hour. By the time this book goes to its next printing, I could be a
true expert on the present Heaven—as a resident. By the time you read it, I may
have died years ago. Our time here is short. But when we consider "here" is

under the Curse and "there" is freedom from that curse, then why would people in their right minds want to be here instead of there?

When I wrote the first edition of this book, Nanci's dear father was dying, falling further and further from his peak of a very strong mind and body. I heard Nanci say to someone on the phone, "Life is closing in on him, but he's headed in the right direction." It's paradoxical, isn't it? But true. The further we drop from our earthly peak, the closer we get to the present Heaven—where Nanci's father now resides—and ultimately to the New Earth. For the Christian, death is the doorway to the Christ who has defeated death and will swallow it up. Therefore, to be headed toward death is to be headed in the right direction. Nanci's dad now has a restored mind, and one day will have a restored body, both far exceeding what he had here in his "best days."

Understanding that our peak doesn't come in this life should radically change our view of deteriorating health, which otherwise would produce discouragement, regret, anger, envy, and resentment. Elderly people could envy and resent the young for what they can do. People handicapped from birth could envy and resent others for what they can do. But when the elderly and handicapped recognize that their experiences on the New Earth will be far better than the best anyone else is experiencing here and now, it brings anticipation, contentment, consolation, and the ability to fully rejoice in the activities of the young and healthy, without envy or regret.

People without Christ can only look back to when they were at their best, never to regain it. Memories are all they have, and even those memories fade. But elderly or bedridden Christians don't look back to the peak of their prowess. They look *forward* to it.

When we Christians sit in wheelchairs or lie in beds or feel our bodies shutting down, let's remind ourselves, "I haven't passed my peak. I haven't yet come close to it. The strongest and healthiest I've ever felt is a faint suggestion of what I'll be in my resurrected body on the New Earth."

This isn't wishful thinking. This is the explicit promise of God. It is as true as John 3:16 and anything else the Bible tells us.

When blind hymn writer Fanny Crosby wrote the lines "His glory we shall see" and "When our eyes behold the city," her thoughts were all the more significant because her eyes had never seen anything. She'd tell people not to feel sorry for her because the first face she'd ever see would be Christ's. Her sight was forever healed in 1915 when she died and left this world.

I had the privilege of spending two hours alone with Campus Crusade founder Bill Bright six months before he died. As he sat there, tubes running to his oxygen tank, he almost jumped out of his chair as we talked about Heaven and the God he loved. This wasn't a man past his peak but one leaning toward it. "The path of the righteous is like the light of dawn, that shines brighter and brighter until the full day" (Proverbs 4:18, NASB). This was true of Bill Bright. Although when I had breakfast with him that morning he was nearing his death, his eyes and smile looked supernaturally young.

Dallas Willard says in *The Divine Conspiracy*:

> I meet many faithful Christians who, in spite of their faith, are deeply disappointed in how their lives have turned out. Sometimes it is simply a matter of how they experience aging, which they take to mean they no longer have a future. But often, due to circumstances or wrongful decisions and actions by others, what they had hoped to accomplish in life they did not. They painfully puzzle over what they may have done wrong, or over whether God has really been with them.
>
> Much of the distress of these good people comes from a failure to realize that their life lies before them. That they are coming to the end of their present life, life "in the flesh," is of little significance. What is of significance is the kind of person they have become. Circumstances and other people are not in control of an individual's character or of the life that lies endlessly before us in the kingdom of God.[328]

The time may come when I won't be able to play tennis, ride bikes, drive, write books, or read them. I may suffer terribly before I die. Someday my wife or my daughters may sit beside my bed, lovingly assuring me that I've been imagining things again. I don't look forward to that. *But I do look beyond it.* I look first to being with my Jesus, second to being with loved ones, third to Christ's return and the bodily resurrection, and fourth to setting foot on my eternal home—the New Earth. It makes me want to shout and cry and laugh just thinking about it.

My waning years or weeks or days won't be the last my wife or daughters see of me. I'll be with them again, and one day we'll all have bodies and minds far better than the best we ever knew here. We'll converse with a brilliance and wit and joy and strength we've never known.

I don't look back nostalgically at wonderful moments in my life, wistfully thinking the best days are behind me. I look at them as foretastes of an eternity of better things. The buds of this life's greatest moments don't shrivel and die; they blossom into greater moments, each to be treasured, none to be lost. Everything done in dependence on God will bear fruit for eternity. This life need not be wasted. In small and often unnoticed acts of service to Christ, we can invest this life in eternity, where today's faithfulness will forever pay rich dividends.

"Thanks, Lord, that the best is yet to be." That's my prayer. God will one day clear away sin, death, and sorrow, as surely as builders clear away debris so they can begin new construction.

HOW CAN ANTICIPATING NEW OPPORTUNITIES CHANGE US?

After Columbus discovered the New World, Spain struck coins with the Latin slogan *Plus Ultra*. It meant "More Beyond." This was a horizon-expanding message to people who'd always believed the world they knew was all there was.

We'll constantly enjoy the wonders of the New Earth, but we're promised the new heavens too, including stars, planets, and cosmic wonders that will thrill us. *Plus Ultra*—there will always be more to discover about our God. In his new universe there will *always* be more beyond.

God is going to enjoy his new universe, and we'll enter into his joy. Since we'll draw from the reservoir of God's being, which never runs dry, we'll never run out of passion and joy. And God's creation will never run out of the beauty that will be the Creator's reflection.

At 2:30 a.m. on November 19, 2002, I stood on our deck, gazing up at the night sky. Above me was the Leonid meteor shower, the finest display of celestial fireworks until the year 2096. For someone who's enjoyed meteor showers since he was a kid, this was the celestial event of a lifetime.

There was only one problem. Clouds covered the Oregon sky. Of the hundreds of streaking meteors above me, I couldn't see a single one. I felt like a blind man

> In heaven 'tis the directly reverse of what 'tis on earth; for there, by length of time things become more and more youthful, that is, more vigorous, active, tender, and beautiful.
>
> **JONATHAN EDWARDS**

being told, "You're missing the most beautiful sunset of your lifetime. You'll never be able to see another like it."

Was I disappointed? Sure. After searching in vain for small cracks in the sky, I went inside and wrote these paragraphs. I'm disappointed but not disillusioned. Why? Because I did *not* miss the celestial event of my lifetime.

My lifetime is forever. My residence will be a new universe, with far more spectacular celestial wonders, and I'll have the ability to look through clouds or rise above them.

During a spectacular meteor shower a few years earlier, I'd stood on our deck watching a clear sky. Part of the fun was hearing the oohs and ahhs from neighbors looking upward. Multiply these oohs and aahs by ten thousand times ten thousand, and it'll suggest our thunderous response to what our Father will do in the new heavens as we look upward from the New Earth.

On the inside of my office door is a beautiful photograph of a menagerie of several hundred galaxies (there are more than three thousand detectable in the full picture), averaging perhaps a hundred billion stars each, never seen with any clarity until photographed by the Hubble space telescope.[329] The photograph represents the deepest-ever view of the universe, called the Hubble Deep Field. In addition to the spiral and elliptical shaped galaxies, there's a bewildering variety of other galaxy shapes and colors. This is a tiny keyhole view of the universe, covering a speck of sky one-thirtieth the diameter of the moon. When I look at this picture, I worship God.

We are *not* past our prime. The earth and planets and stars and galaxies are *not* past their prime. They're a dying phoenix that will rise again into something far greater—something that will never die.

I can't wait to see the really great meteor showers and the truly spectacular comets and star systems and galaxies of the new universe. And I can't wait to stand gazing at them alongside once-blind friends who lived their lives on Earth always hearing about what they were missing, some believing they would never see, regretting the images and events of a lifetime beyond their ability to perceive. The hidden beauties *will* be revealed to them—and us.

Plus Ultra—there is more beyond. If we know Jesus, you and I, we who will never pass our peaks will be there to behold an endless revelation of natural wonders that display God's glory . . . with nothing to block our view.

CHAPTER 44

WILL WE DESIGN CRAFTS, TECHNOLOGY, AND NEW MODES OF TRAVEL?

God will provide for us a renewed natural universe and a new city with the best of human culture from the old Earth. But where will civilization go from there? That will be up to us. For just as God called Adam and Eve, God calls us to develop a Christ-pleasing culture and to rule the world to his glory.

With advanced science and technology, we will build far greater things on the New Earth than we can on the old. Paul Marshall points out, "The Bible never condemns technology itself. . . . It does not make the modern distinction between what is 'natural' and what is 'artificial.' Both are seen merely as aspects of what is 'creational,' a category that includes both the human and the non-human world in relation to each other."[330]

DOES GOD VALUE CRAFTSMANSHIP?

The first person Scripture describes as "filled with the Spirit" wasn't a prophet or priest; he was a craftsman. "Then the Lord said to Moses, 'See, I have chosen Bezalel son of Uri, . . . and I have filled him with the Spirit of God, with skill, ability and knowledge in all kinds of crafts—to make artistic designs for work in gold, silver and bronze, to cut and set stones, to work in wood, and to engage in all kinds of craftsmanship. Moreover, I have appointed Oholiab son of Ahisamach, of the tribe of Dan, to help him. Also I have given skill to all the craftsmen to make everything I have commanded you'" (Exodus 31:1-6).

God gifted and called Bezalel to be a skilled laborer, a master craftsman, a God-glorifying artist. Bezalel and Oholiab were not only to create works of art but also to train apprentices to do so. The gifting and calling were from God: "He has filled them with skill to do all kinds of work as craftsmen, designers, embroiderers in blue, purple and scarlet yarn and fine linen, and weavers—all of them master craftsmen and designers" (Exodus 35:35).

If you don't believe craftsmanship will be an important part of the New Earth, read Exodus 25–40. God tells his people in exquisite detail how to sew clothing, what colors to use, how to construct the furniture for the Ark of the Covenant and Tabernacle, what stones to put on the high priest's breastplate, and so on.

The Master Designer goes into great detail in his instructions for building the Tabernacle: the veil and curtain, the Ark of the Covenant, the table, the lampstand, the altar of burnt offerings, the courtyard, the incense altar, the washbasin, the priests' clothing. The design, precision, and beauty of these things tell us about God, ourselves, and the culture of the New Earth. Those who imagine that spirituality is something ethereal and invisible—unrelated to our physical skills, creativity, and cultural development—fail to understand Scripture. God's instructions and his delight in the gifts he imparts to people to accomplish these tasks make clear what we should expect in Heaven: greater works of craftsmanship and construction, unhindered by sin and death.

It wasn't an accident that Jesus was born into a carpenter's family. Carpenters are makers. God is a maker. He'll never cease being a maker. God made us, his image-bearers, to be makers. We'll never cease to be makers. When we die, we won't leave behind our creativity, but only what hinders our ability to honor God through what we create.

WILL THERE BE TRADE AND BUSINESS?

I believe we will see trade and business in Heaven, although not for all the same reasons we engage in them now. There's much more to business and trade than putting food on the table or repairing the roof, though those are good reasons. Business is the result not of sin but of human interdependence, creativity, and variety. To say we will not "need" money or goods or services on the New Earth doesn't close the discussion. We may not "need" homes, food, and drink either, but we'll enjoy them nevertheless.

When the kings of the nations bring treasures into the city, is it possible that one purpose will be to give tribute to the King and another to exchange treasures with other people groups? Might they then bring back to their own people the cultural splendors, including discoveries and inventions, of other nations? Even now, honest trade brings benefit and pleasure to both parties.

People trade and engage in business for reasons besides survival. It's possible that business as we know it could be replaced by a social structure centered on creating, giving, and receiving. An artist might create a beautiful work and simply give it away for someone's delight, just as Christ freely gives of himself. Jesus said it's "more blessed to give than to receive" (Acts 20:35), so the joy of giving someone else a cultural treasure would exceed even the joy of receiving one.

Whether you work in a bookstore, bakery, or school, don't you experience joy in using your knowledge, skills, services, and products to help and please others? Sure, it's good and often necessary to earn money too, but that isn't the ultimate joy. If we dismiss the likelihood of business and commerce on the New Earth, we send the wrong message: that business and commerce are part of the Curse, inherently unspiritual or unimportant to God. On the contrary, God's Word tells us, "Whatever you do, work at it with all your heart, as working for the Lord, not for men, since you know that you will receive an inheritance from the Lord as a reward. It is the Lord Christ you are serving" (Colossians 3:23-24). We work for him on the present Earth, and we will work for him on the New Earth.

WILL THERE BE TECHNOLOGY AND MACHINERY?

Technology is a God-given aspect of human capability that enables us to fulfill his command to exercise dominion. As we've seen, we will find harps, trumpets, and other man-made objects in the present Heaven. What should we expect to find on the New Earth? Tables, chairs, cabinets, wagons, machinery, transportation, sports equipment, and much more. It's a narrow view of both God and humans to imagine that God can be pleased and glorified with a trumpet but not a desk, computer, or baseball bat. Will there be new inventions? Refinements of old inventions? Why not? We'll live in resurrected bodies on a resurrected Earth. The God who gave people creativity surely won't take it back, will he? The gifts and calling of God are irrevocable (Romans 11:29).

When God gave Eden to Adam and Eve, he expected them to develop it. He'll give us the New Earth and expect the same of us. But this time we'll succeed! This time no human accomplishment, no cultural masterpiece, no technological achievement will be marred by sin and death. All will fully serve God's purposes and bring him glory.

On this earth, we seek comfort and invent ways to get it. On the New Earth, comfort may seek us. It may be built into the environment so that our efforts can be spent on other concerns. Of course, we'll have the technological knowledge and skills to control our environment, so if we can make ourselves more comfortable, we will.

Something in the human constitution loves to create, tweak, experiment, and play with machinery. This isn't a modern development; it was true of ancient people as well. It's inherent in exercising dominion over creation.

If mankind had never sinned, would we have invented the wheel and created machinery? Certainly. On the New Earth, shouldn't we expect machinery made for the good of mankind and the glory of God? On the New Earth people might invent machinery that could take us to the far ends of the New Milky Way, to other galaxies and beyond. Why not? Is this notion more unthinkable than it once was to imagine sailing a ship across an ocean or flying a plane across the world or landing a spacecraft on the moon? Because people in this fallen world have extended their dominion beyond our current Earth, might we not expect people on the New Earth to extend their Christ-exalting reach into the new universe?

WHAT WILL TRAVEL BE LIKE?

Many people have asked how our resurrected bodies will travel on the New Earth, wondering whether we will be able to materialize, as Christ apparently was able to do in his resurrected body (John 20:24-26). Will our bodies become servants to our righteous wills, carrying out their directions? Might we be able to go somewhere simply by thinking or willing it? Possibly. It's also possible that although our bodies will be like Christ's, his ability to dematerialize and materialize and to rise in his ascension could be unique to his deity. We can't be certain on this point.

Philip, after he met with the Ethiopian, was "snatched away" by God's Spirit and found himself at Azotus (Acts 8:25-40). Philip didn't snatch himself away, but perhaps he experienced a foretaste of what a Spirit-empowered person with a resurrection body might do. Since we will rule with Christ over a vast New Earth, and possibly over faraway places in the new heavens, it seems likely that we might be able to be instantly transported great distances.

Perhaps we might be able to be directly in the presence of Christ, worshiping him before his throne in the New Jerusalem, then go off to our duties far away, only to come back to him regularly. Perhaps we will be able to travel to the far ends of the New Earth, or even to the remote parts of the new universe, in the blink of an eye.

We do know, however, that the New Jerusalem will have streets and gates, suggesting conventional modes of travel. If citizens only walked, perhaps paths would be enough. But streets may suggest the use of wagons and horse-drawn carts, or something more advanced. Will we ride bicycles and drive motorized vehicles? Will we travel to other places outside the New Jerusalem in airplanes? We don't know. But we should use the "why not?" test. Is there anything sinful about wheels and motors? Unless you're a Christoplatonist, you realize the answer is no. Therefore, there's no reason to assume we won't enjoy high-tech modes of travel on the New Earth.

Remember, the New Earth isn't a return to Eden in the sense of abandoning culture, including inventions, transportation, and technology. It's a resurrected Earth with resurrected people, who have better brains and will be capable of better inventions. How long would it take brilliant people working in full cooperation to make startling technological breakthroughs? Imagine how quickly the space shuttle could become a relic.

WILL WE TRAVEL AND EXPLORE IN SPACE?

I've explained my understanding of Scripture that God will resurrect nations and cultures and that we'll be able to visit them on the New Earth. This may seem radical, but it's just the beginning. I've also mentioned my belief that we will explore the far reaches of the new universe. Let me further develop that idea.

God promises to make not only a New Earth but also "new heavens" (Isaiah 65:17; 66:22; 2 Peter 3:13). The Greek and Hebrew words translated "heavens" include the stars and planets and what we call outer space. Since God will resurrect the old Earth and the old Jerusalem, transforming both into the new, shouldn't we understand "new heavens" as an expression of his intention to resurrect galaxies, nebulae, stars, planets, and moons in a form as close to their original form as the earth will be to its original form and we will be to ours?

> There will be new planets to develop, new principles to discover, new joys to experience. Every moment of eternity will be an adventure of discovery.
>
> **RAY STEDMAN**

The stars of the heavens declare God's glory (Psalm 19:1), yet how vast and distant they are. God made countless billions of galaxies containing perhaps trillions of nebulae, planets, and moons. Not many in human history have seen more than a few thousand stars, and then only as dots in the sky. If the heavens declare God's glory now, and if we will spend eternity proclaiming God's glory, don't you think exploring the new heavens, and exercising dominion over them, will likely be part of God's plan?

As a twelve-year-old, I first viewed through a telescope the great galaxy of Andromeda, consisting of hundreds of billions of stars and untold numbers of planets, nearly three million light years from Earth. I was mesmerized. I also wept, not knowing why. I was overwhelmed by greatness on a cosmic scale and felt terribly small and alone. Years later I first heard the gospel. After I became a Christian, I found that gazing through the telescope became an act of delighted worship.

From the night I first saw Andromeda's galaxy, I've wanted to go there. I now think it's likely I will.

Many of us have taken pleasure traveling on this earth. What will it be like to travel both the New Earth and the new universe? People didn't venture across oceans and to outer space because of sin. They did so because God made us with the yearning to explore and the creativity to make that yearning a reality. Have you ever read about people who have taken amazing journeys and wished you had the time, money, courage, or health to do the same? In the new universe, none of those restraints will hold us back.

It's hard for me to believe God made countless cosmic wonders intending that no human eye would ever behold them and that no human should ever set foot on them. The biblical accounts link mankind so closely with the physical universe and link God's celestial heavens so closely with the manifestation of his glory that I believe he intends us to explore the new universe. The universe will be our backyard, a playground and university always beckoning us to come explore the wealth of our Lord—as one song puts it, the God of wonders beyond our galaxy.

WILL WE FIND NEW BEINGS ON OTHER WORLDS?

When we travel in the new universe, will we find new beings on other worlds? No Scripture passage proves that God will or will not create new races of intelligent beings, either on Earth or on other planets spread across the new universe. It's not speculative to say there will be a new celestial universe of stars and planets. Scripture is clear on this point; that's what "new heavens" means. Whether God might inhabit them with new creatures is not provable but certainly possible. God is a creator. He'll never stop being what he is. We should expect new and wondrous creations that declare his glory. God hasn't exhausted his creative resources. He never will.

Some people will say, "To imagine that God would populate worlds with new beings is just science fiction." We may have it backward. Science fiction is the result of mankind's God-given sense of adventure, wonder, creativity, and imagination. It emerges from being made in God's image. Like everything else undertaken by sinful humans, science fiction is often riddled with false philosophies and assumptions that glorify mankind and ignore God. But this shouldn't cause us to dismiss its glimpses of what an infinitely creative God might fashion across the broad expanse of the new heavens and the New Earth. Is God's imagination less than that of his image-bearers? Or is the height of human imagination at its best a reflection of the infinite creativity of the divine mind?

Those who consider extraterrestrial creation a foolish notion shouldn't dismiss too quickly the longing and intuitive sense that many people have about intelligent creatures different from ourselves. The worlds of *Star Trek, Star Wars,* and *E.T.* are fictional, as are the worlds portrayed throughout the long history of mythology, fantasy, and science fiction. But if people, created in God's image and endowed with divine creativity, have invented these fictional alien races and have so passionately contemplated them, should it surprise us if God creates the substance of which science fiction, fantasy, and mythology are but shadows?

When we get excited reading Tolkien's The Lord of the Rings trilogy or Lewis's The Chronicles of Narnia, it's not our sinfulness that arouses that excitement. It's our God-given hunger for adventure, for new realms and new beings, for new beauties and new knowledge. God has given us a longing for new worlds.

Give painters a room full of canvases, and they will paint. Why? Because they are painters. It's their nature. When the Creator fashions the new heavens— as we're told he will—whatever he does will be in keeping with his nature. Considering that his higher glory and praise come not from inanimate objects such as stars and planets but from intelligent beings such as people and angels, it's no great stretch to suppose he might create other intelligent beings.

Would I expect the Creator, from whom human artists derive their creativity, to do less to demonstrate his ingenuity in the coming ages than he has in this first age? No. I anticipate an eternity of delight in watching and discovering what he creates to reveal more of himself to us.

WILL WE TRAVEL IN TIME?

If we will travel to other galaxies, will we also be able to travel in time? Even though I believe we'll live in time, God is certainly capable of bending time and opening doors in time's fabric for us. Perhaps we'll be able to travel back and stand alongside angels in the invisible realm, seeing events as they happened on Earth. Maybe we'll learn the lessons of God's providence through direct observation. Can you imagine being there as Jesus preached the Sermon on the Mount? Perhaps you will be.

Want to see the crossing of the Red Sea? Want to be there when Daniel's three friends emerge from the fiery furnace? It would be simple for God to open the door to the past.

Because God is not limited by time, he may choose to show us past events as if they were presently happening. We may be able to study history from a front-row seat. Perhaps we'll have opportunity to see the lives of our spiritual and physical ancestors lived out on Earth.

Usually we're not able to see God's immediate responses to our prayers, but in Heaven God may permit us to see what happened in the spiritual realm as a result of his answers to our prayers. In the Old Testament an angel comes to the prophet Daniel and tells him what happened as the result of his prayers: "As soon as you began to pray, an answer was given, which I have come to tell you" (Daniel 9:23).

Will God show us in Heaven what almost happened to us on Earth? Will he take us back to see what would have happened if we'd made other choices? Perhaps. Will the father whose son had cerebral palsy see what would have happened if he'd followed his temptation to desert his family? Would this not fill his heart with gratitude to God for his sovereign grace?

Will I see how missing the exit on the freeway last night saved me from a crash? Will I learn how getting delayed in the grocery store last week saved my wife from a fatal accident? How many times have we whined and groaned about the very circumstances God used to save us? How many times have we prayed that God would make us Christlike, then begged him to take from us the very things he sent to make us Christlike? How many times has God heard our cries when we imagined he didn't? How many times has he said no to our prayers when saying yes would have harmed us and robbed us of good?

Perhaps we'll see the ripple effects of our small acts of faithfulness and obedience. Like Scrooge in *A Christmas Carol* and George Bailey in *It's a Wonderful Life,* perhaps we'll see how we affected others, and how living our lives differently might have influenced them. (May God give us the grace to see this *now* while we can still revise and edit our lives.)

If we believe in God's sovereignty, we must believe God would be glorified through our better understanding of human history. We'll no longer have to cling by faith to "God causes all things to work together for good to those who love God" (Romans 8:28, NASB). We will see history as definitive documentation of that reality.

Does this discussion seem to you a bit bizarre? Consider it further. Surely you agree that God is capable of sending resurrected people back in time or of pulling back the curtain of time and allowing us to see the past. If he couldn't do this, he wouldn't be God. So the question is whether he might have good reasons to do so. One reason might be to show us his providence, grace, and goodness in our lives and the lives of others. Wouldn't that bring God glory? Wouldn't it cause us to praise and exalt him for his sovereign grace? This is surely a high and God-glorifying response. Couldn't this fit his revealed purpose "that in the coming ages he might show the incomparable riches of his grace" (Ephesians 2:7)?

C. S. Lewis wrote, "Don't run away with the idea that when I speak of the resurrection of the body I mean merely that the blessed dead will have excellent memories of their sensuous experiences on earth. I mean it the other way round; that memory as we know it is a dim foretaste, a mirage even, of a power which the soul, or rather Christ in the soul . . . will exercise hereafter. It need no longer . . . be private to the soul in which it occurs. I can now communicate to you the fields of my boyhood—they are building-estates today—only imperfectly, by words. Perhaps the day is coming when I can take you for a walk through them."[331]

WILL GOD DO MORE THAN WE IMAGINE?

In much of what I've just said, I'm speculating, of course. But because the Bible gives a clear picture of resurrection and of earthly civilization in the eternal state, I'm walking through a door of imagination that Scripture itself opens. If all this seems more than you can imagine, I'd encourage you not to reject it simply on that basis. Our God, after all, is called the one "who is able to do immeasurably more than all we ask or imagine" (Ephesians 3:20). The very next verse gives praise to this God who acts immeasurably beyond our imaginations: "To him be glory in the church and in Christ Jesus throughout all generations, for ever and ever!"

In my novel *Edge of Eternity*, Nick Seagrave beholds the Woodsman (Jesus) and the end of the world—then realizes it's really a beginning:

> I saw a dying cosmos hold out its weak right arm, longing for a transfusion, a cure for its cancerous chasm. I saw the Woodsman, holding what appeared to be a tiny lump of coal, the same size as the blue-green marble he'd held before. The Woodsman squeezed his hand and the world around me darkened. Just as I felt I would scream from unbearable pressure, the crushed world emerged from his grip a diamond. I gasped air in relief.
>
> I saw a new world, once more a life-filled blue-green, the old black coal delivered from its curse and pain and shame, wondrously remade.
>
> It looked so easy for the Woodsman to shape all this with his hands. But then I saw his scars . . . and remembered it was not.[332]

PART III

LIVING IN LIGHT OF HEAVEN

CHAPTER 45

REORIENTING OURSELVES TO HEAVEN AS OUR HOME

I must keep alive in myself the desire for my true country, which I shall not find till after death; I must never let it get snowed under or turned aside; I must make it the main object of life to press on to that other country and to help others to do the same.

C. S. Lewis

When I see ocean fish in an aquarium, I enjoy watching them, but I feel as if something's wrong. They don't belong there. It's not their home. The fish weren't made for that little glass box; they were made for a great ocean.

I suppose the fish don't know any better, but I wonder if their instincts tell them that their true home is elsewhere. I know *our* instincts tell us that this fallen world isn't our home—we were made for someplace better. As we've seen, the Bible repeatedly confirms this instinct.

Theologian Donald Bloesch suggests, "Our greatest affliction is not anxiety, or even guilt, but rather homesickness—a nostalgia or ineradicable yearning to be at home with God."[333]

Christian slaves sang of "goin' home to live with God" and a chariot "comin' fo' to carry me home." Christians have always thought of going to Heaven as going home. When Jesus said he was going to prepare a place for us, he spoke of building us a home. To anticipate Heaven, then, we need to understand the meaning of *home*. Early in the book we touched on it. Now it's time to take a closer look as we move toward our conclusion in the next chapter.

WHAT HOME IS LIKE

Have you ever been on a trip that became miserable, where everybody got sick or everything went wrong? What did you want more than anything? *To go home.* In your imagination you could feel your comfy bed, taste a home-cooked meal, and picture the company of family and friends laughing together in front of the fire, telling stories about what went wrong on your trip.

Home is also about comfort. It's a place where we can put on jeans and a sweatshirt and throw ourselves on the couch to relax. It's a place we *want* to be. As much as I've enjoyed traveling to many different countries, I always *love* to come home. That craving for home is sweet and deep. Home is our reference point, what we always come back to. No matter how much we enjoy our adventures away, we anticipate coming home. Knowing we can come home is what keeps us going—and that's what Heaven should do for us. It should keep us going because it's our eternal home, the welcome refuge that awaits us and calls our name.

Home is where friends come to visit. It's where we putter, plant gardens, read our favorite books, and listen to music we enjoy. Home is where I inhale the wonderful aroma of strong, rich coffee every morning, and where Nanci fixes great meals and her amazing apple pie.

I realize it sounds as if I'm romanticizing home. I know that many people have had terrible experiences at home. But our true home in Heaven will have all the good things about our earthly homes, multiplied many times, but *none of the bad.*

The world says, "You can never go home again." It means that while we were gone, home changed and so did we. Our old house may have been destroyed or sold, been renovated or become run-down. In contrast, when this life is over—and particularly when we arrive on the New Earth—God's children will truly be able to come home for the very first time. Because our home in Heaven will never burn, flood, or be blown away, we'll never have to wonder whether home will still be there when we return. The new heavens and New Earth will never disappear. They'll give a wonderful permanence to the word *home.*

When it comes to our eternal home, we often fail to think biblically in two ways. First, we imagine we won't be fully human and our ultimate home won't be physical and earthly. Second, we imagine that this world as it now is, under the Curse, is our ultimate home. C. S. Lewis wrote, "Our Father refreshes us on the journey with some pleasant inns, but will not encourage us to mistake them for home."[334]

> When I get to heaven, I shall see three wonders there. The first wonder will be to see many there whom I did not expect to see; the second wonder will be to miss many people who I did expect to see; the third and greatest of all will be to find myself there.
>
> **JOHN NEWTON**

If Heaven is truly our home, we should expect it to have the qualities we associate with home. *Home* as a term for Heaven isn't simply a metaphor. It describes an actual, physical place—a place promised and built by our bridegroom; a place we'll share with loved ones; a place of fond familiarity and comfort and refuge; a place of marvelous smells and tastes, fine food, and great conversation; a place of contemplation and interaction and expressing the gifts and passions that God has given us. It'll be a place of unprecedented freedom and adventure.

The unbiblical stereotypes of Heaven as a vague, incorporeal existence hurt us far more than we realize. Among other things, they diminish our anticipation of Heaven and keep us from believing it is truly our home. Bible scholar Graham Scroggie was right: "Future existence is not a purely spiritual existence; it demands a life in a body, and in a material universe."[335] Though many of us affirm a belief in the resurrection of the dead, we don't know what that really means. Our doctrine dresses up men and women in bodies, then gives them no place to go. Instead of the New Earth as our eternal home, we offer an intangible and utterly unfamiliar Heaven that's the *opposite* of home. No wonder there is such ambivalence and uneasiness about Heaven in our churches.

GOING TO THE PARTY

Imagine someone takes you to a party. You see a few friends there, enjoy a couple of good conversations, a little laughter, and some decent appetizers. The party's all right, but you keep hoping it will get better. Give it another hour, and maybe it will. Suddenly, your friend says, "I need to take you home."

Now?

You're disappointed—nobody wants to leave a party early—but you leave, and your friend drops you off at your house. As you approach the door, you're feeling all alone and sorry for yourself. As you open the door and reach for the light switch, you sense someone's there. Your heart's in your throat. You flip on the light.

"Surprise!" Your house is full of smiling people, familiar faces.

It's a party—for *you*. You smell your favorites—barbecued ribs and pecan pie right out of the oven. The tables are full. It's a feast. You recognize the guests, people you haven't seen for a long time. Then, one by one, the people you most enjoyed at the other party show up at your house, grinning. This turns out to be the *real* party. You realize that if you'd stayed longer at the other party, as you'd wanted, you wouldn't be *at* the real party—you'd be *away* from it.

Christians faced with terminal illness or imminent death often feel they're leaving the party before it's over. They have to go home early. They're disappointed, thinking of all they'll miss when they leave. But the truth is, the real party is underway at home—precisely where they're going. They're not the ones missing the party; those of us left behind are. (Fortunately, if we know Jesus, we'll get there eventually.)

One by one, occasionally a few of us at a time, we'll disappear from this world. Those we leave behind will grieve that their loved ones have left home. In reality, however, their believing loved ones aren't *leaving* home, they're *going* home. They'll be home before us. We'll be arriving at the party a little later.

Remember, Jesus said, "Blessed are you who weep now, for you will laugh" (Luke 6:21). He said, "There is rejoicing in the presence of the angels of God over one sinner who repents" (Luke 15:10). Laughter and rejoicing—a party awaits us. Don't you want to join it? Yet even that party, in the present Heaven, is a preliminary celebration. It's like the welcome at the airport for a woman who's come home for her wedding. Sure, she's home now, and it's wonderful, but what she's really looking forward to is the wedding, and the wedding feast, which will be followed by moving into her new home with her beloved bridegroom.

To be in resurrected bodies on a resurrected Earth in resurrected friendships, enjoying a resurrected culture with the resurrected Jesus—now *that* will be the ultimate party! Everybody will be who God made them to be—and none of us will ever suffer or die again. As a Christian, the day I die will be the best day I've ever lived. But it won't be the best day I ever *will* live. Resurrection day will be far better. And the first day on the New Earth—that will be one *big* step for mankind, one giant leap for God's glory.

LONGING FOR RESURRECTION

I've never been to Heaven, yet I miss it. Eden's in my blood. The best things of life are souvenirs from Eden, appetizers of the New Earth. There's just enough of them to keep us going, but never enough to make us satisfied with the world as it is, or ourselves as we are. We live between Eden and the New Earth, pulled toward what we once were and what we yet will be.

As Christians, we're linked to Heaven in ways too deep to comprehend. Somehow, according to Ephesians 2:6, we're already seated with Christ in Heaven. So we can't be satisfied with less.

Desire is a signpost pointing to Heaven. Every longing for better health is a longing for the New Earth. Every longing for romance is a longing for the ultimate romance with Christ. Every desire for intimacy is a desire for Christ. Every thirst for beauty is a thirst for Christ. Every taste of joy is but a foretaste of a greater and more vibrant joy than can be found on Earth as it is now. A. W. Tozer said, "In nature, everything moves in the direction of its hungers. In the spiritual world it is not otherwise. We gravitate toward our inward longing, provided of course that those longings are strong enough to move us."[336]

That's why we need to spend our lives cultivating our love for Heaven. That's why we need to meditate on what Scripture says about Heaven, read books on it, have Bible studies, teach classes, and preach sermons on it. We need to talk to our children about Heaven. When we're camping, hiking, or driving, when we're at a museum, a sporting event, or a theme park, we need to talk about what we see around us as signposts to the New Earth.

When we think of Heaven as unearthly, our present lives seem unspiritual, like they don't matter. When we grasp the reality of the New Earth, our present, earthly lives suddenly matter. Conversations with loved ones matter. The taste of food matters. Work, leisure, creativity, and intellectual stimulation matter. Rivers and trees and flowers matter. Laughter matters. Service matters. Why? *Because they are eternal.*

Life on Earth matters not because it's the only life we have, but precisely because it isn't—it's the beginning of a life that will continue without end. It's the precursor of life on the New Earth. Eternal life doesn't begin when we die—it has already begun. Life is not, as Macbeth supposed, "a tale told by an idiot, full of sound and fury, signifying nothing." Informed by the doctrines of creation, redemption, resurrection, and the New Earth, our present lives take on greater importance, infusing us with purpose. Understanding Heaven doesn't just tell us *what* to do, but *why*. What God tells us about our future lives enables us to interpret our past and serve him in our present.

Consider the old proverb, "Eat, drink, and be merry, for tomorrow we die." It assumes that the only earthly pleasures we'll ever enjoy must be obtained now. As Christians, we should indeed eat, drink, and be merry—and also sacrifice, suffer, and die—all to the glory of God. In doing so, we're preparing for an eternal life in which we will eat, drink, and be merry, but never again die. This present life, then, is not our last chance to eat, drink, and be merry—rather, it is the last time our eating, drinking, and merrymaking can be corrupted by sin, death, and the Curse.

We need to stop acting as if Heaven were a myth, an impossible dream, a relentlessly dull meeting, or an unimportant distraction from real life. We need to see Heaven for what it is: the realm we're made for. If we do, we'll embrace it with contagious joy, excitement, and anticipation.

HEAVEN: OUR SOURCE OF OPTIMISM

Secular optimists are wishful thinkers. Discovering the present payoffs of optimism, they conduct seminars and write books on thinking positively. Sometimes they capitalize on optimism by becoming rich and famous. But then what happens? They eventually get old or sick, and when they die they go to Hell forever. Their optimism is an illusion, for it fails to take eternity into account.

The only proper foundation for optimism is the redemptive work of Jesus Christ. Any other foundation is sand, not rock. It will not bear the weight of our eternity.

However, if we build our lives on the redemptive work of Christ, we should all be optimists. Why? Because even our most painful experience in life is but a temporary setback. Our pain and suffering may or may not be relieved in this life, but they will *certainly* be relieved in the next. That is Christ's promise—no more death or pain; he will wipe away all our tears. He took our sufferings on himself so that one day he might remove all suffering from us. That is the biblical foundation for our optimism. No Christian should be a pessimist. We should be realists—focused on the *reality* that we serve a sovereign and gracious God. Because of the *reality* of Christ's atoning sacrifice and his promises, biblical realism is *optimism*.

Knowing that our suffering will be relieved doesn't make it easy, but it does make it bearable. It allows joy in the midst of suffering. Jesus said, "Blessed are you when men hate you, when they exclude you and insult you. . . . Rejoice in that day and leap for joy, because great is your reward in heaven" (Luke 6:22-23). Paul said, "I rejoice in my sufferings" (Colossians 1:24, NASB), and James said, "Consider it pure joy, my brothers, whenever you face trials of many kinds" (James 1:2). The apostles didn't enjoy suffering, but they rejoiced in the midst of it, because they trusted God's sovereign plan and they looked forward to Christ's return, their bodily resurrection, and the redemption of all creation.

Christ said to his disciples, who would suffer much, "Rejoice that your names are written in heaven" (Luke 10:20). Our optimism is not that of the "health and wealth" gospel, which claims that God will spare us of suffering here and now. Peter said, "Rejoice that you participate in the sufferings of Christ, so that you may be overjoyed when his glory is revealed" (1 Peter 4:13). Christ's future glory, in which we will participate, is the reason for our present rejoicing while suffering.

Anticipating Heaven doesn't eliminate pain, but it lessens it and puts it in perspective. Meditating on Heaven is a great pain reliever. It reminds us that suffering and death are temporary conditions. Our existence will not end in suffering and death—they are but a gateway to our eternal life of unending joy. The biblical doctrine of Heaven is about the future, but it has tremendous benefits here and now. If we grasp it, it will shift our center of gravity and radically change our perspective on life. This is what the Bible calls "hope," a word used six times in Romans 8:20-25, the passage in which Paul says that all creation longs for our resurrection and the world's coming redemption.

Don't place your hope in favorable circumstances, which cannot and will not last. Place your hope in Christ and his promises. He will return, and we will be resurrected to life on the New Earth, where we will behold God's face and joyfully serve him forever.

REEPICHEEP'S QUEST

In C. S. Lewis's *Voyage of the "Dawn Treader,"* a ship sails east in search of lost countrymen and new adventures. But the heart of one passenger, Reepicheep the valiant mouse, is steadfastly set on a greater adventure. He has one destination in mind: Aslan's country.

From his youth, Reepicheep was taught in a poem that one day he would journey to the far east and find what he'd always longed for:

> *Where sky and water meet,*
> *Where the waves grow sweet,*
> *Doubt not, Reepicheep,*
> *To find all you seek,*
> *There is the utter East.*

After reciting the poem to his shipmates, Reepicheep says, "I do not know what it means. But the spell of it has been on me all my life."[337]

Late in the journey, when they have sailed farther than anyone on record, Reepicheep is thrown into the sea. To his surprise, the water tastes sweet. His excitement is unrestrainable. He's so close to Aslan's country, he can literally taste it.

Earlier in the voyage, Reepicheep had expressed his utter abandonment to the cause of seeking Aslan's country: "While I can, I sail east in the *Dawn Treader*. When she fails me, I paddle east in my coracle. When she sinks, I shall swim east with my four paws. And when I can swim no longer, if I have not reached Aslan's country, or shot over the edge of the world in some vast cataract, I shall sink with my nose to the sunrise . . ."[338]

We can identify with Reepicheep's glorious quest, because the spell of Heaven has been on us all our lives, as well, even if we have sometimes confused it with lesser desires. At the end of *The Voyage of the "Dawn Treader,"* Reepicheep's traveling companions watch him disappear over the horizon. Does he make it to Aslan's country? In the final book of the Narnia series, we discover the answer, which confirms what we already knew in our hearts.

THROUGH THE DOORWAY

When five-year-old Emily Kimball was hospitalized and heard she was going to die, she started to cry. Even though she loved Jesus and wanted to be with him, she didn't want to leave her family behind. Then her mother had an inspired idea. She asked Emily to step through a doorway into another room, and she closed the door behind her. One at a time, the entire family started coming through the door to join her. Her mother explained that this was how it would be. Emily would go ahead to Heaven and then the rest of the family would follow. Emily understood. She would be the first to go through death's door. Eventually, the rest of the family would follow, probably one by one, joining her on the other side.

The analogy would have been even more complete if the room that Emily entered had had someone representing Jesus to greet her—along with departed loved ones and Bible characters and angels. Also, it would've helped if the room she walked into was breathtakingly beautiful, and contained pictures of a New Earth, vast and unexplored, where Emily and her family and friends would one day go to live with Jesus forever.

Every person reading this book is dying. Perhaps you have reason to believe that death will come very soon. You may be troubled, feeling uncertain, or unready to leave. Make sure of your relationship with Jesus Christ. Be certain that you're trusting him alone to save you—not anyone or anything else, and certainly not any good works you've done. And then allow yourself to get excited about what's on the other side of death's door.

I've often read at memorial services this depiction of a believer's death:

I'm standing on the seashore. A ship at my side spreads her white sails to the morning breeze and starts for the blue ocean. She's an object of beauty and strength and I stand and watch her until, at length, she hangs like a speck of white cloud just where the sea and the sky come down to mingle with each other. And then I hear someone at my side saying, "There, she's gone."

Gone where? Gone from my sight, that is all. She is just as large in mast and hull and spar as she was when she left my side. And just as able to bear her load of living freight to the place of destination. Her diminished size is in *me*, not in her.

And just at the moment when someone at my side says, "There, she's gone," there are other eyes watching her coming, and there are other voices ready to take up the glad shout, "Here she comes!"

And that is dying.[339]

The place of our arrival will be a beautiful, though temporary, place where we'll await the culmination of history: the return of the risen Jesus, who will resurrect us. When his millennial reign is accomplished (whether that's a nonliteral present reign or a literal thousand-year future reign), we'll join him in ruling the New Earth, free of sin and the Curse.

Five months before he died, C. S. Lewis wrote to a woman who feared that her own death was imminent. Lewis said, "Can you not see death as a friend and deliverer? . . . What is there to be afraid of? . . . Your sins are confessed. . . . Has this world been so kind to you that you should leave with regret? There are better things ahead than any we leave behind. . . . Our Lord says to you, 'Peace, child, peace. Relax. Let go. I will catch you. Do you trust me so little?' . . . Of course, this may not be the end. Then make it a good rehearsal."

Lewis signed the letter, "Yours (and like you, a tired traveler, near the journey's end)."[340]

We see life differently when we realize that death isn't a wall but a turnstile, a small obstacle that marks a great beginning. Calvin Miller put it beautifully:

> *I once scorned ev'ry fearful thought of death,*
> *When it was but the end of pulse and breath,*
> *But now my eyes have seen that past the pain*
> *There is a world that's waiting to be claimed.*
> *Earthmaker, Holy, let me now depart,*
> *For living's such a temporary art.*
> *And dying is but getting dressed for God,*
> *Our graves are merely doorways cut in sod.*[341]

CHAPTER 46

ANTICIPATING THE GREAT ADVENTURE

Can you hear the sighing in the wind? Can you feel the heavy silence in the
mountains? Can you sense the restless longing in the sea? Can you see it in the
woeful eyes of an animal? Something's coming . . . something better.
                                                        Joni Eareckson Tada

When H. S. Laird's father, a Christ-loving man, lay dying, his son sat at his bedside and asked, "Dad, how do you feel?"

His father replied: "Son, I feel like a little boy on Christmas Eve."[342]

Christmas is coming. We live our lives between the first Christmas and the second. We walk on disputed turf, between Eden and the New Earth, not that far from either. The dispute will soon be settled. Christ will forever reign over the universe. And we will reign with him.

In this last chapter, I want to draw us toward Heaven-influenced living, and further prepare us for the adventure that awaits us on death's other side.

CHAPTER ONE OF THE GREAT STORY

In the final book of the Narnia series, *The Last Battle*, C. S. Lewis paints a beautiful picture of the eternal Heaven. Early in the book, Jill and Eustace are traveling on a train, when suddenly they are thrust into Narnia. When their adventure is over, the children—having experienced the joys and wonders of Narnia and the presence of Aslan, the great lion—are afraid they will be sent back to Earth again.

Then, in a section called "Farewell to Shadowlands," Aslan gives the children some good news: "'There *was* a real railway accident,' said Aslan softly. 'Your father and mother and all of you are—as you used to call it in the Shadowlands—dead. The term is over: the holidays have begun. The dream is ended: this is the morning.'"

Then Lewis concludes the story with one of my favorite paragraphs in all of literature:

> And as He spoke He no longer looked to them like a lion; but the things that began to happen after that were so great and beautiful that I cannot write them. And for us this is the end of all the stories, and we can most truly say that they all lived happily ever after. But for them it was only the beginning of the real story. All their life in this world and all their adventures in Narnia had only been the cover and the title page: now at last they were beginning Chapter One of the Great Story which no one on earth has read; which goes on forever; in which every chapter is better than the one before.[343]

At the end of *The Last Battle*, when Lewis refers to the typical fairy-tale ending—"they all lived happily ever after"—some readers may be tempted to respond, "But fairy tales aren't true." However, the Bible *isn't* a fairy tale—it is utterly realistic, devastating in its portrayal of sin and suffering, not at all naive. Nowhere in Scripture do we see sentimental wishful thinking. What we see is mankind's devastating separation from God; the death of countless sacrificial lambs; the hard, agonizing work of Christ's redemption; the tangible nature of his resurrection; and the promise of coming judgment. At last we see the restoration of God's ideal universe, fulfilling his plan of the ages, culminating in a resurrected people living with him on a resurrected Earth. Then, and only then, will we live "happily ever after."

But we *will* indeed live happily ever after!

By God's grace, I know that what awaits me in his presence, for all eternity, is something so magnificent it takes my breath away even now. Job said it most succinctly: "In my flesh I will see God; . . . I, and not another" (Job 19:26-27). The prospect of seeing God eclipsed all of Job's heartaches. Surely it can eclipse yours and mine. Our ship of happiness may not come in today—but it will certainly come in. Meanwhile, laying claim to Christ's bought-and-paid-for happiness brings us joy today.

WHAT CAN DEATH DO TO US?

"To die will be an awfully big adventure," says Peter Pan.[344] But it will be a wonderful, big adventure only for those who are covered by the blood of Christ. Those who die without Jesus will experience a horrifying tragedy.

Of course, *dying* is not the real adventure. Death is merely the doorway to eternal life. The adventure is what comes after death—being in the presence of Christ. Just before he was hanged by the Nazis, Dietrich Bonhoeffer prayed aloud, "Oh, God, this is the end; but for me it is just the beginning." His trust in God's promises served him well in the face of death.

We shouldn't glorify or romanticize death—Jesus didn't. He wept over it (John 11:35). For every beautiful story of people peacefully slipping into eternity, there are other stories of confused and shrunken people, wasting away mentally and physically, leaving behind exhausted, confused, and grief-stricken loved ones. I've often seen death close-up. Unless Christ returns in our lifetime, it's certain that my own death—and that of everyone I love—awaits.

Death is painful, and it's an enemy. But for those who know Jesus, death is the *final* pain and the *last* enemy. "For [Christ] must reign until he has put all his enemies under his feet. The last enemy to be destroyed is death" (1 Corinthians 15:25-26).

Death's destruction was foretold in ancient prophecy: "[God] will destroy the shroud that enfolds all peoples, the sheet that covers all nations; he will swallow up death forever. The Sovereign Lord will wipe away the tears from all faces" (Isaiah 25:7-8).

The apostle Paul echoes Isaiah, saying, "When the perishable has been clothed with the imperishable, and the mortal with immortality, then the saying that is written will come true: 'Death has been swallowed up in victory.' 'Where, O death, is your victory? Where, O death, is your sting?'" (1 Corinthians 15:54-55).

Do you crave God's perspective on the death that awaits you? Reread the previous three paragraphs. Read them aloud. Memorize them. Ask yourself, "What's the worst that death can do to me?" Consider Romans 8:35, 38-39: "Who shall separate us from the love of Christ? . . . Neither death nor life, neither angels nor demons, neither the present nor the future, nor any powers, neither height nor depth, nor

> If there be so certain and glorious a rest for the saints, why is there no more industrious seeking after it? One would think, if a man did but once hear of such unspeakable glory to be obtained, and believed what he heard to be true, he should be transported with the vehemency of his desire after it, and should almost forget to eat and drink, and should care for nothing else, and speak of and inquire after nothing else, but how to get this treasure. And yet people who hear of it daily, and profess to believe it as a fundamental article of their faith, do as little mind it, or labor for it, as if they had never heard of any such thing, or did not believe one word they hear.
>
> **RICHARD BAXTER**

anything else in all creation, will be able to separate us from the love of God that is in Christ Jesus our Lord."

Not only will death not separate us from Christ—it will actually usher us into his presence. Then, at the final resurrection, Christ will demonstrate his omnipotence by turning death on its head, making forever alive what appeared forever buried.

If you believe this, you won't cling desperately to this life. You'll stretch out your arms in anticipation of the greater life to come.

If my descendants, perhaps my grandchildren or great-grandchildren, should read these words after I've died, know this: I'm looking forward to greeting you when you arrive in the intermediate Heaven (unless Christ returns in the meantime and we meet at the resurrection). I'll have some favorite places picked out for you, and we'll go there together. But we won't stay there long. Ultimately we'll travel together to our true home, the New Earth. We'll settle and explore it side by side, as pioneers.

What a world it will be. I'm overwhelmed just thinking of it. What a great God we'll enjoy and serve forever. What a great time we'll have together there. I look forward to seeing every reader who knows Jesus, meeting most of you for the first time, and being reunited with those I've known here on the present Earth. I can't wait for the great adventures we'll have with Christ and each other.

Don't let a day go by without anticipating the new world that Christ is preparing for us. God loves the Heaven bound, but he is proud of the Heaven minded: "They were longing for a better country—a heavenly one. *Therefore* God is not ashamed to be called their God, for he has prepared a city for them" (Hebrews 11:16, emphasis added).

A WORD TO THE DEPRESSED

The fact that Heaven will be wonderful shouldn't tempt us to take shortcuts to get there. If you're depressed, you may imagine your life has no purpose—but you couldn't be more wrong.

As long as God keeps you here on Earth, it's *exactly* where he wants you. He's preparing you for another world. He knows precisely what he's doing. Through your suffering, difficulty, and depression, he's expanding your capacity for eternal joy. Our lives on Earth are a training camp to ready us for Heaven.

I know depression can be debilitating. Many godly people have experienced it. But if you are considering taking your own life, recognize this as the devil's temptation. Jesus said that Satan is a liar and a murderer (John 8:44). He tells lies because he wants to destroy you (1 Peter 5:8). Don't listen to the liar. Listen to Jesus, the truth teller (John 8:32; 14:6). Don't make a terrible ending to your life's story—finish your God-given course on Earth. When he's done—not before—he'll take you home in his own time and way. Meanwhile, God has a purpose for you here on Earth. Don't desert your post. (And by all means, go to a Christ-centered, Bible-believing church, and get help to find a wise Christian counselor.)

If you don't know Jesus, confess your sins and embrace his death and resurrection on your behalf. If you do know him, make your daily decisions in light of your destiny. Ask yourself what you can do today, next week, next year, or decades from now to write the best ending to this volume of your life's story—a story that will continue gloriously in the new universe.

By God's grace, use the time you have left on the present Earth to store up for yourself treasures on the New Earth, to be laid at Christ's feet for his glory (Revelation 4:10). Then look forward to meeting in Heaven Jesus himself, as well as those touched by your Christ-exalting choices.

QUESTIONS IN LIGHT OF HEAVEN

We'll have eternity to celebrate great victories on the old Earth, but we have only this brief window of opportunity now to win those victories. As missionary C. T. Studd said, "Only one life, 'twill soon be past; only what's done for Christ will last."

What will last for eternity? Not your car, house, degrees, trophies, or business. What *will* last for eternity is every service to the needy, every dollar given to feed the hungry, every cup of cold water given to the thirsty, every investment in missions, every prayer for the needy, every effort invested in evangelism, and every moment spent caring for precious children—including rocking them to sleep and changing their diapers. The Bible says we'll reap in eternity what we've planted in this life (Galatians 6:7-8).

Setting our minds on Heaven is a discipline that we need to learn. Pastors and church leaders should train themselves and their people to be Heaven-minded. This means teaching and preaching about Heaven. It means presenting a biblical theology of Heaven that can shape and transform people's lives, liberating them from the shallow hopelessness of life centered on a fallen and failing world. Ask yourself these questions:

- Do I daily reflect on my own mortality?
- Do I daily realize there are only two destinations—Heaven or Hell—and that I and every person I know will go to one or the other?

- Do I daily remind myself that this world is not my home and that everything in it will burn, leaving behind only what's eternal?
- Do I daily recognize that my choices and actions have a direct influence on the world to come?
- Do I daily realize that my life is being examined by God, the Audience of One, and that the only appraisal of my life that will ultimately matter is his?
- Do I daily reflect on the fact that my ultimate home will be the New Earth, where I will see God and serve him as a resurrected being in a resurrected human society, where I will overflow with joy and delight in drawing nearer to God by studying him and his creation, and where I will exercise, to God's glory, dominion over his creation?

INCENTIVES FOR RIGHTEOUS LIVING

Theologian Paul Helm writes, "The goal and end of a person's calling does not terminate in this life, but it makes sense only in the light of the life to come. . . . The basic fact about the present life is that it is important and valuable in all its aspects because it leads to the world to come."[345] The world to come is what we were made for—and it gives shape and meaning to our present lives. If we think regularly of the heavenly and the eternal, we aren't easy prey for Satan's lies and distractions.

Knowing that this present world will end and be resurrected into new heavens and a New Earth should profoundly affect our daily behavior. "You ought to live holy and godly lives as you look forward to the day of God. . . . In keeping with his promise we are looking forward to a new heaven and a new earth, the home of righteousness. So then, dear friends, since you are looking forward to this, make every effort to be found spotless, blameless and at peace with him" (2 Peter 3:11-14).

If we understand what "a new heaven and a new earth" means, we will look forward to it. (And if we're not looking forward to it, we must not yet understand it.) Anticipating our homecoming will motivate us to live spotless lives here and now. Recognizing our future life on a resurrected Earth can help empower us to stick with a difficult marriage, to persevere in the hard task of caring for an ailing parent or child, or to stay with a demanding job. Moses stayed faithful to God because "he was looking ahead to his reward" (Hebrews 11:26).

Christ-centered righteous living today is directly affected by knowing where we're going and what rewards we'll receive there for serving Christ. After all, if we really believe we're going to live forever in a realm where Christ is the center who brings us joy, and that righteous living will mean happiness for all, why wouldn't we choose to get a head start on Heaven through Christ-centered righteous living *now*?

A LIFE THAT GETS US READY

"Everyone who has this hope fixed on Him purifies himself, just as He is pure" (1 John 3:3, NASB). If my wedding date is on the calendar, and I'm thinking of the person I'm going to marry, I shouldn't be an easy target for seduction. Likewise, when I've meditated on Heaven, sin is terribly unappealing. It's when my mind drifts from Heaven that sin seems attractive. Thinking of Heaven leads inevitably to pursuing holiness. Our high tolerance for sin testifies of our failure to prepare for Heaven.

Heaven should affect our activities and ambitions, our recreation and friendships, and the way we spend our money and time. If I believe I'll spend eternity in a world of unending beauty and adventure, will I be content to spend all my evenings staring at game shows, sitcoms, and ball games? Even if I keep my eyes off of impurities, how much time will I want to invest in what doesn't matter?

What will last forever? God's Word. People. Spending time in God's Word and investing in people will pay off in eternity and bring me joy and perspective now.

Following Christ is not a call to abstain from gratification but to delay gratification. It's finding our joy in Christ rather than seeking joy in the things of this world. Heaven—our assurance of eternal gratification and fulfillment—should be our North Star, reminding us where we are and which direction to go.

When we realize the pleasures that await us in God's presence, we can forgo lesser pleasures now. When we realize the possessions that await us in Heaven, we will gladly give away possessions on Earth to store up treasures in Heaven. When we realize the power offered to us as rulers in God's Kingdom, a power we could not handle now but will handle with humility and benevolence then, we can forgo the pursuit of power here.

To be Heaven-oriented is to be goal-oriented in the best sense. Paul says, "But one thing I do: Forgetting what is behind and straining toward what is ahead, I press on toward the goal to win the prize for which God has called me heavenward in Christ Jesus" (Philippians 3:13-14).

Thinking of Heaven will motivate us to live each day in profound thankfulness to God: "Therefore, since we are receiving a kingdom that cannot be shaken, let us be thankful, and so worship God acceptably with reverence and awe" (Hebrews 12:28).

In *Perelandra*, C. S. Lewis's protagonist says of his friend Ransom, who has recently returned from another planet, "A man who has been in another world does not come back unchanged."[346] A man who gives sustained thought to another world—the Heaven where Christ is and the resurrected Earth where we will live forever with him—also does not remain unchanged. He becomes a new person. He'll no longer fill his stomach with stale leftovers and scraps fallen to a dirty kitchen floor. He smells the banquet being prepared for him. He won't spoil his appetite. He knows what his mouth is watering for.

ALL THINGS MADE NEW

Nanci and I have spent some wonderful moments with our family and friends—at Christmas or on vacation or at simple times in the family room after dinner—and we've said those enchanting words: "It doesn't get any better than this."

No matter how difficult your life has been, you've said the same thing about some magnificent moment, haven't you? Maybe it was recently. Maybe it was long ago. Maybe you can barely remember. "It doesn't get any better than this." Can you think of even one time in your life when, even for a fleeting moment, that seemed to be true?

Well, it *isn't* true.

The most ordinary moment on the New Earth will be greater than the most perfect moments in this life—those experiences you wanted to bottle or hang on to but couldn't. It *can* get better, far better, than this—*and it will*. Life on the New Earth will be like sitting in front of the fire with family and friends, basking in the warmth, laughing uproariously, dreaming of the adventures to come—and then going out and *living* those adventures together. With no fear that life will ever end or that tragedy will descend like a dark cloud. With no fear that dreams will be shattered or relationships broken.

If the ideas presented in this book were merely the product of my imagination, they would be meaningless. But here's what the apostle John recorded near the end of the Bible:

> Then I saw a new heaven and a new earth. . . . And I heard a loud voice from the throne saying, "Now the dwelling of God is with men, and he will live with them. They will be his people, and God himself will be with them and be their God. He will wipe every tear from their eyes. There will be no more death or mourning or crying or pain, for the old order of things has passed away." He who was seated on the throne said, "I am making everything new!" Then he said, "Write this down, for these words are trustworthy and true." (Revelation 21:1, 3-5)

These are the words of King Jesus. Count on them. Take them to the bank. Live every day in light of them. Make every choice in light of Christ's certain promise.

We were all made for a person and a place. Jesus is the person. Heaven is the place.

If you know Jesus, I'll be with you in that resurrected world. With the Lord we love and with the friends we cherish, we'll embark together on the ultimate adventure, in a spectacular new universe awaiting our exploration and dominion. Jesus will be the center of all things, and joy will be the air we breathe.

And right when we think "it doesn't get any better than this"—*it will.*

APPENDIX A

CHRISTOPLATONISM'S FALSE ASSUMPTIONS

It's no coincidence that Paul wrote his detailed defense of physical resurrection to the Corinthians, who were immersed in the Greek philosophy of dualism. They'd been taught that the spiritual was incompatible with the physical. But Christ, in his incarnation and resurrection, laid claim not only to the spiritual realm but to the physical as well. His redemption wasn't only of spirits but also of bodies and the earth.

Plato was "the first Western philosopher to claim that reality is fundamentally something ideal or abstract."[347] To think of the spiritual realm in physical terms or to envision God's presence in the physical world was to do it a disservice. Plato considered the body a liability, not an asset. "For Plato . . . the body is a hindrance, as it opposes and even imprisons the soul (*Phaedo* 65–68; 91–94)."[348]

But according to Scripture, our bodies aren't just shells for our spirits to inhabit; they're a good and essential aspect of our being. Likewise, the earth is not a second-rate location from which we must be delivered. Rather, it was handmade by God for us. Earth, not some incorporeal state, is God's choice as mankind's original and ultimate dwelling place.

To distinguish the version of Platonism seen among Christians from secular forms of Platonism, I've coined the term *Christoplatonism*. This philosophy has blended elements of Platonism with Christianity, and in so doing has poisoned Christianity and blunted its distinct differences from Eastern religions. Because appeals to Christoplatonism appear to take the spiritual high ground, attempts to refute this false philosophy often appear to be materialistic, hedonistic, or worldly.

Because of Christoplatonism's pervasive influence, we resist the biblical picture of bodily resurrection of the dead and life on the New Earth; of eating and drinking in Heaven; of walking and talking, living in dwelling places, traveling down streets, and going through gates from one place to another; and of ruling, working, playing, and engaging in earthly culture.

One author writes, "Only our redeemed spirits can live in a spiritual realm like heaven. Therefore, the life we know now as spiritual reality will continue in heaven, but we shall not need or desire the things associated with our present physical bodies, simply because we shall not possess physical bodies in heaven."[349]

This statement constitutes a denial of the foundational doctrine of the bodily resurrection of the dead, and it is utterly contradicted by countless Scriptures. Nevertheless, it's a common perspective among evangelical Christians.

Another writer suggests, "When the material world perishes, we shall find ourselves in the spiritual world; when the dream of life ends, we shall awake in the world of reality; when our connection with this world comes to a close, we shall find ourselves in our eternal spirit home."[350] According to the Bible, however, our eternal home is on the New Earth!

A godly man, a lifelong Bible student, told me that the thought of eating and drinking and engaging in physical activities in Heaven seemed to him "terribly unspiritual."

In Plato's statement, "*Soma sema*" ("a body, a tomb"), he asserts that the spirit's highest destiny is to be forever free from the body. The Bible, however, contradicts this premise from the beginning of Genesis to the end of Revelation. It says that God is the creator of body and spirit; both were marred by sin, and both were redeemed by Christ.

Yes, we need to be delivered from our earthly bodies, which are subject to sin and decay (Romans 7:24). But the promise of Heaven isn't the *absence* of body; rather, it's the attainment of a new and sinless body *and* spirit. In 1 Corinthians 15, Paul regards the new *body*—not simply the new spirit—as essential to our redemption. *If the body isn't redeemed, mankind is not redeemed*, because we're by nature body as well as spirit. A spirit without a body, like a body without a spirit, isn't the highest human destiny. Rather, it's a state of incompleteness, an aberration of the full meaning of being human.

THE INFLUENCE OF PHILO AND ORIGEN

Platonic ideas began making inroads into Christian theology through the writings of Philo (ca. 20 BC–AD 50). An Alexandrian Jew, Philo admired Greek culture and was enamored with Plato's philosophy. He was also proud of his

Jewish heritage. In his desire to offer the Greeks the best of Judaism and the Jews the best of Greek philosophy, he allegorized Scripture. He did so in contrast to the literal interpretation of many rabbis.[351]

Philo's ideas caught on. Alexandria became the home of a new school of theological thought. Clement of Alexandria (150–215), an early church father, was a part of this movement, as was Origen (185–254), an Egyptian-born Christian writer and teacher. Clement embraced Greek philosophy and maintained that Scripture must be understood allegorically. Origen developed an entire system of allegorizing Scripture. His method was to see the Bible as a three-part living organism, corresponding to body, soul, and spirit. The body was the literal or historical sense, the soul was the psychic or moral sense, and the spirit was—by far most important—the philosophical sense.

Educated people were considered more qualified to find the Bible's "hidden" meanings in texts that the average person would take at face value. In other words, Origen's approach meant that ordinary people couldn't understand the Bible without the help of trained, educated people. These enlightened teachers could find and teach the Bible's "true" spiritual meanings, which were usually quite different from its apparent, obvious, and "less spiritual" meanings.

Origen typically dismissed or ignored literal meanings in favor of fanciful ideas foreign to the text. At the time, his modern approach was embraced by Christian intellectuals as a sort of Gnostic and elitist approach that separated the educated clergy from the ignorant laity. This distinction still continues in some circles, with literal interpretations seen as suspect, and allegorical and symbolic interpretations deemed more spiritual and intellectually appealing.

Judged by christoplatonic presuppositions, anytime the Bible speaks about Heaven in plain, ordinary, or straightforward ways, the assumption is that it doesn't actually mean what it says. For example, the plain meaning of living as resurrected beings in a resurrected society in a resurrected city on a resurrected Earth cannot be real, because it doesn't jibe with the Platonic assumption that the body is bad and the spirit good. Consequently, Heaven cannot possibly be like what Revelation 21–22 appears to say. There could not be bodies, nations, kings, buildings, streets, gates, water, trees, and fruit, because these are physical, and what's physical is not spiritual. The prophetic statements about life on a perfect Earth are considered mere symbols of the promise of a disembodied spiritual world.

Tragically, the allegorical method of interpretation—rooted in explicitly unchristian assumptions—came to rule the church's theology. (We'll deal more with this in appendix B.) Even today, commentaries and books on Heaven seem to automatically regard all Scripture about Heaven as figurative. For instance, in his commentary on Revelation, Leon Morris says, "When John speaks of streets paved with gold, of a city whose gates are made of single pearls and the like, we must not understand that the heavenly city will be as material as present earthly cities."[352] But given what Scripture teaches about the resurrection of mankind and the earth, *why not?*

Was the body of the resurrected Jesus as material as our present earthly bodies? Yes. If, in our resurrected bodies—which we're told will be like his—we'll be as material as we are now, why wouldn't the resurrected Earth also be as material as it is now? Likewise, why wouldn't New Earth cities be as material as those on the present Earth? Is there something wrong with material things? To Platonists, the answer was yes—to the apostles and prophets, the answer was no. If our material, resurrected bodies will walk on the ground, why not on streets? And considering God's unlimited resources, is there any reason why those streets couldn't be made of gold?

An allegorical interpretive approach undercuts Scripture's magnificent revelation that there will be one world, both spiritual and material. The two aspects will coexist in perfect harmony, made by a God who forever linked the spiritual and material worlds both by incarnation and resurrection.

ACCOMMODATION

Earth is not the opposite of Heaven. But our christoplatonic assumptions prompt us to polarize Heaven and Earth. Theologians speak of the language of *accommodation*. "The doctrine of accommodation asserts that in the Bible, God, who is spiritual, has accommodated Himself to human understanding by portraying Himself and heavenly reality in humanly understandable images."[353] There is, of course, truth in the doctrine of accommodation. But the Bible explicitly tells us that we'll live forever, in resurrected bodies, on a resurrected Earth. It tells us that Jesus became a man and will be a man forever. It tells us that God will bring down the New Jerusalem from Heaven to Earth, and that's where he will live with us.

The Incarnation wasn't God talking *as if* he'd become a man—it was God actually becoming a man. The doctrine of the bodily resurrection of the dead isn't God telling us we'll have bodies because that's all we're capable of understanding. We really *will* have bodies. The doctrine of the New Earth isn't God acting as if we'll live in an earthly realm—rather, it's God explicitly telling us that we *will* live on the New Earth.

The "New Earth" isn't a figure of speech any more than calling Jesus a "man" is a figure of speech. He *is* a man. The Resurrection was not merely a symbol of God overcoming spiritual darkness; it was an actual, physical resurrection. The New Earth will be a real Earth where mankind and God will dwell together. Therefore, we should be open to taking literally its depiction of earthlike realities.

Jesus really *did* become a man. He really *did* rise from the grave. We really will rise too. The incarnation, life, death, and resurrection of Christ literally happened. The biblical texts aren't merely using the language of accommodation. Likewise, when Scripture speaks of our bodily resurrection and the coming of the New Earth, this isn't accommodation—it's *revelation* that we will spend eternity as physical beings in a physical universe.

If the Bible taught that the present Heaven and the eternal Heaven were both unearthly realms of disembodied spirits, then we should consider as figurative the repeated depictions of Heaven in physical terms. However, if people really will live on the New Earth in resurrected bodies—and if even the current, intermediate Heaven contains physical objects, including the risen body of Christ—then we shouldn't base our hermeneutic of Heaven on the assumptions of Philo and Origen. We should base our understanding on the testimony of Jesus and the apostle John.

Given the weight of biblical revelation, I believe that descriptions of resurrected humanity and the resurrected Earth should be understood as literal, and interpreted figuratively only when a plain literal understanding is impossible or highly unlikely.

For those accustomed to always spiritualizing Scripture when it comes to Heaven, I'd encourage you to ask yourself the following questions: What if the resurrection of the dead is an actual, bodily resurrection? What if the New Earth will be real? What if Heaven will be a tangible, earthly place inhabited by people with bodies, intellect, creativity, and culture-building relational skills? What if a physical Heaven is God's plan and has been all along? What terminology would God have to use to convince us of this? How would it be different from what he has actually used in Scripture?

A BIBLICAL VIEW OF PLEASURE

One of Christoplatonism's false assumptions is that spiritual people should shun physical pleasures. But who's the inventor of pleasure? Who made food and water, eating and drinking, marriage and sex, friendship and games, art and music, celebration and laughter? God did.

The Bible knows only one Creator: God; and only one race of subcreators: mankind. Satan cannot create. Ultimately, he can't even destroy. He can only twist and pervert what God has created, as C. S. Lewis depicts in a correspondence between two demons in *The Screwtape Letters*:

> Never forget that when we are dealing with any pleasure in its healthy and normal and satisfying form, we are, in a sense, on the Enemy's ground. I know we have won many a soul through pleasure. All the same, it is His invention, not ours. He made the pleasures: all our research so far has not enabled us to produce one. All we can do is to encourage the humans to take the pleasures which our Enemy has produced, at times, or in ways, or in degrees, which He has forbidden. Hence we always try to work away from the natural condition of any pleasure to that in which it is least natural, least redolent of its Maker, and least pleasurable. An ever increasing craving for an ever diminishing pleasure is the formula.[354]

"Sin does not create things," writes Paul Marshall. "It has no originality, no creativity, no being in itself. Sin lives off that which is good. It is a parasite, feeding greedily on the goodness of what God has made."[355] God will remove the parasite without killing the patient.

"Nothing is evil in the beginning," says the Elf king Elrond in J. R. R. Tolkien's *The Fellowship of the Ring*. Once that idea is clearly in our minds, we can never again regard mankind or the earth, plants, animals, natural wonders, stars, or planets as lost causes. Created with purpose by an omniscient God, they're not disposable. Because they're part of God's creation, they're fully within the scope of his redemption.

A POSITIVE VIEW OF THE NATURAL REALM

Every belief that would make our resurrection bodies less physical than Adam's and Eve's, or that makes the New Earth less earthly than the original Earth, essentially credits Satan with a victory over God by suggesting that Satan has permanently marred God's original intention, design, and creation.

Anthony Hoekema writes,

> If the resurrection body were non-material or non-physical, the devil would have won a great victory, since God would then have been compelled to change human beings with physical bodies such as he had created into creatures of a different sort, without physical bodies (like the angels). Then it would indeed seem that matter had become

intrinsically evil so that it had to be banished. And then, in a sense, the Greek philosophers would have been proved right. But matter is not evil; it is part of God's good creation. Therefore the goal of God's redemption is the resurrection of the physical body, and the creation of a new earth on which his redeemed people can live and serve God forever with glorified bodies. Thus the universe will not be destroyed but renewed, and God will win the victory.[356]

After reading a first draft of this book, a friend sent me an e-mail. She has attended a Bible-teaching evangelical church for many years, reads widely, and is very intelligent. She wrote, "Because I believed that places didn't matter to God, I didn't want them to matter to me. Because I believed that animals didn't really matter to God, I didn't want them to matter to me. Because I believed that my spirit was really all that mattered to God, I didn't let my body matter to me." She was glad to be free from these christoplatonic beliefs.

If I could snap my fingers and eliminate a single false assumption that keeps us from accurately understanding Scripture's revelation about Heaven, it would be the heretical notion that the physical realm is an obstacle to God's plan rather than a central part of it.

Wayne Grudem argues for the physical nature of the realm we'll live in forever: "God will not completely destroy the physical world (which would be an acknowledgment that sin had frustrated and defeated God's purposes), but rather he will perfect the entire creation and bring it into harmony with the purposes for which he originally created it. Therefore we can expect that in the new heavens and new earth there will be a fully perfect earth that is once again 'very good.' And we can expect that we will have physical bodies that will once again be 'very good' in God's sight, and that will function to fulfill the purposes for which he originally placed man on the earth."[357]

Consider the biblical facts that give us a very positive view of the physical realm:

- God made Adam and Eve to be spiritual *and* physical—they were not human until they were both.
- God often took on human form in Old Testament times. He was also likely in human form as he walked in Eden.
- God took on a human body, becoming a man in Christ, not just temporarily but forever.
- God raised Christ in a human body with physical properties, a body that walked, talked, ate, and could be touched. He explicitly stated he wasn't a ghost.

- God made mankind in his image, and because humans are physical beings—though God is spirit—there must be something in our human bodies that reflects God's identity. Certainly there's nothing about our bodies that repulses God, who created humanity as his crowning achievement.
- God's Holy Spirit indwells human bodies and calls them his holy temples.
- God will raise people with eternal physical-spiritual bodies, then come down to inhabit the New Earth with them.

All seven of these assertions are undeniable to most Bible-believers. Yet somehow, many Christians imagine they will live forever in a disembodied existence in an immaterial realm. As a result, they wear blinders when they interpret Scripture, and they fail to understand the richness of God's revelation concerning the world we'll inhabit forever.

The christoplatonic view of the eternal Heaven is an insult to Christ's redemption and his resurrection. Christ did not die to give disembodied people a refuge in the spirit realm. He didn't rise to offer us a mere symbol of new spiritual life. On the contrary, he died to restore to us the fullness of our humanity—spirit *and* body. He rose to lay claim to and exemplify our destiny, to walk and rule the physical Earth as physical beings, to his glory. He died to lift Earth's curse and rose to guarantee that the earth itself would rise from misery and destruction to be a realm ruled by righteous humanity, to God's eternal glory.

APPENDIX B

LITERAL AND FIGURATIVE INTERPRETATION

If my interpretation is accurate of even one-quarter of the Scripture passages I've cited in this book, then the Bible says a great deal more about Heaven than many Christians have ever considered. How could this be? A major reason is the interpretive assumptions we bring to Scripture.

For years, I taught biblical interpretation at a Bible college. We studied the different types of biblical literature and how to interpret each—including historical narrative, wisdom, poetry, prophecy, and instruction (especially the Epistles). There's considerable overlap between these literary forms. For instance, the Gospels are historical narrative but include Christ's parables. The letters are instructional but include some history and poetry. Biblical poetry often recalls historical events. Historical books contain prophecy. Prophetic books include history and instruction. Daniel and Revelation are apocalyptic books that contain both history and prophecy. Therefore, it's a mistake to say that every statement in a historical book should be taken literally and every statement in an apocalyptic book should be taken figuratively. We must always evaluate meaning in light of immediate context.

In studying biblical interpretation in the classroom, we'd often go to texts commonly understood a certain way, then try to discern what the original writer was conveying to the original readers. Often we found a striking difference between what the texts actually said and how they were popularly understood. We realized that our minds often weren't open to the meaning of the texts because of the preconceived ideas we were reading into them, ideas we'd heard from others or picked up from our culture, but which didn't correspond to Scripture.

This is why we read in Luke 15:7 that Jesus says there is "rejoicing in heaven over one sinner who repents," yet we don't believe that people in Heaven are aware of what's happening to people on Earth. We read in Luke 16:9 that we should "use worldly wealth to gain friends for yourselves, so that when it is gone, you will be welcomed into eternal dwellings," yet we don't believe we'll have homes in Heaven and open those homes to each other. We read passages in the prophets promising that God's people will live forever on a righteous Earth, then assume this must mean a spiritual blessing in an incorporeal Heaven. We read that we will have resurrection bodies and will eat and drink at tables with Christ and fellow believers, yet we don't actually envision this to be true. We read in the last two chapters of Revelation about nations on the New Earth and kings of those nations bringing their treasures into the city, yet we don't believe there will be real nations or kings of those nations. Many doubt there will be a city at all. The examples go on and on—when it comes to the eternal state, we don't let Scripture say what it says.

Then, despite these and innumerable other passages, we say, "The Bible tells us very little about Heaven." The truth, in my opinion, is that we simply don't *believe* the significant amount the Bible tells us about Heaven. Our christoplatonic assumptions have a stranglehold on us and impair our ability to interpret Scriptures that deal with the afterlife. Only by discarding those assumptions and replacing them with the scriptural doctrines of bodily resurrection and life on the New Earth can we interpret Scripture in ways that allow "bodies" to be bodies, "eating" to be eating, and "dwelling places" to be dwelling places. I'm well aware that many readers will question my interpretations in this book, often because they've never heard them before. They sound far-fetched because we're unaccustomed to them. Though some of my hundreds of interpretations are undoubtedly flawed, I believe most of them are sound. I encourage readers to let the texts speak for themselves—let God speak to you without filtering his words through christoplatonic assumptions.

If we abandon the unbiblical assumptions that predetermine our biblical interpretations, the otherworldly house of cards will come crashing down. In its place we'll be able to construct a doctrine of Heaven that's solidly based on revealed Scripture.

To do this, let's further examine what went wrong—how, historically, the church has embraced false assumptions that distort our view of Heaven.

SCHOLASTICISM'S UNEARTHLY HEAVEN

Prior to the Middle Ages, people thought of Heaven tangibly—as a city or a paradise garden, as portrayed in Scripture. But the writings of twelfth-century theologians such as Peter Abelard and Peter Lombard and thirteenth-century theologian Thomas Aquinas led to the philosophical movement known as scholasticism, which came to dominate medieval thought and ultimately took hostage the doctrine of Heaven.

The scholastic writers viewed Heaven in a much more impersonal, cold, and scientific manner than their predecessors. They departed from the Heaven of Scripture that contains *both* the unfamiliar transcendent presence of God, surrounded by the cherubim, *and* familiar earthly objects and personages, including people wearing clothes and having conversations. They embraced a Heaven entirely intangible, immaterial, and hence—they thought—more spiritual.[358] They claimed that Heaven couldn't be made of familiar elements such as earth, water, air, and fire. Instead, they argued, "the empyrean [the highest heaven or heavenly sphere] must be made of a fifth and nobler element, the quintessence, which must be something like pure light."[359] And they ignored almost entirely—or allegorized into oblivion—the New Earth as the eternal dwelling place of resurrected humans living with the resurrected Jesus in a physical realm of natural wonders, physical structures, and cultural distinctives.

The scholastic view gradually replaced the old, more literal understanding of Heaven as garden and city, a place of earthly beauty, dwelling places, food, and fellowship. The loss was incalculable. The church to this day has never recovered from the unearthly—and anti-earthly—theology of Heaven constructed by well-meaning but misguided scholastic theologians. These men interpreted biblical revelation not in a straightforward manner, but in light of the intellectually seductive notions of Platonism, Stoicism, and Gnosticism.

According to Aquinas, neither plants nor animals will have a place in Heaven, the world of light.[360] He argued there would be no active life in Heaven, only contemplation.[361] Because God is the great object of our worship, Aquinas supposed we would think of nothing and no one but God.

Aquinas was absolutely correct that God is the cosmic center. But his faulty logic reshaped our understanding of Heaven by undercutting the biblical doctrines of physical resurrection, Paradise restored on the New Earth, and the redeemed culture and community of the New Earth's holy city and nations. His view neglected the eternal nature of Christ's humanity and immanence, entirely eclipsing them with his deity and transcendence. Scholastic theology requires that we negate or spiritualize countless Scriptures, rejecting the plain meaning.

Though some thinkers later departed from scholasticism, its underlying christoplatonic views never lost their grip on the Western church.

SHOULD WE TAKE LITERALLY WHAT SCRIPTURE SAYS ABOUT HEAVEN?

No one interprets the Bible absolutely literally or absolutely figuratively. Whether we tend more toward the literal or the figurative largely depends on our assumptions. People who believe Christ's body remained in the grave must interpret the Resurrection accounts figuratively. If they believe that Christ literally rose, but that Heaven will be a realm of disembodied spirits, then they will take some of Christ's words literally, but take figuratively Christ's references to Heaven being an actual place, mankind one day inheriting the earth, and the physical universe being renewed. They will take figuratively God's fashioning of the new heavens, New Earth, and New Jerusalem.

Obviously there are many figures of speech in the Bible, such as when Peter is called a rock and Christ is called a door, a lamb with seven eyes, and is said to have a sword coming out of his mouth.

Scripture is also full of accounts that should be taken *literally*, such as Noah's flood and ark, the plagues, crossing the Red Sea, and Christ being born in Bethlehem, calming the storm, healing people, multiplying loaves and fishes, being crucified, physically rising from the dead, and ascending.

I believe that our resurrection bodies wouldn't be called bodies if they weren't actual bodies. They wouldn't be said to be like Christ's body if they won't be, just as Christ wouldn't be portrayed as literally rising from the dead and having a resurrection body if he didn't. Similarly, Paradise wouldn't be called *paradise* if it wasn't Edenlike, at least to a degree. (It need not be identical to Eden, of course.) Similarly, I believe the New Earth wouldn't be called the New Earth if it wasn't earthlike. Kings wouldn't be called kings and ruling wouldn't be called ruling if the meaning didn't largely correspond to those words. (The meaning needn't be *limited* to what these words mean presently, but there must be substantial correlation.)

The detailed literal fulfillment of Christ's first coming and death portrayed in Isaiah 52–53 and 61:1-3 instructs us on how we should interpret Isaiah 60–66's detailed descriptions of a coming life of righteousness and peace on what is called a "new earth." Similarly, I believe that the historical accounts of Christ's life on Earth after his resurrection should instruct us how to interpret Revelation 21–22's account of our lives on the New Earth after our resurrection. It's true that large portions of both Isaiah and Revelation contain figurative and apocalyptic depictions, some of which should *not* be taken literally. Yet we shouldn't make the same mistake many scholars make with Isaiah 52–53, spiritualizing these passages and entirely missing their central—and very literal—points, even in the midst of much that's figurative.

HOW LITERALLY SHOULD WE INTERPRET THE BIBLE AS A WHOLE?

It's demonstrably true that Revelation, as apocalyptic literature, often shouldn't be taken literally. Will the blood literally flow up to the horses' bridles (14:20)? Will Christians become pillars in the temple (3:12)? Is there really a seven-horned, seven-eyed lamb, and are there seven spirits of God (5:6)? If you took their temperature, would the Laodiceans be lukewarm? Does Christ literally spit them out of his mouth (3:16)? Is Christ actually knocking at the door (3:20)? Is he the lion of Judah (5:5) *and* the lamb with seven eyes? Is the woman literally clothed with the sun (12:1)? Does a great prostitute sit on many waters (17:1)? Is there literally a great red dragon with seven heads (12:3)? These are figures of speech. They can't be taken literally without contradicting known facts, both observable to us and elsewhere revealed in Scripture.

It's obvious that certain numbers, especially the numbers seven and twelve, and various multiples of twelve, have symbolic significance in Revelation. As I've developed elsewhere, the thousand years of the Millennium have been understood either literally or figuratively by orthodox Christians throughout history.[362] (However, those who disagree about the Millennium can nonetheless agree on the New Earth.)

When John the Baptist said, "Look, the Lamb of God," no one should (or does) think he was affirming that Jesus had wool and walked on four legs (John 1:29). Rather, John meant, "Look, this man Jesus is the fulfillment of the Old Testament sacrificial system." Note, however, that this figure of speech alludes to realities with physical correspondence—the actual, literal death of Jesus on the cross. So, the figure of speech had an actual (one might say almost literal) fulfillment in Christ's crucifixion.

Christ's words to the seven churches of Revelation 2–3 contain some figurative language. But shouldn't we believe these were actually seven churches, located in the specified geographical locations? In Revelation, didn't the real apostle John witness certain real events, some past, some present, and some future, including the physical return of Christ to the earth? Revelation, like other books of Scripture, contains passages that must be interpreted according to their context.

Peter, in an instructional letter, tells the church about the new heavens and Earth, with no suggestion that he's speaking figuratively. Isaiah spoke of new heavens and a New Earth in very tangible, descriptive, earthly ways. Hence, when we hear of God creating new heavens and a New Earth in Revelation 21, we would be mistaken to assume it doesn't have a literal meaning corresponding to the Bible's previous references to a New Earth.

When Jesus is described as a lamb with seven eyes, it contradicts known facts to take that literally. But would it contradict known facts to believe that on the New Earth there will be a great city with streets of gold and gates made of pearls (Revelation 21:21), and with trees and a river (22:1-2)?

When Christ is described as riding on a white horse (Revelation 19:11), must this be purely symbolic? When he rode a colt into Jerusalem (John 12:12-16), it had symbolic meaning, but it was also literal—*he was actually riding a colt*. If Christ could descend from Heaven at the Second Coming, why couldn't he just as easily come down riding on a horse? Kings often rode horses into vanquished cities. Thus, commentators say that riding a horse symbolizes a kingly entrance. Of course it does. But that's because *kings really did ride horses into cities*. And they really did sit on thrones that had symbolic significance. Christ has a body suited to sitting on a throne and riding a horse, doesn't he? He created horses and exults in their magnificence (Job 39:19-25). Why should we assume he won't actually return on horseback or sit on a throne?

Of course, I recognize that *thrones* and *horses* can be used figuratively, particularly in apocalyptic literature. But if you look at the passages of Scripture I've cited in this book, you'll find that most of them are *not* from apocalyptic literature. Many of them are from epistles and books of historical narrative where the authors normally expect us to take their words literally.

Because we know that Christ's resurrected body is physical and that our resurrected bodies will be like his, there isn't a compelling reason to assume that other physical depictions of the New Earth must be figurative. The doctrine of resurrection should guide our interpretation of texts concerning the eternal state.

When faced with a decision about whether to interpret a passage of Scripture literally or figuratively, how do we know which is right? One way is to interpret based on what the Bible says elsewhere about the same subject. Consider Revelation 2:7, "I will give the right to eat from the tree of life, which is in the paradise of God." A figurative or allegorical interpreter might say that the tree of life stands for eternal life, and its fruit symbolizes that God will spiritually nourish us in Heaven. A literal interpreter would say it means there's an actual Paradise with a real tree bearing real fruit that will actually be eaten by people with real bodies.

In Genesis 1–3, Scripture tells us about mankind's nature and about Paradise. Was Paradise an actual place? Yes. Was the tree of life there actually a tree? Yes. Did it have fruit on it that people could eat? Yes. Did the people have actual bodies with which they took bites of fruit, chewed, and swallowed? Yes. If this tree of life is our reference point when we read Revelation 2:7, I see no reason to believe that the tree of life depicted there isn't a literal, physical tree.

As Francis Schaeffer points out in *Genesis in Space and Time*, it's essential to a Christian understanding of history that we realize the early chapters of the Bible are not allegory or metaphor. It's also important that the final chapters of the Bible, which correspond so closely to the first, aren't stripped of their physical reality.

If after we die we'll never again be physical beings living in a physical place, then by all means we should not take Revelation 21–22—or any of the other passages about Heaven—literally. But because Scripture teaches us that we will be resurrected beings serving God in a resurrected universe, we should take at face value what it says about the New Earth.

CAN SOMETHING BE SYMBOLIC <u>AND</u> LITERAL?

One of the frustrating aspects of christoplatonic interpretation is the tendency of interpreters to assume that because something is symbolic it can't also be literal. Earlier I referred to thrones. A throne is rightly regarded as a symbol of power and authority. When Jesus says that his disciples will sit on thrones and rule a kingdom on the earth (Luke 22:30), some regard this as purely symbolic. But every earthly king sits on a throne. His throne is, of course, symbolic of his power and authority, but it's also *an actual physical object.* Nevertheless, interpreters often understand the throne in the New Jerusalem as purely figurative (Revelation 21:3, 5). They read the word *city* and think "relationship," *walls* and think "security," *gates* and think "access to God." Personally, I believe in all these symbolic meanings, but I also believe there will be a real city (the New Jerusalem) with real walls and real gates.

Suppose you travel to Switzerland. After returning, you tell others about what you saw. You describe the Alps, the jagged peaks and slopes, the beautiful rivers and trees, the shops and the city streets. What would you think if someone said, "When he speaks of the peaks, he's speaking of the lofty, transcendent nature of Switzerland, which he experienced in a disembodied state, floating in the spiritual realm. By *streets*, he means that one may journey there into deeper spiritual truths. By *waters*, he means the place is pure and life-giving, a source of refreshment. By *trees*, he means the place is alive with a beauty which can't be put in human words."

How would you feel? Frustrated? How might God feel when he tells us about the New Earth and the New Jerusalem—a huge city with a river going through it, and the tree of life bearing fruit, and people living there, coming and going through its gates—and we take it as nothing but a collection of symbols, without substance? Both in Genesis 1–3 and Revelation 20–22, in order to generate "spiritual" meanings, interpreters too often strip the text of its literal meanings.

IS THE NEW JERUSALEM A LITERAL, MASSIVE CITY?

In describing the New Jerusalem, the apostle John writes, "The twelve gates were twelve pearls, each gate made of a single pearl. The great street of the city was of pure gold, like transparent glass" (Revelation 21:21). The pearls John describes are gates set in walls that are two hundred feet thick.

Commentators routinely suggest, "Of course, these are not actual streets of gold." But why do they say that? In part, at least, because of their christoplatonic assumptions. Disembodied spirits don't need streets to walk on. Incorporeal realms don't have real cities with real streets, real gates, and real citizens. But isn't John's description of gates and streets further evidence that Heaven is a physical realm designed for human citizens? Why wouldn't a resurrected world inhabited by resurrected people have actual streets and gates?

Likewise, most books on Heaven argue that the city cannot really be the size it's depicted as being in Revelation 21:15-17: "The angel who talked with me had a measuring rod of gold to measure the city, its gates and its walls. . . . He measured the city with the rod and found it to be 12,000 stadia in length, and as wide and high as it is long. He measured its wall and it was 144 cubits thick, by man's measurement, which the angel was using."

Twelve thousand stadia equates to fourteen hundred miles in each direction. According to one writer on Heaven, "It would dishonor the heavenly Architect to contend that its dimensions were meant to be taken literally."[363] He doesn't say *why* it would dishonor God, and I have no idea why it would. But, as usual, taking Scripture allegorically or figuratively is considered the high ground, whereas literal interpretation is considered naive or crass.

If these dimensions are not literal, why does Scripture specifically give the dimensions and then say "by man's measurement, which the angel was using" (Revelation 21:17)? The emphasis on "man's measurement" almost seems to be an appeal: "Please believe it—the city is really this big!"

Suppose God wanted to convey that the city really is fourteen hundred miles wide and deep and high. What else would we expect him to say besides what this passage says? Is it possible for God to make such a city? Obviously— he's the creator of the universe. Is it possible for people in glorified bodies to dwell in such a city? Yes.

I have no problem believing that the numbers have symbolic value, with the multiples of twelve suggesting the perfection of God's bride. However, most commentators act as if we must choose between literal dimensions and ones with symbolic significance. But we don't. My wedding ring is a great symbol—but it's also a real object.

Some argue, "But this city rises above the earth's oxygen level." Can't God put oxygen fourteen hundred miles high on the New Earth if he wishes? Or can't he make it so we don't have to breathe oxygen? Such things are no problem for God.

Some argue that nothing could be that big. It would cover two-thirds of the continental United States. If the great pyramids of Egypt or the Great Wall of China amaze you, imagine a city that extends five miles into the sky—let alone fourteen hundred miles! Envision the city disappearing into the clouds.

Some claim anything that big would weigh so much it would disrupt the earth's orbit. Of course, the New Earth could be much bigger than the present one. In any case, issues of mass and gravity are child's play to the Creator.

That the dimensions are equal on all sides is reminiscent of the Holy of Holies in Israel's Temple (1 Kings 6:20). This likely symbolizes God's presence, because the city is called his new dwelling place (Revelation 21:2-3). By suggesting there's symbolism, am I contradicting my suggestion that the measurements are literal? Not at all. Many physical objects, including the Ark of the Covenant and the high priest's breastplate and its stones, had symbolic significance.

Is it possible that the city's dimensions aren't literal? Of course. The doctrine of the New Earth certainly doesn't stand or fall with the size of the New Jerusalem. However, my concern is this: If we assume the city's dimensions can't be real, people will likely believe the city isn't real. If it doesn't have its stated dimensions, then it's a short step to believing it doesn't have any dimensions at all. Then we think of the New Earth as not being a resurrected realm suited for resurrected people.

Christoplatonism produces certain interpretive assumptions, which in turn reinforce the Christoplatonism that Scripture argues against.

SUBJECTIVE INTERPRETATION

An interpretive approach that makes everything symbolic also makes everything subjective. It will never allow us to break free of our assumptions and see what the Bible really says about Heaven, our bodily resurrection, and life on the New Earth. If we assume that our heavenly bodies won't be real, and Heaven itself won't be a tangible, physical place, and we won't really eat in Heaven, live in physical dwellings, or rule over actual cities or nations, then we'll automatically interpret all Scripture references to these things as figures of speech—which is exactly what interpreters often do.

What happens in figurative interpretation? The river going through the New Jerusalem becomes God's grace, the tree becomes Christ, the city walls become security. Or the river becomes Christ, the tree God's grace, and the city walls God's omnipotence. Or river, tree, and walls all become Christ. Or the fruit from the tree of life becomes the fruit of the Spirit or the attributes of God, and so on. But if the text can be said to mean *everything*, it ceases to mean *anything*. One cannot have serious interpretive discussions with those who interpret all references to the New Earth figuratively. Why? Because as soon as you cite a passage depicting anything tangible, they will dismiss it by saying, "You can't take that literally."

Suppose someone believes that the tree of life symbolizes the cross of Christ, and its fruit is a blood-colored liquid. They decide that the tree bearing fruit means Jesus hangs on the cross every day in Heaven, his blood drips from the fruit and flows into the river, and we go to the river to drink daily of his freshly shed blood.

I don't believe this heresy—I just made it up to illustrate the point that once we allow symbolism and allegory and figurative interpretation to reign, "making it up" becomes routine. Anyone can believe and defend anything they want. Interpreters can twist any passage into heresy, as Origen and those of his interpretive school often did. Cults are built on this approach to biblical interpretation as people are taught "hidden meanings." "Experts" teach people hidden meanings, which conveniently correspond to whatever the expert believes or wants others to believe. Even within the church, people may be intimidated into believing that they're not smart enough to understand a text's "real meaning."

Interpreters end up doing exactly what Revelation warns us not to do—taking away from and adding to the words of the prophecy (Revelation 22:18-19). We take away from Scripture by denying its apparent meaning. We add to it by supplying new meanings not supported by the text. When I mentioned the tree of life in Revelation 22, someone told me, "But the tree of life is Jesus, not an actual tree." Was the tree of life in the Garden of Eden also Jesus, and not an actual tree? When Adam and Eve ate its fruit, were they picking Jesus or eating him? If it was a real tree on the original Earth, why wouldn't it be a real tree on the New Earth? If the rivers that ran through Eden were actual rivers, why wouldn't the river flowing through the city in Revelation 22 also be an actual river?

That we'll forever enjoy a resurrected life on a New Earth isn't true because we want it to be. It's true because God says it is. Paying attention to context and taking other Scriptures into account, we need to draw God's truth from the text, not superimpose our preconceived ideas onto it.

NOTES

INTRODUCTION
THE SUBJECT OF HEAVEN

1 J. Sidlow Baxter, *The Other Side of Death: What the Bible Teaches about Heaven and Hell* (Grand Rapids: Kregel, 1987), 237.

2 Harvey Minkoff, *The Book of Heaven* (Owings Mills, Md.: Ottenheimer, 2001), 87.

3 Edward Donnelly, *Biblical Teaching on the Doctrines of Heaven and Hell* (Edinburgh: Banner of Truth, 2001), 64.

4 Don Richardson, *Eternity in Their Hearts*, rev. ed. (Ventura, Calif.: Regal, 1984).

5 Spiros Zodhiates, *Life after Death* (Chattanooga: AMG, 1977), 100–101.

6 Ulrich Simon, *Heaven in the Christian Tradition* (London: Wyman and Sons, 1958), 218.

7 Aristides, *Apology*, 15.

8 Cyprian, *Mortality*, chap. 26.

9 Basilea Schlink, *What Comes after Death?* (Carol Stream, Ill.: Creation House, 1976), 20.

10 C. J. Mahaney, "Loving the Church" (taped message, Covenant Life Church, Gaithersburg, Md., n.d.); read the story of Florence Chadwick at http://www.vanguard.edu/vision2010.

CHAPTER 1
ARE YOU LOOKING FORWARD TO HEAVEN?

11 Ola Elizabeth Winslow, *Jonathan Edwards: Basic Writings* (New York: New American Library, 1966), 142.

12 Jonathan Edwards, "The Resolutions of Jonathan Edwards (1722–23)," JonathanEdwards.com, http://www.jonathanedwards.com/text/Personal/resolut.htm; see also Stephen Nichols, ed., *Jonathan Edwards' Resolutions and Advice to Young Converts* (Phillipsburg, N.J.: Presbyterian and Reformed, 2001).

13 Blaise Pascal, *Pensées*, trans. W. F. Trotter, Christian Classics Ethereal Library, http://www.ccel.org/p/pascal/pensees/cache/pensees.pdf, section VII, article 425.

14 Barry Morrow, *Heaven Observed* (Colorado Springs: NavPress, 2001), 89.

15 John Eldredge, *The Journey of Desire: Searching for the Life We've Only Dreamed Of* (Nashville: Nelson, 2000), 111.

16 Mark Twain, *The Adventures of Huckleberry Finn* (New York: Fawcett Columbine, 1996), 6.

17 Mark Twain, quoted in Charles Ferguson Ball, *Heaven* (Wheaton, Ill.: Victor, 1980), 19.

18 Charles H. Spurgeon, *Morning and Evening*, April 25, morning reading.

19 J. C. Ryle, *Heaven* (Ross-shire, UK: Christian Focus Publications, 2000), 19.

20 Reinhold Niebuhr, *The Nature and Destiny of Man*, vol. 2 (New York: Scribner's Sons, 1942).

21 W. G. T. Shedd, *Dogmatic Theology*, 3 vols. (Grand Rapids: Zondervan, n.d.).

22 D. Martyn Lloyd-Jones, *Great Doctrines of the Bible*, vol. 3, *The Church and the Last Things* (Wheaton, Ill.: Crossway, 2003), 246–48.

23 A. J. Conyers, *The Eclipse of Heaven* (Downers Grove, Ill.: InterVarsity, 1992), 21.

24 Ibid., 58.

25 K. Connie Kang, "Next Stop, the Pearly Gates . . . or Hell?" *Los Angeles Times*, October 24, 2003.

26 Ibid.

27 John Baillie, *And the Life Everlasting* (London: Oxford University Press, 1936), 15.

28 C. S. Lewis, *The Silver Chair* (New York: Collier Books, 1970), 151–61.

CHAPTER 2
IS HEAVEN BEYOND OUR IMAGINATION?

29 Alister E. McGrath, *A Brief History of Heaven* (Malden, Mass.: Blackwell, 2003), 5.

30   Gerhard Kittel and Gerhard Friedrich, eds., Geoffrey W. Bromiley, trans. and ed., *Theological Dictionary of the New Testament* (Grand Rapids: Eerdmans, 1964–76), 2:288.

31   C. S. Lewis, *Mere Christianity* (New York: Collier Books, 1960), 118.

32   C. S. Lewis, "Bluspels and Flalanspheres: A Semantic Nightmare," quoted in Walter Hooper, ed., *Selected Literary Essays* (Cambridge: Cambridge University Press, 1969).

33   Francis Schaeffer, *Art and the Bible* (Downers Grove, Ill.: InterVarsity, 1973), 61.

CHAPTER 3
IS HEAVEN OUR DEFAULT DESTINATION . . . OR IS HELL?

34   K. Connie Kang, "Next Stop, the Pearly Gates . . . or Hell?" *Los Angeles Times*, October 24, 2003.

35   Dante Alighieri, *Inferno*, canto 3, line 9.

36   Clark Pinnock, "The Destruction of the Finally Impenitent," *Criswell Theological Review* 4 (1990): 246–47, 253.

37   W. G. T. Shedd, *The Doctrine of Endless Punishment* (1885; repr., Edinburgh: Banner of Truth, 1986), 153.

38   C. S. Lewis, *Letters to Malcolm: Chiefly on Prayer* (New York: Harcourt Brace Jovanovich, 1963), 76.

39   Dorothy Sayers, *A Matter of Eternity*, ed. Rosamond Kent Sprague (Grand Rapids: Eerdmans, 1973), 86.

40   C. S. Lewis, *The Problem of Pain* (New York: Macmillan, 1962), 118.

41   E. Allison Peers, trans. and ed., *The Complete Works of St. Teresa* (London: Sheed and Ward, n.d.).

CHAPTER 4
CAN YOU KNOW YOU'RE GOING TO HEAVEN?

42   Ruthanna C. Metzgar, from her story "It's Not in the Book!" copyright © 1998 by Ruthanna C. Metzgar. Used by permission. For the full story in Ruthanna's own words, see Eternal Perspective Ministries, http://www.epm.org/articles/metzgar.html.

43   Ron Rhodes, *The Undiscovered Country: Exploring the Wonder of Heaven and the Afterlife* (Eugene, Ore.: Harvest House, 1960), 39–40.

44   C. S. Lewis, *The Problem of Pain* (New York: Macmillan, 1962), 147.

CHAPTER 5
WHAT IS THE NATURE OF THE PRESENT HEAVEN?

45   Wayne Grudem, *Systematic Theology: An Introduction to Biblical Doctrine* (Grand Rapids: Zondervan, 1994), 1158.

46   Anthony A. Hoekema, "Heaven: Not Just an Eternal Day Off," *Christianity Today* (June 6, 2003), http://www.christianitytoday.com/ct/2003/122/54.0.html.

47   Salem Kirban, *What Is Heaven Like?* (Huntingdon Valley, Pa.: Second Coming, 1991), 13.

48   "Sight Unseen," *World* (November 8, 2003): 13; see the article "One Unseen Divinity? Ridiculous! Billions of Unseen Universes? Sure, Why Not?" discussed at "Easterblogg," *The New Republic Online*, http://www.tnr.com/easterbrook.mhtml?week=2003-10-21.

49   Grudem, *Systematic Theology*, 1159.

CHAPTER 6
IS THE PRESENT HEAVEN A PHYSICAL PLACE?

50   John Milton, *Paradise Lost*, bk. 5, lines 574–76.

51   C. S. Lewis, *Letters to Malcolm: Chiefly on Prayer* (New York: Harcourt Brace Jovanovich, 1963), 84.

52   Randy Alcorn, *Safely Home* (Wheaton, Ill.: Tyndale House, 2001), 376–77.

53   Peter Toon, *Heaven and Hell: A Biblical and Theological Overview* (Nashville: Nelson, 1986), 26.

54   Alister E. McGrath, *A Brief History of Heaven* (Malden, Mass.: Blackwell, 2003), 40.

55   Gerhard Kittel and Gerhard Friedrich, eds., Geoffrey W. Bromiley, trans. and ed., *Theological Dictionary of the New Testament* (Grand Rapids: Eerdmans, 1964–76), 5:767.

56   Ibid., 9:654–55.

CHAPTER 8

THIS WORLD IS NOT OUR HOME . . . OR IS IT?

57 Douglas Connelly, *The Promise of Heaven: Discovering Our Eternal Home* (Downers Grove, Ill.: InterVarsity, 2000), 120.

58 Ibid., 121.

59 Paul Marshall with Lela Gilbert, *Heaven Is Not My Home: Learning to Live in God's Creation* (Nashville: Word, 1998), 11.

60 Gary Moon, *Homesick for Eden* (Ann Arbor, Mich.: Servant Publications, 1997).

61 John Eldredge, *The Journey of Desire: Searching for the Life We've Only Dreamed Of* (Nashville: Nelson, 2000), x.

62 Ibid., 104–5.

63 Millard Erickson, *Christian Theology* (Grand Rapids: Baker, 1998), 1232.

64 Donald Guthrie, *New Testament Theology* (Downers Grove, Ill.: InterVarsity, 1981), 880.

65 Walton J. Brown, *Home at Last* (Washington, D.C.: Review and Herald, 1983), 145.

66 Marshall with Gilbert, *Heaven Is Not My Home*, 247, 249.

CHAPTER 9

WHY IS EARTH'S REDEMPTION ESSENTIAL TO GOD'S PLAN?

67 C. S. Lewis, *Christian Reflections*, ed. Walter Hooper (Grand Rapids: Eerdmans, 1967), 33.

68 Albert M. Wolters, *Creation Regained: Biblical Basics for a Reformational Worldview* (Grand Rapids: Eerdmans, 1985), 58.

69 Philip P. Bliss, "Hallelujah, What a Savior!" *International Lessons Monthly*, 1875.

70 Wolters, *Creation Regained*, 62.

71 Ibid., 58–59.

72 Gerhard Kittel and Gerhard Friedrich, eds., Geoffrey W. Bromiley, trans. and ed., *Theological Dictionary of the New Testament* (Grand Rapids: Eerdmans, 1964–76), 1:686.

73 J. R. R. Tolkien, *The Hobbit* (Boston: Houghton Mifflin, 1966), 300–301.

74 David Chilton, *Paradise Restored* (Fort Worth: Dominion Press, 1987), 23, 25.

75 The Westminster Shorter Catechism may be viewed online: "Westminster Shorter Catechism with Proof Texts," Center for Reformed Theology and Apologetics, http://www.reformed.org/documents/WSC_frames.html?wsc_text=WSC.html.

76 In my summary of Isaiah 60, I am indebted to Richard Mouw's *When the Kings Come Marching In* (Grand Rapids: Eerdmans, 1983).

77 Mouw, *When the Kings Come*, 5–21.

78 Ibid., 12–15.

79 A. A. Hodge, *Evangelical Theology: A Course of Popular Lectures* (Edinburgh: Banner of Truth, 1976), 399–402.

CHAPTER 10

WHAT WILL IT MEAN FOR THE CURSE TO BE LIFTED?

80 Anthony A. Hoekema, *The Bible and the Future* (Grand Rapids: Eerdmans, 1979), 277.

81 Maltbie D. Babcock, "This Is My Father's World," 1901.

82 Albert M. Wolters, *Creation Regained: Biblical Basics for a Reformational Worldview* (Grand Rapids: Eerdmans, 1985), 64, 71.

CHAPTER 11

WHY IS RESURRECTION SO IMPORTANT?

83 Marcus J. Borg and N. T. Wright, *The Meaning of Jesus: Two Visions* (San Francisco: HarperSanFrancisco, 1998), 129–31.

84 *Time* (March 24, 1997): 75, quoted in Paul Marshall with Lela Gilbert, *Heaven Is Not My Home: Learning to Live in God's Creation* (Nashville: Word, 1998), 234.

85 R. A. Torrey, *Heaven or Hell* (New Kensington, Pa.: Whitaker House, 1985), 68–69.

86 Anthony A. Hoekema, "Heaven: Not Just an Eternal Day Off," *Christianity Today* (June 6, 2003), http://www.christianitytoday.com/ct/2003/122/54.0.html.

87   Herman Bavinck, *The Last Things: Hope for This World and the Next*, ed. John Bolt, trans. John Vriend (Grand Rapids: Baker, 1996), 157.

88   Ibid., 158.

89   Anthony A. Hoekema, *The Bible and the Future* (Grand Rapids: Eerdmans, 1979), 251.

90   Hank Hanegraaff, *Resurrection* (Nashville: Word, 2000), 68–69.

91   Peter Toon, *Longing for Heaven: A Devotional Look at the Life after Death* (New York: Macmillan, 1986), 141.

92   The Westminster Confession of Faith, Chap. XXXII, "Of the State of Men after Death, and of the Resurrection of the Dead," http://www.pcanet.org/general/cof_chapxxxi-xxxiii.htm.

93   Joni Eareckson Tada, *Heaven: Your Real Home* (Grand Rapids: Zondervan, 1995), 39.

CHAPTER 12
WHY DOES ALL CREATION AWAIT OUR RESURRECTION?

94   Albert M. Wolters, *Creation Regained: Biblical Basics for a Reformational Worldview* (Grand Rapids: Eerdmans, 1985), 11.

95   Cornelius P. Venema, *The Promise of the Future* (Trowbridge, UK: Banner of Truth, 2000), 461.

96   Wolters, *Creation Regained*, 59.

97   Frank S. Mead, ed., *Encyclopedia of Religious Quotations* (London: Peter Davies, 1965), 379.

98   John Calvin, *Commentary on Romans*, Romans 8:19-22, Christian Classics Ethereal Library, http://www.ccel.org/ccel/calvin/calcom38.all.html#xii.

99   This explanation of a uniformitarian view was adapted from *Merriam Webster's Collegiate Dictionary*, 11th ed., s.v. "uniformitarianism."

100 Erich Sauer, *The King of the Earth* (Grand Rapids: Eerdmans, 1962), 97.

101 I am indebted here to some thoughts expressed in an e-mail to ChiLibris (an online association of Christian novelists), posted by Dave Jackson, March 5, 2004. Used by permission.

102 John Piper, *Future Grace* (Sisters, Ore.: Multnomah, 1995), 377–78.

CHAPTER 13
HOW FAR-REACHING IS THE RESURRECTION?

103 J. B. Phillips, *Letters to Young Churches: A Translation of the New Testament Epistles* (London: G. Bles, 1947), 66.

104 Bruce Milne, *The Message of Heaven and Hell* (Downers Grove, Ill: InterVarsity, 2002), 257.

105 Randy Alcorn, *The Law of Rewards* (Wheaton, Ill.: Tyndale, 2003).

106 Randy Alcorn, *Safely Home* (Wheaton, Ill.: Tyndale, 2001), 394–95.

CHAPTER 14
WHERE AND WHEN WILL OUR DELIVERANCE COME?

107 Wayne Grudem, *Systematic Theology: An Introduction to Biblical Doctrine* (Grand Rapids: Zondervan, 1994), 1111–14.

CHAPTER 15
WILL THE OLD EARTH BE DESTROYED . . . OR RENEWED?

108 Albert M. Wolters, *Creation Regained: Biblical Basics for a Reformational Worldview* (Grand Rapids: Eerdmans, 1985), 41.

109 Wayne Grudem, *Systematic Theology: An Introduction to Biblical Doctrine* (Grand Rapids: Zondervan, 1994), 1160–61.

110 Anthony A. Hoekema, *The Bible and the Future* (Grand Rapids: Eerdmans, 1979), 280.

111 John Piper, *Future Grace* (Sisters, Ore.: Multnomah, 1995), 371, 376.

112 Wolters, *Creation Regained*, 57.

113 Piper, *Future Grace*, 376.

114 Cornelius P. Venema, *The Promise of the Future* (Trowbridge, UK: Banner of Truth, 2000), 468.

115 Albert M. Wolters, quoted in Venema, *The Promise of the Future*, 468.

116 Venema, *The Promise of the Future*, 469.

117 E. J. Fortman, *Everlasting Life after Death* (New York: Alba House, 1976), 304.

118 Walter Bauer, *The Greek-English Lexicon of the New Testament and Other Early Christian Literature*, ed. Frederick W. Danker, 3rd ed. (Chicago: University of Chicago Press, 2000).

119 Hoekema, *The Bible and the Future*, 280.

120 Greg K. Beale, "The Eschatological Conception of New Testament Theology," *Eschatology in Bible and Theology*, ed. Kent E. Brower and Mark W. Elliott (Downers Grove, Ill.: InterVarsity, 1997), 44.

121 Ibid., 50.

122 Ibid., 21–22.

CHAPTER 16
WILL THE NEW EARTH BE FAMILIAR . . . LIKE HOME?

123 René Pache, *The Future Life* (Chicago: Moody, 1971), 68.

124 Randy Alcorn, *Edge of Eternity* (Colorado Springs: WaterBrook, 1998), 309.

125 Walter Bauer, *The Greek-English Lexicon of the New Testament and Other Early Christian Literature*, ed. Frederick W. Danker, 3rd ed. (Chicago: University of Chicago Press, 2000).

126 Paul Marshall with Lela Gilbert, *Heaven Is Not My Home: Learning to Live in God's Creation* (Nashville: Word, 1998), 32–33.

127 C. S. Lewis, *Mere Christianity* (New York: Collier Books, 1960), 120.

128 Augustine, *Confessions*, trans. Henry Chadwick (Oxford: Oxford University Press, 1991), 257.

129 C. S. Lewis, *The Problem of Pain* (New York: Macmillan, 1962), 115.

130 G. K. Chesterton, *Orthodoxy* (Chicago: Thomas More Association, 1985), 99–100.

CHAPTER 17
WHAT WILL IT MEAN TO SEE GOD?

131 Randy Alcorn, *Edge of Eternity* (Colorado Springs: WaterBrook, 1998), 317.

132 Jonathan Edwards, *Misc.* 777, quoted in John Gerstner, *Jonathan Edwards on Heaven and Hell* (Grand Rapids: Baker, 1980), 48.

133 Augustine, *The City of God*.

134 Herman Bavinck, *The Last Things: Hope for This World and the Next*, ed. John Bolt, trans. John Vriend (Grand Rapids: Baker, 1996), 162.

135 J. I. Packer, "Incarnate Forever," *Christianity Today* (March 2004): 72.

136 Jonathan Edwards, *The Sermons of Jonathan Edwards: A Reader*, ed. Wilson H. Kimnach, Kenneth P. Minkema, and Douglas A. Sweeney (New Haven, Conn.: Yale University Press, 1999), 74–75.

137 Augustine, *The City of God*, 22, 30 and *Confessions* 1, 1, quoted in John E. Rotelle, *Augustine Day by Day* (New York: Catholic Book Publishing, 1986).

138 The Westminster Shorter Catechism may be viewed online: "Westminster Shorter Catechism with Proof Texts," Center for Reformed Theology and Apologetics, http://www.reformed.org/documents/WSC_frames.html?wsc_text=WSC.html.

139 Sam Storms, "Joy's Eternal Increase," an unpublished manuscript on Jonathan Edwards's view of Heaven.

140 Augustine, *The City of God*, chap. 29, "Of the Beatific Vision," Christian Classics Ethereal Library, http://www.ccel.org/fathers/NPNF1-02/Augustine/cog/t127.htm.

141 Augustine, *The City of God,* quoted in Alister E. McGrath, *A Brief History of Heaven* (Malden, Mass.: Blackwell, 2003), 182–83.

142 J. Boudreau, *The Happiness of Heaven* (Rockford, Ill.: Tan Books, 1984), 15–16.

143 Ibid., 33–34.

CHAPTER 18
WHAT WILL IT MEAN FOR GOD TO DWELL AMONG US?

144 Dallas Willard, *The Divine Conspiracy: Rediscovering Our Hidden Life in God* (San Francisco: HarperSanFrancisco, 1998), 392.

145 Ibid.

146 Steven J. Lawson, *Heaven Help Us!* (Colorado Springs: NavPress, 1995), 142.

147 J. Boudreau, *The Happiness of Heaven* (Rockford, Ill.: Tan Books, 1984), 95–96.

148 Mitch Albom, *The Five People You Meet in Heaven* (New York: Hyperion, 2003).

149 Jonathan Edwards, "The Christian Pilgrim," sermon preached in 1733, quoted in Alister E. McGrath, *A Brief History of Heaven* (Malden, Mass.: Blackwell, 2003), 115.

150 Teresa of Avila, *The Way of Perfection*, chap. 28, par. 2, Christian Classics Ethereal Library, http://www.ccel.org/t/teresa/way/chapter28.html.

151 John Milton, quoted in James M. Campbell, *Heaven Opened: A Book of Comfort and Hope* (New York: Revell, 1924), 75.

152 Samuel Rutherford, quoted in Charles H. Spurgeon, *Morning and Evening*, January 17, morning reading.

153 Martin Luther, quoted in James M. Campbell, *Heaven Opened: A Book of Comfort and Hope* (New York: Revell, 1924), 148.

154 John Piper, *Desiring God: Meditations of a Christian Hedonist* (Sisters, Ore.: Multnomah, 1996), 50.

155 I am indebted to Marshall Beretta for these insights on the Holy Spirit.

CHAPTER 19
HOW WILL WE WORSHIP GOD?

156 Cornelius P. Venema, *The Promise of the Future* (Trowbridge, UK: Banner of Truth, 2000), 478.

157 John G. Elliot, "The Praise Goes On and On" (Grapevine, Tex.: Galestorm Music, n.d.).

158 J. C. Ryle, *Holiness: Its Nature, Hindrances, Difficulties, and Roots* (Welwyn, UK: Evangelical Press, 1985), 40.

159 Jonathan Edwards, *The Works of Jonathan Edwards*, ed. Perry Miller, vol. 13, *The Miscellanies*, ed. Thomas A. Schafer (New Haven, Conn.: Yale University Press, 1994), 105, 275–76.

160 Venema, *The Promise of the Future*, 487–88.

CHAPTER 20
WHAT DOES GOD'S ETERNAL KINGDOM INVOLVE?

161 David Chilton, *Paradise Restored: A Biblical Theology of Dominion* (Fort Worth: Dominion Press, 1987), 49.

162 R. L. Harris, *Theological Wordbook of the Old Testament* (Chicago: Moody, 1980), 60.

163 Herman Ridderbos, *Paul and Jesus: Origin and General Character of Paul's Preaching of Christ*, trans. David H. Freeman (Philadelphia: Presbyterian and Reformed, 1958), 77.

164 Anthony A. Hoekema, *The Bible and the Future* (Grand Rapids: Eerdmans, 1979), 33.

165 Bruce Milne, *The Message of Heaven and Hell* (Downers Grove, Ill.: InterVarsity, 2002), 321.

CHAPTER 21
WILL WE ACTUALLY RULE WITH CHRIST?

166 Richard Mouw, *When the Kings Come Marching In* (Grand Rapids: Eerdmans, 1983), 30.

167 Wayne Grudem, *Systematic Theology: An Introduction to Biblical Doctrine* (Grand Rapids: Zondervan, 1994), 1158–64.

168 Dallas Willard, *The Divine Conspiracy: Rediscovering Our Hidden Life in God* (San Francisco: HarperSanFrancisco, 1998), 378.

CHAPTER 22
HOW WILL WE RULE GOD'S KINGDOM?

169 Jonathan Edwards, "The End for which God Created the World," *The Works of Jonathan Edwards* (Edinburgh: Banner of Truth, 1974), 2:210.

170 Erich Sauer, *The King of the Earth* (Grand Rapids: Eerdmans, 1962), 80–81.

171 Wilbur M. Smith, *The Biblical Doctrine of Heaven* (Chicago: Moody, 1968), 220–21.

172 Dr. and Mrs. H. Grattan Guinness, *Light for the Last Days: A Study in Chronological Prophecy*, chap. 31, "The Rulers in the Coming Kingdom," (1888), Historicism.com, http://www.historicism.com/Guinness/Light/light21.htm.

173 Bruce Milne, *The Message of Heaven and Hell* (Downers Grove, Ill.: InterVarsity, 2002), 326.

174 Blaise Pascal, *Pensées*, para. 398, 425, quoted in John Eldredge, *The Journey of Desire: Searching for the Life We've Only Dreamed Of* (Nashville: Nelson, 2000), 12–13.

175 Dallas Willard, *The Divine Conspiracy: Rediscovering Our Hidden Life in God* (San Francisco: HarperSanFrancisco, 1998), 398.

CHAPTER 23
WILL THE NEW EARTH BE AN EDENIC PARADISE?

176 This comment is made by the character Dani in my novel *Dominion* (Sisters, Ore.: Multnomah, 1996), 99.

177 Albert M. Wolters, *Creation Regained: Biblical Basics for a Reformational Worldview* (Grand Rapids: Eerdmans, 1985), 64.

178 Cornelius P. Venema, *The Promise of the Future* (Trowbridge, Wilts, UK: The Banner of Truth Trust, 2000), 482.

179 David Chilton, *Paradise Restored: A Biblical Theology of Dominion* (Fort Worth: Dominion Press, 1987), 33.

180 Anthony A. Hoekema, *The Bible and the Future* (Grand Rapids: Eerdmans, 1979), 276.

181 Alister E. McGrath, *A Brief History of Heaven* (Malden, Mass.: Blackwell, 2003), 70.

182 C. S. Lewis, *The Weight of Glory and Other Addresses* (Grand Rapids: Eerdmans, 1949), 13.

183 Edward Thurneysen, quoted in J. A. Schep, *The Nature of the Resurrection Body* (Grand Rapids: Eerdmans, 1964), 218–19.

184 C. S. Lewis, *The Last Battle* (New York: Collier Books, 1956), 168–71.

185 Ibid., 181.

CHAPTER 24
WHAT IS THE NEW JERUSALEM?

186 Edward Donnelly, *Biblical Teaching on the Doctrines of Heaven and Hell* (Edinburgh: Banner of Truth, 2001), 112.

CHAPTER 25
WHAT WILL THE GREAT CITY BE LIKE?

187 Steven J. Lawson, *Heaven Help Us!* (Colorado Springs: NavPress, 1995), 131.

188 William Hendriksen, *More Than Conquerors: An Interpretation of the Book of Revelation* (Grand Rapids: Baker, 1961), 249.

CHAPTER 26
WILL THERE BE SPACE AND TIME?

189 David Winter, *Hereafter: What Happens after Death?* (Wheaton, Ill.: Harold Shaw, 1973), 67.

190 Randy Alcorn, *Dominion* (Sisters, Ore.: Multnomah, 1996), 307–8.

191 George MacDonald, quoted in John Eldredge, *The Journey of Desire* (Nashville: Nelson, 2000), 123.

192 Ulrich Simon, *Heaven in the Christian Tradition* (London: Wyman and Sons, 1958), 236.

193 Peter Toon, *Heaven and Hell: A Biblical and Theological Overview* (Nashville: Nelson, 1986), 157.

194 Isaac Newton, *Sir Isaac Newton's Mathematical Principles of Natural Philosophy and His System of the World*, trans. Andrew Motte (Los Angeles: University of California Press, 1966), 2:545.

195 René Pache, *The Future Life* (Chicago: Moody, 1971), 357.

196 Salem Kirban, *What Is Heaven Like?* (Huntingdon Valley, Pa.: Second Coming, 1991), 35.

197 John Newton, "Amazing Grace," *Olney Hymns* (London: W. Oliver, 1779).

198 N. A. Berdyaev, *Dream and Reality*, quoted in Hendrikus Berkhof, *Christ the Meaning of History*, trans. Lambertus Buurman (Richmond, Va.: John Knox, 1966), 184.

199 Winter, *Hereafter*, 68.

200 Berkhof, *Christ the Meaning of History*, 188.

CHAPTER 27
WILL THE NEW EARTH HAVE SUN, MOON, OCEANS, AND WEATHER?

201 Steven J. Lawson, *Heaven Help Us!* (Colorado Springs: NavPress, 1995), 108.

202 Ibid.

203 Ray C. Stedman, "The City of Glory," sermon preached on April 29, 1990, available from Discovery Publishing, Palo Alto, Calif., or at Peninsula Bible Church, http://www.pbc.org/dp/stedman/revelation/4211.html.

204 C. S. Lewis, *The Voyage of the "Dawn Treader"* (New York: Scholastic, 1952), 184.

CHAPTER 28
WILL WE BE OURSELVES?
205 Adapted from Charles Dickens, *A Christmas Carol*, part 3, st. 1.
206 C. S. Lewis, *The Problem of Pain* (New York: Macmillan, 1962), 147.
207 Walton J. Brown, *Home at Last* (Washington, D.C.: Review and Herald, 1983), 192.
208 Randy Alcorn, *Safely Home* (Wheaton, Ill.: Tyndale, 2001), 377.
209 C. S. Lewis, *The Last Battle* (New York: Collier Books, 1956), 137.
210 Augustine, quoted in Michael Horton, *The Agony of Deceit* (Chicago: Moody, 1990), 144.
211 Bruce Milne, *The Message of Heaven and Hell* (Downers Grove, Ill.: InterVarsity, 2002), 194.
212 C. S. Lewis, *Mere Christianity* (New York: Macmillan, 1972), 190.

CHAPTER 29
WHAT WILL OUR BODIES BE LIKE?
213 Augustine, *The City of God*, 22:19, 2; 22:20, 3 (PL 41:781.783).
214 H. A. Williams, *True Resurrection* (New York: Holt, Rinehart, Winston, 1972), 36, quoted in Arthur O. Roberts, *Exploring Heaven* (San Francisco: HarperSanFrancisco, 1989), 119.
215 A. B. Caneday, "Veiled Glory," in John Piper, Justin Taylor, and Paul Kjoss Helseth, *Beyond the Bounds* (Wheaton, Ill.: Crossway, 2003), 163.
216 Joni Eareckson Tada, *Heaven: Your Real Home* (Grand Rapids: Zondervan, 1995), 53.
217 Arthur E. Travis, *Where on Earth Is Heaven?* (Nashville: Broadman, 1974), 24.
218 Ibid., 30.
219 James M. Campbell, *Heaven Opened* (New York: Revell, 1924), 169.
220 Randy Alcorn, *Deadline* (Sisters, Ore.: Multnomah, 1994), 238.
221 Alister E. McGrath, *A Brief History of Heaven* (Malden, Mass.: Blackwell, 2003), 37–38.
222 Thomas Aquinas, *Summa Theologica*, supplement, q. 81, art. 1.
223 Hank Hanegraaff, *Resurrection* (Nashville: Word, 2000), 133–34.
224 C. S. Lewis, *The Great Divorce* (New York: Macmillan, 1946), 29–30.
225 Jonathan Edwards, quoted in John Gerstner, *Jonathan Edwards on Heaven and Hell* (Grand Rapids: Baker, 1980), 39.

CHAPTER 30
WILL WE EAT AND DRINK ON THE NEW EARTH?
226 Harvey Minkoff, *The Book of Heaven* (Owings Mills, Md.: Ottenheimer, 2001), 143.
227 Wayne Grudem, *Systematic Theology: An Introduction to Biblical Doctrine* (Grand Rapids: Zondervan, 1994), 1161.
228 Spiros Zodhiates, *Life after Death* (Chattanooga: AMG, 1977), 148.
229 John Calvin, quoted in Paul Marshall with Lela Gilbert, *Heaven Is Not My Home: Learning to Live in God's Creation* (Nashville: Word, 1998), 164.
230 Lee Irons, "Animal Death before the Fall: What Does the Bible Say?" The Upper Register, http://www.upper-register.com/other_studies/animal_death_before_fall.html.

CHAPTER 31
WILL WE BE CAPABLE OF SINNING?
231 Paul Helm, *The Last Things* (Carlisle, Pa.: Banner of Truth, 1989), 92.
232 Jonathan Edwards, *Heaven: A World of Love* (Amityville, N.Y.: Calvary Press, 1999), 16.
233 Frederick Buechner, quoted in *A Little Bit of Heaven* (Tulsa, Okla.: Honor Books, 1995), 118.

CHAPTER 32
WHAT WILL WE KNOW AND LEARN?
234 Walton J. Brown, *Home at Last* (Washington, D.C.: Review and Herald, 1983), 73.
235 Wayne Grudem, *Systematic Theology: An Introduction to Biblical Doctrine* (Grand Rapids: Zondervan, 1994), endnote on 1162.
236 Gerhard Kittel and Gerhard Friedrich, eds., Geoffrey W. Bromiley, trans. and ed., *Theological Dictionary of the New Testament* (Grand Rapids: Eerdmans, 1964–76), 1:692.
237 Dave Hunt, *Whatever Happened to Heaven?* (Eugene, Ore.: Harvest House, 1988), 238.

238 Colleen McDannell and Bernhard Lang, *Heaven: A History* (New York: Vintage Books, 1988), 307.

239 Kittel et al., *Theological Dictionary*, 1:703.

240 Jonathan Edwards, *The Works of Jonathan Edwards*, ed. Perry Miller, vol. 13, *The Miscellanies*, ed. Thomas A. Schafer (New Haven, Conn.: Yale University Press, 1994), 483.

241 Ibid., 275; I'm indebted to Andrew McClellan for several citations from his seminary paper "Jonathan Edwards's View of Heaven," August 15, 2003.

242 William Shakespeare, *Hamlet*, act 3, scene 1, line 87.

243 Jonathan Edwards, quoted in John Gerstner, *Jonathan Edwards on Heaven and Hell* (Grand Rapids: Baker, 1980), 24.

244 Ibid., 26.

245 Jonathan Edwards, "The End for which God Created the World," quoted in John Piper, *God's Passion for His Glory* (Wheaton, Ill.: Crossway, 1998), 37.

246 Ibid., 160.

247 Ibid., 251.

248 J. Boudreau, *The Happiness of Heaven* (Rockford, Ill.: Tan Books, 1984), 120–22.

249 Philip Melanchthon, quoted in W. Robertson Nicoll, *Reunion in Eternity* (New York: George H. Doran, 1919), 117–18.

250 C. S. Lewis, *God in the Dock* (Grand Rapids: Eerdmans, 1970), 216.

CHAPTER 33
WHAT WILL OUR DAILY LIVES BE LIKE?

251 J. Boudreau, *The Happiness of Heaven* (Rockford, Ill.: Tan Books, 1984), 107–8.

252 Charles Spurgeon, "Foretastes of the Heavenly Life" (1857), quoted in *Spurgeon's Expository Encyclopedia* (Grand Rapids: Baker, 1951), 8:424.

253 Donald A. Carson, *The Gospel According to John* (Grand Rapids: Eerdmans, 1991), 489.

254 Joseph M. Stowell, *Eternity* (Chicago: Moody, 1995), 239.

CHAPTER 34
WILL WE DESIRE RELATIONSHIPS WITH ANYONE EXCEPT GOD?

255 Bede, a sermon preached on All Saint's Day ca. 710, quoted in William Jennings Bryan, ed., *The World's Famous Orations* (New York: Funk and Wagnalls, 1906).

256 John Calvin, quoted in Colleen McDannell and Bernhard Lang, *Heaven: A History* (New York: Vintage Books, 1988), 155.

257 Jonathan Edwards, *Heaven: A World of Love* (Amityville, N.Y.: Calvary Press, 1999), 18.

258 Richard Baxter, *The Practical Works of Richard Baxter* (Grand Rapids: Baker, 1981), 97.

259 Salem Kirban, *What Is Heaven Like?* (Huntingdon Valley, Pa.: Second Coming, 1991), 8.

260 J. Boudreau, *The Happiness of Heaven* (Rockford, Ill.: Tan Books and Publishers, 1984), 117.

261 George MacDonald, quoted in Herbert Lockyer, *Death and the Life Hereafter* (Grand Rapids: Baker, 1975), 65.

262 J. C. Ryle, *Heaven* (Ross-shire, UK: Christian Focus Publications, 2000), 34–35.

263 Amy Carmichael, *Thou Givest . . . They Gather*, quoted in *Images of Heaven: Reflections on Glory*, comp. Lil Copan and Anna Trimiew (Wheaton, Ill.: Harold Shaw, 1996), 111.

CHAPTER 35
WILL THERE BE MARRIAGE, FAMILIES, AND FRIENDSHIPS?

264 Drake W. Whitchurch, *Waking from Earth: Seeking Heaven, the Heart's True Home* (Kearney, Neb.: Morris, 1999), 95.

265 C. S. Lewis, *Miracles* (New York: Collier Books, 1960), 159–60.

266 Charles H. Spurgeon, "Infant Salvation," sermon 411, September 29, 1861, The Spurgeon Archive, http://www.spurgeon.org/sermons/0411.htm.

267 Randy Alcorn, "Do Infants Go to Heaven When They Die?" Eternal Perspective Ministries, http://www.epm.org/articles/infant.html.

268 Augustine, quoted in Colleen McDannell and Bernhard Lang, *Heaven: A History* (New York: Vintage Books, 1988), 58.

269 Ibid., 60.

270   Augustine, *On the Christian Doctrine,* 1:32–33.

271   Augustine, quoted in McDannell and Lang, *Heaven: A History,* 64–65.

CHAPTER 36
WHOM WILL WE MEET, AND WHAT WILL WE EXPERIENCE TOGETHER?

272   J. I. Packer, "Hell's Final Enigma," *Christianity Today* (April 22, 2002): 84.

273   Jonathan Edwards, "The End of the Wicked Contemplated by the Righteous," *The Works of Jonathan Edwards* (Edinburgh: Banner of Truth, 1974), 2:207–12, emphasis added.

274   C. S. Lewis, *The Last Battle* (New York: Collier Books, 1956), 139.

275   C. S. Lewis, *The Magician's Nephew* (New York: Collier Books, 1978), 98–116.

CHAPTER 37
HOW WILL WE RELATE TO EACH OTHER?

276   Jonathan Edwards, *Heaven: A World of Love* (Amityville, N.Y.: Calvary Press, 1999), 27–29.

277   Jonathan Edwards, quoted in John Gerstner, *Jonathan Edwards on Heaven and Hell* (Grand Rapids: Baker, 1980), 21–22.

278   C. S. Lewis, *The Problem of Pain* (New York: Macmillan, 1962), 150–51.

279   Author unknown, *Theologica Germanica,* trans. by Susanna Winkworth, chap. 51, Believer's Web, http://www.believersweb.net/view.cfm?ID=254.

280   Author unknown, *Theologica Germanica,* chap. 51.

281   I wrote about my relationship with Jerry in the nonfiction companion to my novels that deal with Heaven. See *In Light of Eternity* (Colorado Springs: WaterBrook, 1999), 66–72.

282   Elisabeth Elliot, *Through Gates of Splendor* (Wheaton, Ill.: Tyndale, 1981).

283   *Babette's Feast,* directed by Gabriel Axel (Panorama Film, 1987).

284   J. C. Ryle, *Heaven* (Ross-shire, UK: Christian Focus Publications, 2000), 84.

CHAPTER 38
WHAT WILL NEW EARTH SOCIETY BE LIKE?

285   Abraham Kuyper, *The Revelation of St. John,* trans. John H. de Vries (Grand Rapids: Eerdmans, 1963), 122.

286   Herman Bavinck, *The Last Things: Hope for This World and the Next,* ed. John Bolt, trans. John Vriend (Grand Rapids: Baker, 1996), 160.

287   Richard Mouw, *When the Kings Come Marching In* (Grand Rapids: Eerdmans, 1983), 47.

288   Dave Hunt, *Whatever Happened to Heaven?* (Eugene, Ore.: Harvest House, 1988), 236.

289   Cornelius P. Venema, *The Promise of the Future* (Trowbridge, UK: Banner of Truth, 2000), 481.

290   See discussion at Eternal Perspective Ministries, http://www.epm.org/articles/characters.html.

291   Anthony A. Hoekema, "Heaven: Not Just an Eternal Day Off," *Christianity Today* (June 6, 2003), http://www.christianitytoday.com/ct/2003/122/54.0.html.

292   Ibid.

CHAPTER 39
WILL ANIMALS INHABIT THE NEW EARTH?

293   Gary R. Habermas and J. P. Moreland, *Beyond Death: Exploring the Evidence for Immortality* (Wheaton, Ill.: Crossway, 1998), 106.

294   John Gilmore, *Probing Heaven* (Grand Rapids: Baker, 1991), 132.

CHAPTER 40
WILL ANIMALS, INCLUDING OUR PETS, LIVE AGAIN?

295   Steve Wolberg, *Will My Pet Go to Heaven?* (Enumclaw, Wash.: WinePress, 2002), 57.

296   C. S. Lewis, *The Problem of Pain* (New York: Macmillan, 1962), 139–41.

297   C. S. Lewis, *The Great Divorce,* quoted in Wayne Martindale, ed., *Journey to the Celestial City: Glimpses of Heaven from Great Literary Classics* (Chicago: Moody, 1995), 140.

298   Joni Eareckson Tada, *Holiness in Hidden Places* (Nashville: J. Countryman, 1999), 133.

299   John Piper, *Future Grace* (Sisters, Ore.: Multnomah, 1995), 381.

300   This and subsequent quotations in this section from John Wesley's sermon "The General

Deliverance, Sermon 60" can be found, with comments by Randy Alcorn, at Eternal Perspective Ministries, http://www.epm.org/articles/wesleysermon.html.

301 C. S. Lewis, *The Magician's Nephew* (New York: Collier Books, 1978), 167.

302 Ibid., 172.

CHAPTER 41
WILL HEAVEN EVER BE BORING?

303 Mark Buchanan, *Things Unseen* (Sisters, Ore.: Multnomah, 2002), 76.

304 James M. Campbell, *Heaven Opened* (New York: Revell, 1924), 123.

305 Victor Hugo, "The Future Life," quoted in Dave Wilkinson, "And I Shall Dwell," sermon preached at Moorpark Presbyterian Church, February 18, 2001, "Sermons from Moorpark Presbyterian Church," Moorpark Presbyterian Church, http://www.moorparkpres.org/sermons/2001/021801.htm.

306 Wilbur M. Smith, *The Biblical Doctrine of Heaven* (Chicago: Moody, 1968), 195.

307 Campbell, *Heaven Opened*, 123–24, 190.

308 Anthony A. Hoekema, "Heaven: Not Just an Eternal Day Off," *Christianity Today* (June 6, 2003), http://www.christianitytoday.com/ct/2003/122/54.0.html.

309 Cornelius P. Venema, *The Promise of the Future* (Trowbridge, UK: Banner of Truth, 2000), 481.

310 Bruce Milne, *The Message of Heaven and Hell* (Downers Grove, Ill.: InterVarsity, 2002), 321–22.

311 Paul Marshall with Lela Gilbert, *Heaven Is Not My Home: Learning to Live in God's Creation* (Nashville: Word, 1998), 30.

312 Ibid.

313 Ibid., 30–31.

314 Hoekema, "Eternal Day Off."

315 Marshall with Gilbert, *Heaven Is Not My Home*, 173.

316 Arthur O. Roberts, *Exploring Heaven* (San Francisco: HarperSanFrancisco, 2003), 148.

CHAPTER 42
WILL THERE BE ARTS, ENTERTAINMENT, AND SPORTS?

317 C. S. Lewis, *The Great Divorce* (New York: Macmillan, 1946), 80.

318 Arthur O. Roberts, *Exploring Heaven* (San Francisco: HarperSanFrancisco, 1989), 63–64.

319 Colleen McDannell and Bernhard Lang, *Heaven: A History* (New York: Vintage Books, 1988), 47.

320 John Gilmore, *Probing Heaven* (Grand Rapids: Baker, 1991), 252.

321 C. S. Lewis, *Letters to Malcolm: Chiefly on Prayer* (New York: Harcourt Brace Jovanovich, 1963), 92–93.

322 C. S. Lewis, *The Last Battle* (New York: Collier Books, 1956), 179.

323 *Chariots of Fire*, directed by Hugh Hudson (Warner Bros., 1981).

CHAPTER 43
WILL OUR DREAMS BE FULFILLED AND MISSED OPPORTUNITIES REGAINED?

324 Randy Alcorn, *Safely Home* (Wheaton, Ill.: Tyndale, 2001), 378–79.

325 Joni Eareckson Tada, quoted in Douglas J. Rumford, *What about Heaven and Hell?* (Wheaton, Ill.: Tyndale, 2000), 31.

326 Peter Toon, *Heaven and Hell: A Biblical and Theological Overview* (Nashville: Nelson, 1986), 204.

327 This principle is explained more fully in my book *The Treasure Principle* (Sisters, Ore.: Multnomah, 2001), 48.

328 Dallas Willard, *The Divine Conspiracy: Rediscovering Our Hidden Life in God* (San Francisco: HarperSanFrancisco, 1998), 376.

329 To see the Hubble Deep Field image, go to "Image: Hubble Deep Field North," Eternal Perspective Ministries, http://www.epm.org/hubbledeep.html.

CHAPTER 44
WILL WE DESIGN CRAFTS, TECHNOLOGY, AND NEW MODES OF TRAVEL?

330 Paul Marshall with Lela Gilbert, *Heaven Is Not My Home: Learning to Live in God's Creation* (Nashville: Word, 1998), 176.

331   C. S. Lewis, *Letters to Malcolm: Chiefly on Prayer* (New York: Harcourt Brace Jovanovich, 1963), 121–22.

332   Randy Alcorn, *Edge of Eternity* (Colorado Springs: WaterBrook, 1999), 311.

CHAPTER 45
REORIENTING OURSELVES TO HEAVEN AS OUR HOME

333   Donald Bloesch, *Theological Notebook* (Colorado Springs: Helmers and Howard, 1989), 183.

334   C. S. Lewis, *The Problem of Pain* (New York: Macmillan, 1962), 115.

335   W. Graham Scroggie, *What about Heaven?* (London: Christian Literature Crusade, 1940), 93–95.

336   A. W. Tozer, *The Size of the Soul* (Harrisburg, Pa.: Christian Publications, 1992), 17–18.

337   C. S. Lewis, *The Voyage of the "Dawn Treader"* (New York: Scholastic, 1952), 24.

338   Ibid., 180.

339   Variously attributed to Henry Scott Holland and Henry Van Dyke; source uncertain.

340   C. S. Lewis, *Letters to an American Lady* (Grand Rapids: Eerdmans, 1967), 117.

341   Calvin Miller, *The Divine Symphony* (Minneapolis: Bethany, 2000), 139.

CHAPTER 46
ANTICIPATING THE GREAT ADVENTURE

342   Jack MacArthur, *Exploring in the Next World* (Minneapolis: Dimension Books, 1967), 16.

343   C. S. Lewis, *The Last Battle* (New York: HarperTrophy, 1994), 228.

344   Sir James M. Barrie, *Peter Pan*, in *Peter Pan, and Other Plays* (New York: AMS Press, 1975), 94.

345   Paul Helm, *The Last Things* (Carlisle, Pa.: Banner of Truth, 1989), 10.

346   C. S. Lewis, *Perelandra* (New York: Simon & Schuster, 1996), 10.

APPENDIX A
CHRISTOPLATONISM'S FALSE ASSUMPTIONS

347   Luciano Floridi and Gian Paolo Terravecchia, eds., *The Free On-line Dictionary of Philosophy* (FOLDOP), version 2.4, SWIF, http://www.swif.uniba.it/lei/foldop.

348   Plato, *Phaedo*, quoted in Walter A. Elwell, ed., *Evangelical Dictionary of Theology* (Grand Rapids: Baker, 1984), 859.

349   Arthur E. Travis, *Where on Earth Is Heaven?* (Nashville: Broadman, 1974), 16.

350   James M. Campbell, *Heaven Opened* (New York: Revell, 1924), 114–15.

351   John A. Sarkett, "How Did We Lose the Rest of the Story?" chap. 9 in *After Armageddon: A Bible Study on the World Wide Web*, 1996, http://208.234.11.183/aa/9.shtml.

352   Leon Morris, *The Book of Revelation: An Introduction and Commentary*, vol. 20, Tyndale New Testament Commentaries, rev. ed. (Grand Rapids: Eerdmans, 1987).

353   Leland Ryken, "The Rhetoric of Transcendence," in Wayne Martindale, ed., *Journey to the Celestial City: Glimpses of Heaven from Great Literary Classics* (Chicago: Moody, 1995), 19.

354   C. S. Lewis, *The Screwtape Letters*, rev. ed. (New York: Macmillan, 1982), 41–42.

355   Paul Marshall with Lela Gilbert, *Heaven Is Not My Home: Learning to Live in God's Creation* (Nashville: Word, 1998), 32–33.

356   Anthony A. Hoekema, *The Bible and the Future* (Grand Rapids: Eerdmans, 1979), 249.

357   Wayne Grudem, *Systematic Theology: An Introduction to Biblical Doctrine* (Grand Rapids: Zondervan, 1994), 1158–64.

APPENDIX B
LITERAL AND FIGURATIVE INTERPRETATION

358   Colleen McDannell and Bernhard Lang, *Heaven: A History* (New York: Vintage Books, 1988), 80–81.

359   Ibid., 82–83.

360   Ibid., 84.

361   Ibid., 89.

362   Randy Alcorn, "Additional Thoughts on the Millennium," Eternal Perspective Ministries, http://www.epm.org/millennium.html.

363   John Gilmore, *Probing Heaven* (Grand Rapids: Baker, 1991), 114.

SELECTED BIBLIOGRAPHY

Alcorn, Randy. *Deadline*. Sisters, Ore.: Multnomah, 1994.

———. *Dominion*. Sisters, Ore.: Multnomah, 1996.

———. *Edge of Eternity*. Colorado Springs: WaterBrook, 1999.

———. *In Light of Eternity*. Colorado Springs: WaterBrook, 2000.

———. *The Law of Rewards*. Wheaton, Ill.: Tyndale, 2003.

———. *Safely Home*. Wheaton, Ill.: Tyndale, 2001.

———. *The Treasure Principle*. Sisters, Ore.: Multnomah, 2001.

Alighieri, Dante. *The Inferno*.

Augustine. *The City of God*.

———. *Confessions*. Translated by Henry Chadwick. Oxford: Oxford University Press, 1991.

———. *On the Christian Doctrine*.

Baillie, John. *And the Life Everlasting*. London: Oxford University Press, 1936.

Ball, Charles Ferguson. *Heaven*. Wheaton, Ill.: Victor, 1980.

Bauer, Walter. *The Greek-English Lexicon of the New Testament and Other Early Christian Literature*. Edited by Frederick W. Danker. 3rd ed. Chicago: University of Chicago Press, 2000.

Bavinck, Herman. *The Last Things: Hope for This World and the Next*. Edited by John Bolt. Translated by John Vriend. Grand Rapids: Baker, 1996.

Baxter, J. Sidlow. *The Other Side of Death: What the Bible Teaches about Heaven and Hell*. Grand Rapids: Kregel, 1987.

Baxter, Richard. *The Saints' Everlasting Rest*, in *The Practical Works of Richard Baxter*. Grand Rapids: Baker, 1981.

Berkhof, Hendrikus. *Christ the Meaning of History*. Translated by Lambertus Buurman. Richmond, Va.: John Knox, 1966.

Blanchard, John. *Whatever Happened to Hell?* Wheaton: Crossway, 1995.

Bloesch, Donald. *Theological Notebook.* Colorado Springs: Helmers and Howard, 1989.

Boudreau, J. *The Happiness of Heaven.* Rockford, Ill.: Tan Books and Publishers, 1984.

Brower, Kent E., and Mark W. Elliott, eds. *Eschatology in Bible and Theology.* Downer's Grove, Ill.: InterVarsity, 1997.

Brown, Daniel. *What the Bible Reveals about Heaven.* Ventura, Calif.: Regal, 1999.

Brown, Walton J. *Home at Last.* Washington, D.C.: Review and Herald, 1983.

Buchanan, Mark. *Things Unseen.* Sisters, Ore.: Multnomah, 2002.

Bunyan, John. *Pilgrim's Progress.*

Campbell, James M. *Heaven Opened: A Book of Comfort and Hope.* New York: Revell, 1924.

Carson, Donald A. *The Gospel According to John.* Grand Rapids: Eerdmans, 1991.

Chesterton, G. K. *Orthodoxy.* Chicago: Thomas More Association, 1985.

Chilton, David. *Paradise Restored: A Biblical Theology of Dominion.* Fort Worth: Dominion Press, 1987.

Connelly, Douglas. *The Promise of Heaven: Discovering Our Eternal Home.* Downers Grove, Ill.: InterVarsity, 2000.

Conyers, A. J. *The Eclipse of Heaven.* Downers Grove, Ill.: InterVarsity, 1992.

Copan, Lil, and Anna Trimiew, comps. *Images of Heaven: Reflections on Glory.* Wheaton, Ill.: Harold Shaw, 1996.

DeStefano, Anthony. *A Travel Guide to Heaven.* New York: Random House, 2003.

Donnelly, Edward. *Biblical Teaching on the Doctrines of Heaven and Hell.* Edinburgh: Banner of Truth, 2001.

Edwards, Jonathan. *Heaven: A World of Love.* Amityville, N.Y.: Calvary Press, 1999.

———. *The Sermons of Jonathan Edwards: A Reader.* Edited by Wilson H. Kimnach, Kenneth P. Minkema, and Douglas A. Sweeney. New Haven, Conn.: Yale University Press, 1999.

———. *The Works of Jonathan Edwards.* Edited by Perry Miller. Vol. 13, *The Miscellanies.* Edited by Thomas Schafer. New Haven, Conn.: Yale University Press, 2000.

———. *The Works of Jonathan Edwards.* Edinburgh: Banner of Truth, 1974.

Eldredge, John. *The Journey of Desire: Searching for the Life We've Only Dreamed Of.* Nashville: Nelson, 2000.

Elliot, Elisabeth. *Through Gates of Splendor*. Wheaton, Ill.: Tyndale, 1981.

Erickson, Millard. *Christian Theology*. Grand Rapids: Baker, 1998.

Fortman, E. J. *Everlasting Life after Death*. New York: Alba House, 1976.

Gerstner, John. *Jonathan Edwards on Heaven and Hell*. Grand Rapids: Baker, 1980.

Gilmore, John. *Probing Heaven*. Grand Rapids: Baker, 1991.

Grudem, Wayne. *Systematic Theology: An Introduction to Biblical Doctrine*. Grand Rapids: Zondervan, 1994.

Guinness, Dr. H. Grattan and Mrs. H. Grattan Guinness. *Light for the Last Days: A Study in Chronological Prophecy*. 1888.

Guthrie, Donald. *New Testament Theology*. Downers Grove, Ill.: InterVarsity, 1981.

Habermas, Gary R., and J. P. Moreland. *Beyond Death: Exploring the Evidence for Immortality Beyond Death*. Wheaton, Ill.: Crossway, 1998.

Hanegraaff, Hank. *Resurrection*. Nashville: Word, 2000.

Harris, R. L. *Theological Wordbook of the Old Testament*. Chicago: Moody, 1980.

Helm, Paul. *The Last Things*. Carlisle, Pa.: Banner of Truth, 1989.

Hendriksen, William. *More Than Conquerors: An Interpretation of the Book of Revelation*. Grand Rapids: Baker, 1961.

Hodge, A. A. *Evangelical Theology: A Course of Popular Lectures*. Edinburgh: Banner of Truth, 1976.

Hoekema, Anthony A. *The Bible and the Future*. Grand Rapids: Eerdmans, 1979.

Hunt, Dave. *Whatever Happened to Heaven?* Eugene, Ore.: Harvest House, 1988.

Kendall, R. T. *When God Says Well Done*. Ross-shire, UK: Christian Focus Publications, 1993.

Kittel, Gerhard, and Gerhard Friedrich, eds. *Theological Dictionary of the New Testament*. Translated and edited by Geoffrey W. Bromiley. Grand Rapids: Eerdmans, 1964.

Kreeft, Peter. *Everything You Ever Wanted to Know about Heaven*. San Francisco: Ignatius, 1990.

———. *Heaven: The Heart's Deepest Longing*. San Francisco: Ignatius, 1989.

Kuyper, Abraham. *The Revelation of St. John*. Translated by John H. de Vries. Grand Rapids: Eerdmans, 1963.

Lawson, Steven J. *Heaven Help Us!* Colorado Springs: NavPress, 1995.

Lewis, C. S. *Christian Reflections.* Edited by Walter Hooper. Grand Rapids: Eerdmans, 1967.

———. *God in the Dock.* Grand Rapids: Eerdmans, 1970.

———. *The Great Divorce.* New York: Macmillan, 1946.

———. *The Last Battle.* New York: Collier Books, 1956.

———. *Letters to an American Lady.* Grand Rapids: Eerdmans, 1967.

———. *Letters to Malcolm: Chiefly on Prayer.* New York: Harcourt Brace Jovanovich, 1963.

———. *The Magician's Nephew.* New York: Collier Books, 1978.

———. *Mere Christianity.* New York: Macmillan, 1972.

———. *Miracles.* New York: Collier Books, 1960.

———. *Perelandra.* New York: Simon & Schuster, 1996.

———. *The Problem of Pain.* New York: Macmillan, 1962.

———. *The Screwtape Letters.* New York: Macmillan, 1982.

———. *The Silver Chair.* New York: Collier Books, 1970.

———. *The Voyage of the "Dawn Treader."* New York: Scholastic, 1952.

———. *The Weight of Glory and Other Addresses.* Grand Rapids: Eerdmans, 1949.

Lloyd-Jones, D. Martyn. *Great Doctrines of the Bible.* Wheaton, Ill.: Crossway, 2003.

Lockyer, Herbert. *Death and the Life Hereafter.* Grand Rapids: Baker, 1975.

Lotz, Anne Graham. *Heaven: My Father's House.* Nashville: Word, 2001.

MacArthur, Jack. *Exploring in the Next World.* Minneapolis: Dimension Books, 1967.

MacArthur, John. *The Glory of Heaven.* Wheaton: Crossway, 1996.

Marshall, Paul, with Lela Gilbert. *Heaven Is Not My Home: Learning to Live in God's Creation.* Nashville: Word, 1998.

Martindale, Wayne, ed. *Journey to the Celestial City: Glimpses of Heaven from Great Literary Classics.* Chicago: Moody, 1995.

McDannell, Colleen, and Bernhard Lang. *Heaven: A History.* New York: Vintage Books, 1988.

McGrath, Alister E. *A Brief History of Heaven.* Malden, Mass.: Blackwell, 2003.

Miller, Calvin. *The Divine Symphony*. Minneapolis: Bethany, 2000.

Milne, Bruce. *The Message of Heaven and Hell*. Downers Grove, Ill.: InterVarsity, 2002.

Milton, John. *Paradise Lost*.

Minkoff, Harvey. *The Book of Heaven*. Owings Mills, Md.: Ottenheimer, 2001.

Moon, Gary. *Homesick for Eden*. Ann Arbor, Mich.: Servant Publications, 1997.

Morris, Leon. *The Book of Revelation: An Introduction and Commentary*. Tyndale New Testament Commentaries. Rev. ed. Vol. 20. Grand Rapids: Eerdmans, 1987.

Morrow, Barry. *Heaven Observed*. Colorado Springs: NavPress, 2001.

Mouw, Richard. *When the Kings Come Marching In*. Grand Rapids: Eerdmans, 1983.

Nicoll, W. Robertson. *Reunion in Eternity*. New York: George H. Doran, 1919.

Niebuhr, Reinhold. *The Nature and Destiny of Man*. New York: Scribner's Sons, 1942.

Pache, René. *The Future Life*. Chicago: Moody, 1971.

Pascal, Blaise. *Pensées*. Translated by W. F. Trotter. Christian Classics Ethereal Library. http://www.ccel.org/p/pascal/pensees/cache/pensees.pdf.

Peterson, Robert A. *Hell on Trial*. Phillipsburg, N.J.: Presbyterian and Reformed, 1995.

Piper, John. *Desiring God: Meditations of a Christian Hedonist*. Sisters, Ore.: Multnomah, 1996.

———. *Future Grace*. Sisters, Ore.: Multnomah, 1995.

———. *God's Passion for His Glory*. Wheaton, Ill.: Crossway, 1998.

Plato, *Phaedo*.

Rhodes, Ron. *The Undiscovered Country: Exploring the Wonder of Heaven and the Afterlife*. Eugene, Ore.: Harvest House, 1960.

Richardson, Don. *Eternity in Their Hearts*. Ventura, Calif.: Regal, 1984.

Ridderbos, Herman. *Paul and Jesus: Origin and General Character of Paul's Preaching of Christ*. Translated by David H. Freeman. Philadelphia: Presbyterian and Reformed, 1958.

Roberts, Arthur O. *Exploring Heaven*. San Francisco: HarperSanFrancisco, 2003.

Rotelle, John E. *Augustine Day by Day*. New York: Catholic Book Publishing, 1986.

Rumford, Douglas J. *What about Heaven and Hell?* Wheaton, Ill.: Tyndale, 2000.

Ryle, J. C. *Heaven*. Ross-shire, UK: Christian Focus Publications, 2000.

———. *Holiness: Its Nature, Hindrances, Difficulties, and Roots*. Welwyn, UK: Evangelical Press, 1985.

Sauer, Erich. *The King of the Earth*. Grand Rapids: Eerdmans, 1962.

Sayers, Dorothy. *A Matter of Eternity*. Edited by Rosamond Kent Sprague. Grand Rapids: Eerdmans, 1973.

Schaeffer, Francis. *Art and the Bible*. Downers Grove, Ill.: InterVarsity, 1973.

Schep, J. A. *The Nature of the Resurrection Body*. Grand Rapids: Eerdmans, 1964.

Schlink, Basilea. *What Comes after Death?* Carol Stream, Ill.: Creation House, 1976.

Scroggie, W. Graham. *What about Heaven?* London: Christian Literature Crusade, 1940.

Shedd, W. G. T. *The Doctrine of Endless Punishment*. Edinburgh: Banner of Truth, 1986.

———. *Dogmatic Theology*. Grand Rapids: Zondervan, n.d.

Simon, Ulrich. *Heaven in the Christian Tradition*. London: Wyman and Sons, 1958.

Smith, Wilbur M. *The Biblical Doctrine of Heaven*. Chicago: Moody, 1968.

Spurgeon's Expository Encyclopedia. Grand Rapids: Baker, 1951.

Stowell, Joseph M. *Eternity*. Chicago: Moody, 1995.

Tada, Joni Eareckson. *Heaven: Your Real Home*. Grand Rapids: Zondervan, 1995.

Toon, Peter. *Heaven and Hell: A Biblical and Theological Overview*. Nashville: Nelson, 1986.

———. *Longing for Heaven: A Devotional Look at the Life after Death*. New York: Macmillan, 1986.

Torrey, R. A. *Heaven or Hell*. New Kensington, Pa.: Whitaker House, 1985.

Travis, Arthur E. *Where on Earth Is Heaven?* Nashville: Broadman, 1974.

Venema, Cornelius P. *The Promise of the Future*. Trowbridge, UK: Banner of Truth, 2000.

Whitchurch, Drake W. *Waking from Earth: Seeking Heaven, the Heart's True Home*. Kearney, Neb.: Morris Publishing, 1999.

Wiersbe, Warren, ed. *Classic Sermons on Heaven and Hell*. Grand Rapids: Kregel, 1994.

Willard, Dallas. *The Divine Conspiracy: Rediscovering Our Hidden Life in God*. San Francisco: HarperSanFrancisco, 1998.

Williams, H. A. *True Resurrection.* New York: Holt, Rinehart, Winston, 1972.

Winslow, Ola Elizabeth. *Jonathan Edwards: Basic Writings.* New York: New American Library, 1966.

Winter, David. *Hereafter: What Happens after Death?* Wheaton, Ill.: Harold Shaw, 1973.

Wolberg, Steve. *Will My Pet Go to Heaven?* Enumclaw, Wash.: WinePress, 2002.

Wolters, Albert M. *Creation Regained: Biblical Basics for a Reformational Worldview.* Grand Rapids: Eerdmans, 1985.

Yancey, Philip. *Rumors of Another World.* Grand Rapids: Zondervan, 2003.

Zaleski, Carol, and Philip Zaleski. *The Book of Heaven.* Oxford: Oxford University Press, 2000.

Zodhiates, Spiros. *Life after Death.* Chattanooga: AMG, 1977.

SCRIPTURE INDEX

NAME INDEX

SUBJECT INDEX

ABOUT THE AUTHOR

 **DR. RANDY ALCORN** is the founder and director of Eternal Perspective Ministries (EPM), a non-profit ministry devoted to promoting an eternal viewpoint and drawing attention to people in special need of advocacy and help.

A pastor for fourteen years before founding EPM in 1990, Randy is a popular teacher and conference speaker. He has spoken in a number of countries and has been interviewed on more than 600 radio and television programs. Holding degrees in theology and biblical studies, he has taught biblical interpretation, theology, and ethics on the adjunct faculties of Multnomah University and Western Seminary in Portland, Oregon.

Randy is the author of more than thirty books (4 million copies in print), including *Tell Me About Heaven*; *Wait Until Then*; *Heaven for Kids*; *50 Days of Heaven*; *TouchPoints: Heaven*; *The Treasure Principle*; *The Grace and Truth Paradox*; *The Purity Principle*; *In Light of Eternity: Perspectives on Heaven*; *ProLife Answers to ProChoice Arguments*; *Money, Possessions, and Eternity*; *The Law of Rewards*; and *Why ProLife?* His novels include *Deception, Deadline, Dominion, Edge of Eternity, Lord Foulgrin's Letters, The Ishbane Conspiracy* (coauthored with his daughters), and the 2002 Gold Medallion winner for best novel of the year, *Safely Home*.

Randy lives in Gresham, Oregon, with his wife and best friend, Nanci. They have two grown daughters, Karina Franklin and Angela Stump, and several precious grandchildren.

Eternal Perspective Ministries Contact Information:

Web site: www.epm.org
E-mail: info@epm.org
Phone: 503-668-5200
Mail: 39085 Pioneer Blvd., Suite 206, Sandy, OR 97055

Follow Randy Alcorn online:
www.epm.org/blog
www.facebook.com/randyalcorn
www.twitter.com/randyalcorn

OTHER BOOKS BY RANDY ALCORN

FICTION

Deadline
Dominion
Deception
Edge of Eternity
Lord Foulgrin's Letters
The Ishbane Conspiracy
Safely Home

NONFICTION

Heaven
Touchpoints: Heaven
50 Days of Heaven
In Light of Eternity
Managing God's Money
Money, Possessions, and Eternity
The Law of Rewards
ProLife Answers to ProChoice Arguments
Sexual Temptation booklet
The Goodness of God
The Grace and Truth Paradox
The Purity Principle
The Treasure Principle
Why ProLife?
If God Is Good
The Promise of Heaven

KIDS

Heaven for Kids
Wait Until Then
Tell Me About Heaven

LOOK FOR THESE TYNDALE BOOKS
BY RANDY ALCORN
AT YOUR LOCAL BOOKSTORE

MONEY, POSSESSIONS, AND ETERNITY

This classic best seller provides a thoroughly biblical perspective about money and material possessions. Includes a study guide and appendix with additional resources.

THE LAW OF REWARDS

Using excerpts from his classic *Money, Possessions, and Eternity*, Randy Alcorn demonstrates that believers will receive differing rewards in Heaven depending on their actions and choices here on Earth.

SAFELY HOME

"Not only is *Safely Home* a first-class story, it's also a bracing wake-up call about Christian persecution in China. You'll be challenged."
—CHARLES COLSON

"This brilliant story mixes the warmth of a good novel with the harsh reality of the persecuted church."
—DR. TIM LaHAYE

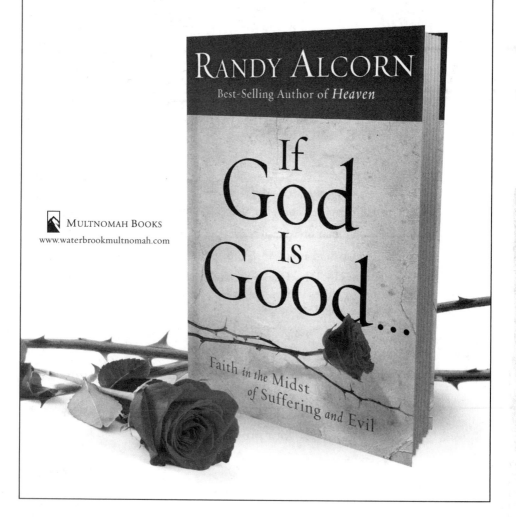